BOONE AND CROCKETT CLUB'S

20TH BIG GAME AWARDS

Boone and Crockett Club's 20th Big Game Awards

A BOOK OF THE BOONE AND CROCKETT CLUB
CONTAINING TABULATIONS OF OUTSTANDING NORTH AMERICAN
BIG GAME TROPHIES ACCEPTED DURING THE
20TH AWARDS ENTRY PERIOD OF 1986 - 1988

EDITED BY WM. H. NESBITT AND
JACK RENEAU

1990
THE BOONE AND CROCKETT CLUB
DUMFRIES, VIRGINIA

Boone and Crockett Club's 20th Big Game Awards

Copyright © 1990 by the Boone and Crockett Club.
All rights reserved, including the right to
reproduce this book or portions thereof in any form
or by any means, electronic or mechanical, including
photocopying, recording, or by an information storage
and retrieval system, without permission in writing
from the Boone and Crockett Club.
Library of Congress Catalog Card Number: 90-82934
ISBN Number: 0-940864-16-9
Published 1990

Published in the United States of America
by the
Boone and Crockett Club
241 South Fraley Boulevard
Dumfries, Virginia 22026

FOREWORD

Once each three years, the staff of the Boone and Crockett Club has the task, and the pleasure, of putting together the Awards records book. The three years of trophy entry are summarized, the results of the Awards Judging of invited top trophies are factored-in, the stories of the hunt are solicited from the owners of the invited trophies, and the photos and additional information are assembled. Then, the work begins. From this mound of raw material emerges finally a collection of hunting stories and photos that are unmatched in depicting the current conditions of hunting in North America today. The trophy listings show graphically the trophy quality of animals taken today, but it is the stories that reflect the ongoing conditions found by the trophy hunter. These stories are an excellent primer for the beginning or novice hunter, or for "boning-up" on the characteristics of a particular category that you have not hunted before. They are also just plain good reading and an enjoyable way to spend an evening during the off-seasons.

This is the third in the series of Awards records books, and it is a whopper. This book has more trophies listed and ranked (over 2,100) for a three-year period of trophy entry than ever before. More trophies were received at the 20th Awards Final Judging and Display (96) than ever before, and in terms of pages, this book, at 496 total pages, easily tops the previous two of the series. Put another way, trophy hunting, in terms of popularity and in terms of quality trophies being taken, has never been better. This book is a reflection of that.

As the Awards records book series has progressed, there has been an obvious evolution in the contents of each book. This book is the best illustrated to date, with more than 200 photographs. The photos range from portraits of the award-winners to field photos that capture the essence of the successful chase. They nicely complement the hunting stories for the award-winners, providing an excellent review of big-game hunting today in North America.

The beautiful bison on the dust jacket of this book is by well-known wildlife artist Bob Kuhn. The scene is from the Boone and Crockett Club's 1987-88 Centennial Edition Conservation Stamp Print, the latest in the stamp print series started by the Club in 1982. The American bison was chosen for the centennial year stamp print because of its obvious ties to the early days of the Club and the fact that it is an excellent symbol of the success of conservation. The plains bison were once reduced, by market hunting and slaughter to remove them as competitors with domestic livestock, to a few hundred animals, and a genuine fear was held by many observers that they would not recover but would become extinct. That has not happened, with both conservation and modern wildlife management combining to give bison populations that are healthy and at capacity for the currently available habitat.

Since the Boone and Crockett Club was founded in 1887, with the first called meeting on February 29, 1888, the choice of a bison for the 100th year stamp print was a natural. And, with net revenues from the Conservation Stamp Print series going to the Club's Centennial Project, the Theodore Roosevelt Memorial Ranch (6,000 acres of prime big-game wintering habitat on the east slope of the Rockies, near Dupuyer, Montana), again, the bison was a most appropriate subject. If you might be interested in the stamp print series, contact the Club office relative to available print numbers and sets. It's a fine way to help support an important conservation work and also enjoy some outstanding wildlife art.

Thanks are due to several folks for their hard work on this volume. Jack Reneau has directed the daily staff work of reviewing trophy entries, following up on needed additional materials and details, and he conducted the final proofing of the trophy data listings in addition to being co-editor of this book. Walter H. White and the members of his Records of North American Big Game Committee have worked tirelessly in setting and reviewing standards and making final decisions when questions have arisen that require policy change or interpretation. C. Randall Byers, Chairman of the 20th Awards Judges Panel, and each of the Judges and Consultants, all spent a solid week, without pay, to carry out the judging activities. As always, a "bottom-line" thanks goes to our 650 Official Measurers who make the program possible by volunteering their time to measure the trophies that this and the other records books are based upon.

As you enjoy this book, you'll notice the strong emphasis in the records keeping that is placed upon Fair Chase and sportsmanship. These are cornerstones of the Boone and Crockett Club and all of its activities, including the records keeping. They have never been more important than today when increasingly strident voices of the anti-hunting and anti-use groups are trying to curtail such activities. I challenge each of you to behave afield in such a manner that will bring credit to our fine sport and help insure that our descendants will be able to enjoy sport hunting in the centuries ahead. It is one of the finest legacies that we could leave to them.

Good hunting.

Wm. H. Nesbitt
Executive Director
Boone and Crockett Club

CONTENTS

Foreword v
List of Illustrations xi
The Story of This Book 1
An Overview of the 20th Big Game Awards 3
The Stories Behind the Award-Winning Trophies
    Whitetail Deer, Typical Antlers, Goldie Haske 11
    Whitetail Deer, Non-Typical Antlers, Duane R. Linscott 15
    Coues' Whitetail Deer, Typical Antlers, Robert G. McDonald 19
    Coues' Whitetail Deer, Typical Antlers, Larry Vance, Jr. 25
    Coues' Whitetail Deer, Typical Antlers, Mike Kasun 31
    Coues' Whitetail Deer, Non-Typical Antlers, William B. Bullock 33
    Coues' Whitetail Deer, Non-Typical Antlers, Eric M. Thorsrud 39
    Coues' Whitetail Deer, Non-Typical Antlers, Walter H. Pollock 41
    Coues' Whitetail Deer, Non-Typical Antlers, Ronald D. Hyatt 45
    Coues' Whitetail Deer, Non-Typical Antlers, Harry P. Samarin 47
    Mule Deer, Typical Antlers, John K. Frei 49
    Mule Deer, Typical Antlers, Shelly R. Risner 51
    Mule Deer, Typical Antlers, David V. Collis 53
    Mule Deer, Typical Antlers, John T. Sewell 57
    Mule Deer, Typical Antlers, Nelson Harding 61
    Mule Deer, Non-Typical Antlers, Artie McGram 65
    Mule Deer, Non-Typical Antlers, Brett J. Sauer 69
    Mule Deer, Non-Typical Antlers, Michael A. Siewert 73
    Columbia Blacktail Deer, Douglas L. Milburn 77
    Columbia Blacktail Deer, Keith A. Heldreth 79
    Columbia Blacktail Deer, Bruce and Scott Wales 83
    Columbia Blacktail Deer, Dick Allen 87
    Sitka Blacktail Deer, Harry R. Horner 89
    Sitka Blacktail Deer, William B. Steele, Jr. 93
    Sitka Blacktail Deer, Daniel J. Leo 95
    Sitka Blacktail Deer, Kenneth W. Twitchell 97
    Sitka Blacktail Deer, Donald E. Thompson 101
    Sitka Blacktail Deer, Craig Allen 105
    American Elk, Typical Antlers, Bruce R. Keller 107

American Elk, Typical Antlers, Martin Braun 111
American Elk, Non-Typical Antlers, Jerry J. Davis 115
American Elk, Non-Typical Antlers, James L. Ludvigson 119
American Elk, Non-Typical Antlers, Lou A. DePaolis 123
American Elk, Non-Typical Antlers, Joe W. Carroll 127
American Elk, Non-Typical Antlers, Ernie M. Bernat 131
American Elk, Non-Typical Antlers, Fred S. Scott 135
American Elk, Non-Typical Antlers, Donald A. Roberson 141
American Elk, Non-Typical Antlers, Fred Thorkelson 147
American Elk, Non-Typical Antlers, Camron Paxton 149
Roosevelt's Elk, James H. Flescher 151
Canada Moose, Donald F. Blake 155
Canada Moose, Robert G. Burkhouse 159
Canada Moose, Nick Denecky 163
Canada Moose, H. Chapman, C. Chapman, M. Chapman, and J. Anderson 167
Alaska-Yukon Moose, Myron A. Peterson 171
Alaska-Yukon Moose, Vol S. Davis, Jr. 175
Alaska-Yukon Moose, Brian C. Ziegenfuss 179
Wyoming Moose, Marion J. Fonville 183
Mountain Caribou, James C. Johnson 187
Woodland Caribou, Harry L. Gunter 189
Woodland Caribou, Thomas W. Triplett 193
Woodland Caribou, Fred Waite 197
Barren Ground Caribou, Roger Hedgecock 199
Barren Ground Caribou, James W. Vorhease 203
Central Canada Barren Ground Caribou, Toby J. Johnson 207
Central Canada Barren Ground Caribou, Jon Vanderhoef 211
Central Canada Barren Ground Caribou, Dale L. Zeigler 215
Central Canada Barren Ground Caribou, Joseph Pinkas 221
Central Canada Barren Ground Caribou, Patrick H. Ackerman 225
Central Canada Barren Ground Caribou, Paul Wisness 227
Quebec-Labrador Caribou, Carol A. Mauch 231
Quebec-Labrador Caribou, David Walker 235
Quebec-Labrador Caribou, Bernard W. Masino 237
Pronghorn, John P. Grimmett 245
Pronghorn, James W. Barrett 249
Pronghorn, William W. Diekmann 255
Pronghorn, Bruce L. Zeller 259
Pronghorn, Grant L. Perry 265
Pronghorn, Daniel E. McBride 267
Bison, Gerald H. Phillips 269
Rocky Mountain Goat, Dan Stobbe 273

Rocky Mountain Goat, Wallace E. Sills 277
Muskox, Donald Nicholson 281
Muskox, Robert D. Jones 289
Muskox, Tom Gross 293
Muskox, Richard A. Jones 295
Muskox, Don L. Corley 297
Muskox, Steve Munier 301
Muskox, Douglas G. Williams 305
Bighorn Sheep, Mitchell A. Thorson 307
Bighorn Sheep, Chris L. Mostad 311
Desert Sheep, Beverly M. Nuessle 315
Dall's Sheep, Emil V. Nelson 319
Stone's Sheep, Cliff C. Cory 323
Cougar, Gene R. Alford 325
Cougar, Richard C. Farthing 329
Cougar, Harold J. Coult 333
Black Bear, Larry W. Cox 337
Black Bear, Pennsylvania Game Commission 339
Grizzly Bear, Thomas E. Smith 341
Grizzly Bear, Peter Martinson 345
Grizzly Bear, William A. Brooks, Sr. 347
Alaska Brown Bear, W. Ted Burger 351
Alaska Brown Bear, John L. Largura 355
Alaska Brown Bear, Ron D. King 358
Alaska Brown Bear, Joe B. Brewster 362
Tabulations of Trophies Accepted for the 20th Awards Entry Period 365
Trophy Boundaries 366
    Black Bear 367
    Grizzly Bear 370
    Alaska Brown Bear 372
    Cougar 374
    Pacific Walrus 376
    American Elk, Typical Antlers 377
    American Elk, Non-Typical Antlers 379
    Roosevelt's Elk 380
    Mule Deer, Typical Antlers 382
    Mule Deer, Non-Typical Antlers 384
    Columbia Blacktail Deer 386
    Sitka Blacktail Deer 389
    Whitetail Deer, Typical Antlers 391
    Whitetail Deer, Non-Typical Antlers 402
    Coues' Whitetail Deer, Typical Antlers 408

Coues' Whitetail Deer, Non-Typical Antlers 409
  Canada Moose 410
  Alaska-Yukon Moose 412
  Wyoming (Shiras) Moose 414
  Mountain Caribou 416
  Woodland Caribou 418
  Barren Ground Caribou 419
  Central Canada Barren Ground Caribou 423
  Quebec-Labrador Caribou 426
  Pronghorn 428
  Bison 432
  Rocky Mountain Goat 433
  Muskox 435
  Bighorn Sheep 438
  Desert Sheep 440
  Dall's Sheep 442
  Stone's Sheep 443
Charts of the Official Scoring System for North American Big Game 445

ILLUSTRATIONS

Boone and Crockett Big Game Awards Certificate xvi
R. Hedgecock and P. Deuling With Their Caribou 4
D. Nicholson and R. Williams With Their Trophies 8
Whitetail Deer, Typical Antlers, Certificate of Merit 10
B. Perry, B. Knadle, and G. Brataschuk With Their Whitetails 13
Whitetail Deer, Non-Typical Antlers, First Award 14
Members of the 20th Awards Judges Panel 17
Coues' Whitetail Deer, Typical Antlers, First Award 18
J. Schnider, M. Gatlin, and S. Sperl With Their Whitetails 23
Coues' Whitetail Deer, Typical Antlers, Second Award 24
G. Haske and W. Pollock Accepting Trophy Awards 29
Coues' Whitetail Deer, Typical Antlers, Certificate of Merit 30
Coues' Whitetail Deer, Non-Typical Antlers, First Award 32
B. McGann, R. Osborne, and F. Safford With Their Whitetails 37
Coues' Whitetail Deer, Non-Typical Antlers, Second Award 38
Coues' Whitetail Deer, Non-Typical Antlers, New World's Record 40
J. Machac and G. Martin With Their Coues' Whitetails 43
Coues' Whitetail Deer, Non-Typical Antlers, Certificate of Merit 44
Coues' Whitetail Deer, Non-Typical Antlers, Certificate of Merit 46
Mule Deer, Typical Antlers, First Award 48
Mule Deer, Typical Antlers, Second Award 50
Mule Deer, Typical Antlers, Third Award 52
J. Luterbach and T. Thiel With Their Mule Deer 55
Mule Deer, Typical Antlers, Fourth Award 56
Mule Deer, Typical Antlers, Honorable Mention 60
B. Conley and J. Wagner With Their Mule Deer 63
Mule Deer, Non-Typical Antlers, First Award 64
H. Jons, M. Arkins, and L. Brady With Their Mule Deer 67
Mule Deer, Non-Typical Antlers, Second Award 68
J. Bechtel, A. Selzler, and T. Hundley With Their Mule Deer 71
Mule Deer, Non-Typical Antlers, Honorable Mention 72
R. Sibley, G. Rocha, and B. Freed With Their Deer 75
Columbia Blacktail Deer, First Award 76
Columbia Blacktail Deer, Second Award 78
Columbia Blacktail Deer, Certificate of Merit 82

L. Johnson and T. Prechter With Their Columbia Blacktails 85
Columbia Blacktail Deer, Certificate of Merit 86
Sitka Blacktail Deer, First Award 88
A. Johnson and R. Shumate With Their Sitka Blacktails 91
Sitka Blacktail Deer, Second Award 92
Sitka Blacktail Deer, Third Award 94
Sitka Blacktail Deer, Fourth Award 96
C. Hastings, R. Jones, and S. Merrill With Their Sitka Blacktails 99
Sitka Blacktail Deer, Certificate of Merit 100
Sitka Blacktail Deer, New World's Record 104
American Elk, Typical Antlers, First Award 106
American Elk, Typical Antlers, Second Award 110
G. Long, R. Pickett, and B. Keller With Their American Elk 113
American Elk, Non-Typical Antlers, New World's Record 114
C. Paxton and W. Diekmann Accepting Trophy Awards 117
American Elk, Non-Typical Antlers, Second Award 118
J. Ludvigson and S. Atwood With Their American Elk 121
American Elk, Non-Typical Antlers, Third Award 122
L. DePaolis and L. Williams With Their American Elk 125
American Elk, Non-Typical Antlers, Fourth Award 126
F. Fortier and R. Jochim With Their American Elk 129
American Elk, Non-Typical Antlers, Fifth Award 130
J. Carroll, D. Schmitz, and D. Parks With Their Elk 133
American Elk, Non-Typical Antlers, Honorable Mention 134
F. Scott, M. Braun, and R. Stamps With Their Elk 139
American Elk, Non-Typical Antlers, Honorable Mention 140
D. Dunson and S. Jamieson With Their Roosevelt's Elk 145
American Elk, Non-Typical Antlers, Honorable Mention 146
American Elk, Non-Typical Antlers, Honorable Mention 148
Roosevelt's Elk, Certificate of Merit 150
M. Jacobson and D. Welch With Their Canada Moose 153
Canada Moose, First Award 154
Canada Moose, Second Award 158
Canada Moose, Third Award 162
S. Stewart and K. Bonnett With Their Wyoming Moose 165
Canada Moose, Fourth Award 166
W. Yamashita, D. DiBetta, and B. McLay With Their Moose 169
Alaska-Yukon Moose, First Award 170
Alaska-Yukon Moose, Second Award 174
Alaska-Yukon Moose, Third Award 178
Wyoming Moose, First Award 182
Mountain Caribou, First Award 186

Woodland Caribou, First Award 188
R. Byers and L. Schmaus With Their Mountain Caribou 191
Woodland Caribou, Second Award 192
W. Shaw and G. Thompson With Their Woodland Caribou 195
Woodland Caribou, Third Award 196
Barren Ground Caribou, New World's Record 198
M. McCormick and H. Moore With Their Barren Ground Caribou 201
Barren Ground Caribou, Second Award 202
J. Rohrer and D. Richards With Their Barren Ground Caribou 205
Central Canada Barren Ground Caribou, New World's Record 206
S. Brown and G. Truitt With Their Barren Ground Caribou 209
Central Canada Barren Ground Caribou, Second Award 210
B. Sippin, R. Kiessel, and R. Hazlewood With Their Caribou 213
Central Canada Barren Ground Caribou, Third Award 214
S. Godfrey and T. Gildersleeve With Their Caribou 219
Central Canada Barren Ground Caribou, Honorable Mention 220
Central Canada Barren Ground Caribou, Honorable Mention 224
Central Canada Barren Ground Caribou, Honorable Mention 226
E. Luce and T. Rue With Their Quebec-Labrador Caribou 229
Quebec-Labrador Caribou, First Award 230
C. Mauch and B. Masino Accepting Trophy Awards 233
Quebec-Labrador Caribou, Second Award 234
Quebec-Labrador Caribou, Honorable Mention 236
Pronghorn, First Award 244
Pronghorn, Second Award 248
J. McCasland, R. Cunningham, and P. Dreeszen With Their Pronghorns 253
Pronghorn, Third Award (Tie) 254
T. Williams, N. Sutherland, and R. Hinze With Their Pronghorns 257
Pronghorn, Third Award (Tie) 258
B. Mueller, W. Spahn, and C. Grimmett With Their Pronghorns 263
Pronghorn, Honorable Mention 264
Pronghorn, Certificate of Merit 266
Bison, First Award 268
Rocky Mountain Goat, First Award 272
M. Gaede, M. Cook, and D. Pankoski With Their Rocky Mountain Goats 275
Rocky Mountain Goat, Second Award 276
Muskox, New World's Record 280
Muskox, Second Award 288
Muskox, Third Award 292
Muskox, Honorable Mention 294
Muskox, Honorable Mention 296
S. Sherer, J. Lees, and A. Quimby With Their Muskoxen 299

Muskox, Honorable Mention 300
Muskox, Honorable Mention 304
Bighorn Sheep, First Award 306
Bighorn Sheep, Second Award 310
K. Throckmorton, V. Pugnea, and N. Gianopoulos With Their Sheep 313
Desert Sheep, First Award 314
A. Maynard, J. Wallis, and W. Williamson With Their Sheep 317
Dall's Sheep, First Award 318
Stone's Sheep, First Award 322
Cougar, Sagamore Hill Award and First Award 324
D. Artery and G. Kudrick With Their Cougars 327
Cougar, Second Award 328
M. Barthelmess and R. Dugas With Their Cougars 331
Cougar, Third Award 332
R. Wolfel and B. Gilbert With Their Black Bears 335
Black Bear, First Award 336
Grizzly Bear, First Award 340
V. Pisani and B. Morgenstern With Their Grizzly Bears 344
Grizzly Bear, Third Award 346
W. West and A. O'Neil With Their Alaska Brown Bears 349
Alaska Brown Bear, First Award 350
P. Iverson, R. Hancock, and E. Dobler With Their Alaska Brown Bears 353
Alaska Brown Bear, Second Award 354

BOONE AND CROCKETT CLUB'S

20TH BIG GAME AWARDS

BOONE AND CROCKETT CLUB
NORTH AMERICAN BIG GAME AWARDS

This is to certify that the

World's Record barren ground caribou 465-1/8

entered by

Roger Hedgecock

in the 20th North American Big Game Awards was awarded

First Award

this 10th day of June 1989

_____
Jack Reneau
Director, Big Game Records

_____
Walter H. White
Chairman, Records of North American Big Game Committee

The Boone and Crockett Club Big Game Award Certificate. The Certificate and the Boone and Crockett Club Medal (pictured at the top of the Certificate) are both given to those trophies certified by the Final Awards Judges Panel for a place award. The Certificate only is given to trophies qualifying for other awards such as the Certificate of Merit and Honorable Mention.

THE STORY OF THIS BOOK

Wm. H. Nesbitt
Executive Director
Boone and Crockett Club

Over the past half-century, the name "Boone and Crockett" has become synonymous with trophy big game of North America. The all-time records book, *Records of North American Big Game*, is the "bible" for many serious big-game hunters, and it is the universally recognized source of data for native big-game animals. Not surprisingly, many sportsmen know the Club only for the big-game records, being unaware of the storied history of the Club as a major force in developing the conservation ethic and well-maintained natural resources of today. That story, a fascinating and informative one in itself, is well-told in the Club's book, *An American Crusade for Wildlife* (available from the Club and from most book stores).

The all-time records book is published on roughly a six-year schedule, beginning with the first edition that was printed in 1932. Since then, there have been eight additional editions (1939, 1952, 1958, 1964, 1971, 1977, 1981, and 1988), and the tenth edition will be published after the close of the 21st Awards entry period (1989-1991). On the current schedule, the all-time records book is published after completion of two Awards entry periods (each three years long), adding the new entries accepted during these two periods to the previously published listings.

From the standpoint of producing a major reference book, a six-year schedule is just about right. A huge amount of work goes into each edition of the all-time records book, with endless checking and verification to give the most accurate result humanly possible. But, to sportsmen, especially those fortunate enough to kill a records-book trophy, six years is a <u>long</u> time to wait to see results in print. For this and several other good reasons, the Awards records books were started in 1984 with the publication of *Boone and Crockett Club's 18th Big Game Awards*. It covered the 18th Awards entry period of 1980-82, and it listed and ranked nearly 1,000 trophies in 27 categories.

The concept was immediately popular, offering choice reading and a review of current hunting conditions on the North American continent. The second Awards records book was *Boone and Crockett Club's 19th Big Game Awards*, published in 1986. It covered the 19th Awards entry period of 1983-85, and it listed over 1,400 trophies in 32 categories. This volume that you are holding in your hands is then the third of the Awards records books. It covers the 20th Awards entry period of 1986-88, and it continues the well-accepted features of the first two books of the series. The popularity of the records-keeping and the excellent big-game habitat condition of North America are underscored by the number of trophies in this edition: over 2,100 trophies in 32 categories. Tell that to your non-hunting friends when they question the role of hunting and wildlife management in today's world.

One of the best-received features of the Awards records books is the lower scores required for entry. Simply stated, the lower scores allow recognition for a much larger segment of the better big-game trophies taken each fall. The lower entry scores are not so low that an "ordinary" trophy can be entered, but they do make the odds of seeing a "book" animal much better. A 160-point typical whitetail is a real trophy in any part of its range, and 160 points is the minimum entry score for a whitetail to make the Awards book.

Trophies that score at or above the Awards book minimums, but below that required for the all-time book, are published only the single time in the Awards book. Those that score at or above the all-time minimums are listed in both books. This opportunity to provide additional recognition for fine trophies was a major reason for development of the Awards records book concept. If the minimum entry scores for the all-time records book had been lowered to accomplish the same objective, the result would have been a much bigger book, and listings that would soon take on the appearance of a "yellow pages." With the Awards book approach, the all-time book is not materially increased in size, but the possible recognition of fine trophies is greatly increased via the one-time listings in the Awards records book.

The Awards records book is then an excellent complement to the all-time records book editions. For data on long-term trends, the greatest expression of trophy character (number of points, greatest horn length, etc.), the all-time records book is the obvious choice. But for determining current hunting conditions, and enjoyable hunting stories of the top few trophies accepted during a three-year period of trophy entry, the choice is the Awards book.

The final scores and data shown in this book supplement those of the latest edition of the all-time records book, *Records of North American Big Game*, 9th Edition, 1988. In the case of asterisked trophy scores, the asterisk indicates that the score shown is tentative, subject to final confirmation by either an Awards Judges Panel or additional verifying measurements. Such asterisked trophies are listed at the bottom of their category, unranked. The asterisk can be removed by the trophy owner complying with the requirement of additional measurements, and the trophy can then be shown, at the revised score, in future publications and ranked by that score.

There's some fine reading in this book, and more than a few good tips on how trophy animals are taken. We've tried to keep editing at a minimum, so you can enjoy the hunt in the hunter's own words. Of course, some hunters are obviously better at hunting than at writing. You'll therefore notice a considerable variation in story length and details. But in all of them, you'll be at the hunter's side as the finest trophies of North America are taken in Fair Chase. It's an "armchair safari" that I know you will enjoy.

AN OVERVIEW OF THE 20TH AWARDS

Walter H. White, Chairman
Records of N.A. Big Game Committee

Boone and Crockett Club's 20th Big Game Awards is the third book in the series begun in 1984 to recognize the trophies entered during a single Boone and Crockett Club big-game Awards entry period. This book lists *only* those trophies entered and accepted during 1986, 1987, and 1988, the years of the 20th Awards entry period.

The 18th Awards book, which covered the years 1980, 1981, and 1982, listed 951 trophies and featured the 68 trophies sent in for final judging by the 18th Awards Judges Panel along with photographs and the story of their hunts. The 19th Awards book, which covered the years 1983, 1984, and 1985, listed 1,447 entries (a 50 percent increase over the 18th Awards book), and featured 87 trophies with photographs and the story of the hunt for those trophies that received awards at the 19th Awards final judging held in Las Vegas, Nevada, during the summer of 1986.

This book lists and ranks the 2,138 trophies accepted during the 20th Awards entry period. This is once again nearly a 50 percent increase of entries over the previous three-year Awards entry period. Like the two previous Awards books, this book features all the trophies sent-in to the 20th Awards Judges Panel (96 of them), with the story of the hunt and a full-page photograph of each trophy.

This book is solid proof that big game management is working and that trophy hunting is a popular activity for increasing numbers of sportsmen. Of the 2,138 trophies listed in this book, 1,708 exceed the all-time records book minimums and will be listed in future editions of the all-time records book, beginning with the 10th edition that will be published after 1991. The remaining 430 trophies exceed the Awards minimums and are featured in this book for this one-time listing.

In the black bear category, there are 101 trophies listed from 17 states and six provinces. While 67 of these bruins exceed the all-time minimum score of 21 points for listing in future editions of the all-time records book, six rank in the all-time top 10. The largest black bear is from Lycoming County, Pennsylvania, scoring 23-7/16 points. This skull, owned by the Pennsylvania Game Commission, ranks as the second-largest black bear ever recorded since the records keeping was begun.

Photograph Courtesy of Roger Hedgecock

Roger Hedgecock (l) took the New World's Record barren ground caribou, scoring 465-1/8 points, in 1987 along the Mulchatna River, Alaska. The rear points are more than 20 inches on each antler.

Photograph Courtesy of Paul T. Deuling

Paul T. Deuling's 1988 mountain caribou entry scored 458-3/8 and is a potential World's Record but must come before an Awards Judges Panel to determine final score and rank.

The two top black bear trophy producing states during the 20th Awards were Arizona, with a total of 14, and Alaska with 13. The top areas in Arizona and Alaska were Gila County (five) and Prince of Wales Island (five), respectively. The top provinces were Saskatchewan and Manitoba, which respectively produced 11 and 10 trophies each.

Of the 43 grizzlies listed in this book, 19 each came from Alaska and British Columbia. The remainder came from Alberta (four) and Yukon Territory (one). Forty-one of these trophies exceeded the all-time minimum score and will be listed in the next edition of the all-time records book. The largest boar, scoring 26-9/16 points, was taken near Bella Coola, British Columbia, in 1986. Because it ranks in the top-10 all-time and it was not sent-in for Final Judging by the 20th Awards Judges Panel, it is asterisked and unranked in this book, and it will be asterisked and unranked in future editions of the all-time records book until its final score is verified by the stated alternative of submission of two additional scorings (total of three; original entry scoring plus the two additional).

Forty-five trophies were entered in the Alaska brown bear category. Interestingly, Kodiak Island continues to be the top brown bear producing area. In spite of its comparatively small size, 26 record book animals were taken there, while 14 came from the Alaska Peninsula and five from other areas of the mainland recognized as brown bear territory. Even though there were none in the top-10 all-time, 26 trophies exceeded the all-time minimums.

There were no polar bear or jaguar trophies entered in the 20th Awards. Even though these species can currently be hunted in certain areas of Canada and Mexico, respectively, it is not currently possible to import specimens of either category into the United States except under certain, special Federal permits.

Sixty-nine cougar were entered in the 20th Awards from 11 states and two Canadian provinces. Forty-seven trophies exceeded the all-time minimum entry score of 15 points. The top three trophy cougar producing areas were Colorado (13), Idaho (13), and Montana (9). Three cougar were accepted that placed in the all-time top-10, including the monster tom taken by Gene Alford (score of 16-3/16) in Idaho County, Idaho, in 1988 to become the new No. 2 in the category. Alford's fine, Fair Chase hunt merited the highest award of the Club, the Sagamore Hill Award, given for only the 14th time for a trophy. Alford has graciously donated his trophy to the Boone and Crockett Club's National Collection of Heads and Horns, on continuing display at the Buffalo Bill Historical Center, Cody, Wyoming.

Only two Pacific walrus were entered in the 20th Awards. (There is no legal sport hunting for Pacific walrus in Alaska at this time.) One of them was picked-up along the beach on Nelson Island in 1987 and the other was legally taken in the 1978 hunting season.

A total of 50 American elk was accepted in the 20th Awards. Thirty-three were entries in the typical category and 17 were entered in the newly established non-typical category. They came from 11 states and four Canadian provinces. While none of the trophies accepted in the typical American elk category replaced trophies in the all-time top-10, the top 10 trophies accepted in the non-typical American elk category set a standard against which all future trophies entered in this category will be measured. Arizona and New Mexico continue to be the current hot spots for trophy elk, with 12 trophies being accepted from the former and six from the latter. Five typical trophies came from Colorado, one of the traditional trophy elk producing states. In the non-typical category, six trophies were accepted from Montana, with five having been taken many years prior to the 20th Awards entry period.

The 20th Awards Judges Panel declared a first-time World's Record for the new non-typical American elk category. This exceptional bull, scoring 445-5/8 points, came from the White Mountain Apache Indian Reservation in Arizona.

There were 34 Roosevelt's elk trophies accepted in the 20th Awards, an increase of 26 percent over the entries accepted in the 19th Awards. Four of these accepted trophies fall in the all-time top-10.

A record number of 103 mule deer (70 typical and 33 non-typical) was entered in the 20th Awards from 13 states and two provinces. This is an increase of 42 (69 percent) over the 19th Awards. This total includes trophies from virtually every state and province where mule deer exist in significant numbers and are hunted. The top-two mule deer trophy producing states were Utah and Colorado, with 27 and 25, respectively. If our entry statistics are a barometer of the condition of the mule deer herds in the western states, I'd say that mule deer populations appear to be recovering from the die-offs that occurred in several areas of the west in the late 1970's.

Three entries in the non-typical mule deer category replaced trophies in the all-time top-10. A massive buck, scoring 305-6/8 points, was taken by Artie McGram in 1987 in northern California and now ranks as the eighth-largest mule deer ever recorded.

With a total of 39 entries from California, that state was the top Columbia blacktail deer trophy producing state. A total of 95 trophies was accepted in this category during the period. Only one came from British Columbia. The largest rack, with a final score of 163-7/8 points, was picked up in Lincoln County, Oregon, in 1987. It now ranks as the seventh-largest ever entered.

The 46 entries accepted in the Sitka blacktail deer category more than doubled the 17 trophies entered in the 19th Awards, the first Awards to recognize these small deer from Coastal Alaska and the Queen Charlotte Islands of British Columbia. An exceptional trophy that scores 128 points was taken by an unknown hunter on Kodiak Island, Alaska, in 1985, is the New World's Record for this category. A total of 29 entries came from Kodiak Island, making this the most productive area for trophy-class Sitka blacktail deer. Eight of the remaining trophies came from Prince of Wales Island, and the rest were from coastal Alaska.

Without doubt, whitetail deer continue to be the most popular trophy entered in the records keeping. A total of 607 trophies was entered, with 396 in the typical category and 211 in the non-typical. They came from 34 states and seven provinces. Minnesota and Wisconsin continue to be the top trophy producing states for both categories. Minnesota produced a record number of 112 trophies that exceeded the Awards minimum score of 160 points and Wisconsin produced 62 trophies. The two top trophy producing provinces were Manitoba and Alberta, with 36 and 25 respectively. Alberta has long been known to the world as a top trophy producing area in Canada, while only 22 trophies had been entered from Manitoba prior to 1985. One reason for the few trophies previously from Manitoba was that there were no Official Measurers in Manitoba for many years. In late 1986, a workshop held in Winnipeg appointed 15 new Official Measurers. The world will now discover that Manitoba produces trophy whitetail deer.

Record numbers of trophies are being entered in the typical and non-typical Coues' whitetail deer categories, with 40 trophies accepted, a 67 percent increase over the 19th Awards. The finest Coues' whitetail entered was a non-typical rack scoring 158-4/8 points that was picked up by Walter H. Pollock during a quail hunt in Santa Cruz County, Arizona, in 1988. It exceeds the previous World's Record by seven inches and is the New World's Record. Mr. Pollock has generously placed his trophy on a continuing loan basis in the Boone and Crockett Club's National Collection of Heads and Horns.

There were record numbers of moose in all three categories. The greatest increase was in the Alaska-Yukon moose category, with 50 trophies accepted (a 213 percent increase over the 19th Awards). Much of this increase is due to 21 trophies that exceed the Awards minimum but not the all-time minimum. There were seven Canada moose trophies entered from the lower 48 states, and British Columbia and Alberta produced 25 and 11 entries, respectively. Three-fourths of the Canada moose entries met or exceeded the all-time minimum score of 195 points. Wyoming and Utah were the top Wyoming moose producing states, with 19 and 18, respectively. Idaho produced 13 trophies. Three trophies were entered in the Wyoming moose category that scored in the top-10. None of them were sent to the Final Awards, but the scores of two of them were verified by additional measurements and now rank as the fifth and ninth largest Wyoming moose ever recorded.

There were record numbers of caribou entered in all five categories. Roger Hedgecock's barren ground caribou, scoring 465-1/8 points and from Mosquito Creek, Alaska, replaced the former World's Record by 1-3/8 points. Mr. Hedgecock has generously placed his trophy on a continuing loan basis in the Boone and Crockett Club's National Collection of Heads and Horns, where this New World's Record is a major attraction.

The Central Canada barren ground caribou category was established in 1983 to recognize the caribou that occur on the mainland (excluding the Mackenzie Mountains) of Northwest Territories and Baffin Island, with these animals having smaller antlers in general than the barren ground caribou of Alaska and other Canadian provinces. There were 52 trophies accepted, including a New World's Record. This is a 225 percent increase over the number of trophies accepted during the 19th Awards. The New World's Record, scoring 416 points, was taken by Toby J. Johnson near Courageous Lake, N.W.T., in 1987.

A potential World's Record mountain caribou was taken by Paul T. Deuling that entry scores an impressive 458-3/8 points, 6-3/8 points greater than the current World's Record. Since this massive trophy did not come before the 20th Awards Judges Panel, it is asterisked and unranked in this book and it will continue to be asterisked and unranked in future editions of the all-time records books until it is sent-in to a Final Awards Judges Panel. Only a Final Awards Judges Panel can declare a New World's Record. This is the only situation where a trophy entered in an Awards entry period can receive an invitation to more than one Final Awards Judging session.

The pronghorn category is one of only a few categories that showed a decrease in the number of entries over the previous entry period. With 126 entries, there were 27 fewer (18 percent) trophies entered. Pronghorns were accepted from 11 states and one province. .pa

Photograph Courtesy of Donald Nicholson

An obviously very satisfied Donald Nicholson with his New World's Record muskox that scores 125-2/8 points. He took this bull in 1988 near Bay Chimo in Northwest Territories.

Photograph Courtesy of Robert B. Williams

Robert B. Williams hunted the Henry Mountains, Utah, for this bison 118-4/8. During the 20th Awards, the Records Committee designated several new areas as acceptable for bison entries.

Wyoming and New Mexico were the two top trophy pronghorn producing states with 30 and 26, respectively. The finest pronghorn entered scores 90-6/8 points and was taken by John P. Grimmett in 1986 in Catron County, New Mexico.

Hunter-taken bison from the lower 48 states are acceptable for listing in the records books only from areas where they are considered game animals and a hunting license is required. (Bison from free-ranging herds in Alaska and Canada are fully eligible for listing and possible award.) The two most productive states for bison hunting were Utah and South Dakota, with eight bison taken in each state. During the 20th Awards entry period, several new areas were designated as acceptable areas for bison entries. These areas include an area north of Great Slave Lake, N.W.T.; Antelope Island, Utah; the Crow Indian Reservation in southern Montana; and portions of Wyoming and Montana adjacent to Yellowstone National Park where bison commonly migrate out of the park during winter.

British Columbia continues to be the top Rocky mountain goat producing area, supplying 29 of 58 trophies (50 percent) accepted in this category. The remaining 29 trophies came from six states, including Alaska which produced 12 trophies.

Muskox entries totaled 78, an increase of 34 trophies (77 percent) over the total for the 19th Awards. Alaska and the Northwest Territories are the only two areas where muskox hunting is currently available to the sport hunter. The muskox trophy listings were rewritten during the 20th Awards. There were many trophies accepted that were larger than the all-time top-10 for the category. In fact, the top two trophies replace the top two listed in the 9th edition of the all-time records book, *Records of North American Big Game*, that was released in 1988. Don Nicholson took the New World's Record, scoring 125-2/8 points, near Bay Chimo, Northwest Territories, in 1988. Starting with the 21st Awards entry period, that began on January 1, 1989, the minimum score for muskox was raised to 105.

Montana and Alberta remain the top bighorn sheep producing areas with 33 and 11 trophies, respectively. The finest sheep entry is arguably a desert sheep taken by Samuel S. Jaksick, Jr., in Gila County, Arizona, in 1988 with an entry score of 189 points. This trophy potentially ranks in the all-time top-10 but it did not come before the 20th Awards Judges Panel and it is asterisked and unranked in this book and later records books. Of all the sheep categories, Dall's sheep posted the greatest increase in number of entries over the 19th Awards, with 20 trophies for a 67 percent increase. A Dall's sheep taken by Charles W. Troutman in 1987 is only the second Dall's sheep from the Brooks Range of Alaska to make the all-time records.

In summary, the 20th Awards was the most active entry period ever, with 2,138 trophies accepted during 1986, 1987, and 1988. It included five New World's Records and 161 trophies (eight percent of the total) accepted that did (or could potentially after additional, verifying scorings) place in the all-time top-10 of their categories. It's a <u>great</u> time to be a trophy hunter. Start making plans for this fall now.

Photograph by Wm. H. Nesbitt

WHITETAIL DEER, TYPICAL ANTLERS
CERTIFICATE OF MERIT
SCORE: 197-5/8
Locality: Wood Co., Wisc.   Date: November 1945
Hunter: Joe Haske   Owner: Goldie Haske

WHITETAIL DEER, TYPICAL ANTLERS 197-5/8

Joe Haske, hunter
Goldie Haske, owner

[This story is told in the words of Joe Haske's son.]

I am writing this story about my dad's large whitetail deer. My dad passed away in 1979, so I will tell the story in my own words.

While small game hunting in the fall of 1945, I saw something that was out of this world. I noticed some movement in the heavy brush. The first thing I thought was that some animal had a stump caught on top of its head. The animal was about 400-500 feet away from me. When the deer came out of the heavy woods, I found it hard to believe that there was anything like that here in Wood County.

Some weeks later, I saw a deer across a 40 acre area. It was easy to determine that this animal had a very large rack on top of its head. My dad, my uncle, and I talked about this animal a number of times between us.

When gun season opened in November 1945, we all hoped to get a chance at the big buck. We had a meeting before opening day to have everything planned for the start of the deer hunt.

We decided to drive a 40 acre area, about a quarter-mile from my grandparent's farm. My uncle thought this 40 acres would be the best area to start.

My dad, mother, and I got up at 4:30 a.m. My dad and I did most of the farm chores, then my mother finished the chores after we left for my grandparent's place to meet with my uncles. They were Herman, John, William, Sr., and Frank Haske, all my dad's brothers.

We all walked to the north side of the forty to make our first drive. The drivers would wait until the posters were around the forty. The east poster had to walk around the forty. The wind was from the east, so we did not want any deer to get our scent or hear us. We posted one on the west, one on the south, and my dad went around the forty and came about halfway back north to stand on the east side, a spot that was called Speed Hill. Many deer were missed on the hill. There was a small clearing on the east side of this hill, and the deer usually went across this with great speed.

On the way around, my dad met Joe Becker, a close friend. He visited with him a few seconds, then walked on. Before reaching the top of the hill, he had to take a "call of nature," then he proceeded to the top of the hill. While he was going there, the drive began without him in his spot on the crest of the hill.

As my dad reached the crest, the buck was coming up the opposite side. They both saw each other at about the same time. My dad shot quickly, as the animal turned around and headed back toward the drivers. The shot knocked the buck down, but then he got up, trying to run again. Dad shot once more and finally bagged his trophy.

There was a fair amount of snow, so two men could drag the deer. Dad and John were nominated to drag the deer back to my grandparent's farm. As a rule, we would dress the deer and let it lay until later in the day. Then we would drag them out around quitting time. We had good neighbors and no one would take any deer that didn't belong to them.

The rest of us kept on hunting. Dad and uncle John joined us, as soon as possible. At day's end, Will, Frank, and I had also downed our bucks.

My mother, Goldie, kept a diary of almost every day's happenings. She has it in her diary that Joe shot a big buck. Little did anyone know his deer was such an outstanding animal that would later be recognized.

Our area that we hunt is about eight miles northwest from the exact center of Wisconsin. In those years, it was not unusual to see four or five bucks a day, with six to 10-point racks, running around. I feel very lucky to have enjoyed all that fine hunting, and to have seen this outstanding whitetail two times in the wild. We do wish that Dad was here to enjoy the final scoring of this fine rack.

Happy hunting to all.

Photograph Courtesy of Buford Perry and Bob Knadle

(l) Buford Perry and grandson, Josh Payne, with typical whitetail Perry killed in Madison Parish, Louisiana, in 1961, that was scored in 1986 at 180-4/8 points. (r) Bob Knadle with typical whitetail that he shot on the first day of South Dakota's 1986 deer season. It scores 161-2/8 points.

Photograph Courtesy of Greg Brataschuk

Meeting Lake, Saskatchewan, produced this non-typical whitetail for Greg Brataschuk during the 1987 deer season. It has a total of 56-2/8 inches of abnormal points and scores 244-1/8 points.

Photograph by Wm. H. Nesbitt

WHITETAIL DEER, NON-TYPICAL ANTLERS
FIRST AWARD
SCORE: 259-5/8
Locality: Chariton Co., Mo.   Date: November 1985
Hunter: Duane R. Linscott

WHITETAIL DEER, NON-TYPICAL ANTLERS 259-5/8

Duane R. Linscott

November 16, 1985 was a day that I'll remember the rest of my life. Some say it only happens once in a lifetime; I've had several people tell me that anyway. So I guess I've used my one chance-in-a-lifetime, to bag one of the largest non-typical whitetails ever taken. Actually there are a few hunters that will get a chance at a deer of this magnitude.

During the four years since November 16, 1985, I've been fortunate enough to see two different typical whitetails with world-class dimensions. I attribute this to spending every spare minute in my deer woods, especially during the rut and late season. The latter pertains to periods of snow or ice and bitter cold weather. It also takes a grain field that hasn't been fall tilled. These conditions will congregate the deer, and usually there will be at least one big, mature buck staying close by.

Mostly, I hunt two different farms in Chariton County, near my home town of Mendon, Missouri. Both farms border a wildlife refuge. To most trophy hunters, this spells mature, big-racked whitetails. It was on one of those farms that I found my non-typical whitetail.

The fall of 1985 was very wet; 70 percent of the row crops had not been harvested by the firearms deer season. I felt that a lot of deer were still on the small drainages. I also thought this would have the deer scattered throughout the hill ground. Most years, the crop fields are usually harvested by gun season, putting most of the deer back in the larger woodlots. On November 15, I saw a very nice buck crossing a bean field adjacent to one of these small drainages. At that point, it was a toss-up as to where I would hunt the following morning, the opening of firearms season. I wanted to look at my regular hunting spot, so I bow-hunted there that afternoon.

I had two stand sites. One stand was on the creek side of a levee. Thanks to the flood water, my favorite stand was in three feet of water. The other stand was on the protected side of the levee. From this stand I could see anything crossing the property, and there was only about 30 yards of timber between the stand and flood water. Right before dark, I spotted a big buck at about 75 yards, but he saw me first. As he turned away, his rack looked large, but he was in real thick brush, so it was hard to see how big. With all the flood water on the refuge, and having spotted the buck, I decided to hunt this stand the next morning.

Next morning went like so many other openers. I was on my stand 45 minutes before daylight and, as usual, the half-mile wade through mud and water got me hot and soaked. The morning wasn't cold, just cool. It was one of those bluebird days with a light breeze.

I hadn't seen anything by 8:30 a.m. But being wet and cold, I decided to get down and still hunt a small patch of brush. I had just reached the ground when a real nice buck exploded into a run down the levee. He was no more than 30 yards away, but there was no chance for a shot.

I hadn't hunted very far when I jumped a fork-horn from his bed. He ran from the brush, out into a harvested corn field where he made a short circle and ended-up 40 yards away, facing me. He stood there, bobbing his head up-and-down, while stomping the ground occasionally. After what seemed like 10 minutes, I noticed a movement behind the forkhorn. There, 150 yards out, was the biggest set of antlers I'd ever seen and they were walking straight toward me. He walked to within 100 yards. All I had to do was move my line of sight three or four inches and then touch it off. When I moved, the forkhorn spooked and ran, with the big buck chasing him. There was too much brush to shoot.

They entered the same patch of brush I was in, about 100 yards from me. When I couldn't shoot, I ran to a ditch that I thought they might cross, possibly giving me a shot. After a few seconds I hadn't seen the big buck and I thought it was all over. About this time, I heard a deer grunting. It was coming from the area the two deer had run into, so I still hunted toward the sound. Thirty minutes later, after covering 50 yards, I spotted an antler tine. He was bedded down, not more than 35 yards away. All I could do was wait and hope for a shot. So, I sat at the base of a pin oak tree from 10 a.m. to 2:05 p.m.

There were many "ups and downs." He would stand up and move around, but never offer a clear shot. At one time, there were two small bucks within 15 yards. I think back how many times I've had deer that close that didn't see or smell me. It hasn't happened very many times hunting from a tree, let alone being on the ground. Anyway, about 2 p.m. the buck stood up and started working in my direction, finally giving me a clear shot at 20 yards. It took one round from my 6 mm Remington to down the buck.

After crossing shoulder-deep water, I got my first clear look at the rack. Before, I had just thought it was a rack big enough to mount. It was huge! There were points going up and down; I counted 27 of them. I had never seen anything like it before. After 20 years of deer hunting, I FINALLY got one big enough to mount. It's also the No. 2 non-typical whitetail for Missouri, following the current World's Record.

The 20th Awards Judges Panel. Standing, (l-r): Bob Hults, Wisconsin; Jack Graham, Alberta; Dennis L. Shirley, Utah; William C. MacCarty III, Virginia; Philip L. Wright, Montana; Eldon L. Buckner, Oregon; Robert E. Estes, New York; George K. Tsukamoto, Nevada; Elvin Hawkins, Oregon; Jesse E. Williams, New Mexico; Wm. H. Nesbitt, Executive Director, Virginia. Kneeling/sitting (l-r): Jack Reneau, Director Big Game Records, Virginia; Tim E. Kelly, New Mexico; John G. Stelfox, British Columbia; Walter H. White, Chairman of Records Committee, Wisconsin; C. Randall Byers, Chairman of Judges Panel, Idaho. Photograph taken by James J. McBride who assisted the panel.

Photograph by Wm. H. Nesbitt

COUES' WHITETAIL DEER, TYPICAL ANTLERS
FIRST AWARD
SCORE: 126-1/8
Locality: Pima Co., Ariz.   Date: December 1986
Hunter: Robert G. McDonald

COUES' WHITETAIL DEER, TYPICAL ANTLERS 126-1/8

Robert G. McDonald

Want to kill a record Coues' deer? Buckle on your backpack, lighten your rifle, and hunt the wilderness of Arizona's mountains for 20 years. I did! It wasn't easy, and there were times when I wanted to give up, but the rewards were many, many more than I envisioned in the beginning. Let me begin this story at the start of my last hunt.

My muscles tensed, then recoiled upwards, propelling me to a standing position with the pack. The first steps were a bit awkward, then my strides began to flow rhythmically toward the mountain. I looked up and it seemed to lie there, tantalizingly hiding my quarry in jumbled topography. "The climb will be tougher this year," I thought, "With food for 17 days in the pack. How many hunts have I made for these Coues' deer? It has to be close to 20. This is my 17th consecutive hunt since I killed the big mule deer in 1969, and I hunted them three other years, so this is the 20th one."

"Rrrrip," a catclaw grabs a thread from my wool pants. "Too bad I can't wear blue jeans," I thought, "But if it rains or snows, jeans are wet and cold compared to wool. And, it probably will rain; look at the clouds scudding across the desert to the southwest."

I pick up the fallen sprout of a flowering yucca and use it as a walking staff. Later, it will double as a support for my binoculars, so I can glass while standing. Now the mountain steepens, so that each step is labored. "Don't think about how far it is, just keep trudging up the mountain; it seems quicker that way," I tell myself.

Now, I am above the cholla and catclaw. But, I can never make the climb without a stab in the calf from a shindagger.

At the first live oak, I am heartened because I remember that the ridge is less steep and it is not far to the campsite. As I set up camp, the clouds pile up against the mountain above and a drizzle begins. Hurriedly, I tie off the fly so I have shelter in front of the tent to cook and eat.

It rained all night and is still coming down in the morning. The canyons roar with runoff and I'm glad the season doesn't open for five days. That will give me time to wait out the storm and then scout for my elusive buck. The tent hasn't leaked a drop, and it is warm and cozy inside. I put down the book I am reading and I begin thinking of my first hunt for Arizona whitetail.

I met my brother Fred in Springerville, Arizona. It took us an hour, driving south on the Coronado Trail, to get to the Rim road. We turned and bumped down that road for two miles to its end. From there, only a trail tracked the Rim for eight miles west to Rose Spring. And that is what fascinated us about the area, no roads. Neither of us had made a backpack hunt before and we were excited with senses of discovery and exploration. Three miles down the trail (and down 600 feet elevation to 8,500 feet), pine, fir, and aspen forested the top of the Rim. On its steep southern face (a 2,000 foot drop, slightly less steep than bluff), Gambel and live oak, juniper, and mountain mahogany were thick. During our three-day hunt, we saw does and bucks, a cougar, and elk, but not another hunter. We were disappointed after missing shots, but the experience was so satisfying that I knew wilderness hunting would become a way of life for me.

Two years later, I shot my first Coues' buck on the Rim. It was a mature buck and for the moment I was satisfied. While packing out, however, I thought, "Can I find a really big buck? One that will make the Boone and Crockett records book? Possibly, if I persist and don't shoot the little ones." Those thoughts spawned a change in my hunting ethic that led me down a difficult, yet rewarding, trail for the next 20 years.

I continued to hunt the Rim for several years. Every hunt there turned up a good buck, but I never saw one that met my standards. Then, I turned my focus to the mountains of southeastern Arizona. I scrutinized maps and records books. My Tucson hunting friends (and venerable Coues' deer hunters) John Doyle and Jim Levy gave me advice. After digesting it all, mountain ranges with names of Indian and Spanish origin (like Chiricahua, Santa Catalina, San Cayetano, and Tumacacori, to name a few) beckoned to me because of their roadless areas and frequent listings in the Boone and Crockett Club records book.

I hunted these territories, with my oldest son, Jon, sharing my campfires for three hunts. Then, he moved from my home and I lengthened my hunts to a full week, later to two weeks and more. Then Cosine, my Labrador retriever, became my only hunting companion, as my other friends couldn't spend that much time.

With Cosine's company I hunted the southern ranges for five years without finding a record rack. But I can't say the hunts were unsuccessful; discovering the mountains and their wildlife was my reward. On my 15th hunt I finally saw what I now think was a buck well above B&C minimum. But, he was walking at a steady pace and I couldn't be sure of his score, so I didn't shoot. From my backpack camp, I hunted for another eight days, but I couldn't relocate him.

Now the rain has stopped. The silence abruptly halts my reminiscing and, after lunch, this hunt begins. Taking only the camera until opening day, a routine is developed. After an evening meal of freeze-dried dinner, I pack a lunch; go to bed; leave camp before dawn; and make a different circle each day, returning at dark. Deer are seen, but the mountain successfully hides the big one.

Opening day arrives and I take the .223 Ruger single-shot rifle. (I know its limitations: running or long-range shots must not be taken. However, it is worth the handicaps because the 5-1/2 pound weight, helped by a lightened barrel, is hardly noticed in the pack.) My routine continues for an additional five days, then I decide to move camp to new territory. Although the distance is not far as the crow flies, a labyrinth of a canyon intervenes and the hike takes three hours.

That afternoon, with the sun waning on the western horizon, a thunderstorm building in the foothills suddenly blossoms to full strength. It is as if a curtain is pulled across the sky, and twilight engulfs the area. The distant lightning and choruses of thunder mesmerize me; then, my trance is broken by the tinkle of a rock rolling to my left.

Looking in that direction for a minute or two, I see only empty landscape. My focus wavers, then wanders to a mesquite-dotted slope below. Again to my left, with startling suddenness, a buck is there. He stepped from behind an oak less than 20 yards away. Mutual recognition is almost instantaneous. Like a tyro, I am pinned with my rifle lying on the rock beside me.

His rack looks awesome as he stands silhouetted against burnt red clouds; for the second time ever, a sure record-book deer is in front of me. Saying a few silent epithets about the hopelessness of my situation, I s-l-o-w-l-y move my hand toward the rifle. The deer snorts, runs, and is swallowed by the boiling black clouds as the storm moves in.

That evening, while lightning bolts dance across the desert to the south, I note in my diary that the big buck's inside spread was about 16 inches, exceptionally wide for a Coues' deer and very likely of records book dimensions. I stare into the flickering campfire and recall the probable record rack I saw on my 15th hunt. I hope that I will be luckier this year and relocate this big buck.

The next day, I hunt in the direction the big buck went, but I see only two does and a small buck. Time is running out. Tomorrow will be the 13th day of the hunt, and only three days supply of food remains.

The eastern sky is colored with pink pastel, but Venus still flickers visibly in the western horizon when I leave camp the following morning. I sit down on a knob east of my camp and glass a small buck meandering down a gently sloping ridge. I watch him for a while, then look elsewhere. I sweep the binoculars back to the buck and I am unnerved to see a huge buck a few yards below the small one. A doe is with the big one.

They are a half-mile away, so I set up my spotting scope. Turning the focus sharp, I gasp. The big buck is the one that pinned me on the rock two days ago. My blood pressure ratchets up several notches, but years of acquired patience soon settles me down to watch until they bed. Soon they do, the small buck about 25 yards up the ridge from the doe and big buck.

The canyon runs to the desert floor to my left, and it rises to its source to my right. The opposite side of the canyon is a jumble of terrace steps punctuated with granite chimneys marching up to the ridge to where the deer are. I reject a direct approach; the deer will immediately see me. I rule out a couple of other possibilities and elect to go to my right, down the ridge of the knob until I am able to drop into the canyon, out of sight of the deer.

I walk down the canyon to a sharp bend (a pre-planned spot) and climb to a lip of a terrace. I can see the deer, but I am not within range of the .223. The only way to get closer is to crawl, so I shed my pack. Then, with rifle on my belly, I slither down a rocky swale on my butt. Soon I am low enough so that a chimney rock conceals me from the deer. I climb the rock and peer over its top.

The obscure outline of the big buck is seen through a mesquite bush. The small buck is in plain view, higher up the ridge, so I can't get any closer. But, at 120 yards, I am within range of my rifle. I decide to wait for the big guy to stand and give me a clear shot.

Maybe 30 minutes pass, then the little buck gets up and strolls over the ridge, out of my sight. "Now's my chance," I think, and I stealthily advance to another chimney. I peek over it and suffer mixed emotions. The big buck is in plain view at a distance of about 60 yards but he is facing directly away from me. I don't want to risk a shot into his rear or head, so once again I restrain myself and hope the deer will soon stand. Carefully, I ease into a sitting position. The wait begins.

Time interminable passes. The rocks I sit on gouge and torture my motionless figure while I anxiously watch the buck nod his great head. Then, with the suddenness of a flash of lightning, the buck is up and out of sight. My confidence plummets into despair. However, a flicker of hope returns when the doe walks up the ridge. Then she looks directly my way. Sensing danger, she snorts and stomps the ground, bringing the small buck to his feet.

Exercising powers of will unknown to me, I sit, hardly twitching an eyelash. Finally the doe relaxes and ambles back down the ridge. A shadowy movement from behind a leafless mesquite alerts me that the big buck is still here. I recall leaving my extra cartridges in the pack; this must be a one-shot kill. The buck steps into a clearing and I squeeze the trigger. He staggers two or three steps, then goes down. One would expect me to give a big "whoopee," but I didn't. It was 2:40 p.m., more than five hours since I saw the deer, and I had been sitting on the rocks for two or three hours. I stand up and it feels so good that I don't get very excited.

I walk over to the deer and I am overcome with contradictory emotions of elation and remorse that perhaps only a hunter can have after making a kill. I look at his rack and it is bigger than I thought. I also look at his teeth and guess his age as between six and eight years, an old-timer.

Some two months later, I took the skull and cape to John Doyle, a master taxidermist, for mounting and measuring. The rack was scored at 128 for the entry measurement. As I told the story of the hunt to this long-time friend, it was also with mixed emotions. I thought of the pride of accomplishment, yet I sensed the end of an era.

For 20 years, I had annually looked forward to these exciting and spiritually rewarding hunts. Now my enthusiasm is diminished by the loss of two friends: Cosine died a year later and I have learned of the passing of John Doyle. But when I walk back over the wilderness, feel the warm desert breeze on my back and watch the sunset in the west, I think of the memories, wonderful memories, of Cosine and John Doyle, who now do their hunting in the great beyond; of the camaraderie of my son Jon; and of the immeasurable pleasure of my association with the wilderness and its wildlife.

Photographs Courtesy of John W. Schnider, Jr., and Michael D. Gatlin

(l) John W. Schnider, Jr., took this typical whitetail while bowhunting in Lake County, Illinois, in late 1987. It scores 161-1/8 points. (r) Michael D. Gatlin with typical whitetail he took in Seward County, Kansas, in 1987. With six abnormal points, it scores 185 points in the typical category.

Photograph Courtesy of Steven J. Sperl

Steven J. Sperl bagged this 206-7/8 point non-typical whitetail with a 15 yard shot from his 12 gauge shotgun. He took it in 1987 in Stearns County, Minnesota.

Photograph by Wm. H. Nesbitt

COUES' WHITETAIL DEER, TYPICAL ANTLERS
SECOND AWARD
SCORE: 123-6/8

Locality: Cochise Co., Ariz.   Date: December 1985
Hunter: Larry Vance, Jr.

COUES' WHITETAIL DEER, TYPICAL ANTLERS 123-6/8

Larry Vance, Jr.

There was a foot of snow on the ground, but we could see stars all across the sky. The time was about 5:45 a.m. The coffee sure hit the spot as my partner, Mike Daugherty, and I sat at the foot of a high ridge, near the south end of the Chiricahua Mountains, waiting for daybreak. We were going to separate and hunt the northeast side, while my friends, Lenard Maddux and his son Jimmy, would hunt the southwest side. Lenard and I had done some scouting in the area with spotting scopes and we had decided that the area was a good bet for a late season whitetail. The country is extremely steep and rough, with heavy scrub brush patches here and there, and oak, juniper, and pinon pine trees. The higher ridges, where I was now headed, gave good visibility back down into some of those brush patches and trees, from hundreds of yards to over a thousand yards away.

As I crossed through some brush on a small ridge about two thirds of the way to the top, I jumped three does and a fawn. They weren't really spooked, as they kept stopping to look back. I held still and watched them. It wasn't quite light enough, or late enough, to legally shoot, so I watched those four deer feed over a ridge about 600 yards above me. About 30 minutes later, I was looking at eight more deer, about 400 yards away across a big canyon. One of them was a small buck. The rest were all does.

I wasn't interested in the buck as I had already killed a "meat" buck on the early hunt near Patagonia, Arizona, with my other tag. These deer were in rut, so I figured my best bet was to sit tight for a few minutes and see if a big buck was interested in those does. Sure enough, there he was, about 25 yards above the does. I couldn't believe how big his rack was. I positioned myself behind an old stump for a shot, as there wasn't any practical way of getting closer. I had my Remington 700 ADL .30-06, so the range wasn't a real problem.

Suddenly, the big buck took off like a bat-out-of-hell, and then I heard a shot. I led the deer by about a body-length-and-a-half and squeezed off my shot. Bolting another round as another shot went off about 45 degrees to my right, I tried another shot at the buck. My partner Mike shot again, as did I. The big buck, who had been joined by the smaller one, disappeared over the ridge, and the does crossed a few hundred yards further to the west. I quickly picked up my brass and put three fresh rounds into the magazine.

About 45 minutes later, after an exhausting march through the loose rock covered by 12-

18 inches of snow, I was looking at a small spot of blood in the snow where the two bucks had crossed the ridge. Mike finally got there about five minutes later and he was as excited about that deer's rack as I was. He explained that he had spotted the deer the same way I did, and he was about 300 yards from them when he shot.

Both Mike and I have killed big whitetails, and we have seen many others, but nothing like that. There was no way of knowing which one of us drew blood on that buck, but we were both certain, judging from the small, far-apart specks of blood, and the way the buck ran off, that he wasn't seriously hurt. I decided that with all the snow on the ground I should be able to find the buck again. We took off on the tracks as fast as possible, but we were slowed way down by the route the bucks took. After crossing the ridge heading west, they had made an abrupt turn and headed northeast, into and across one of the steepest and roughest canyons in the area. It took us about two hours to cross that canyon and get to the top of the next ridge.

Mike had decided to work his way to a saddle further up so that he might cut the tracks if the deer headed back west when they crossed the ridge I was on. They took another sharp turn to the right, crossing another small ridge, and turned hard left. The tracks indicated that they were beginning to feed and they had split up, the bigger buck continuing on to higher ground and the smaller one to my right.

It was about noon, and I was almost to the top of the canyon, when I took a break. While I was drinking juice and eating my peanut butter sandwich, a small buck showed up across the canyon. I watched him feeding to my left and into a small clump of brush. I made some noise with my gear as I got up to get back to the task at hand. All of a sudden, the old boy I was after jumped up about 15 yards in front of me and headed toward the bottom of the canyon (about 100 yards below me). I sat down quickly, knowing that when he crossed the canyon, he would be mine. He sailed across the canyon bottom and started up the other side, and I proceeded to empty my rifle at him. Quickly I yanked my cartridge pouch open and shot four more times at him as he went up the opposite canyon wall.

I grabbed two more rounds out of my pouch. Realizing something must be wrong with my scope, I looked along the barrel and pulled the trigger. The range was probably about 300-350 yards. Damned if that bullet didn't hit the rock the buck was jumping, and then hit him. He lost his footing in the mud and slush of the now rapidly melting snow. It took the buck a minute to get back on his feet. I fired another along-the-barrel shot as he slowly made his way up the ridge and into some brush.

About that time, Mike came over the ridge and asked me where the buck was. I told Mike the buck was hit hard, but my rifle was off and I couldn't hit him again. I pointed out the spot where I last saw the buck. As Mike watched, I noticed the smaller buck had reappeared farther along the ridge, looking at something about where the big buck disappeared.

The small buck's gaze shifted slightly higher and, finally, he quit looking at his side of the mountain and was looking back at us. I thought maybe the old boy was down, so I sat there and watched as Mike went across to the spot where I last saw the big buck. The buck wasn't there, but there was some blood, and tracks, to follow.

The temperature had risen to about 60 degrees and the snow was quickly turning to muddy slush. By the time I got to Mike, tracks and blood were almost a thing of the past. We crisscrossed the area for about an hour, with not a hint of where the buck had gone. I decided to work my way across some little shady spots where there was still some snow, and then to the bottom of the main canyon, in case the buck headed down the hill. Mike said he would stay on top, so that he wouldn't have to climb out of that canyon again.

After about three hours of crisscrossing the bottom of the canyon I was beginning to doubt that I would find the old boy, and I was afraid that he would die a painful and lingering death.

I was mentally kicking myself every step I took for not shooting my rifle after the first hunt. While dragging my other buck down a steep, slick slope, I lost my footing and fell pretty hard. My tail end absorbed most of the shock, and my rifle didn't seem to hit anything. I just took for granted that all was well, but here it was about to cost me the trophy of a lifetime and leave a wounded animal in the field.

As I hiked back up and out of the canyon, I decided to take the long way back to swing by the canyon where I had first seen the old boy so that I could glass the canyon at dusk. As I neared the top of the ridge, I started glassing. About 1,000 yards away, on the very far side of the canyon, I spotted a huge buck standing in a small patch of snow under an oak tree. I couldn't believe there was another buck like the one I was chasing in the same area. After a few minutes, the buck started moving down into the canyon and I'll be damned if he wasn't limping. There he was, and I had another chance at him.

It took me a few minutes to calm down and decide how best to approach the buck. I knew that I had to get close without spooking him, yet cover close to 1,000 yards before the sun went down. My best bet was to let him go for now; he was headed down hill to a small seep. I gave him about five minutes, then I took off for the edge of the canyon as fast as I could move, without waking the dead.

When I reached the edge, I let my breathing return to normal, then I chambered one of my last seven rounds. Peeking over the edge, I saw him about 100 yards below me, still limping slowly along the opposite side of the canyon and headed for the seep. I moved quickly to a dead century plant stalk below me, and I laid my pack on it for a rest. The buck noticed the commotion and tried to run, but he was too stiff to run.

My first shot hit about a foot high and a foot behind him. My second and third shots hit about the same spot, so I held under and in front of him by about a foot. He was now over 150 yards away when I squeezed the trigger. His front legs went out from under him, but he got back up and continued. I knew that if I went straight at him, he would probably give me the slip again as I couldn't catch up with him after crossing the canyon. The sun was almost behind the mountains now.

I stayed on my side of the canyon and yelled at the buck several times. I figured that if he realized that he couldn't outrun me, then he might just decide to brush up and hide. If he once lay down to hide, I could probably walk right up on him. Finally, after about five minutes of my yelling, and his stumbling, he went into a thick patch of bear grass and mountain mahogany and disappeared.

After yelling a few more times at him, and throwing some big rocks into the bottom of the canyon, I was convinced that he would hold tight and try to hide. I had taken about a dozen steps toward the bottom of the canyon when another buck jumped out of a brush patch not five feet from me, just like a cottontail, and high-tailed it. I think that probably took five years off my life. After collecting my wits, I crossed the canyon and found my buck's tracks above the spot where I had fired my last shot at him. About 10 yards further, I found where he had gone down. He was now bleeding heavily and was easy to follow.

I put one of my last four rounds into the chamber. I had eased along the buck's trail for about 200 yards when I spotted his antlers sticking up through some bear grass, about 25 yards in front of me. I eased along until I was about five yards behind him and then stopped. He slowly turned his head toward me. As we made eye contact, he jumped to his feet and I broke his back. That was the 17th shot and it finally killed him. I stood there for about 10 minutes, admiring him. Finally, I heard Mike coming and I yelled for him to tell him that I had finally nailed the big old boy.

While examining the deer, we discovered that the first blood had been caused by a bullet that had just grazed the navel. No damage was done to the muscle tissue, but a subcutaneous vein had been cut. When I had hit the deer about noon with the ricochet, the bullet had flattened out on the rock, hitting him in the right hind hock and traveling up the leg bone, stopping on the top of his hip. The third hit broke his right front leg below the knee.

We took some pictures in the last few minutes of light and then dressed the buck. Mike headed out of the canyon with my rifle and most of my gear. As I headed to the bottom of the canyon with my prize, it finally dawned on me that this buck died just before sunset, not 300 yards from where I saw him shortly after sunrise.

I packed the big buck down the bottom of the canyon until about 8 p.m. This canyon wound its way out of the mountain, opening up near where my truck was parked. At about 8 p.m., I realized that I could go no further, as I was stumbling in the near pitch black. I knew that Mike would be coming back up the canyon with flashlights. The temperature was dropping fast now, so I built a small fire to keep warm until I could start moving again.

About the time I started to hang the deer in a tree, Mike and Lenard showed up. I was sure glad to see them, as fatigue was beginning to set in. After admiring the buck and talking about the day's hunt, we decided to leave the buck hanging overnight. I would come back in the morning and finish packing him out. Lenard told me that Jimmy had killed a big buck with a weird rack early that morning.

It was midnight when I finally got to bed, but I was on my way up the canyon with my 10-year-old-daughter Darlyne by 8 a.m. I was so sore and stiff that it took me 3-1/2 hours to finish packing the deer out. On the way home we stopped by Southwestern Taxidermy. Richard Bates, my friend and taxidermist, weighed the buck at 105 pounds.

After 60 days, I sent the rack to John Doyle in Tucson, Arizona, and he officially scored it at 122-5/8. That score put it number 8 in the Arizona Wildlife Federation Records. I took the rack back to Richard and he mounted the head for me. It now hangs on my living room wall, with my other antlers.

This buck is not only the most outstanding trophy I have ever taken, it is by far the hardest earned.

Photograph by Scott Brown

At the 20th Awards, 1989, Goldie Haske accepts a Certificate of Merit for her late husband's typical whitetail from Dr. Philip L. Wright, Chairman Emeritus of the Records Committee.

Photograph by Scott Brown

At the 20th Awards, Walter H. Pollock accepts a Certificate of Merit for his New World's Record non-typical Coues' whitetail from Dr. Philip L. Wright, Chairman Emeritus, Records Committee.

Photograph by Wm. H. Nesbitt

COUES' WHITETAIL DEER, TYPICAL ANTLERS
CERTIFICATE OF MERIT
SCORE: 126-5/8

Locality: Cochise Co., Ariz.　Date: October 1959
Hunter: Mike Kasun　Owner: Mike Kasun, Jr.

COUES' WHITETAIL DEER, TYPICAL ANTLERS 126-5/8

Mike Kasun, hunter
Mike Kasun, Jr., owner

Before dawn one morning, I took off from the truck and walked up a canyon I named Cold Canyon. This was in the Chiracahua Mountains in southeastern Arizona, in October of 1959. I stayed in the bottom of the canyon for about two miles, until I got to a place where I had seen whitetail activity when I was scouting earlier in the year. I was alone this particular morning.

I had jumped a few does on the way up Cold Canyon. After I got to a place that I wanted to watch, I sat down and glassed a draw about 250 yards away. About 40 minutes had gone by when I decided to make a move. As I got up, I immediately sat back down because I thought I saw some movement near a saddle on the opposite side of the draw I was in. It looked like a deer was in a juniper bush. I glassed the bush for 10 more minutes, finally deciding that I was seeing things.

I got up to move, and then the buck stepped partially out from behind the bush. I could tell he had antlers, but I couldn't tell how big because his head was partly in the bush. I carefully raised my .30-06, put the dot in my scope on his neck, and squeezed the trigger. With the shot, he dropped in his tracks. I could see the buck lying on the ground from where I was standing. I started rimming around the draw and over to the area where the deer was. But when I got there, there was no deer, no blood, nothing. I looked for 20 minutes. Then, I had this fear that he had gotten up and run off; that I had just nicked his antler since it was a head shot.

I finally decided to go back over to where I had shot from. I walked to the exact spot, seeing the spent shell on the ground. I looked up, and there he was, down and in the same spot. What a relief!

This time, I walked as the crow flies, straight to the deer. I had no idea the size of the antlers. What a nice surprise! After field dressing the deer, I packed him back to the truck.

When I got back to town, I weighed the buck. He weighed 107 pounds. I also had no idea that he was big enough for Boone and Crockett until years later, when my son got hooked on hunting and had it measured.

Photograph by Wm. H. Nesbitt

COUES' WHITETAIL DEER, NON-TYPICAL ANTLERS
FIRST AWARD
SCORE: 134-2/8
Locality: Yavapai Co., Ariz.   Date: December 1986
Hunter: William B. Bullock

COUES' WHITETAIL DEER, NON-TYPICAL ANTLERS 134-2/8

William B. Bullock

I'm no different from any other trophy hunter. I hunt to see game and enjoy it, not to just fill a tag and go home. I enjoy the country and the aspects of hunting: glassing, stalking to get a closer look, studying the prey, enjoying the incidental wildlife, and simply experiencing natural treats that most non-hunters never even know exist. I'm usually successful at eventually filling my tag, but I most always know that I could have filled it sooner, had I wanted to do only that. However, I must honestly admit that I'm usually just a touch disappointed when I approach my freshly downed quarry; maybe I should have taken the one yesterday, or held out a little longer. Sure he's a nice one, but maybe, just maybe, there's a B&C trophy was out there somewhere.

In the late 1970's, my dad and I began to hunt Coues' whitetails, before they became popular. It seemed that every time we went hunting javelina, quail, mountain lion, or whatever, we found whitetails. Not lots of whitetails, just enough to make us think about a new hunting spot come fall.

Dad had taken a dandy buck in 1973. At 107-1/8, it made the Arizona Records Book, just missing the B&C minimum of 110. Every time I looked at that buck, I began to dream. There had to be bigger ones out there, and most people didn't really care about them.

We found a spot just north of Roosevelt Lake that had a fairly good Coues' deer population. While Arizona hunters must wade through a drawing process to hunt deer in the fall, this particular area was a cinch to get a permit for whitetails only. We had to pack in about three miles, carrying our own water and food. After the first year or two, we had our packing down to a science. While we saw bucks every year, and only one or two other hunters, we actually took only four deer in six years. None scored above the 90's. In the meantime, new hunts were being opened up during the late December rut in north-central Arizona, closer to home. A few bigger bucks were being taken, some approaching, and a few even making, the "book."

In 1985, we both drew permits and decided to give it a try. Dad took a buck midway through the season that was respectable, although still in the 90-point range. I passed up about a dozen decent bucks, looking for that rare exception. I finally took a smaller one to fill my tag on the season's final day. The sound of my rifle had just completed its final echo when I heard rocks roll and then watched a real nice Coues' buck trot off. Of course, he had to stop and look back at 80 yards. I think he even smiled. His beautiful rack would have crowded the "book." If a lion didn't get him, he would probably be there next year. But, would I?

Permits were getting tough to come by. Coues' whitetails had become popular, and not just to trophy hunters. Someone decided that those cute little deer were good eating. I eat wild game year round, and the fact is that they're really not all that good. They're usually tough and dry, and they're strong from being in the rut. But, Lady Luck again gave me a permit in 1986. Maybe this year would be different.

By opening day my hunting partner and I were excited. We still remembered the buck that trotted off on the last day of the year before. We turned on the last two-track road that would lead to "our" favorite country. As we topped the last ridge, we counted three sets of taillights a half-mile or so ahead. Two more vehicles were leaving camps not far ahead of us and heading in the same direction. Since I didn't feel properly invited to that party, I spun the Bronco around and we headed for some "new" country that we had casually looked at while scouting.

An hour later we were looking at a series of rolling pinon pine and juniper ridges that we had never been on before. Glassing looked to be much more difficult than where we had hunted the year before, and we now had a very late start. But something about new country and opening day really gets the juices flowing. It felt good to be hunting whitetails again. It turned into quite a day. As well as seeing several bull elk, we saw over 20 Coues' deer, far more than I normally see in my style of hunting. We saw no respectable bucks, but we did see several smaller ones. We got a "feel" for the country that turned out to be valuable.

The next day, we had a plan of attack. We climbed to a fairly high vantage point that gave us about a 200 degree view, including the heads of two juniper-covered basins. Glassing was tedious. My partner (Steve) and I would spot a deer. That same deer would vanish in the thick trees in seconds, leaving us with strained vision while trying to detect even parts of other deer in that area. I studied likely looking places for as much as 30 minutes, only to see a deer that had been there all along step into view and then disappear again in seconds, leaving me to wonder if I had really seen him at all. Meanwhile, Steve had spotted three does in the open, feeding near a rocky outcropping some distance away.

While Steve is a good hunter, he chose to stay with hunting mule deer for meat. Blessed with an exceptional set of eyes, and being a good friend, I have found him to be very helpful in looking for that special buck and in keeping the hunt lively. I'm sure that many times he has asked himself what in the world I'm waiting for. Moments later, he knew.

It was Steve who spotted the buck. I quickly set up the spotting scope. The eyepiece showed a mass of antlers. I didn't know how many points. I simply stated, "That's him." My next move is normally a stalk.

Steve and I discussed it. We could get to the rocky outcropping, but we would take a chance of spooking the three does and probably never see the buck. The other direction was out of the question, too low. Due to the lay of the land, a move in any direction to shorten the distance would cut off our view. We had to try it from there. We guessed the distance at 450 yards.

I knew that the Remington 7 mm Mag could do the job, I just didn't know if I could. I have to admit I was nervous. I found a rest, and Steve set up to call the location of my shots, should I miss. I settled the cross hairs until they lay right on the buck's back. My instincts told me to hold higher, but I have always believed that I should never hold off an animal on the first shot. I squeezed. The buck jumped forward, toward us by about five yards, and stood dead-still. I thought I had hit him. Steve had flinched at the blast and wasn't sure what had happened. As I chambered another shell, the buck disappeared. Seconds later, Steve spotted him again, slowly moving uphill.

When the buck stopped again, I raised my hold slightly and fired. "You're low! Below his feet," Steve said. Again the buck was on the move. When he finally stopped, I held four feet above him and fired again, and again. "You're still low," was all I heard. The buck topped the ridge and disappeared over it, pausing just long enough for Steve to gasp at the antler structure. Meanwhile, I desperately tried to reload.

We spent the next two hours trying to find blood, tracks, or any sign of the deer, but to no avail. On the ride home, we tried to assess the situation. We decided that my first shot must have been barely low; it probably sprayed the deer's back with rocks or brush on impact. My last shot was at least 200 yards longer than my first shot. But, the season was young and there were plenty of does around. We hoped we could find the buck again. I was definitely after only one deer.

We had planned to skip the next day, but the thought of that buck was more than I could take. I called Steve that night and he was ready to go. My 12-year-old son went along the next day. He watched with his mouth open as a high-90 to low-100 point buck lay down about 500 yards away. He was a nice 3-point (actually an 8-point by eastern count). Arizonans have a funny habit of ignoring the first point on any deer, calling it an "eye guard." In many cases, that's the biggest point on a Coues' deer. At any rate, my buck was not to be seen on that day, or on the next three hunting days I had over the next week-and-a-half. With each day, I learned more about the country. Occasionally I spotted some large tracks that I hoped were his, but I really believed that they were made by a passing mulie.

In the meantime, word had gotten out that I had missed a huge, non-typical whitetail. Luckily, no one else was hunting the area, since the country really doesn't look like typical whitetail country. My dad had gotten a nice buck that scored about 97. He had over-estimated it in the field, mostly due to foggy conditions. But that had me convinced that "my" buck wasn't as big as I had first thought.

By 7:15 Christmas Eve morning, Steve and I were heading back to our vantage point. Two deer were working the hillside to the right of the rocky outcropping. I set up the spotting scope and looked. It was HIM! In our earlier confrontation he had been to the left of the outcrop. The previous outings had served as an education. I felt that I could make a stalk this time.

We dropped down to our left and, in minutes, we were completely out of any sightline to the deer, who were about 500 yards away. The doe was feeding, and the rut had begun.

The buck couldn't take his eyes off the doe. We moved along quickly and quietly, Steve staying about 30 yards behind. If anyone was going to blow it, Steve was making sure it would be me. As I approached the outcrop, I eased up behind a small cedar tree. I couldn't see the deer or find the right spot. I backed off and moved further up the ridge. As I moved to the edge again, I reached down for my field glasses and eased them up to my eyes. They came to focus right on the buck. He was about 200 yards out, still watching the doe. I put my hand down and Steve stopped, recognizing my signal.

I had nowhere to take a rest. I couldn't risk another move until both deer were out of sight again in the brush. Finally, they moved and so did I. I found an open spot behind a huge juniper tree and sat down, exposing just enough of myself so that I could see clearly. Another doe appeared from above, walking downhill toward the other two. I breathed a sigh of relief that she had not seen me, even though I never knew she was there.

When the doe disappeared, I stood and positioned myself behind a chest-high rock. I decided to start glassing with my scope instead of my binoculars. As I patiently watched, the first doe moved from behind a giant patch of prickly pear. As she did, the buck stepped into view, slightly quartering away from me. I positioned the cross hairs right behind his right shoulder and squeezed.

This time, there was no doubt. I recovered from the recoil in time to see the buck somersault down the hill and land under a big cedar tree. Steve was at my side in seconds. I held the gun, with the scope fixed on the tree where I'd last seen the buck. I had been shooting across a shallow ravine. As we moved toward the deer, I could see the spot clearly until we bottomed-out. From then on we hurried until we came to the big patch of prickly pear. From there, we circled around for what seemed like minutes, although I'm sure it was only seconds until I spotted the back of one huge antler in the brush beneath the cedar tree.

As Steve and I hauled the buck from beneath the tree, I was completely amazed. I had never dared to imagine that the buck was actually that big. The big tracks we had seen were his. His front feet were as big as a good mule deer. I guessed his score to be about 135, non-typical. He weighed 117 pounds. By Boone and Crockett standards, he had nine measurable points on his right antler and seven on his left. He was very heavily palmated and webbed, unlike any pictures I had ever seen. A 2-3/4 inch drop point was on his right antler, and his left antler sported a forked point that stuck straight out to the side.

I thoroughly enjoyed the next few hours. Dressing the buck and dragging him out was a pleasure. The following morning (Christmas), we green scored him at 137-7/8. Two-and-a-half months later, Mike Cupell officially scored him for entry at 138-7/8. Steve wrote an article capturing his views of the hunt titled "Trophy Buck For Christmas" that was later published in the Christmas edition of the Arizona Hunter and Angler Magazine. The Arizona Republic newspaper made mention of the buck the following spring. That beautiful buck was definitely a trophy hunter's dream, not taken strictly by chance, but with a measure of persistence and patience. He was my buck-of-a-lifetime.

Photographs Courtesy of Bryan J. McGann and Ronald K. Osborne

(l) Bryan J. McGann killed this non-typical whitetail that scores 220-7/8 points in Sauk County, Wisconsin, in 1986. (r) Mahoning County, Ohio, was the location of Ronald K. Osborne's 1986 whitetail hunt that yielded this non-typical that scores 243 points.

Photograph Courtesy of Frank E. Safford

Frank E. Safford used mules to pack into a remote area of the Chiricahua Mountains of Arizona where he took this non-typical Coues' whitetail that scores 111-6/8 points.

Photograph by Wm. H. Nesbitt

COUES' WHITETAIL DEER, NON-TYPICAL ANTLERS
SECOND AWARD
SCORE: 131-3/8
Locality: Cochise Co., Ariz.   Date: December 1986
Hunter: Eric M. Thorsrud

COUES' WHITETAIL DEER, NON-TYPICAL ANTLERS 131-3/8

Erik M. Thorsrud

Arizona has many delights to offer the big-game sportsman. One of the most delicate of these is the tiny Coues' whitetail deer. Found only in a few desert areas of the southwest, this miniature replica of the common whitetail is avidly sought by those who know it, and it rewards hard hunting with a chase full of pleasant memories.

Erik M. Thorsrud lives in Tucson, Arizona. Not surprising, he hunts in his home state. In 1986, he had one of his most memorable Coues' whitetail deer hunts. On that hunt, he was hunting in Cochise County near Klondyke.

Thorsrud's hunt took place in mid-December, with weather that was good hunting, but rough on hunters. He arrived at his hunting area on the 17th of December, and he took his fine trophy on December 20th. On that day, the sky was heavily overcast and it was lightly raining. Those are good conditions for stalking most any kind of game. Thorsrud caught up with his trophy at 2 p.m., at a distance of 100 yards. He used a .270 with a 130 grain bullet.

Thorsrud knew that he had a fine trophy, but he didn't expect that it would be one of the finest taken in the three years of the 20th Awards entry period. It made this hunt truly one to remember always.

Photograph by Tim E. Kelly

**NEW WORLD'S RECORD COUES' WHITETAIL DEER, NON-TYPICAL ANTLERS
CERTIFICATE OF MERIT**

SCORE: 158-4/8

Locality: Santa Cruz Co., Ariz.   Date: Prior to 1988
Picked up by Walter H. Pollock   On Display: B&C National Collection

COUES' WHITETAIL DEER, NON-TYPICAL ANTLERS 158-4/8

Walter H. Pollock, owner

Little did I know what lay in store for me when I left my home in Boulder, Colorado, on the 2nd of January 1988. My friends, Joe Ruwitch and John Kline, and I had been planning our annual bird hunting trip to Arizona ever since we had returned from the previous year's hunt. Joe and I have been hunting quail in Arizona for the last six years.

We arrived in the small town of Patagonia, where we had reservations to stay at the small casita of Dennis and Laura Parker. They have been our hospitable hosts for the last five years. After checking in with Dennis and Laura, we visited with Steve and Beth Hopkins. Steve is a local taxidermist, well versed in the ways of the Mearns' quail, the species that we had come south to hunt. Steve filled us in on the conditions to expect in hunting this year. It seems they had a smaller than average hatch; hunting would be harder than usual.

True to Steve's word, we did find the hunting slow but none-the-less exciting. We were hunting behind three English setters and one pointer, and all the dogs were finding birds. We had hunted for seven days when Joe said we should go to his number one place, where we always found birds. So, off we went to the Patagonia Mountains. We had hunted most of the morning, with some success, and we were returning to the vehicles when, as I was walking through a little glen, something lying on the ground caught my eye.

I walked over and saw small deer antlers lying on the ground, just waiting to be picked up. All that remained, besides the skull and antlers, was a small amount of hair that formed an outline of the deer's body. I thought these were small antlers because I am used to looking at mule deer antlers back in Colorado. I remembered that Steve had told me that if I ever found any Coues' deer antlers, he could always use them in his practice.

I picked them up and started back. Meanwhile, Joe and John had come up and were admiring my find. They asked what I was going to do with it. I said, "Take it back for Steve to look at." On the way back, the dogs found two coveys. Each time, I dropped the antlers so I could take a shot. Each time, I would go back and pick up the antlers. I thought to myself, "I sure hope Steve appreciates this."

We had to cross a couple of fences; each time, I would drop the antlers on the other side and pick them up, then proceed toward the truck. When we arrived at the truck, we needed some wood, so we gathered some limbs that were lying under the tree we had parked under.

I then threw the rack in and Joe said, "Maybe we need some more wood." We got out and threw on more wood, over antlers and all.

On the way back, John kept making remarks about how nice the rack was, and I sensed that maybe he would like them, so I asked him if he'd like to have them. He excitedly said, "Yes." I replied that he probably could.

After we arrived back in Patagonia, I was unloading the wood when Dennis drove up and asked how we did. I told him that we had found five coveys and a deer rack. He took a look at the antlers and his eyes got big. He said he had been looking for a rack like this for ages. He said it probably would place in the Boone and Crockett records. I turned to John and told him I was a "taker-backer," and I had better keep the rack until I found out more about it.

Dennis asked if he could take the rack to his friend, Ross, and they would measure it. When he returned later in the night, he and Ross thought that the rack would go in the top three of the non-typical division. Meanwhile, Steve got word that I had found something and he came over to look. He concurred with Dennis that it was a nice rack and we should take it to John Doyle, who had a shop in Tucson and who could measure it. Since I had to leave for Boulder the next day, Steve said that he would take the rack to John for a measurement. John measured the antlers at around 159 points and said it was a magnificent specimen.

When Steve called me in a couple of days with the news, I knew I had literally stumbled into the records book.

Note: This New World's Record non-typical Coues' deer is now on continuing display in the Boone and Crockett Club's National Collection of Heads and Horns in the Buffalo Bill Historical Center, Cody, Wyoming. Walter Pollock came to an agreement with Wm. H. Nesbitt during the 20th Awards activities to make a continuing loan of this trophy to the Club's collection so that the vast numbers of hunters and others who visit the BBHC each year can enjoy seeing the finest known specimen of this category.

Photograph Courtesy of James M. Machac

James M. Machac proudly displays the typical Coues' whitetail that he shot in the Baboquivari Mountains of southern Arizona in 1985. Machac's buck scores 114-4/8 points.

Photograph Courtesy of George Martin

George Martin struck "gold" in the Superstition Mountains of Arizona when he found this typical Coues' whitetail that scores 115 points. He dropped it with his .284 Winchester in 1983.

Photograph by Wm. H. Nesbitt

COUES' WHITETAIL DEER, NON-TYPICAL ANTLERS
CERTIFICATE OF MERIT
SCORE: 134-2/8

Locality: Sonora, Mexico   Date: Prior to 1986
Hunter: Unknown   Owner: Ronald D. Hyatt

COUES' WHITETAIL DEER, NON-TYPICAL ANTLERS 134-2/8

Ronald D. Hyatt, owner

Ron Hyatt started hunting whitetail deer in old Mexico several years ago. Through contacts, Ron met a rancher by the name of Carlos Morales who has property in the states of Coahuila and Sonora. Mr. Morales is president of the Coahuila Cattlemen's Association.

Ron hunts whitetail deer on Mr. Morales' ranch near Sabinas in Coahuila State. There are no Coues' deer on Mr. Morales' property in Coahuila. The only deer from Mexico eligible for entry in the Coues' whitetail deer category are those taken in the states of Sonora and Chihuahua.

Since Ron knows very little Mexican, and Mr. Morales only knows broken English, they communicated through sign language and the few words each knows in the other's language. However, Ron understood Mr. Morales quite clearly when the latter told him on Ron's second trip to Mexico that he had a nice Coues' deer rack. Mr. Morales had received the rack from a ranch hand who manages his Sonora property.

When Ron asked if he could see the big rack for the "little" deer, Mr. Morales retrieved the antlers from a storage shed. After admiring the rack, Ron asked if he could have them. Since they were taking up valuable space in the storage shed, and he didn't have any interest in them, Mr. Morales told Ron he could keep the rack.

While Mr. Morales may not have fully appreciated the massive size of this rack, Ron had no doubt that it was trophy quality. He got in touch with one of the Club's Official Measurers in Texas and had the rack scored. It was good enough to be invited to the Final Awards of the 20th Awards entry period.

Photograph by Wm. H. Nesbitt

COUES' WHITETAIL DEER, NON-TYPICAL ANTLERS
CERTIFICATE OF MERIT
SCORE: 132
Locality: Sonora, Mexico   Date: Prior to 1988
Owner: Harry P. Samarin

COUES' WHITETAIL DEER, NON-TYPICAL ANTLERS 132

Harry P. Samarin, owner

I wish I could write you a beautiful story about hunting the Coues' deer buck that I submitted for your records book. But, the only thing that I can say is that this rack was given to me.

In January 1988, Baldimar Salinas was going on a trip to buy cattle in Hermasillo, Mexico, from a cattleman named Jesse Acheta. While visiting the ranch and inspecting the cattle, the conversation turned toward deer hunting. Mr. Acheta informed me that it was not allowed on the ranch, but the cowboys had been picking up deer heads as they were found. He also told me of a real nice antler set about an hour's drive away. Being on a working vacation, I drove up to look at them.

To say I was impressed with those antlers is an understatement. I brought them back to show Alan Jensen and Baldimar. I then informed Jesse that they were a very nice set of antlers. Jesse said that since I liked them so much, he would give them to me as a gift.

I took them home knowing that they were a nice set, but I never imagined that they would score as high as they did. It would have been a real pleasure to have gotten them hunting, but just to make the book is an honor in itself.

Photograph by Wm. H. Nesbitt

MULE DEER, TYPICAL ANTLERS
FIRST AWARD
SCORE: 207-4/8
Locality: Washington Co., Utah   Date: October 1987
Hunter: John K. Frei

MULE DEER, TYPICAL ANTLERS 207-4/8

John K. Frei

It was deer hunting season 1987. My hunting partners, Wayne Wittwer and Kevin Lounsbury, and I drew licenses in a Southern Utah area. We had scouted the area prior to the hunt, spotting only a few deer. We left town on the 16th of October, destined for our hunting camp.

The morning of opening day, we saddled our horses and got an early start, each of us going in different directions so that we could cover more ground. We had no luck the first day, although Kevin came back to camp saying that he had spotted a big buck he called "Blackhorn." Not thinking much about Blackhorn, we all awaited a new day.

The second day, we went our separate ways again and Kevin headed for the area where he had seen Blackhorn. Kevin did spot the deer again, but he could never get close enough to him to get a clear shot. Kevin did spot another excellent buck in the area and followed it until he could get a good shot that succeeded. When he returned to camp, he told us his success story and that Blackhorn was in the area where he had shot his buck.

On the 19th of October, the third day of the hunt, Wayne and I saddled up and took off. Wayne wanted to ride higher up on the mountain but his horse was showing signs of a sore back. So we traded horses and I set off for the area where Blackhorn had been spotted.

The day was crisp and clear. I was riding along without a clue to what I was about to encounter. I spotted the deer below me. I followed him until I could get a clear shot. As I continued to follow him, the adrenalin was pumping faster and excitement rising higher. I finally got a clear shot with my .30-06.

Riding back into camp, I told my partners that Blackhorn was dead. Getting the deer out was no easy task. We had to carry the deer to where we could load it on horses. While loading it on my horse, he got spooked and took off, heading back to camp. We did eventually get the deer out.

I never realized how large this buck was until I got it into town and people there kept telling me that it would score high points. I knew that it was a nice-sized buck, but I didn't think it would score as high as it did. Now I know different.

Photograph by Wm. H. Nesbitt

MULE DEER, TYPICAL ANTLERS
SECOND AWARD
SCORE: 205-2/8
Locality: Carbon Co., Wyo.   Date: October 1986
Hunter: Shelly R. Risner

MULE DEER, TYPICAL ANTLERS 205-2/8

Shelly R. Risner

The 1986 deer hunting season was about over. My husband and a couple who had camped with us had all taken really nice bucks, but I hadn't gotten a chance at a good one, even though I had seen a lot of deer. (I won't shoot at anything unless it is standing still; because of this, I had passed on some nice bucks.) We had come home to get ready for elk season. We hunt deer and elk out of the same camp, in the Medicine Bow National Forest.

My husband (Jack) and son (Travis) went back to camp to cut firewood. When they came home that night, they said that they had seen a Boone and Crockett buck that day and to get ready and we would go back in the morning to see if we could find him. It was the last day of deer season, so at 4 a.m. the next morning we headed back up the mountain.

It was before daylight when we got to where they had spotted the buck, so we waited until we could see good before starting out to a point to see if we could see something. We didn't spot anything out there, so we got back in the pickup to go around to another point to look. The road went around the head of a little draw. We were past the draw when Jack looked back toward the draw and saw the buck standing there on the edge of some quakies.

I didn't realize how big the buck was, but I should have because Jack usually bugs me, telling me to hurry, and anything else to fluster me. All Jack said was, "There he is." He was at a bad angle (looking back over his back at us), so I asked where should I aim? Again, Jack was a lot of help; he said, "Right in the biggest part." So, I aimed at the back of the ribs (which was in the middle, because of the angle the buck was at).

When I shot, we heard a "whop," but the buck took off like he wasn't hit and disappeared into the trees. It was wet and it had gotten really cold the previous night, with the ground frozen as hard as rock. We found some hair and that was it; no track, no nothing. We looked for about an hour, still nothing. We almost gave up, but we looked some more.

We split-up and kept looking. It was still cold, so I went back to the truck to warm up. I was sitting there, warming up, when here comes Jack, all out-of-breath and saying, "You killed the BIGGEST BUCK ON THE MOUNTAIN." Jack had found the buck about a half-mile down the canyon. I still didn't believe the buck was that big until we finally got down to him. Then I sat down and cried. When we finally got him loaded, it took us a half-day to get back home; we had to stop and show him off at all the elk camps on the way.

Photograph by Wm. H. Nesbitt

MULE DEER, TYPICAL ANTLERS
THIRD AWARD
SCORE: 204-3/8
Locality: Sonora, Mexico   Date: December 1986
Hunter: David V. Collis

MULE DEER, TYPICAL ANTLERS 204-3/8

David V. Collis

The trip from my home in Sarasota, Florida, to Tucson was uneventful, with the usual wait in Tucson for the always late Aero Mexico flight to Hermosillo, Sonora, Mexico. I was met at the airport by my good friend and guide, Leon Hoeffer. It was late evening by the time we finished picking up our supplies and made the two hour drive to camp.

Four other hunters were already there in Camp El Oasis. All of us were looking forward to the start of our hunt, to begin the next morning. After a few nightcaps and some hunting stories, we hit the sack.

The camp was an old ranch house with two bedrooms, a kitchen, and a bath. I had hunted there several times before and always loved every bit of it. Breakfast call was at 4 a.m. After ham, eggs, and fresh fruit and coffee, prepared by our lovely cook Rosecita, we were ready and eager to go hunting.

We had a 30 minute drive to the area where the guides had earlier spotted some large-racked mulies. In the previous three years of hunting with Leon, I had taken several deer in the 30-inch class (a 30-inch, a 32-inch, and a 35-inch deer), so I was excitedly looking for a big deer. The way one hunts this area is to find some large tracks and walk the deer down. While doing this, one often jumps a lot of other deer.

This first day out we found a lot of tracks and walked until about noon, when we ate our lunch of sandwiches, oranges, and pop. We were back at it in a hour. With this method of hunting, the whole day can be utilized. We tracked and jumped many deer during the first three days of this hunt but none of the caliber that I was seeking.

On the fourth day, we decided to hunt in a different area. The new area had a few more hills, rather than the desert and dried-up river bottoms. It was mostly flat, with lots of cactus and some hills about 200 feet tall. In the morning, we successfully tracked several bucks in the 28 to 30-inch group. Not shooting a 30-inch buck takes a lot of will power, but I knew the bigger bucks were there, so I decided to wait.

We stopped to have lunch on top of one of the hills. After we ate and had a short rest, I heard a domestic bull bellowing. He kept it up for about five minutes, getting my attention. I glassed in the direction of the bull, about 600 yards away. Noticing that he was looking away from my direction, I caught a glimpse of movement about 30 yards from the bull. Two outstanding bucks were looking for a place to bed down for the afternoon.

By this time, Leon was as ecstatic as I. The smaller of the two bucks was 34 inches wide and a 4x4. I knew at this time the other buck was the one I had always dreamed about. We started after the two deer at once, going as slowly and quietly as possible. I was behind Leon, trying to stop my heart from coming out of my rib cage, when he stopped and pointed in the direction of some brush. He whispered to me to make sure I took the big one, which had considerably larger forks and five points on a side. As yet, I hadn't seen the big buck's antler spread.

After glassing the bush with my scope, I could pick out the large, branched antlers. When I spotted his neck, I squeezed the trigger. Leon slapped me on the back as the buck went down. But while we were trying to settle our nerves, my buck jumped up and bolted away. We examined the spot and found some blood. We quickly started on the tracks, finding that the bucks were together again and headed in a northerly direction into the wind, which was to our advantage.

After about 20 minutes of fast walking, we spotted the bucks, again in heavy brush. The smaller buck was the first to leave, and he went to his right, through an opening about 50 yards away. I swung my rifle to the opening, hoping the wounded buck would follow the same escape route, which he did. But, when he got to the opening, he stopped and looked directly at me. This was the first time I had a chance to see his spread, and I was overwhelmed. I couldn't believe it, 37 or more inches of antler spread. I steadied the cross hairs on his front shoulder and watched him run away.

By this time Leon was shouting, "What's the matter? What's the matter?" I told him I had no explanation for not shooting the buck then. The next tracking wasn't as easy. The bucks were split-up, leaving only half as many tracks to follow. About 45 minutes later, we jumped our buck and I had a running-away shot at 125 yards. He was now mine to keep.

Michael Valencia, who was in the same hunting area, heard the shooting, and our whooping and hollering, so he came over to investigate. Again more celebration and pictures, as we finally put a tape on him and measured the antlers at 37-1/2 inches wide.

After a 60-day drying period, the buck was officially scored for entry at 216-1/8 gross, and 208-2/8 net. This great mule deer now graces my trophy room in a life-size mount.

Photograph Courtesy of Joseph J. Luterbach

A hunting trip to Sonora, Mexico, in 1986 proved to be the ticket to success for Joseph J. Luterbach who poses here with his 189-6/8 point typical mule deer.

Photograph Courtesy of Thomas N. Thiel

There was snow on the ground in Bonneville County, Idaho, in 1987 when Thomas N. Thiel located this typical mule deer with two abnormal points that scores 198-2/8 points.

Photograph by Wm. H. Nesbitt

MULE DEER, TYPICAL ANTLERS
FOURTH AWARD
SCORE: 203-4/8
Locality: Garfield Co., Colo.   Date: November 1985
Hunter: John T. Sewell

MULE DEER, TYPICAL ANTLERS 203-4/8

John T. Sewell

It was my first trip out west in four years and the excitement was building with each day. We were headed for the western slope of the Rockies in Colorado. There were eight of us on this hunting trip. It was the first time in this particular area for three of us. The other five had hunted the area in years past and had many stories of large mule deer missed and killed. The year before, all the tags had been filled with deer in the 25 to 30-inch spread category. Stories were told and retold in the airport and on the plane. Everyone had high expectations, and we were ready for some cool weather when we reached Denver. On October 30, 1985, we left a balmy 82 degrees in Tallahassee, Florida, and were met with a light snow in Colorado.

The next two days were spent in preparation for the 10-day hunting season. We leased two four-wheel drive vehicles and headed for Glenwood Springs, Colorado. There we split into groups and began gathering supplies. Seven of our eight-man group were from Tallahassee. My dad (John T. Sewell, Jr.), Rob Carter, Jack Rick, and John Waddill had all been here before. Jim Henry Slappy, who had been from Tallahassee but was now living in Fort Collins, had also hunted this area. But this was the first time for me, Wyatt Taylor, and Paul Rayborn. The three of us spent most of our time looking at the scenery and asking the same questions over and over. We wanted to know every crook and cranny about the mountain we would be hunting.

We were hunting on a private ranch just out of New Castle, Colorado. We were above Canyon Creek, on 400 acres that border the White River National Forest. The canyon provides a natural migration route for both deer and elk when the heavy snows begin at the higher elevations.

On the first day of hunting, we had about 12 inches of snow on the ground. Many deer were seen, but none were killed. Everyone was waiting for a real trophy. Some of the men hunted at lower elevations where many elk had been seen, but the deer were staying at the higher elevations.

On the second day of the hunt, two large bull elk were spotted bedding down at midmorning. That afternoon was spent stalking the animals, and it ended successfully with Paul and me killing 5-point bulls. Now I had one tag filled and could concentrate on mule deer.

The third day was work day. It took us all day to pack-out the two elk. Both were at the bottom of a creek draw. The weather was beginning to warm a bit, and the snow was beginning to melt fast. Only a few small bucks were spotted by the other hunters in our party.

On the fourth day, Paul and I hunted the highest peak in the area. We saw many deer but nothing of the trophy size we wanted. The full moon was approaching and the deer were beginning to get more active. One of the other hunters, Wyatt Taylor, saw several trophies but he was unable to get a good shot. That afternoon, my Dad took a nice mule deer with a 25-inch spread. That night the temperature dropped sharply. Although we had not had any new snow, we hoped the deer would be more active during the day.

The next morning, Paul and I decided to hunt an area where we had seen a large buck with some does on the day before. With the colder weather, and the full moon getting close, the deer had become more active. About midmorning the buck we had seen the day before ran a doe right by Paul. The buck made a close circle to Paul and he was able to get a shot. He killed his first mule deer. It was a nice 5-point, with a 25-inch spread. He was proud. We took pictures and then began the work. We were uphill from the road and were able to carry the deer down the hill without any aid from the horses. But it sure did wear us out. I rested most of the day and did not go back to hunting until late that afternoon.

I left the truck and decided to make a short circle down the mountain and back to the road, where I could be picked up at dark. I started down one ridge where I could see into a draw on both sides and up the side of another ridge. I approached an area where I had seen a large buck on the first day we were there and stopped to view the draw below. I had only been there a few seconds when I spotted a large deer on the opposite side of the draw, standing in a small clearing. When I looked through the scope, all I could see were antlers. I instantly knew this was my trophy.

I began to get excited, but tried to plan an attack route. There were only small aspens between me and the deer. This did not provide much cover. I eased down the side of the draw and managed to get within what I thought was 500 yards of the deer. I had killed the elk at long range and was over-confident. I found a prop in the fork of a tree and began to shoot. The first shot I aimed over the deer and he did not move. The second shot I aimed at meat, still the deer did not move. By now I was a nervous wreck. I am not sure where I aimed on the third, but I must have been closer because he did raise his head and look around. This was not working and I had to get closer. I was shaking so badly that I could hardly reload my gun. The sun was about to disappear behind a distant mountain and soon it would be dark, so I had to act fast. I decided to move swiftly down the hill toward the deer and hope he would not see me. I marked him near a small group of spruce, because the trees would block my view of him as I dropped down the slope.

When I reached the bottom of the draw I began to work closer to the spruce. I was shaking so badly I felt that every animal on the mountain was watching me. There was a slight breeze coming from the direction of the deer, so at least he could not smell me. Just then, I saw his antlers moving through the spruce. I found a prop against an aspen and waited. When the deer reached an opening, I shot him behind the shoulder. The deer just stood there. Instantly, I fired another shot into his neck. This time he just dropped. When I reached him he was dead. I just stood there in awe. I knew he was a good buck. I field dressed the deer and then headed for the road.

It was dark when I got to the road. My dad and Paul were waiting there. They both began to harass me about all the shooting. They wanted to know why I had to shoot so many times. When I told them they could put both of their deer's racks inside my deer's rack, it got quiet. Of course I exaggerated.

The next morning, Paul, Dad, Rob Carter, and I went to pack the deer out. Rob made a circle in case we spooked some others on the way to the deer. When we reached the buck, Dad and Paul were astonished. Dad said that he was a nice one and Paul was speechless. We had begun to take pictures when Rob walked up. He began to get excited and said it was the biggest mule deer he had ever seen. He said it would definitely make Boone and Crockett. Rob had killed a couple of deer over 30 inches and his statement got me excited.

We later showed the deer to the rest of our hunting party and took it to the camp. We then packed meat and antlers and headed for New Castle. We dropped the meat off at the meat packing plant and headed for Elk Creek Taxidermy. The owner of the taxidermy shop went crazy when we took the head out of the truck. He ran inside and got a tape measure and began to take measurements. He said it was the largest mule deer he had ever seen and it would surely make Boone and Crockett. This was when I was sure I had a real trophy.

The next day, the heavy snows began to fall and hunting became difficult for the rest of our party. Paul and I headed for Aspen to do a little sightseeing. No one else killed anything the rest of the season, but we sure had one to talk about.

It took 11 months for the taxidermist to return the head to Tallahassee. There we had it officially scored. It was a dream come true. I had finally made the Boone and Crockett Club records book.

Photograph by Wm. H. Nesbitt

MULE DEER, TYPICAL ANTLERS
HONORABLE MENTION
SCORE: 200-2/8
Locality: Montrose Co., Colo.   Date: November 1985
Hunter: Nelson Harding

MULE DEER, TYPICAL ANTLERS 200-2/8

Nelson Harding

Each year, Nelson Harding hunts with the same four individuals that he has hunted with since grade school. They are Jerry Smith, Jim Barbour, and Buddy Meyer. All four men are from California. The year that Harding took this trophy mule deer, they were accompanied by two other hunting companions.

Every year, Nelson and his hunting party plan a hunting expedition out-of-state. In the past they've hunted in Colorado (twice), Oregon (once), Nevada (once), and Idaho (four or five times). Jerry Smith is responsible for planning the hunt, collecting the money, and sending in the applications.

On Nelson's second trip to Colorado, they hunted a couple of different areas in the vicinity of Dark Canyon in Montrose County. (Dark Canyon is the area where the current World's Record typical American elk was taken by John Plute in 1899.)

The first day, the group split-up into two groups of three hunters each and headed for the high country. All day long, they worked their way to the top of one of the highest peaks in the area. The higher they went, the deeper the snow and the more fatigued they became. They saw a lot of sign, especially elk, but very few animals. After a brief rest at the top, they worked their way back to the truck, arriving at dark.

The next day, they selected a different area to hunt, at a much lower altitude, near Crawford Reservoir. Nearly everyone was dragging from the previous day's climb and they didn't want to go back to the same area.

On this day, the hunters broke up into groups of two, with Nelson and Jerry hunting together. They began working a few of the many draws that intersect the area, making a big loop that would eventually get them back to the vehicle.

The area looked good and they figured it should produce a few good deer for hunters willing to get out and work. It appeared, however, that the area had received a considerable amount of hunting pressure and they didn't see anything.

Around 3:30 p.m., Nelson started to play-out. He suggested to Jerry that they start working their way back to the vehicle. Nelson was so worn-out that he simply wanted to make a beeline for the trucks. Jerry agreed to head back, but he suggested they check a few promising looking areas on the way back to the vehicles. Nelson agreed.

They had not gone more than 100 yards when they came upon a brush thicket about 25 yards across that looked like a good spot for a buck to bed down during the afternoon. They split-up, about 15 yards apart, and headed into the thicket. They hadn't gone more than a few paces when, to their surprise, a buck popped out of the other side of the thicket. It was immediately obvious to both hunters that they were looking at a truly exceptional trophy.

As the buck headed away from them, each hunter immediately jacked a round into the chamber of their firearms. (Neither Nelson nor Jerry carries a loaded firearm when they are hunting so close together.) A few yards out, the buck began hooking to Nelson's right. At that point, Jerry did not have a shot because Nelson was in the line of fire.

Nelson shouldered his Ruger Model 77 in .270 caliber, sighted on the buck, and let one round go. The buck dropped, stone-dead in its tracks.

Nelson could tell the buck was big when it first got up. However, the size of the massive antlers did not really sink-in until he walked up to it. Jerry was tickled pink and carrying on. Nelson had never seen him that excited before. Jerry probably couldn't have been more excited if he had shot the buck himself.

Nelson said he had a very nice buck that he took in Idaho many years prior to this hunt. The antlers on that buck didn't seem much larger than the one he had just dropped. Jerry kept assuring Nelson that this buck was much bigger and in a class all by itself.

While Nelson field dressed the animal, Jerry went back for the truck. By the time Jerry got back with the truck and help, it was dark. They loaded the buck into the pickup and headed back to camp, where they had a tasty dinner and a well-deserved night's rest.

Photograph Courtesy of Barbara M. Conley

Barbara M. Conley's 1987 deer hunt ended when she took this typical mule deer in Washoe County, Nevada. She dropped it with her .270 Winchester from nearly 400 yards away. It scores 193-3/8.

Photograph Courtesy of James D. Wagner

James D. Wagner killed this typical mule deer while bowhunting in Coconino County, Arizona, in 1986. It entry scores 196-6/8 points.

Photograph by Wm. H. Nesbitt

MULE DEER, NON-TYPICAL ANTLERS
FIRST AWARD
SCORE: 305-6/8
Locality: Shasta Co., Calif.   Date: October 1987
Hunter: Artie McGram

MULE DEER, NON-TYPICAL ANTLERS 305-6/8

Artie McGram

It was Sunday, October 4th, 1987. It was a very hot and dry fall. I had been hunting some ridges near a remote canyon, outside of town by about ten miles. The area I had been hunting was really thick and brushy; with it so dry, it made it very difficult to hunt.

I had hunted the same area several times. I had jumped a number of deer but I was not able to see them, as it was so thick with brush. On Sunday, October 4th, I had planned an afternoon hunt on one ridge, overlooking another, hoping to see a few deer that afternoon.

I was sitting on a rock, around 4:30 p.m., when I saw two does feeding on the opposite ridge. I sat watching a couple of active squirrels running below me in the brush.

With the sun starting to set, watching the shadows rise on the hill opposite me, I was thinking I should start back to the truck before dark. Then I noticed yet another deer, about 200 yards away. It was above the two does that were feeding. I decided to watch the deer a little longer.

With the shadows rising, I heard a noise below me. Thinking the noise was made by the squirrels, I didn't pay much attention to it. I was still watching the deer across the ridge when I heard the noise again. It was then that I decided it wasn't the squirrels, it was bigger and moving in my direction.

I picked up my gun and waited. Out through the brush walked a small 3-point. With my heart pounding with excitement, I decided it was not what I wanted. I watched the small buck walk through the clearing I was sitting in, soon disappearing into the thick brush again. I remember telling myself that would probably be the last legal buck I would see this season. It was just not what I wanted.

I settled back down on the rock and picked up my binoculars to look at the deer on the opposite ridge, thinking I should call it quits. I heard yet another noise. Thinking it was still the 3-point that had moved through the clearing, I paid little attention. Then, all of a sudden, I looked to my left and there in the clearing stood a buck. He was apparently following the 3-point. From the side view, he had an unbelievably heavy antler mass, with a hanger point down below his ear. I quickly grabbed my gun, knowing that was the one. Through my scope, all I could see was hair. I pulled the trigger and the buck humped as if he had been hit good. The buck twirled as if to run away.

Thinking he was going to fall any moment, I froze in amazement of that rack. In one swift bounce, he was gone. I thought I'd lost him. Running over to where he had been, I could not find any blood. With my heart racing out of control, I moved in the direction that he had disappeared.

Trying to get my senses, I watched the ridge above me, hoping he would appear; nothing! So I continued to follow. Coming upon his trail, I found a fine spray in the dust that I thought might be blood. I kept on going. Crossing some dead branches, I found more blood. As I went on, the blood trail became very apparent.

All of a sudden, I came around a bush and there, lying in the trail, was the biggest thing I could ever imagine. I ran up to the buck and grabbed the antlers, shaking them. It was apparent that he was dead. I sat down near him, thinking, "What have I got!"

It was beyond my wildest dreams. When I gathered my senses, I saw the bullet wound in his lower chest. With dismay, I realized how close I had come to missing him. At that point, I also realized I had killed my dream buck!

Photographs Courtesy of H. Ritman Jons and Matthew J. Arkins

(l) H. Ritman Jons connected with this typical mule deer in 1987 while still hunting on the Deseret Ranch in Morgan County, Utah. It scores 199-1/8 points. (r) Matthew J. Arkins was mule deer hunting in Archuleta County, Colorado, in 1986 when he shot this typical that scores 195-5/8 points.

Photograph Courtesy of Leslie M. Brady

Leslie M. Brady used his .30-06 to drop this typical mule deer in 1986 that scores 186-6/8 points. He took his buck 15 miles north of John Day in Grant County, Oregon.

Photograph by Wm. H. Nesbitt

MULE DEER, NON-TYPICAL ANTLERS
SECOND AWARD
SCORE: 300-7/8

Locality: Bonneville Co., Idaho   Date: November 1985
Hunter: Brett J. Sauer

MULE DEER, NON-TYPICAL ANTLERS 300-7/8

Brett J. Sauer

Around October of every year, my friends and I would plan a hunting trip together. I was a construction worker at the time, and hunting season seemed to be the busiest time. I never knew exactly when I could go.

I ended-up working on opening day of the deer season. After work, all week long, a friend from work and I went out looking around. All we could find were does. On the weekend, I went to Crooked Creek, near Howe, Idaho, with a friend from work. We saw a lot of does, and one buck, but he was too far away to shoot. There were only two days left of the season and I was starting to think I was going to get skunked this year. My friends that I usually go hunting with every year had gone on opening day and hadn't seen much either. They were planning on going near Bone, Idaho, just southeast of Idaho Falls, Idaho.

On November 10th, 1985, Ron, Jim, Cody, Nick, and I left at about 7 a.m. for Bone, Idaho. We found an area that wasn't posted or on private property at McCoy Creek (Unit 66A). We split-up, in sets of two, and went different directions. Ron and I headed up the canyon, over the ridge. After a few minutes of walking, we ran into a herd of moose. They made such a loud noise running through the trees that I headed up the next canyon to get away from where they were.

I had walked for two or three miles when I reached the top of the ridge. From there, I could see three or four deer across the canyon. They were in the trees, so I couldn't really tell if there was a buck or not. I sat down and watched for about ten minutes, to see if maybe one was a buck. I thought there was a buck, but while he was in the trees, I couldn't be sure. Then he stepped out into the clearing and there was no doubt.

I remember thinking of my 5-point the year before, from Challis, Idaho. I knew this one had to be at least that big.

I was using my Dad's Winchester bolt-action .30-06, with a Weaver scope. I thought it would be an easy shot, but I guess I know now what they mean when they say, "Buck Fever." I'm not sure to this day where I aimed but the bullet hit him right in the antlers. He stumbled, shook his head, and then leaped over to the other side of the ridge.

I now think that I probably was aiming right at his antlers. I started down the canyon toward him. At that time I was thinking about all of the hunting stories I've heard. Those where someone would walk up on a deer and it would run away and then circle back to see what was there. About halfway up the side of the canyon, I decided that if the buck did run away from me, he was long-gone. So, I had the choice to go either right or left. To the left, the ridge went for about a quarter-mile, gradually tapering into another canyon. I followed it over. When I reached the top, I saw the buck walking, just on the other side of the ridge, about 100 yards away.

Remembering the bad shot I had made previously, I pulled up and shot quickly. He ran into the trees and down to the bottom of the canyon. I then ran down the ridge to a clearing where I could see him climbing the other side of the canyon, about 250 yards away. I shot two more times and he stopped going up the hill. He turned to the side, going across the hill. I fired two more times as he ran down the hill. He fell at the bottom of the canyon. I sat and watched for awhile, while reloading my gun. I was sure he would get up.

After awhile, I went down. I never had any idea the buck was that big. I counted his points and he had 43. He only had three teeth in his mouth and they were worn to nothing. I tagged and cleaned him. I then left my coat hanging in a tree so I could find him again.

Down the canyon, I found Mr. Fisher and his boys. One went to find Ron, to get the pickup down to the bottom of the canyon. The other one carried our guns while Mr. Fisher and I dragged the deer down the canyon. It was about 2 p.m. when we started down the canyon, and about 5:30 when we reached the pickup. I'm very thankful to my friends for helping me that day. I would hate to have done it by myself.

Photographs Courtesy of Jeffrey A. Bechtel and Allan J. Selzler

(l) A guided hunt in the Great Bear Wilderness Area of Flathead County, Montana, produced this typical mule deer with a score of 187-5/8 for Jeffrey A. Bechtel in 1983. (r) Allan J. Selzler with non-typical mule deer 268-1/8 that he took 15 miles southeast of Elbow, Saskatchewan, in 1986.

Photograph Courtesy of Thomas S. Hundley

Thomas S. Hundley killed this non-typical mule deer that scores 244-2/8 points on the Grand Mesa National Forest in Colorado. He took this buck in 1986.

Photograph by Wm. H. Nesbitt

MULE DEER, NON-TYPICAL ANTLERS
HONORABLE MENTION
SCORE: 265-7/8
Locality: Powder River Co., Mont.   Date: November 1987
Hunter: Michael A. Siewert

MULE DEER, NON-TYPICAL ANTLERS 265-7/8

Michael A. Siewert

Hunting in southeastern Montana, with its numerous deep ravines, draws, and rolling foothills, can be quite an experience. It was November 12, 1987, a crisp Montana morning. The day before, my father and mother had driven the 350 miles from Helena, Montana, to Colstrip, a boomtown about 35 miles from Forsyth.

We were excited about our hunting trip and we were up before dawn, preparing for the big day. We saw several deer feasting on the farmers' haystacks on our way to the hunting grounds. It was still dark, so we didn't disturb them.

Just before dawn, we saw some deer feeding about 600 yards out in an open field. We stopped to scope them. There were 20 does and one small, 2-point buck in the herd. We watched them feed for about five minutes. Then we proceeded on to our hunting area. We drove about 50 feet and saw more deer come running out of a hidden draw, heading for the trees. We stopped again to scope them, and we got a quick glimpse of an enormous buck with antlers going in every direction. I knew it was a trophy! We jumped out of the truck. I was so excited that I left the door to the truck wide open and took off running up the hill.

I went up one draw and my father took another, in hopes of cutting the buck off. We ran over fields, up hills, and through draws for about a mile. I thought my lungs would burst as I topped the hill. All I could see were those antlers and about half of his neck as he was watching me come up the hill. Breathless from the climb, I fired my first shot, and he just stood there.

I bolted-in another round and settled down enough to shoot again. Down the buck went, to his knees, but immediately he jumped up and started running. As he was flashing through the trees, I shot again, just as he disappeared from sight. I went to where I last saw him and found the buck lying 50 feet away, over a small knoll. I went over to my trophy and discovered that in my excitement, I had left my knife in the truck. Luckily, my father came along just at that time and he had his knife with him. As we dressed the deer, we noticed that he was hit twice, once in the trachea and once in the lungs.

The day had warmed up by then and there was very little snow. We really worked to drag that deer out of the woods, up the hills, through brush, and down hills. He got his last licks in as we were dragging him down a hill. He got away from us and his antler caught my ankle as I was trying to get out of the way. He dragged me down the hill with him. I sprained my ankle, but I didn't notice it until I got home. But, I still feel it once in a while. All I could think about then was my luck in finding this enormous deer.

The rack had 16 points on one side and 21 on the other. It scored 273-6/8 for entry, which was good enough to get it invited to the 20th Awards in Albuquerque, New Mexico.

The gun I was using was a .22-250. This may seem like a small gun for deer hunting, but I usually carry it in case I run into a coyote. Word spread quickly around Colstrip and the state, and I received a call to have my picture taken for the local paper. I also had many callers wanting to see the deer. This was the biggest thrill of my hunting experience, even topping my first elk.

Photographs Courtesy of Ralph I. Sibley and Greg Rocha

(l) Ralph I. Sibley with the Columbia blacktail deer he took with his 7 mm B.A.R. in 1986 in Mendocino County, California. It scores 145 points. (r) Greg Rocha was hunting on the Baxter Ranch in Northern California in 1985 when he shot this Columbia blacktail deer that scores 141-4/8 points.

Photograph Courtesy of Bert L. Freed

Bonneville County, Idaho, was home to this non-typical mule deer with 13 abnormal points that scores 237-3/8 points. It was killed by Bert L. Freed in 1987.

Photograph by Wm. H. Nesbitt

COLUMBIA BLACKTAIL DEER
FIRST AWARD
SCORE: 159-6/8
Locality: Jackson Co., Oreg. Date: November 1985
Hunter: Douglas L. Milburn

COLUMBIA BLACKTAIL DEER
159-6/8

Douglas L. Milburn

My wife and I usually hunt around China Gulch, which is near the town of Ruch in Southern Oregon.

The first day of our season was unsuccessful, but by late evening it was starting to snow. The second day was November 10th, 1985, and about six inches of snow covered the ground. It was shortly after daylight when we arrived and parked the truck.

We started walking the old roads. My wife, Sherie, decided to go down one road, while I walked the other one. I had been walking for about 15 minutes when I noticed a set of large deer tracks. The deer had come down the hill, and then he had continued walking down the road. I followed the tracks for some time. Then I noticed that the tracks left the road and went down the other side. I crept to the edge and looked down the mountainside. About 35 yards away, I could see the head and neck of a buck. The rest was obscured by a tree. He was looking right at me. I quickly raised my gun, aimed about six inches under his chin, and fired.

There was a cloud of smoke and when it had cleared, I couldn't see the buck. As usual, when this happens, a million things start going through a person's mind. Did I miss completely and it ran away? Did I wound it and need to track it? Well, I soon found out. I headed down to where I had last seen the deer. There he was. I had dropped him dead in his tracks with a bullet hole just where I had hoped it would be. This was my tenth and best deer to be shot with my muzzleloader.

Later, when I finally met up with Sherie, she helped me get the deer up the hillside, which was quite difficult. It was slippery and Sherie had to dig in and hold the deer's rump while I found new footholds and yanked it up, a few inches at a time. It took us about an hour of this push-and-pull effort to get the buck that 35 yards.

It wasn't until two days later, after the urging of friends and relatives, that I took my deer in to get the head mounted. It was at that time that I discovered that it was big enough to get into Boone and Crockett.

Photograph by Wm. H. Nesbitt

COLUMBIA BLACKTAIL DEER
SECOND AWARD
SCORE: 158-2/8
Locality: Lewis Co., Wash.   Date: November 1984
Hunter: Keith A. Heldreth

COLUMBIA BLACKTAIL DEER
158-2/8

Keith A. Heldreth

The sun, now just a dull glimmer on the horizon, had long since taken its final bow. As the shadows from the dark timber gradually consumed the field, the two bucks moved out further and further, finally stopping to feed on a particularly succulent stand of red clover.

This general area had always been good for observing deer in past years. It provides just the right mix of fields, water, logged areas, and mature timber that our coastal blacktails thrive on. Over the years our family has taken several nice blacktails out of this secluded corner of Lewis Co., Washington. Although some of the deer we have taken have been very good by blacktail standards, I knew that even the best of them would pale in comparison to one of the bucks I was now watching.

As the smaller of the two bucks (a spike) fed beside his older companion, I was finally able to get a look at the larger buck's velvet-clad antlers. Although the glimpse of the buck's antlers silhouetted against the smaller deer was fleeting at best, I knew this was, by far, the best blacktail buck I had ever seen. He was definitely worth a second look.

As the weeks crept by, I continued my early evening vigil whenever time allowed. By late August, the buck had filled-out to be quite a tremendous specimen. He was deep and heavy through the body, but the remarkable thing was his antlers. With an outside spread that I guessed to be over 20 inches, and four long, symmetrical points on each side, he was definitely the buck-of-a-lifetime.

Throughout the month of September, we gradually started to see less and less of the two bucks. By this time, the fields had been stripped of their crop of hay. The short stubble provided no cover for the deer and, gradually, their early evening forays became later and later. By the first of October, the large buck had disappeared completely. Although I continued to see the spike occasionally, he was always by himself. With the general buck season a short two weeks away, I began to fear that something had happened to the old buck.

Opening morning of Washington's 1984 general deer season was met by me with the same sort of anticipation and excitement that grips hunters the world over at this time of year. After an early morning breakfast at my mom and stepfather's home, we were ready to go. Although we hunted hard, opening morning left us with nothing to hang on the meat pole but a few stories. That evening everyone's consensus was the same. All of the large tracks in the old buck's domain were weeks old and rapidly disappearing under the almost-daily rain. One by one, the days slipped by. Each one held new surprises, but one story was always the same; the large, blunt-toed tracks that had been so familiar a few short weeks before had completely vanished.

By the time the general season ground to a halt, I had grudgingly given in to the fact that the big old buck no longer haunted the same piece of swamp and timber that he had earlier called home. It was a bitter pill to swallow but I eventually put my thoughts of the buck on the back burner and began to look ahead to the late November season. This season coincides with the rut here in western Washington and generally it is a hunter's best bet for tying his tag on a true trophy deer.

Toward the middle of November, two things happened that directly affected the rest of my story. The first came in the form of six inches of new snow, three days before late season opened. The second happened the very next evening when my wife Lisa came in the door and excitedly told me she had just seen my big buck! He had crossed the road in front of her car after dark, narrowly missing the opportunity of gaining hood ornament status. As I quizzed Lisa about where she had seen the buck, and how large he was, I became more excited and convinced that this was the same deer I had watched the summer before, more than a mile-and-a-half away. There just couldn't be two bucks that were that large in the same general area.

Early the next morning I hiked into a small, logged-off basin a short distance from where my wife had seen the buck the previous night. The area had been planted back to Douglas fir seedlings about five years before. It seemed to be the logical choice for spotting the buck, if he was chasing does in the area. These logged areas are full of natural feed and act as a magnet, drawing deer from a large radius. Although I only saw one doe that morning, my spirits soared with the discovery of those same old, familiar hoof prints cut deeply into the snow. I couldn't be positive that this was the same buck, but I felt that it was my best bet for the next morning.

Opening morning of late buck season dawned clear and cold. Daylight found me with binoculars glued to my eyeballs as I tried to separate deer-sized shadows from the stumps and brush in the logged area. As the gray light slowly pushed back the shadows, I began to see deer. I had already spotted two does and a precocious young spike buck when movement near a stand of fire-killed timber caught my attention.

I trained my binoculars in that direction and was immediately rewarded as two more does came into focus. A few seconds later, they were followed by a third, smaller deer. I had watched the three deer for a minute or so when one of the does snapped her head erect and stared down the hill to her left. Sweeping my binoculars in the direction she was gazing, I quickly located the object of her attention. Fifty yards down the hill a fourth doe climbed a low bank and paused nervously at the top for a second before threading her way up toward her waiting companions. She had barely cleared the low swell when an impossibly large buck, his rut-swollen neck stretched out and his nose into the wind, scrambled up the bank close behind her.

One quick look was all I needed. I swiftly exchanged the binoculars for my old Winchester Model 70 and eased off the safety. With my heart hammering wildly in my chest, I located a corner of an old root wad for a rest. When the cross hairs finally settled for a moment at the base of the buck's neck, I slowly took the rest of the slack out of the trigger. I was surprised a split second later by the BOOM-Whuump of a solid hit. I quickly worked the bolt to feed a fresh cartridge up the spout of the old .300 Mag. It wasn't needed. At the first shot, the buck had collapsed in a cloud of snow and had slid down the slight incline, coming to rest against a small fir tree.

As I ran my hand down his sleek side and admired his massive, mahogany-colored antlers a few moments later, I was touched with a mixture of accomplishment and sorrow that can only come at a time like this. I had won the game ... but I had lost a little bit as well. No one can claim such a magnificent trophy and not feel a wee bit of remorse.

As I walked back to my truck later that morning, I thought about the space left by the buck's passing. It was a hard space for any other deer to fill for sure, but then my thoughts brightened as I remembered the small buck that had been his companion all summer. Who knows? With the right genetics and a few lucky years behind him ... who knows?

Photograph by Wm. H. Nesbitt

COLUMBIA BLACKTAIL DEER
CERTIFICATE OF MERIT
SCORE: 163-7/8
Locality: Lincoln Co., Oreg.   Date: Picked Up 1987
Owners: Bruce and Scott Wales

COLUMBIA BLACKTAIL DEER
163-7/8

Bruce and Scott Wales, owners

My son, Scott, and I are accustomed to walking in the woods for hunting, fishing, or just enjoying nature, and this particular afternoon was no different. I had returned home from work early that day and Scott was anxious to do something. So I suggested that we walk down into the North Fork of the Yachats River to do some fishing.

We packed our gear quickly, as we were both eager to start fishing in this secluded area, an area that only hunters visit during hunting season, and this was not hunting season. As we climbed into the truck, Scott asked to hear more about what had happened the previous day at the Flescher Ranch, just eight miles up the Yachats River from our house.

On Sunday, hunters from all over central Lincoln County had gathered at Jim Flescher's Ranch for an antler measuring extravaganza. Since Rusty Lindberg, an Official B&C Measurer had received several phone calls from hunters in the Yachats area, he and Jim decided to set a date on which Rusty would come down and measure qualified Roosevelt's elk and Columbia blacktail deer. The date chosen was July 19, 1987.

Lots of hunters and spectators showed up to witness and observe the many trophy elk and deer. When the food was all gone, the stories told, the tape measure put away, and all the calculating done, there were five elk and two deer that met the all-time records book requirements, with quite a few more that met the awards book minimum. Among them was my own blacktail deer. I had gotten him after hunting for days during the last week of the 1985 deer season. It scored 156-4/8.

The more I talked about the event at Flescher's Ranch, the more Scott wished that he could have been there to see all those magnificent trophies and listen to some of the eye-opening stories. But he had made plans to visit a friend that day and he wasn't willing to change them.

As we drove up to the gate on the old logging road, we decided that we would start fishing where Earley Creek entered the North Fork of the Yachats River. From the truck, this was a short walk down the old logging road that had been closed at both ends to motor vehicles for many years as a wildlife habitat. We figured that we would fish down the river to Williamson Creek. Not only should the fishing be good, it was a long hike and would be a great opportunity to start scouting for the next elk season.

As we continued down the old logging road, I mentioned to Scott that it seemed a perfect day for fishing; the sun was out, there were a few intermittent clouds, and there was absolutely no wind. The alder trees were spaced close enough together so that Scott could not find any of his familiar landmarks to get his bearings, so I reminded him that we were south of Burnt Timber Mountain and west of Howell Ridge.

As the old logging road entered the bottom of the canyon and started to cross Earley Creek, we found a well-used game trail full of fresh elk tracks. Thinking this was the easiest route to take to reach our destination on the river, we left the logging road and followed the game trail down to where it entered a small meadow, some 30 to 40 yards from the north fork of the Yachats. Upon entering the small meadow, and looking for more elk sign, we noticed a pile of bones. After examining the pile, we immediately started searching for the skull of the animal to help us determine if it was a buck or a doe; we guessed it to be a deer by the size of the bones and pieces of lower jaw.

We discovered the skull at the edge of the meadow, lying upside down on a large sword fern. We ran over to the edge of the meadow and pulled the skull off the fern. As we turned it over, we realized we had found a truly huge blacktail buck rack. Excited, we sat staring at the skull, trying to guess what fate this mighty buck had encountered, but we will never know. Even though the native cutthroat were not biting as much as we would have liked that day, it was a day that father and son will remember for a long, long time.

Photograph Courtesy of Les Johnson

Les Johnson was hunting along the "Go Road" in Del Norte County, California, in 1986 when he shot this Columbia blacktail deer that scores 141-4/8 points.

Photograph Courtesy of Terence K. Prechter

This tall-racked Columbia blacktail deer was taken on San Hedron Mountain in Mendocino County, California, in 1986 by Terence K. Prechter. It scores 133-6/8 points.

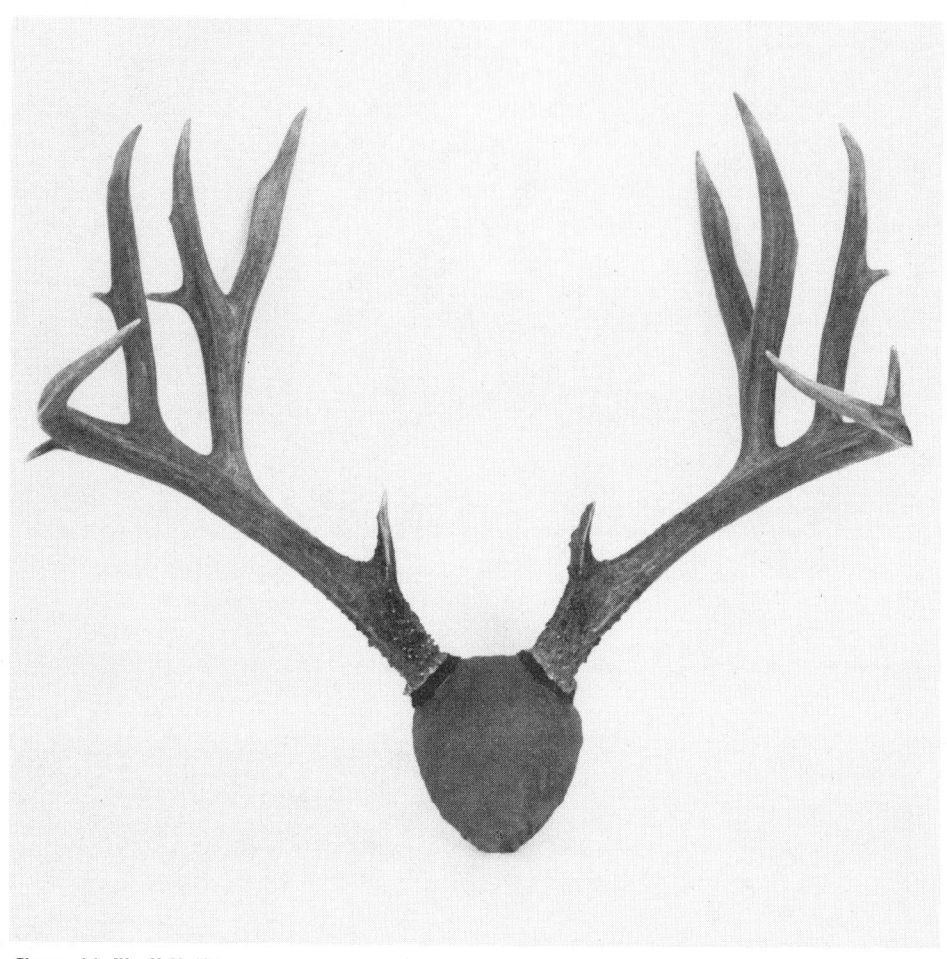

Photograph by Wm. H. Nesbitt

COLUMBIA BLACKTAIL DEER
CERTIFICATE OF MERIT
SCORE: 162-6/8
Locality: Pierce Co., Wash.   Date: 1952
Hunter: Dick Allen   Owner: Craig Allen

COLUMBIA BLACKTAIL DEER
162-6/8

Dick Allen, hunter
Craig Allen, owner

Several years ago Dick Allen was visiting his son Craig in Murray, Utah. Both men are long-time hunters and their conversation eventually turned to hunting, as it normally does when they get together. Dick has hunted most of his life and he introduced Craig to hunting when Craig was a young boy.

Dick told Craig of a trophy Columbia blacktail deer that he had taken many years previously. Dick was 20 years old at the time and was stationed in the army at Fort Lewis, Washington. Dick had made arrangements to take annual leave to go on a deer hunt with relatives and friends. This was the last chance Dick had to go hunting before being transferred overseas to serve in the Korean Conflict.

It was the fall of 1952. Dick's hunting party arrived at their favorite hunting site in Pierce County, Washington. Shortly after that, Dick shot the first buck that walked by with his .30-06. Dick's hunting companions admired his tremendous trophy and congratulated him on his good fortune. Dick was not too impressed at the time with his buck's antlers. Coming from Utah, he was more familiar with the much larger cousin of the Columbia blacktail deer, the mule deer. His buck's antlers simply didn't match up.

With his leave running out, Dick packed the antlers away, under the stairs in a cellar storage area of his grandmother's home. The antlers remained there, nearly forgotten, for over 30 years. Dick told Craig that he would drop the antlers off the next time he visited.

True to his word, Dick presented Craig with the set of Columbia blacktail deer antlers from 1952 on his next visit. Craig "freaked out" when he saw the antlers. He realized immediately that his father had taken a tremendous Columbia blacktail deer trophy those many years before. Craig had his father's rack officially scored, resulting in an invitation to the 20th Awards Final Judging and proper recognition of a great trophy. The antlers today occupy a place of honor in Craig's home.

Photograph by Wm. H. Nesbitt

SITKA BLACKTAIL DEER
FIRST AWARD
SCORE: 126-3/8

Locality: Sunny Hay Mt., Alaska   Date: November 1987
Hunter: Harry R. Horner

SITKA BLACKTAIL DEER
126-3/8

Harry R. Horner

The morning of Oct. 17, 1987 was clear. It had snowed a light skiff at higher elevations the night before, but it promised to be a perfect hunting day. I picked up my hunting partner, Jim See, and we headed out about 5:30 a.m. Jim had gone out the day before, bagging a beautiful 5-point, so our hopes were high. The rut was just beginning and nice bucks were being taken each day. I was using a 6 mm Parker Hale bolt-action rifle with Remington 100 grain ammo. Jim was packing his Ruger Model 77 in .25-06 caliber.

It took us about 30 minutes to reach our chosen area via logging roads. We left the truck and started up the back side of Sunny Hay Mountain, located just behind the town of Craig on the West Coast of Prince of Wales Island, in the Panhandle Region of Alaska.

We hiked up a ridge, through broken timber, for about an hour-and-a-half, seeing no fresh sign or game. When we reached the muskeg, we decided to split-up. Jim took the higher side, while I chose the lower. We hunted for quite a while, with no success, and then met on the far side, back in the timber. Jim had encountered a sow black bear and her two cubs. She was not happy with the intrusion and she huffed and gnashed her teeth to speed him on his way. He had seen three more bear than I, as the area I had chosen was apparently deserted.

We rested for a bit, then decided to head back for the rig. We had covered about a quarter-mile of the broken muskeg when I noticed a flicker of movement behind a bull pine. My first thought was that it was a bird. When it flicked again, I realized that it was a deer, and a nice buck at that. His red antlers were visible through the trees. I turned to Jim and said, "There he is!" The buck chose that moment to step from behind the tree. I pulled down, fired, and missed clean!

The buck began to run across the muskeg at top speed. I fired four more shots and hit him just behind the last rib on the left side with the final shot. He continued to run and disappeared from sight. We found no blood, but we could follow his tracks in the moss as he was running hard. When he slowed down, the tracks were no longer visible in the moss. We then split-up and began to search the area. Jim followed a lower deer trail, while I took the higher one. When the trail reached a spot where it went over a steep bank, I could see no fresh tracks on that trail, so I returned to where Jim was and asked him what he had found.

His trail was as cold as the one I had been on.

At this point I began to wonder if I had hit him at all. But a hunter knows these things! On a hunch, I walked over to a nearby ravine and looked down to see the buck lying quietly at the bottom. It didn't take long for us to join him. We could tell by the size of his rack that this was a definite head mount, so we finished him off with a shot in the heart.

We dressed him, took pictures, admired him, had lunch, took more pictures, admired him even more, and then we began to realize that this was indeed a trophy buck! We were very generous with our praises to each other about what fine hunters we were, and we also whooped and hollered like a couple of kids with our first spike on the ground!

We spent the next two hours packing the buck out. He was in prime shape, fat and ready for the coming rut. His neck was swollen and he was truly a magnificent animal. Upon our arrival back in Craig, it didn't take long for the word to get around. The rest of the evening was spent leaning on the rig, retelling the tale to "forty-leven" envious hunters.

Bob Woods, a game Biologist with the Alaska Department of Fish and Wildlife and an Official Scorer for Boone and Crockett, measured the antlers the next time he was in town. He came up with an entry score of 126 points, which placed it in the potential World's Record class. I had already made arrangements with Brad Moore of Bear and Claw Taxidermy in Craig to do a shoulder mount for me. Bob's scoring made it even more of a trophy worth saving. I've shot many fine bucks in my time, but this fellow was the one I had been looking for all along!

Photograph Courtesy of Andrew G. Johnson

Andrew G. Johnson with the Sitka blacktail deer he took on Kodiak Island, Alaska, in 1986. It scores 107 points and easily qualifies for the book.

Photograph Courtesy of Randy S. Shumate

Karluk Lake on Kodiak Island, Alaska, was the location where Randy S. Shumate took this Sitka blacktail deer in 1988 that scores 101-6/8 points.

Photograph by Wm. H. Nesbitt

SITKA BLACKTAIL DEER
SECOND AWARD
SCORE: 126-2/8

Locality: Control Lake, Alaska   Date: August 1987
Hunter: William B. Steele, Jr.

SITKA BLACKTAIL DEER
126-2/8

William B. Steele, Jr.

    I was very eager to explore the area to which we were transferred seven short months ago. My freezer was quite empty. Deer being a staple part of our diet, our stomachs would also be empty, not to mention our wallets, if we had to buy winter meat!

    So, a day trip was planned after I studied many maps and walked many miles. I had many areas chosen, but one was of great interest to me. This time I would go alone, being my all-time favorite companion was pregnant with our son, Matthew.

    The day looked very promising, clear and cool, much like any August day. As I began my two-hour drive, the fog rolled in. Being able to see only 100 feet in front of me, I began to climb the steep ravine. Nearing the top, I hiked across the ridge. The fog was lifting, slowly. It was time to begin the hunt.

    I scanned the valleys with my binoculars, spotting a few deer bedded down and a few more browsing across the valley, about a half-mile away. On the chance one was a buck, I got closer. And as I did, I noticed two large bucks standing together. I slowly worked my way up to the treeline, and then stalked my way even closer to them. A small stand of trees stood between us. They had been occupied with what the muskeg had to offer their empty stomachs, not paying much attention to anything else. As I proceeded out into the open, the smaller of the two bucks stepped out and was looking directly at me! I froze in my tracks, knowing that I wanted nothing to do with this one. And that is the way we stood for quite some time, frozen in our tracks. One of us would conquer the other, but whom?

    I watched as the other buck slowly made his way in-and-out of view. Raising my rifle as he moved into my range, I slowly leaned to the right, and as the other one watched, I fired. I hit him in the chest, and both bucks bounded off. To my surprise, four does joined them! I tracked him 80 yards and found him lying silently on the forest floor. He was still in the velvet. I could not get over his enormous size, I was in awe of him. It was 11 a.m., so there was no need to hurry back down; I had plenty of daylight left. I dressed and quartered him, then tied it all to my packframe. I could call it a day after an eight-hour hunt, a very successful hunt. I did not realize the potential of the buck becoming part of the Boone and Crockett trophies until much later.

Photograph by Wm. H. Nesbitt

SITKA BLACKTAIL DEER
THIRD AWARD
SCORE: 124-2/8
Locality: Exchange Cove, Alaska   Date: October 1986
Hunter: Daniel J. Leo

SITKA BLACKTAIL DEER
124-2/8

Daniel J. Leo

Our deer hunting plans for 1986 began coming together in early September. We'd spent numerous evenings discussing our hunting successes from previous years, and we had decided on a mid-October, week-long hunt on Prince of Wales Island, in southeast Alaska.

Prince of Wales is the third largest island under the U.S. flag, and it is located in the Tongass National Forest. It is 2,000 square miles of pristine wilderness beauty, accessed by 700 miles of logging road.

We departed our home in Ketchikan (also on an island) on the Alaska State ferry, the "Aurora." We were bound for Hollis, a small logging community on the east side of the island. My son Mark, age 14, and I would travel to Whale Pass, a former logging community 100 miles from Hollis. There, we would stay with my hunting companion Ed Cochran.

Ed is a home-grown Oregon man, with legs clean to his chest and the eyes of an eagle. We have shared hunting experiences in this Great Land that most can only dream about.

It was typical southeast Alaska weather: rain showers, rain squalls, and WET! We got up at 4:30 a.m. on most mornings, and we were out by first light, looking for that "big one." Or, as the day wore on maybe just "something with antlers." We traveled to different areas with our four-wheel drive pickup, spotting numerous deer (17 the first day), but no bucks. On the afternoon of the 16th, we had moved into an area called Exchange Cove to hunt an old clear-cut. Contrary to what the preservationists are telling us, these logging sites provide excellent browse for deer and black bear. We had just headed up a short spur road when Ed spotted a buck on a hillside, some 225 yards across a ravine. He began sputtering adjectives, describing the size of this buck and would I please shoot!

I realized after looking at this beauty through my rifle scope that he was really special. It was the largest-bodied blacktail we had ever seen. Realizing that made me reluctant to squeeze the trigger, wanting to just watch this guy.

Instinctively, I knew that it was time, and I made an easy, one-shot kill. The deer dressed out at over 200 pounds. He sported a nearly perfect set of antlers, with four points on each side. Well, that is one day the three of us will share with each other for the rest of our lives, and those bonds of family and friendship that are born of these hunting experiences and adventures into this Great Land, Alaska!

Photograph by Wm. H. Nesbitt

SITKA BLACKTAIL DEER
FOURTH AWARD
SCORE: 123-2/8

Locality: Prince of Wales Island, Alaska   Date: August 1987
Hunter: Kenneth W. Twitchell

SITKA BLACKTAIL DEER
123-2/8

Kenneth W. Twitchell

On August 31, 1987, my six hunting companions and I met at the site from which we were to embark on our annual, opening-day hunting trip to an un-named mountain, 10 miles north of Craig, Alaska. The hike up the 3,000 foot mountain is through some of the most beautiful alpine meadows of any I have seen in my 10 years of hunting in southeast Alaska. But after seven hours of clawing and clinging to bushes, grass clumps, devils club, and getting separated from two of our party (who caught up with us the next morning), we finally reached the top at 8:30 p.m. If it did not cloud up and rain (which it does faithfully in southeast Alaska), opening morning would be great.

After camp was set up, we cleaned our fingernails, picked devils club out of our hands, and sat down to drink a much deserved Pepsi. While quenching our thirst we observed some 20 bucks, ranging from forkhorns and spikes to several nice 4-points. We watched until it got dark and hoped that we would see some of these nice bucks, which more than likely had never seen a human, again.

Around 4:30 in the morning, shortly after dawn made its first crack, the three boys (Kent, Kory, and Sean; ages 15 to 17) took off. They had not slept much, kind of like six-year-olds at Christmas. They rolled back into camp about 2-1/2 hours later, reporting to us what they had seen. As Dennis and I rolled out of our beds, we made a pot of hot coffee and discussed our hunting plans. With plenty of ground to hunt, we took off, seeking the hunter's dream. After a seven-hour hike up the mountain, I was after anything that would beat Kory for the case of Pepsi that we had bet. The year before, he had won the same bet with a 2x3 buck.

At eight that morning I heard the sound of Kory's .300 Win. Mag and his hollering, "All right, Boone and Crockett!" I was sure that he had a nice one and, after I saw it, I knew he had won the bet again.

After we boned-out Kory's 4-point and were packing it back to camp, we heard more shots. Sean, who was on another ridge, was downing a nice 3x4. Then, as Kory, Kent, Dennis, and I were about half-way back to camp, we spotted a nice buck on a knob, lying down. I could tell through the 2x7 scope on my rifle it was a big deer. I shot two times, offhand at about 350 yards, with my .30-06 pump, hitting low both times.

As Kent and I ran over to where the buck was lying, we split and circled the knob. As I went around the back-side, I saw the deer stop and look at me. I raised my gun and shot him in the neck. He had dropped just 10 feet shy of going into no man's land where the big bucks go and not even the bugs can find them. I then realized that perhaps I had won the Pepsi bet.

When we arrived back at camp, we found Speed and Shane (Sean's dad and ten-year old brother) had arrived. They were the two party members that had become separated from our group the night before. They had spent the night on the ridge that we had come up.

We continued to hunt the rest of that day but didn't see anything to shoot at. The next morning offered just as much as the previous morning. Kent shot a 3x5, and Dennis got a nice 3-point on the backside of the farthest ridge from camp. Speed shot a big 3-point on the same ridge and almost on the same spot where his son, Sean, had gotten his 4x3 buck. Shane, Speed's youngest son, didn't get a deer. But, after a 6-1/2 hour hike back down the mountain, he was glad he hadn't gotten one. After we got back to our pick-ups, we were thankful that the weather had been nice because in this country it can be real dangerous if the fog sets in and you're not prepared for it.

After hunting for years to get a nice 4-point in velvet, I finally did, only to have to remove the velvet to get it entered in the records book.

Photographs Courtesy of Charlie W. Hastings and Robert C. Jones

(l) Uyak Bay, Kodiak Island, Alaska, produced this Sitka blacktail deer scoring 111-3/8 points for Charlie W. Hastings in 1986. (r) Robert C. Jones hunted all day in a light rain on Kodiak Island, Alaska, before he took this Sitka blacktail deer in 1987 that scores 107-2/8 points.

Photograph Courtesy of Allan C. Merrill

Sharla L. Merrill was only nine-years-old when she dropped this Sitka blacktail deer that scores 109 points on Dall Island, Alaska, in 1985, with one shot.

Photograph by Wm. H. Nesbitt

SITKA BLACKTAIL DEER
CERTIFICATE OF MERIT
SCORE: 125-7/8

Locality: Tenakee Inlet, Alaska   Date: November 1964
Hunter: Donald E. Thompson

SITKA BLACKTAIL DEER
125-7/8

Donald E. Thompson

November in southeast Alaska is a bleak month ordinarily. Usually, you can be assured the wind will howl. As I write this piece, I recall a bit of doggerel that was penned long ago that sums up November perfectly. It says, "First it rained, then it blew, then it friz and then it snew."

The one redeeming feature of this month is the fact that the Sitka blacktail deer are in the peak of the annual rutting season. When they are about with amorous intent, the buck's behavior can border on the verge of stupidity.

The date was November 11, 1964, and I was employed by Island Logging Company of Sitka, Alaska. They were engaged in a massive clear-cutting operation involving acres of prime old-growth Sitka spruce and western hemlock in Tenakee Inlet, Alaska. They had a floating camp that was a compact affair, situated atop logs that were cabled together with support for a cook house, office, bunk house, and other buildings integral to the logging show needs.

I was employed as a back rigger, a very vital job. When I had completed the rigging, I often had several hours of free time to pursue my own interests. Much of this time was spent glassing the surrounding mountains for big game. Deer were abundant, and often the great coastal grizzly was spotted making his rounds. The area that I was hunting is located on a magnificent, scenic inlet that pierces the heart of Chichagof Island.

As I set out on the morning of the 11th, my chief concern was for the weather as a brisk southeaster was whipping up the inlet. I was enroute by boat to an area that had always been generous in providing big bucks for the logger table. I fondly called the area "Valley of the Kings." Most logger-hunters were interested in the tasty steaks and tenderloins, and the antlers usually ended-up atop the gut piles, miles from camp. I have always remarked that you can barbecue, boil, bake, and make soup of these antlers, but I had never yet discovered the secret to making them a gourmet's delight. Consequently, many an antler ended-up supplying calcium to the mice.

In the incredible quiet that lies over a pristine wilderness, sound carries remarkably well in the still air. No sooner had I secured my boat in the lee of a sheltering point than I heard the sound of two bucks in battle. In my excitement I forgot what a miserable thing an Alaskan mountainside could be. As I tried to scurry upwards, I would often slide back two steps for every one I advanced. In my eagerness, it seemed hours before I came onto the scene of the conflict. There, the one level spot in the area was ripped and torn as the bucks had fought for the favors of the does.

The climb up the mountainside had taken its toll on me. At the time I was six foot one and weighed a solid 200 pounds. I had toiled over windfalls, plowed through thickets of the spiny devils club, and clung to the berry brush, to reach the battlefield. As I brushed the moisture from my streaming face, I wondered if it was all worth it.

As I surveyed the scene I was cradling my favorite weapon. It was an ancient Winchester Model 1894 in .30 caliber centerfire, with an octagon barrel. Little chance of this piece running low on bullets, it held 10 rounds. In spite of the ever-present threat of bears, I had chosen the .30 caliber over a veritable arsenal in the bunkhouse. Those weapons included a .300 Magnum, a .308 Norma Magnum, a .338, and a .348 Winchester.

I had picked my favorite firearm that I fondly dubbed "Old Meat Getter". I have always had many uses for this old gun, as a walking stick, a paddle, and bringing home the bacon.

The sounds of combat had ceased, but I was nearly as excited as the combatants. Although I had killed countless deer in my long career, each hunt still contained the anxiety and anticipation of my first deer. As I paused for breath and peered intently up the wooded slope, I saw a blacktailed rump disappear behind a stand of spruce. Raising the old rifle to my shoulder, I waited. Just then a deer's muzzle poked tentatively from the cover. Like an anxious nimrod, I nearly squeezed off on a big doe. For a shaky second I mentally castigated myself for my tension and then settled back to watch.

As the doe cast coy glances behind her, the brush parted and the great stag with his massive rack gleaming in the pale light emerged. He appeared to be in a state resembling shell-shock. He was so intent on the doe that he was oblivious to anything but her.

I placed the sight on his swollen neck and squeezed the trigger. My brass was loaded with 190 grains of powder, and when the lead hit the buck's neck, he pitched forward and was dead as he struck the ground. Racing over to my prize, I could scarcely believe the size of the animal lying before me.

The neck was enormous and the entire carcass gave off the sickening stench that only rutting bucks possess. I was quick to emasculate the buck and slice off the scent glands on his hind hocks. Alaskans say, "When you pull the trigger the fun is over." How true.

The massive animal emptied of his viscera was still more than I could hoist on my back and carry down the mountain. The only other way to transport the animal was to drag him by the antlers. Anyone familiar with the procedure of retrieving your prize from an Alaskan mountain knows that sooner or later (usually sooner), you will have problems. The very terrain is the enemy. With a giant body in tow down the steep grades, you will become entangled in brush and often the tow picks up speed and runs over you. After being run down several times with bruising consequences, I was able to fling myself sideways as the trophy once again came plunging down at me. The deer went rocketing down the grade, unhindered, and when I caught up to it, it was piled up at the bottom of a deep draw.

By now being a weary hunter, I almost wished that buck was alive and well and back with his lady love. I was scratched, bruised, and sopping wet from my exertions. All for an old buck that I figured was so tough that you'd have a hard time sticking a fork in the gravy at dinner.

Now it was decision time. The options were to cut off the head and abandon it; butcher the animal and make several trips; or find another way. (You must remember daylight in Alaska's fall is brief and fleeting.) As I paused, a light flashed in my brain and I knew how the deer was going to remain intact (well not quite intact) as I reached down with my hunting knife and severed the lower jaw at the hinge. In some long ago jungle survival school when I was a Green Beret, I learned a trick that I had never before used but now I put it to very good use.

Going in front of the huge beast, I put my foot on his nose and pressed the upper teeth firmly into the grade; then I grasped the antlers and leaned backwards and felt the animal move upward a few inches. It was working! Sometimes I gained a foot; at other times only inches, but the buck was moving upwards and out of the hole. Finally, a tremendous tug brought the buck over the top and I sank down atop the heavily haired carcass.

Few packs off the mountains of Chichagof are trouble-free, and the remainder of the trip was a continuation of the nightmare. Spiny brush, windfalls, brush, and muck underfoot made it interesting. The last 100 yards through the thinning timber to the beach seemed endless, and as I stumbled onto the graveled shore, I was numb with fatigue.

Even though I was at the skiff, there was still the problem of hoisting the big body on board. I wasn't a rigger for nothing. I gathered piles of rounded drift logs and, using a pole as a pry bar, I eased the head and shoulders aboard. Little by little, the rest of the deer finally settled onto the bottom of the boat. A world class blacktail was headed for glory at last!

At the floating camp, I nosed the skiff up to the brow log and dumped the buck unceremoniously onto the deck. I then took a hand saw and removed the rack. I compared it to the buck I had taken earlier. I found that the early buck was larger, but it had an odd point protruding off the main beam that destroyed its symmetry, so I luckily decided to keep the prize of the day.

In 1965 I returned to Juneau area and married. My new bride preferred the comforts of the Juneau-Douglas area, and soon I was enroute to camp to pick up my belongings and settle down to domestic bliss. Later, the rack was put on a plaque, but the years brought it close to disaster many times. As my house lacked a den, the rack had often brushed the garbage collection. Once when a teen-age son was taking shop, it was in imminent danger of being converted into bone handles for hunting knives. But at long last, its true destiny has been found as a world-class trophy.

Photograph by Wm. H. Nesbitt

NEW WORLD'S RECORD SITKA BLACKTAIL DEER
CERTIFICATE OF MERIT
SCORE: 128

Locality: Kodiak Island, Alaska   Date: 1985
Hunter: Unknown   Owner: Craig Allen

SITKA BLACKTAIL DEER 128

Craig Allen, owner

There is not too much of a story. I just got interested in antlers after years of buying them for my business. Then, I had to have the bigger and the harder to find ones.

This Sitka blacktail deer I got from a taxidermist in Anchorage, Alaska. He got it from an Eskimo that killed it on Kodiak Island during the 1986 deer hunt.

Photograph by Wm. H. Nesbitt

AMERICAN ELK, TYPICAL ANTLERS
FIRST AWARD
SCORE: 401-7/8

Locality: Apache Co., Ariz.   Date: September 1987
Hunter: Bruce R. Keller

AMERICAN ELK, TYPICAL ANTLERS 401-7/8

Bruce R. Keller

Every hunter has felt it, that strange, magical sensation. Whether it's when perched in an oak tree overlooking a whitetail scrape in Michigan, or surveying an elk meadow in Arizona as I was, the location is of little importance. Maybe this day we shiver a little more and shrug it off as the pre-dawn chill, but this shaking doesn't sneak-in through our heavy wool coats. For this is the first day of the hunt, and with it a special thrill and anticipation that never diminishes, no matter how many times the scene is repeated or rehearsed. But still I tried to convince myself that it was the frosty morning that caused my hands to shake so badly as my binoculars scanned the meadow in front of me. My eyes tested the first hint of light, wishing life into the ghostly shadows. But this morning my eyes weren't playing tricks on me; trees were trees, rocks were rocks, but elk were there too! Lots of elk.

A fickle wind may have betrayed our presence. Before Tom, my Apache guide, or I could determine if any of these elk were worthy of taking, they were again melting back into the protective darkness of the surrounding forest. Yet one bull, following a sizable harem, caught our attention.

Tom and I stayed just inside the trees and hustled around the meadow to where the bull had disappeared. Luck was with us as we nearly ran smack into the small herd. A screaming bugle brought us to a halt, not 20 yards from the rut-crazed bull. We watched in amazement, evaluating this majestic 6x7 as he put on a heck of a show for us and his girls. Tom and I must have looked questioningly at each other a dozen times in the short five minutes the bull was in sight, deciding if I should end my hunt here and now. This was the first bull we'd seen, scarcely 30 minutes into the hunt, and surely he was the biggest bull I'd ever seen alive.

Prior to my trip to the White Mountains I'd made myself a promise that I'd take the first 350 point bull I saw. Now here I was, sliding the safety back on a monster that would gross score over 375 Boone and Crockett points, and score well up in SCI too. I'm still not sure why I turned him down, or how many times I questioned my decision on the way back to the truck. But heck, I was finally at the White Mountain Apache Reservation, the mecca of elk hunting. And as my good friend and elk hunting mentor, Howard Gilmore, coached me the prior evening, most people shoot too quickly and regret it the rest of the week as they watch the patient hunters drag monster after monster into camp. But, does "quickly" mean passing up the elk of my dreams?

Though we saw several bulls during the next few hours, nothing approached the grandeur of the leviathan I had turned down. On the drive back to camp for lunch I was proud of my decision and restraint. That is I was proud until I told Howard what I had done. "You WHAT? How BIG?"

Later that afternoon, I resumed my elk hunting education a much wiser and more circumspect pupil. But unfortunately, there was no opportunity to test my resolve. That night a congenial group of hunters and guides greeted each party of hunters as they returned from the field. Two jubilant hunters ended their hunts on the first day with outstanding bulls. John Church of California bagged a wide-spread 6x6, while Jackie Brittingham of Texas took a high-scoring, non-typical 7x7. Even in an area like this, these bulls were exceptional and cause for great celebration.

Like many other elk hunters, I cut my teeth packing into the back country of Montana and Wyoming year after year, rarely seeing, much less taking, anything over five points to a side. I treated myself to an elk hunt on a huge ranch in New Mexico a few years back, and although I took a fine 6x6, I still longed to hunt the bulls of the White Mountains, the heads of which I had seen displayed over the years at the Safari Club Convention in Las Vegas.

Finally, with the help of John Griffith and Howard Gilmore, great friends from previous hunts to other places, I was able to join them on the first trophy hunt of the 1987 season. The White Mountain Apache Reservation covers 1,700,000 acres of virtually roadless wilderness in the northeast corner of Arizona. The hunting season and bag limits are set by the Apache Tribe, and all guiding is done by tribal members. Under the guidance and direction of Phil Stago and John Caid, hunting at White Mountain has become one of the greatest game-management success stories in our country today. They have resisted the temptation to over-harvest the herd for the obvious short-term financial gain, preferring the long range goal of producing the finest elk trophies to be found anywhere in the wild for years to come.

If sleep comes hard the night before the hunt begins, try ignoring a records book bull that keeps parading through your mind as you watch the late hours slip by. But hope springs eternal, and long before dawn I was up and ready to recoup my flagging self-respect and bag a bull that was big enough to prove that the youngster I had turned down the day before was really no "mistake."

But as day two melted into day three, and then four, I still hadn't seen a bull to equal the "mistake" bull, though each day Tom and I pondered over at least one "if only" candidate. This coupled with the fact that the other hunters were seeing good bulls, and two more monsters were brought into camp, made it impossible not to remain in high spirits.

During lunch on day five, another guide, Greg, whose hunter had filled-out the previous day, told Tom and me of a bull they had seen just at dusk. Though too dark to see well, it appeared worthy of a better look.

Following the rough map and directions, we left the truck at 2:30 that afternoon and headed up the mountain above the designated meadow. Though Greg had seen him in this meadow, we figured a smart old bull wouldn't show himself in an open field until right at dark, so we hoped to intercept him on his way down. A few hundred yards inside the timber, the stillness was broken by a bugle, followed by two answering challenges. The bull on our right sounded young (too high pitched) while the one straight ahead of us sounded the worthier of the other two, with a deeper, wheezing call.

An hour's slow stalk through the black timber brought us to within 100 yards of the enraged bull. For several minutes we watched his antler tops bob between trees, frustrated by not being able to get a clear look at the rest of his head gear. He fed slowly through a small opening, although never raising his head. The interloper to our left answered our prayers and squealed a challenge, not 200 yards across the mountain. The big boy responded with a screaming warning, tilting the massive rack toward his flanks, revealing incredibly long front tines. For the first time in five days of hunting with Tom, I didn't have to turn to him for approval or confirmation. I can't say that I tried to figure exactly how big the bull really was, but I knew I wanted him.

Hoping the bull would continue downhill and pass a scant few yards from our position, I quietly got in a good sitting position and waited. But again the challenger called from the timber above us. This proved too much for our bull's territorial pride and he disappeared into the timber to confront this intruder to his kingdom. Slowly and very quietly, we advanced to the left, expecting to catch him stealing through the thick timber. Within 50 yards, Tom and I saw a flash of brown heading back toward the small opening we had come from. Fearing we had blown the stalk, we hurried back to catch him crossing the clearing.

As I was about to break into sight of the opening, I felt Tom's hand grab my shoulder. There, above the tops of the bushes, were the tips of the bull's antlers. He let out a scream at the fleeing mule deer buck that we had spooked, thinking it to be our bull. He then stepped into the clearing and started walking directly away from us. As I was armed with a .270 Weatherby Mag, I was hesitant to take the rear shot. Finally, just as he was about to disappear into the timber, he quartered slightly to his right. Knowing this would be my best and possibly only chance, I angled a shot behind his ribs, toward the far shoulder. Tom, who had up to this point been silent, thought I had missed when the bull didn't immediately go down; he swore and broke his walking stick over a big log in disgust. Before his words died though, the bull sagged to his knees and two more rounds put him down for good.

He fell with his antlers in some low bushes, so it wasn't until we wrestled him free that we realized how good he really was. Though I never seriously believed I'd take a records book bull, I didn't need a tape to verify what I'd done.

With darkness nearly upon us, and the truck and my cameras a mile down the mountain, I asked Tom's indulgence one more time to take a few quick measurements before starting out. On the way, I had to mentally calculate and recalculate my figures several times to convince myself that not only had what I suspected of the bull's records book quality been correct, but I had also done what fewer than 20 hunters have done since the first elk was entered into the Boone and Crockett records book. I also know that this is the place to do it. John Caid showed us a shed antler he picked up. If both sides of that elk were similar, it would score in the 440's, making it a contender for the new world's record!

Photograph by Wm. H. Nesbitt

AMERICAN ELK, TYPICAL ANTLERS
SECOND AWARD
SCORE: 388-2/8
Locality: Sentinel Mt., B.C.   Date: September 1986
Hunter: Martin Braun

AMERICAN ELK, TYPICAL ANTLERS 388-2/8

Martin Braun

In 1986 I drew a limited entry permit for elk. Having lived in the area all my life, and knowing that it had large elk, Dad and I decided we would give it our all for a granddaddy. September 10 (opening morning) found Dad and I on the mountain, bugling and getting answers from four different directions. We had one 6-point come in, but nothing impressive. That evening we tried again, but it seemed that most of the bulls were reluctant to show or come in, maybe because a lot of hunters practice bugling and have made them cautious.

The next morning we tried a different approach. Dad bugled, and when we got an answer, I (with my felt liners on my feet) would stalk in on the bull, which worked. Unfortunately, the thick jack pine made it difficult to get a good look at the antlers. After wearing the bottoms completely out of the felt liners, and having to return in bare feet, we decided to try a higher, more open area.

The next weekend we spotted a huge bull in the evening. He had a bunch of cows that he was trying to keep two other bulls away from. It was great to watch. He would stand on a rock outcrop over the harem, and when one of the bulls would get too close, he would take off after him, then return to the same rock. We watched this through the spotting scope until dark.

That evening my friend Donald arrived from Fort St. John in time to help celebrate my birthday on September 28, the next day. That night we studied forestry maps and talked it over. We decided we would have to try to get on top of that mountain so we could hunt downhill, giving us the advantage.

The next morning we tried to get up a couple of roads that were shown on the map. They were made for the fire that had burned there several years earlier. The roads were all washed-out and grown-up, so we drove around to the other side of the mountain range. We went up a road that used to service a lookout tower. We arrived at an area where we thought the elk might be. Donald tried bugling. After a length of time with no response from elk, we kept on going.

On the way to the lookout tower we came to another old, grown-up road. It was about 4 o'clock, but we decided to walk down the road a bit and try bugling. When we got to the open country, Donald bugled and we got a reply from across the draw. We got into position, then Donald bugled again. We got another reply that seemed closer.

We started glassing the area where the elk was bugling, hoping to pick up movement. Just then, about 500 yards away, the bull walked out of the jack pine and onto a flat rock bluff. We didn't have to wonder about his size, only if I should take a chance at that range. Knowing that he could step into the jack pine and possibly not be seen again, I shouldered my 7 mm Remington Mag rifle and shot. The shot was just a bit low, going under his belly. The bullet hit a rock on the far side of him. The elk looked at the spot where the bullet hit the rock, then he turned and headed straight down in our direction.

At about 300 yards, he was about to get out of sight when I shot a second time, hitting him in the antler. That turned him into the open again, long enough for me to get a third shot. On this shot, Donald yelled, "He's down." After watching the area for a few moments we saw a small tree shake. Dad and Donald watched the area, while I worked my way down to where the elk was. When I got there, the elk was lying behind a blown-down tree. I then took my fourth and final shot.

When Dad and Donald got down to where I was, they saw how big the elk really was. They then turned to me, shook my hand and said, "That's a birthday present that will be hard to beat."

Photographs Courtesy of George E. Long and Robert H. Pickett, Jr.

(l) George E. Long hunted the Hualapai Indian Reservation, Arizona, in 1985 and intercepted this bugling, typical American elk scoring 381-5/8 points. (r) Robert H. Pickett, Jr., dropped this 6x7 typical American elk with his .54 caliber muzzleloader in 1987. It scores 360-2/8 points.

Photograph Courtesy of Bruce R. Keller

Bruce R. Keller with typical American elk he shot on White Mountain Apache Indian Reservation, Arizona, in 1987. It scored 401-7/8 points and received the First Award at the 20th Awards.

Photograph by Wm. H. Nesbitt

NEW WORLD'S RECORD AMERICAN ELK, NON-TYPICAL ANTLERS
FIRST AWARD
SCORE: 445-5/8

Locality: Apache Co., Ariz.   Date: October 1984
Hunter: Jerry J. Davis

AMERICAN ELK, NON-TYPICAL ANTLERS 445-5/8

Jerry J. Davis

I'll begin with a note of thanks to J.M. Hoke and K.L. Davis who helped me write this story. Trophy hunting has been a personal goal I have developed over the past 45 years. South Texas is where I began hunting at age seven with a BB gun in hand. My hunting experiences include ducks, quail, deer, pronghorn, and elk across the United States. My most rewarding hunting trip was to the White Mountain Apache Indian Reservation in Arizona during the fall of 1984.

I decided to venture back to the Reservation after careful coaxing by my hunting partner, Joe Carroll. We began the trip from Katy, Texas, filled with pure anticipation and excitement as my hunting partners and I discussed thoughts about killing some of the largest elk in the world.

Upon arrival at the Reservation, I was impressed with the rich, green forest just ahead of me; in a few short hours my dreams of hunting on this game-filled land would come true.

The first step in hunting on the Reservation is matching the hunter with an experienced Apache guide. I was fortunately paired with Phil Stago, the director of hunting and fishing on the Reservation, who would lead me on the hunt-of-a-lifetime.

The hunters and their guides exchanged a few greetings and briefly got to know each other. Eagerness to hunt on this land was meanwhile filling my every thought. I began recalling the first time I hunted elk at the Fort Apache Indian Reservation. On the first day of hunting, I was too quick to shoot an elk that scored 350 plus Boone and Crockett. This size elk is considered small for the Reservation, and based on this experience, I decided not to shoot any elk on the first day of the hunt. Moreover, the most experienced hunters at the Reservation advised me to use my seven days of hunting to view and consider several bulls before shooting the optimum elk. Patience seemed to be an ever-present virtue.

Time passed slowly as I examined my gun and made sure all my supplies were close at hand. The time was now 4:30 a.m. on October 1, 1984, and the venture to find my elk was finally beginning. Phil and I started out into the cool, early morning that, at 8,000 feet, seemed prime conditions for hunting.

After driving about 15 minutes, we decided to park the truck on a logging road. We searched for elk on foot for some time in the hours before daybreak. Phil and I walked carefully through the brush, with our ears alert to any sounds or slight movements. Finally, about one mile away, we detected the faint sound of a bull's bugle. The guide then led me in the direction of the elk's sound. We were two hunters walking with a definite purpose.

As we steadily moved toward the elk's bugling, our visibility of the land was becoming clearer and sharper. The sun's rays began peering through the tree branches about 7 a.m. We came on five bulls, milling around the lower mountainside, about 600 yards away.

Our eyes carefully focused on each bull, searching for the largest set of antlers. Phil then said in a hushed voice, "Get down on your hands and knees and get rid of that noisy jacket." Understanding the sense of the guide, I did as he said. We carefully crawled to a dead snag just ahead.

Looking up the mountain, we could see a bull finding his way down, but neither Phil nor I could see his antlers. Determined to see the full size of the elk's rack, we followed his shape carefully with our field glasses. After what seemed like an hour, the herd bull came into full sight on the logging road and stopped in his tracks. No sounds but our own hearts could be heard. I stood in amazement as the elk's large rack encompassed the width of the nearby, eight-foot-wide logging road. With assurance and confidence Phil commented, "That is a good elk."

Within a heartbeat, I realized what an opportunity I had before me and I took the shot with my 7 mm Mag. The sound of the single shot echoed over the mountainside, and I watched as the elk went down immediately.

With my gun at my side, Phil and I approached the animal with caution. Phil watched me as I took inventory of the dead elk that lay before me, and he asked, "Do you like the elk?" With no hesitation I replied, "Yes! It's the biggest elk I have ever seen!"

I then remembered my thoughts of not shooting any elk on the first day, and I realized my actions spoke louder than words. However, my instincts allowed me to feel good about what I had just shot.

With those feelings in mind, we retrieved the truck. Phil and I attacked the cumbersome job of winching the elk into the back of the truck. We relived the moment of shooting the elk several times on our way to reconvene with the other hunters and guides. We were among the last to return to the camp around noon.

Energetic conversations about the hunters' experiences filled the air, and I was no exception to this activity. Joe Carroll came up to the truck, looked at what I had shot, and said wide-eyed, "This is a record elk."

As I ran my hands over the smoothness of the antlers, I was beginning to feel some ownership of the dominating elk. I did not know or think it was a record until Joe put the measuring tape to the rack to show a score of 447-7/8 non-typical for Boone and Crockett. I was astounded at the size of the elk's antlers and I still am to this very day. This hunt will always be a welcomed memory.

In conclusion, I would like to thank the Fort Apache Indian Tribe and Phil Stago's guiding expertise for providing me with this great experience. The Reservation is a once-in-a-lifetime hunt. Last, but most of all, I give thanks to The Lord Jesus for letting me kill this record elk.

Photograph by Scott Brown

At the 20th Awards (Albuquerque, 1989), Camron Paxton accepts Honorable Mention for his non-typical American elk from Dr. Philip L. Wright, Chairman Emeritus of the Records Committee.

Photograph by Scott Brown

At the 20th Awards (Albuquerque, 1989), William W. Diekmann accepts Third Award for his pronghorn from Dr. Philip L. Wright, Chairman Emeritus of the Records Committee.

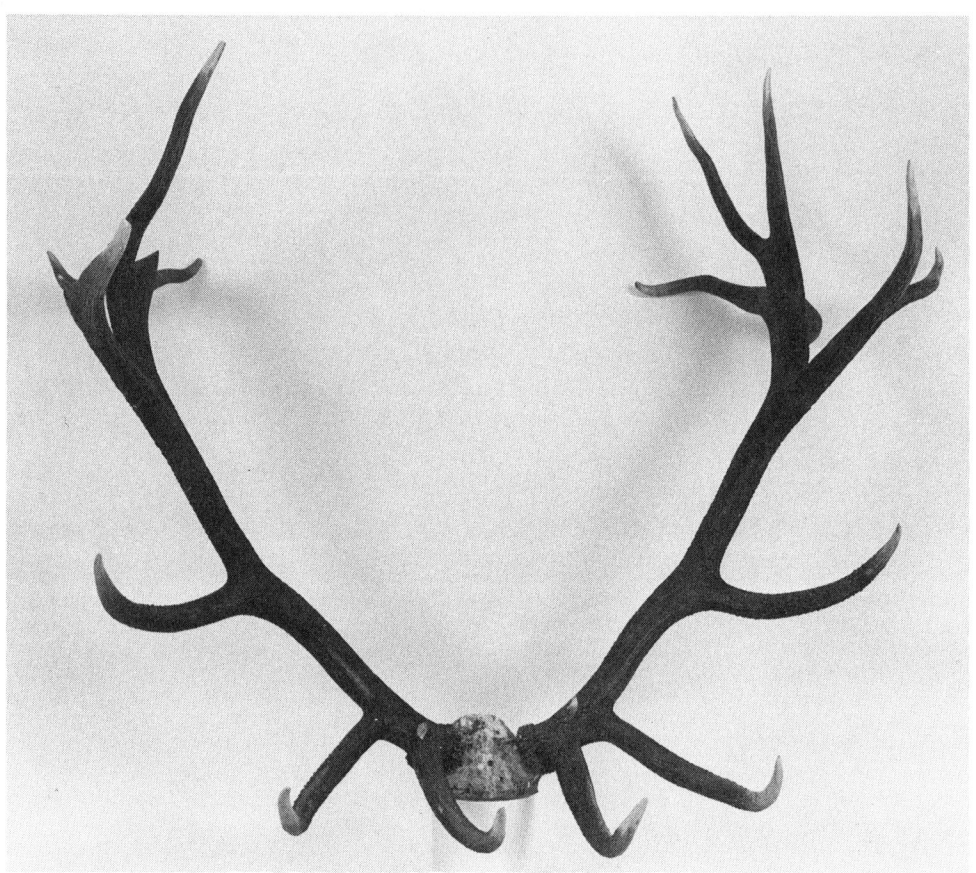

Photograph by Wm. H. Nesbitt

AMERICAN ELK, NON-TYPICAL ANTLERS
SECOND AWARD
SCORE: 423

Locality: Coconino Co., Ariz.   Date: September 1985
Hunter: James L. Ludvigson

AMERICAN ELK, NON-TYPICAL ANTLERS 423

James L. Ludvigson

Just south of the Grand Canyon, on Friday the 13th, the Arizona archery elk season started and a very lucky season it was for me.

On the first day I sat by a little trickle tank and, as the morning progressed, I tried my bugle. I got an answer from up the canyon. The bull would not come to me, so I slowly stalked my way closer to him, bugling occasionally. I ended-up in a stand across a little clearing, with a little red truck between us.

On the way back to camp, I found a fresh wallow and rebuilt a ground blind I had placed there two years before.

On the second morning of the hunt, I approached the blind at the wallow and whistled with my mouth to make sure no one else was there first. To my surprise, I got an answer to my whistle from what sounded like the bull I had been bugling with a half-mile farther down the canyon on the previous day. I slipped into the blind and sat quietly waiting.

Then, from down a trail leading to the wallow, came a magnificent elk with antlers that seemed to be coming out all over the place. He stopped and watched the wallow before coming in. As he moved the rest of the way to the wallow, I moved to my knees and got ready to shoot. He stopped and started to throw mud with his antlers. I had a shot, but I decided not to take it, because there were a few small oak branches I might hit with the arrow.

I waited and he moved farther out into the wallow, turned, and gave me a broadside shot at 25 yards. All I had to do was just nick the ends of some pine needles of a tree that was hiding a part of his shoulder. My heart was pounding, but to my surprise when I glanced down at my hands, they were not shaking. I drew back on my 72 pound Jennings Model T bow and put the 25-yard pin a third of the way up his chest, behind the shoulder. I said a little prayer to God to guide the arrow to where he wanted it to go. I then released the MA3-tipped, 2219 Gamegetter arrow that I had four-fletched with feathers.

The arrow hit the chest four inches from the point of aim and penetrated all the way through to the skin on the far side. The bull bolted away from the wallow, going through a barbed wire fence and laying one post over to the ground. I waited 45 minutes to start trailing him, and it seemed like eternity. I had an easy trailing job. He ran 300 yards and then walked for 100 yards before keeling over.

When I got to him, I made sure he was dead and thought, "He is big and he is mine when I place my tag on him." I made a fast trip back to camp. On the way, I met up with hunting friends Wayne Holt and Dave Deacon. We went to camp where my Dad was waiting for us.

After pictures were taken, and the gutting and boning finished, the meat was on its way to the processing plant in Flagstaff. I received several awards for this animal and I can say after 30 years of practicing and hunting with a bow, it has all paid-off for me with this truly magnificent bull elk that I will never forget.

Photograph Courtesy of James L. Ludvigson

James L. Ludvigson shot this non-typical American elk with a bow on the Kaibab National Forest in 1985. It scores 423 points and received the Second Award at the 20th Awards.

Photograph Courtesy of Stanford H. Atwood, Jr.

The White Mountain Apache Indian Reservation, Arizona, produced this typical American elk for Stanford H. Atwood, Jr., in 1987. It was 10-1/2 years old and scored 378-1/8 points.

Photograph by Wm. H. Nesbitt

AMERICAN ELK, NON-TYPICAL ANTLERS
THIRD AWARD
SCORE: 414
Locality: Taos Co., N.M.   Date: October 1974
Hunter: Lou A. DePaolis

AMERICAN ELK, NON-TYPICAL ANTLERS 414

Lou A. DePaolis

The hunt for Lou DePaolis' non-typical American elk took place on the famed Vermejo Ranch in northern New Mexico in 1974. However, the story for this hunt actually began in New York State, where Lou and his hunting companions still live.

Lou's regular hunting companions include Don Peters (brother-in-law), Don Moyer, and Bill Richardson, a former guide in British Columbia and Quebec. Lou made all the arrangements for their hunt, and they left for New Mexico on a Friday in October 1974, after everyone got off work. The four men met at their designated meeting area, made one last check of their equipment, and then they headed west at 5 p.m. Lou's party took two pickup trucks. One was a 4x4 for getting into the more difficult hunting areas and the other was a standard pickup.

Two men went in each truck. They alternated sleeping and driving all night the first night. They had breakfast the next morning in Indiana, then they continued on to Texas where they spent their second night. After a well-deserved night's sleep, and a hefty breakfast, they headed for Raton, New Mexico. Following Raton, they continued on to the ranch headquarters, where they checked-in.

Once they were signed-in, Lou and his companions were on their own. They took the back roads they had been assigned into the high country. The elevation of the ranch starts at 6,500 feet and goes to well over 9,000 feet at State Line Cabin, which they used as their base camp. State Line Cabin is 100 yards from Colorado on Vermejo Creek.

According to Lou, Vermejo Creek is the key secret to hunting Vermejo Ranch. When the weather gets bad, elk migrate through Vermejo Creek to their wintering grounds.

Lou's hunting party usually splits-up and hunts in pairs. Each day they switch companions so that they're hunting with someone different. Each group goes to a different area where they bugle and evaluate the trophies that respond to their calling. Lou's group learned many years earlier that the herd bull wasn't necessarily the bull they were always after. Sometimes the older bulls that have been drummed out of the herds are the bigger bulls.

On this day Lou hunted with Bill Richardson in the Costilla Meadow area. Late in the afternoon they positioned themselves on a hummock to glass the area before nightfall. They had already looked over a couple of herds that had 5x5 bulls, but they passed them up because they were looking for 6x6 bulls.

Bill was glassing through a spotting scope and Lou, about 10 feet to Bill's left, was looking down a draw when he spotted a small herd of elk near the treeline. Lou evaluated them and determined that the bull was a nice 6x6. He got ready to take it. While Lou was positioning himself, Bill whispered excitedly, "Get over here right now." With that tone of voice, Lou knew Bill had spotted something exceptional and he rolled over. Bill told Lou to take a look through the spotting scope. Lou looked and whispered to Bill, "It looks like a darn caribou."

The bull was so big that Lou did not believe Bill when he told him it was over 400 yards away. Lou got comfortable and in position to shoot. He touched off the first round. The cows and the big bull milled around, trying to decide which way to go. Apparently they couldn't determine where the shot came from.

Bill told Lou that he had missed, the bullet had hit right at the bull's feet. By this time it was getting dark and Lou was having a hard time isolating the bull again. Suddenly, the bull presented itself and Lou touched off a second shot, aiming a little higher to allow for the distance. At the crack of the rifle, all the elk disappeared and the meadow was empty.

Bill was upset and told Lou that he had missed the big bull. Lou marked the area where the bull was last seen by means of a large tree. All the way to the spot where the bull was last seen, Bill told Lou that he had missed the bull.

When they got to the site where they had last seen the bull, Bill told Lou it was 437 paces. By then it was almost pitch dark. They were groping their way from tree to tree when Lou tripped right over his bull. Lou never had such a thrill in his life. Bill, a big guy and naturally calm, grabbed Lou and threw him up in the air in his excitement.

Lou was reluctant to leave his trophy but Bill insisted they had to go back and get some lights and help before they could get the animal out of the field. Eventually, Bill convinced Lou he knew exactly where they were and that they could find his trophy again. They hiked the half-mile back to the pickup truck in record time and drove back to the cabin. There, they got their lights and hunting companions and returned to dress the animal.

Not only was Lou successful on this hunt, so was everyone else in his hunting party. Don Peters took a tremendous 7x7 bull, and Don Moyer and Bill Richardson each took respectable 6x6 bulls. The excitement and success of their hunt helped keep Lou and his friends awake on the return drive home.

Photograph Courtesy of Lou A. DePaolis

Lou A. DePaolis killed this non-typical American elk on the famous Vermejo Ranch in northern New Mexico in 1974. It scored 414 points and received the Third Award at the 20th Awards.

Photograph Courtesy of Laura R. Williams

Laura R. Williams took this typical American elk bull at daybreak on the White Mountain Apache Indian Reservation, Arizona, in 1986. It scores 384-5/8 points.

Photograph by Wm. H. Nesbitt

AMERICAN ELK, NON-TYPICAL ANTLERS
FOURTH AWARD
SCORE: 406-7/8
Locality: Apache Co., Ariz.   Date: October 1982
Hunter: Joe W. Carroll

AMERICAN ELK, NON-TYPICAL ANTLERS 406-7/8

Joe W. Carroll

Friday, October 1, 1982, was the last day of a trophy elk hunt on the Apache Indian Reservation at White River, Arizona. By noon, only two of the eight hunters in camp had not taken a bull. The two were Mike Chirpich (a hunting buddy) and me. As Mike and I hurriedly ate lunch, we shared our morning hunt experiences. Mike had seen several bulls but none met his high standards. My morning hunt had been a disaster! While my guide, Daniel Parker, and I were traveling from one hunt area to another, our truck hung "high-center" at a bad spot on an old logging road. Forty-five minutes after radioing camp for help, John Caid and his successful hunter, Hermann Meyer (with a 384-6/8 scoring bull) found us. With the help of a winch, we were off again.

After two hours and several miles of following and stalking three or four average bulls with a small herd of cows, we made our way back to the truck to head for another area. After driving a few miles, the frustration mounted when the transmission went out. Again, we made a radio call for help and, 1-1/2 hours later, we arrived back at camp.

After lunch, Mike and I made a small wager on the outcome of the last evening's hunt. We wished each other good luck and, with our guides, headed separate ways into the mountains. The afternoon was on the warm side and the bulls weren't talking very much. Time was flying, and by 4 p.m., all we had seen was one 5x5 that Daniel had lured-in by beating a fence-post-sized limb against a small pine tree. The young bull came within 30 feet of us before we decided he wasn't big enough. We decided to work our way to an area where, days before, we had seen a bull that I estimated to be between 360 and 370 points. The bull and six cows had moved into a small, high-mountain meadow to feed just before dark, but they had spooked when the wind changed and they got our scent.

By the time we reached the meadow, the sun was behind the mountain and it was cool, with a slight breeze blowing. We took a stand in a small clump of aspen in the middle of the meadow and Daniel sounded a bugle call. Almost immediately, a bull answered. After several exchanges, we could tell the bull was moving our way. Out into the open he marched, mad as he could be. As the 6x6 moved toward us, at 100 yards, I knew this was not the bull we had seen here before. He had long main beams, average point lengths, and the entire right side of his body was covered with mud. Daniel must have interrupted him at his wallow. With only 40 minutes of daylight left, Daniel knew the pressure was on me. The bull was within 40 yards when I said, "He's not what I'm looking for." Daniel asked if I was sure and I said, "Yes, let's go." I wonder what that bull thought when he saw us leave his territory at a fast walk.

One mile and 20 minutes later, we reached the end of a small ridge above a small open valley. Across the valley were two small timbered peaks. Bulls were bugling on both peaks when we spotted a bull crossing the saddle in scattered timber between the peaks. Looking through binoculars at over 300 yards, my adrenalin started to flow. A great bull with average front points, but many long top points, was crossing from the left peak to challenge the bull on the right peak. As I hurriedly positioned myself on a large boulder for a shot, I knew that with 15 minutes left on this hunt, this would be my only chance.

The bull disappeared in the dark timber. My aim was directed at a small opening at the bottom of the saddle. The bull trotted across the opening and out of sight quicker than I had expected and headed uphill toward another opening. I picked him up in my scope as he entered the next opening. The cross hairs were at the top of his back and front of his shoulders when the .270 roared. As the sound of the shot echoed through the valley, the bull walked into the timber. I quickly bolted another round into the chamber, at the same time wondering if I was underestimating the distance. As I waited and watched the opening, I saw a sight I can never forget. The bull staggered backward into the opening where I had shot, reared up on his hind legs, and then fell over backward, dead! After I recovered from that stunning sight, I let out a victorious whoop, and then I ran to Daniel to accept his handshake of congratulations.

While Daniel went to find the truck, I hustled down the ridge and across the valley, wondering if what I saw in the binoculars could be true. Up the other side I went, over downed timber and through scattered pine, stopping occasionally to glance back to the ridge from where I had shot to verify my location. I climbed a steep bank and there, in the middle of an old logging road, was my bull. I could hardly believe my eyes! An 8x7 with matching side points parallel to his fourth (royal) points. Of the six points consisting of the fourth, fifth, and side points, five are over 20 inches long and the other is 17 inches. The 130 grain soft-point had entered at the back of the ribs and angled through the lungs.

After Daniel made his way up the logging road to the elk, we whooped and hollered, took pictures, then hollered some more. We decided to radio camp with the good news and also ask for assistance in loading. While on the radio with camp, Mike cut-in to say that he had take a fine 6x6. Within one hour, Phil Stago, Jr., the tribal Director of Fish and Game, showed up and offered his congratulations and shared our excitement. Phil ran his winch line over a spare tire placed on the cab of our truck, attached the line to my bull's hind legs, and winched the bull into our truck. We followed Phil back to camp where the end of a great hunt was celebrated well into the night by all hunters, guides, and skinners.

Photograph Courtesy of Fred Fortier

Fred Fortier with his typical American elk that scores 389-6/8 points. It was shot on the White Mountain Apache Indian Reservation in Arizona in 1985.

Photograph Courtesy of Robert H. Jochim

Robert H. Jochim killed this non-typical American elk along Dogrib Creek in Alberta in 1984. Its entry score is 402-2/8 points.

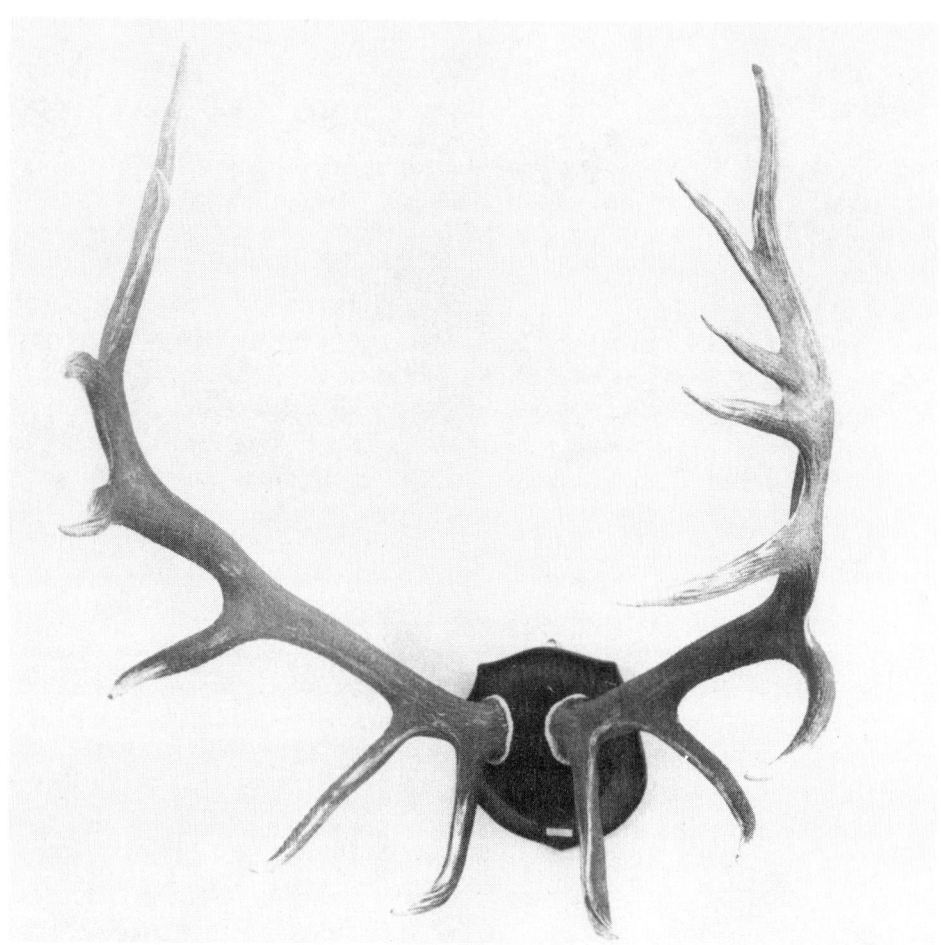

Photograph by Wm. H. Nesbitt

AMERICAN ELK, NON-TYPICAL ANTLERS
FIFTH AWARD
SCORE: 405-3/8

Locality: Vermillion River, Man.   Date: December 1986
Hunter: Ernie M. Bernat

AMERICAN ELK, NON-TYPICAL ANTLERS 405-3/8

Ernie M. Bernat

The morning of December 6, 1986, the opening day of the first elk season, my partner and I set out anticipating an exciting morning of hunting. Armed with my .30-06 semi-automatic, even the cold temperature (minus thirty degrees) couldn't prevent us from participating in the hobby we most enjoyed. Approximately eight inches of snow covered the ground and I felt fortunate to be out on the first calm, crisp morning of the season.

When we reached our destination (a meadow situated between two bluffs), we immediately noticed the numerous sets of tracks leading from one bluff across the meadow to where the elk seemed to have fed, and then on to a second bluff. Sometime after we arrived, at approximately 9 a.m., my partner, Terry Kolida, had shot an average 6x6 bull elk. Just after the kill, we field dressed the bull and, seemingly on cue, a Game Warden came by on a ski-doo and assisted us in moving the animal to our vehicle.

On our way home, both of us pleased with the morning's hunt, we discussed the morning's happenings. However, I kept picturing the abundant tracks we had seen, and the fact that we had only found one elk bothered me greatly. But home, seven miles away, was waiting for us and farm chores still had to be done. Later that day, we skinned and hung the bull, then decided to return to the bluff and check things out.

At 3 p.m. that same afternoon, Terry and I returned to the location. The many tracks both mystified and confused us. Anxious to get to the bottom of it all, my partner followed the tracks around the 15 acre bluff, leaving me to inspect even more tracks in the meadow.

In the silent air, I heard a loud snap that caused me to jump and make a 180 degree turn to face the source of the noise. It sounded like a young sapling breaking, so I stopped and listened intently. Immediately after, the snap matured into loud rattling and trees breaking. The sounds were getting louder by the minute. My heart raced; by all the noise I thought, "This must be one huge animal!" Feeling the intensity build, my heart beat faster and faster. I knew this would be an important shot and I prepared myself, with my gun aimed. The big bull broke through the thick bush at quite a speed, spotted me, and veered to the right. Being about 150 yards away, the bull continued to bolt and I saw the great clearance between the snow and the elk's belly. Instantly, I knew it was the largest elk I had ever seen, and the desire to attain the bull was almost overwhelming.

I aimed and pulled the trigger, and the monstrous elk fell to the ground. It was a clear hit, behind the left shoulder. Relief swept over my trembling body and I lowered my gun, amazed at my aim, and even more amazed at the size of the bull. I slowly walked up to my bull and realized how massive he truly was.

My partner, who had heard the shot, rushed over to me and verified that the elk was the largest he had ever seen. We then field dressed the elk, excitedly exchanging words about the hunt. Both of us knew that we couldn't possibly lift the huge elk, and we decided to return home to find a neighbor as a third man to help us load the bull.

Soon after, three of us reported to the site and attempted to load the elk. Taking over an hour to accomplish the loading of the bull, it was obvious that the weight of the animal had to be unbelievable. We would get enough steam to actually lift the carcass to the level of the truck box, and then all three of us would "power-out," and down to the snow the elk would go again. This happened several times. We finally loaded him, his rump tight against the truck's cab window and with his head and rack still resting on the ground. It was unreal! We then tied the head and antlers up on top of his wide, massive body and journeyed home.

After sending the lower jaw away to determine the age, it was found that this big boy was 14-1/2 years old. We hope that he fathered many BIG BOYS for future generations of hunters to be in awe of. I guess the area along the Riding Mountain National Park, just south of Dauphin, Manitoba, is ideal habitat for these big, beautiful animals. The abundant vegetation within the park itself, and the grain farm land and pasture along the outskirts of the park, provides these animals with adequate food. The fact that I farm just seven miles away makes me realize how truly lucky I am.

Photographs Courtesy of Joe W. Carroll and Denis Schmitz

(l) Joe W. Carroll with his non-typical American elk 406-7/8 killed in 1982 on the White Mountain Apache Indian Reservation, Arizona, that received Fourth Award at the 20th Awards. (r) Denis Schmitz killed this Roosevelt's elk near Tillamook, Oregon, in 1987. It scores 279-7/8 points.

Photograph Courtesy of Donald Parks, Jr.

Donald Parks, Jr., bowhunted for this typical American elk in Catron County, New Mexico, in 1988. It scores 380-3/8 points.

Photograph by Wm. H. Nesbitt

AMERICAN ELK, NON-TYPICAL ANTLERS
HONORABLE MENTION
SCORE: 403-7/8
Locality: Shoshone Co., Idaho   Date: October 1964
Hunter: Fred S. Scott   Owner: Mannie Moore

AMERICAN ELK, NON-TYPICAL ANTLERS 403-7/8

Fred S. Scott, hunter
Mannie Moore, owner

Note: this story originally appeared in Boone and Crockett Club Associates Newsletter for May 1988.

It was October of 1964 in Shoshone County, Idaho. At four o'clock in the morning, I was up, as all people who work for a living get into the habit of doing. I was trying to decide if I should go elk hunting or just sit around the house all day. I couldn't go to work, as I had injured my left hand in an accident at the local silver mine where I was employed as a miner. Due to the dirty environment underground, it was not possible to work with an open wound because of the danger of infection.

It wasn't a hard decision; I decided on the elk hunt. It was just a matter of gathering the things I would need to take for a day of hunting: my rifle, ammo, bone saw, knife, rope, binoculars, lunch, and a pack to carry it all in.

I arrived at the trailhead at about 6 a.m., half-an-hour later than I would like to have gotten started. I was on Sunset Peak, which rises 6,424 feet in elevation. My hunting plan for the day was to take the trail out to Pony Peak, then go around into the head of Pony Gulch, where I would hunt the water holes and wallows in the early morning. In the afternoon, I would move onto the Idaho Gulch side to hunt the bedding areas on the north side of the main ridge. This would put me at approximately 4,000 feet in elevation. So, come night fall, I would have a good climb to get back to my vehicle.

I left Sunset Peak on a north-south ridge for the first quarter-mile, then turned off on the main east-west ridge. I was out on the main ridge about a quarter-mile, dog-trotting to make up for my late start, when a bull bugled just below the crest of the ridge. I knew he had to be close, because I heard him clearly even with my hearing impairment. I stood real still, listening for the bull to bugle again. He did! I then realized that he could be no more than 50 yards away, and just out of sight. I bugled back at him, using a short squeal to make him think that I was a small bull that needed to be put in his place with a whippin'.

Up onto the ridge came a bull like nothing you have ever seen in your life, or I in mine. He looked like a cross between a caribou and an elk. His hair standing on end, he was broadside to me, walking stiff-legged like they do when they are showing another bull just how "big and bad" they are. Posturing, I believe the game biologists would call it.

The bull didn't see me as he crossed at about 50 yards, perfectly broadside. I dropped to the seat of my pants and held for a heart shot, right at the point of his "elbow." At the shot, the bull jumped forward and raked his antlers through a small evergreen on the ridge top. I shot again, with the same point of aim. He jumped again, turned to his left, and began to walk away. I aimed at his neck and shot for the third time. To my surprise, the bull continued over the side of the ridge and out of sight.

I could not believe this was happening! This would be my fifth elk, and all the others had dropped in their tracks with the first shot. What could be wrong? I was using a model 721 Remington in .270 Winchester caliber, with a handload that Jack O'Connor had recommended for elk. It was a 150 grain Nosler partition bullet ahead of 59-1/2 grains of Hodgden 4831 military powder. This load gave an approximate velocity of 3023 feet per second at the muzzle. With the rifle sighted dead-center at 25 yards, it was right on again at 275 yards, giving the hunter a simple, "dead-on" hold on shots out to 300 yards. Shooting my rifle from a bench rest, I could keep my shots on a six-inch bulls eye at 275 yards. But, not this time.

I knew I had a wounded bull on my hands. I checked the ground for signs of blood where the bull had walked off the ridge. There were just a few drops here and there. I started tracking him down the side and over to a north facing slope. Imagine, if you can, a hillside about as steep as the bottom half of a barn roof, covered with hemlock trees and an understory of huckleberry brush about chest high. (That's right, I was in the "thick of things.") Because the ground was covered with huckleberry leaves and other debris, it was difficult to follow the signs. I would go until I lost the track or blood sign, then mark the spot and start making circles until I found another sign. I jumped the bull several times without seeing him. Finally, about the third or fourth time that I jumped him, I saw my elk. He was standing in a hole where an uprooted tree had left a deep depression.

The bull didn't jump or run, so I aimed to hit him under his ear. (He was only 50 feet away!) At the shot, I saw a piece of antler tine fly off his rack. This made me suddenly aware that my gun was not shooting where I was aiming it. Using some "Kentucky" windage and a whole lot of luck, I managed to hit my bull in the head and kill him (after two complete misses).

After I got over the excitement of the kill, I sat down for a smoke and a good look at this bull that I had just bagged. Boy, this bull had been in one hell of a fight, with his shoulders and ribs covered with scrapes and puncture wounds. Since then, I have often wondered just how big the bull must have been to put such a whippin' on my big old bull. I estimated my elk to weigh about 900 pounds, with about 40 of that being the antlers. The antlers were real heavy, with long tines and points going in every direction. There were 1-2-3-4-5-6-7-8-9; Wow! There were 9 points on each antler! This bull was certainly a trophy-of-a-lifetime.

By this time, it was 10:30 am. Being nice "Indian Summer" weather, it would get into the high 70's before the day was over. I would have to get that meat taken care of fast. It was hard to believe that I had been tracking this bull for more than 3-1/2 hours. I field dressed the elk without delay, then skinned and quartered him so I could get the meat off the ground. This allowed the air to circulate around the meat and thus disperse the body heat more quickly. I hung the quarters from a tree, then sprinkled the moist areas with black pepper to take away the moisture that the blow flies would need to lay their eggs.

All these precautions were taken to ensure that I would have good-tasting meat for the following winter, not just a freezer full of "wild meat."

After skinning the elk, I was able to determine where my bullets had hit. The first shot had hit right in the point of the brisket, and the second went in under the near leg and shattered the other leg. This was what probably caused the bull to turn left. The third shot hit in the left side of the neck, and my final shot hit the brain. I later determined that the problem with my shooting had been caused by the reloads, which had been manufactured by a local gun shop. After pulling the bullets from the remaining cases, I found that there was a difference of 5-15 grains of powder from one shell to another. This explained the different points of impact from one shot to the next. There also might have been just a touch of "buck fever." This was the only time in 35 years of hand-loaded rifle ammo that I have ever had such a problem.

With the meat taken care of, I had to get back to town and get the horses ready to pack out my elk. By the time I arrived home, caught the horses and saddled and loaded them on my truck, it was 3:30 p.m.

I drove around to the hotel where my brother Don lived, and waited for him to come home from work. I wanted him to go with me, as he had always been a better packer and "rank-horse hand" than me. Besides, one of the horses I had loaded was Don's. Both of the horses were just starting to be trained to ride and pack. My brother's horse was a 4-1/2 year-old Montana range horse of unknown breeding, and the other wasn't any better. It was a half-crazy, hot-blooded crossbreed of some sort that a friend had given me to attempt to calm it down to where someone could ride or pack him in safety.

We were just about to leave town when another friend, Frank, decided to come along for the ride. We arrived at Sunset Peak, unloaded the horses, and started down the trail without further delay. Don was in the lead, following the trail that I had blazed on the way out. We were in a hurry to get the elk out before dark, as the last quarter-mile coming up to the peak is a steep, narrow, rocky trail. It was not the best place to be with a green bronco after dark.

Once we had arrived at the elk, Don thought the quarters were covered with blow flies until he got a closer look and realized that it was just the black pepper that I had put on them. We put meat sacks on the quarters, wrapped each in a canvas manta, and then loaded the quarters on the horses. Because of the excitable and unsteady nature of the horses, it was not practical to pack the antlers on them. It was likely to lead to accident or injury to the horses or to us. Don and I would be occupied with handling the horses, so that left friend Frank to pack the antlers. We padded the skull plate and antler bases well with our jackets, and Frank put them on his shoulders and followed the horses up the trail. We certainly wouldn't need our jackets on the steep climb back to the peak. We made it back to the truck and then on to town without incident.

Back in town, the antlers caused quite a stir. No one had seen any antlers of this type before. Our local game warden, Wes McKeever, had been made aware of the kill and he contacted me to take the antlers to the regional office of the Fish and Game Dept. in Cour d'Alene, Idaho, to have them measured for Boone and Crockett. The antlers were measured by Jack McNeel, the regional public relations man for the department and also an Official Measurer for the Boone and Crockett Club. Both Wes and I were disappointed when the antlers, being so un-symmetrical, were scored below the minimum final score necessary for the records book.

Over the years, several different local business establishments have borrowed my antlers for display, and several people have offered to buy them. Although I never thought there would be a non-typical elk class, I kept the antlers for my own satisfaction.

You can imagine my surprise when I received my Fall 1986 issue of Bugle magazine, published by the Rocky Mountain Elk Foundation, of which I am a member. This issue contained an article about the Boone and Crockett Club's consideration of starting of a category for non-typical elk. The article requested that entries be made to establish if there were enough trophies to warrant a non-typical elk class. I at once contacted Jack McNeel to have him measure my antlers. Yes, the same Jack McNeel who had measured them as "typical" 22 years earlier. Jack scored the antlers at 401-2/8 points. The completed score chart was then sent to Dr. Philip L. Wright, Chairman Emeritus of the Records of North American Big Game Committee for his review.

In December 1986, the non-typical elk category was approved by the Records Committee. In February 1987, Phil Wright contacted me to get a remeasurement of the second tine on the right antler. In March of 1987, the Inland Big Game Council sponsored a Bighorn Show in Spokane, Washington. I entered the antlers in that show and they were given a score of 402-7/8. This score sheet was sent to Dr. Wright. After reviewing all the data, Dr. Wright sent in the official entry scoring of my elk as 404-3/8 points to the Club's office.

There ends my very non-typical elk story.

Photographs Courtesy of Fred S. Scott and Martin Braun

(l) Fred S. Scott shot this non-typical American elk in 1964 in Shoshone County, Idaho. It scored 403-7/8 points and received Honorable Mention at the 20th Awards. (r) This typical American elk scoring 388-2/8 points was taken by Martin Braun on Sentinel Mountain, B.C., in 1986.

Photograph Courtesy of R.L. Stamps

R.L. Stamps and hunting companions pose with Roosevelt's elk he shot from eight yards away in thick undergrowth in Polk County, Oregon. It was taken in 1985 and scores 322-1/8 points.

Photograph by Wm. H. Nesbitt

AMERICAN ELK, NON-TYPICAL ANTLERS
HONORABLE MENTION
SCORE: 402-7/8
Locality: Powell Co., Mont.   Date: October 1987
Hunter: Donald A. Roberson

AMERICAN ELK, NON-TYPICAL ANTLERS 402-7/8

Donald A. Roberson

Hunting has been something I have enjoyed since I was a boy, but elk hunting in the West was just a far away dream, a dream that continued into my manhood.

At age 35, my dream became reality on an elk hunt with an outfitter in Belgrade, Montana. Unfortunately, my reality was just an expensive nightmare. (However, just seeing elk and the sound of a bull bugling kept calling me back to the Big Sky Country.)

With my dream still alive, I went back to Pennsylvania, saved some money, and with the understanding and support of my wife, Emma, I was able to book a first-class hunt with K Lazy 3 Ranch and Outfitters, Kenny and Mary Faith Hoeffner of Lincoln, Montana. I was introduced to these fine people by my brother-in-law, Sonny Templeton, also of Lincoln. It was during my successful hunts with K Lazy 3 that I met my good friend Mark Young, who was guiding for them at that time. Mark and I have since made many journeys into the mountains in search of the majestic wapiti. Due to Mark's knowledge of the mountains and of the wapiti's habits, I have been very successful in taking some fine bulls with my custom built 7 mm, a gift from my wife. Along with the privilege of taking such a wonderful animal during these wilderness journeys, and being Mark's friend, I have experienced the sounds of nature filling my ears, the beautiful sunsets that guided me into camp, and the millions of stars in the sky that served as my night-lite.

Just before every hunting season, I would reflect on all of my previous experiences, the exhilaration and excitement of bagging the elusive elk, and how exhausted I felt after bringing this large, four-legged mammal back to camp. Thinking of this would be enough to motivate me into grabbing my running shoes and beginning my Scapegoat Wilderness conditioning program. This quest for physical fitness began with jogging, followed by hiking up a grade that could never compare to the mountains of Montana.

However, in spite of my conditioning, the mountains seemed to be getting steeper with every year. It was for these reasons, and the fact that my hunting buddy was getting busier with his ranching and outfitting, that Emma suggested I take up bowhunting and hunt the lower country when the elk were rutting. This sounded like a good idea and I decided to give it a try.

The bow I had at that time was no longer suitable, so at the 1987 Rocky Mountain Elk

Foundation banquet in Virginia, my wife successfully bid on a certificate to purchase a compound bow. With this certificate in hand, I headed for Courtney's Archery in Quakertown, Pennsylvania, to purchase my bow. I took my son Jay along for advice, as he is a avid bowhunter. Jay and Al Courtney explained to me the different choices I needed to make regarding my bow, choices such as pulley or cam system, the kind of arrows and heads, and did I want to use a release or sight pins? With their help, and the advice of people who had tried both the pulley and the cam system, I decided on a pulley. They said that this would give me a much smoother release and more accuracy. I also decided on the release and sight pins. Practice was all that was left if I was to be successful in an early season hunt for elk.

After a week or two of practicing, I found that the release was very beneficial in improving my accuracy. I also eliminated all but one sight pin. When people asked why, I replied, "I get confused easily." One evening my brother-in-law called from Montana, curious as to how I was doing with my new bow. I must tell you that he is very successful with his bow and has seven whitetails in the Pope and Young Club records book. He has also bagged lots of elk. I told him I was doing fairly good, but once in a while I had a flyer. My range was 30 yards and under, fairly consistent, but not perfect.

In early September of 1987, Emma and I loaded our motor home with hunting gear for both of us, including her rifle and my new bow and arrows. Once through packing, there was only enough room for the two of us to sit and prepare ourselves for the 2,100 miles westward to Lincoln, Montana.

The day we arrived in Lincoln, my brother-in-law, Sonny, was pronghorn hunting with our friend Mark Becker. This left me to roam the vast mountain wilderness in search of the elusive elk with only my bow for companionship. I saw several cows and one bull during those hunts alone but wasn't able to get a shot.

When Sonny and Mark returned from their hunt, they took Chris (Sonny's son-in-law) and I to their favorite elk hunting spots and, due to their great knowledge of those areas and their bugling ability, they provided us with several action-packed elk hunts.

At the end of September, Chris, Mark, and I went on an afternoon hunt. We heard a faint bugle as we walked along an old logging road. This hair-raising sound stopped us dead in our tracks. Then Chris and I got in position, while Mark bugled to lure this creature in to us. Within seconds, I was faced with a 6-point, records-book bull prepared to defend his domain. Although I have taken a few bulls with my 7 mm, this was my first encounter with a bull with only a bow for a weapon. Entranced by this animal, I forgot everything I had taught myself while practicing. As a result of my blackout, the arrow did not connect with the elk, and it might have even gone straight up in the air. It was a very bad shot. However, this mistake was a blessing in disguise.

Several days after this monstrous mistake, Sonny and Mark decided they would go deer hunting. This left Chris and I on our own. Time was of the essence now, as the elk were almost out of rut. We thought it would be best if we could catch them coming in to feed at Sonny's suggested hot spot. After a few days Chris decided to hang up his bow and call it quits. I was now hunting alone, using a portable tree stand strategically placed near a well-used elk trail. The only action I encountered during five days of solitude was when I spooked some elk on my way out of the dark timber.

With my spirits dampening, I continued to return. On Sunday, October 4th, as I was walking in the timber to set up my tree stand, I saw four cows in a small park. As there was plenty of daylight left, I quietly slipped the tree stand off my back and intently watched the cows as they fed and moved down a well-used trail. With the wind in my face, I positioned myself about 25 yards off the trail. I decided to stay on the ground, as to ready a tree for my stand would be too noisy. I figured that if any more elk came through, they would probably follow the cows.

This plan, unlike many others, appeared to be falling into place as in the distant trees across from the park I saw movement. With binoculars, I could see elk, and one was sporting a large set of antlers. When they entered the open park, my heart raced. My bow began to shake (as well as the ground beneath my feet, it seemed) as the giant bull fed about 75-100 yards from me. At first I wished for my 7 mm, then I calmed down and convinced myself that there was no need for excitement; I would never be able to take this magnificent bull with a bow. Once calmed, I began rehearsing in my mind where I would position the kisser button in my mouth and where I would place the pin on the bull if he continued on the trail in my direction, as I knew the distance from where I stood to the trail. During this rehearsal, my eyes remained glued on the huge bull.

All at once I realized that an old cow had worked her way down the trail and was standing less than 25 yards from me, intensely evaluating her surroundings. There were only a few scattered lodge pole pines between us and I couldn't even blink an eye. At this point, the bull decided to join her. He came up behind her and they both started to move. I knew it was now or never.

As the bull quartered away from me, I turned, drew, and released, all in one fluid motion. The arrow penetrated deeply into his chest, with little more than the fletching exposed. My past experience told me this was a fatal shot. But due to the angle of the shot, the blood trail would be minimal because I suspected the arrow did not exit the other side. The elk then ran in a circular pattern, with only the cows retreating to the mountains. Daylight was burning fast and tracking would be difficult, so I marked the trail he used, gathered up my stand, and started for my pickup truck. There was one thing on my mind and that was to get help to find this prize-of-a-lifetime. As I made my way out in the darkness, I spotted some fresh elk tracks that weren't there on the way in. By their size, I felt and hoped that it might be the tracks of my trophy.

It seemed to take forever to return to Sonny's house, where Emma and I were staying. As usual, the first question asked as I walked inside was "Did you see anything?" My reply, unlike so many times before was, "Yes." Then more questions followed, "Did you get a shot?" My reply was, "Yes." "Did you hit it? Was it a good hit?" Again I answered, "Yes." "How Big?" Bigger than a spike was all I cared to answer. As excited as they were, they insisted I eat, but I found myself not hungry for the first time in my life. Sonny called Mark Becker, who was staying nearby, and asked him to help track. Sonny, his wife, Darlene, and Mark rode in one rig; Emma and I rode separately. As we drove back to the spot where we could park our trucks, I told Emma that I knew I made a killing shot and if we didn't find this animal, I would be devastated and it would haunt me forever.

We began tracking from where I shot. Since there was very little blood to be found, Mark, Sonny, and Emma led the tracking expedition with their keen eyesight. Darlene and I brought up the rear, armed with flashlights. I remained in the back as I am color blind and did not want to jeopardize my chances of finding this bull. As our search for any minute speck of red on the ground continued, I began to think of the possibility that we might never find this trophy. During this night-time rendezvous, the only sounds heard were those of coyotes yipping and a voice declaring, "We found another drop." The night air was heavy with the smell of a bull, and this would make it easy for those yipping coyotes to home-in on a bull that was in one spot for very long. I suspect the coyotes were hoping we would not find the bull, as there would be plenty of fine meals for them.

When we came to the end of the blood trail, my hopes began to fade. But, Sonny said, "Don't worry, we'll find him within 50 yards or less." I still had not revealed how big this bull was; but once Mark's flashlight shone on the massive, motionless bull and he shouted, "You S.O.B.," I knew he had found my trophy and my dream of a lifetime was now reality!

I asked Sonny, as we stood and admired my 8x9 non-typical bull in the dead of the night, if he thought it would make the records book. He replied, "You bet!" You bet was right. The bull scored 403 for the Pope and Young Club, the world's second largest in its class, and 402-7/8 for Boone and Crockett entry. My trophy will be mounted, life-size, by my son Jay and it will be on display at JR's Taxidermy in Lincoln, Montana.

Photograph Courtesy of Dean Dunson

Dean Dunson was bowhunting in Coos County, Oregon, when he dropped this Roosevelt's elk in 1986. It does not have crown points but still scores 308-3/8 points.

Photograph Courtesy of Shane Jamieson

Shane Jamieson says that he got 650 pounds of excellent-tasting meat when he killed this Roosevelt's elk in an old clear-cut on Vancouver Island, British Columbia. It scores 373-3/8 points.

Photograph by Wm. H. Nesbitt

AMERICAN ELK, NON-TYPICAL ANTLERS
HONORABLE MENTION
SCORE: 402
Locality: Lundar, Man.   Date: Picked Up 1980
Owner: Fred Thorkelson

AMERICAN ELK, NON-TYPICAL ANTLERS 402

Fred Thorkelson, owner

Until recently, Manitoba wasn't known to many non-resident hunters as a trophy producing province. The trophies, however, have always been there and the residents have always known it.

Fred Thorkelson and his cousin, Donny Lindell, are farmers in south-central Manitoba. They are avid deer hunters and pursue their favorite pastime whenever the opportunity presents itself. In fact, Fred took a unique 17 point <u>typical</u> whitetail deer in 1986 that scores 177 points. It is listed in the typical whitetail deer listings of this book. Fred is also the owner of an outstanding non-typical elk rack. The story goes like this.

One day, after Fred and Donny had finished mowing some natural slough grass areas they own, they decided to check out a new deer hunting area they wanted to get to know a little better. Fred was walking along when he happened to notice something unusual about a deadfall in the brush. He walked over and checked it out a little closer. He found that it wasn't a deadfall at all. Instead, it turned out to be a tremendous set of elk antlers. Fred took them home and threw them in a work shed where they became buried under a pile of other trophies Fred has taken over the years.

A couple of years later, Fred loaned his typical whitetail deer 177 to the Manitoba Habitat Trust Program. The Trust had hired an artist to create a limited edition whitetail deer print and they used Fred's rack as the model for the print. The print was sold to raise funds for the Habitat Trust Program.

When Randy Bean of the Trust returned Fred's whitetail antlers, Fred wanted to show him the other trophies in his antler collection. As Randy and Fred walked into Fred's work shed, the trophy that really caught Randy's attention was not a set of whitetail antlers; it was the odd-ball set of elk antlers at the bottom of a pile of moose antlers. Randy told Fred that he believed the elk rack might make the Boone and Crockett Club's new category for non-typical American elk. In fact, Randy said that he wouldn't be surprised if it scored close to 400 points. Fred let Randy borrow the rack so that the antlers could be officially scored for the records books.

Fred was later pleased to find out that Randy's assessment of his non-typical American elk was correct. That picked-up set of elk antlers made the records books easily.

Photograph by Wm. H. Nesbitt

AMERICAN ELK, NON-TYPICAL ANTLERS
HONORABLE MENTION
SCORE: 398-4/8
Locality: Morton Co., Kan.   Date: September 1987
Hunter: Camron Paxton

AMERICAN ELK, NON-TYPICAL ANTLERS 398-4/8

Camron Paxton

My elk hunting adventure really began sometime in August of 1987 when I was notified by phone that my name was among those that had been drawn for an elk permit.

The area we were hunting is located in the extreme southwestern corner of Kansas near Elkhart. This area consists of about 100,000 acres of grassland, trees, and the Cimarron River bottom.

The season was to open on September 26, so my father and I set up camp at a site where the wagon trains stopped for water when the old Santa Fe Trail was being used. In some places you can still see the old wagon trails a short distance away from the river bottom. The River itself has a lot of tree and bush cover, with little meadows sprinkled about.

We found the most elk activity during early mornings and late evenings. One morning, a very large bull followed his harem of cows and calves along the edge of the river cover, while about 500 yards back, another 6x6 bull followed, making up his mind about challenging. It was a very beautiful sight. After three days of observing, we had our general area picked-out.

On opening morning we were in the field about three hours before sunrise. After walking for some time, we heard a coyote barking a short distance away. Almost immediately, we heard a bull bugle back. We were directly between bull and coyote, but we definitely knew where we wanted to head. Things got very exciting when we could hear tree limbs snapping and, after very hard looking, we finally spotted the old lead cow. When they came through a clearing, there were six cows and several calves before the bull made his appearance. We had to wait for what seemed like an eternity for the bull to move into an area for a good enough shot. We could see lots of antlers, but not enough of the body because of the tall grass and brush.

Finally, we could see enough of the upper body for a 150 yard shot. The 140 grain bullet from a .264 Mag found home in the spinal column and the bull dropped instantly. We had dressed out other elk, but this one was a lot more work because of his size. After giving some of the processed meat away, we still put 550 pounds in the deep freeze.

We were very grateful to John Parsons of Parsons Taxidermy in Derby, Kansas, who donated his time and materials to mount the head for us.

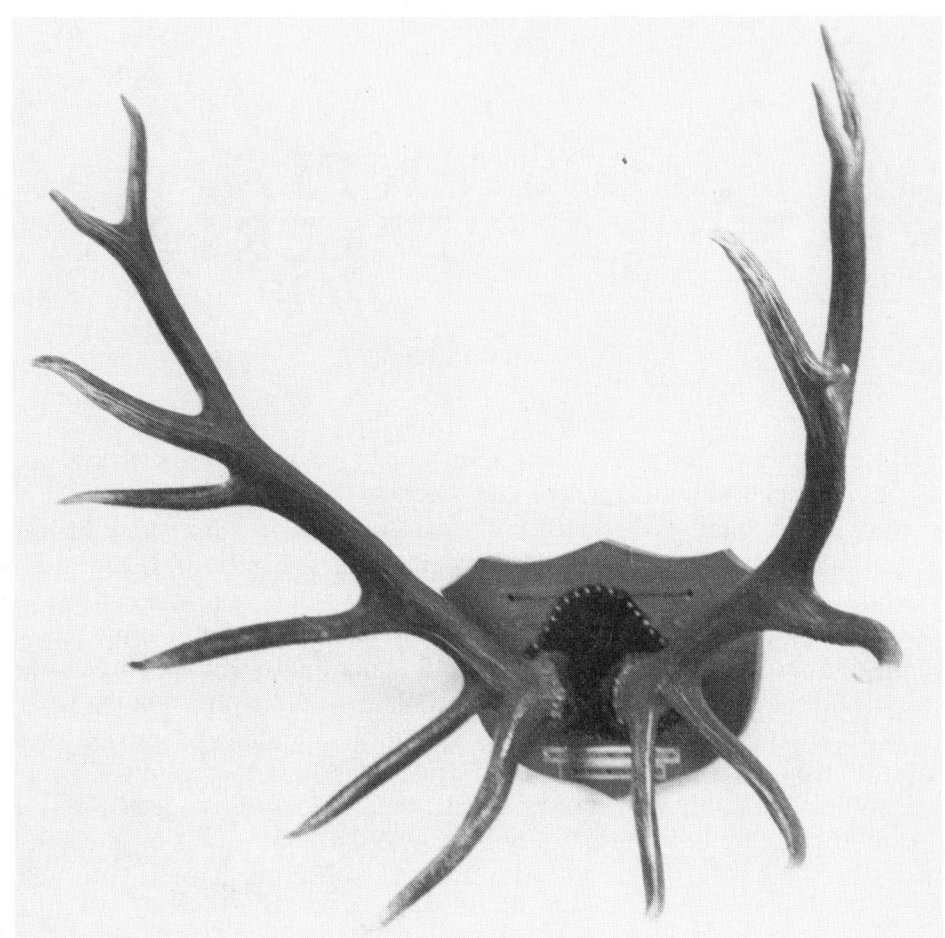

Photograph by Wm. H. Nesbitt

ROOSEVELT'S ELK
CERTIFICATE OF MERIT
SCORE: 362-6/8

Locality: Lincoln Co., Oreg.   Date: November 1955
Hunter: James H. Flescher

ROOSEVELT'S ELK 362-6/8

James H. Flescher

My cousin (Ed Kyniston), his two boys (Gene and Marvin), and I were hunting the "Howell Homestead" late one afternoon, early in the elk season of 1955. I had bought the 160 acres on which the homestead was located some years earlier, and I was familiar with the area as well as the Roosevelt's elk of the central Oregon coast.

For many years I packed a Winchester Model 94 in .30-30 caliber, with a side-mounted Weaver scope. The side-mounted scope was handy not only to allow spent cartridges to eject up out of the old carbine, but since I lost my right eye in a logging accident about three years before, I could still shoot right handed and aim with my left eye.

We had ventured about a mile from my house, up a crooked and overgrown crawler tractor road toward the long-since abandoned homestead, where I suspected there'd be elk. Nearing the fern openings and meadows that were scattered with Douglas Fir and dense underbrush, we winded the unmistakable smell of elk.

Though there was no sign, we planned our hunt on the barnyard odor, hoping to find a bull in the meadows we knew lay ahead. Ed would sit tight with one of his boys for a couple of minutes, while I circled downhill and to the left with his other boy.

The underbrush was noisy, and my concern was too often focused on the placement of my feet and the sometimes difficult task of weaving my arms and legs quietly through the bushes. As an opening came into view, I was still contentedly involved with my perfect sneak. My young companion whispered something from behind and to my right. I turned to see him pointing directly ahead of us. We had exposed ourselves almost entirely to probably the biggest bull elk I'd ever seen. He was uphill and over a slight rise at the edge of the meadow, about 40 yards away. As I saw him, he was turning and stepping into the brush. He trotted off to our left. I watched excitedly through my scope as he gradually disappeared into the maze of vine maple and salmon berries, unable to get off a clean shot.

"There's another one!," I recall hearing in a much more urgent tone of voice. To take the first bull's place was a much larger one, a monster. Immediately my cross hairs were between his eyes, and I "let him have one." He dropped. Though we were meat hunting, I shamed myself under my breath for possibly splitting such a rack of antlers.

Almost before I completed my thought, he was up, shaking his head crazily and coming right at us. I concentrated my aim on his neck and let go with another. The old bull was mad and dazed, and he continued wallowing his head, bleeding from his nose and one ear and blowing bloody foam all over the place.

He went down at least once more as he was hit in the neck, but I obviously was missing bone and he was up, charging at a little-faster-than-a-walk pace.

I was on the retreat, with my "tail between my legs," when the big boy stopped briefly and turned to his left. He was about 50 feet away, and close to where I stood originally. It actually seemed as though his head and neck were bullet-proof, and I was damn shook up. Out of sheer desperation to break him down, I pulled down on his back bone just forward of his hindquarters and touched off another shot. He went down again. Still trying to crawl with his front legs, and undoubtedly at this point trying to flee, he was bleeding heavily from his neck and much weaker. I approached cautiously. About that time, Ed and his other boy joined the party. The big bull quietly laid his head to the side and gave up.

Still trembling, I jacked out the empty shell with a mind to unload the gun, finding I'd unknowingly shot all seven shells. We field dressed the bull and then headed for my place, talking it up the whole way.

Once full of food, and equipped with packboards and a single-cell flashlight, about eight of us returned to the bull, shortly before nightfall. While boning-out meat, we found four bullet holes in his neck, all of which missed bone. There was one, of course, in his back. Apparently, it was my first shot that left a .30 caliber bullet that is still there today, embedded below the burr of his right antler. It was a slow, difficult pack in the dense brush and dark of night.

For over 30 years, "them old antlers" hung on the wall. I had no idea of what caliber they really were until my friend Mike McQuaw helped me touch base with Charles "Rusty" Lindberg of St. Helens (a Boone and Crockett Club Official Measurer).

After the measurement and having been exposed to the measuring system, Mike and I became somewhat obsessed with searching the area's barns and attics for other possible records book elk and deer antlers. After six months of rummaging and hundreds of conversations, we located roughly 20 racks of blacktail deer and Roosevelt elk antlers, near or just above the minimum entry scores.

Rusty, who was accompanied by his friend Tom Eilertson, was excited about being the honored guest at an informal antler measuring gathering and potluck dinner at my place on the Yachats River. There, at least eight other deer and elk heads rated above the minimum score, and 50-75 people had a great time.

Thanks go out from all of us to Rusty for the dedication and good will it requires to take off two days from work as a Police Officer, sacrifice a day of vacation time, and drive 200 miles one way, to measure antlers all day long for free.

Photograph Courtesy of Michael J. Jacobson

A very happy Michael J. Jacobson with the Canada moose he shot in 1986 in the Cassiar Mountains in British Columbia. It scores 197-4/8 points.

Photograph Courtesy of Delmar W. Welch

Delmar W. Welch and friend with Welch's Canada moose that he took in the Snowden Mountains of British Columbia. It has 28 countable points and scores 195-1/8 points.

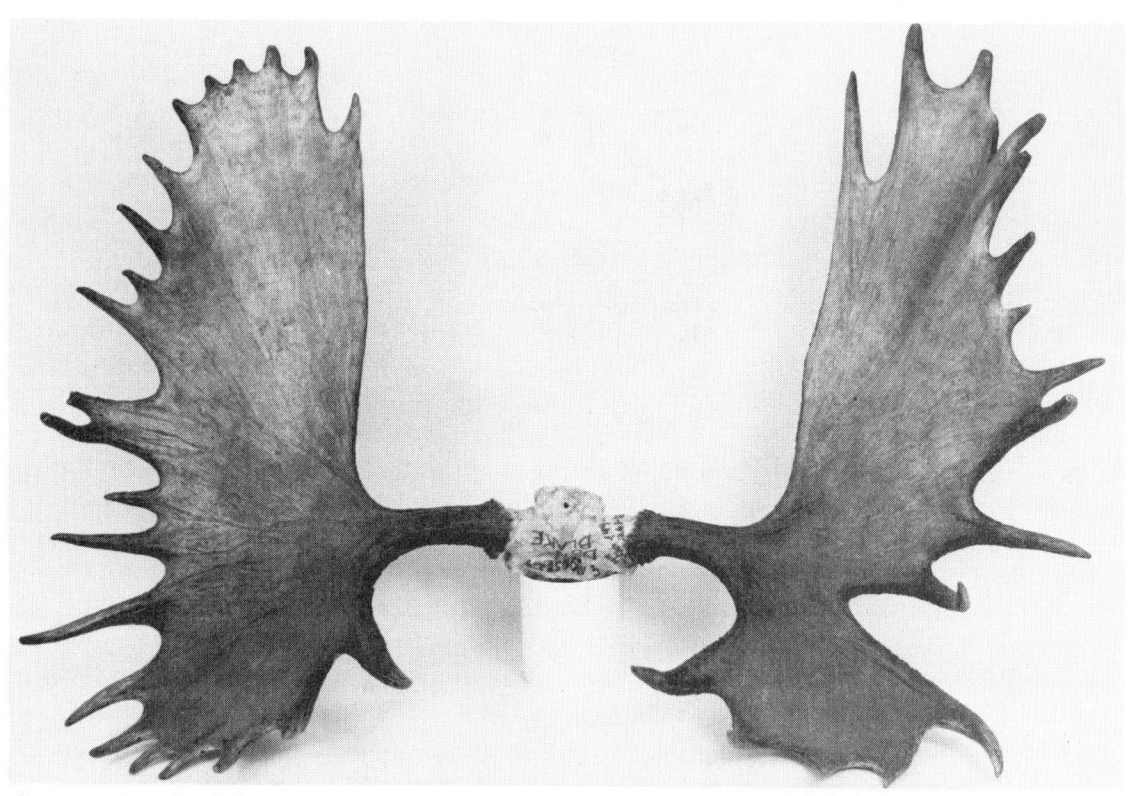

Photograph by Wm. H. Nesbitt

CANADA MOOSE
FIRST AWARD
SCORE: 227-4/8
Locality: Cook Co., Minn.   Date: October 1985
Hunter: Donald F. Blake

CANADA MOOSE 227-4/8

Donald F. Blake

My moose hunt started during the summer of 1985 when I found out that I had been drawn for a coveted Minnesota state moose license. Roughly four percent of the applicants are successful in the alternate, odd-year hunts. Minnesota assigns four hunters to the single license for one moose. On my license were my wife, Darlene, and two close friends.

Preparations for the hunt started at this time. Darlene and I decided that if we were fortunate enough to take a moose, to have a plaque mount made rather than full head mount. We felt that most moose mounts are rather ugly and very imposing on a room. Two scouting trips were made by Darlene and me. Even being in this area of the Superior National Forest (less than five miles from the Boundary Waters Canoe Area) is exciting; one never knows what will be found around the next corner, deer, black bear, or a moose. For the five years previous to my moose hunt, I had been hunting grouse and black bear, and encountering moose in this area. Encounters with bull moose at this time of year are not always the most pleasant, such as being forced to drive backward down a one-lane logging trail with a moose chasing you.

We started the hunt (October 1985) with very high hopes but we were down to three hunters (one friend could not make it) and after the first weekend, we were down to two hunters, Darlene and me. Our hopes were high but after nine solid days of hunting, both Darlene and I had to return to our jobs; I planned to return, by myself, by mid-week.

I was feeling highly frustrated, as we had not yet filled our tag. We had passed up a cow, had been within 30 yards of a moose in a spruce bog and were not able to see it, and we blew a stalk on two bulls with 50-inch plus racks that were having a fight in a swampy area during a snow squall. I had tried many different types of hunting: still, stand, drives, grunting, and rattling of antlers (I had found an antler in a spruce bog) without success. At this point, I was feeling so frustrated that if I had thought that it would help, I would have sat down and cried.

On Wednesday, I returned to the Baker Lake campsite by myself, too late to hunt. Thursday, the weather was the best of the whole hunt, bright sunshine, gusty winds, and temperature in the 60's. After hunting all morning, I drove 20 miles to the Minnesota Department of Natural Resources Moose Registration Station in Tofte Minnesota to check the status of the hunt. Fourteen of the 16 tags in the zone had been filled. I also called my wife to let her know that I had arrived okay. She told me that our dog, Floyd, had died the night before. This did not help my enthusiasm. I made a decision to check an old clear-cut area, 20 miles up the Caribou Trail. We had not hunted this area, but we had scouted there and had seen a lot of sign. It looked like a wintering area for moose. Time was running out, as only 3-1/2 days of hunting were left. All these things were weighing on me as I started to still hunt the edge of the clear-cut.

Suddenly, to my left, something caught my eye, white on black and about two hundred yards out. Grabbing my binoculars, I muttered "Oh my God he's huge." Here was the largest bull I had ever seen. Before I could react, the bull disappeared. Running up a hill, I came out about 75 yards above him. Shaking, I took a shot and heard my .30-06 handloaded bullet impact. The bull started to run and, in two steps, disappeared into the brush. Later, I found that the bullet had entered the left side, breaking a rib on the way in, had gone through the heart, both lungs, and had shattered the upper leg bone on the opposite leg, before stopping under the skin. It was a wonder that he could travel the 200 yards that he did, after being hit so solidly.

Running after him, I was so excited I didn't even know that I had run through a creek until later when I found I had wet pants and shoes. Seeing him standing, I shot again. This time he ran off, favoring his right front leg. Approaching the area where I saw him last, I could hear the rasping breath of a dying animal. I decided to wait a while longer. After it got quiet, I circled around and approached from the back side and put another round into the spine when I saw hair rising and falling (the bullet didn't even go through the spine).

Sitting down, I was admiring this beautiful animal when I imagined that I could hear God saying, "You prayed for a big moose, now here is a big moose," and then peals of laughter. Right then I knew that I had a big job ahead of me. I was able to get my four-wheel drive pickup about 800 feet from the moose. Of course, I had to cross a bog, a creek, and numerous downfalls to get to my moose. I started field dressing him about 3:30 p.m. and quit about midnight. Exhausted, I collapsed into bed in the back of the pickup.

Waking at sunrise, and seeing a heavy frost on the ground, I decided to stay in bed a little longer. Around 8, I was startled awake by timber wolves howling about 100 yards away. I was rather hoping that they would help themselves, saving me a lot of work that I knew lay ahead. I began boning-out the meat into portions small enough to pack out on my pack frame. It took the entire day to bone and pack out the meat and the hide, along with some teeth and the antlers. During the last trip out with the hide, I heard a ripping noise that I hoped wasn't my back, then, all-of-a-sudden, my pack frame broke. I could not remember being so tired from a hunt before.

At the DNR Moose Registration Station, the game biologists were excited by the size of the antlers and said that it was the largest antler set they had ever seen. The antlers were green scored at 229 Boone and Crockett points. The antlers have 36 scoreable points, and they are greater than 59 inches wide and 47 inches long, with the distinctive brow palms of a mature bull and a fold in the left antler. My moose was the 16th and last moose registered in that zone. During the five-hour drive home I alternated between euphoria and exhaustion.

After the required 60 day drying period, Bernie Fashingbauer scored the antlers at 229 for the entry measurement. The Minnesota DNR aged my moose at 7-1/2 years old from an examination of the teeth.

After finding out how high in the records books my moose scored, Darlene and I decided to have a full head mount done by Mid-America Taxidermy in Savage, Minnesota. Brad Reddick, the taxidermist, found a cape from an Alaskan moose and used that for our mount. There is a joke about the hunt not being the most costly part, it's the addition needed on the house to hold the trophy. Well, we could not get the mounted moose through the doors into our old house until we put in a patio door. We had the hide tanned with the hair on for a rug that we use as a comforter on our bed.

Coincidentally, during the 1987 Minnesota moose season a moose was taken within 20 miles of where I took mine that has the same distinctive fold in the left antler. That moose scores 209. Also in the fall of 1986, while grouse hunting, I met two couples that had, ironically, taken their bull moose (in the early 1980's) in the same exact place where I had taken my moose.

While I did not set out to take a trophy animal, I have been blessed with a hunt, memories, and an animal-of-a-lifetime. My moose has won the NRA's highest hunting award, the prestigious 1986 Leatherstocking Award, the Minnesota Deer Classic award for the largest moose taken in Minnesota, my story of the hunt was published in Outdoor Life's 1988 Annual, and my antlers were part of the Boone and Crockett Club's 20th Big Game Awards.

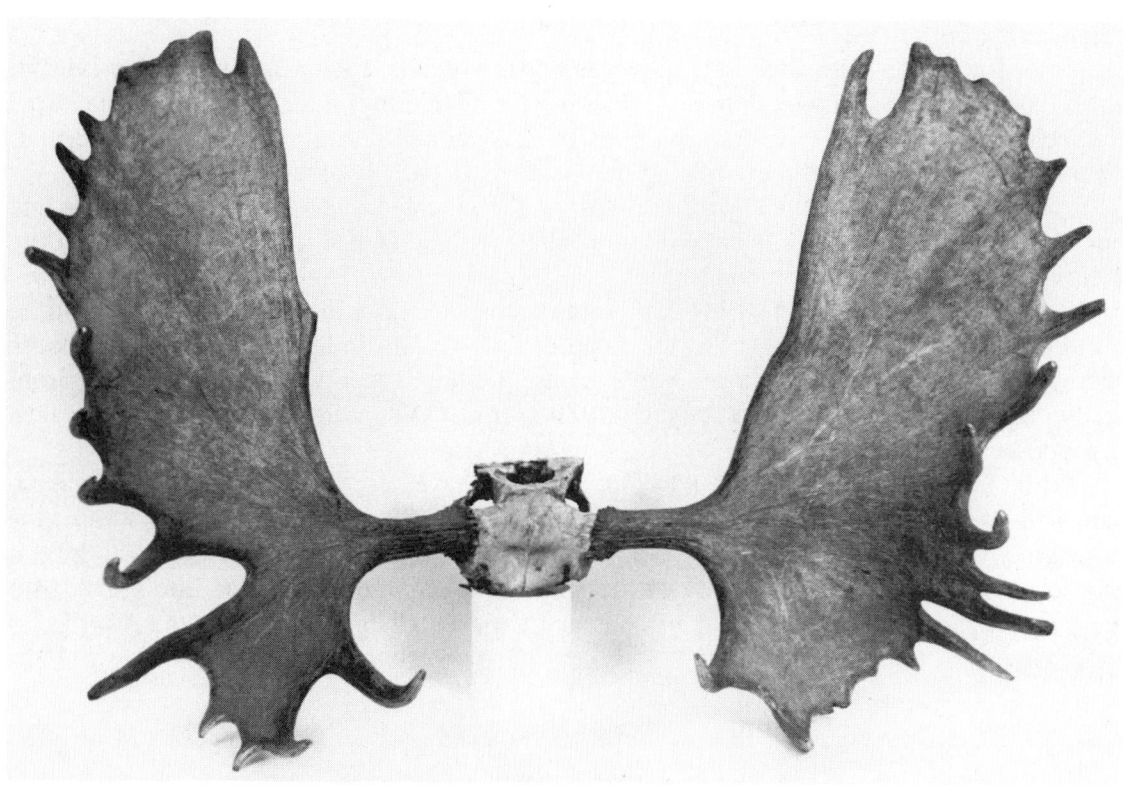

CANADA MOOSE
SECOND AWARD
SCORE: 214-6/8
Locality: Kennicott Lake, B.C.   Date: October 1988
Hunter: Robert G. Burkhouse

CANADA MOOSE 214-6/8

Robert G. Burkhouse

My hunting partner, Wayne Kingsley, and I have been hunting together for over 25 years. We had planned a sheep hunt to British Columbia for the fall of 1988, but last minute complications with the outfitter caused us to call off the trip.

Wayne said that he was going to contact Jack Atcheson and Sons, to see if they might still have any openings or cancellations for two hunters. We had previously used their services and were well satisfied with the results. Since we are both retired, the dates for the hunt were not critical, but it looked like a long shot at best. Several weeks passed and it began to look like Wayne and I would be doing all our fall hunting in the hills of north-central Pennsylvania that we call home.

On September 19, 1988, the phone rang and Wayne was on the other end. Atcheson's had just contacted him about an opening for a combination moose and goat hunt with W.E. Moynihan of Skyline Outfitters, Ltd. The hunt location was northern British Columbia.

On a fall 1987 hunt in Alaska I had seen a tremendous bull moose, but lacking the proper tag, I could only watch him. That incident had remained etched in my brain and I had been slowly cultivating a case of moose fever! I immediately told Wayne I would love to go, and the moose hunt sounded especially good to me.

Wayne and I had tried a combination black bear and mountain goat hunt in Alaska several years before. The bear portion of the hunt was successful, but five straight days of rain and fog had put the dampers on the goat hunt. Wayne apparently still had goats on his mind because he said his top priority for the hunt would be a mountain goat.

It sounded too good to be true. Our last-minute hunt was shaping into a reality. Wayne finalized the arrangements and the hunt was on. The hunt was scheduled for October 4th through the 14th, and the base camp was set up west of Telegraph Creek.

Our flight from Toronto to Vancouver, and then on to Smithers, went as scheduled. Complications arose, however, in our commercial flight from Smithers to Telegraph Creek. The schedule had been changed and the next available flight to Telegraph Creek would be in two days! After a brief consultation, Wayne and I decided to charter a private flight rather than lose two days of our hunt. It proved to be a very wise decision! We phoned our outfitter, Bill Moynihan, to advise him of our plans. He said he would meet us at the airstrip in Telegraph Creek.

When we touched down at Telegraph Creek, Bill was waiting with his Piper Cub. Incidentally, Wayne and I reside near Emporium, Pennsylvania, and the Piper Aircraft Manufacturing Plant was located about 60 miles east of our hometown.

We transferred our duffel and equipment to Bill's plane and were off for base camp. As we approached the camp, we could see the guides and wranglers chasing the horses off the landing strip so we could touch down.

Base camp was a renovated log cabin, with tents set up for sleeping quarters. Ann Moynihan, Bill's wife, was the camp cook. After settling-in and dining on an excellent supper that included homemade pie, I knew the eating portion of our hunt was in good hands. The horses were in good shape and the beautiful alpine setting looked like terrific hunting.

The following day was spent looking over the area around the base camp. Several bulls had been seen near camp and, the day before we arrived, a nice bull had even visited the camp! It sounded good.

About mid-afternoon our guide, Darcey Praud, suggested that we take a hike down the old telegraph line and look over an area about two miles from camp.

We approached a large swamp that merged into a small lake with eager anticipation, proceeding along the trail for another mile. Moose sign was evident, and Darcey decided we should retrace our steps for the return trip. As we approached the upper end of the lake, Darcey spotted a moose standing on the opposite shore of the lake. Binoculars were put to work and I could immediately make out the reflection of the sun from a huge set of antlers. The bull was about 600 yards away and walking toward the swamp. Needless to say, we quickly closed the distance by moving at a fast trot to our edge of the lake.

The bull had left the shoreline and was walking through a 300 yard swamp that gave way to heavy timber. Darcey said, "That's a dandy moose, you had better start shooting." I judged the distance at about 250 yards. I knew my .270 handloads, sighted-in three inches high at 100 yards, should be right on the nose.

I leaned against a tree to give me some support but I could only make out the bull's antlers and about half of his body as he trotted through the swamp. I preferred a standing shot, but since the distance was getting greater all the time, I decided I had better not wait. I tried to knock him down with a shot in the shoulder area. As the gun recoiled, I immediately saw chunks of mud and moss explode over his back and I knew I had shot high. As I picked up the bull again he stopped, but I could only see a portion of his head and neck, so I tried to lay one at the base of his skull. He started running again, and he was rapidly nearing the timber. My shooting score was 0 for 2!

Suddenly, he stopped and turned broadside. Perhaps he thought I was harmless! It was a big mistake, as he was perfectly stationary and his entire body was exposed. The cross hairs steadied, high in the chest, and I carefully squeezed. I heard the 130 grain Sierra boat-tail strike home. What a welcome sound! As the scope settled down, I was amazed to see he was still standing, so I quickly put another shot into the same area. That did the job. The last thing I remember seeing were huge antlers disappearing and legs sticking up in the air.

After a round of congratulations, Darcey said, "We might as well go back to camp. He isn't going anywhere and there is no way to get at him from this side of the lake."

The main topic of conversation that night involved two questions. How big was the bull, and how do we get him back to camp? A decision was made that Wayne, his guide, and wrangler would leave in the morning with the horses to see if they could get Wayne a goat. Darcey, Bill, and I would deal with the moose.

Later the next morning, I fully developed an appreciation for what Bill meant when he said, "The only place to shoot a moose is on hard bare ground." The entire day was spent getting the quarters out of the swamp and the antlers carried back to camp. It took the better part of the next day to retrieve the quarters with the pack horses.

Bill and Darcey were both immediately impressed with the size and mass of the antlers, and Bill felt certain it was a Boone and Crockett rack. I told Bill I was elated with my trophy and anything beyond that would be an added bonus.

Darcey and I spent the next two days on a pack trip for goats. We sighted about a dozen goats, but none that met Bill's specifications. Bill had stressed that our first choice should be to shoot a nice billy, and our second would be an old, dry nanny with nice horns. Under no circumstances were we to shoot a nanny with kids, even though it would have been legal to do so.

On returning to base camp, Wayne was there with his billy. His story revealed that he had passed up a nice bull moose while stalking the goat. He did not want to take a chance on the moose for fear it might spook the goat! Wayne did, however, get the bull to pose for his camera, at 40 yards! The picture was enlarged and now adorns his trophy room, accompanied by the unfilled tag.

The remaining three days of our trip were spent on a pack trip to another area for my goat and a bull for Wayne. Neither of these goals was achieved, but we did see several small bulls and a number of goats. We did see one nice billy, but he had about half of one horn broken-off and we decided to pass him up. We returned to camp, well satisfied with our hunt. Upon our return to base camp, we were excited by the news that, according to Bill's measurements, Wayne's goat would also make the Boone and Crockett records books.

As we parted ways for our trip home, Bill's last words were, "Don't let anyone split that skull!" When we arrived in Smithers and the natives all began talking about the "big horns," I really began to believe how really lucky I had been.

After we got home, Wayne measured the rack several times and assured me that Bill had been correct. The antlers would indeed make the Boone and Crockett Club records book. After the required waiting period, we had both animals officially measured and scored. Both heads made the records book!

How lucky can you get? Two outstanding trophies on a last-minute hunt by two old hunting-buddies!

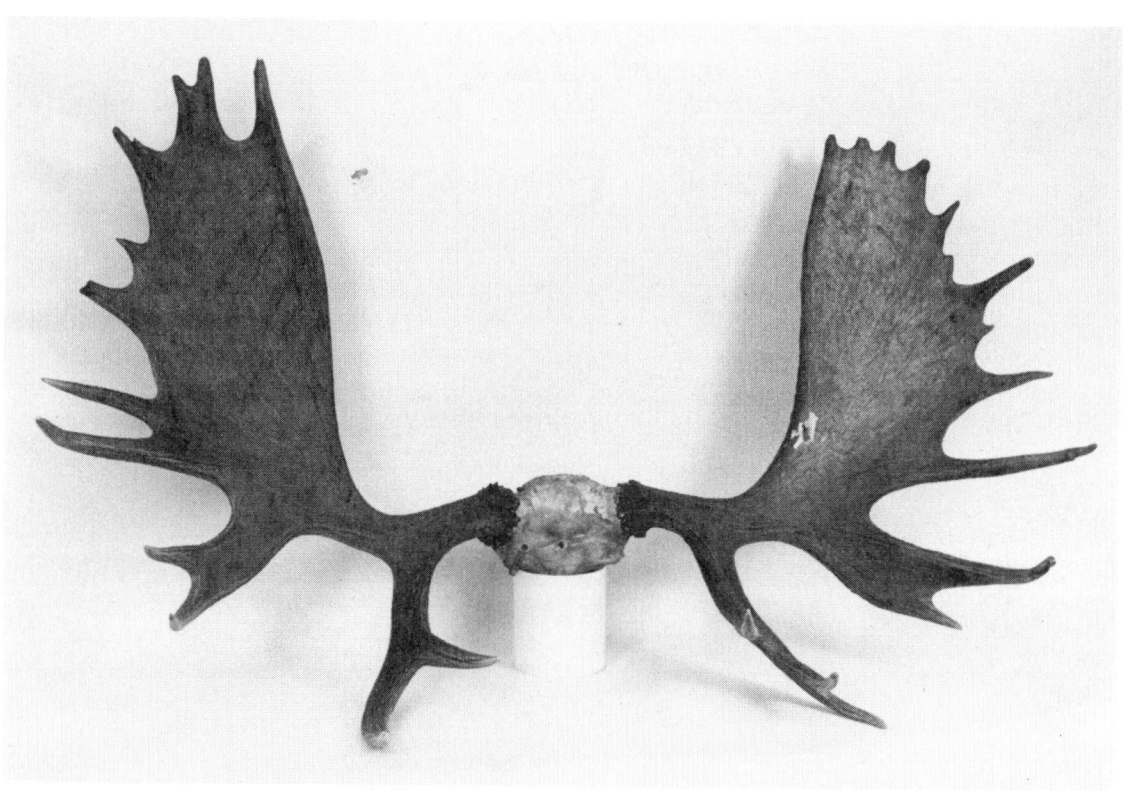

Photograph by Wm. H. Nesbitt

CANADA MOOSE
THIRD AWARD
SCORE: 206-2/8
Locality: Manning, Alta.   Date: October 1988
Hunter: Nick Denecky

CANADA MOOSE 206-2/8

Nick Denecky

This would be my fifth trip to northern Alberta for trophy moose. Brent Sparks, a taxidermist friend from Coalhurst, first mentioned that Dennis Potter of Chinchaga River Hunts was getting some pretty decent moose for his clients. Upon investigation, my hunting partner, Helmutt Fomradas, and I found Dennis booked during the rutting season, so we booked a November hunt.

On September 29, Dennis phoned; the rut was on, moose were plentiful and, due to a cancellation, the following week was now open. On such short notice, I could find no one who could join me. So next morning, I left alone for the all-day drive from my home in Lethbridge to Manning, where I would spend the night.

At Saturday noon, I was to meet Dennis at his designated pick up point where his sign reads, "Dennis Potter - 3 miles south, 1 mile west." I would be picked up by an eight-wheeled Argo, about the only way to get to the camp and home where Dennis and his wife Joanne live year-round, trapping and guiding hunters in a huge area consisting mainly of large muskeg swamps and peat bogs.

After introductions, we discussed moose in general and 50-inch or better moose in particular, as I was not interested in anything smaller. Dennis agreed our chances were excellent. After a second cup of coffee we set out, crossing the Chinchaga River to the south. What I saw was not only reassuring, it promised to be different from my other trips. Moose sign was everywhere and moose scrapes were quite frequent. We stopped at a fresh scrape that looked promising and the first call from Dennis was answered by a grunting bull. A few minutes later a cow came out, looked us over and slowly circled us at close range, then went back to the bull. The bull was not to be lured out, so we moved on.

To me this is forbidding country; one would have difficulty walking any distance as the country is mostly swamp. Beaver ponds bar the way of travel on many seismic lines. The winches seem a necessary part of the Argo's equipment.

Our destination was an old trapper's cabin on an unnamed lake. With some winching and detouring, we arrived to find the resident moose quite vocal. We could hear at least four bulls grunting in different directions.

A few calls from Dennis caught the attention of two different bulls that started coming in, giving the illusion this was going to be too easy. It was not to be, however, as the two bulls noisily circled us, met, had a short sparring match, then with occasional clashing of antlers, moved further and further away. As we prepared for our journey back to camp in near darkness, the bulls were still raising quite a fuss in the bush. It had been a very interesting day.

A frosty Sunday morning found us taking the camp's jet boat up the Chinchaga River to a spot Dennis knew to contain some big bulls. As we thawed out on shore, a grunting bull could be heard in the distance. We attempted to stalk him, as he would not come to us and seemed to be moving away from us. Anyway, the walk was welcome as it gave us a chance to warm up. After about a half-hour or so, a shot rang out. We had pushed him too close to one of the few roads in the area.

After lunch, for our third attempt, Joanne, Dennis, and I headed back to the trapper's cabin from the day before to see if we might now find a bull willing to apologize. Two of the Argos were readied, as we planned to spend the night at the cabin, a two hour drive.

Dennis and I took a canoe and rowed the better part of a mile across the lake as the wind from the east was wrong to hunt from the cabin side. We landed on a seismic line where we found a fresh, smelly scrape containing the size tracks we were looking for. While examining the scrape, we started hearing faint grunts coming from the bush upwind of us; but try as he might, Dennis could not get the bull to move. Then, after a stalemate of about a half-hour or so, we got a break. Two cows from the bull's vicinity came out and started feeding in the lake, taking no notice of us. Further down the lake, other moose were appearing on the lakeshore for their evening feed.

A few calls later, it seemed that Dennis had said something with his moose call that lost the bull's temper. The bull was now preparing to fight, at first moving around in the bush, then, no question now, he was coming.

We listened silently to his every move. Then suddenly, there he was. Not the whole moose, only the rack was visible and none too clearly as our attention was drawn to a tree being torn apart. The view was not great, but it was enough to tell us this was a big moose.

Then he came for Dennis. I was a bit ahead and to one side. When the bull was within 100 yards or so, I got a reasonably clear shot at his left shoulder. The 175 grain bullet from my 7 mm stopped but did not drop him. He managed to get his left antler in the way of my second shot at his shoulder. After two more shots in the lungs, he made it about 20 feet, then slowly collapsed.

After congratulations, we walked to the bull and, amazingly, the rack had grown considerably since I first saw him. Here lay the trophy of a lifetime!

In the fading light, we caped and dressed him. Leaving the carcass to cool until morning, we loaded the cape and head into the canoe and, in the darkness, began the long row back to the cabin.

It was over supper that Dennis first suggested the antlers probably would make Boone and Crockett. Next morning, the Argos, with some difficulty, were driven right to the moose, saving us considerable work. A rough measurement of the rack assured us that indeed it would make the book. After five years, it was my turn.

I thank you Dennis and Joanne! I thank you Lord!

Photograph Courtesy of Shawn G. Stewart

Shawn G. Stewart with Wyoming moose he killed with his .30-06 in Madison County, Montana, in 1987. It scores 155-1/8 points.

Photograph Courtesy of S. Kim Bonnett

Lost Creek Canyon in Morgan County, Utah, produced this Wyoming moose scoring 164-2/8 points for S. Kim Bonnett in 1986.

Photograph by Wm. H. Nesbitt

CANADA MOOSE
FOURTH AWARD
SCORE: 205-7/8

Locality: Cook Co., Minn.   Date: October 1987
Hunters: H. Chapman, C. Chapman, M. Chapman and J. Anderson

CANADA MOOSE 205-7/8

H. Chapman, C. Chapman, M. Chapman, and J. Anderson

Our moose story began in the spring of 1987. Minnesota only has moose hunting every other year, and an individual is only allowed to apply for a permit every 5th season. Even then, it is a permit for a party of four with one animal (bull, cow, or calf) being allowed to be taken. Since I had been on a hunt in 1977, I was eligible again in 1987. I thought that a hunt with my son (Craig Chapman), brother (Mike Chapman), and son-in-law (Jeff Anderson) would be great. I wanted to see these young guys on a real big game hunt since they are all deer hunters.

We applied and were lucky enough to be drawn. We then began our plans for the hunt in October. We invited a friend of mine, Darrel Dobe, to come along and videotape the trip. He thought it sounded like a great trip and was excited to do the video for us, since he has been on many hunts but not with a camera.

We made a scouting trip to the area in northern Minnesota one week before the actual hunt. This was the same area that I had hunted 10 years before. The area is being logged and had really changed in that time. We were able to find the exact spot I had hunted before, and we decided where we wanted to camp and hunt. We also talked to some grouse hunters who had a video camera with them and had photographed a large moose that day. We checked out this area as an alternate and it looked real good. This really got us excited for the hunt.

Jeff, Darrel, and I left Friday morning to set up camp. Craig and Mike came later, after attending the seminar required of Minnesota moose hunters. We saw a large bull that evening and we could barely wait until morning.

We were up early on Saturday. After breakfast, we drove to the area we had decided upon for our hunt, only to find that another group of hunters was already there. So, we went to the area where we had checked out the report from the grouse hunters the week before. We got out of our trucks and decided which hunter would go in what direction.

We had barely moved from our trucks when we spotted a bull moose. Craig and Jeff moved quickly to get closer and both shot. The moose moved away from them and they (along with Darrel, who was filming) ran after the animal in order to prevent him from getting away. Mike was also able to take a shot at the bull as he moved away. We lost sight of the bull and had to track him. We caught sight of him a short distance away and the final shots were fired. Our moose was down at 7:30 a.m. The hunt had taken less than one hour.

Upon approaching our moose, we found that he had gone down over the edge of a ravine. We were concerned that he might slide down further and make getting him out of the woods more difficult. As we stood around, back-slapping and toasting our successful hunt, we began to realize that he was indeed very large.

Getting him out was really a struggle. Because of his size, we decided to only keep the rack for mounting, and the best way to move our moose was in two halves. Darrel had offered the use of his Honda four-wheeler and it certainly is an asset to any big game hunt. However, the Honda was barely able to pull each half out. Someone had to sit on the front of the Honda to hold it down because of the extreme amount of weight it was pulling. It took 4-1/2 hours to get everything back to our campsite. We spent that evening reliving and celebrating our successful moose hunt.

On Sunday, we packed up and drove to Tofte, Minnesota, to register the moose. When the DNR officials saw the rack, they said that they figured we had a record-sized animal. We then really started to realize that this was indeed a special hunt we had been on.

We had the moose measured by a Boone and Crockett Club Official Measurer and it is the second largest moose taken in the State of Minnesota.

Needless to say, the video that Darrel made of our trip and the actual hunt has been shown many times and enjoyed by many friends and other hunters. It is a priceless part of the trip and a great remembrance to have.

To say this was the greatest hunt of my lifetime would be putting it mildly. I wanted the boys to be part of a moose hunt, since I have been on hunts in Minnesota and Canada. I could have only dreamed that they would each have an opportunity to get a shot at a moose, to say nothing of a trophy such as we were lucky enough to get. I hope to have an opportunity for other big game hunts in the future, but this one will always be special because of the fact that these young men had such a great experience.

Photographs Courtesy of Wayne J. Yamashita and Dennis H. DiBetta

(l) Wayne J. Yamashita and friend with the Wyoming moose Yamashita took in 1985 in Weber County, Utah. It scores 165-6/8 points. (r) Dennis H. DiBetta was hunting along the Innoko River in Alaska in 1988 when he took this Alaska-Yukon moose scoring 221-7/8 points.

Photograph Courtesy of John H. McLay

This Alaska-Yukon moose was shot by the late Bert A. McLay in 1986 on the Alaska Peninsula. The rack scores 238-2/8 points and has a greatest spread measurement of 73-2/8 points.

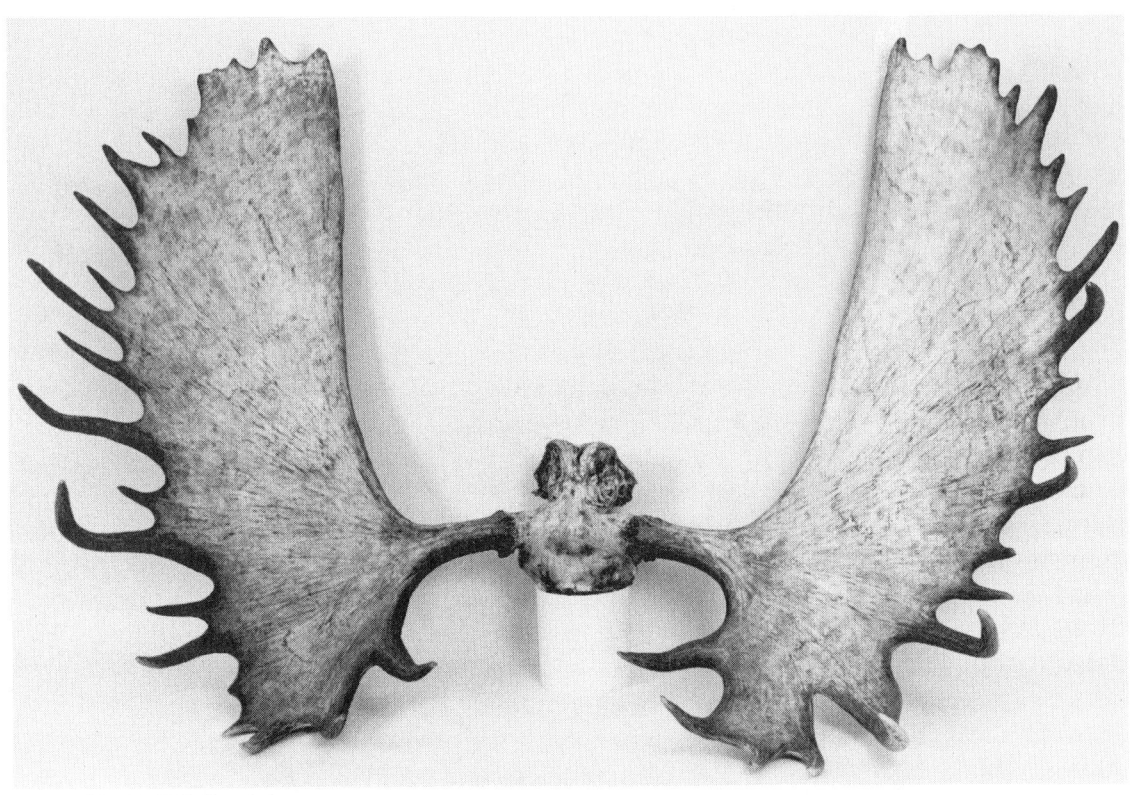

Photograph by Wm. H. Nesbitt

ALASKA-YUKON MOOSE
FIRST AWARD
SCORE: 248-3/8
Locality: Natla River, N.W.T.   Date: September 1988
Hunter: Myron A. Peterson

ALASKA-YUKON MOOSE 248-3/8

Myron A. Peterson

As my guide, Duane Nelson, and I rode down the bench above the Natla River, we kept a sharp eye out for any sign of moose there. The preceding day we had trailed-in from base camp on Divide Lake, and as we arrived at spike camp late in the day, we had seen a monster moose. Through the spotting scope we counted 15 or 16 points to a side and he had great width and symmetry. He had been above us and down river slightly. If we had arrived at camp a little sooner, we might have tried for him; but darkness was coming quickly and we had to use the remaining light to take care of the horses and set up camp. Besides, we figured a moose that big couldn't hide from us for long.

I was hunting the Mackenzie Mountains in the Northwest Territories with N.W.T. Outfitters Ltd., operated by Duane and Darrell Nelson. They have an excellent big game area where they hunt Dall's sheep, caribou, moose, wolf, and wolverine. I had been on a combination sheep-caribou hunt with the Nelsons in 1980, taking a nice 38-1/2 inch Dall's ram and a mountain caribou that made the records book. On my moose hunt in the fall of 1988, I was hunting with my father-in-law, Foster Bectell, who also had been with N.W.T. Outfitters on previous hunts, taking a nice caribou and a beautiful 43-1/2 inch Dall's sheep that scored 169-4/8.

Foster and I had left our home in southern Alberta early on September 13th and had driven to Edmonton, then along the Alaska Highway as far as Watson Lake, Yukon. We arrived late in the next afternoon. Our floatplane flight into our hunting area would be on the 15th. The next morning, light rain and fog delayed our flight with Watson Lake Flying Service, but the afternoon brought clearing skies and we were able to wing our way northward to base camp on Divide Lake.

At base camp, we were met by Duane and Darrell, Darrell's wife Rose (who is base camp cook), and Foster's guide, "Doc" French. We enjoyed a delicious meal of roast sheep and caribou, oven-fresh biscuits, and all the trimmings before crawling into our sleeping bags in anticipation of the next day's ride into the area we would hunt. After a hearty breakfast, we packed our horses and trailed through a beautiful valley and over a mountain pass, down into the Natla River. We saw caribou and moose intermittently throughout the day, and as we arrived in spike camp, we spotted the big moose above us on the mountain side. Our spirits were high as we anticipated the next day.

In the morning, after graining the pack horses and eating breakfast, Doc and Foster decided to go west, up a nearby tributary of the Natla, in search of that big bull we had seen the evening before. Duane and I rode downstream, moving along the bench above the river and stopping at good vantage points to glass the river bottom and the slope of the opposite mountain side. After about two hours, we saw a cow moose in the bottom. We decided to watch for a while, since the moose were in the rut and we thought there might be a bull nearby. After another 20 minutes or so, we saw the flash of a wide, flat antler palm back in the tall pines. The bull was definitely watching the cow, but he was not about to show himself completely and we couldn't get a good look at him to tell if this was the big one.

We caught glimpses of the bull through the trees for the next half-hour or so, then both he and the cow moved back into the trees close to the river. Several more minutes passed, then we heard several loud crashes as two bull moose started sparring together. Two bulls! It would be nice to have a choice! We still could not see them, but the clashing and grating of antlers continued. Duane suggested we try a stalk while they were occupied fighting one another, hoping they would not hear our approach. We tied the horses in a depression, then started down, being guided through the head-high brush in the bottom by the loud antler crashing. All went well until they stopped fighting. With no further sounds to guide us, we did not know exactly where they were, so we then backed-off and returned to our previous viewing point.

We spotted an open knob above the river on the other bank that we felt would give us a good look, so we mounted and made our way down river a half-mile or so and crossed over. We tied our horses in the bottom, then climbed the hill to take a look. Nothing! But since we had a good view of the area, we settled down to wait. The river bottom had lots of game. While we waited for the next couple of hours, we saw a cow moose with her calf and another cow accompanied by a smaller bull, further downstream. We also spotted a nice grizzly working his way down river along the river bank, digging for roots as he went. I wished the Northwest Territories had a grizzly season, as this would have been a fine trophy.

By this time, it was mid-afternoon and as the sun burned through the clouds, I began to get drowsy in its warmth. I was jolted back to wakefulness when a cow moose came out on the river bank, then went down to the water for her afternoon drink. She was followed in the next few minutes by four more cows. Then again, through the trees, there was the flash of white antlers of a bull. And since this one was guarding the cows, he had undoubtedly won the shoving match with the other moose and was the dominant bull. Through the trees, we got glimpses of his rack with a spotting scope, first one side, then the other. Finally, his full head came into view and my guide said, "You've got to take this one!"

I chambered a round in my Ruger Model 77 in .338 Winchester Mag and steadied it across my rolled-up coat, ready for the opportunity for a clear shot. The big bull turned broadside and was feeding slowly down stream, about 20 yards back in the cover of the willows and pines. We had estimated the range at 300 yards and I knew my 210 grain Nosler partition bullets would drop only a few inches below the point of aim at that distance, as my rifle was sighted in for 250 yards. After what seemed like an eternity, he paused in an opening and I steadied on a spot slightly behind his front shoulder and sent the bullet on its way. The unmistakable whump of a solid hit came back to us, yet the bull hardly flinched. A second, hurried shot spooked him and he ran about 25 yards, then paused. (I found later that this second shot had pierced the large bell under his neck. My guide says this was due to the severe shaking of my legs as I was shooting!) A third, more steady shot again sent back the sound of a solid hit. Then, the bull lay down and I knew he was mine. But his head was still up, and since he was in a very favorable spot for access, I put another bullet through his shoulder and he was finished.

Whoops and handshakes were exchanged, then we gathered our gear and went back down to the horses and crossed the river. As we approached the downed bull, I marveled at his immense size. I had shot bull moose in the foothills of Alberta, but they were small compared with this big fellow. I asked Duane to get his tape out to take some quick measurements, but when he reached in his pack for it, he remembered that he had put it in his duffel and hadn't transferred it to his pack. So, we could only estimate the spread of the rack. We guessed it at 64 or 65 inches and I felt very lucky as before the hunt I had set a goal of taking a 60-inch moose on this trip.

After clearing away the brush for photographs, and after more admiring, we started the task of caping the trophy. After we got the antlers and head off, Duane continued skinning the skull while I started butchering the meat. I got the backstraps off first, then the front and hind quarters, the tenderloin, and finally the ribs and neck meat. No usable meat was left to waste, as all meat must be checked out of the Northwest Territories through game check stations upon departure. After finishing the one side, it was all we could do to roll the carcass over to get at the other side. Darkness was falling as we finished laying the meat out to cool. We then made our way back to camp to tell my partner and his guide of our success. They had seen four bulls during their day's hunt but had passed on them all. A day later, Foster connected on a nice bull.

The next day, after breakfast, we rode back to our kill site. Using a horse and a lariat, we were able to get all the meat up in trees, away from predators, to await the pre-arranged arrival of Darrell's floatplane two days later to check on our success and to fly-out the meat. Luckily, the plane was able to land on the river only 300 yards from the kill. When we returned for the meat, the carcass had been covered over by a grizzly but fortunately he wasn't there at the time. We quickly cut the untouched meat down from the trees and got it out of there before the bruin returned.

When we finally put a tape to those great antlers, it stretched over 69 inches, with a green score of 250-2/8. What a trophy! The final Boone and Crockett measurement at the 20th Awards put my bull at 248-3/8, the largest moose ever to come out of the Northwest Territories.

The remainder of the 12-day hunt was very relaxing. I can't think of a more beautiful spot to spend a few days. Several more bears were sighted, and lots of caribou and even some wolves were seen at long distances. The memories of my hunt will long be with me, and whenever I gaze at those great antlers, I can go back in my mind to the Natla and that special experience there.

Photograph by Wm. H. Nesbitt

ALASKA-YUKON MOOSE
SECOND AWARD
SCORE: 247-5/8
Locality: Bering River, Alaska Date: September 1984
Hunter: Vol S. Davis, Jr.

ALASKA-YUKON MOOSE 247-5/8

Vol S. Davis, Jr.

What does it really mean to kill a top, records-placing animal? It means a lot to any hunter. I refer to mine as a "Campfire and Parlor Special." You will recount that hunt the rest of your life.

I left San Antonio, Texas, five days before the season opened on September 1, 1985. I spent the night in Anchorage, Alaska, then left for Cordova the next morning. Sam Fejes, my outfitter, met me at the airport. I had talked to Sam several times before the hunt. We talked about the unpredictable September weather, the type of gear I was to bring, and what kind of terrain we would be hunting in. Like a lot of flat-land hunters going to Alaska, I took more gear than I needed. However, if you forget something, there are not many places to shop in the wilderness. On our flight from Cordova to Sam's headquarters, I learned that Sam had been a hunter since he was nine years old. This is very important, as there are outfitters who are no more than promoters.

When we arrived at headquarters, I quickly took a visual inventory. The camp was clean and well-organized. The chief cook and guides were very friendly, the equipment looked like it was in good shape and well maintained, and to find out we had hot water for showers really pleased me.

Our moose hunting area was about 125 miles southeast of Cordova. We would hunt the flatlands between the Bering Glacier and the Gulf of Alaska. During the three days prior to opening of the season, Sam and I flew over his entire hunting area. To prevent airsickness, I brought along those commercial tabs that you stick behind your ears. While I did not get airsick in Sam's Super Cub, I did experience a side effect of dehydration and extreme thirst. I drank everything from glacier water to swamp water. When I finally removed the patches, the symptoms disappeared.

Sam wanted to find out where the game was located and if they were on the move. In this area, you either fly or walk. There are no horses. Bears eat horses and horses know it. The antlers on bull moose are easy to see from the air, particularly with sunlight. Sam told me to watch for the "head lights." The palms of the bull's antlers reflect the sunlight. I quit counting bulls when I reached 65 in a three-day span. There was about a 5,000 acre area that was all swamp. This is where we found the bull I really wanted.

Sam and I had discussed what kind of a bull I was looking for. As long as I had come this far, I wanted to get a records book type animal. We also discussed where Sam felt I should shoot my bull. Most outfitters and guides would like to see a clean heart shot. In large game like moose and bear, the heart rides low in the body. With this discussion out of the way, I was ready for a serious hunt.

As we flew over the swamp, we spotted a huge bull whose antlers lay flatter than the typical moose whose palms tilt upward. His 38 points on a 76-inch spread made him stand out over any of the other bulls I had already seen. The day before the season opened, Sam flew our gear to the closest place he could land and be near the area where we last saw my bull. He then flew me down. After a good, spike-camp supper, we prepared for the first day's hunt. I had brought along a pair of waders. It's a good thing Sam had brought an extra pair of hip boots that fit me, because waders would have eaten me up.

After a good breakfast, we left the spike camp at daylight. The swamp water was anywhere from 12 inches deep to chest-high when you hit a low place. I saw right quick that I would really earn my trophy, if we could find him in this large area. It took four hours, the first time, to get to the general area where Sam thought we last saw the bull. There are some tall trees that survived the swamp water but mostly it is alder brush. The roots of the alder brush are extensive and lay mainly on the bottom, on top of the sticky mud. Now where I come from, there are thorns on nearly every green thing and you must be careful of snakes too. There are no thorns on any of the brush I saw in Alaska and no snakes. I really enjoyed this part of the stalk.

After three to four hours of stumbling on submerged roots, literally having to stop and pull one foot after the other out of the sticky mud, we finally got to a drier area on higher ground. This was the first time I could sit down and pour the water out of my hip boots.

I had worked out for over two months before I left home. A lot of leg and breathing exercises, plus jogging and walking. This helped, but I had not exercised the muscles on the inside of my thighs. I'll never forget that swamp as long as I live.

We hunted for about four hours before we had to leave to get back to camp before dark. Another four hours of misery in the swamp going to camp.

The second day, I was sore inside my thighs and had to treat a few blisters on my feet, but I figured misery was the cost to get my bull and I was ready to pay the price. The second day was a repeat of the first. We saw several good bulls in the 60-inch class, but not the one I wanted.

The third day, I didn't think I could crawl out of my sleeping bag. I ached in every bone in my old body. I was surprised I didn't have dysentery from drinking the swamp water. I told Sam that "my get up and go had got up and left." I just couldn't see fighting that swamp for another eight hours. Maybe I could kill one of those other big bulls we saw on dry ground. This is where having a guide that is a true hunter really paid off. Sam said we had one area that we had not covered. He felt the bull had not moved far from where we saw him, all three days, before the season. He felt this was our day and the bull was really worth one more try.

When we finally got to the drier land, Sam would climb one of the tall trees and glass the surrounding area. After a couple of hours of this, and several trees later, I heard him snap his fingers. I looked up and saw the prettiest smile I have ever seen. He pointed to the north, then came down.

We worked our way for about a quarter-mile through the alder brush until we were safely downwind from the bulls. I slowly parted the brush and what did I see? Three bull moose, standing nearly antler-tip to antler-tip, looking in my direction. The bull on the left was about a 60-inch bull. Mine was in the middle, and the bull on the right was a monster. His antlers would easily go in the high 60's, they were heavy and he would easily weigh over 1,500 pounds.

Not being mentally ready for a frontal shot, I had to ponder where I was going to place my shot. I decided to get close to his dewlap and at the top of his brisket. This should be right about where his heart was. The bulls were approximately 80 yards away. I figured my 180 grain bullet from a .300 Weatherby Mag should do the job.

I squeezed off a good, off-hand shot and heard it hit. The bulls on either side ran off. My bull never moved. I shot twice more, as fast as I could. The bull still didn't move. I whispered to Sam, "Am I missing this dude or am I shooting blanks?" Sam said he saw water fly off the bull's chest after all three shots; shoot him again. By this time I was reaching for more shells. I looked up and the old bull slowly fell over. Sam ran around the alder brush to be sure the bull was dead and I proceeded to reload.

About this time, I heard Sam holler several times. I didn't think much about this until I walked over to where he was kneeling down. Sam motioned me to kneel down. He said the bigger of the other two bulls had come back, then ran off into the brush about 80 yards away. Sam told me to get ready because the bull would come charging back. The bull would stop about 15-20 yards away, do a little dance, hook his antlers and grunt. He would then make up his mind if he was going to charge us or turn and run off.

Sam asked me if my gun was loaded. I laughed softly. I said "Hell, what makes you think I can stop a charging bull when it took three shots to drop the first one. The important thing is whether your .375 H&H Mag with the 300 grain bullets is loaded." He smiled and patted his rifle.

It wasn't two or three minutes and here came this charging monster. He did just what Sam said he would do. With my safety off, I put the cross hairs on the center of his neck. This would be my best and probably only shot I could get off if he charged. Sam was ready too. After what seemed to be a long time, the bull turned and ran off. What a relief!

After several rolls of pictures, Sam and I caped him and cut off those beautiful antlers. We would carry the antlers back to our camp, fly back to headquarters, and then Sam would bring two packers back to cut up the meat, sack it, get the hide, and return to headquarters.

Sam Fejes is about 5 feet, 10 inches tall and weighs about 170 pounds. He strapped the antlers, which were awkward and very heavy, to his back pack and carried them out, by himself, walking back through the swamp for four hours. I offered to help or spell him, but he said it would be quicker if he did it himself.

During one of our rest stops on the way back to our spike camp, I asked him how he figured he could carry those antlers out and I couldn't? He smiled and said, "Well it's the difference between me being 29 years old and you being 53 years old." I agreed.

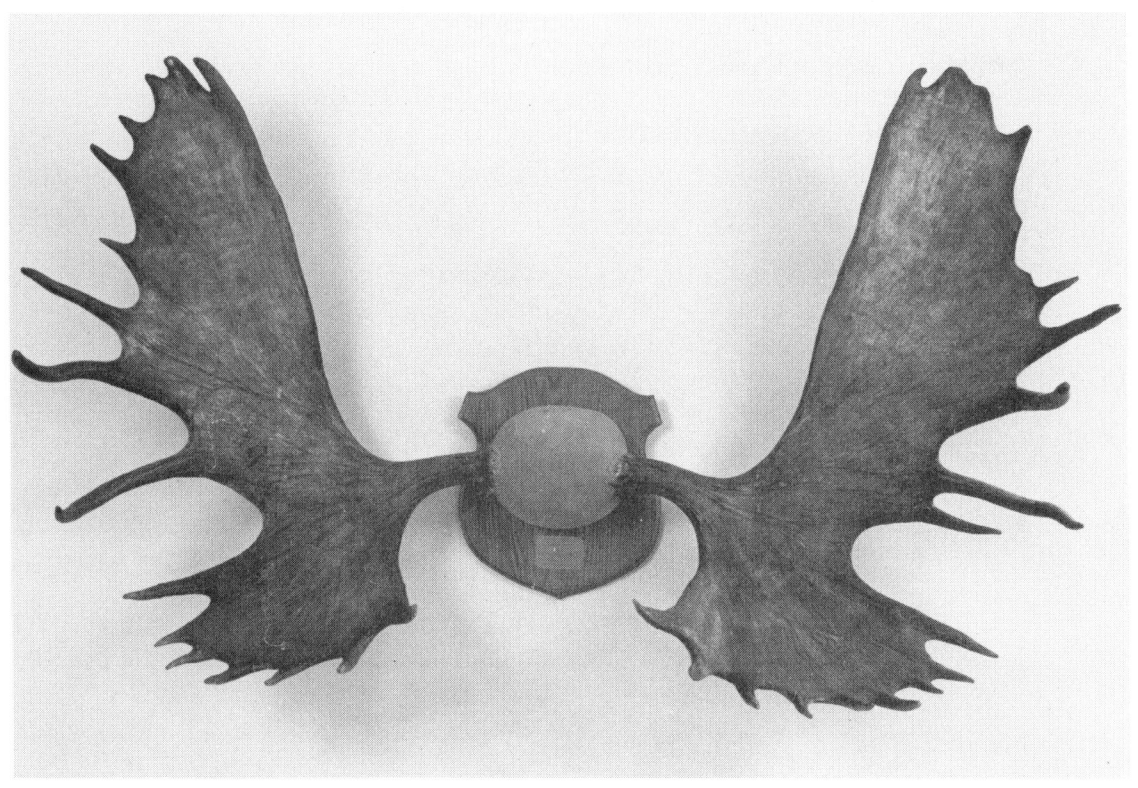

ALASKA-YUKON MOOSE
THIRD AWARD
SCORE: 235-5/8
Locality: Nowitna River, Alaska Date: September 1988
Hunter: Brian C. Ziegenfuss

ALASKA-YUKON MOOSE 235-5/8

Brian C. Ziegenfuss

My moose hunt was a well-planned and thought-out hunt. I reenlisted in the Army just to be stationed in Alaska, so I could hunt big game. A few months after I arrived in Alaska, I met Paul Crisman at the local German club. He has been hunting, fishing, and trapping in Alaska for over 30 years. The third member of the hunting party was Clay King, a fellow worker at the Army airfield. The planning and preparation of the hunt started in April 1988. The first week, Paul and I talked about hunting procedures, supplies, transportation, preparation of boat and trucks, setting-up the camp, the time, and finally the dates. We made lists, then went over them again and again, making plenty of revisions. I've seen military operations that weren't planned as well as this hunt.

After the planning stage, the inventory of existing supplies such as tent, cooking hardware, cots, tools, etc. started. Our resources were pooled and we then came up with yet another list of things that we needed to purchase for the hunt.

An extensive preparation of the boat started after that. We installed a new canvas top, an electric windshield wiper, CB radio, and repainted the boat inside and out. The boat was owned by Paul. It is a 28-foot, flat-bottomed river boat, powered by two 60 horsepower Mercury engines. Paul and I also did a really good servicing of the engines. You don't want to be stuck floating powerless on the Yukon River in the middle of nowhere. Paul even had the two stainless steel props rebuilt in Seattle. We also brought along two more brass props, and an extra lower unit, just in case. The Alaskan wilderness can be unforgiving.

The moose hunt took place 12 miles up the Nowitna River. This river is located approximately 300 miles down the Yukon River from the Yukon River bridge. I was the pilot of the boat and it was a very exciting drive down the Yukon River. We carried along three 55-gallon drums of fuel for the 600 mile round-trip. We still had to stop in the village of Rampart to pick up a little extra fuel on the trip back.

Our camp was set up very well and elaborately. The tent was 18 by 16 feet and made of white canvas. We carried along some plywood to build a kitchen table and a dining table. To heat the tent, we brought along a new, large Alaskan wood stove and stove pipe. Clay and I cut a cord of wood, dug a large deep garbage pit away from the camp, built a covered latrine, and then built a smoking pit for the plentiful fish Paul said we were going to catch. Also constructed were three meat hanging racks. We were thinking positive.

The preparation of the camp took three days. During the breaks, we caught plenty of pike and shot some grouse and a duck. We were catching so many pike that any under 26 inches were thrown back. There were so many grouse in the area that we had to chase one out of our tent one day. I was the camp cook, so we ate a lot of smoked pike and grouse stew (later in the hunt we had a lot of moose ribs, heart, and Mulligan Moose stew and moose steaks).

On September 9, we decided to start hunting for moose. Clay was stationed a half-mile down river from the camp where we'd seen numerous moose tracks crossing the river. I was going a half-mile upriver from the camp. Paul, being the experienced moose hunter, decided to wait for the moose to walk into the camp. Paul told Clay and I to shoot our moose on the banks of the river to avoid packing it a long distance, and to shoot them 13 inches below the hump on their backs. That puts the bullet straight through the spine for a sudden halt of the central nervous system.

After I dropped Clay off at his spot, I drove the boat up to my area, side-washed, and picked a good place to sit and watch the river banks for signs of a moose. After 15 minutes, I got a little restless about sitting there waiting for a moose to cross the river so I decided to walk down a game trail that was directly behind me.

The rifle I was using for this hunt was a Spanish Santa Barbara .300 Winchester Mag with a Mauser action and Barnes 250 grain bullets. I also carried a Ruger Redhawk .44 Mag revolver on my side.

It was a beautiful morning that day of the 9th, a little chilly but not uncomfortable. The scenery was picture perfect. There were geese flying overhead, the sound of ducks in the distance, and I even watched some great horned owls swooping down to catch red-backed voles. Before you'd know it, I'd walked in about a mile. Realizing how far I'd walked, I sat down to take a break before turning around to go back to the river bank.

When I got up, I looked down the slough toward the original direction I was walking and saw a bull moose standing in the middle of the slough, around 250 meters away. I was surprised to see him standing there looking at me. I put my cross hairs on him but I could not get a steady sight picture, so I reached down to get a stick to use to steady my rifle.

When I looked up, the large moose was walking back into the woods. I decided to walk down to where he went into the woods and see where he went. After about 10 minutes, I heard his rack crashing through the brush, approximately 150 meters up the dry slough. The bull then walked out into the slough and I immediately aimed 13 inches below the hump and fired. The moose just flinched. I fired again and he stumbled into the brush where I couldn't see him any more.

I knew I hadn't missed him because I'm an expert shot and had even shot a whole box of ammo to familiarize myself with the weapon. As I walked up to where I'd last seen him, I suddenly saw him 20 feet to my left and on his knees, not on his side. My immediate reaction was to pull my pistol and shoot him twice in the chest area, thinking he was going to rush me and stick me with his antlers. The moose finished getting up and then walked 10 feet before falling down dead. This was some tough animal.

Now the work began. I went back and got Paul and Clay, plus the tools to skin, gut, and quarter the moose. Paul also had a few choice words for me for shooting the moose so far inland. Being prepared as we were, we had everything you would need to skin an Alaskan bull moose. That included four big skinning knives, an ax, hand saw, chain saw, "come-a-long," half-inch nylon rope, and a US Army surplus stretcher to transport the meat. We used the come-a-long [hand winch] to position the moose for gutting. We had to remove the head before we could even turn the moose over. It was really large and weighed a lot. The half-inch rope was used to hold up the legs as we did the skinning. I have skinned and gutted whitetail deer before, but doing this moose was a real experience. His gut pile alone weighed as much as a whole whitetail deer.

Once we had the moose quartered, it was time to haul it to the boat. Clay and I made 10 trips back-and-forth to the boat, stopping every 300 meters or so. The hind quarters weighed at least 200 pounds apiece. Now I realize we should have boned-out the animal like most experienced moose hunters do. It got dark, so we had to finish it the next day. After we got the boat loaded with the last stretcher load, we sat down to take a break. Clay noticed a large moose about 100 yards across the river. It probably had a 45-inch rack on it, but we decided to let it pass because we were so exhausted from hauling my moose. When we reached camp a few minutes later, Clay and I found out that Paul had shot a bull right at camp. It was then Clay's turn to have a few choice words for me.

So, after 15 hours of hauling moose and hanging it on the rack we'd built, we then had another moose to skin, gut, and quarter. Luckily, it wasn't very far from camp. Needless to say, Paul's shot was 13 inches below the hump when we measured it, going straight through the spine. Clay and I were totally exhausted and sat around the next day. Clay ended-up shooting his moose six days later, about 300 meters from camp. Clay's had a 34-inch rack and Paul's was a 35-inch.

We stayed in camp four more days before deciding to leave. Our departure from the camp was two days early due to the extreme lowering of the river level. The water had dropped two feet in depth during the time we were there. Leaving the Nowitna River, we plowed through a small sand bar. Then, half-way up the Yukon River, we became stuck on a gravel bar. We pulled out the pike pole, raised the engines almost out of the water, and poled out of there. I was finally able to get us back to the bridge and our trucks. We made it back to Fairbanks without meeting any speeding large trucks heading for the North Slope that could have run us off the road. Unfortunately, I ran out of gas just about 10 miles out of Fairbanks.

My bull moose weighed at least 1,800 pounds and had a rack that measured 69-1/2 inches. When my moose was officially scored for entry by Dr. David Klein, an official Boone and Crockett Club scorer at the University of Alaska, it scored 243. That roughly put it in a tie for 21st place according to the all-time records book.

This adventure was a real experience that I shall never forget.

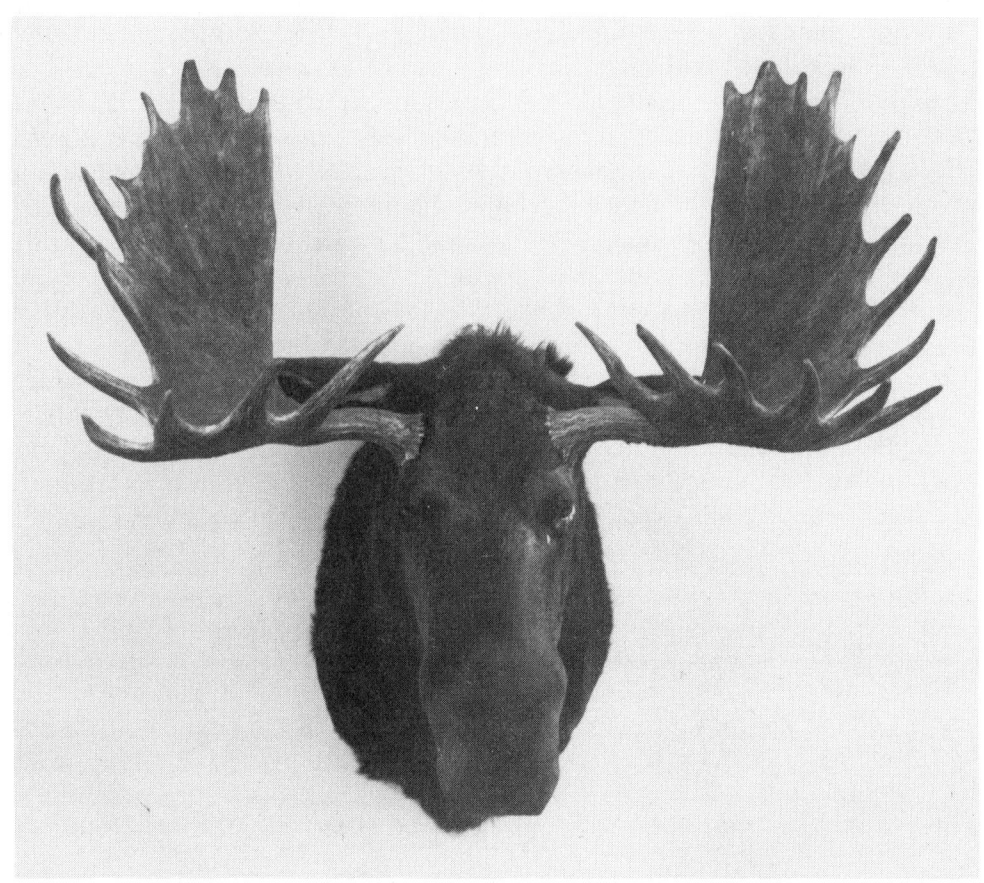

Photograph by Wm. H. Nesbitt

WYOMING MOOSE
FIRST AWARD
SCORE: 179-1/8
Locality: Teton Co., Wyo.   Date: September 1987
Hunter: Marion J. Fonville

WYOMING MOOSE 179-1/8

Marion J. Fonville

What a deal! The idea of a Wyoming moose seemed worlds away! The very idea of planning one's hunt before applying for a permit, that seemed presumptuous indeed. Putting it in layman's language, and to be exact, the words of Brian Welker, co-owner of Teton Crest Outfitters, "If you draw a permit, Marion, on your first try, I'm going to know that you've had supernatural help!" So what, let's go for it! That's when it all began, back in January of 1987.

So, when we arrived in Jackson in mid-September, it was almost too real to be true. There we were, Jack McDaniel and I, without our two hunting buddies, Dr. Fred Turner and Ed Richardson, who opted out at fate's last minute, even though they had elk permits and were willing to sacrifice reservation deposits with Teton Crest. Met by Phil Major, respected guide and co-owner of the Wilson, Wyoming outfit, we embarked upon a week of outstanding highs.

Having unloaded our gear and settled in, we took one of those customary strolls to relax our legs and get some bearing on the area surrounding the base camp. Though rustic and housed in new canvas tents (Brian and Phil had just purchased the outfit in 1986 and had begun to expand from the ground up), the setting was picturesque. Located by a well-known creek, we had been told that game could be spotted as near as the door of the tent, and yet, one could drive to the corral in good weather.

Discovering hunting country really begins at daybreak. In fact, we had waited considerably longer than expected even though the generator started promptly at 3:30 a.m. It was Phil's style to start his day well in advance of our 4:30 a.m. wake-up. The stock was saddled and everything made ready before we walked into the beautifully floored cook tent. What a beginning! Even without Chef Tell, that breakfast spread on the first day was a predictor of good things to come.

Mounting a strange horse (or familiar one, for that matter), is just not my cup of tea! And, I asked the usual question, "Is this thing gentle? You know I don't have much experience riding a horse!" With incidental instructions, we started up Moose Creek under the cover of darkness. Without the beams of a flashlight, but accompanied by two knowledgeable guides, we embarked upon what would be a rather routine day.

Jack and Phil would leave us about a mile into the trek, heading up a long canyon known for above-average bull elk. When we first crossed the creek, criss-crossing back and forth as we made our way toward the head-waters, it was a gray-brown world that introduced the new day. As we managed to slide past tight passages between trees and rocks, we caught glimpses of what seemed to be wildlife, or perhaps a moose, only to discover a stump, or some other inanimate object. How disappointing until we came round a sharp z-turn to find a cow moose with a calf, munching in the edge of the dammed creek. The beavers really know how to do their work. Lewis Sharpe (my guide) remarked that it was often in the shallows that you will find that prized moose, just reviving his appetite after bedding down for the night.

We finally reached the large lake toward which we had been moving, after having passed the spike camp along the trail. The camp is positioned in a perfect place to accommodate the hunter who really wants to get an early start on the game, or for the party that gets caught in a driving snow storm. As Lewis reminded me, "You need to be prepared." Having hunted so much of my life since being introduced to the outdoors back in Mississippi, that work of preparation needed to be mentioned only once as it came from Phil in his packet of materials in preparation for our hunt. In fact, the down jacket had to be shed about 30 minutes into our climb; the temperature was unseasonably hot, 75-80 degrees.

How big is a good moose? I'd never seen one before, and when we rounded a sharp turn, Lewis spotted one at the edge of the big lake, but far across from where we stopped. Lewis agreed to stay with the horses while I went ahead to get a better view. The binoculars revealed good palms, but at more than 400 yards, we needed to get a bit closer. Moving quietly, I arrived at a position where he should have been easy to judge for size. As I peered into the slash of conifers meeting the lake, he had disappeared! Lewis arrived soon after and concluded that the bull was just moving across the slash and might have gone into the thick timbers. Sure enough, we found his trail as he disappeared into the timber, even the smell of the ungainly creature, but not another glimpse.

We returned to the north side of the lake and spent the better part of the afternoon waiting for perhaps another appearance. We left in time to arrive back in camp before dark. After the full day, my fanny looked forward to relaxing and leaving that mount. I can't say enough about Phil's stock, inexperienced horsemen really would appreciate his painstaking effort at finding the right kind.

Janie's food that night really hit the spot! We needed that lift; Jack and Phil also "struck out." They had heard some bulls bugle, but no response. The weather had been terrible; just a bluebird day! But with choice sirloins on the plate, my memory of the first day, a disappointing one, quickly disappeared. Over dinner, Lewis remarked, "We'll get him preacher, we'll start earlier in the morning!" With that in mind, we turned-in, anticipating we would have a better day.

Next morning at dawn, we were well ahead of the schedule of a day ago. In fact, I could hardly see more than a huge blob of black when I dismounted to get a better look at that object in the edge of the first lake that we passed. It was the same lake where we saw the cow and calf a day earlier. I didn't have time to tell Lewis I was dismounting. I just unsheathed my 7 mm Mag and hit the ground in one movement. The horse continued to follow Lewis as I looked the bull over. He was looking down the trail that we had come up. He was a mass of moose! And, until he turned to his right and faced me with both palms showing their size, I could only guess. But then I knew, it had to be that monster they had seen back during the summer when they had trekked up Moose Creek on their pack trips. No time for me to ask Lewis, "Do you think he's good enough?" I knew!

The rifle roared as the bullet lodged just below the backbone and directly into the lung. He bolted, but stopped short of 50 yards away when I slammed another, and yet another, of my 175 grain handloads. The Noslers found their mark. As the bull toppled to the ground, there stood Lewis, nearly trembling with his question, "How big is he?" After tying the horse, we ambled over to see his monstrous antlers. "That's him, yep, that's him. That's the one they've been seeing up here all during the summer."

We waited and celebrated, and finally, there was enough light to allow for pictures. And then the work began. We made it back in time for lunch; in fact, Jack and Phil had gathered, sensing we had scored. After lunch, a long lunch indeed, they started back with three fresh horses in their pack string.

Phil was right too! I remember him saying, "There's one of them moose up the creek that I believe will make the book! He's a good one!" When we carried my moose to the locker, we stopped by the museum taxidermist, and after a quick, rough score of 181, there was but one explanation. "What a deal!"

Photograph by Wm. H. Nesbitt

MOUNTAIN CARIBOU
FIRST AWARD
SCORE: 444
Locality: Kechika Range, B.C.   Date: August 1988
Hunter: James C. Johnson

MOUNTAIN CARIBOU 444

James C. Johnson

In 1988, Jim Johnson signed up for a 12 day Stone's sheep hunt with Jerry Gerraci, an outfitter in Smithers, British Columbia. The area he planned to hunt was in the Kechika Range, at the upper end of the Kechika River. Jim wanted Jerry to guide him into the remote area in search of a trophy Stone's ram. Jim was not a novice to hunts of this nature since he had hunted in the north country on at least 10 previous occasions. Jim also bought caribou and goat tags for the hunt, in case he filled-out his sheep tag early in the hunt and wanted something else to hunt.

Jim and Jerry flew into the hunting area and packed into sheep country. They had hunted for 10 days, but they had not seen a sheep that Jim wanted to take. At 3 p.m. on the 10th day, they were heading for an area to glass for sheep that evening. They were walking across an open area where the grass was only about four inches high when they spotted a caribou bull about a mile away and heading in their direction. The bull wasn't at a dead run, but it was moving at that gait characteristic to caribou when they want to cover country. When the bull was approximately 1,000 yards away, both men realized that they were looking at a very respectable bull, one that got bigger and better the closer it got. The bull was heading straight at them, and they were still standing out in the open with absolutely no cover and no place to go.

Since there were only two days left of Jim's hunt, Jim and his guide began considering their options. They could continue their fruitless search for a trophy Stone's sheep, or they could take a mountain caribou that might just make the records book. Jim had already taken three caribou during previous hunts, and he really wanted a nice ram.

As the bull continued to head straight for them, they did some quick calculations to determine whether or not it was caribou season. They had been out ten days and had lost track of time. However, they quickly determined that it was actually the first day of the caribou season and Jim could harvest the bull, if he wanted it.

When the bull was 300 yards away, Jerry began getting excited. Jerry had seen many trophy bulls over the years, but this was certainly the best one he had ever seen. They could tell it had tremendous top palms, but they could not tell if it had well-developed shovels on both antlers. The brow palms were so close together that it looked like it had only one brow palm. Still, they figured that this bull would easily score for the book and Jim took it. It's not every day that a "skunked" sheep hunter gets such a marvelous consolation prize.

Photograph by Wm. H. Nesbitt

WOODLAND CARIBOU
FIRST AWARD
SCORE: 341-2/8
Locality: Barachois Brook, Nfld.   Date: October 1986
Hunter: Harry L. Gunter

WOODLAND CARIBOU 341-2/8

Harry L. Gunter

A short whistle caught my attention. It was my guide, Henri Payne, motioning down the ridge to where he had taken a stand. We had left camp at Southwest Brook Pond at daybreak and had taken a boat across the lake to Henri's chosen site to hunt caribou. After hiking uphill and away from the lake for about a quarter of a mile, we split-up at a long ridge to better glass the vast tundra that had opened up before us. I had been sitting and watching with awe the mixture of grass, low hills, ponds, and small pockets of evergreens for no more than a half-hour, when Henri's whistle awoke me from my reverie.

I hustled down the ridge to see what he wanted. Henri motioned to a small pond about a half-mile distant and said that a real nice stag had just walked up to it. I put my binoculars on the caribou and we agreed that he warranted a closer look. As the stag was moving into the wind and almost parallel to the ridge, we headed-off through the waist-high tundra brush to intercept the stag for a closer evaluation.

I already had a gut feeling that the stag was a good one and the moment of truth was about to arrive. Henri and I made for a small pond in the general direction that the stag was believed to be traveling, to set up an ambush. As we arrived at the edge of the pond, the surprise was on us. Less than 100 yards across the pond, our caribou had beaten us to the punch. We had underestimated his speed, as the stag had been moving at a rapid pace.

As often happens in a pressure situation, time stood still. Henri said it was a good stag; I thought he was magnificent! There was time for a quick, broadside shoulder shot before he walked out of sight behind a low hill. I dropped to one knee, centered the cross hairs high on the shoulder, took a deep breath, relaxed, and then squeezed the trigger. Click! My heart stopped! My mind had thought of everything but the empty chamber that the guide required except when ready to shoot! (I think it is a good idea for safe gun handling, but it was my first experience with the rule, and to say the least, a less than auspicious beginning.) I swear the caribou heard the sound, because he took a long look at us before he disappeared behind the hill.

I was nervous, heartsick, and conscious of many other emotions that manifest when failure seems imminent. Henri was unflappable. He said not to worry, that we would catch up with the stag.

As we scurried around the pond, Henri said the caribou would be bedding down soon on one of the small hills and we would get another chance at him. I wasn't so sure. We covered about a quarter-mile, half-walking and half-trotting, in the direction our stag had taken, always looking at the tops of the little hills to see if he had indeed bedded down. When we did spot him, dead ahead, he was still moving into the wind.

Henri explained our options. I could either take the shot or we could try to flank him and hopefully get a little closer. As the range was not more than 125 yards, I decided on the quartering shot. There was a nice rock, perfect for a prone rest, so I threw my old Stetson on it, settled my Ruger 7 mm Mag on it, remembered to chamber a round this time, made a steady, easy squeeze of the trigger, and the stag was history.

As the stag collapsed, Henri started shaking my hand and telling me how lucky we were and how good an animal it was. I was still floating on adrenalin and would be the rest of the day. Although we would see plenty of caribou as we fought the inclement weather in an unsuccessful attempt to find a bull moose, this was the first caribou on the first morning of the hunt, and by far the largest.

The rest of the day was spent getting the trophy back to camp. The rest of the week was spent hunting moose and lamenting the weather. My hunting partner, Tom Triplett, would get a real nice stag on Wednesday. On Sunday, our outfitter, Angus Wentsel, came to fly us out and, as often happens, the sun came out for the first time.

As we left Corner Brook, Newfoundland, on our 1,600 mile drive home, I looked in the back of the camper shell at our racks and reminisced about our adventure that had included: New England in the fall (the colors are brilliant); the coast of Maine (friendly people and great seafood); the ferry ride from North Sidney, Nova Scotia (the North Atlantic can get rough); and the hunt (comfortable cabins, competent guides, good food, plenty of game).

Sometimes you wonder why you hunt, because as good as it gets, it is still hard work. But, looking at the racks, I knew the answer. It is for adventure that is otherwise missing from our everyday lives. Also, we hunt for the memories; one look at my caribou rack and I am sitting on the ridge once again, feeling the wind against my face and smelling the tundra. And even though both stags scored well enough to make the Boone and Crockett records book, just the adventure of the hunt and the thrill of the kill were enough to make it all worthwhile to me. As Henri said when he shook my hand, "Yes, sir, we were sure some kind of lucky."

Photograph Courtesy of C. Randall Byers

C. Randall Byers (l) and guide Duane Nelson with mountain caribou Byers took with a bow in the Mackenzie Mountains, N.W.T., during the 1988 caribou season. It scores 377-2/8 points.

Photograph Courtesy of Leo M. Schmaus

Leo M. Schmaus is congratulated by his guide for the mountain caribou he took near the Arctic Red River in Northwest Territories in 1986. It scores 392-5/8 points.

Photograph by Wm. H. Nesbitt

WOODLAND CARIBOU
SECOND AWARD
SCORE: 336-1/8

Locality: Barachois Brook, Nfld.   Date: October 1986
Hunter: Thomas W. Triplett

WOODLAND CARIBOU 336-1/8

Thomas W. Triplett

When we started out on our 1,600 mile drive from Virginia to Newfoundland, Harry Gunter, my hunting partner, and I had no idea of what an enjoyable trip we would experience. We drove all night to start this trip, and we were greeted with some beautiful fall colors when the sun rose. New England and the maritime provinces of Canada are absolutely beautiful in the fall.

Leaving the mainland and arriving in Newfoundland was quite a contrast. We met our outfitter, Angus Wentzel, near Corner Brook. From there, we flew by floatplane to our hunting site on southeast Brook Pond. From there we would hunt moose and caribou. The Newfoundland landscape is harsh and wet. Having never seen tundra before, I was not prepared for what I found. When we arrived at our camp, the only dry places were the walkways around the site. I was soon to learn that almost everywhere you walked, you were either on rock or on the very wet, sponge-like ground.

Our first full day in camp was Sunday. There was no hunting allowed on Sunday in Newfoundland in 1986; it is now allowed. So, Harry and I decided to go for a walk. We traveled only about a mile when we spotted out first caribou. He was a very nice trophy that, if hunting had been permitted, would probably now be hanging on a wall. He approached to within 50 yards and got some great pictures. We did see other game that day, so when we turned in that night, our thoughts were in anticipation of our first day hunting.

The first day out, Harry was guided by Henry Payne and I went with his brother, Bryant. We left camp just before sun-up and spotted caribou soon after. Bryant and I saw probably a dozen stags and cows that morning, but none were as big as the stag Harry and I had seen the previous day. About 11:30, we decided to head back to camp for lunch. When we arrived, there was a huge set of antlers outside the cabins. Harry had already scored, and his was a once-in-a-lifetime trophy. The antlers were about 40 inches wide, with over 30 points and a nice double shovel.

That afternoon was not nearly as eventful. We saw only a few, distant caribou. That night after dinner, Harry was still glowing about his trophy, and justifiably so. I just hoped to see something even close to being as nice as Harry's.

The second day we woke to find that rain and fog had moved in. Those elements make hunting in Newfoundland very difficult. You simply cannot spot game at any distance in the fog. We drank a lot of coffee that morning. Finally, about mid-afternoon, the weather broke, so Bryant and I set out to try a new area. We spotted a nice stag after being out only 30 minutes but he was not what I was looking for. About an hour later, we spotted a small bull moose and a cow, about 400 yards away. Since I also had a moose tag, we decided to try to close the distance. However, the pair soon disappeared in the timber and we never saw them again. We then returned to camp.

Wednesday morning, the third day of the hunt, was a carbon copy of Tuesday with rain and fog. That afternoon, the wind picked-up and the skies began to clear. Bryant and I headed out to the same area we had hunted the first day. With the wind blowing and the damp air, I was very uncomfortable sitting at our stand. It wasn't really cold temperature-wise, but the wind just penetrated to the bone. We spotted one very small stag and decided to move to another high spot. I was happy to move, knowing that the hike would warm me up. I was not cold again that afternoon.

We had traveled only a half-mile when Bryant and I spotted a stag to our left, about 200 yards away and traveling parallel to us. I knew immediately that this was the one I wanted. His antlers seemed huge. There was some cover between us, so we used it to get about 75 yards closer. I found a good vantage point and tried to catch my breath. The stag never knew we were there. All of a sudden, he changed directions and headed straight toward us. This allowed me to calm down, since I knew that time was on my side and I would not have to take a rushed shot.

When the stag was about 60 yards away, he stopped and seemed to know something was wrong. The wind was in our favor and, in a few moments, he was again proceeding toward us. Just before he entered a thick path, I held my Remington Model 700 in 7 mm Mag on his shoulder and squeezed the trigger. He fell in his tracks without a step.

Bryant got to him first. I was delighted when I first saw my downed stag. He only had one shovel, but his antlers were beautiful to me. Now the work began. After caping-out the head, we started for camp. There was not enough daylight to make another trip, so we would return the next morning for the meat. Bryant carried the cape and I carried antlers.

When we arrived at the site of the kill next morning, a bald eagle had already located the carcass. It was the first bald eagle I had ever seen and I was in awe of its beauty. While we packed the meat, another stag watched us from about 300 yards away.

On Friday and Saturday we continued looking for moose but we never saw any. The rut had been over for a week or so and they seemed to disappear into the timber. Though the weather was still foggy, we continued to see caribou. None were as nice as the two Harry and I had taken. I felt really fortunate to get the biggest trophy I had seen.

As most vacations end, our fly-out day (Sunday) came and the sun showed itself for the first time in a week. It was by far the prettiest day.

The drive home was long, but pleasant. The trees were a treat to see as we drove along the beautiful coast of Maine. One of our last stops in Maine was made at a small fishing village where Harry and I bought a cooler full of fresh lobsters to take home.

Though we didn't fill our moose tags, our caribou trophies made up for them. I would have never believed that both Harry and I would get trophies that would qualify for the Boone and Crockett Club records. It was the end of a fantastic trip.

Photograph Courtesy of William A. Shaw

William A. Shaw hunted along Lloyds River in Newfoundland in 1987 to find this woodland caribou that scores 298-4/8 points.

Photograph Courtesy of George C. Thompson, Jr.

George C. Thompson, Jr., and the woodland caribou that he took in the Port aux Basques area in Newfoundland in 1987 that scores 310-3/8 points.

Photograph by Wm. H. Nesbitt

WOODLAND CARIBOU
THIRD AWARD
SCORE: 319
Locality: Fishels Brook, Nfld.   Date: September 1986
Hunter: Fred Waite

WOODLAND CARIBOU 319

Fred Waite

My caribou hunt took place in Newfoundland with outfitter Don MacInnis and his guide Joseph Hynes.

On September 20, 1986, while in the field hunting, we spotted a fairly nice moose. As we were watching this moose, we spotted a caribou about a mile away that looked to be pretty nice. We decided to move closer and got to within 200 yards. We both decided this was a very nice caribou. In fact, Joe (my guide) thought maybe there were two caribou standing side by side. As it turned out though there was only one.

I was using my .340 Wetherby with a Zeiss 3x9 scope. My first shot downed the caribou, but it got up on its feet, fell back down, and then floundered around on the ground. Joe yelled for me to shoot it again, so I shot it a second time. Then, it was down for good.

My guide said this was the nicest caribou that they had ever taken. He counted 41 points on the rack. This caribou was taken near Old Country Pond, in area 61, which is in the southwestern part of Newfoundland.

Two days later, I was able to take a fairly nice moose, putting an end to a very successful hunt and a great time.

Photograph by Wm. H. Nesbitt

NEW WORLD'S RECORD BARREN GROUND CARIBOU
FIRST AWARD
SCORE: 465-1/8

Locality: Mosquito Creek, Alaska   Date: September 1987
Hunter: Roger Hedgecock   On Display: B&C National Collection

BARREN GROUND CARIBOU
465-1/8

Roger Hedgecock

On one hand, I can say Boone and Crockett has never really been the objective of any of my hunting trips. But on the other hand, I can never remember sitting on a cold deer stand, rifle in hand, that thoughts of a record whitetail didn't cross my mind. In fact, on my second elk hunt, I felt the rush of adrenalin on a Wyoming mountain. But that big bull, the largest one in the whole world to me at the time, measured 320 unofficially and it takes 375 to make the book.

That elk hunt was back in 1986, and I figured that was the biggest of big game for me. There's an old adage about not knowing what the future holds. I believe in it.

At the time of the elk hunt, I had never seen a barren ground caribou. I had never seen a caribou of any kind. To be perfectly clear on the matter, I had never seen a caribou until September 25, 1987, the day we flew into a base camp that was located about 80 miles north of Nondalton, Alaska.

The next day, about two miles from camp, I squeezed the trigger on my .300 Weatherby. It was nearly 1 o'clock, an hour-and-a-half after the guide, Bob Tracy, had spotted the animal and said we were going after it. I could detect some excitement in his voice as he pointed it out in a herd of about 20. As we slowly worked our way from Mosquito Creek across barren tundra, using ridges as shields, trying to reach the highest point nearest the herd, I kept remembering what Bob had said, "If you have to look twice at the size of the rack, it ain't worth going after."

We were going and going hard. We crawled the last 200 yards. The cows, apparently sensing something was wrong, got up and started moving from left to right. Flat on my stomach, I was watching through my 3x9 Nikon scope. My eyes were watering, my vision was blurred, and I raised my head to wipe my eyes. At this point, I got my first really good look at the rack. Rack was all I could see. Quickly I put my Leitz binoculars before my eyes to take another look. I saw the rack, the head, and then the body. He was walking slowly behind the cows.

As I eased the rifle into a shooting position, Bob was whispering, "Wait. Wait. Give him just a little more time, and you, take your time. Make the first shot a good one."

Finally, after what seemed longer than the trip from North Carolina to Alaska, the big bull was clearly straight away, showing me his right shoulder. I fired! The animal spun completely around and just stood there. I fired again, and he spun completely around once again. Each time I could hear the impact of the 220 grain bullet. The novice of my caribou hunting came out. I asked Bob, "Did I hit him?" He nodded his head and added, "He'll die standing. Just wait, you have placed two bullets right on target."

The cows ran and the bull didn't, and I began feeling comfortable. Finally, the huge body crumbled to the tundra. At such a time I guess most hunters find something to worry about. I knew the hip boots were lighter as we walked the 200 yards, but I was worried about a broken tine, or just simply broken antlers. You allow a lot of things to pass through your mind. Bob's first words were comforting. "It's a really big one," he said, "And it may make the book."

Of course we took a lot of pictures before caping the animal out and quartering the meat and packing it out, but my real excitement didn't come until we were back at camp. We did not score it at camp, but Bob talked seriously with my wife Molly and me about the possibility of a records book caribou.

Bob packed the meat and antlers and sent them back to Nondalton. I knew it was a super way to begin a hunt. For the next nine days, we hunted moose and brown bear. It was the kind of hunt you dream about. I was able to fill both tags, a moose that rough scored 218 and a bear measuring 9-1/2 feet. Molly bagged a moose, caribou, and brown bear.

After the hunt, we returned to Nondalton and began rough scoring the caribou. Three people scored it from 470 to 477. Bob told me that after the 60 day drying period, he felt sure the animal would score close to the current World's Record. This makes you get a lot more excited about records than you ever have been.

After the drying period, an Official Measurer for the Boone and Crockett Club records scored the antlers at 465-1/8. Then, D&C Expediters of Anchorage shipped the cape to Cody Taxidermy, Cody, Wyoming, where the trophy was mounted and then shipped to North Carolina.

It's been a long year-and-a-half, waiting to know if this trophy will go in the records book, and how it will rank. That's why we are here. June 10, 1989 [20th N.A.B.G. Awards, Albuquerque, N.M.] is a day I have been eagerly waiting for. It's like Christmas morning for a 45-year-old farm boy from the foothills of the Blue Ridge Mountains in North Carolina, who until recently seldom dreamed of a records book trophy, especially a records book caribou.

Note: This New World's Record barren ground caribou is now on continuing display in the Boone and Crockett Club's National Collection of Heads and Horns in the Buffalo Bill Historical Center, Cody, Wyoming. Shortly after the 20th Awards of June 10, 1989, Roger Hedgecock agreed to a continuing loan of this trophy to the Club's collection, where it can be enjoyed by the vast throngs of hunters who visit the BBHC each year. Interestingly, Roger lived for a number of years near Cody while ranching, moving back to his boyhood state of North Carolina shortly before his memorable hunt.

Photograph Courtesy of Monty D. McCormick

Shotgun Hills, Alaska, was the site of Monty D. McCormick's 1987 hunt that resulted in this barren ground caribou scoring 400 points.

Photograph Courtesy of Harold L. Moore, Jr.

That's a big Texas grin Harold L. Moore, Jr., is sporting with the barren ground caribou he shot near Port Heiden, Alaska, in 1985. It scores 408-3/8 points.

Photograph by Wm. H. Nesbitt

BARREN GROUND CARIBOU
SECOND AWARD
SCORE: 440-3/8

Locality: Lake Clark, Alaska   Date: September 1988
Hunter: James W. Vorhease

BARREN GROUND CARIBOU 440-3/8

James W. Vorhease

What began as the hunting-trip-of-a-lifetime proved to be even more fantastic as I stared through my scope at an enormous trophy caribou. The trip had begun months earlier when I had been invited by Lance McCandless from Ashdown, Arkansas, and some friends to go to Alaska for a caribou and moose hunt. Lance had been to Alaska two years prior, and he and Bill Aitken had taken two very nice bull caribou.

Lance had arranged for an unguided trip with Rust Flying Service in Anchorage to begin the second week of September 1988. I was the novice "Big Game Hunter," so everyone checked to be sure I was properly outfitted for the trip. We were on an unguided trip to the tundra, so we would have to be self-sufficient for one to two weeks. As we accumulated all of our gear, freeze-dried food, medical supplies, tents, sleeping bags, and heavy clothing, it seemed it would be impossible to stay under the 70 pound limit per person required by the bush plane.

Lance had told us we might be taking shots of 200 yards plus, so Butch Miller asked if I would like to take his Winchester Model 70 rifle in 7 mm Mag. I had been shooting my semi-automatic .30-06 for whitetail, but on my last hunt, it had hung, so I was gratefull to accept his offer. Lance had developed a load for his 7 mm Mag that uses a 160 grain Spitzer boat-tail. This turned out to be an excellent round, with a one-inch pattern at 100 yards.

We arrived in Anchorage on Friday afternoon, prepared to fly out the next morning. We were to hunt the Clark Lake area, which meant we had to fly through a pass in the Alaska Range. On Saturday, the weather turned bad and the pass quickly became impassable.

After listening to the radio all day, and hearing of many close calls of bush pilots attempting to fly the pass and having to turn around, I quickly understood why Rust Flying Service had a perfect record. Even though he knew we were extremely disappointed, Hank would not take a chance on flying in bad weather. The next day, as we flew out through the tight pass, I understood his concern.

We set up camp late Sunday afternoon on the crescent lake. We had divided our group of 10 into three camps. I was with Dan York and Don Wallingfford. Don is an Alaskan transplant of 20 years, whose experience on the tundra proved invaluable.

Late that afternoon, a nice bull and two cows walked past the camp, within 300-400 yards. Since we could not hunt the day we had flown in, all we could do was sit and watch.

The next morning I was up before daylight. I had decided to climb the mountain near the camp in order to have a good view of the valley. I climbed halfway up and took a seat on a ledge. Don had insisted that we would find the caribou high on the mountain, not in the valley. But all I could remember was a National Geographic series of hundreds of caribou traveling across the low, flat tundra.

Around 8 a.m., I decided to move up the mountain since I had not seen any movement. I had walked less than a quarter-mile when I noticed a large group of caribou coming over the crest of the mountain toward me. They were approximately 1,000 yards away. But even at that distance, it was apparent that there was an enormous bull in the group. I scanned the herd with my binoculars. It appeared to be just one bull with about 20 cows. As the group moved down the mountain, I moved up the slope toward them. The mountain had a natural terrace shape that gave good cover as I ascended. For 20-30 minutes, we gradually moved towards each other. They grazed slowly down the mountain, and about 300-400 yards between, I topped the slope and saw them across an open, grassy flat. The cows had split-up, half moving down past me on the left and half feeding out to my right.

As I made my last move for position, one of the cows to my right saw a movement and ran back up the mountain past the bull. He turned and ran approximately 50 steps up the mountain and stopped on a ledge. He looked out over the flat, trying to see what had disturbed the cow. Then he turned and looked up the mountain. I knew this would be my only chance at such a massive trophy. I estimated he was 350-400 yards away. I placed the cross hairs on the top of his shoulder and fired. I heard a dull thud and the bull dropped his head but stood fast. I reloaded and fired again. Another dull thud. This time he slumped to his right, but to my amazement, he continued to stand. I wasn't sure how much lead this big bull could carry, so I chambered another round and fired again. As the third shot found its mark, the bull fell forward, motionless. We then spent the rest of the day packing meat off the mountain.

The next two days, we experienced torrential rains and winds that nearly blew our tents away. Finally, on Thursday, the weather broke and Dan and Don were able to take two large bulls. On Friday, the bush plane returned and was a welcome sight, since the weather had turned bad again that night. The trip back through the pass was like a roller coaster ride.

Overall, we had an extremely successful trip, with seven caribou and two moose, thanks to Hank and the pilots at Rust Flying Service. Also, a special thanks goes to Don and Kathy Wallingford for their hospitality to our group.

Photograph Courtesy of John S. Rohrer

John S. Rohrer did not need a guide in 1987 to locate this barren ground caribou that scores 426-4/8 points. He killed it on the Alaska Peninsula in Alaska.

Photograph Courtesy of David L. Richards

This barren ground caribou was still in velvet when David L. Richards located it in the Talkeetna Mountains in Alaska in 1987. It scored 411-7/8 points with the velvet removed.

NEW WORLD'S RECORD CENTRAL CANADA BARREN GROUND CARIBOU
FIRST AWARD
SCORE: 416
Locality: Courageous Lake, N.W.T.   Date: September 1987
Hunter: Toby J. Johnson

CENTRAL CANADA BARREN GROUND CARIBOU 416

Toby J. Johnson

Our guide Bobby Algona (an Eskimo from Pellet Lake, N.W.T.), my hunting partner Dave Collis (from Florida), and I were stalking a caribou that Dave was interested in getting a better look at. I looked off to our right, over a little rise, and all I said was, "I see the one that I want."

Our hunt started on September 12, 1987. Dave and I left my home in Sheridan, Wyoming, and flew to Edmonton, Alberta, where we spent the night. The next day we headed for Yellowknife, the capitol of the Northwest Territories in Canada. We would be hunting Central Canada barren ground caribou with Fred Webb and Mike Freeland of Webb Qaivvik Ltd. Dave and I were met at the airport by Fred.

The following morning, September 14, we went to purchase our hunting licenses before we were flown in a Twin Otter to Courageous Lake, which lies about 150 miles north-northeast of Yellowknife. We were met at the camp by Fred's son Martin, who runs the camp. The camp had very comfortable accommodations. Our sleeping quarters were tents with wooden frames and plywood floors. We had foam mattress pads for beds, and oil burning stoves for heat. The meals prepared by the camp cook, Pascal Lleres, were excellent.

We could see the caribou right from our camp which sure gets you excited. Dave and I couldn't hunt the first day because the law states that a person cannot hunt within the 12 hours following being flown into camp. That afternoon, we sighted-in our rifles. That first night in camp, I went to bed with great anticipation of what the next day would bring.

The following morning was somewhat of a letdown, as it was rainy and very windy outside. It was too windy to take the boats out on the lake to hunt for caribou. Bobby, Dave, and I walked out from camp and hunted all day. We saw a total of about 250 caribou that day. Of the caribou we saw, we thought we had seen only one that would make the records book. Maybe tomorrow would bring a better day.

The next day, the weather was even worse. The wind was blowing harder, with a few snow squalls. So Bobby, Dave, and I walked out from camp again that day. We didn't see as many caribou as we had the previous day, maybe about 50 head. But we did see a cross fox, short-eared owl, gyrfalcon, some ptarmigan, and a group of whistling swans.

The following morning, September 17, we awoke to a better day. The winds were calm, but it was a little rainy and foggy. We were able to take the boat that day, which enabled us to get into some new hunting country, far from camp. This brings us back to the start of this hunting story.

The caribou I was watching was in a group of several other good bulls. My caribou really didn't stand out in this bachelor group of bulls. As I think back on it now, there were probably several other bulls in the herd that may have scored 400 plus Boone and Crockett points. But the caribou I was watching was a bull that I thought had everything it takes for a caribou to score really well on the Boone and Crockett Club's system of scoring.

I immediately took my day pack off and laid it on the ground. I used my pack to rest my rifle on as I got into a prone position for the shot. With one shot at about 150 yards, I had taken what I thought was a tremendous caribou.

As we walked up to the caribou, my first thought was that I had shot a runt. This caribou was small-bodied in comparison to its cousin, the barren ground caribou. Here I was, thinking that I had just collected an average-sized caribou. But our guide kept talking about the size of my caribou's antlers. I tried telling Bobby that the caribou's antlers only appeared big because his body was so small. Then, Dave decided the best way to settle this discussion was to score the head. We didn't have paper or pencil to add up the score so we just kept track of the score in our heads. We came up with a score of 423. I figured we had not added correctly, so we rescored it and again came up with a score that was 15 points greater than the existing World's Record.

As we took pictures of my caribou, caped out the head, boned-out the meat, and packed it all back to the boat, I think it was at this point I finally realized that I had in fact collected a potential New World's Record Central Canada barren ground caribou.

Photograph Courtesy of Shawn T. Brown

Hoholitna River, Alaska, was the site of Shawn T. Brown's hunt for barren ground caribou in 1988 that resulted in this trophy that scores 406-7/8 points.

Photograph Courtesy of Gary L. Truitt

Gary L. Truitt killed this barren ground caribou at Mt. Harper, Alaska, in 1987. It scores 411 points for entry into the records keeping.

Photograph by Wm. H. Nesbitt

CENTRAL CANADA BARREN GROUND CARIBOU
SECOND AWARD
SCORE: 408-3/8

Locality: Courageous Lake, N.W.T.   Date: September 1987
Hunter: Jon Vanderhoef

CENTRAL CANADA BARREN GROUND CARIBOU 408-3/8

Jon Vanderhoef

We received a call in June 1987 from Glenn St. Charles of Seattle that he had a super bowhunt lined up for Central Canada barren ground caribou in the Northwest Territories. After talking it over with my dad, we called Glenn back and told him to count us in.

The hunt was to consist of Glenn, his son Jay, two of Jay's hunting friends, Jack Joseph from Nebraska, and my dad, Bill Vanderhoef. Jack drove to Boise from Nebraska, and the three of us drove to Seattle to meet the rest of the party. After a fine dinner and evening as guests of the St. Charles family, we left the next morning, driving to Vancouver, B.C., to catch our flight to Yellowknife, N.W.T.

The next morning, we met our guide and went to the Fish and Game Department and bought our caribou tags, as well as wolf tags. We had heard there was a chance to take a wolf. Later in the day, we loaded all our gear, together with four other hunters, into the Twin Beaver plane and flew to the camp on Courageous Lake.

After getting our gear put away, we went fishing for lake trout (you can't hunt on the day you fly). Such fishing I had never experienced. Dad and I caught and released at least 15 lake trout each. They ranged in size from 18 to 24 inches.

The next morning, the hunt started. Our head guide said he knew just the place to take us bowhunters, a place away from the rifle hunters in the camp. It was flat as a table top! We saw a few caribou bulls within rifle range, but no way to stalk within bow range.

Our means of transportation was a 14 foot aluminum boat with a 15 horsepower outboard, so Dad and I decided to boat along the shore, looking for some mature bulls that we could stalk for a shot. We hadn't gone far when we spotted some antlers sticking above some rocks on the shore. The wind had come up, which made it a little difficult for the guide to get us ashore within 150 yards of the bull. Dad stalked to within 35 yards and dropped the bull in his tracks with an arrow in the neck.

The wind was really blowing by now and the guide thought we should be heading for camp. When we got out in the lake, we had about three-foot-high whitecaps, and we were bobbing around like a cork. I asked the guide if he thought this was a safe thing to be doing and he said, "No, I don't think so." I suggested we go back to an inlet and wait until the storm blew over, which we did.

While we were fixing something to eat, the other five hunters and their guide pulled into the cove for shelter too. After waiting several hours, the wind died down a little. We decided that since the other boat was larger (18 feet long, with two 25 horsepower outboards), they could lead and we would follow in their wake. After a breathtaking, hair-raising, experience, we arrived at camp wet and cold, but safe.

That evening, while sitting in "Van's Bar & Grill" (that's what we called Dad's tent) drinking vodka and Tang, we decided that on the next day we would go to the lake where we had caught the lake trout since it was hilly country with rocks and pockets. That would make it easier to stalk within bow range. Besides, we had seen more caribou in that area.

This was my lucky day, September 10, 1987! I spotted a herd of caribou: cows, calves, two mature bulls, and one huge bull in the rear. When I glassed him, I could not believe the length of his rear points on each side. I knew I had to take him. I glassed the area and sighted a basin with lots of big rocks in the direction the caribou were heading. It would make a good ambush for a bowhunter. My guide and I circled around and got in place in the rocks and waited. Cows and calves came by about 20 yards away. The big bull was last in line. The two mature bulls came by the rock and stopped broadside, but I was sure I wanted the "granddaddy." Then the guide, who was kneeling behind me, said, "Shoot!"

The two bulls didn't hesitate; they whirled around and blew out of there, taking old "Rear Points" with them. Another 30 seconds and I could have had a 20 yard shot at him with my bow. Grabbing my rifle that the guide was carrying in the event we saw a wolf, I ran out of the rocks and, finding the bull in the cross hairs, I touched one off. He didn't slow down. I fired again. Nothing. At the third shot, down he went. I thought the scope had gotten off target, bouncing around in the boat, but when I got to him, there were three holes in his rib cage. Old Rear Points was every bit the trophy bull I had thought him to be during the stalk.

While all this was going on, Dad was out fishing. He caught a 40 inch, 29 pound lake trout, which he kept to have mounted.

Jay and his friend Tye each took nice bulls with their bows that made the Pope & Young Club records book, as did Dad's bull. Of the seven hunters in our party, we had four bow kills and three rifle kills for 100% success.

I was elated with taking my trophy bull, but the thought comes back many times that I could have had a World's Record Pope and Young Club caribou trophy as well as a Boone and Crockett bull.

Photographs Courtesy of Bernard Sippin and Randall J. Kiessel

(l) Bernard Sippin with his Central Canada barren ground caribou from 1988 from Parry Peninsula, N.W.T. It scores 386 points. (r) Randall J. Kiessel hunted out of Cape Dorset, N.W.T., in 1986 and took this Central Canada barren ground caribou that scores 390-5/8 points.

Photograph Courtesy of Robert M. Hazlewood

Rendez-vous Lake, N.W.T., produced this Central Canada barren ground caribou for Robert M. Hazlewood in 1986. It scores 398-4/8 points.

Photograph by Wm. H. Nesbitt

CENTRAL CANADA BARREN GROUND CARIBOU
THIRD AWARD
SCORE: 400-6/8
Locality: Rendez-vous Lake, N.W.T.   Date: September 1986
Hunter: Dale L. Zeigler

CENTRAL CANADA BARREN GROUND CARIBOU 400-6/8

Dale L. Zeigler

One day in August of 1986, a friend of mine called and advised me of a possible hunting trip to the Northwest Territories that turned out to be a once-in-a-lifetime experience for me. I've lived in Helena, Montana, for the past 18 years, being a transplant from the west side of Washington state. I grew up there and started hunting with my dad as soon as I was of sufficient size to carry a 12 gauge shotgun or a .30-30 Winchester rifle. I'll never forget my first experience of shooting a 12 gauge shotgun at a passing duck on Bud Inlet and finding myself sitting in a mud puddle directly behind me. We weren't what you would call avid hunters; however, my dad would take me out whenever possible during pheasant and deer hunting season and later for waterfowl. However, as my teen years came along, a few other things seemed to be somewhat more important, and it seemed that the hunting pressure in that area increased at such a drastic rate that I lost a considerable amount of interest.

In my late 20's, the company I was working for had an opportunity to open an office in Montana. I had a new young family, and I decided there were too many people where I was living and we packed up and moved to Montana. It didn't take long to realize the tremendous fishing and hunting possibilities in my new home. As the years went on, both my wife Diane and I began to more and more take advantage of the great outdoors in Montana. Some very close friends of ours from Helena bought a business in Harlowton, Montana, and moved there near the Musselshell River. Each year, Diane and I look forward to the coming of pronghorn season so that we can go to the Harlow area and hunt pronghorn and then later, hunt whitetails along the Musselshell. I go elk hunting every year, but I'm not really what you would consider an avid elk hunter.

When my friend John gave me a call in August 1986, I was a little apprehensive at first, but as the conversation went on, it became more and more exciting. It seemed that a native Eskimo living in Tuktoyaktuk, Northwest Territories, had expressed an interest to the Canadian Fish and Wildlife Service in starting a guiding service in the Rendez-vous Lake area of the Northwest Territories. The Canadian Fish and Wildlife Service took an interest in Billy Jacobson since he had demonstrated a hard-working attitude and genuine desire to succeed in an enterprise of his own. During the summer months, he would work for the Canadian Fish and Wildlife Service on bear studies, tagging the grizzly bear in the area around Rendez-vous, approximately 200 miles southeast of Inuvik. During the winter months, he spent his time in that same area trapping for fox, marten, and arctic hare.

In response to Billy's inquiry, the Canadian Fish and Wildlife Service made contact in the states to see if a group of hunters would be willing to travel to Rendez-vous on a hunt for caribou from the Blue Nose Herd. It was our understanding that very few non-natives had ever hunted that herd. When John called me, he told me the trip was in the planning stages; however, if I had the time and could come up with the cost, there was an opening and I was welcome to tag along. As the time for our departure came nearer, my excitement continued to rise.

On September 14, we left Helena, Montana at approximately 8:30 a.m., planning to drive straight through to Edmonton, Alberta, where we would catch our plane ride to Inuvik. I found myself with Dr. Phil Wright (emeritus chairman of the Boone and Crockett Club's Records Committee), Robby Hazelwood (owner of Cedar-Hill Game Calls and also a biologist for the U.S. Fish and Wildlife Service), and my friend John, who is a vice president of the Boone and Crockett Club. Needless to say, in this group I felt somewhat inadequate. I more or less likened myself to the water boy with the Green Bay Packers. Very shortly into the trip, these fellows made me feel right at home and very comfortable.

We arrived in Edmonton about 7 p.m. We stayed overnight at the Convention Center after we visited with Sam Berry. Sam is a son of Mr. Tom Berry, owner of the number one Central Canadian barren ground caribou rack. Sam had spent some time at Billy Jacobson's camp on Rendez-vous, and Sam had given us somewhat of a run-down on what sounded like an absolutely beautiful area. After a very nice evening meal, we hit the rack, planning on rising early to catch our plane from Edmonton. We left at 7:15 a.m. on Pacific Western Airways. We flew on a 737 into Yellowknife, then onto Norman Wells, and finally into Inuvik at approximately 1:30 p.m. It wasn't nearly as cold as I had anticipated, approximately 40 degrees. The sun was shining and it was a little breezy.

We went to the Fish and Game Department and picked-up our tags and regulations. We flew out of Inuvik in two floatplanes, a Cessna 185 and a 210. We arrived at Rendez-vous at approximately 4 p.m. We got set up in our quarters, which were not really what I had expected, given the remoteness of the area. Billy had converted a building that had been left behind by the seismic oil exploration companies after the bust of the oil boom in that area. We ended-up with very comfortable quarters, well-heated and even electric lights provided by a small generator. Since at that time of the year we had daylight well into the evening, we took about a mile walk from camp to look over the country. Just a very short distance from camp we came upon an arctic fox, several ptarmigan, and, within a half-mile, saw a number of very fine caribou. At this point I have to tell you that on the very first sighting of a caribou bull, it takes considerable restraint to keep yourself from taking one the first day. When you are used to hunting whitetail deer or mule deer, antlers of a bull caribou seem massive. I could very easily have shot a bull that first night and been extremely pleased.

We returned to camp about 8 and had a delicious meal of barbecued caribou steak, baked potatoes and biscuits. Billy's wife, Ilean, can turn out some of the most delicious camp food you will ever taste. Shortly after dinner we went to bed. We awoke the next morning to temperature of about 35 degrees and the prospect of a beautiful, sunny day. John and I went behind camp, toward the area that we had seen the caribou the night before, while the others took a boat trip down Rendez-vous Lake to the east end, where the caribou frequently cross. While walking around the lake, we came within 40 to 50 yards of an old muskox bull. We took numerous pictures until he finally decided to saunter off.

As we continued around the lake, we saw a herd of caribou that at a distance seemed to have several very fine bulls in it. After about an hour-and-a-half stalk, we decided that one bull definitely was in the records class and John and I continued to stalk him. After John decided not to take that animal, I had a very large decision to make; however, it didn't take long to make it. It was only about a 75 yard shot. As we approached the animal, John's comment was, "That one's going to score high."

After taking several pictures and skinning and caping the animal, we set-out with skin and head on the pack board, leaving the rest to return for later. We packed for approximately a mile to the lake. Believe me, packing the head and cape of a caribou on a pack board in the far north tundra is a feat in itself. John is considerable smaller than I, but in much better physical condition, and he gave me quite a workout. We were eventually picked up by Billy in the boat and taken back to camp. When we arrived at the camp, Robby had a magnificent set of antlers sitting on the bank of the lake, and I couldn't help but be a little bit disappointed. John merely smiled and said, "Wait 'til you see the numbers." Phil Wright made green scores of the racks, at that time placing mine at 401-5/8 and Robbie's at 399-3/8. We had yet to fill tags for John and Phil.

That night we were all quite tired. We had another tremendous meal of caribou steak, mushrooms, and potatoes, and we hit the beds early. The next day, Robby and I fished around camp while John and Phil went in the boat down the lake with Billy. We caught some very fine fish and then spent the better part of the afternoon cleaning the capes and antlers. Later that evening, Rob and I went to watch my kill site to see if by chance a bear or wolverine might feed on the remains of the field dressing but darkness came before we saw any signs of life.

The next morning, John and I took the same route around the lake as we had Tuesday but we only saw four caribou. We met Rob and Phil and Billy after we had walked from camp down to the end of the lake. Phil had shot a nice bull but didn't feel that it would score as high as the other two taken previously. We spent several hours at the end of the lake, having tea and sandwiches over a campfire and catching several fish ranging from six pounds up to 10. Phil and I took the boat back to camp, while John and Rob tried for John's caribou that afternoon.

Back in camp, Phil scored his caribou at 378 points. Phil showed me how to turn ears and split the lips on my cape. That night, Phil and I feasted on caribou steak, chili, and a delicious piece of yellow cake. Ilean has to be one of the finest camp cooks in the Northwest Territories. It started to rain that evening, and when Robby and John returned it was raining quite hard. They hadn't had any luck. On Friday, Phil and I stayed in camp and worked on capes and antlers. John, Rob, and Billy left in the boat after a filling breakfast of sourdough pancakes and bacon. I took Billy's young son Berry fishing, just a short way from camp.

Once again, we caught several very fine fish. That evening, about 8 p.m. when the fellows returned, John had taken his caribou that Phil green scored at 398.

The next day was fairly lazy since we had all filled our caribou tags. We spent considerable time fishing on the banks and hunting for ptarmigan. The ptaramigan in September are a beautiful white, with a spattering of brown left over from their summer colors. Phil had expressed a desire to bring back several ptarmigan for his zoology classes at the university in Missoula, so we quickly froze several of the complete birds so that he could take them with him.

That morning, I had commented to Ilean that it would be nice to have some fish that night. When we returned to camp she had nice, thick trout steaks, fried to a perfect golden brown with baked potatoes and a delicious lemon meringue pie to top it off.

Since we had only a half-day left before the planes were to come to pick us up the next day, we spent it relatively close to camp. We had picked up one grizzly bear tag in Inuvik before flying out, but we decided there wasn't going to be much chance of filling it. According to Billy, the weather had just been too nice and it was a little too early in the year for the grizzlies to come in from the barrens. We had seen one grizzly track on the beach when John and I were walking back to camp one day, but it was fairly small and we saw no signs of grizzly in the area.

Before leaving, Billy took us to the west end of the lake and showed us some artifacts left by the Indians who, apparently until the 1930's and '40's, had traveled into the area trapping and trading with the Hudson Bay Company. There were still several tepee poles, the remnants of a boat, and what appeared to be part of a lodge remaining.

Shortly thereafter, the planes arrived and flew us back to Inuvik. Getting four hunters and four sets of caribou antlers and capes, along with the two pilots, in these two airplanes was another feat. We spent Sunday night in Inuvik. The following morning, we flew to Edmonton and then drove back to Helena, Montana, all four of us with records book caribou.

This trip, from the beginning moment to the end, was truly an experience-of-a-lifetime for an amateur hunter.

Photograph Courtesy of Stanley Godfrey

Official measurer Stan Godfrey (r) and guide with Central Canada barren ground caribou Godfrey took near Warburton Bay, N.W.T., in 1988. This bull scores 355-6/8 points.

Photograph Courtesy of Timothy D. Gildersleeve

Timothy D. Gildersleeve with Quebec-Labrador caribou he took in 1987 near Wayne Lake, Quebec. The well-developed brow and bez palms helped this trophy score 382-3/8 points.

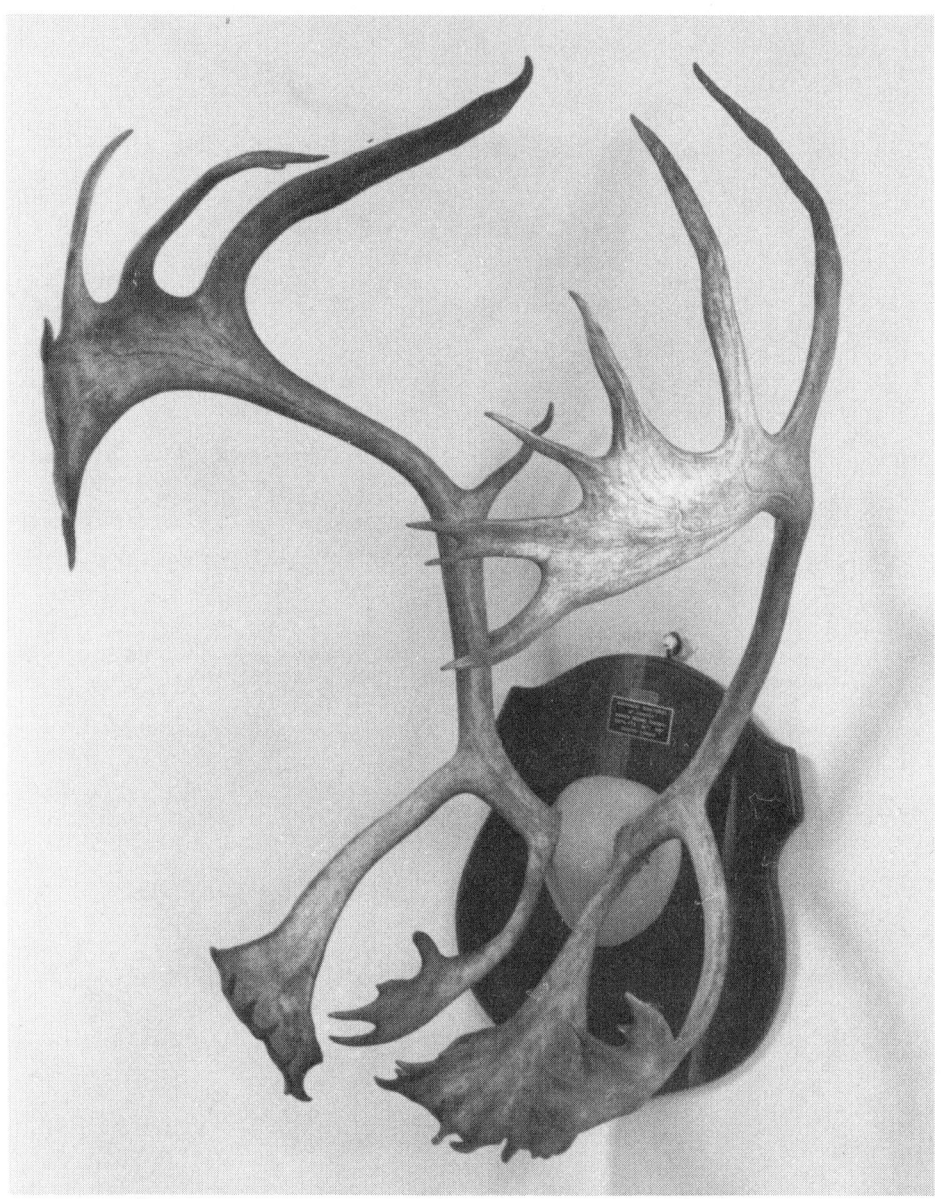

Photograph by Wm. H. Nesbitt

CENTRAL CANADA BARREN GROUND CARIBOU
HONORABLE MENTION
SCORE: 390-4/8

Locality: Courageous Lake, N.W.T.   Date: September 1987
Hunter: Joseph Pinkas

CENTRAL CANADA BARREN GROUND CARIBOU 390-4/8

Joseph Pinkas

After several months of planning, it finally became apparent that our caribou hunt was going to be on. We were informed by our outfitter, Fred A. Webb, that our group would be the last one to hunt the Courageous Lake camp that season. We knew quite well this was "The" area for Central Canada barren ground caribou, and the top three caribou in the Boone and Crockett Club's 19th Awards records book came out of Webb camps. Summer seemed to be just beginning, but our minds were already on September.

Besides the usual planning and preparation, my attention was focused on target range practice, and especially on working-up a proper handload for my .270 Winchester. Since this was to be my first caribou hunt, I was trying to do my utmost to prepare. I read a great deal about the arctic in general, but I concentrated on the Northwest Territories, caribou, Indian and Eskimo hunters, and guides. Many hours were spent talking to my good friend and mentor, and a trophy hunter of 30 years, Collins F. Kellogg. At last, September had finally arrived and the date of departure was getting closer. The anticipation was growing by the minute.

Our flight from Toronto to Edmonton was quite routine, as expected, since many people fly this route, but the flight from Edmonton to Yellowknife was much more exciting. This is not a common destination and we were finally getting closer to the capital of the Northwest Territories. Located on the north arm of Great Slave Lake, Yellowknife is touted as the "City in the Wilderness." Yellowknife is a city of contrasts: log cabins; pastel-colored, tiny houses, not far from modern downtown buildings; fashionable boutiques; and other unquestionable signs of civilization. Certainly not the rowdy frontier town we expected to see.

To obtain the necessary licenses and tags was quite simple, and in no time we were heading to the floatplane base in Yellowknife's Back Bay. It was quite an experience to see the DeHavilland Twin Otter aircraft being loaded with drums of gasoline, assorted supplies, baggage, and our hunting party. It seemed that plane would never be able to take off, but it did and quite easily. In a few moments, the shining surface of Great Slave Lake was fast disappearing and we were amazed to see the multitude of glacier-made lakes, occasional stands of stunted spruce, and some birch and pine. As we were heading north toward Courageous Lake, the trees fairly quickly gave way to the tundra. One could only begin to comprehend the vastness of this region.

After touching down on the slightly choppy surface of Courageous Lake and taxiing to a nearby sandy beach, it was time to disembark and to help unload the plane. Finally, we saw the tent camp that would be our home for the next several days. We couldn't wait to explore the surrounding area and we were immediately overtaken by the strange beauty of this barren land. Scattered outcroppings of rock, some covered with colorful lichens, yellow and white arctic grasses, red bearberries, and purple cranberries, covered the tundra. Standing on an esker not far from the camp, one can look over a vast area of wilderness and realize it is not barren of life but quite the opposite.

Our first day's task was to scout the area with our Indian guide Noel. It was a dreary, cloudy, and foggy day, with occasional drizzle falling from the steel-gray skies. To say that one appreciates the extra senses of your guide steering the boat over the miles of lake in a fog is a clear understatement, and he did it with ease, grace, and a smile. I will never forget my first encounter with caribou. After walking a couple of miles, we were sitting next to a big rock, preparing to glass, when suddenly out of the mist emerged a group of five bulls. We were downwind from them, but I was convinced they could see us clearly. They quite inquisitively came closer to investigate. Suddenly, the wind changed and they darted away, back into the mist.

For the next couple of days we scouted the most promising areas, around the western region of Courageous Lake. We could see herds of caribou of varying size and composition. Some herds consisted mostly of cows, calves, and bulls that were either too young or too old. On a few occasions, we approached the caribou very closely and were able to view them and count the points of their racks without binoculars. The incredible eyesight of our guide was a constant source of amazement.

On September 23, 1987, the day appeared to be "just right." The lake was calm, the day was mild, and the skies were slightly overcast. We selected an area adjacent to our previous exploration. Soon after leaving the boat, we came across fresh grizzly tracks. About 100 yards further, we saw freshly dug ground, a large hole that was a few feet deep, and several overturned boulders, each probably weighing several hundred pounds. The guide suddenly became very quiet and extremely alert. He had a loaded gun ready in his hand and, needless to say, I was doing exactly the same thing. We did not see the grizzly, but we certainly gained an extra measure of respect. The bear was obviously digging for ground squirrels, and in the process, had pushed aside huge rocks.

Our plan was to climb the nearby ridge and overlook the small stream that was on the other side. Walking was difficult; the ground was a wet and spongy bog. From the top of the ridge, we could see a small group of caribou about a mile-and-a-half away. Suddenly, the guide became quite excited, saying that the beautiful bull leading the small herd was the biggest one that he had seen in a few years. Finally, the hunt was really on.

We tried to get closer to the herd, which was moving parallel to us. The wind was in our favor, but the surrounding area resembled the surface of the moon. The ground was almost bare except for a few scattered small rocks. It was very difficult to take cover. And at this point, we had to run in crouched position just to keep up with the herd. I did not even want to think what kind of shot I might take, should I get a chance at a shot, after running that distance.

In a few minutes, the herd stopped moving and started to feed. This gave us the chance to catch our breath and start selecting our approach. Luckily, in this area there were some larger rocks so we had adequate cover. At this point, we were about 180 yards away. I saw the big lead bull only occasionally feeding because he was constantly watching the area. I was observing him through my rifle scope, and for the first time could actually see how magnificent an animal he was. Suddenly, something spooked the herd. They immediately stopped feeding, their heads went up, and I knew I had to shoot immediately. I did not even hear the sound of the shot from my Weatherby. The bull had taken two steps, and the herd had started to run in an opposite direction, when he went down.

By the time we reached the animal, the herd was gone and the entire area was strangely quiet, except for two ptarmigans crying overhead.

Photograph by Wm. H. Nesbitt

CENTRAL CANADA BARREN GROUND CARIBOU
HONORABLE MENTION
SCORE: 390-3/8
Locality: Courageous Lake, N.W.T.   Date: September 1988
Hunter: Patrick H. Ackerman

CENTRAL CANADA BARREN GROUND CARIBOU 390-3/8

Patrick H. Ackerman

Our hunt started on September 19, 1988, with the outfitters, Fred Webb and Mike Freeland, transporting us to the Fish and Game Department for licenses and tags. Then, it was on to the bush plane for the 1-1/2 hour flight to Courageous Lake, Northwest Territories.

The next day, we scouted and saw several hundred caribou but no bulls that were of the size we wanted. On September 21, 1988, my partner, Alan Bell of Stayton, Oregon, took his nice bull about 10 a.m., after glassing a herd of about 200 bulls, cows, and calves.

We moved to another location, approximately a half-mile away, and began glassing a large herd of caribou. We watched this herd for two hours and passed up many respectable (and possible Boone and Crockett) heads. The last of the herd was about to pass, 200 yards away, when this big bull appeared. We knew he had good tops, double shovels, and back points, but we could not make out the bez very well. After watching him for another 15 minutes, I decided to go ahead as he looked good and there were no other bulls in sight. I settled into a sitting position with my 7 mm Remington Mag and took him with a shoulder shot at 200 yards.

As we approached the bull, I could see how magnificent he was and how truly spectacular his antlers were. My Dene Indian guide ("Noel") did a great job in helping me to determine his size and get into position for a good stalk.

The camp of Webb-Freeland at Courageous Lake was great. We had delicious hot meals, hot showers, oil-heated wall tents, good conversation, and very qualified guides from the Dene Indians or from the Inuit Eskimos.

Photograph by Wm. H. Nesbitt

CENTRAL CANADA BARREN GROUND CARIBOU
HONORABLE MENTION
SCORE: 385-1/8
Locality: Lake Providence, N.W.T.   Date: September 1987
Hunter: Paul Wisness

CENTRAL CANADA BARREN GROUND CARIBOU 385-1/8

Paul Wisness

"Paul, how would you like to go to the Northwest Territories up in Canada for a caribou hunt?" This question, posed by a hunting buddy of mine here in North Dakota, started it all in May, 1987.

Now, I had done a fair bit of hunting locally, and every fall had seen me loading the horses for an annual trip to Montana for elk, but this would be something entirely different! Well, as it worked out, six of us headed-out in a motor home, bound for Yellowknife, the capital of the Territories.

September 7th found us in a twin-engine Otter plane, heading further north to Lake Providence and the main camp for Arctic Safaris, where we'd be spending the week hunting and fishing.

After landing, introductions were made, we got settled-in, and then we headed for the gun range to check our rifles. In the Territories, there is a 12 hour wait after flying before you can hunt, so most of us opted to try fishing for some big trout for supper.

Barry Taylor, our outfitter, headed down the 45-mile-long lake with a couple of the guides to see where the caribou were moving through, in preparation for the next day. They were back in time for the fish supper, announcing that there were lots of animals moving into the area a couple of miles south of the camp. The next day would see us in the midst of them.

Morning saw everyone up and eager to go, after a hearty breakfast. Mark Thompson and I paired-up and headed out with Barry and Vicki St. Germaine as guides.

Only five minutes out, we were forced to crouch down while 80 or so bulls paraded in front of us, headed to the lake crossing at Obstruction Rapids north of us. This was unbelievable and some were big, with racks at least four feet long. Each was scrutinized with binoculars and turned down. I'd never observed caribou before, so I trusted our guides who explained that none of these animals had the right combination of shovels, bez, and tops to be outstanding.

We pressed on, every now and then glassing an animal or two or three. About an hour later, as we crested a ridge, we hit pay dirt. Below us were 200-300 caribou in the valley, and off in the distance was an endless dark mass detouring a lake. We lay there for at least an hour, commenting on this one and that one, taking turns with the spotting scope. The guides were quite excited about a half-dozen of the big bulls. But the problem was getting within range without being spotted. Finally, realizing that most caribou were bedded and would stay put, the decision was made to check-out the next valley.

Noon hour saw us overlooking camp from a high outcrop of rock, munching sandwiches. Interruptions were constant, as caribou were everywhere. One even walked out of a small dip in the rocks 40 feet behind us, totally unconcerned.

Gradually, we worked our way back toward the first valley. About a quarter-mile short of it, a line of bulls was seen coming our way, slowly but surely. Without hesitation, the decision was made to waylay them as they came through a small gap into a wet flat. We found concealment in the midst of a small clump of dwarf spruce and waited. Cautiously, we waited, watching the narrow gap and knowing they had to come to us. And come they did, ever so slowly. Just like cattle, browsing along the way.

Vicki and Barry fixed their attention on each and every one, with critical comments on each. "The second point's too small," or "That one's got a deformed bez." Finally they arrived at a consensus, "The third one is the best. No, now he's the fourth."

Mark and I looked at each other. It was the first day of hunting and neither of us was in a hurry. We had flipped a coin for first shot and I had won. But, I had to ask, "You want to take it, Mark?" He declined, saying, "Go for it!"

The pack was on the ground in front of me for a rest and I knew my .270. Barry confirmed the distance, about 150 yards. The caribou were now lined-out, and as they hit the flat, I felt the recoil. But that caribou just stopped, nothing else. Twice more I hit him, each time with no visible effect. Gradually he turned around, obviously with broken shoulders. The other caribou walked on by, indifferent to his stumbling or the shots. Finally, he caved over in the long grass until only the antlers were visible.

As we approached the fallen animal, it became evident why this bull was so outstanding. The beams were over five feet long and in the classic heart shape, with good palmation on top, excellent bez, and a huge shovel. Barry and Vicki were full of congratulations and confident that this would break the existing record.

The next evening the rack was green scored at over 417! By this time, everyone in the group had taken a trophy and they'd all made the book, even the bowhunters. We were an ecstatic bunch to say the least. Four months later, I picked up my mount in Edmonton, officially scored for entry at 406 after drying. It now hangs as the main feature of my trophy room at the ranch.

In 1989, it was sent to the 20th Awards, where the Judges Panel was forced to make a judgment call on the palmation. This resulted in a final score of 385, still a fine example of the species.

Photograph Courtesy of Elmer R. Luce, Jr.

Elmer R. Luce, Jr., with one of two records book Quebec-Labrador caribou he took on the same hunt along the Baleine River in Quebec in 1987. This bull scored 384-4/8; the other scored 384-2/8.

Photograph Courtesy of Thomas A. Rue

Thomas A. Rue with Quebec-Labrador caribou he took at mid-afternoon in 1988 near Narcy Lake, Quebec. It scores 406 points.

Photograph by Wm. H. Nesbitt

QUEBEC-LABRADOR CARIBOU
FIRST AWARD
SCORE: 431-6/8

Locality: Tunulik River, Que.   Date: September 1984
Hunter: Carol A. Mauch

QUEBEC-LABRADOR CARIBOU
431-6/8

Carol A. Mauch

It was the second day of our second caribou hunt with Arctic Adventures on the Tunulik River in northern Quebec. My husband Dick and I were on our first outing with the camp's senior guide, Elijah. Also accompanying us was Edward Snowball, who at 11 years old, was an apprentice guide and interpreter. Elijah only spoke Inuit, his native language. We had become acquainted with Edward two years before and insisted he hunt with us.

In the morning, we headed up the river in a large, outboard canoe to a place my husband had remembered. He liked the lay of the land, which worked to funnel a series of worn and rutted migration trails to a single caribou highway and river crossing.

Dick had gone up the shoreline to glass for animals and still hunt on his own. Elijah sat on a high point to glass across the river landscape, while Edward and I started a fire for tea. Before long, Elijah shouted and waved to us. Through Edward, I learned Elijah had seen three bulls enter the river, beginning their swim for the far shore.

The crossing site was a mile or more wide, like a huge lake. Approximately 1/4 to 1/3 of the way across was a very long, narrow, rocky, and rough island. Edward and I ran for the canoe that Elijah had ready to go. We jumped in and headed for the island.

Caribou have thick, hollow hair that makes them very buoyant. We could see the bulls swimming high in the water. Even their tails were poked above the surface. Every time I see caribou swimming with their huge racks in the air, they remind me of the old sailing ships gliding along.

Meanwhile, the caribou had reached the island, crossed it and reentered the water. The guides took me two-thirds of the way down the backside of the island and dropped me off there. Edward and Elijah went on to the far shoreline. Earlier in camp, Glenn St. Charles, Jack Joseph, and Dick, all Pope and Young Club members and scorers, had been discussing with the guides fair chase and herding caribou in the water with boats. Edward had been a very intent listener, with many questions. Now he was determined to "do it right" so the trophy could qualify.

When they had gotten the boat past the caribou and near the far shore, Elijah stopped the outboard and sat dead in the water. The caribou soon saw the boat and began a large circle, changing direction. Because the island was long and narrow, with a high, rocky crown down the center, I was able to situate myself in the shrub brush and rocks on the high middle, therefore enabling me to shoot either left or right should the bulls come ashore at my end of the island.

The bulls did exactly as I had hoped. It was warm and almost still, with a hazy sun. I could easily hear their feet clicking on the stones along the rocky beach, approaching on my right side. As I pulled my bow once to loosen my arms, I thought, "Keep calm and wait for the big one." I was excited but ready.

The two smaller bulls came first and passed undisturbed, the herd master soon was broadside. I released my arrow. The caribou broke into a run and I quickly lost sight of them due to the rough terrain. A hit on the left side of the neck, just in front of the shoulder, produced a blood trail easy to follow.

I ran down the beach, climbing over and around rocks. Finally, I saw the end of the island, but no caribou. Not in the water, not on the island. Had they gone down the other side, back in the direction they had come from?

Quickly, I ran back down my side to approximately where I had made the shot and climbed up over the crest. There stood the three bulls, with my big one facing me. I released another arrow that went straight into his chest. My license was filled; it was time to find Dick to show him this beautiful animal I had taken by myself.

Elijah crossed the river to our campsite. He couldn't locate Dick, but he did bring back my camera and supplies we left behind. We took pictures, caped the trophy, and dressed-out the meat. It's delicious and we planned to take all we could home.

Once again, we returned to the campsite and there was Dick, smiling. During the whole chase, he had been sitting on a hill a mile or so away, watching the chain of events through his binoculars. Only, he didn't have the slightest idea who the bowhunter was. (Wives are supposed to be making tea.) It never occurred to him that it was me until he returned to our empty campsite.

Back at main camp, Dick and I gave Edward my bow and some arrows. Was he ever eager to learn to shoot, and he was the envy of the other young guides. Although Dick did not have a caribou yet, he took time to teach Edward some bowhunting basics on our outings. I went along to photograph and enjoy the beautiful tundra.

The hunt ended all too soon. Edward presented us with a gift of friendship and a carving of a seal he had made from soapstone. Someday, I would like to go back, but Dick says I only get to fish.

At the 1987 Pope and Young Club Banquet in Tulsa, Oklahoma, this caribou was recognized as a World's Record in its category. As far as I know, it still is. Also, I am the first woman to hold a World's Record in the Pope and Young Club.

Photograph by Scott Brown

At the 20th Awards (Albuquerque, 1989), Carol A. Mauch accepts First Award for her Quebec-Labrador caribou from Dr. Philip L. Wright, Chairman Emeritus of the Records Committee.

Photograph by Scott Brown

At the 20th Awards, 1989, Bernard W. Masino accepts Honorable Mention for his Quebec-Labrador caribou from Dr. Philip L. Wright, Chairman Emeritus of the Records Committee.

Photograph by Wm. H. Nesbitt

QUEBEC-LABRADOR CARIBOU
SECOND AWARD
SCORE: 427
Locality: Ungava Bay, Que.   Date: September 1984
Hunter: David Walker

QUEBEC-LABRADOR CARIBOU 427

David Walker

David Walker is a resident of Alberta, Canada. He is a big game hunter and he is aware of the bounty that his country offers, including the romantic Quebec-Labrador caribou. He decided to take a Quebec-Labrador caribou hunt in 1984.

Walker's choice of a hunt location was the George River, famed as a fine locality for big caribou. His one-week hunt began on September 17, 1984, when he was transported by airplane to the hunting camp, located about 120 miles northeast of Fort Chimo on the Keg River. From the base camp, freighter canoes would be used to transport hunters and guides to the hunting area and back.

The first few days of Walker's hunt were unsuccessful in finding the big bull that he was looking for. Finally, on September 22, he found his trophy.

It was a beautiful day for caribou hunting, sunny and clear with only a 15 mile-per-hour wind. The time was 12:15 a.m. and the distance was 380 yards. Walker used his Remington Model 700 in .270 caliber to take his trophy with a 130 grain bullet. It was a huge bull, one that Walker knew would have a excellent chance of post-season recognition. It was a fine ending to a memorable hunt.

Photograph by Wm. H. Nesbitt

QUEBEC-LABRADOR CARIBOU
HONORABLE MENTION
SCORE: 408
Locality: Caniapiscau River, Que.   Date: September 1987
Hunter: Bernard W. Masino

QUEBEC-LABRADOR CARIBOU 408

Bernard W. Masino

"Take him, he's a real good bull," our guide, Gordon Belvin, said to me in a hoarse whisper. I wasn't about to argue. At 200 yards, my scope at full magnification of 4.5x enabled me to see the huge rack clearly, with a magnificent double shovel on the bull caribou.

It was late September of 1985, and I was prone on a sandbar in the Caniapiscau River of northern Quebec, scoping a bull caribou that had been the object of dreams ever since my brother, Tony, had booked this caribou hunt. Lying prone in the sand with me on my right side was our guide, Gordon Belvin, and on my left, also belly-down in the sandbar, was brother Tony Masino. Gordon was busy with his binoculars, and Tony had his hands full with a Pentax 35 mm camera with a 200 mm lens.

For the past 40 minutes, the three of us had been lying on this sandbar, taking advantage of the occasional oversized rock and contours in the sand, watching a large herd of caribou cross from the west bank to the east bank of the Caniapiscau River. Caribou were crossing south of our position and in front of us, with a few stragglers even coming onto the sandbar with us, passing within 40 yards. Needless to say, our eyes were straining from the careful scrutiny of the many good bulls that were in this herd.

This extraordinary hunt had its beginning in December of 1986. My brother Tony is an enthusiastic hunter and he had been in correspondence with Jack Hume of Jack Hume Adventures, Inc. (operating Laurentian Ungava Outfitters Ltd.). Tony was familiar with Jack Hume's reputation, and after speaking with numerous references, was eager to book a hunt with him. Tony told me of his intentions and before long, we were booked with Hume's Outfit on the last hunt of the 1987 season, in the last week of September at the Main Camp.

I'm 40 years old and an insurance company manager in my home state of Maryland. Tony is 25 and a Corporal with the Prince George's County (Maryland) Police Department. Both of us have hunted since we were six years old, mostly small game, deer, and turkey, in Maryland and Pennsylvania. In the last few years however, we have enjoyed hunting trips to British Columbia and Alaska. Prior to our hunt, we both put in a good amount of time at the rifle range, sighting-in our rifles with the ammunition we were intending to hunt with. Both my brother and I were using Remington Model 700 bolt-action rifles shooting Remington factory ammo, soft-point, Core-Lokt in 180 grain. The only difference was in our scopes.

Tony's is a Bushnell 3x9 with see-through mounts and mine is equipped with a variable 1.75x4.5 Bushnell. My brother and I have enjoyed excellent performance with Remington ammunition in the past on moose, bear, and deer, and we expected the same performance for caribou.

We drove the ten hours from Maryland to Montreal in my Chevy Blazer, loaded with our hunting gear for the six day hunt. We had no trouble finding lodging for the night at a very comfortable motel in Brossards, just outside of Montreal. We were scheduled to depart from the Dorval Airport in Montreal to fly the approximately 900 miles north to Schefferville, jumping-off point for caribou hunters in Quebec and referred to as the "Caribou Capital of The World." We flew on a four-engine DeHavilland plane to Schefferville and we got to know the other hunters we would be sharing camp with. The other six hunters going to the Main Camp were sportsmen of exceptional character and humor, and by the end of our hunt, we had all become good friends.

The small and rustic, but efficient, Schefferville airport was busy with other hunters, their gear, and trophies, preparing to fly back to Montreal. Excitement continued to build as we looked over departing hunter's trophies and some of the mounted heads in the airport.

We were soon greeted by Jack Hume's son, Richard, who assisted us in getting our gear together for the short ride to Squaw Lake, where Jack Hume maintains his base of operations. Wendell Hume and his delightful wife, Martine, were at the office and assisted us in obtaining licenses and information. From Wendell, we learned that the weather had been very warm and, as a result, the caribou herds were not moving well. Hunters that were now in camp had experienced a difficult hunt for big bulls. We all hoped that the weather would turn colder.

In the afternoon, our party of hunters was driven back to the airport at Schefferville. Before long, we were airborne on a twin-engine Otter going due north to the Main Camp on the Caniapiscau River. The thing that strikes you most when flying over this country is that there is water everywhere. Rivers, streams, and lakes lie like jewels reflecting the sunlight as they wind and flow along the rocky, tree-studded landscape.

Captain Pat Patterson touched down on a large, sandy beach on the Caniapiscau, right near the Main Camp. All hands pitched in and the Otter was soon free of our gear. We were informed by the guides who met us that two bull caribou had crossed the beach about a mile from the airstrip, and not five minutes ago to boot. Of course, binoculars seemed to materialize instantly as everyone thoroughly scanned the area in hopes of catching a glimpse of the beautiful, white-maned bulls.

Camp was a short walk from the river and proved to be very comfortable. The kitchen and dining area is the only structure that stays up year-round. The guest and guide quarters are break-down metal frames over which sturdy nylon tarps are fastened. Inside are bunk frame beds with foam mattresses, and oil stoves and lanterns.

There was another group of hunters still in camp, with two more days of hunting. After that, our group of eight hunters was it for this camp for the season. We felt that the two bulls sighted on the beach upon our arrival was a good omen. The other hunters leaving in two days said that the weather had been unseasonably warm and the hunting difficult. But already the temperature seemed crisp and there were dark clouds moving in.

After stowing our gear in our quarters, we met our guide for the next six days of hunting, Gordon Belvin. Gordon and three of his brothers, who were also guiding in this camp, along with the rest of the camp personnel, were all from the village of St. Augustin on Quebec's north shore. "Get your rain gear and guns and let's see if we can see a few caribou before dinner at six o'clock," Gordon said to Tony and me. Moments later, we were in an 18 foot canoe, wearing life jackets, and cruising the Caniapiscau in search of caribou. Motorized canoes are utilized to travel up and down the river to select locations where the river and both banks can be watched for caribou. When animals are spotted crossing the river, the canoe can be used to narrow the often long distance between you and the caribou, and once beached, a stalk is planned.

We traveled south on the Caniapiscau but saw no caribou. Upon our return to camp, however, I spotted a black bear feeding on the rocky hillside of the east shore. Even at 400 or more yards, we could see with the naked eye a white blaze on the bear's chest as he stood up, investigating the sound from the river that had disturbed his evening foraging. Neither Tony nor I had a bear license. But soon, we saw another canoe approaching, occupied by Dr. Phil Warner, Rich Uhlman, and their guide. We excitedly waved them over, because we knew that Phil had a bear tag. Both canoes were beached downwind and Phil and his guide set off after the bear. After a 45 minute stalk, the bear was wise to the situation and had vanished into the cover of the lichen-covered boulders, scrub growth, and pine trees. This was the first of three individual black bears that Tony and I would see over the next six days. A total of five bears altogether was seen by our hunting party; however, due to distance or no bear license, none were taken.

We arrived in camp hungry and excited, to tell the tale of the bear sighting. We were greeted by the wonderful aroma of dinner wafting out of the cook tent. We had been warned by the other party of hunters that unless we were careful, we'd surely gain 15 pounds from the delicious meals. Three meals a day, each one a feast, were prepared by Donna, the camp cook. Eggs, toast, pancakes and syrup, homemade bread, juices, and hot tea got everyone fortified for a day in the field. Lunches were carried into the field in waterproof containers and thermos, or if you were in camp at noon, hot and hearty soups, thick sandwiches, and desserts were always ready. And after a full day of hunting in sun, sleet, snow and rain (it depended on what time it was, as the weather seemed to change several times a day), dinner was truly welcome. Turkeys, hams, roasts, chicken, potatoes, vegetables, hot bread, butter and jellies, and desserts were standard fare.

The first full day of hunting found Tony, Gordon, and me several miles north of camp on the west bank, glassing for caribou. We were on a bank about 12 feet high, above the Caniapiscau. Our canoe was beached on the sand below us. The weather was crisp and slightly overcast. The first game that was spotted was by Tony. It was a huge, almost-white wolf on the opposite bank of the river. He was standing on a large rock, surveying his domain and no doubt eager to see some caribou also. By the time Tony got his camera out of its case, the wolf was slipping away through the rocks and trees. It was a rare treat to see one of these elusive predators. Over the next six days, we would find no shortage of wolf, bear, and caribou tracks throughout the area.

Excitement came late in the afternoon. We had just finished a snack and some hot tea when Gordon stared and pointed behind us, away from the river. I followed his gaze and saw a large herd of caribou that had wandered into our area. Some bulls were as close as 30 yards and they all looked like trophy class bulls to me. Tony had won the coin toss for the first shot and he chambered a round in his rifle. Gordon said to wait, as the herd spooked and ran up and over the mountain. After the herd had gone from our sight, the three of us set off at a quick, hunched-over trot to stalk the herd. As we crested the mountain, we could see the opposite mountainside dotted with caribou, most of them big, white-maned bulls.

We took advantage of boulders and trees to conceal our stalk. We finally got up with the herd, about a mile-and-a-half from the river. We were in a low, boggy area and we climbed up the side of a huge granite boulder to where we were able to watch the herd. Directly in front of us in the pines, and up on the mountainside, were dozens of caribou. We were resting our upper bodies on the top of the boulder while our legs hung over the back, our boots dug into any crevice possible. It would have been a 12 foot drop from the boulder into wet muskeg if we slipped. There were small pine trees growing on top of the boulder and these provided some concealment. The caribou that were in the pines in front of us were constantly moving and feeding, making it difficult to judge the racks. At the top of the mountain, some bulls had settled down for a rest and others had fed into relatively open areas.

Gordon asked Tony if he was ready to shoot. Tony had decided on a good bull that was feeding near the crest of the mountain, about 300 yards away. Tony had a good rest and he squeezed off a shot at the bull. The bull was anchored in his tracks, but still standing. Tony immediately put another shot into the bull and he staggered forward a few feet. Tony quickly put a third and final bullet into the bull and he collapsed immediately. The rest of the herd was off and running. The bull that Tony had shot was down for keeps. Tony, still allowed one more caribou, reloaded his rifle.

We stood up on top of the boulder and began to negotiate a route down into the muskeg and forest to Tony's bull. Caribou were still running past us. Behind me, I heard Tony say, "Look at the shovel on that bull!" Tony was aiming at a nice bull that was running broadside, about 40 yards from him. At Tony's shot, the bull lurched forward but kept running. The bull was now quartering away at a 45 degree angle and Tony put another shot into him, just behind the last rib and up into the chest cavity. The bull stopped in a small clump of pine trees and lay down facing Tony's direction. An offhand shot at 80 yards into the bull's shoulder finished him quickly.

While Gordon and I made our way to the first bull Tony had shot, Tony made for the second bull, which was closer. Both were fine bulls, the first one being a double shovel with a beautiful rack. All of Tony's shots were winners, each one in a vital area. After admiring the two fine bulls, it was time for some pictures. Tony then realized that in the initial excitement of the herd coming upon us, the camera was back at our vantage point near the canoe, a mile-and-a-half away. It was getting late, so Tony set off at a good trot. Before too long, Tony had returned with the camera, breathing heavily and soaked with sweat. The country is not as flat as it appears from the air.

Caribou truly are beautiful animals. The thick white mane of the older bulls is especially attractive. We estimated that these bulls would have gone around 400 pounds on the hoof. The two bulls were caped and the meat of each animal laid on beds of pine boughs. This kept the meat clean and allowed for ample air circulation. As it was getting late, we would return the next day to pack-out all of the meat. In fact, the last part of our hike out with the two trophies was made in darkness. We arrived at the canoe tired but still exhilarated from the fine stalk, good shooting, and the grand adventure the day had brought. Dinner was eaten amidst the chatter of each hunter's tale of the day's events, the talk lasting into the night.

The next morning found us busily quartering Tony's two bulls and wrapping them in cheesecloth. Six trips, to and from the canoe, each of us carrying a back pack full of caribou meat, completed the job. While we were high up on the ridge where Tony had shot his first bull, we spotted a lone bull caribou crossing the Caniapiscau. He was about three-fourths of the way across when a large black bear appeared on the beach that the caribou was swimming toward. The bear watched the bull intently until the bull, apparently deciding that the side of the river from which he came was a nice place to be, made an about face and swam to the other bank. When we arrived in camp, the meat was promptly hung in the meat locker on the beach. Lunch was eaten in camp and some time was spent resting and taking care of the trophies.

Afternoon found us canoeing south on the Caniapiscau, with me riding the bow and all of us keeping a sharp lookout for caribou while enjoying the beautiful scenery. Since Tony had filled both of his caribou tags yesterday, he would be attempting to photograph my hunt, if we were fortunate enough to cross paths with some bulls.

About an hour out of camp, we came across a herd of about 20 caribou, crossing the river from west to east. The herd consisted mostly of bulls, with a few cows and calves. Tony was able to get some pictures and we left them to finish their crossing. Almost immediately, Gordon saw caribou moving in the forest on the west bank, about 1,000 yards away. Tony and I fixed our eyes on the mountainside too, which appeared alive with caribou. Hundreds were winding their way through the trees, rocks and boulders, following age-old trails worn deep into the land by generations of caribou from years gone by. We quickly made for the east side of the river, beaching at a sandbar close to the river bank, but separated by a channel of water about 150 yards wide. The three of us did a quick, bent-over walk onto the sandbar, trying to stay inconspicuous. We lay down prone in the sand, taking advantage of contours in the land and rocks for concealment. My heart was pounding in my chest and I was certain that Tony and Gordon could hear it, as I watched one of nature's wonders unfold on the opposite shore.

The caribou made their way out of the forest and onto the broad beach, pausing for only a moment before entering the cold water of the river and swimming for the opposite bank. Hoarse whispers passed between the three of us as we exclaimed about some of the racks that the bulls were sporting. Some of the herd finally made their way across, and some passed south of us and to the north. Several even made their way onto the sandbar. At first, all of the bulls appeared to be trophy class. But after scrutinizing so many, I became aware of what to look for in a really good rack, and I followed Gordon's advice to wait a bit, that there were many bulls to glass yet in this herd.

There was a slight pause in the action when no more caribou were gathering on the far shore to cross. But shortly, we could see many more caribou cresting the mountain and making their way to the river. When this herd began to cross, they veered slightly north of our sandbar. We did a shuffling, hands-and-knees, low-crawl to the far tip of our sandbar, finishing the last few yards on our bellies. We were now as far as we could go without exposing ourselves to the caribou.

Gordon said, "I think there is a good bull in this bunch," referring to a group of caribou that was fast approaching the shore. We all focused our attention and, by comparing movements and position of the animals, we all had our eyes on the bull Gordon had spotted. Tony agreed with Gordon that this bull was by far the best we had yet seen and he certainly appeared to be so to me. The big, white bull cleared the river and shook himself off in a fine mist that seemed to hang about him momentarily like a shroud. He began to move slightly ahead of the other animals, but his position remained closest to us in relation to the other caribou. In my scope, I saw the big bull look directly toward us. That is when I saw the magnificent double shovel and decided to take this bull.

Using Tony's camera bag and knit cap as a rest, I settled the cross hairs just behind the bull's right shoulder and slowly squeezed the trigger of my .30-06. The rifle boomed and I automatically chambered another round. My first shot anchored the bull in his tracks; he stood there with his head hanging low and hindquarters sagging, while the other animals trotted off toward the brush. Tony said, "Hit him again!" I put another shot just in front of the right shoulder/neck area and the big bull crashed to the ground. We watched the bull for a few moments, but he was down for keeps. We were ecstatic, the patient waiting and discipline culminating in the taking of a truly outstanding animal. But Gordon remarked that there could very well be another good bull in the still crossing herd and it would be a good idea to sit tight and watch.

Not five minutes had passed when Tony, photographing and glassing the animals with his telephoto lens, said that he had spotted a rather large-racked bull still in the water. I found the large, dark-racked bull in my scope. He was huge, his rack standing out from bulls that any sportsman would have been proud to hang on the wall. Gordon agreed too that the bull was a keeper. When the bull cleared the river and was apart from his comrades, I put a 180 grain bullet just behind his shoulder and into the lungs. A stream of blood appeared and the bull staggered a few steps and then collapsed with a splash in the river. Gordon pounded my shoulder, exclaiming, "You got him right in the boiler room!" I felt numb. There were two magnificent bulls down within yards of each other. Just how good the bulls were, I would find out shortly.

The remainder of the herd was still crossing as we made for the canoe. The second bull was dead in the water. I got out of the canoe at that point and made for the first bull that was lying a short distance away on the beach. Tony grabbed hold of the bull's rack in the water and he and Gordon pulled the animal up to the beach where I now stood with the big, white double-shovel. With much huffing and puffing, we finally managed to drag the one bull out of the river and onto the beach next to the first bull. I couldn't believe the size of these two animal's racks. Gordon's smile was ear-to-ear. He said that these were the biggest bulls that he had seen taken out of the Main Camp. Tony said that he felt both bulls would make Boone and Crockett, and I was certain that the big double-shovel bull would. Caping and quartering of the bulls was done with much excited chatter, as we were already replaying the excitement of the hunt.

Pictures were taken and soon our canoe, laden heavily with trophy caribou and happy hunters, was headed for camp. There was a certain sadness in leaving this spot, and I'm sure Tony felt it too. There were the mixed emotions that one feels after taking a game animal, but there was more. I felt that what had taken place on that sandbar and beach was truly a once-in-a-lifetime experience, and as we pulled away from the shore, I couldn't help but feel that a small part of each of us would remain forever in that spot.

The remainder of our hunt was spent hiking and enjoying the beautiful north country, along with delicious meals in the company of good friends and enjoying the tales of other hunter's success. By the end of the hunt, all eight hunters in camp had bagged two fine bull caribou each. Tony was able to photograph a black bear at close range when the bear appeared suddenly while on a hike up the river

Hunters in camp were permitted to take a good portion of the meat home. It was hung in camp and then boxed in wax-lined containers for the trip home. We all enjoyed an evening in Schefferville, having dinner and drinks afterward at the hotel there. The Main Camp staff joined us for some cold beers at the bar, and we all prepared for our trips home, guides and hunters alike.

Just how good the two caribou bulls I had taken was revealed a few months later. On December 20, 1987, well after the required 60 day drying period, my two caribou trophies were officially scored for entry at 414-6/8 and 403-3/8 respectively. This was thrilling news for Tony and I. Neither of us could recall ever reading or hearing about one hunter taking two records book animals on the same day, within minutes of each other. All four of our caribou were put in the capable hands of our taxidermist, Albert Stone, of Frederick, MD.

For us, the hunt will live on in memory and with the beautiful photographs Tony took and in a video that Al Rood (a hunter from Pennsylvania) took while hunting and in camp. In addition, there were many fine roasts, steaks and chops to enjoy for months to come.

Photograph by Wm. H. Nesbitt

PRONGHORN
FIRST AWARD
SCORE: 90-6/8
Locality: Catron Co., N.M.   Date: September 1986
Hunter: John P. Grimmett

PRONGHORN 90-6/8

John P. Grimmett

The year of 1986 was a big one for us. My brother Tony and I were determined to hunt pronghorn. Tony had already taken three nice pronghorn in Arizona, but I had applied unsuccessfully for 20 years. I had taken a couple of small bucks on the Hualapai Indian Reservation in northern Arizona several years ago, but I just couldn't get drawn in the general Arizona hunt.

Needless to say, I was feeling frustrated and depressed. We got our usual rejections for the Arizona hunt in early August, but Tony, who had received a tip on a "hot spot" from a New Mexico game officer, had covered his bet by applying in New Mexico. But he had no luck in the New Mexico draw either. Undaunted, my brother got on the telephone and located two ranchers in Catron County, New Mexico (near Quemado), with permits for sale. We mortgaged the family jewels and bought them. Finally, I had a pronghorn tag!

Since I am a teacher, and Tony owns and operates Elkhorn Taxidermy, August is the perfect time for us to scout. Determined to find some long, heavy-horned pronghorn, we made several trips from our homes in Phoenix to the beautiful, high plateau country of western New Mexico. It is quite different from the pronghorn country we know in Arizona; wide, vast, open country. Our New Mexico unit was juniper country, with rolling hills and high, open mesas. It is definitely God's country.

Our scouting trips excited us so much that we thought September 27th would never come. While driving into the ranches on our first trip, we saw several very nice bucks. We could hardly wait to see what each ranch had. When we got to my ranch, we took a little, bone-jarring road to the east. We immediately spotted a couple of 15-inch bucks, but we were looking for something bigger. And then we saw him, a 16-inch buck with very heavy horns! But he was hard to judge; his horns seemed to be only 1-1/2 times the length of his ears, and he would never stand still long enough for us to get a good look with the spotting scopes before he high-tailed it into the junipers. We saw him twice more on subsequent trips but we could never agree as to just how big he was. But I decided I wanted him, so we spooked him into the surrounding trees figuring out his escape routes and "scared tactics."

In the meantime, we were busy scouting my brother's ranch. We also scouted the surrounding ranches, because in New Mexico's two-day hunt, you are allowed to hunt the adjacent ranches on the second day. We wanted to cover all our bases. Tony's rancher had told him about a pronghorn on his ranch with horns three time the length of his ears. This buck we had to see! But either the rancher was mistaken, or the big buck was a ghost, because we never found him. But, we did find many exceptional bucks, including four or five records class bucks. We even had names for the larger ones, so that when we discussed the animals around camp at night, we knew which was which. Tony even went so far as to sketch them out in a notebook he carried! We were obviously very serious about taking Boone and Crockett bucks. We spent many long hours glassing pronghorn and many more long hours at the rifle range to make sure we were ready when the season opened.

Finally it was time; once more we took the long drive. We arrived a day early so that we could find our pronghorns and "bed" them down for the next morning. But while looking for our number one choices, we glassed a big buck we hadn't seen before. After driving a couple of miles around a giant mesa, we stalked into the wind and were able to get within 150 yards of the big boy and his harem. Through the spotting scope we estimated his horns at 17-18 inches, with 5-inch prongs, a definite records book buck. When he turned, however, we noticed that his left prong was broken. But he still seemed to be the largest buck we had seen. After a long discussion at the truck, Tony decided that this was the buck he wanted, in spite of the broken prong.

We then drove to my ranch to find the heavy-horned 16-incher I had decided on. But we could not find him anywhere! Needless to say, I was very nervous about locating him on a two-day hunt. Sleep was hard to come by that night.

The next morning, I decided to help Tony with old "Broken Prong" since we knew where he was. We drove from camp before daylight to the big mesa where we had left him. But after a long hike into the wind and over a couple of hills, we could not find the buck where he was supposed to be. After a frantic search with the spotting scopes, we found him about a mile-and-a-half away, in the valley below the mesa. Although I thought there was no way to approach him, Tony decided to give it a try. I went back to drive the truck around. When I got to our meeting place, I found a very upset brother. Tony had got close enough for a shot, but he had missed because of a heavy crosswind. Good-bye, "Broken Prong!"

We then decided to try to find my buck. We took our nasty little road east, left the truck, and climbed to a better vantage point. We still could not find old Heavy Horns in the junipers. We gave up and went back to the truck; but, as we started to drive away, Tony looked over his shoulder and spotted a herd of pronghorn a half-mile away, dropping out of sight behind a ridge. "I'll bet that's him," Tony yelled, as he jammed the truck into gear so that we could get to a high spot. We bailed out and started scanning the area for movement.

The pronghorn had dropped into a rolling basin that was thickly covered with junipers. We finally spotted the pronghorn running through the brushy trees, about 500 yards away. I took off on a dead run at an angle to them in order to cut the distance, hoping they might stop long enough for a shot. I raced down a hill and into a ravine for cover. I stopped to catch my breath and looked up. The big buck and three of his does had stopped to look around! I knew I had to shoot quickly, in spite of the fact that my long sprint had left me gasping for breath. I quickly estimated the range at 300 yards, knowing my Lawson-built .270 would do the job if I could hold it still. I knelt down, took a quick deep breath, centered the cross hairs on his heavy chest, and squeezed the trigger. Down he went!

Now my knees no longer seemed to want to work. But I had to get to him and see just how big he was. I raced up the hill. Tony, who watched the whole thing through his binoculars, reached the buck before I did. "It's a monster!" he shouted. My heart was racing as I reached this magnificent animal. A moment of quiet admiration was quickly followed by whooping, hollering, back-slapping, and handshaking. Tony whipped out his trusty measuring tape. I waited with quiet anticipation. Tony's long, low whistle told me it was going to be good. He announced, "93 points and 18 inches in length, John." We didn't have long to celebrate, however. I had hit the buck in the neck, so we had to cape him quickly so we could clean off the blood. It was only 10:30 in the morning, and my hunt was finished, but the memories are forever.

Now it was back to Tony's ranch for his buck. An hour later, we had found one of our big bucks in thick junipers. We crept through the woods, and Tony dropped him with a 70 yard shot with his Browning 7 mm Mag (an 1885 single-shot, "long-tom"). A quick tape job confirmed another Boone and Crockett buck, 84 points green. What a thrill and the hunt-of-a-lifetime. Two brothers taking records book animals on one glorious New Mexico morning.

After the required 60 day drying period, Tony's was well above the 82 point minimum at 83-6/8. My buck was scored for entry at 92 points. Earlier this year, I received another honor, that of being named the recipient of the NRA's 1988 Leatherstocking Award for modern long gun.

After everything that has happened, all those long scouting trips and the weekends at the rifle range certainly paid-off. We'll be back!

Photograph by Wm. H. Nesbitt

PRONGHORN
SECOND AWARD
SCORE: 89-6/8
Locality: Coconino Co., Ariz.   Date: September 1987
Hunter: James W. Barrett

PRONGHORN 89-6/8

James W. Barrett

Pronghorn hunts in Arizona are on a drawing basis. I put in for the hunt with my stepbrother, Aaron Haught. We put in for Unit 5B as first choice, and Unit 5A as second choice. I had hunted Unit 5B in 1981 and I killed a respectable buck that scored 82-6/8. It was entered in the state records book, but not Boone and Crockett. As luck would have it, we were drawn in Unit 5A as second choice, permit numbers 21 and 22, out of a 25 permit unit. I knew the unit fairly well since I was stationed in Winslow for three years with the Arizona Game and Fish Department (from 1961 to 1963) as a Wildlife Manager, but I have since retired after almost 27 years.

I called Ken Clay, who is the current Wildlife Manager for the unit, and told him we had gotten drawn. He told us where he had seen some decent bucks. Also, he informed me that part of the unit was behind locked gates of the Clear Creek Land and Cattle Company. There was no problem hunting their land if you contacted the ranch and filled out a form that asked for your name, address, dates you would be hunting, and vehicle descriptions. In return, they gave permission to hunt their land and the combination to the lock. I called a good friend of mine in Winslow, Nick Paul, and told him I would be hunting Unit 5A. He said he would get me permission from Clear Creek Cattle Company and would hunt with Aaron and me if he got the chance.

Two weeks before the hunt, Aaron, my 7-year-old boy Cody, and I left Payson about 3 a.m. to do some scouting in Unit 5A. We first looked at some areas that were on the Coconino National Forest, then later at the Clear Creek Cattle Company in an area known as Dick Hart Pasture. Here we found a herd of approximately 25 pronghorn, with a couple of respectable bucks in it. We decided to camp at Boundary Well since it had corrals and water for our horses. The cattle were to be gathered and shipped from this pasture in just a week.

The pronghorn hunt in Unit 5A was from September 18 to September 21, 1987. The dividing line between 5A and 5B is the Meteor Crater, Chavez Pass to Highway 87 south to Coconino-Tonto National Forest Boundary. The unit is characterized by two long, flat mesas that rise above the flats and are known as East and West Sunset. We were going to hunt the country between Boundary Well and East Sunset.

Two days before the hunt, I loaded my 30 foot, fifth-wheel trailer with all the necessary supplies and equipment for the hunt and traveled to Boundary Well. Aaron was to bring my horse, Keno, and his horse that afternoon. I parked approximately a quarter-mile from the corrals and right on the edge of a prairie dog town. That afternoon, Aaron came with the horses and they were put in the corrals. The next day, Aaron and I got up before daylight and proceeded to scout Dick Hart Pasture. We found one herd of approximately 12 pronghorn, with one decent buck of about 15 inches. We checked-out some other areas but saw no pronghorn. That afternoon, Nick Paul and his wife, Claudine, came to camp with the papers to hunt on Clear Creek Cattle Company and the combination to the locked gates. He also would be there before daylight with his horse. Leonard Cooper, Wildlife Manager from Roosevelt Lake who was assigned to work the hunt in 5A and 4A, camped with us the next two nights.

Before daylight on opening day, Nick Paul pulled-in and loaded our horses into his four-horse trailer. We traveled around a couple of miles and then rode to a high point where we could see a fair portion of Dick Hart Pasture. We spotted the same herd we had seen the previous day. They were over two miles away, so we figured out a plan of attack. We got tied up on a fence line and had to ride almost back to camp to get through the fence at a gate. Needless to say, by the time we got back into the area where we had seen the pronghorn, they were gone. When we did finally find them, they spotted us and took off. We did not find them again the rest of the day. Scratch Day One.

Day Two, same plan as Day One except we located a gate we could get through so we would be on the same side of the fence as the pronghorn, if they were roughly in the same area. Leonard Cooper drove to the base of the high point and walked up to it. We did likewise, tying our horses and walking to the high point. We spotted about 50 or more elk toward the base of East Sunset that another hunter had spooked. We again spotted the herd of pronghorn we had seen the day before, only closer. We made our stalk, tied the horses, and after the pronghorn saw us, they took off but did not go far. Aaron was able to get behind piles of pushed cedar trees and make his way toward them, while Nick and I stayed back. He finally shot, then shot again. The result: one 15-inch pronghorn buck.

We gutted the buck, then rode back to camp to get my pick-up truck to drive to the kill. We returned to camp, hung the buck up in a tree, and while Aaron skinned it, I took Nick back to his truck and we all returned to camp. Nick and I then trailered down to the highway approximately five miles and rode back to camp. We did find two small bucks and made stalks on them, but we finally lost them.

That evening, Nick and I went toward Winslow and took a road that is on the north and east side of East Sunset. Nick showed where the road was to go up on East Sunset, but it was behind a locked key gate. I debated riding up there on horseback and hunting the top of this mesa. On the way back to the highway, at almost dark, we spotted a herd of about 25 pronghorn with several bucks in it. Two of the bucks were nice trophies. We started stalking these pronghorn and were within about 600 yards when we heard gunshots being aimed at this same herd. Numerous shots were fired and we watched these pronghorn run off as it was almost dark. Plan for Day Three was as follows: I would trailer my horse out and try to find this herd of pronghorn again. Aaron was to take his pronghorn back to Payson and put it in a cooler, since the weather was clear and warm. Nick Paul was unable to hunt with me the next day.

Day Three. I loaded my horse into my horse-trailer before daylight, Aaron loaded his pronghorn into his truck and headed for Payson. I trailered my horse down the highway, went through a locked gate and then down the two-track road for approximately a half-mile. I saddled-up and rode up on the side of East Sunset, then glassed back toward the rising sun. After about an hour, seeing nothing, I decided to make a big circle in this pasture that, at the least, covers a township. After about two hours, I spotted a small herd of pronghorn. I made a stalk of them and got within 250 yards, overlooking them. There were five does, two fawns, no buck. I watched them graze, then I went back to my horse and hunted the pasture for a couple of hours before returning to my truck and back to camp. That evening, I took my truck and went back toward East Sunset where I did spot a small buck (13 inch horns) and, after a short stalk, I missed two running shots at him at about 350 yards. That night, I decided that I would take my horse trailer and hunt the last day on top of East Sunset.

Day Four, last day of hunt. I got up at 4 a.m. and drank some coffee, then loaded my horse, and trailered back to the two-track road I was on the previous day. It was still almost completely dark when I turned onto the road. I decided that I would pull-off a little way up this road and wait until it got light enough to see, as there was some good pronghorn country before I got to the gate for the ride on top of East Sunset. I stopped after approximately three-quarters of a mile to wait for sunlight. I started glassing. When I glassed back toward where the sun would come up, I could see something moving about at 600-700 yards, so I got out my spotting scope. With it, I could barely make out three pronghorn, one a buck with horns longer than the ears. I figured-out a stalk and slipped my .25-06 out of the scabbard. I exited from the other door, went around the horse trailer and down the backside of a small ridge. I then crawled over the top of the ridge and located the three pronghorn. They had grazed out in the flat from where I originally had seen them. I could barely see their heads and backs over the sagebrush. They were approximately 400 to 500 yards from me. I finally could see enough of the buck to get a shot; just as I was about ready to pull the trigger, the sun popped up and I was looking into the sun with my scope cranked to nine power. Needless to say, I could not see as my right eyeball was sucked back into my head.

After a while, I got my sight back but I was still looking into the rising sun and the three pronghorn had grazed out farther from me. Then one of the does decided to trot-off and the other doe and buck followed. As all three disappeared over the rise, I decided to follow them afoot. I was two-thirds of the way across the flat when I looked up and saw all three of them sky-lined and looking at me. I glassed them and I could tell this buck had a very nice set of heart-shaped horns. Needless to say, they took off running, out-of-sight. I walked back to my truck and debated whether to go hunt the top of East Sunset as originally planned or hunt this buck. I decided to hunt this one, so I unloaded my horse, saddled her, clipped on my scabbard and gun, and set off.

I went in the direction they were running and toward a high point where I could see a lot of country. Just as I got to the high point, I could see all three pronghorns running back toward the east, going full-bore. I got off my horse and watched them to where they finally slowed down and all but stopped. I watched the buck chase one doe around and around. They finally stopped and went back to grazing. They were about a mile-and-a-half away, so

I made another plan of attack. I rode about halfway there, and then I walked and crawled to where I had last seen them, but no pronghorn. I glassed and glassed, but to no avail.

I went back to my horse and made a big circle by a water tank and back to my truck. I unsaddled my horse and pondered what to do next. I was to meet Aaron back at camp around noon to haul the horses back. Since it was already past 10 a.m., I decided to go back but by a different way and come out to the highway on the road to Clear Creek Cattle Company headquarters. I loaded my horse into the horse trailer and proceeded south until I came to a stock tank and the road that turned back to the ranch headquarters. This two-track road runs along a fence line and goes by a couple of tanks. I stopped periodically to glass. I went by one tank that I had been by earlier that day. I was within a half-mile of the second tank when the three pronghorn that I had hunted stood up near the fence. One doe took off to my left; the other doe and the buck ran down the fence, turned and came toward me. I lost sight of them due to the terrain.

I drove down the road so I could see which way they would run. If the buck crossed under the fence, I would get at least one shot. I stopped at the top of the rise and could see the remaining doe running across the flat to my right, but no buck following her. The buck had crawled under the fence and hung his horn on the lower strand of wire. I had just enough time to slip my .25-06 out of the scabbard, step-out and kneel, and fire as the buck got free and turned to run. The buck jumped forward and back into the fence, but up higher. I went to the buck to make sure he was dead. The bullet struck the buck in the left shoulder and exited in the front of the right leg. I went back and got my truck. A ranch hand, Dennis Echos, came by and helped me load the buck into the truck. I took a quick measurement of his horns and got a little over 18 inches. I trailered back to camp where Aaron was waiting. We hung the buck in a tree and skinned it, leaving all the skin attached to the head. We then loaded-up and returned home to Payson.

Photographs Courtesy of James K. McCasland and Robert Cunningham

(l) James K. McCasland killed this pronghorn in 1987 while hunting in Yavapai County, Arizona. It scores 84 points. (r) Robert Cunningham hunted in Carter County, Montana, in 1986 to take this pronghorn that scores 84-2/8 points.

Photograph Courtesy of Patricia M. Dreeszen

Fergus County, Montana, yielded this pronghorn to Patricia M. Dreeszen in 1988. It scores 80-2/8 points to qualify for the 20th Awards book.

Photograph by Wm. H. Nesbitt

PRONGHORN
THIRD AWARD (TIE)
SCORE: 88-6/8

Locality: White Pine Co., Nev.   Date: August 1987
Hunter: William W. Diekmann

PRONGHORN 88-6/8

William W. Diekmann

My family and I operate an old-time general store in a small town in California. I'm 42 and have been around guns and hunting since I was five. At 12, I took the NRA Hunter Safety Course. It was one of the highlights of my life.

Deer and ducks were my primary game for years. I soon learned of Jack O'Connor and "the book." When I was 14, I got a Winchester Model 70 in .270 caliber. I still shoot the same gun. It now has a stainless steel barrel and a Precision stock (my friends call it "Old Betsy"). When California had its first drawing for pronghorn permits, I applied. It took 20 years to draw a tag.

My California pronghorn hunt was a disaster. The first and only time in my life that I did not shoot some targets before the hunt, Old Betsy let me down.

When I decided to apply for a Nevada pronghorn permit, the drawing had already been held. There were, however, two non-resident tags left in one of the lower hunter-pressure areas. My wife and I were ready for a vacation, so I got one of the tags. We drove our truck to the high desert country in Nevada. The terrain was quite desolate, with temperatures in the 90's.

During the first two days, we saw several small bucks and one fair buck that I tried to sneak on. The wind changed and we never saw him again. The next day, I stopped to ask some surveyors about going deeper into the valley. When they said, "There's nothing there but snakes and scorpions," my wife Melinda looked a little pale. It sounded good to me because I've always liked hunting where other people aren't.

The next day I talked Melinda into braving the snakes and scorpions and we headed deeper into the valley. The following morning we decided to take the small motorcycles that we had brought to conserve gas. After four or five miles, we spotted a small bunch of pronghorn with a really nice buck. As we approached, they ran into the hills. We watched them through the spotting scope for several hours. At one point Melinda asked, "How long are we going to watch them?" I think my reply was, "As long as it takes." Finally, it seemed that they had all bedded down in the shade of some small trees.

I circled way-up above where "Big Sam" and his does had bedded down. When I got there, the does were there but Big Sam was not. As I walked back to the truck, Big Sam was standing on the skyline, looking down at me as if to say "nice try." I watched him for several minutes before he headed up the hill to his does.

The next morning we drove the truck up into the hills. After glassing for some time, we spotted Big Sam below us, about a mile away and heading toward us. I grabbed my gun and started up the canyon. I thought he would be there. After waiting for what seemed to be forever, there was still no buck. All of a sudden, I saw Melinda way down the canyon. I immediately thought that she wouldn't be out there if something wasn't wrong. Either the buck didn't come back up the mountain, or he came up a different canyon. I lit-out for the adjoining canyon, stopping only to catch my breath and be relaxed before I went over the top of the ridge.

As I crested the ridge, I spotted two pronghorns, but no Big Sam. I went a little farther down the canyon and there he was. None of the pronghorns had seen me and the wind was right. Not too far to shoot, but I'd like to be closer. The sagebrush here is about ankle high, not much in the way of cover for a sneak. As I decided what to do, I noticed a large, flat-topped rock down the canyon. It was the only rock on the entire hillside, and it was between Big Sam and me. I crawled up to the rock and peeked over the top. There he was, about 85 yards away! As I put the cross hairs on him and started to squeeze, a doe stepped in front of him and just stared in my direction. Finally, she moved away and I finished my squeeze. Big Sam is mine!

We knew we had a nice buck, but we didn't know how nice until we got back to town. Several people thought it would make "the book." After the 60 day drying period, "Big Sam" was entry scored at 91 points. I find it very comforting to know that it is still possible to hunt some place on your own and bring home a records book trophy.

Photographs Courtesy of Thomas F. Williams and Neil G. Sutherland II

(l) Thomas F. Williams holds up the head of pronghorn he took in Johnson County, Wyoming, in 1986. It scores 82 points. (r) This pronghorn was taken by Neil G. Sutherland II in Cochise County, Arizona, in 1986. It scored 83-2/8 points, in spite of a broken prong.

Photograph Courtesy of Ronnie L. Hinze

Ronnie L. Hinze was hunting in Hudspeth County, Texas, in 1988 when he killed this pronghorn that scores 85 points.

Photograph by Wm. H. Nesbitt

PRONGHORN
THIRD AWARD (TIE)
SCORE: 88-6/8
Locality: Washoe Co., Nev.   Date: August 1986
Hunter: Bruce L. Zeller

PRONGHORN 88-6/8

Bruce L. Zeller

Like so many other Nevada big-game hunting addicts, I annually crave the results of the trophy tag drawing. When I checked the mailbox on that fateful day in 1986, I was elated to see two envelopes, a sure sign I had drawn a tag of some kind. Now the unanswered question was for which species: elk, bighorn sheep, or pronghorn. After ripping open the one without my usual refund check in it, I must admit that I was quite disappointed to see a pronghorn tag. I had my heart firmly set on going on my first sheep hunt.

Other than possibly Arizona, Nevada has some of the best trophy pronghorn hunting to be found anywhere. With this in mind, my disappointment quickly waned and I eagerly began preparing for the hunt. This included re-scoping one of my Ruger rifles, practicing at the Boulder City silhouette range, and discussing field-scoring techniques with friend and part-time outfitter Wilford Allen. Calls were also made to two friends intimately familiar with the area I'd be hunting (1B). These were Nevada Department of Wildlife Biologist Mike Dobel and Gerlach trapper, outfitter, and photographer Tony Diebold. Since my wife would be out of town during the season, arrangements were made to fly-out my mother-in-law. (Only something as important as hunting Nevada's trophy pronghorn warranted an act as irrational as inviting my mother-in-law for an extra visit.)

Having drawn the early season, time passed quickly and before I knew it, I was packing the trailer for the trip north. With copilot Patches (my Brittany spaniel), we arrived the Wednesday before the opener. The following day was spent scouting nearby Hog Ranch Mountain. After lunch, I saw what appeared to be an outstanding buck feeding below some rimrock, a mile or so east of camp. The temperature was nearly 100 degrees and the heat waves made any attempt to zoom-in with my scope futile. Consequently, I donned my pack and headed cross-country for a closer look. Though I searched for most of the afternoon, I was never able to locate him again.

Arriving back at camp hot and tired, I jumped in the 4x4 and headed to Gerlach for some extra supplies. Tony Diebold had returned home from Tahoe that day, and he invited me over for supper with him and his wife, R'deen. After the meal, and a cold brew or two, I asked Tony where else near my present campsite I might look for a respectable head. After expressing his disappointment over my choice of areas to base from, Tony suggested I do some glassing on the west side of Lost Creek Road. Taking Tony's advice, the following morning I climbed to a mesa top overlooking Cottonwood Creek. My vantage point was ideal. I was directly above a waterhole, the sun was at my back, and a large, sage-covered basin to the west was clearly visible.

I located several good bucks in the basin almost immediately. I continued to watch these until mid-morning when I noticed a lone buck coming to water below. Viewed through the scope, the "Loner's" massive horns, with long prongs, were clearly visible. Although the length was difficult to judge from my steep overhead position, this was definitely an exceptional pronghorn. After observing this buck for quite some time, I slipped quietly off the mesa and returned to camp for lunch. The rest of the afternoon was spent scouting north of camp. I saw other bucks, but my mind was already made-up to try for the Loner on opening morning of the hunt.

I reached the mesa top before sunup, slipped off my pack, and set up the scope. As I sat there in the pre-dawn darkness, catching my breath and enjoying a cup of coffee, the anticipation of the hunt began to build. Shortly thereafter, I began seeing pronghorn across the creek with my binoculars. I checked each animal closely with the scope, but none was the large, lone buck I'd seen the previous day. After several hours had passed, I still had not located him and my hopes began to fade. Then, out of the corner of my eye, to my left and on top of the same mesa upon which I was sitting, I caught sight of a lone pronghorn. Swinging the scope in his direction, I soon realized it was the buck I'd been waiting for. I was expecting him to approach the creek from the other side.

After allowing him to feed over the top, I carefully backed off the mesa, leaving all my gear except the rifle behind. Circling in his direction below the rim, I quickly closed the distance between us. When I slipped back over the top, he was looking directly toward me at a distance of approximately 200 yards. Knowing I could get no closer, I eased to the prone position. The ground sloped sharply off in front of me, so I gathered up some rocks within arm's reach to form a rest for the fore-end of my rifle. All the while, the buck continued to stare in my direction.

Although the rock pile was rather unstable, as were my nerves, I managed to center the cross hairs on his brisket. I kept repeating to myself, "Now wait till he turns broadside." Seconds seemed like hours and my patience quickly wore thin. Before I really realized what was happening, I had squeezed the trigger and missed him cleanly. As he took off running downhill, I frantically emptied my rifle without so much as drawing a hair. I was so disgusted with myself, I seriously considered packing the trailer and going home. Then I remembered a saying Wilford Allen so often uses, "The Lord hates a quitter."

Out of ammo, I walked dejectedly back along the mesa top to my gear. Before long, I located the buck in the basin to the west. I spent four more hours trying unsuccessfully to crawl into rifle range before eventually spooking him over the edge to parts unknown.

That evening, I hiked into an area further west of Cottonwood Creek. I saw a number of pronghorn, and one that may have been this same buck; however, I was never close enough to be certain. I saw one other hunter that evening, sitting on the hillside a short distance from his truck. That was the only person I encountered during this entire hunt that ventured into this roadless section of the unit.

Sunday morning at sunrise, I was once again glassing Cottonwood Creek. Although I counted nearly 80 head of pronghorn in the basin to the west, the "Loner" was not among them. Convinced he would still be in the area, I packed my gear and eased along the mesa top. As I neared the south end, I peeked over the eastern edge only to come face to face with him. He bolted out of sight behind the crown of the hill, and try as I might, I could not locate him again.

That afternoon, for a change of scenery, I road-hunted north of camp, around Yellowjacket Canyon and Indian Springs. When I returned to camp at sundown, Patches was nowhere to be found. Backtracking my route, I found her at the nearest camp, five miles to the north. She had apparently followed me, and after becoming dehydrated, went to camp for water. Thankful for not having to spend the night worried and looking for my old buddy, I retired early with plans to return to the mesa above Cottonwood Creek.

On Monday morning, after glassing for an hour or so, I spotted the Loner herding his harem toward a large pool in the creek below. Immediately I gathered up my gear and began carefully working my way downhill. Although the vegetation was sparse, I was able to use the shadow of the mesa to conceal my movements. Upon reaching the edge of the shadow, I was afraid to move for fear he or the others would spot me. If he continued on his present course for water, I figured he would approach to within a little over 300 yards. Shedding my pack, I used it to form a rest on top of the sage in front of me. Then, I waited and watched.

There was a young buck in the group and his presence clearly annoyed the Loner. When the group was approximately 100 yards from the creek, the Loner chased the youngster away. When he returned, much to my disappointment, the big buck began herding the does downstream toward a different spot on the creek. Although the shooting distance made me uncomfortable, I had no choice and I opened fire. On the second shot, I broke a front leg. By the time I'd chambered another round, he was beyond my range. Try as I might, I was unable to anchor him with a better placed shot.

After climbing back up the steep slope that I had descended, I began glassing the basin to the west. Before long, I observed him going up the south side. I waited and watched until he bedded down several yards below the rim. Weighing my options, I decided to circle around behind from the north. This 270 degree route of several miles would be longer, but it would allow me to relocate him on the way in.

As I looped around behind the crest of the basin, a heavy-horned buck emerged in my path. I quickly jacked a round into the chamber and began looking him over with the glasses. He did not appear to be the same pronghorn; but, to make sure, I approached for a closer look. When he finally bolted at a distance of less than 100 yards, it was quite clear that he had four good "wheels." I've met some hunters, and I use that term loosely, who would have busted that pronghorn rather than taking their chances on catching up to a cripple on foot. With that thought in mind, I continued my wide arc to my quarry.

Stopping to catch my breath under the hot, noonday sun, I took aim at a distant rock for some dry-fire practice. To my amazement, the gun went off. After assuring myself that my heart had not stopped, I realized what I had done. I had forgotten to remove the round I had put in during the encounter with the heavy-horned buck. The shattered rock was little consolation for this act of stupidity. A group of pronghorn to the west had not reacted to the shot, so I reasoned the Loner, who was over the rim, had not either.

About 30 minutes later, I slipped over the top at a point directly above where I thought he'd be. My sense of direction was good and he bolted out of his bed from 200 yards below. I dropped him stone-dead with a shot through the neck. At that point in time, the only thing that went through my mind was, "Thank God he's dead and out of his misery."

Other than on Friday before the opener, I'd really not spent a lot of time closely studying the horns of this buck. As I approached, they seemed to grow larger with every step. Upon reaching him, I was in shock. Had I known he was this good, I probably never would have hit him. Out of water and tired, I quickly caped and field dressed him. Shoving the punched tag in my pack, I picked up my rifle and the head and began hiking down to the truck. Upon my arrival, I noticed I had left the pouch with the tag in it open, and everything, knife, watch, tag and toilet paper, had fallen-out.

When I went back for the meat, I retraced my steps looking for the tag. I found only one of the lost articles. You guessed it: the toilet paper. Upon returning to the truck with the meat, I dug my tape measure out of the tool box and took some measurements. The rough B&C score totaled over 92. Having not measured a pronghorn before, I thought maybe I'd made a mistake. At any rate, I sure didn't want to get this trophy confiscated and I breathed a lot easier when I finally got a duplicate tag.

This magnificent pronghorn now adorns the family room wall. My measurements were very close, with the entry B&C score being 91-4/8. Each time I look at the mount, or wear the buckle I was awarded for breaking the state record, the thrills (and blunders) of this hunt come racing back to mind.

Photographs Courtesy of Ben L. Mueller and W. Wayne Spahn

(l) Ben L. Mueller was hunting on the Cansler Ranch north of Fort Sumner, New Mexico, in 1986 when he shot this pronghorn scoring 83-6/8 points. (r) W. Wayne Spahn with the 7-1/2 year old pronghorn he took in Hudspeth County, Texas, in 1988. It scores 84 points.

Photograph Courtesy of Charles A. Grimmett

Charles A. Grimmett was in hunting Mohave County, Arizona, in 1984 when he shot this pronghorn that scores 80-4/8 points.

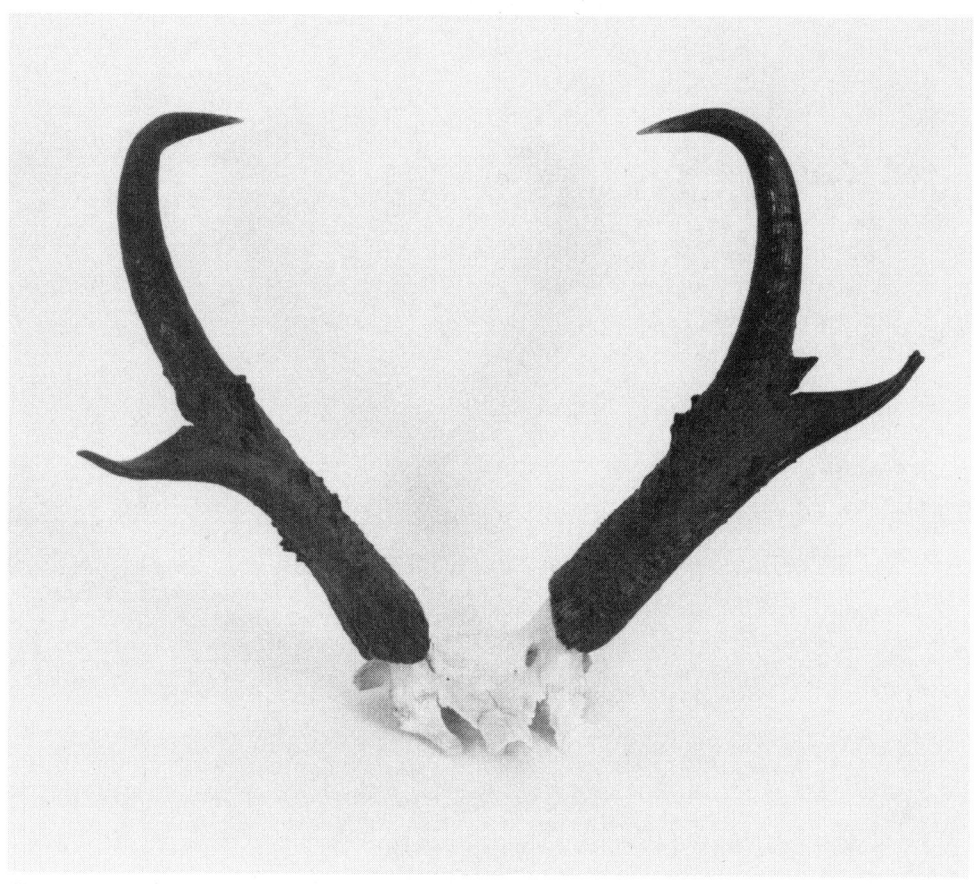

Photograph by Wm. H. Nesbitt

PRONGHORN
HONORABLE MENTION
SCORE: 88
Locality: Chaves Co., N.M.   Date: September 1988
Hunter: Grant L. Perry

PRONGHORN 88

Grant L. Perry

Grant L. Perry is a resident of Higley, Arizona. Arizona is a fine big-game hunting state and it borders another mecca for the sportsman, New Mexico. For the 1988 hunting season, Grant Perry decided to hunt pronghorn in New Mexico. As things turned out, he's mighty glad that he did.

Perry's hunt took place in Chavez County, New Mexico. He arrived at the hunting area on the 23rd of September 1988. After utilizing the remainder of that day to familiarize himself with the hunting area, Perry turned-in for a good night's sleep.

September 24th was a sunny and clear day. Hunters who got out early were rewarded by seeing pronghorn bands. But, Perry didn't see the pronghorn he wanted until later in the same morning.

It was 10 a.m. when Perry finally shot his big buck at a distance of 225 yards. Perry used a Remington Model 700 in .30-06 caliber with a 150 grain, soft-point bullet. One shot was all it took.

Perry knew his pronghorn was big, but little did he realize that it was big enough to qualify for the 20th Awards Final Judging. That was a fine ending to the hunt.

Photograph by Wm. H. Nesbitt

PRONGHORN
CERTIFICATE OF MERIT
SCORE: 86-6/8
Locality: South Dakota   Date: Prior to 1940
Hunter: Unknown   Owner: Daniel E. McBride

PRONGHORN 86-6/8

Daniel E. McBride, owner

Dan McBride owns and operates a large-animal veterinary clinic in Texas. While working in the office one day in 1980, one of McBride's clients stopped by on his way out-of-town. The client owed money to McBride for past services rendered and wanted to settle his debt. He knew McBride was an avid pronghorn hunter and he asked McBride to follow him outside. There, at the top of the gentleman's belongings, in an open rental trailer, was a very old mounted pronghorn. The client climbed onto the trailer to retrieve it. He grabbed the mount by one horn and prepared to pass it down to McBride, but the horn came-off in his hand. McBride could see immediately that the trophy mount was in poor shape.

Once the trophy was on the ground, the client informed McBride that he could not pay his bill and offered the head as payment. McBride reluctantly accepted the head as payment-in-full, feeling that it was better to get something for his efforts than nothing. McBride's client told him that the pronghorn was taken by his grandfather in the 1930's in South Dakota.

McBride took the trophy inside the clinic and placed it on a nail in the operating room next to a trophy bass he had taken several years earlier. McBride always knew that his pronghorn was an excellent trophy, but it wasn't until seven years later that he had it officially measured for the records book.

At its entry score, the pronghorn was large enough to be invited to the 20th Awards Final Judging. However, between the time it was officially measured for entry and the time it was invited, the trophy was damaged in the clinic.

It happened on a day that McBride was working outside the clinic. He heard a tremendous crash and the building shook. His assistant and receptionist rushed outside to tell him that a horse coming out of anesthesia had fallen against the outside wall and had knocked his pronghorn and bass off their nails. McBride hurried inside to find the horse in fine condition, but the pronghorn severely damaged. The 10-foot fall from its nail to the floor had cracked a portion of the skull plate.

McBride knew that if he sent his trophy to the 20th Awards Final Judging it might be rejected by the Judges Panel if the judges determined the skull plate was completely split between the horns. However, he took the chance in the spirit of true sportsmanship and sent it in for the Judges' examination. The Judges Panel had the skull plate X-rayed and determined that the damage to the skull plate was not as significant as it appeared. This trophy now takes its rightful place in the Awards and all-time records books.

Photograph by Wm. H. Nesbitt

BISON
FIRST AWARD
SCORE: 123-2/8
Locality: Chitina River, Alaska   Date: September 1987
Hunter: Gerald H. Phillips

BISON 123-2/8

Gerald H. Phillips

Some things are just meant to be. This whole adventure began when I discussed buying a high-powered rifle with my wife, Lue, who is also known as "secretary of the treasury" in our home. "Are you sure you will be going hunting this year," she asked? I had often talked about hunting large game but had always put it off for one reason or another. Growing up in the city as part of a non-hunting family, I had only vicarious experiences and dreams prompted by outdoor magazines. Shortly, my wife and I agreed that "if" I was drawn for one of the limited registration permit hunts, I could buy an appropriate rifle.

In June 1987, while completing the registration permit forms for winter hunts, an associate recommended that in addition to caribou and moose, I apply for a bison permit as well. I remember his words well, "You'll never get drawn for it but you need to pay your dues if you want to get drawn for it in the future." So, I applied for hunt areas I knew, and some I didn't know. To my amazement, I was selected for a bison permit at Chitina. I couldn't quite pronounce Chitina right. (Pretend that the second "i" isn't there when you say it.)

Now Alaska is a big place, and in four years of living here, with the exception of a fly-in fishing trip and travel on the Alaska Marine Ferry System, my travel was largely limited to where there were roads. There are not that many roads in Alaska, so in essence I hadn't seen very much of this great state. Those of you familiar with Alaska know that the airplane is the way to get around and into the bush.

I was soon to learn that of the various bison herd areas in Alaska, the Chitina was more difficult to access and harder to hunt. According to friends, I had applied for the "wrong" area. Interest from several associates initially eager to go on such a hunt quickly waned as they learned the difficulties in hunting this area. The Chitina region is next to the Wrangell Mountains and St. Elias National Park. This borders on Kluane National Park of Canada. River airboat or light plane would be what was needed to get in.

Now, to find help in getting there. Expense for bush planes varied with the number of trips, if I got an animal, and the number of additional meat trips. This was discouraging. The financial projections for this escapade were far exceeding the cost of any rifle I initially had in mind. I even called a biologist at The Alaska Department of Fish and Game and asked if their harvest numbers were correct, or would it be better if I didn't hunt?

I was having grave doubts about still trying to go. I am happy to say that doubt gave way to determination. It finally hit me that I had an opportunity afforded to very few to hunt in the wilds of the "Last Frontier" for the bison, an awesome animal of heritage and folklore. It is indeed a credit to conservation efforts that this is even possible.

After what seemed to be several dead ends, I called the local Chitina cafe and explained my situation. I heard discussion on the other end of the receiver, followed by my being told that Paul and Donna Claus did some guiding in the area. They flew-in for their mail in Chitina every week or two. I wrote to Paul Claus of my situation and my plans to buy a .338 rifle. I asked him if this projected hunt was something he could help me with.

About 10 days later, Donna Claus called me while she was in Anchorage, getting supplies, and we made initial plans. Expense was still considerable, and if I went, I probably couldn't afford the new rifle. Donna related that Paul had several rifles to use and their DeHavilland Beaver airplane could take four people and gear into their place, about an hour flight out of Chitina.

Since I had long been deserted by others, I now sold the trip to the wife and kids, inviting them along. What would be better than a trip-of-a-lifetime with your family along. The wife and kids accepted and dates for the hunt were set in late September, to follow the end of moose season.

Paul rendezvoused with us at Chitina airstrip and we had a beautiful flight back to their camp. The hospitality, care, and meals given us were superb. You don't have to hunt to enjoy this place. The kids and my wife were having as fantastic a time as I was.

Paul and I hunted for five days. From my letter, he had been expecting me to come equipped with a new .338. In the interest of economy and selling the trip to the wife and kids, I planned to borrow one of Paul's guns. In the interval since I spoke with Donna, Paul had experienced one rifle broken and had loaned another. A .270 and .300 Winchester Mag remained. We quickly settled on the .300 Winchester Mag and 180 grain bullets.

Our first night out, we were awakened by a snort behind and to the right of our tent but it was still black outside. In the daylight we found several bison tracks, possibly of a group of eight to 10 that we had seen when flying-in. Also, within 20 yards of the tent, along the left side, were fresh tracks of a grizzly and her cub.

The bison seemed to be staying in the deeper wooded areas rather than any of the river bottoms of the braided Chitina River. They may have been seeking more cover, having been made wary during the moose season that was now over.

There was an abundance of fresh sign, and more than once we stalked a fallen dead tree, thinking it was a bison. Signs of grizzly were also fresh and abundant. We came to one area that appeared to have had a bulldozer turning over the ground and was no doubt the site of a bruin's search for ground squirrels or mice. Yet, no bison were sighted. Tracks and signs, but no animals. Paul would, on occasion, climb a tree much higher than I would want to for that extra good look ahead. We hiked a lot. Each day as it warmed-up, we shed our multiple layers of clothing. The mountains around us were snow-capped but the valley stayed dry during the hunt.

While Paul and I were out hunting, Lue tutored the kids with their school assignments at the dinner table at the lodge. They also hiked the trails to nearby streams and waterfalls with Paul's mother, Eleanor.

The fifth day out, we were accompanied part of the time by a young eagle that had not yet acquired the fine points of flying. Three times, it literally seemed to crash into trees within a few yards of us. Its flying was majestic, only the landings were spastic. We were about to give-up on the hunt when we came across deep bison tracks that were fresh. None of the previous tracks were this deep, and these tracks headed toward the river and out of the woods. We followed them. As we peered out of the trees, there was a single bull in the low brush, about 250 yards ahead. The wind was directly in our faces at 12-15 miles per hour and the bison was grazing from right to left. Without saying a word, Paul and I exchanged glances that said, "I'm not believing this." Because there were shallow, interconnecting drainage areas of three to five feet deep, we could approach and yet remain low and out-of-sight of the bull.

We reached a drop-off with our heads at grass level, within 100 yards of the animal. The bison had worked its way behind a small clump of alders but we could hear it tear at the horsetails it was eating. I was sure my heartbeat may have been equally as loud. The slight rustle of brush with that favorable wind helped to calm me and give me confidence that I could go on breathing and the bull might not hear me.

As we eased up to look through the grass, we couldn't see the bull as it was in a depression of its own, with only part of the hump showing. Head down, the bull moved parallel to us. There was one more small clump of trees for it to get past and it then would be in a clearing. He entered the clearing and was broadside, my dreamed-of shot.

Paul, I'm sure, was wondering when I would shoot as I seemed to methodically calculate placement of the sights. I fired, looked, and fired again. The animal started to walk away. Paul assured me it was hit well, though I was not as confident. Within the next 30 yards, the animal collapsed. Paul, who has tremendous enthusiasm, said, "Its size makes it look prehistoric." The two of us couldn't even roll the bison over.

It was particularly good fortune that Paul was able to maneuver the plane into an area where he could land and taxi to within 200 yards of the animal. Several Super Cub flights were needed to pack-out the meat to the cabin. The meat dressed 900 pounds when weighed in Anchorage. Eleanor Claus made us a bison feast to top off that night.

Weather can change fast in Alaska and it often alters plans. When we left the lodge, two trips were needed in Paul's Beaver. One to fly the meat out to our four-wheel drive Suburban and the second for family and gear. This was a one-hour flight each way. The meat trip was unremarkable. While loading gear and family, some clouds were building. About 15-20 minutes in the air, we began to encounter snow flurries and then blizzard conditions that forced us to fly lower. Eventually, because of near white-out conditions, Paul made a riverbar landing to wait-out the storm. Over the previous several days I had become accustomed to the landings without runways with the Super Cub, though Lue relates this as a faith-building flight. The Beaver, with its greater size, did seem to handle like the lighter Super Cub with Paul's talents. Upon landing in Chitina, we found six inches of snow on the ground.

We will never forget this trip, the adventure, the conservation efforts, and the wonderful hospitality of the Claus family. You ask about "my rifle." Well, I thought I would put in for another permit, and if I get drawn, the wife says . . . .

Photograph by Wm. H. Nesbitt

ROCKY MOUNTAIN GOAT
FIRST AWARD
SCORE: 53-6/8
Locality: Sheslay River, B.C.   Date: September 1987
Hunter: Dan Stobbe

ROCKY MOUNTAIN GOAT 53-6/8

Dan Stobbe

For many years I have been big game hunting, and for most of those years, my activities were confined to guiding and finding trophy animals for hunters from all parts of North America. I served my apprenticeship with the late Frank Stewart, working for him from 1969 to 1975 in the Cassiar area.

In August of 1987, I received a call from a friend at Telegraph Creek, British Columbia, advising that "trophy" mountain goats had been spotted north of the Telegraph Creek area; was I interested? I made a quick call to my hunting partner, Ken Moffat, and the expedition was launched.

We drove from our homes in Kamloops, British Columbia. After two grueling days on the road, we arrived at Telegraph Creek. The weather did not cooperate for the first two days, so we spent the time exploring the old and abandoned miner's cabins. These gave a glimpse of the miner's lives, as many of the cabins still gave the impression that the return of the occupants was expected, with all of their personal belongings still in place.

On the third day, the weather cleared and we flew into our base camp situated in the Cassiar Mountains. Camp was a half-hour flight north of Telegraph Creek and situated on a lake at about the 4,500 level. We each carried about 65 pounds of gear, including our down sleeping bags and a two-man tent that was not required as we found a perfectly serviceable cabin, complete with a functional propane stove, that we commandeered for the duration of our hunt.

The next morning, we started scouting the various ridges. On the second day we spotted a large "billy" on the other side of the ridge above our base camp. The ridge was approximately 7,000 feet in elevation. Rather than go after the goat at that time, we decided to work our way along the various ridges. During the next few days we spotted about 30 more goats, but none of them appeared to be as large as the goat we spotted on the second day.

On our fifth day, we climbed over the ridge again. After 4-1/2 hours, we spotted our large "billy" about three miles away on the edge of a draw. He was about 300 feet above the tree line and the ground between us was extremely exposed. It took approximately three hours to get into position for the shot.

By keeping the wind coming from the goat, I was able to get into a position about 200 yards from the goat, but directly above, which forced me to sight without being able to get my eye up to the scope. My shot was right on the mark, through the shoulder blades, and he didn't fall from the ridge that he had been lying on.

The problem we now faced was getting our prize back to camp. The kill was made at the 5,500 foot level, and it was due to Ken's brawn that we got the approximately 350 pounds of goat over the 7,000 foot ridge and back to our camp.

On the next day, Ken shot a goat that was shorter in horn length but massive. Our time was up, so the red signal tarpaulin was placed on the ground and our pilot landed to fly us to Telegraph Creek. On the flight back we were told that a large grizzly had been spotted on the Stikine. When we arrived at Telegraph Creek, I phoned home to check on the possibility of extending the trip for a day or so to try for the grizzly. I was advised that if I wanted to hunt bear I could do so at home as there was a large black bear taking up permanent residence in our orchard. So much for grizzlies!

My mountain goat was officially measured for entry with horn length of 10-6/8 inches, a base of 6-2/8 inches, and a total score of 54-6/8. At the 7th Big Game Trophy Competition for British Columbia, held at Trail, B. C., my mountain goat was awarded First Place.

Photographs Courtesy of Mark A. Gaede and Mark Cook

(l) Mark A. Gaede took this Rocky Mountain goat in Alaska in 1988 within a few feet of Skilak Galcier (visible in background). It scores 51 points. (r) Mark Cook holds up the Rocky Mountain goat he killed in Okanogan County, Washington, in 1987 that scores 47-6/8 points.

Photograph Courtesy of Danny W. Pankoski

Danny W. Pankoski was hunting the craggy peaks near Day Harbor, Alaska, in 1987 where he killed this Rocky Mountain goat that scores 48-2/8 points.

Photograph by Wm. H. Nesbitt

ROCKY MOUNTAIN GOAT
SECOND AWARD
SCORE: 53

Locality: Sheslay Mt., B.C.   Date: September 1985
Hunter: Wallace E. Sills

ROCKY MOUNTAIN GOAT 53

Wallace E. Sills

My three friends and I left Atlanta on September 8, 1985, and flew Delta Airlines to Seattle. We connected on another flight to Terrace, B.C., arriving in the late afternoon. Ray Davidson, Bill McLennon, Larry Womack, and I went to the hotel and met two other guys from North Carolina. Later that night, we met our outfitter, Odell Dorsey, and settled our account for the hunt. He informed us that we would be split into two groups, with Ray going with the two N.C. guys to one camp, and Bill, Larry, and I would go to a new camp with his new guide, Dan LaFrance.

The next morning, we all flew to a little town in B.C. with a population of 12, but they had a motel and a post office. We spent the night there. I had the cook bake Bill a cake for his birthday. I had carried the cake mix and pecans for this great event.

The next morning, we ate cake and then divided-up to take our floatplane ride to the new camp. We landed on a small lake and unloaded our gear, and the plane took off. After a two-hour wait in this wilderness, three guys and our cook turned up. We carried our gear about three miles to base camp where we found there were no horses. Larry was worn-out after carrying his 20 pounds of candy three miles. Of course, he ate a half-pound on the way to lighten his load.

After waiting that day and another, the head guide and two other guides (Bill and Mike Stini) and the horses arrived. They had lost three horses and were worn-out.

Finally, on the next day, we left for Sheslay Mountain. Bill and I caught the flu; I got thrown from the horse that had just been broken; and we all got to sleep under the stars that night. Dan LaFrance had been in this area years ago but he had to find his way through the so-called trails.

The next day, we finally arrived at an old mine cabin and set up camp. Halfway up the mountain, I went out glassing and spotted goats down low. Mike also spotted a grizzly on the side of the mountain.

The next day, Bill went after the grizzly and I told Womack to go after the goats down low, figuring that his large stature and 20 pounds of candy would never make it to the top.

Ron and I started for the top of the mountain on foot. We stopped about halfway up and watched LaFrance lead Bill straight to the grizzly. I knew this was wrong because of updrafts early in the morning. Sure enough, the old bear stuck his head up and sniffed them. He took off across the mountain, so Ron and I began to climb again.

After 3-1/2 hours of climbing, we reached the top and Ron spotted a goat. I told Ron that I wanted to go over the mountain where probably no one else would go, hoping to find a large goat. I told him that I usually get real close on animals (within 50 yards) and he laughed. We crossed over the mountain and stopped at a spring to eat an orange. I told Ron to look over this little knoll while I filled my canteen. He came back quickly and said there were two goats lying down on the grass over the knoll. I grabbed my Ruger .270 and we eased to the top of the knoll.

There lay these two goats, about 40 yards away. One stood up and he looked big. I asked Ron if it was a nanny or a billy. He said that he didn't know, that he had never seen one that close. I asked him how far away they had to be for him to tell. He lay on his back and laughed. I told him that a lot of good he was, because this was the first goat I had ever seen and I was not going to shoot a nanny goat and have Bill and Womack laugh at me.

The goat stood and looked around, facing us, and his horns looked awfully big, but we could not tell if it was a billy. He finally turned around and I knew right away that this goat was no nanny. The other goat got up and the wind shifted, causing them to get nervous.

They took-off, running to the cliffs. I raised my .270 and shot the billy in the chest. He then leaped from the cliff. We got-up and ran to the edge, and there he lay, in a rock slide. Ron said we could not go after him because the rocks looked loose and we might end-up at the bottom, so we headed back to camp.

We took a short-cut down the side of the mountain, where I proceeded to slide 100 yards down a rock slide. We finally arrived back at camp around 7 p.m. and began telling our story. Of course, no one believed that we got that close, but Ron backed me up. We had no rope, so I found wire and pieces of rope to make 100 feet of rope/wire. Womack had killed his goat, a nice one with horns of 9-1/2 inches.

The next morning, Womack spotted a small grizzly in camp and took off after him in his slippers and boxer shorts. Snow had fallen during the night and it was a sight to watch.

Ron, Mike, and I left to go over the mountain after my goat, while Bill, Womack, and LaFrance broke camp to return to main base. Four hours later, we topped the mountain that was covered in fog and began to look for my goat. Mike and Ron went left, and I went right to where I thought we had been. After a while, I found the spring and my orange peelings and seeds. I called Ron and Mike and we went over to the cliff and there was my goat.

Mike is a taxidermist, so he and Ron went down the rock slide after my goat while I held the rope-wire, if needed. They skinned the goat and returned to the top with few problems. We took pictures and joked, and I showed Mike where I shot from. He concurred that we were close to the goat. He measured the horns at 11-1/8 inches and we knew then that this was a trophy "old goat." The goat had only three lower teeth on one side. Mike said that the goat probably would not last through the winter with so few to pull grass. We headed back to camp, arriving around 7 p.m. again. Mike finished caping the goat while Ron and I fixed dinner.

The following morning we broke camp and headed back to meet Bill and Womack at base camp. We got in around 8 p.m. that night, worn-out.

After a night's rest, we started around noon for Level Mountain with Bill and Womack.

From here, the hunt went bad. It rained, it snowed, and we did not find the supplies that were supposed to be on Level Mountain. Six of us were sleeping in a two-man tent. We got wet and cold, so Bill, Womack, and I decided to leave and go home even though our hunt was not over.

We got back to base camp and radioed Odell. We told him we were going home. We then radioed a bush plane. It came the next day and we left.

Odell Dorsey made up for our bad trip by giving us a good deal on a spring bear hunt in 1986 on the Stikine River. It was a great trip for us, but unfortunately Odell, his wife, and son-in-law died in an airplane crash after we left. We were all saddened by this tragedy.

This goat is a great honor for me and a tribute to my good friends Bill, Ray, Womack, Mike, Ron, Dan, and Odell.

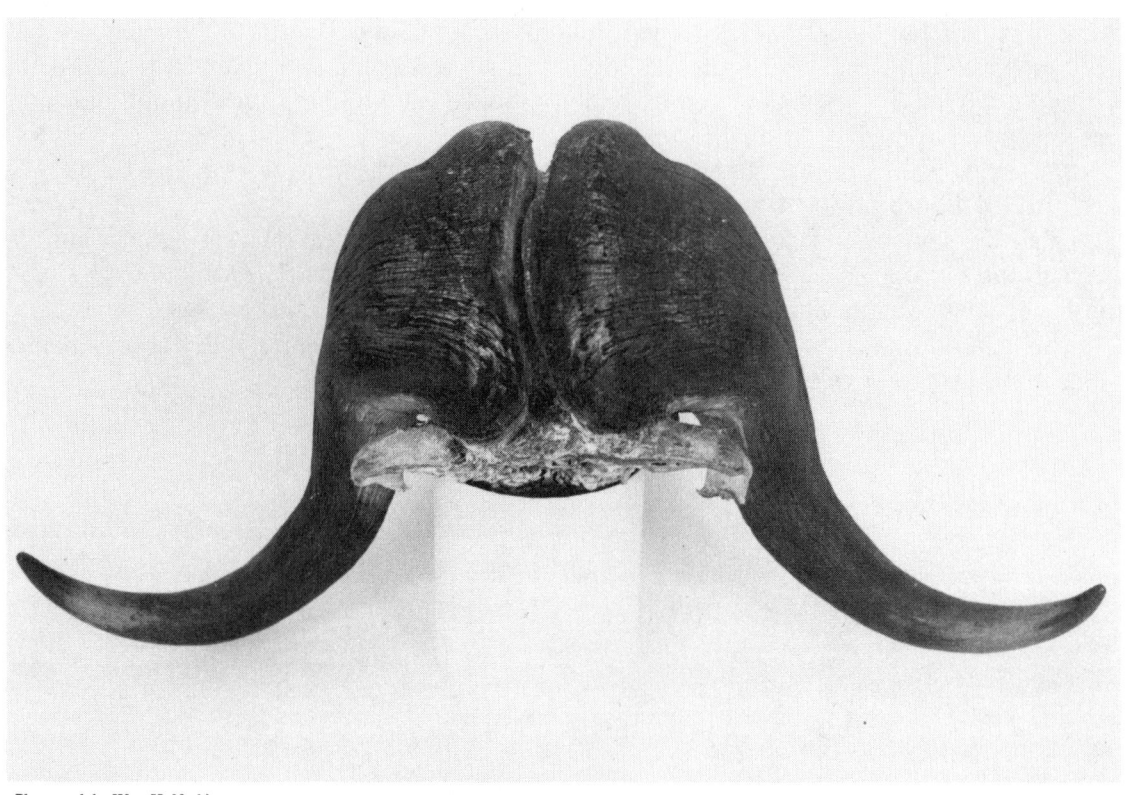

Photograph by Wm. H. Nesbitt

NEW WORLD'S RECORD MUSKOX
FIRST AWARD
SCORE: 125-2/8
Locality: Bay Chimo, N.W.T.   Date: August 1988
Hunter: Donald Nicholson

MUSKOX 125-2/8

Donald Nicholson

[This story is edited exerpts from Don Nicholson's hunting journal]

THURSDAY, 8/18/88: The 1-1/2 hour drive from home to DFW Airport and the flight to Edmonton, Alberta, Canada, were pleasantly uneventful and I reminisced the many enjoyable hours I had spent gathering and testing my equipment and physically conditioning myself for this Arctic experience.

FRIDAY, 8/19/88: Up at 5 a.m. I met Steve Cooke in the lobby of the Edmonton Inn Hotel, and he introduced me to George Skaggs and Allen DeArmond, the other hunters. Shortly, we went to the air terminal to catch our 7:30 a.m. flight to Cambridge Bay, N.W.T. located on the southeast coast of Victoria Island. We arrived there at 1:40 p.m. after another pleasant flight on an old, prop-driven Electra. Our hunting licenses and additional food and supplies were purchased before boarding our chartered floatplane for flight to Daniel Moore Bay where Phillip, Jack, and Clarence, our cheerful, energetic, and competent Inuit guides, were waiting. Camp consisted of a large tent for the four of us, a smaller tent for the food and supplies, and another small tent for the guides, all new, but not a single chair, stool, or even a large rock to sit on. Inuits, like Africans and many other people, simply have no need for anything to rest on; they squat on their haunches and rest, an enviable ability I could never master!

SATURDAY, 8/20/88: When I awakened at 5 a.m., George and Allen were snoring loudly, but Steve was sleeping rather quietly. Outside the tent, the peaceful serenity of the endless wilderness was breathtaking, with neither sign nor sound of civilization. Even though the sun had not risen above the eastern skyline, there was ample light to see far up the wide valley to the south across the calm waters of the bay; but even with my 10x40 Leitz binoculars, I saw nothing stirring, a bit disappointing and quite surprising. From all appearances, the weather would be as warm as yesterday, so I went back into the tent and put on a cotton T-shirt and coveralls, a pair of light wool socks and my Browning lightweight boots, and went down to the cook tent to make coffee on the Coleman gas burner. Not a sound was coming from the guide's tent nearby, so I decided to wait until 6 a.m. to awaken everyone. It was near 8 a.m. before Phillip and I left camp and began making our way up the rock ridge that divided the big valley at the south end of the bay and the adjoining valley to the east; the others were still in camp.

Phillip and I continued toward the southeast, along the ridge, periodically stopping and glassing in every direction until 9:40 a.m. when searching with my 25 to 45 power Swarovsky spotting scope, Phillip located a bear crossing the second valley to the East. The bear was so far away that I was unable to locate it, but Phillip assured me that if it continued on its present course, and we hurried like Hell down the ridge, we might get a shot, or, at least a better look at it. We walked for about 25 minutes, as fast as possible, before stopping to try to again locate the bear. Old Griz was still coming and had now entered the valley to our immediate left, but was still two miles away. Through the scope he did not appear to be moving fast, but he was certainly covering a lot of real estate; Phillip and I were quickly losing the race!

The footing was pretty good on the ridge we were following, so we began to trot at a pretty fast pace and continued on for what seemed like an eternity but was actually only about 20 more minutes before we stopped again and set up the scope. I felt a bit of panic creeping into my mind when we could not see old Griz anywhere. Had he changed his course and turned up the valley? Had he laid down in the tundra for a nap? If so, we would never see him again unless he moved for some unknown reason. Our only hope was that he had managed to reach the pass between the valley on our left, where we had last seen him and the big valley on our right. That pass was, at the very least, three-quarters of a mile further down the ridge we were following.

"No way that bear could have gone that far that fast," I kept saying to myself as we raced to the end of the ridge and began frantically glassing the vast expanse below us. Bitter disappointment permeated my mind when we failed to locate that beautiful chocolate-and-cream colored grizzly during the next few minutes. Phillip went back 100 yards to a large knoll in an effort to get a better view of the area where we had last seen the bear near a distinctive rock formation, while I continued to search the pass and the big valley on the right. Another eternity passed, and then, there it was! Three-quarters of a mile beyond the pass, a bear was moving toward the high mountains on the far side of the big valley on the right. It had just emerged from the willows that skirted the small river in the bottom of the valley.

Phillip immediately saw the bear, as the bright sun reflected from it. Now what? If we moved into the pass from our position in the rocks, the bear would surely see us, just as we had seen him. We had no other choice. We would simply have to remain where we were and hope that old Griz stopped when he reached the rocks instead of just going right on over the mountain. Impatiently, I watched as the bear reached the base of the mountain and began to make his way up through a narrow chute in the nearly vertical rock wall. My adrenalin was really pumping as he steadily climbed 60 feet, 100 feet, 200 feet, 400 feet, and then it happened. He suddenly turned out of the chute onto a moss covered ledge and began ripping up the moss, dirt, and loose rocks with his powerful front claws. Phillip's entire face seemed to smile as he turned and said quietly, "He's going to sleep now." Sure enough, after looking over the valley below, Old Griz lay down with his massive head toward the valley, so he could easily see anything that moved below him, and soon appeared to be sleeping. If we could cross the open valley to the base of the mountain adjacent to our position on the ridge without him seeing us, we could then climb up through a rather broad opening in the rocks about 140 yards to the North of the bear's bed, get well above him, and then work our way to an over-hanging rock about 20 yards immediately above him.

We made our way to the rocks at the base of the mountain, then worked our way up until we were well above the elevation of the bear's position, and moved again to the south before very carefully descending to the over-hanging rock above the bear's bed. Phillip stayed back as I inched my way to the edge of the huge rock and peered below. Not 20 yards away and almost directly under me between the rocks, I could see the cream colored shoulders of the sleeping grizzly. As the rifle roared, the bear jerked as if it had received a large charge of electricity, and never moved again. Our later examination revealed that the 200 grain Nosler partition bullet from my .30-338 had entered the animal's back 20 inches behind the foreleg, broken the spine, punctured the upper lungs, and destroyed the heart as it coursed down and forward before coming to rest against the skin of the lower neck.

Phillip and I were both elated with the bear. After taking the hide, eating a sandwich, and drinking Tang, we rested a while and then started the long, but happy, trek back to camp in the hot afternoon sun. We arrived there at 5:20 p.m. Allen had missed several shots at a bear, but had later taken a nice caribou bull still in velvet. George and Clarence had seen five caribou bulls, but none of them was what George wanted.

SUNDAY, 8/21/88: I awakened at 5 a.m. but did not get up until 6:16 a.m. Clouds had blown in during the night, and a light rain began at 6:30 a.m., so I let everyone continue sleeping. I ate a few sausages and drank hot chocolate for breakfast, packed some gear, and Phillip and I started for Bay Chimo at 9 a.m. We traveled 50 miles across the open sea in Phillip's 18 foot aluminum boat with a 40 horsepower Yamaha motor, stopping only once on an island to stretch our legs and refuel the motor. The sun was shining when we left camp, but there was a solid overcast at noon when we arrived in Bay Chimo. We were greeted by most of the 60 residents as we beached the boat.

We were in the boat at 3:40 p.m. to go hunt for a muskox. A few miles up the coast, I noticed a dark spot in the center of a huge meadow adjacent to the rocky coast. I did not know what it was, but I did know that it was too black to be a rock, so I said, "Phillip, I am not sure, but I may have just seen a muskox in that big meadow back there." Turning the boat around, he replied, "We better go back and look."

After finding a place to beach the boat, we took the rifle and spotting scope for a look at the distant object. It was indeed a muskox, and when I viewed it through the 45 power glass, I was reminded of a remark that Jack O'Conner had once made about field judging the horns of wild sheep: "When you see a ram that will rank high in the Record Book, nobody has to tell you that he is big!" Even though this was the first live muskox I had ever seen, nobody had to tell me he was big! After studying him carefully for a few minutes and recalling what I had read in an article I had recently perused about muskox, I said quietly to Phillip, "He looks good to me!" After taking a quick look through the scope, Phillip replied, "He looks good to me, too! He is probably going to join the others over by the rocks." I was so engrossed with the size of the bull that I had failed to notice three other muskox bedded near the end of a rock formation that extended out into the vast basin more than a mile away.

For two or three more minutes, I continued to watch the bull as he moved toward the others. "Can we cross this valley to that rock formation far enough up there to the north so he can't see us?" I asked. "Yes, let's go," Phillip replied with a smile. Twenty minutes later we had beached the boat in an inlet up the coast a couple of miles, and we were crossing the end of the meadow to the mile-long rock formation. Less than an hour had passed as we eased up on a very large boulder overlooking the muskox bedded 150 yards away. The big bull was now resting 20 yards to the right of the other large bull, cow, and young bull. The huge stature of the older muskox was even more apparent when one compared him to the others. Knowing full well that I was about to shoot anyway, I whispered, "Phillip, are you sure this is the bull we want?" He had hardly finished saying, "He looks good," when the 200 grain Nosler pushed the old monarch flat on his left side. One futile reflexive attempt to raise his massive head, and it was over.

We lay still on the rock for several minutes, hoping the others would wander away without further alarm, but they did not. We were less than 50 yards away before the cow and young bull ran 30 yards and turned again to watch us. The other large bull moved to the side of his fallen elder and snorted defiantly at us until we were less than 10 yards away; he then turned and led the others toward the distant mountain to the south. The great bull was so much larger than a fully mature muskox was said to be that I just stood and looked at him with amazement for several minutes while Phillip was closely examining the heavy horns and nodding his head with approval.

It was all we could manage to position the huge animal for the pictures, and even more difficult to move it as the skinning job progressed. I wanted to take the full skin, but there was simply no way that we could pack it out. I had serious doubt about carrying only the huge head and shoulder skin, but that strenuous work was completed near midnight when we reached the water's edge, only a few yards from the spot where we had beached the boat in our first effort to identify the black spot in the sea of green. After resting little more than 10 minutes, Phillip went to get the boat while I waited in the dark and cold rain that had continued to fall intermittently since we had begun the caping chore. Upon our return to the village at 12:45 a.m., Aggie prepared a much appreciated hot meal that we promptly devoured, and then we went to bed.

MONDAY, 8/22/88: At 5 a.m., it was raining lightly when I awakened from a deep and refreshing sleep. I wrote in my journal and pondered my run of good fortune until 9 a.m. when Phillip, Aggie, and Christopher (their energetic six-year-old son) climbed from the small bed they all had slept in. I had slept in Christopher's small bed! Through the entire day we spent working on the muskox head and hide, most of the other Inuit hunters of the village came and looked at it, spoke briefly in Inuit with Phillip, smiled and shook my hand, and went on. It seems they all agreed that this bull was Omingmaktok, "The Bearded One." They had seen him periodically in the area for several years and they were glad that his long life had come instantly and painlessly to its close by my properly placed bullet, rather than by the vicious teeth of the hungry wolf pack in the deep winter snow. I had mixed feelings of both pride and remorse when Phillip explained what they had been saying, but I got the distinct impression that as fellow hunters, they were undeniably expressing their genuine pleasure with my good fortune.

At 9:30 p.m., we returned to the muskox carcass to get a load of the meat and to cache the remainder. Phillip would return for the frozen meat when it was needed during the long, dark winter. Back at home, we found that Aggie had begun the long and arduous chore of "fleshing" the green hide. Phillip and I planned to go up the coast to an area about 35 miles to the north and hunt caribou the following morning if the weather permitted.

TUESDAY, 8/23/88: The weather became colder and more blustery during the night, and we were forced to remain in the village. I spent a very enjoyable and educational day going about the village visiting with the genuinely pleasant people, young and old alike, and taking many exceptional pictures.

WEDNESDAY, 8/24/88: By 11 a.m., the early winter storm had passed and Phillip and I were making our way up the coast in the choppy sea to the area we hoped would produce the caribou we wanted. Lady Luck was again with us, for as we entered the small bay at the end of which we would make camp, I saw two fine caribou bulls near the water's edge, no more than 300 yards from our intended campsite. By the time we had reached the shore, I had already decided that, if possible, I would take the smaller of the two because his pelt was simply gorgeous and his headgear carried more weight, though smaller than that of his darker-colored buddy.

As the rifle roared, the lovely bull dropped as if hit by a cannon ball. The other bull did not linger to see if his fate would be the same; in less than a minute he vanished behind the rocks from which he and his late partner had so recently appeared. As I was returning from the boat with my daypack and camera, I could hardly believe my eyes as I watched the "dead" caribou struggle to his feet. Another carefully placed shot, and he was never to move again. Examination later revealed that the first shot had entered immediately in front of the left front shoulder, angled slightly forward, and exited the opposite side of the neck, thus severing the major artery but failing to break the neck. Though most likely he could not have taken a single step, I was amazed that he had even mustered enough strength to regain his feet.

We made our camp, cared for the strikingly beautiful caribou, and just enjoyed the remainder of the fine and sunny, but chilly, day that was the most pleasant one we had during the entire hunt. More good news came over the radio when we learned that both George and Allen had taken bears and caribou and were moving camp to Bay Chimo to hunt muskox.

THURSDAY, 8/25/88: Though the night was calm, everything on our table had frozen during the night, even the five inches of water in our water pail, when I awakened a bit before 5 a.m. After getting up at 8, Phillip had eaten a bowl of oatmeal, drunk a cup of coffee, and then worked to remove the bones from the caribou hooves. We then hiked along the rocky ridge behind our camp, heading east for two miles to a point overlooking a valley that stretched as far as the eye could see toward the south, and to the ocean on the horizon to the north, and bound by distant mountains to the east. I was in awe of the grandeur of this magnificent Arctic wilderness; a feeling equaled in magnitude only by my dismay at not being able to see a single living creature except a soaring hawk and few lesser birds. Surely they were there, but I could not see a single solitary one!

After returning to camp and eating a bit of lunch, we took the boat and crossed the channel to a very large island to the west. After climbing to the highest point on the island, some 2-1/2 miles inland, we scoped the terrain as far as the 45 power glass would allow, and again saw no wildlife except two soaring eagles that came under attack by an obviously disgruntled hawk. Through my binoculars, I watched and thoroughly enjoyed that magnificent display of flying skills until the participants disappeared in the evening haze. This was one of the most memorable single days in my entire 48 years of hunting, a day remembered not for the game that I did see, but rather for that which I did not see! We would go farther up the coast in the morning.

FRIDAY, 8/26/88: It had rained lightly during the night. Some way, Phillip must have known that the weather would change, for before going to bed, he had tightened the tent ropes and covered our supplies and the caribou hide with a tarp outside the tent. After breakfast at 7 a.m., Phillip just sat drinking coffee and listening on the radio until 8:45 a.m. when we left camp, hiking north. After crossing three valleys, we moved to a high point on the fourth ridge and glassed for miles in every direction but saw nothing. I was wondering if today would be a "repeat" of yesterday, when Phillip suggested that we should move down the ridge toward the big valley to the east. Just as we were nearing the end of the ridge we had been skirting on the south side, Phillip dropped to his knees and pointed toward five caribou bulls that were grazing 350 yards below and to the left of us. I slipped off my pack and moved up behind the rocks, where Phillip knelt watching the grazing animals dispersed among the scattered rocks. One of the bulls was, by far, the best of the lot, and it did not take long to pick him out!

Moving to a large rock in front of Phillip, I waited for the chosen bull to move from behind some rocks. An eternity seemed to pass before he appeared beyond the rocks. As I squeezed the shot off, he jerked his head up and turned at such an angle that the shot passed through the upper brisket and lower neck, failing to put him down. He was running toward the big valley when my second shot entered slightly in front of his right hindquarter, broke the spine, and exited immediately behind his left front shoulder. He collapsed and was dead within seconds. My hunt was finished. "Good shooting," Phillip exclaimed as we paced the 350 steps to the motionless animal. The antlers were not so widespread, but had very fine bezes and many long and impressive upper points, truly a fine trophy. Phillip and I were both very happy hunters.

By the time we reached camp at 4:30 p.m., the sun was once again beaming down, but a cup of hot tea was quite refreshing. The caribou hide was lightly salted with the last of our supply. If the good weather held, we would return to Bay Chimo in the morning. At 10 p.m., I watched the full, golden, and absolutely gorgeous, moon rise from behind the mountains to the East, and then went to bed.

SATURDAY, 8/27/88: Jack told Phillip on the radio that he was afraid the muskox had returned to the mountains to the south of Bay Chimo, and neither George nor Allen had taken one. Their hopes were waning.

SUNDAY, 8/28/88: The wind continued to blow through the night and it rained lightly for more than three hours in the early morning. The wind had shifted to the northwest, and for all appearances, winter had arrived; but by 6 p.m., the wind had subsided to a gentle breeze, and Phillip chimed, "Let's go to Bay Chimo!" By 6:35 p.m. we were headed that way in the rough, but traversable, sea. After observing Phillip for the past 10 days, I felt as safe as any rational man could under the circumstances! At 8:05 p.m., we beached the boat adjacent to the large tent at the northern edge of the village where we four foreigners were to reside the next few days. I must confess I was rather glad to be there after spending the previous 42 hours inside the small tent.

At 10:30 p.m., Steve and Allen returned from a visit with Jack's family and I learned that George and Clarence had started up the coast to the north, apparently about the same time that Phillip and I had started our trip south. Jack and Allen were planning to head South in the morning to hunt muskox, if the weather permitted, so I agreed to awaken Allen at 6:30 a.m.

MONDAY, 8/29/88: The strong wind returned during the night and continued the entire day and following night.

TUESDAY, 8/30/88: At 10 a.m., Jack came to our tent and told Allen to get his gear and come with him, a muskox bull was staying near a camp 15 miles south of the village. They left at 11:15 a.m., with Allen protesting, "But I haven't had my breakfast!" Shortly after 2 p.m., George and Clarence returned with a fine muskox bull they had taken a few miles up the coast from the bay where Phillip and I had made our little caribou camp. And at 9 p.m., when Allen and Jack returned with their muskox bull, there was jubilation in our camp! We all had taken the animals we had traveled so far to hunt, and no one had gotten sick or injured in the process.

As it later turned out, had George and Allen not gotten their muskox when they did, they would have had to get them on another hunt, for the weather became more severe with each passing day. We were quite fortunate to get back to Cambridge Bay to catch our flight back to Edmonton on the fifth day of September! This was one of those truly exceptional hunts never to be forgotten!

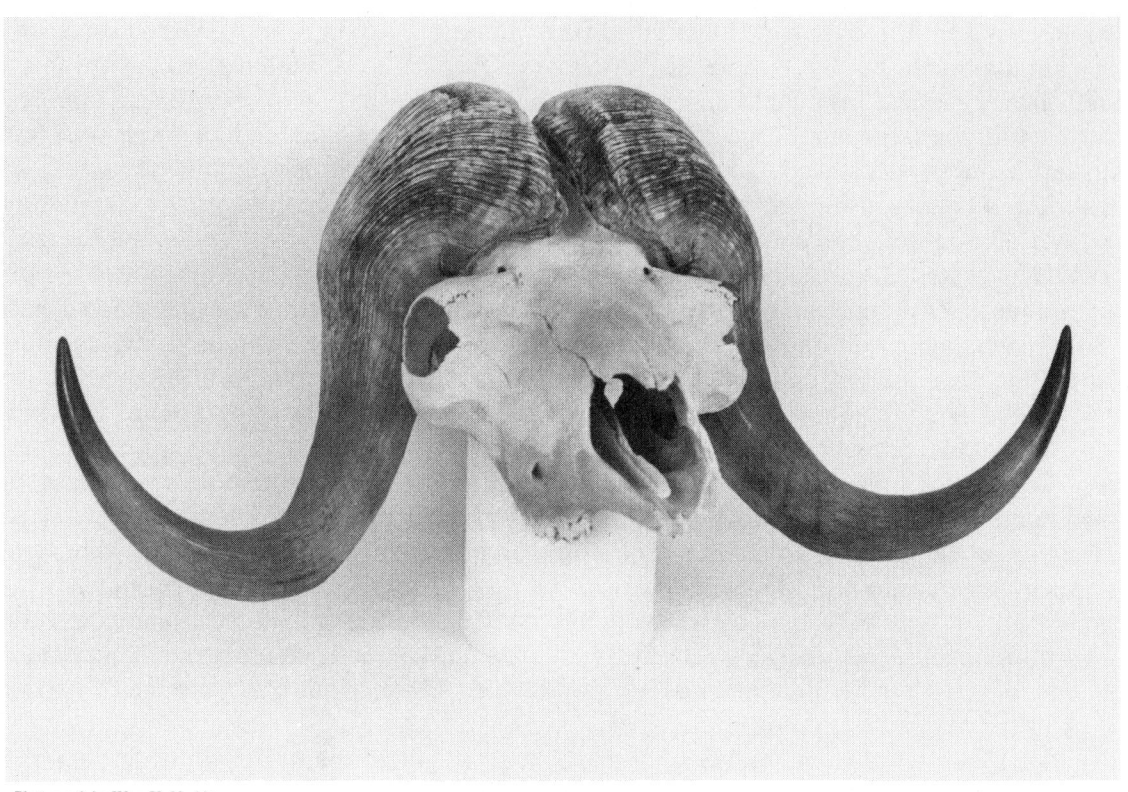

Photograph by Wm. H. Nesbitt

MUSKOX
SECOND AWARD
SCORE: 124-6/8

Locality: Perry River, N.W.T.   Date: April 1988
Hunter: Robert D. Jones

MUSKOX 124-6/8

Robert D. Jones

Two things immediately come to mind when a hunter first observes the North American muskox in a bleak and barren winter environment. First, this is an animal that shouldn't be there at all. Second, whoever hung the names "musk" and "ox" on this tremendous animal did it an extreme injustice. A much more dignified and appropriate name would have been the "Arctic buffalo."

During March of 1988, a party of six of us traveled from northeastern Washington to the lonely little village of Cambridge Bay on Victoria Island, Northwest Territories, Canada. From there, we flew south across the frozen Arctic ocean to our ultimate destination, the ancient and long-abandoned Eskimo and Hudson's Bay outpost camp at Perry Island. The nearby Perry and Ellice River drainages were reputed to be home to the largest race of muskox on the continent, and we would be among the first sport hunters to have the opportunity to sport hunt muskox there.

A half-dozen plywood shacks made a very comfortable winter camp on the island, and each hunter was furnished a native guide. For reasons of safety and efficiency, we were to hunt in pairs. Each guide was equipped with a snowmobile and would tow his hunter on a "komatik," the Eskimo term for a 16 foot wooden sled. My son, Dick Jones, and I chose to hunt together. We would be capably guided by George Angiotok and John Matsiliak.

There were several definite advantages to hunting muskox in the winter season. First, the animals were congregated along the Arctic coast where more forage was available. Secondly, the entire country was frozen harder than a brick, allowing excellent access with the snowmobiles. And thirdly, the weather was generally excellent. The coldest temperature we experienced was minus 34 degrees Fahrenheit, and that was only for one night. Snow depth never exceeded six inches. The days were long and there were about 12 hours of daylight. The cold, dry climate was invigorating, and it was nearly impossible to get wet. It was a great place to be.

Dick and I have each done a considerable amount of do-it-yourself wilderness hunting, and we have always considered the wilderness experience itself to be the greatest reward a hunt can offer. Any trophies taken were always the frosting. And we also knew that no matter how well you were prepared, how well you were equipped, or how hard you worked, there was absolutely no substitute for the most important facet of any hunt: blind luck!

We made it clear to our guides that the wilderness experience this hunt would provide would be its own greatest reward. We also made it clear that we wanted only big, old, trophy bulls. In the event they didn't come along, we would be satisfied with the experience.

We hunted hard for the first three days of the seven-day hunt. A couple of the other members of our party took nice bulls, and we passed up some very respectable trophies. On the fourth day, from the crest of a low, rocky ridge, we spotted seven black objects bunched-up in a little white bowl about three miles distant. The spotting scope revealed seven bull muskox, and two of them were dandies. George and I watched as Dick and John circled with the snowmobile to within a mile. A low, rocky ridge provided cover for a stalk on foot, and two hours later we heard the crack of a lone shot.

Dick's .270 had done its job well, and he and John were a couple of happy hunters. A nice stalk had resulted in a clean, one-shot kill, and the muskox was a giant. We took pictures, skinned and quartered the carcass, loaded up the komatiks, and prepared to follow the rest of this herd. Dick's animal had been the one with the longest horns in the bunch, but I had my mind set on another bull that had tremendous bosses.

I know this will be hard to believe, but we followed the tracks of these bulls in the snow for 26 miles on the odometer. At dark, we climbed a hill and glassed miles into the distance. No muskox could be seen. We arrived in camp long after dark, after having covered the 65 return miles.

We green-scored Dick's muskox at about 117-4/8, and we figured it was the largest head ever taken by a sport hunter! Only two other heads were larger, and they were both pick-ups from this same area.

Early the next morning, we fired up the snowmobiles and got ready to go. We wanted to have a better look at the bull with the big bosses, which we figured could score even more than Dick's trophy. We rode the 65 miles out to the ridge of the night before and then began to follow the tracks in the snow. We actually followed these tracks for another 35 miles before losing them in a great concentration of muskox tracks and sign that blotted them out. Our bunch of bulls had actually run over 60 miles, virtually non-stop!

George unhooked my sled and told me he would ride a great circle around this larger herd in an attempt to pick up the original tracks. In about an hour, he came back, rode up to me, got off his snowmobile, and said very clearly and calmly "The biggest muskox I have ever seen is over there. He has great, wide bosses, and the longest horns I have ever seen. They come way down past his chin, and then sweep way up past the eye. They are huge." I asked George if this bull was bigger than the one that Dick had taken yesterday and he replied, "Much bigger." Dick said, "Nice going George! I kill the best muskox ever taken by a sport hunter one day, and the very next day you find my dad a bigger one! You could have looked for the second-best you know!"

We rode to the base of a long, low rocky ridge and started after the animal on foot. The giant bull was with five other bulls and they were spooky. The squeaking of our feet on the snow kept them about 500 yards ahead of us for most of three hours. Huge boulders and cliffs on the ridge gave us some cover, and the terrain was perfect for our stalk. Finally, after more than four hours, the bulls had hesitated in a small draw running up onto our ridge. Good grass provided them with a little lunch, and they were taking advantage. The wind was straight into our faces as we made our way across bare bedrock and finally worked our way to within 250 yards of the herd. I rested my rifle over a chest-high boulder as George made me a shooting pad out of his pack and gloves. I waited until I had a perfect broadside shot at the big bull. His horns stuck out like a frost-bit thumb, and he was at least a half-foot taller than the other bulls. One 150 grain Nosler bullet from my .270 did the job, and we ran to see just how big he really was.

One look was enough! We had something very special on our hands: a potential World's Record muskox, and a unique background of snow, cliffs and boulders. We took lots of pictures in the late afternoon light, then caped and dressed the bull. We got into camp far after dark again that day, and anxiously got out the tape, pencil, and score sheet. Both horns were over 30 inches long, which was the longest ever recorded. The bosses were very large, the circumference measurements were outstanding, and the head was very symmetrical. The final field score was 128-5/8, more than 6-1/2 inches larger than the World's Record! What was perhaps even more incredible was that Dick and I, as a father and son combination, had on the same hunt and on consecutive days, killed the two largest muskox ever taken by sport hunters. And one of these was a potential New World's Record! Now there was luck with a capital L.

Four months later, we had our bulls officially measured for entry. At that time, mine scored 127-4/8 and Dick's scored 117. We were invited to bring our trophies to the 20th Awards Program in Albuquerque, New Mexico, in June of 1989. The Panel of Judges adjusted our scores to 124-6/8 and 115-2/8. These new scores placed my bull in the No. 2 spot, and placed Dick's somewhere in the top 10 ever recorded.

I won't soon forget the incredible experiences we had on the frozen slopes of the Canadian Arctic. There is an animal there that looks like a buffalo, acts like a buffalo, and thinks like a buffalo. And in my book he should have a better name: the Arctic buffalo.

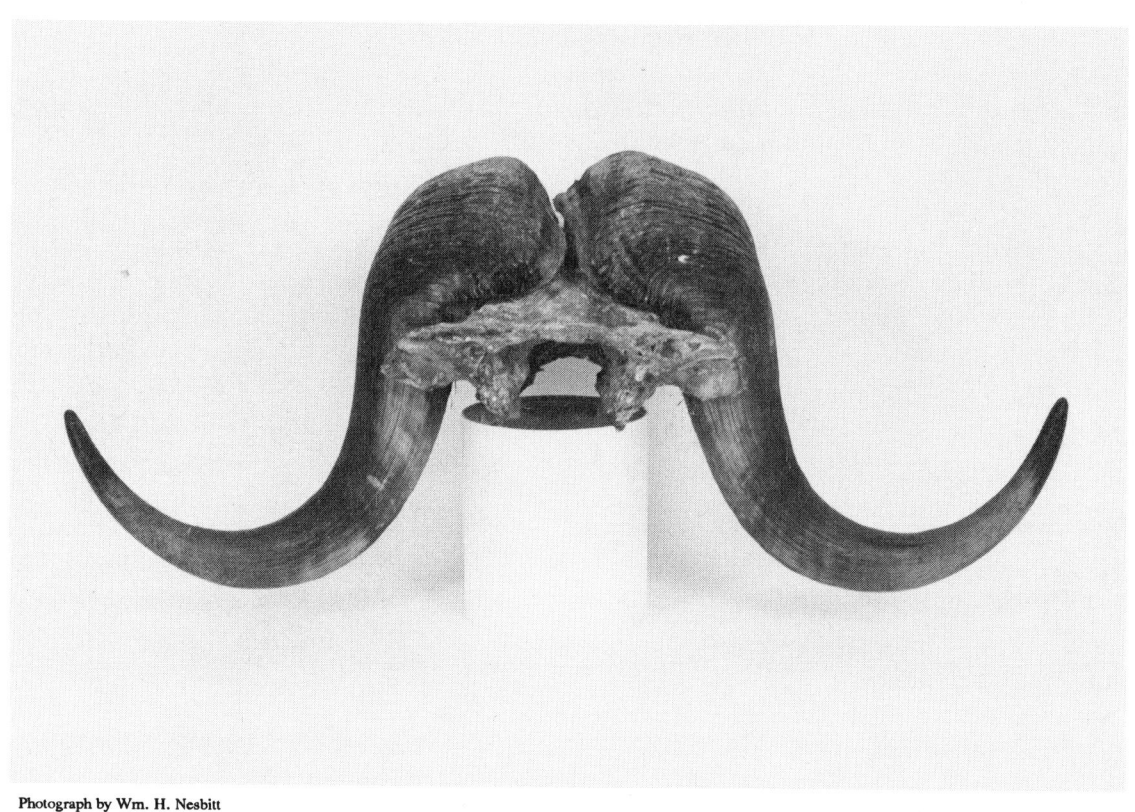

Photograph by Wm. H. Nesbitt

MUSKOX
THIRD AWARD
SCORE: 121-6/8
Locality: Cambridge Bay, N.W.T.　Date: March 1986
Hunter: Tom Gross

MUSKOX 121-6/8

Tom Gross

It was the last weekend in March, the time of year that the weather in the Arctic becomes unpredictable. My two hunting companions, Don and George, and I packed-up our sleds and headed across the frozen sea from our homes in Cambridge Bay, Victoria Island.

We were on our way to an area about 65 miles south, Foggy Bay, to hunt muskox. In a few hours, we found ourselves standing on the north shore of the North American continent. It was close to noon and the weather was clear and cold, about minus 35 degrees Celsius.

We found a nice river valley and followed it inland. We stopped a few miles in when we came across some old muskox sign. Leaving our equipment, we walked up into the rocky hills that surrounded us. Once up top, we could see for a long way but the only sign of life was two ravens whose cries could be heard for miles.

It was almost two hours later that we returned to our snowmobiles and sleds. After a quick lunch, it was decided that we would head further inland to try our luck. The valley began to widen into a large lake, and we saw a small herd of caribou.

Several hours had gone by and still no fresh sign of muskox. Our hopes of finding some were fading. Don had spotted some more caribou and had decided to stalk them, determined not to return home empty-handed. Soon, in the distance, George and I watched as two caribou fell from the bewildered herd. Leaving Don to butcher his animals, George and I headed toward another lake that was to the northeast of our location. Upon reaching the lake, I spotted three muskox running across it. The animals were moving quickly, heading for the rocky hills that surrounded the lake.

Leaving George, I headed across the ice on foot. At that point, the animals had disappeared over a hill. Once I reached the hilltop, there was nothing in sight except one lone bull grazing in a small valley to the south. I quickly moved down the hill and along a small ridge that separated the animal and me. Upon reaching the point that I felt would give me a good shot, I loaded my Ruger Model No. 1 in .30-06 and advanced slowly over the rise.

I was about 200 yards from the bull when he came into view, and he immediately started running up the hill. Aiming just behind the left front shoulder, I squeezed the trigger. The muskox stopped and turned slightly. I reloaded and fired again. The animal jumped forward, then dropped on his knees, digging his horns into the snow. It was a long job of skinning and cutting up the meat. We finally got loaded and started home in the dark, only to get ourselves lost on the sea ice. We waited there until daylight and then returned home.

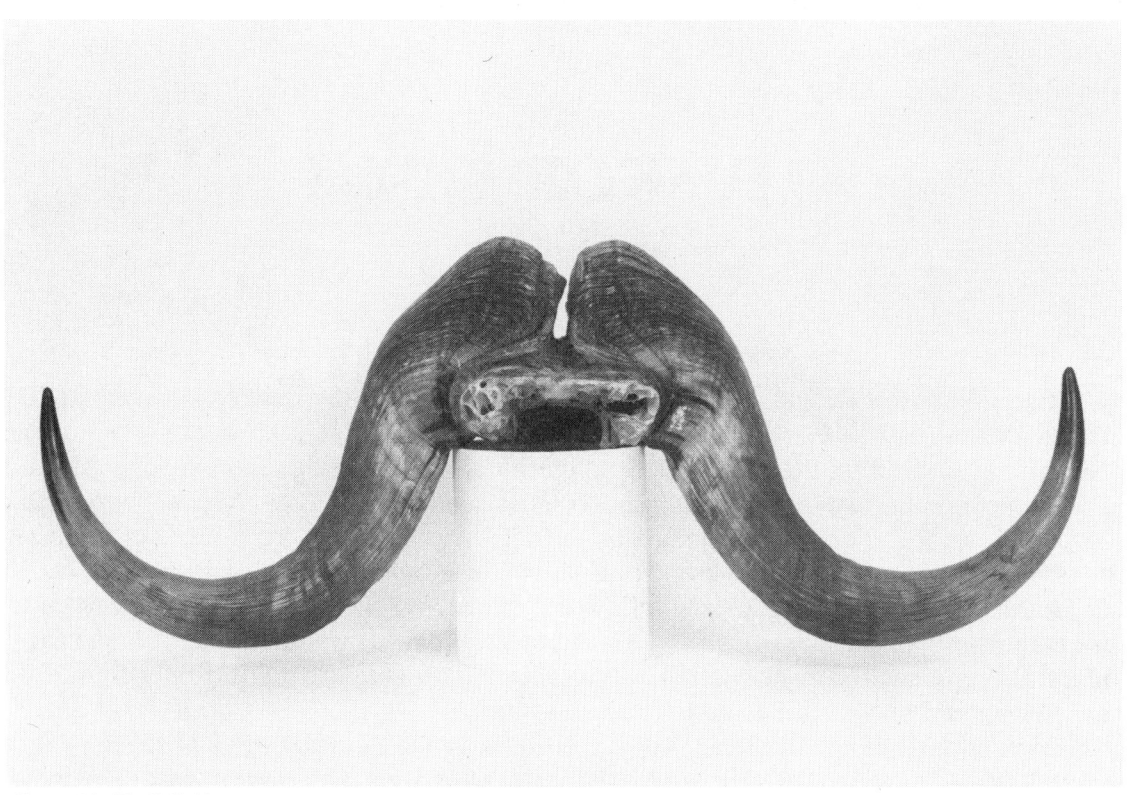

Photograph by Wm. H. Nesbitt

MUSKOX
HONORABLE MENTION
SCORE: 115-2/8
Locality: Perry Island, N.W.T. Date: April 1988
Hunter: Richard A. Jones

MUSKOX 115-2/8

Richard A. Jones

There is always a bit of rivalry between a father and son, and with Dick Jones and his father, Bob Jones, there is no exception to this rule. Their muskox hunt to Victoria Island, Northwest Territories, in March of 1988, produced two exceptional trophies for them, with Dad Jones' trophy becoming the all-time number two ever taken, and son Richard's being recognized as one of the finest in the three-year entry period of the 20th Awards.

The hunt took place during the first week of April 1988. There were six hunters in the party, and several of them took nice bulls almost immediately. Dick and his father held-out for larger trophies. In fact, they had instructed their guides that they wanted big, old trophies, or none at all. They would either have a real trophy, or just happy memories of the experience.

Dick and his father had elected to hunt together. On the fourth day of the hunt, they spotted a band of seven muskox in a white bowl, about three miles from them. Careful evaluation of them through the spotting scope showed that they were all bulls, and two of them were very good trophies. Dick and his guide elected to try to stalk them, while Bob and his guide watched through the spotting scope. There was a low, rocky ridge that would provide cover for the stalk.

The stalk took two hours, and it was ended by the crack by Dick's .270. One shot was all it took. He had taken the largest bull in the bunch and he was very happy indeed.

The green score of Dick's muskox showed it to be over 117 points, likely to end-up being one of the best muskox ever taken, and perhaps the largest one taken by a sport hunter in that area. It was a fine ending to a classic father-son hunting trip.

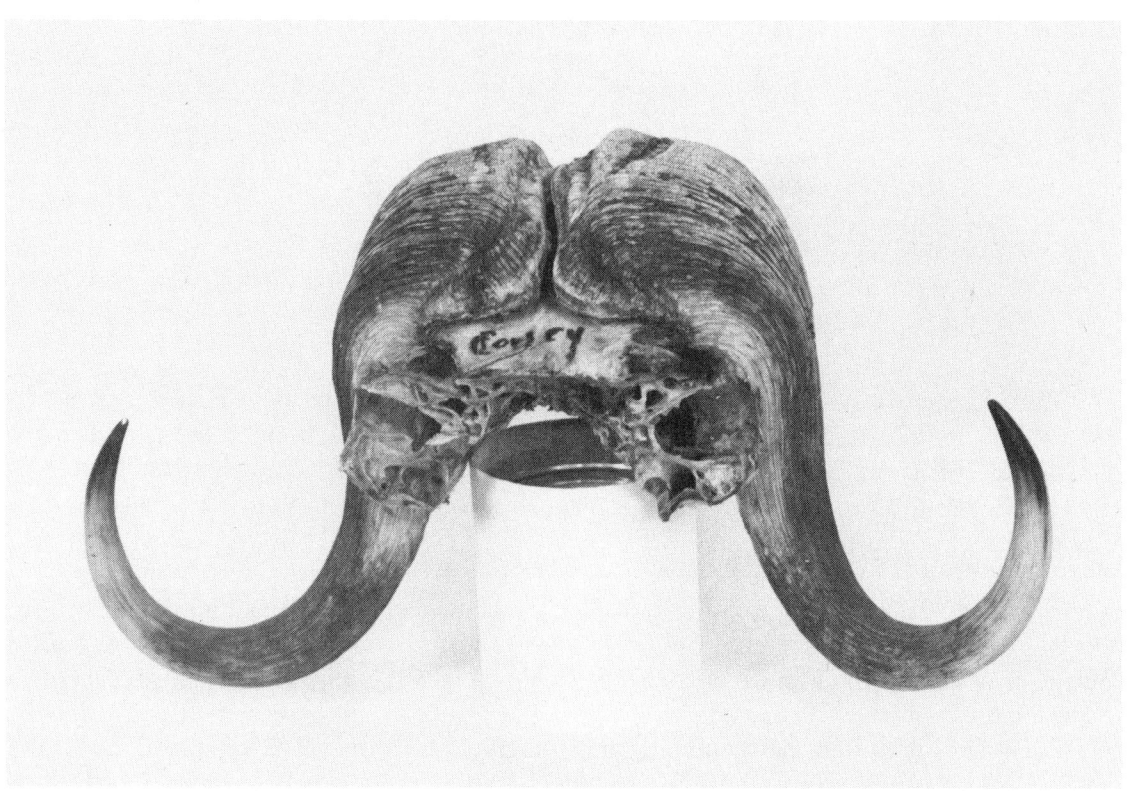

Photograph by Wm. H. Nesbitt

MUSKOX
HONORABLE MENTION
SCORE: 114-4/8
Locality: Banks Island, N.W.T.   Date: November 1985
Hunter: Don L. Corley

MUSKOX 114-4/8

Don L. Corley

I arrived in Sachs Harbor late in October, 1985, on a hunting trip for Peary's caribou and muskox. The Peary's only needed to be respectable, but the muskox was a totally different story. After a half-dozen hunts out of Sachs with Henry Nasogaluak, John Lucas, and Roger Kuptana for polar bear and muskox, this was "old-hat" to me.

A year earlier, Roger and I decided to go after a new World's Record muskox. After lots of looking and doing my homework, I had learned to score muskox at a glance.

First thing to do was to pack supplies for a long trip. Our game plan from the year before was to get the caribou as quickly as possible, which we did. Then we headed out for Masick Pass. No sport hunter had ever gone that far north!

Roger knew that in late October and early November, herds of muskox congregate in the Masick Pass area by the hundreds. Our strategy was to go there, set up camp on a high cliff, then use our spotting scopes to look for a monster.

We traveled around the pass to come up on the high cliff from the back side. When we arrived, we saw an unbelievable sight. As far as the eye could see, straight ahead, to the right, and to the left, were herds of muskox. We immediately set up our double-wall tents, put down caribou skins inside, and started the kerosene heater. By now, it was close to dark, so we just glassed a little and then retired in the tent for the night.

Early next morning, we set up two spotting scopes and started looking. I now knew how the Indians felt when they rode up on a high cliff and saw thousands of bison down below. We were looking at hundreds of muskox, stretching as far as we could see, probably five miles in three directions.

Down in the bottom of the pass were dozens of 8 to 10-foot-wide dry creeks running every direction, making stalks easy. As long as we stayed 300 yards away and downwind, the muskoxen wouldn't spook. If they did, they would only go a few hundred yards to stop and settle down.

On the third day of looking, and after several dozen stalks, we came upon five old bulls in a creek bottom. We crawled to within 50 feet of them. These five looked different from all the others; they were a different color, had dull gray horns, and twice the amount of hair on their necks. John said, "Look at that one!" Roger said, "Yeah, but look at that one!" All of a sudden I yelled, "Yes, but look at that monster!" It was "Ole Evil Eyes!"

The first four were in the 100 to 115 point range, but Ole Evil Eyes was 125 points plus. We had crawled 10-15 yards, so my gun lay 10 yards behind us in the snow. I asked John Lucas to get my gun.

This muskox looked like a cape buffalo in the eyes. I told Roger not to take his eyes off Ole Evil Eyes. As John crawled back with my rifle, a sudden snow flurry hit us! All five bulls went into a small circle and changed places. Trying to find the big one again was tricky as they were stirring around. Suddenly, they burst out like a covey of quail. Two went to the right, two to the left, and one straight out.

We tracked them for several hours and found three of the five, but not Ole Evil Eyes. He was long-gone! Just before dark, we returned to camp, ate, had tea, and went to bed.

Next morning, up early and looking again, we had to make a decision. I was supposed to be back in Anchorage in three days to meet Bob Kubick, who was taking me for my no. 30 of the North American 30, Sitka blacktail deer. I could either be late meeting Bob or hunt only one more day. It was now November 3, 1985. By noon, we hadn't seen what we were looking for, so we stopped for lunch. By one o'clock, we were back looking again.

About an hour later, and one mile below us, out of the creek came eight or 10 bulls. One looked extra large, so we all studied him and agreed that he was the best we had seen since we spotted Ole Evil Eyes the previous day. We figured he was around 115 in score.

It took us about an hour to work our way down behind the muskox and also stay downwind. About 100 yards from them, at 3:30 p.m., I decided to take him. The .270 put him down and I followed up with one more in the neck. Sure enough, by rough score we added up 116. No, it wasn't Ole Evil Eyes, but it was a bull that should go in the top ten, and that's quite a trophy, eh?

For the next two days, Mother Nature was good to me. I made all the flights and met Bob Kubick in Anchorage right on time. The Sitka hunt was fantastic, but that's another story. It did finish my North American 30 Collection!

Photographs Courtesy of Susan D. Sherer and Jerry D. Lees

(l) A bowhunting trip to Banks Island, N.W.T., in 1986 yielded this muskox for Susan D. Sherer. Her bull scores 104-6/8 points. (r) The temperature was five degrees below zero when Jerry D. Lees took this muskox in 1988 along the Canning River in Alaska. It scores 100-2/8 points.

Photograph Courtesy of Alan J. Quimby

Alan J. Quimby shot this muskox in 1987 on Twin Mountain in the southeastern corner of Nunivak Island, Alaska. It scores 102-6/8 points.

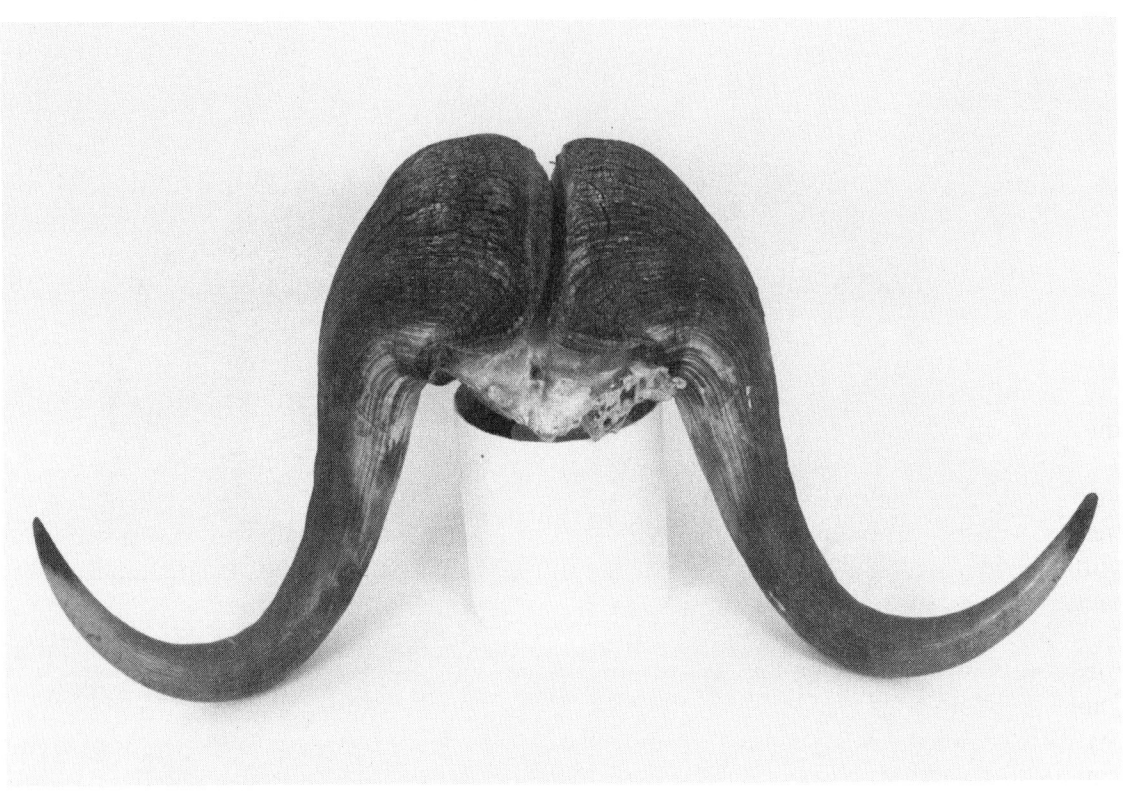

Photograph by Wm. H. Nesbitt

MUSKOX
HONORABLE MENTION
SCORE: 113-4/8
Locality: Ellice River, N.W.T.   Date: September 1988
Hunter: Steve Munier

MUSKOX 113-4/8

Steve Munier

September 11, 1989, is certainly a day that I will never forget and one that will go into the books (the Boone and Crockett books that is.)

My name is Steve Munier and I've been bowhunting for 16 years or so, and I have been very fortunate to bowhunt most of the North American big-game animals. The whitetails here in south-central Michigan have been giving me the biggest education in how to hunt with bow and arrow, and I've had more than my share of luck with them, so I figured a muskox should be a cake walk.

I read an article written by Chuck Adams about muskox hunting in the Northwest Territories. It was more than just interesting to me. In his article, he included the name and phone number of the outfitter. After a few phone calls, the hunt was booked and, much to my surprise, they had a fall hunt instead of the typical March, minus-70-degree hunts, and you could also hunt the Central Canada barren ground caribou at the same time. Boy, was my blood boiling and again my wife heard, "It's a hunt-of-a-lifetime."

This trip was in the making for about a year, and after all those dreams of those big, hairy, prehistoric-looking animals, our Twin Otter plane was making our final approach to land on the soft tundra, turning those dreams into reality. We were at the Ellice River in the Northwest Territories.

After two full days of airline travel to reach Cambridge Bay, I was on our final commercial flight when I met the other members of the hunting group. All of them were gun-hunters and true sportsmen.

I was a minority, hunting with bow-and-arrow, and they razzed me a bit, especially upon getting-off the plane. At camp, it was FLAT ground with no apparent cover and the wind blowing 40 to 50 mph. One of them said, "You can use the spare rifle I brought if you would like." Not wanting to show my real fears, I stated, "It may still work out," not wanting to agree with him.

Upon arrival at the camp, we were greeted by our camp manager, Tudor Howard Davies. He filled us in on the previous hunters' success and the current weather reports. Rain and snow with high winds kept us in camp for three days. It gets a bit much after one day, much less three. Day four was much different, calm weather and sunny.

Cal and I were paired-up to hunt with "Allen," our Inuit guide. The plan was that if I could not get close enough for a shot at a muskox or caribou and it was a trophy, Cal would try for it. As it turned out, we spotted a muskox about noon. When you see a muskox, you know that you are in the North Country. WOW, what a sight! It's almost as if you are in a time warp.

There was no cover available, so I manned the video camera and got excellent footage of Cal downing his trophy. In the same frame, you could see caribou everywhere. Then the work started. It took us two hours just to skin the beast. The wet hide seemed to be 200 pounds alone. It was a good experience, as there wasn't much pre-hunt reading material available on muskox. I had the opportunity to see how thick the hair really was and how big the animals really are. With printed material stating that muskox weigh between 450 and 1,200 pounds, my best estimate is that they weigh approximately 700 pounds, but no more than 800 pounds for the biggest bull. It was nightfall by the time we got back to camp. Four of the other hunters had filled-out on trophy muskox, all scoring around 110.

That night, the winds and rain came back and once again we stayed in our sleeping bags for two more days. We were on a 10 day hunt and we were already seven days into it and I hadn't even had a chance to hunt yet.

Day eight wasn't too appealing weather-wise, but I was determined. I stalked-up on three muskox, with each one resulting in no arrows being shot. On the last stalk, I crawled almost a half-mile only to discover that the last 200 yards had a lake between us. The fog rolled-in, which finalized that day. Upon our return to camp, everyone was anxious to find out how I did. They were all rooting for me and it brought my enthusiasm back.

After four lengthy stalks on other muskox, this one was coming together much better. I had spotted the animal sleeping near a large boulder on a ridge, approximately a mile away. The plan was to circle the ridge and come over the top on the back side to where it appeared to be about a 30 yard shot. The wind was in my favor, and in about an hour, I was at the top of the ridge looking down at him.

The bull was awake and looking at the flatlands below. Not satisfied with a 40 yard shot, I crawled closer, with the boulder partially between us. At about 30 yards, the big muskox's sixth sense kicked-in. He stood up and started to trot off, quartering away from me. I stood up, instinctively drew, and released. The muskox caught the arrow at about 50 to 55 yards in the derriere, with the broadhead severing the femoral artery. The bull ran to another hill about 200 yards away and lay down. I sneaked around the back side of him and buried one to the feathers through the liver and one lung; it wasn't even needed. I had connected on a fine trophy, but little did I know at the time how big his horns really were.

What adds to the hunt for me is that one hour earlier I turned-down a muskox at 20 yards. We had walked-up on that one and it would have been an easy shot, but Allen, my guide, said we could do better. After the animal spooked, I was thinking to myself "a bird in the hand."

On the last day of the hunt I decided to take Cal up on that spare rifle and I collected two magnificent Central Canada barren ground caribou.

During my 3-1/2 days of hunting, I saw about 22 bull muskox (no cows or yearlings), about 10,000 resident caribou, and 10 wolves, ranging in colors from white to black. The muskox and caribou records book possibilities are unreal. The outfitter, Canada North Outfitting, Inc. was very professional. If I had to do the hunt over, I would not change a thing and I highly recommend the hunt.

For the archery tackle buffs, I was shooting a custom-made Cascade Archery/Steve Gorr take-down recurve that I've been shooting for several years. It has brought me a lot of confidence. String it up and go hunting. It's extremely light weight and takes more abuse than any weapon should. I have to give credit to where it is deserved; if it were not for this bow, I probably would not have gotten this trophy.

Photograph by Wm. H. Nesbitt

MUSKOX
HONORABLE MENTION
SCORE: 111-2/8
Locality: Perry River, N.W.T.   Date: March 1987
Hunter: Douglas G. Williams

MUSKOX 111-2/8

Douglas G. Williams

My muskox hunt arrangements were made through Jerome Knap with Canada North Outfitting, Inc. I left Denver, Colorado, on March 12, 1987 at 9:10 a.m., and after five plane changes, I finally arrived in Cambridge Bay, Yukon Territory, on March 13, 1987, at 1:20 p.m. At the airport in Cambridge Bay, I met Bill Cobb from Cody, Wyoming; Bob Hansen from Greenwich, Connecticut; and Greg Shaw from Garden City, Kansas, with all of them scheduled for the same hunt. We were met at the airport by Bill Tarr, Manager of the Hunters and Trappers Association. He took us to our hotel and, after a one day wait in Cambridge Bay, we purchased our license and tag for the muskox hunt. At this time, we were given a full set of caribou-skin clothes to use for the hunt.

On March 15th, we took a bush plane to Perry River. Perry River is an old Hudson Bay Trading Post that has been closed for many years. When I stepped off the plane, I did not have a face cover on and my cheeks immediately froze, with the skin rising-up like boils. We stayed in a couple of old, empty shacks that had been abandoned when the trading post had closed.

On March 16th, we were divided into two groups, with two hunters and two guides per group. We spent the day preparing for the hunt on the following day.

On March 17th, we finally got to hunt. At 7:30 a.m. we were taken afield on sleds drawn by snowmobiles. After glassing numerous muskox, caribou, wolves, and even one wolverine, I found the muskox I wanted about 10:30 a.m. Since you cannot stalk from the sled, I started off on foot and finally made the kill at 4:30 p.m. My muskox's entry score for the records was 116.

Photograph by Wm. H. Nesbitt

BIGHORN SHEEP
FIRST AWARD
SCORE: 192-1/8

Locality: Deer Lodge Co., Mont. Date: September 1987
Hunter: Mitchell A. Thorson

BIGHORN SHEEP 192-1/8

Mitchell A. Thorson

It was truly the luck of the draw! I have been trying to draw a bighorn sheep tag for over 20 years in Montana and other states. It starts out when I picked up the mail on August 17, 1987. When I opened up the letter from Montana, I let out a hoot. First thing I did was to call all of my hunting buddies to tell them of my good fortune. Next I called Jim Ford in Missoula, Montana, who was then western region director for the Montana Fish, Wildlife and Parks Department. We talked for over an hour about the area that I had drawn (area 213 Anaconda) and about the rams that Jim and others had been seeing. Jim told me that there were about 12 rams that would score over 180 Boone and Crockett points and about five rams over 190 points. Boy, I was ready to leave right then. I asked Jim if he could put me in touch with a guide; he said that he would see what he could do and that he would call me back the following evening.

I hardly slept a wink that night, and I drove my wife Vennie nuts. Well, Jim called and said for me to call a sheep hunting buddy of his, Jerry Hurni. I called Jerry and we made our deal. Jerry jacked-me-up even more, telling me about the huge rams that are in area 213. He also told me that Jim Ford would like to go along. The season started the 15th of September, so he wanted me there on the 10th.

I hunt as much as I can get away with, so I had all of my gear ready by the next day. Jerry and Jim both told me that it should be a good possibility that I would harvest a book ram. I have been lucky enough to take three book blacktail deer and one book mule deer and this last December a book Coues' deer.

A week before I was to go, I came down with blood poisoning. So, I called Jerry who said no problem. Well, the next day I received a call from Jerry's daughter and she told me that her dad, Jerry Hurni, and Jim Ford were killed in a plane crash early that morning. I was in shock; these were two avid sportsmen and a real asset to all of the fine work to make the Montana sheep herds what they are today.

After a couple of days I called a sheep hunter friend of mine, Don Turner of Santa Rosa, Caifornia, and asked him what he thought I should do. He said to call Jack Atcheson, Jr.; that Atcheson is an excellent guide and he lives in Butte, Montana. Well, I called him and we talked; he said the same thing: lots of big rams. He said to let him call a friend of his, Tim Magness, who is a sheep hunter who lives at the base of the mountain range that we were going to hunt and that he would get back to me the next day. Well, Jack called back and told me that he and Tim had looked at 55 rams that day and they had spotted at least six that would make the book. Jack and I had made our deal and, being that I was still under the weather with blood poisoning, the doctor would release me on Sept. 18, 1987. I would meet Jack Jr. on the 19th.

I left Santa Rosa at 1 p.m. on Sept. 18th. I drove straight through and got to Butte about 3 p.m. on the 19th. Jack had already left for Anaconda. So I headed for Anaconda, about 45 minutes from Butte. I called Tim's house and his wife Mary said to come out as Jack and Tim were setting-up a camp. They live right at the base of the mountain in the most fantastic setting that you have ever seen. Jack and Tim still were not back yet, so I set up my spotting scope in Tim's yard and saw 12 ewes and lambs and six mule deer does. I told Mary that I was going to head back toward Anaconda and glass from the main road. I stopped and set up the scope again, spotting five rams in an upper basin, with one of them looking pretty good. I glassed till dark and then went back to Tim's house. As I pulled-in, so did Jack and Tim. We introduced ourselves, told a few stories, and then took off for Jack's camp.

We got to camp and got ready for the next morning and told some more stories. Jack had already taken four sheep hunters and harvested four bighorns in the unlimited area. I was to be his fifth hunter. I drew the only non-resident sheep license in area 213, and there had already been six of the 11 sheep tags filled and three of them were over 180 points. Man, oh man, was I ready! I hardly slept a wink. We got up at 3:30 a.m. Jack asked if I was hungry. I said, "No, let's do it." We packed lunch, candy bars, some trail mix and jerky from home, and took off.

We put our packs on and started going up the mountain. After four sheep hunts, I guess you can figure that Jack was in "sheep shape;" in fact, I think that he is half-sheep himself. I have hunted all over our western states and Canada, so my 48-year-old body was ready for this hunt.

We got about two-thirds of the way up the mountain and waited until daylight. About the time that we could see, Jack spotted 12 rams in a basin, so we set up our spotting scopes and took a look. Out of the 12 rams, there were four good ones, with two in the records book class. We bailed-off the ridge that we were on and went up the next one, below where the 12 rams were feeding. After about an hour, we worked ourselves within 50 yards of the rams. We were in the timber and the rams were still feeding, not knowing that they had some company. There were sheep beds and droppings all around us in the timber. We lay there, looking and scoring all of the rams; one we figured would go about 184 points and the other about 188. We figured the largest to have horns of 39 and 40 inches and 17 inch bases, and probably 9-1/2 years old. There were 4-1/2-year-old rams that went 40 inches in that bunch. Jack asked what I thought. I said that this was the first day and the first two hours; we should pass on them. I was hoping that I had not made a big mistake.

We went on up and over the top, into a drainage from Lost Creek that Tim Magness called the Rams Hole, where he had guided for rams that had scored up to 197 points. It was a fantastic basin: alpine lakes, shale slides, big head-walls, and lots of timber.

We spent the rest of the day walking, glassing, and covering the whole area. There were sheep signs and ram tracks everywhere. But, we did not see any sheep. I had looked at a pass with a sheep trail that just looked like you would see something at any moment from about 20 different places. At a lunch stop at one of these locations, I had left my fanny pack, so Jack went back to look for it. He jumped the five rams that I had seen from the main road the previous day. Jack got back with my pack. It was getting late, so Jack suggested we head back and go back over the mountain to look for the 12 rams that we had passed up early that morning.

On the way back, we stopped one last time to glass the Ram Hole. Well, we were sitting in a shale slide in the timber, glassing, and Jack was about 10 feet below me. I looked back at that same sheep trail again and I spotted a ram that would go about 170. I kept glassing and spotted a keeper! Jack was looking in the same area, so I figured that he was sizing him up. This went on for a couple of minutes until I asked if the upper one was a shooter. Jack asked, "What upper one?" Jack moved back up to me and then saw the rams. There was a tree in the way before and that's why he had not seen the rams.

Jack said it was my choice but the bigger ram would go about 195 points. I said, "Let's harvest him!" We were about 550 yards from the ram. In the meantime, the big ram bedded-down and the other one was still feeding. Jack said he did not think that we could get any closer and he asked me if I could take the ram from where we were. I said that I could but that it was a bad shot and I would prefer to get closer. We made a classic stalk and got within 225 yards. I shoot a .270 built on a Springfield action that I call "My Old Rusty Pipe." I load my own shells with 60 grains of IMR 4831 with a 130 grain Nosler partition bullet.

Well, it was 6:30 p.m. and we were about 225 yards from a trophy-of-a-lifetime, and the ram had gone to sleep. I couldn't believe it. I got set up and Jack was glassing. I put a bullet from my Old Rusty Pipe right behind his wing, the ram jerked his head and rolled over. The other ram was gone in a flash. Jack and I both let out a whoop and took-off toward the ram. Well Jack (as I said before, he is half-sheep himself) got to the ram in about 15 minutes; it took me about 30 minutes. Jack was yelling, "You won't believe the size of this puppy." When I got to the ram, I was in shock. I pulled out the tape and he went 43-1/4 by 43-1/2 and 17 inch bases. What a ram! It was getting dark, so we took pictures and started caping. We took the head and cape out with us and hung the meat up to come back for the next morning.

We got to Tim's house about 12:30 a.m., measured the ram again, had a cold beer, and went back to camp. We didn't sleep a wink. This was the biggest bighorn that Jack had ever guided for, and a trophy-of-a-lifetime for me. We got to Tim's at 4 a.m. and started up the mountain for the meat. On the way up, we spotted 25 rams, with the two big ones that we had passed-up the day before. Tim asked if I wanted to get a little closer and watch them. I did. Jack, Tim, and I got within 200 yards of them and set up the scopes. We watched them for about two hours; it was great. We then packed-out the meat. On the way back, we ran into about 75 ewes and lambs.

I would like to thank Jack Atcheson, Jr., Tim Magness, the Anaconda and Butte Sportsman Assoc., and the Montana Dept. of Fish, Wildlife and Parks for all of their work to put these bighorn sheep back on the mountains and manage them for all the lucky hunters that draw a tag. We who take from the mountains should help to put back on the mountains.

Photograph by Wm. H. Nesbitt

BIGHORN SHEEP
SECOND AWARD
SCORE: 190-5/8
Locality: Missoula Co., Mont.   Date: September 1986
Hunter: Chris L. Mostad

BIGHORN SHEEP 190-5/8

Chris L. Mostad

Chris Mostad was successful in drawing one of Montana's coveted bighorn sheep permits the first year that he applied, 1986. Chris knew an individual's odds for drawing a sheep permit were not good and he did not even consider applying until he was encouraged to do so by John Ottman, a taxidermist and long-time friend.

John had drawn a permit the year before for Petty Creek in Missoula County and had taken a nice trophy. At the time, John was a forester and he knew where the sheep were in Petty Creek, and how to hunt them. John agreed to guide him if Chris drew a permit.

Once Chris had his permit in hand, he and John planned their sheep-hunting strategy. They planned to glass the sheep area in Petty Creek from logging roads on U.S. Forest Service and Champion timber lands. Once they spotted a herd of decent rams, they would plan their stalk. Chris planned on hunting at least 17 days during the season. If he didn't have his ram by the last week of sheep season, he planned to take a week's vacation. John advised against hiking into the area and scouting prior to sheep season, since he already knew where the sheep were and did not want to spook them. So Chris and his wife, Jamie, spotted sheep from logging roads prior to the season to get familiar with the sheep in Petty Creek.

The first weekend of the season, the area was "socked-in" by the weather. The clouds were so low and so dense that Chris and John could not see more than a few yards, let alone glass sheep on the opposite hillside. Chris knew the weather conditions were poor before he left home, but he just wanted to get out and do some walking in the hills. That afternoon, they spotted a few young rams in Horse Gulch but decided to call it a day.

On the second weekend, the weather was much nicer. There was no fog and the temperature was in the mid to low 40's. Around 2:30 p.m., they were packing-up and planning their hunt for the next day. Before they left, they went back to Spring Creek, an area they had glassed earlier in the day, and spotted four rams. Instead of quitting, they reassessed their situation and figured that they could cover the distance to the rams and be back by dark if they didn't see anything worth taking.

They got within range of the rams about 6 p.m. The rams hadn't moved more than 20 yards since they were first spotted and they were bedding down for the night. Two rams were already bedded down and the other two appeared to be looking for the right spot. Two of the rams were in the low to mid-180 point range. Certainly they were trophy sheep, but both John and Chris felt they could do better in Petty Creek if Chris held-out a little longer. Besides, he still had most of the season to hunt.

As they turned to head back to the vehicle, they spotted two more rams bedded down near the tree line. In short order, John and Chris worked their way to within 250 yards of the bedded rams.

Chris selected the larger ram and touched-off his first shot. Both rams jumped up but were unable to determine where the shot came from. They milled around for a moment before the larger ram took the lead across a large rock slide. Chris moved a little closer and took his ram on the third shot. With that third shot, the ram bolted for cover where Chris found it a short time later. They had just enough time to cape-out the ram and get it on pack boards before it got dark. They made their way down the mountain in the dark, using their flashlights, and arrived back at the truck about midnight.

Chris considers himself really lucky. Not only was he able to draw the coveted permit and take a trophy sheep, he was especially lucky to have John guiding him into the hunting area. He's certain that he could not have taken such a magnificent ram without John's help.

Photographs Courtesy of Karen Throckmorton and Valentino J. Pugnea

(l) Karen Throckmorton took this bighorn sheep in 1987 in Rock Creek, Montana. This ram scores 183-4/8 points. (r) Valentino J. Pugnea and heavily-broomed desert sheep that scores 170-2/8 points. He took this ram in 1987 in the Kofa Mountains in Arizona.

Photograph Courtesy of Nick J. Gianopoulos

This bighorn sheep was taken by Nick J. Gianopoulos in the Wallowa Mountains of northeastern Oregon in 1986. It scores 188-7/8 points.

Photograph by Wm. H. Nesbitt

DESERT SHEEP
FIRST AWARD
SCORE: 182-2/8
Locality: Graham Co., Ariz.   Date: December 1986
Hunter: Beverly M. Nuessle

DESERT SHEEP 182-2/8

Beverly M. Nuessle

There he was, with my cross hairs right on him. He was the biggest and prettiest ram I had ever seen. I didn't realize at the time that being drawn for a desert bighorn sheep was cause for such a big celebration. I was told that many hunters have waited a lifetime for the opportunity to hunt this particular animal. In spite of the highest drawing odds in the state per unit, I was drawn for the Aravaipa Canyon Wilderness Area. My husband, Mark, and I were elated, to say the least.

Mark quickly set about securing the best bighorn sheep guide possible. After much research, we found Floyd Krank to be our choice because of his reputation for record rams.

The next step in preparation included climbing Squaw Peak to get in shape, and time spent at the range to practice with my rifle. During this time we, with our sons Gentry and Ty, started going with Floyd on scouting trips. Of course, we were out to find the largest and prettiest ram in the area. On two early season scouting trips, we saw more than 100 sheep, many of them rams. We took many rolls of pictures for careful examination.

Two days prior to the hunt, we met with the full hunting party to make camp. The party included Floyd, his wife Mary, his three assistant guides, Mark, and me. All of us were excited. We soon were to find the true meaning of Mark's favorite saying, "What's the worst that can happen?"

On opening day, I became very ill but I wasn't about to pass up a once-in-a-lifetime sheep permit. We decided that day to pass up a top ram in hopes of finding a big ram that we had scouted. Then, a weather front moved in.

We continued looking in vain until the third day. It was a cold and rainy afternoon at camp. A rancher rode into our camp with the big ram we wanted hung over his saddle. The ram had tried to get through the original sheep enclosure fence, became hung in the fence by his hind leg, and died. We were happy for the rancher, although disappointed, since the ram scored 180 points.

The fourth evening, in a hail thunderstorm, lighting struck a few yards from our cook tent while we were all in it. This was just moments after Mark's, "What's the worst that can happen?" was repeated. To make matters worse, I was being followed everywhere by several men we thought to be from the Game and Fish Dept. They used spotting scopes to watch our every move. When we confronted them in the field, they were rude, belligerent, and downright nasty. On the sixth day of the hunt, Floyd made complaints to Game and Fish

Dept. officials. Fortunately, Area Manager Collins Cochrane came to our aid. We asked him to accompany our group for the remainder of the hunt. The men with the spotting scopes disappeared.

On the fifth day, we found the ewes and lambs that our second-choice ram had been travelling with. The sixth day, I was feeling better. Snow and high winds stayed with us. By 2:30 p.m., we located the ram I wanted. He was with a large band of sheep that had a couple of other rams in the 170 point class. It was too late to chance a shot. Floyd and Mark thought it best to bed him down and try in the morning. I was so nervous and worried that I would blow this one-and-only chance, I didn't sleep all night.

We woke up to find a beautiful, clear, star-filled sky. It was very cold; ice everywhere and the ground was frozen. Mark had the video camera, catching the beauty of the morning.

In all the practice I had done from all different positions, I was not prepared for this. I had never practiced on my stomach on the edge of a canyon that was at least 300 yards across. There he was. I placed the cross hairs on the ram and slowly squeezed the trigger. The shot was true. Waiting a few minutes, and looking through spotting scopes, we saw the ram slowly roll over and, with all four legs in the air, drop about 15 feet to a ledge. After several moments of anxiety, it got rather emotional. After two hours of descent, I could finally place my hands on my trophy. The Boone and Crockett green score at the Game and Fish Dept. was 184-6/8 points. What a neat feeling.

This has been the most wonderful experience for me. Getting a beautiful desert bighorn, meeting wonderful people, and making good friends. Hunting has become a part of my life now, something I can enjoy with my husband and our family.

Photographs Courtesy of Alan D. Maynard and Jeffrey D. Wallis

(l) Alan D. Maynard killed this desert sheep that scores 168 points near McPherson Pass in Yuma County, Arizona, in 1987. (r) Jeffrey D. Wallis perched in the craggy reaches of the Talkeetna Mountains in Alaska with his Dall's sheep that scores 168-6/8 points.

Photograph Courtesy of William P. Williamson

The horns on this Stone's sheep that William P. Williamson took in 1987 on Rose Mountain, Yukon Territory, measure 44-7/8 inches on each side. The ram scores 178 points.

Photograph by Wm. H. Nesbitt

DALL'S SHEEP
FIRST AWARD
SCORE: 171-1/8

Locality: Chugach Mts., Alaska   Date: August 1988
Hunter: Emil V. Nelson

DALL'S SHEEP 171-1/8

Emil V. Nelson

On August 17, 1988, my teenaged son, Tom, and I were happily headed up the Glenn Highway toward the sheep hills of the eastern Chugach Range. We had put away our commercial fishing gear about a week earlier than usual and could therefore take advantage of a good weather streak that south-central Alaska was currently experiencing. Our destination was a section of the mountains known as the "Tonsina Walk-In Area," where hunter access is limited to human foot travel only, no horses, ATV's or airplanes allowed. I had hunted this area the previous four years and I had learned a lot about the best way to get in and out, plus where the best rams seemed to be located.

Two years ago, I had seen a ram during an aerial reconnaissance. It looked a solid 40 inches and heavy, with a very even "standard" type curl. My oldest son, Rob, and I spent five days trying to find the ram from the ground, but the cloud cover never raised above 4,000 feet. When the weather decided to turn really nasty, we reluctantly hiked on out. The next year we were unable to locate him at all, though son Tom took a nice 39-1/2 by 13 incher in the same location where the big one had been.

The summer of 1988 was a slow year for salmon fishing in Prince William Sound and I had a lot of time to think about where that big ram might have moved if he was still alive. There was one section of canyons and glaciers that we never seemed to get to in our aerial surveys. It was just too out-of-the-way and seemed to be marginal sheep habitat. I asked Terry Holliday, a salmon spotter pilot, to be sure to check that area over if he got near it in his travels.

On our arrival back in Homer at the end of the fishing season, I was met with the urgent message "Call Terry immediately, he's found the big one." A quick phone call revealed that he had seen a big ram, a really big ram, in the area we hadn't gotten to in previous years. His description of the horn characteristics made it seem plausible that it could be the same ram we had seen two years prior. This information really got us charged-up and in a few hours, Tom and I had our gear packed and were making the 10 hour drive to Chitina.

The next morning showed a few clouds moving in as we left our roadside campsite to begin the long, brush-strewn trek into the mountains. The alders formed an ocean of greenery that resisted our advance with its tangled mats of intertwined limbs. Occasional feathery game trails provided relief at opportune times but always seemed to lead us deeper into the thickets. We finally turned uphill and at about 3 p.m. broke out of the alders and onto a steep, rocky slope. We made better time sidehilling from there and at dusk we set up camp within a few miles of the drainage where we believed the ram was living.

When the sky began to lighten-up at daybreak, we could tell that our good weather might not last. Little gusts of wind buffeted our dome tent as clouds rushed by from peak to peak overhead. No rain yet but maybe soon. We picked up camp and moved it about two miles further to the head of the valley. Taking just our packs and guns, we scaled the hogback ridge that shielded us from the basin where the big ram had been seen. We eased over the ridge, ever so slowly, carefully scanning the hillside as it opened up before us. The bottom of the basin was a gigantic snowfield surrounded on three sides by steep slopes of broken rock with patches of feed here and there. Not a sheep did we see as we stood discussing what our next move might be, Tom suddenly said, "Dad! Down there!" Far below us, in the middle of the snowfield lay four rams, all watching us very intently. We could see that one was a real soaker, and as they rose and began moving away, I could see the horn tips of the big one flip well out of his head.

When the last ram went out of sight, I knew there was a good chance they would double back into the high peak to our left, since it had been the best escape terrain. Tom went storming up the slope to intercept them but came back down shortly saying they had indeed doubled back but had beat him over the slope.

About a half-hour later, the rams popped-out on a steep face across from our camp, then moved over the top of that mountain into the next drainage. We immediately dropped back down into the valley, then began climbing the 6,500 foot peak that overlooked the head of the other drainage. Three hours later, we peeked over the top and there they were, bedded down about 600 yards below us, just above a sheer dropoff to a glacier. They were three drainages away from where we spooked them and they seemed to be pretty relaxed. There was no way to approach them, so we decided to wait them out, hoping they would move to a more vulnerable position later in the afternoon.

We spent an enjoyable three hours lazing on the mountaintop, marveling at the big ram through the spotting scope and enjoying the fantastic scenery. The only problem was a dark storm front moving steadily closer from the south. By 5 p.m., they still had not moved and the sky was getting threatening. With no sleeping bags or shelter with us, I decided to force the action. I dropped about 200 feet downslope to the last remaining cover, then fired a shot off over the ram's back. At the report, he leaped to his feet, then hesitantly began working uphill, quartering toward me. Tom and I stayed quiet and in 10 minutes time, the ram was 300 yards away and almost even with me.

About then, the ram turned on a new tack, quartering away, so on his next hesitation, I lined-up on him with my .257 Roberts and touched one off. The 100 grain Nosler Ballistic-Tip, pushed by 40 grains of 4320 at about 3,100 fps, dropped him in his tracks and he began slowly tumbling downslope. Luckily, he hung up in a rockpile and we got to him with two hours daylight to spare.

He was an absolutely magnificent animal, with horns measuring 43-1/2 by 13-1/2 with perfect tips. After some quick photos, we got him caped and boned-out and we tried to beat the storm back to camp. The final descent into our camp valley was made in semi-darkness with a few raindrops pattering about.

That night, the wind gusted and the snow flew, but we were snug in our tent and happy to be there. The morning revealed six inches of snow on the ground around camp but it disappeared after an hour of losing elevation on the way out.

This sheep was entry scored at 173-2/8 and it won First Place in the 1988 FNAWS ram contest. It is truly the ram-of-a-lifetime and a wonderful culmination to my 10 year quest for a big sheep in the glacier country of Alaska.

Photograph by Wm. H. Nesbitt

STONE'S SHEEP
FIRST AWARD
SCORE: 179-1/8
Locality: Muskwa River, B.C.   Date: September 1987
Hunter: Cliff C. Cory

STONE'S SHEEP 179 1/8

Cliff C. Cory

In September of 1987, I had planned a Stone's Sheep hunt in the Muskwa River watershed, in northeast British Columbia. Being a B.C. resident, I've hunted the area for a number of years on my horses and have come to know the area quite well. I have taken a couple of Stone's Sheep that have made the British Columbia records book. (The minimum score for the B.C. Records is 165.)

However, knowing that there were bigger rams in the area, I had to go back. This time, I only had a week to hunt so I made arrangements to fly there. I flew-in the first week of September, from Fort Nelson with three hunting buddies who also wanted sheep.

The first day of our hunt, one of the three took a nice ram. The second day we saw twelve rams, although nothing spectacular. The following day my partner and I spotted some caribou. We decided to stalk them and we both took a couple of nice bulls. Our other two partners were successful in taking a couple of nice, 36 inch rams.

I still didn't have my sheep, so the next couple of days I had some hard glassing to do. On the sixth day, it paid off. I spotted the ram I wanted. He was in a large basin and hard to stalk. He was feeding his way up in the rocks and he was alone, which was a good thing. I knew I had to move fast, as it was late in the day and bad weather was moving in. When I got to where he had been feeding, he was no longer there. I carefully walked over the next knoll and we saw each other at the same time. He was about 20 yards away. He went down with one shot from my .300 Winchester (180 grain Nosler bullet). To put it mildly, I was one happy man!

Photograph by Gene R. Alford

COUGAR
SAGAMORE HILL AWARD
FIRST AWARD
SCORE: 16-3/16

Locality: Idaho Co., Idaho   Date: February 1988
Hunter: Gene R. Alford   Owner: B&C National Collection

COUGAR 16-3/16

Gene R. Alford, hunter
B&C National Collection, owner

For 40 years, I have hunted cougar with hounds; and, hopefully, my 1988 hunt will not be my swan song. The last 30 years, I have hunted in the Selway Bitterroot Wilderness in Idaho each winter, trying to kill a Boone and Crockett record lion. Each winter for the last 20 years, I have hired a ski plane to fly me, my dogs, and camp, into the back country where I hunt for a month or longer. I prefer to start hunting about the first of February, as the weather tends to improve rather than deteriorate after that time.

That was my thought on February 3, 1988. The day dawned clear and cold, and since I had loaded my pickup the day before, all I had to do was to phone the local commercial flyboy and make arrangements for the flight. I called Frank Hill, of Hill Aviation in nearby Grangeville, and told him I was ready to go.

After a 30 mile drive, I arrived at the airport around 9 a.m. and started loading my gear into a 180 Cessna ski plane. I'd done this many times, so I had a pretty good idea of what I was doing. When the load got to within a foot of the headliner, I stuffed my two hounds on top and we were ready for takeoff. The airstrip we were using was long and black, so there was no problem getting airborne. The strip we were going to, however, would be different.

Forty-five minutes later, and 100 miles east, we came to the snow-covered, 900-foot, private airstrip with a double dog-leg. Frank extended the skis below the tires and powered-in around the ridge to the final approach and we splashed down in 18 inches of fresh snow. My work was just beginning.

After unloading the plane, I packed all my gear 200 yards to the campsite. I had to clear snow for a place to set up my tent, then get the stove in place, and cut a good supply of wood. It was dark by the time I was finished, and the stars were out. The night was going to be real cold.

I'm 65 and have been a senior citizen for 10 years already. While I spend most of my life outdoors and take long summer and fall pack trips with my horses and mules, I wasn't ready to run up and down the mountains as I once did. Consequently, I spent the first week getting in condition and breaking the trails. The first three weeks, my dogs started and treed several lions, one of them a big tom and the rest females. None were big enough to consider taking. I was enjoying the action and the solitude.

Then came the morning of February 26th. It was clear and cold, and the snow was hard and crusted. After a good breakfast, I turned the hounds loose and headed for a saddle in a ridge a mile from the river. My dogs reached the saddle first and had a track started by the time I got there. But they'd trailed-off the other side of the ridge, down into the canyon, then up the other side and over the end of a ridge that came down from the high country. Not knowing if they were trailing forwards or backwards on the track, my only choice was to try to stay within hearing of them. In the steep Selway Bitterroot, that's not always easy. I headed up, staying on top of the ridge they'd crossed. From there, I could hear them well enough to know the direction they were going.

Three hours of uphill climbing later, I found where the dogs and lion had crossed the ridge that I was on. After another hour of steep climbing on snow that was getting soft, I could hear the dogs barking treed. They were still a long way off.

When I finally got to the scene, I found the cougar treed on a steep, north-facing hillside, in a tree that had fallen downhill and was not lying in the tops of others. When I saw it, I realized for the first time that my dogs had treed the cougar that I had spent most of 30 years looking for. It had been a long time since 1961, when the lion I killed that year had challenged Teddy Roosevelt's record cougar. I would take this cat.

The big lion was nervous and wanted to get out of the tree. I was nervous and didn't want him to jump. I had already gone farther down the mountain than I'd wanted, and I did not want him to jump and go even farther down into the canyon. It was already going to be a long trip out.

Light conditions for picture taking were very poor but I tried a few photos anyway, while the cat was still in the tree. Then I tied-up my dogs in case I had a cripple, a situation that can get dogs hurt or killed. The shots were at close range and the two slugs in the ribs from the .357 Mag (Model 19 Smith and Wesson pistol) put an end to the excitement.

Skinning the heavy cat on the steep hillside in two feet of snow was no small job. An hour later, I had his hide and head on my back and had started up the mountain. In another hour it was growing dusk and I was only on top of the first ridge. Camp was still miles and hours away.

I can only estimate the cat's live weight, but from experience and the size of the hide (laid-out on a log, it was 9 feet, 7 inches long) I'd put it at 225 pounds. While I would later find that the hide and head weighed 42 pounds and my backpack 18, the entire load felt like it weighed 100.

It was dark when I hiked into camp three hours later and the stars were out again. It had been a long 27 years.

Note: This outstanding trophy, taken on an excellent example of the epitome of a Fair Chase hunt, was awarded the coveted Sagamore Hill Award at the 20th NABG Awards. While at the Awards, in the spirit of sharing this exceptional trophy with all sportsmen, Gene Alford donated this skull to the Boone and Crockett Club's National Collection of Heads and Horns, with the collection on continuing display at the Buffalo Bill Historical Center, Cody, Wyoming.

Photograph Courtesy of Dan B. Artery

Dan B. Artery with cougar he took while hunting in Hot Springs County, Wyoming, in 1986. This tom scores 15-3/16 points.

Photograph Courtesy of George L. Kudrick

George L. Kudrick's cougar was taken in Lemhi County, Idaho, in 1987 and it qualified for the Awards records book with a score of 14-13/16.

Photograph Courtesy of Richard C. Farthing

COUGAR
SECOND AWARD
SCORE: 15-11/16

Locality: Idaho Co., Idaho   Date: January 1988
Hunter: Richard C. Farthing

COUGAR 15-11/16

Richard C. Farthing

I could hear the hounds clearly barking "treed" as I climbed nearly vertically out of the deep canyon. My heart was racing with excitement and anticipation as I neared the tree. The hounds were barking at full lung capacity so that you could hardly hear yourself think. Hop and Jeff were already there, staring up through the falling snow flakes as I approached the tree. Hop pointed upward and said, "There he is!" My eyes were straining, trying to penetrate the limbs that obstructed my view.

As I shifted for a better viewpoint, I could hardly believe it had been two years since I first saw the giant lion rug hanging on the cafe wall. I had been elk hunting that fall near Grangeville, Idaho, where we stopped at a cafe for a hot meal. Owning a taxidermy business, I always notice any trophies displayed, and it was very obvious the mountain lion rug I was admiring was the largest I had ever seen. My friend Dave and I taped the cat at over 10 feet from nose to tip-of-tail. After a few hours of visiting with some of the locals, I was pointed in the right direction for a future hunt for a trophy cat.

My dream came true in January of 1988. I put the hunt together with my old friend Gideon "Hop" Jackson, a well known hunter and "houndman" from southern Oregon. I have known Hop for years and have heard people say that, "Where his dogs bark a track, the critter is as good as up the tree." We were to meet Jeff Funke, a young lion hunter from Moscow, Idaho, in a small town on the Clearwater River. After a long and grueling 16 hour drive on snow and ice, we met Jeff. After some introductions and "dog talk," he informed us the weather conditions were perfect. He had cut a large lion track up a deep canyon, three or four miles off any road. He said the cat had made two kills, both being large whitetail deer bucks, and the lion had a foot the size of a small platter.

At this point in the story, I had better go no further without letting you meet the heroes of the hunt. They are: "Tick," a seven-year-old Walker hound, "Hammer," a five-year-old Plott hound, and "Kudor," Jeff's young black-and-tan pup. Anyone who has ever hunted lion knows that without the hounds, there is no lion hunt at all. The dogs and their trainers deserve all the credit.

We started our hunt early the next morning, going up the South Fork of the Clearwater River, out of Elk City. By 9 a.m. of the first morning, we had already turned down two small lions. While looking for tracks, I daydreamed about the lion I had seen in the cafe, wondering what his foot prints would look like in the soft powder-snow. After checking several more lion crossings that Jeff knew of, he said, "Let's go see if that old platter-footed lion has made his circuit again."

When we got to the canyon that the big cat had been working, we decided to split-up and check for tracks. I took the west side of the creek, Hop the east, and Jeff was to work his way up the mountain face to the old buck kills. We were to return within the hour. I had only been gone from the truck about 40 minutes when I spotted the track of a huge lion. I knew it had to be the platter-foot Jeff had told us about. I tried to signal Hop with my whistle, but to no avail. So I decided to mark the tracks and head for the rig. I came off that mountain as if a bear was nipping at my heels.

As I rounded the last switchback in the trail, looking down the canyon, I could see Hop and Jeff were already back. When I reached them, I was gasping for air, trying to breathe and talk at the same time. After a few stuttered, mumbled words, it finally came out. "Big lion and the trail is hot!" In a matter of minutes, the hounds were out of their boxes and Hop and Jeff were being towed up the side of the mountain by the anxious hounds. After gulping down a soda and a candy bar, I was also in hot pursuit.

By the time I reached the first switchback in the trail, I could faintly hear the dogs halfway up the other side of the mountain. Leaving the trail, I dropped straight-off into what some might think was some sort of Hell, for the canyons in the "bitterroots" are deep, dark, and brushy mean. Finally reaching the bottom, I began climbing nearly vertically out of the deep, rugged canyon. I could hear the hounds clearly barking "treed." Standing at the base of the lion's tree, the bitter-cold snow hitting me in the face, I stared upward into the treetops, hoping this cat might equal the great size of the cafe tom. Shifting from side to side, and then backing uphill five or six feet, I could finally make out the shape of the giant cat. His massive head looked like a basketball with fur. The barking dogs filled the canyon silence like thunder. Then, above all the noise, I heard Hop yell, "He's a dandy, take him out; the dogs are tied back and he's all yours!"

After wiping the snow from my scope, I placed the cross hairs on the giant lion's chest. I slowly pulled the trigger of my .243 Remington and, at the crack of the shot, the huge cat tumbled out of the tree, hitting the ground where he lay motionless. As I looked at this magnificent cougar, I somehow knew he was a lion-of-a-lifetime.

The big tom was officially weighed and, with nothing in his stomach, tipped the scales at 184 pounds. His hide measured 9 feet, 10 inches from nose to tip-of-tail, un-stretched. He scored 15-11/16 points for entry into the records.

I would like to say thanks to my good friends Hop, Jeff, Tick, Hammer, and Kudor for making this all possible.

Photograph Courtesy of Mike Barthelmess

Lewis and Clark County, Montana, was the location of Mike Barthelmess' cougar hunt in 1987 that produced this fine tom that scores 15-7/16 points.

Photograph Courtesy of Richard J. Dugas

This cougar scores 15 points to qualify for the all-time records book. It was taken by Richard J. Dugas while bowhunting in Rio Grande County, Colorado, in 1986.

Photograph Courtesy of Harold J. Coult

COUGAR
THIRD AWARD
SCORE: 15-10/16
Locality: Tatla Lake, B.C. Date: January 1986
Hunter: Harold J. Coult

COUGAR 15-10/16

Harold J. Coult

It was mid-morning on the 26th day of January, 1985, when I first sighted my quarry. I will never lose this memory. After stepping on 40 miles of his oversized snow prints for three-and-a-half days, I now faced him at short range. As he stood at a half-crouch, a tangle of deer hair drifted slowly down from a huge jowl. At Doug Schuk's signal, his two dogs, Sooner and Sally, charged wildly, as they voiced four days of suppressed excitement. Doug had made them follow silently behind him until this very moment.

By the time I reached the dead mule deer, the cat and dogs were playing tag several hundred yards away on the edge of an older pine grove. I took only a moment to witness the prime buck, to touch his warm body and observe the method by which a cougar starts its weekly meal.

Doug's 10-year-old son, Edward, had been instructed to stay within 20 feet of me, but now he longed to run headlong after his father, who was attempting to stay in rifle range of the dogs until the cat was treed. Although this was a bow hunt, I knew Doug would shoot to protect us or his two dogs. I just hoped this would not be necessary.

What had begun a month ago in the lunchroom where I work was nearing a climax. I began to put the lid on my emotions and gathered my thoughts for the final act. Here I was, over 650 miles from home near a place called Tatla Lake, B.C., approaching a mountain lion that could easily become a new Pope and Young Club World's Record, armed with a 55-pound, old-style Jennings "T" Star Bow. What stood out was the fact that I had never killed an animal with an arrow, although I had hunted deer and elk for five years and had practiced faithfully.

A coworker, Keith Heldreth, had been after this cat for two years. He convinced me to try this hunt, as he could not possibly take it. When Keith said that his friend, Doug Schuk, had taken the all-time No. 1 Boone and Crockett cougar in this area and had sworn that this cat had a larger body, I was impressed. Added to that, Doug's fee was one-third the going U.S.A. rate for a cougar hunt. This was it! My first, perhaps my only, once-in-a-lifetime guided hunt!

By now, Edward and I had reached the pine grove. Gone were the three-foot snowdrifts and brush tangles of the clearing. As we eased through the forest, Sally began barking treed. Then we saw the cat, about 200 yards ahead and 50 feet up in the largest pine in the area.

When I reached the tree, Doug took Sally and Edward to a vantage point some 50 yards away, leaving Sooner, the more experienced dog, and me to claim the trophy. I will not describe the next half-hour except to say that both dogs were raked but not seriously hurt, I gained new insights, and the old lion gave up his nine lives to the bow-and-arrow.

When I finally touched the cat's ears, which had been tattered and frozen over the years to half-size, and I saw and felt the ridges from bones broken and healed and muscles ripped and regrown, I was struck by the realization of the countless life-or-death challenges he had encountered and endured. At that moment, I decided that this old veteran, who had probably killed and eaten 1,000 deer or moose and sired many kittens in his 12-15 years, must have his image preserved. His likeness, seldom seen even by those of us who love and frequent his domain, would be shown to others as a prime example of the raw and rugged beauty that still exists in the wilds of North America. Keith Heldreth, whose hunt I had taken, is a part-time taxidermist. He was thrilled to take on the mounting of this magnificent monarch, and his involvement was the link that completed the circle. The hunt ended where it had begun.

Two cougars are tied for first place in the Pope and Young Club records at 15-11/16 inches. My cat scores 15-10/16 inches.

Photograph Courtesy of Richard L. Wolfel

Richard L. Wolfel (l) and his guide, Nathan Ellison, with black bear 20-1/16 taken on the White Mountain Apache Indian Reservation, Arizona, in 1987.

Photograph Courtesy of Bruce F. Gilbert

Bruce F. Gilbert was hunting Canyon Creek in British Columbia in 1986 when he shot this black bear that scores 20 points.

Photograph Courtesy of Larry W. Cox

BLACK BEAR
FIRST AWARD
SCORE: 22-2/16
Locality: Sanpete Co., Utah   Date: June 1987
Hunter: Larry W. Cox

BLACK BEAR 22-2/16

Larry W. Cox

My interest in bear hunting began while my family was camping in the mountains during the summer months in the La Sal Mountain Range. This happened in the canyons near our home town of Manti, Utah, and it was quite a rare experience. We spotted the bear feeding on ants by an over-turned log, and we enjoyed watching him finish the rest of his feast from a safe distance. I was intrigued by the black bear after that and made my mind up to pursue bear hunting.

My knowledge of bear hunting was minimal and my first experiences at stalking a bear were almost comical. Several times after that, I returned to the same area where we had seen the bear while I was spotting for elk. I did encounter the bear once in this area, but distance and darkness made it impossible to stalk him then.

Between then and the time I actually took my bear, I hunted and took two cougars in this mountainous area of Sanpete County. I hunted with Mike Young during this time, using dogs on both hunts. Since I had known him since grade school, my confidence was already with him. I called Mike and told him I wanted to pursue a bear hunt.

The next three years were spent following Mike Young and Scott Beck and their pack of dogs into three different states, trying our luck at bear hunting. Every spare weekend and holiday was spent traveling to New Mexico, Colorado, and around the State of Utah. The majority of our time was spent in Utah and its various mountain ranges. The *Records of North American Big Game* indicates the Sanpete and Sevier Counties have produced many trophy bears. However, they are scattered and this area has a low bear population.

The out-of-state hunts produced only saddle sores and many scenic horseback rides, and they were filled with hard work and much disappointment. All of which I learned to appreciate more as this hunt went on. Mike Young had been successful on many out-of-state hunts previously, but I was unable to connect on any that we pursued. Mike and I decided that if we were to succeed at this hunt, it would be in our own area where we were familiar with the terrain. We were aware of several bears within our area, possibly two that were of large size. I must admit at this point just seeing a treed bear would have been fine for me. Several times while hunting, we chased bears but were unable to cover enough ground to keep up with the dogs.

Mike and Scott had to spend two weeks during the spring hunt of 1987 hunting without me because of my commitments. They kept in close contact during that time, telling me of their success and failures at seeing bear signs. At one point during those two weeks, they told me things were different and they sensed they were onto a good bear. They told me they had run a bear often, and the dogs would return whipped and in pretty bad shape. They felt they were on the trail of a walking bear that did not want to tree, and he was definitely not afraid of dogs.

The morning of June 12, 1987, proved to be a morning I will never forget. It was just three days before the spring bear hunt would end for our area. This was the day we were to tree my bear. Mike Young, Scott Beck, and a friend, Kevin Rasmussen, were along with me on our chase. During this chase, Mike had actually come upon the bear while it was fighting the dogs on the ground. It was his presence that finally forced the bear to climb the tree.

The excitement of the dogs barking and baying under the tree was unbelievable, as we made our way through the thick deadfalls. Any hound dog owner who has worked with these dogs can appreciate the thrill and excitement of this moment. There was no doubt the dogs had done their job well. Upon arriving at the huge pine tree, we found, approximately three-quarters of the way up, a large male bear glaring down upon the intruders of his territory. No one present was aware of the size of the animal we had treed, and it didn't really matter at this point.

I positioned myself on the steep embankment and waited for the bear to turn slightly to present a shoulder shot. Immediately after the first .44 Mag round struck the bear, he began circling the large pine tree. He climbed to the top, thrashing and breaking tree limbs as he circled. As the bear passed my side of the tree, I shot again, trying to pick a vital spot. The gnashing of his teeth and jaws, the deep groans, and the huge limbs falling to the ground made me wonder if this bear could ever be stopped.

The entire tree began shaking as the bear threw his fit of rage. Temporarily out-of-sight, the bear turned and began backing down the tree. I tried to position myself for a better shot while Mike was yelling, "Shoot again, shoot again, he's coming down." I shot repeatedly as the bear descended the tree. The cylinder of the pistol was empty and the bear finally lay at the bottom of the tree. What had seemed like hours had happened in few short minutes. The excitement of this moment was tremendous. The hard work and patience of the past had paid off in spades.

Upon close inspection of the bear, it was revealed that he had been hit at least five times with the .44 Mag during the ordeal. Recalling all of the events that took place over that three-year period, and since the bear was taken in Manti Canyon, I feel strongly that this was the same bear my family and I had first encountered while camping in the area.

What had taken me many miles from home on several occasions, had actually ended on the mountain where I had grown up and where many memories of good times and hunting other game animals had occurred. At last I had my bear, and a trophy one at that.

BLACK BEAR 23-7/16

CERTIFICATE OF MERIT

Pennsylvania Game Commission, owner

With the recognition of this trophy, Pennsylvania's secret is out. Not only does the Keystone State have a healthy black bear population from which they harvest a large number each year, there are also a good number of trophy-sized specimens taken each year. (In 1989, the harvest was 2,213 black bear.) This bear was aged at 19 years old and it weighed more than 700 pounds.

The bear harvest for 1989 was an increase of 599 bears, or 37 percent, over the previous season when 1,614 bears were taken. Bear hunting is generally by means of bear drives or by hunting areas frequented by bears. The use of dogs and bait is illegal in Pennsylvania. Pennsylvania's black bear population is expanding its range and growing rapidly each year. Research by Gary Alt, Pennsylvania Game Commission, has shown that black bear in Pennsylvania grow faster, reproduce younger, and produce more cubs per female than most black bears in other states or provinces. Twins are common and triplets have been reported.

In addition to producing this trophy, which is the second-largest black bear skull ever recorded in North America, Pennsylvania produces a number of other trophy black bear each year. During the 1989 season, there were approximately 100 bear taken that weighed more than 400 pounds live weight, and several weighed in excess of 600 pounds. Many of the larger bears have been scored at the request of the Pennsylvania Game Commission. Most of them score in excess of 20 points. Several have scored more than 21 points, and a few scored over 22 points. So, don't be surprised if a New World's Record black bear comes out of Pennsylvania in the future.

Photograph Courtesy of Thomas E. Smith

GRIZZLY BEAR
FIRST AWARD
SCORE: 26-1/16

Locality: Camelback Mt., Alaska   Date: September 1985
Hunter: Thomas E. Smith

GRIZZLY BEAR 26-1/16

Thomas E. Smith

My dream began in the early 1980's. Having made a couple of hunting trips to the western states for pronghorn and mule deer (and having good success), my dream started to expand to bigger game. Ever since I was a teenager in rural Pennsylvania, the idea was in the back of my mind to go to Alaska to hunt the grizzly bear. Having friends who have gone to Alaska, and hearing their experiences, I knew that I must share in that experience if at all possible. Ben Handa, a friend of mine from Flint, Michigan, told me about an outfitter that had good success with a mixed-bag hunt and very good luck with grizzly bears. We decided that we would make reservations for a hunt that would be September 1 through September 15, 1985. The party would include Ben, his friend from Bancroft, Michigan (Leon Van Agen), and me. The game hunted would be black bear, caribou, moose, and grizzly.

The year prior to departure was constantly occupied with hours spent walking hillsides with a weighted pack, assembling gear, target practice, and of course, dreaming. Flying to Anchorage, we chartered a flying service to take us to the bush country, approximately 150 miles northwest to Stoney River. We met the master guide, M.J. (Curly) Warren, and he explained what his plans were for us. But he told me that I had another 100 miles of flying to do before I could hunt. He had a distant location chosen that demanded a spartan and a rigorous daily routine. I was thankful for my conditioning program. So after a beautiful scenic flight, I arrived at my new home for the next 14 days. My "home" consisted of a 6-foot-square survival tent, gas camp stove, coffee pot, and a sleeping bag. I was introduced to my guide, Russ Shrear. Russ was a laid-back type of person, age 32, 6 feet tall and 210 pounds. I knew immediately that he was very knowledgeable about guiding and a good judge of sizing-up animals. I would soon witness his superior skill at preparing hides.

After a light lunch, we went for a walk to get familiar with the area. As you are not permitted to hunt on your day of arrival, we decided that we would unpack and rest for the time remaining and get a good night's sleep so we would be ready to go in the morning.

The first few days would be concentrated on moose, as some had been sighted approximately four miles from camp. In order to reach them, we had to walk through tundra, which is difficult when wearing hip boots and carrying a full pack. After 2-1/2 hours of walking in rain and rugged terrain, we startled a black bear. Having a good shot, I killed it. I used a Remington Model 700 BDL in 7 mm Mag, with 165 grain Core-Lokt shells. Three shots were fired, with two hits. This gave me my first black bear of all my years of hunting.

The next couple of days were partly sunny and rainy, 30 to 50 degrees temperature, and foggy at times. We went back to the same area, hoping to find a moose. On the fourth day, mind willing but body weak, we were in no hurry to go hunting. But that changed in an instant when the guide told me, "Tom, there is a grizzly walking by the camp." Opening the flaps of the tent, I could not believe what I was seeing! There, within 150 yards of our camp, was the biggest bear I had ever seen. Grabbing my gun and boots, I rushed out to pursue the bear. By this time, the bear was 300 yards away. Russ told me that I would get no closer and that I should give it a try. Lying down and taking careful aim, I shot and the bear started to run away. I shot three more times, but he never stopped. I told Russ that I thought I hit the bear, and he said that we sure did not need that, a wounded bear around our camp. He assured me that there was a good chance that this bear would return and that we should be prepared at all times. With this in mind, Russ thought that we should have our loaded guns at our sides while we slept.

After I shot, I knew that I had rushed myself into shooting. I was very excited and after I saw that I had missed, I was mad at myself. I think deep-down, Russ knew that I had missed, but I thought I had hit the bear and we would follow-up on the shooting site and find the bear dead. We walked up to the site and found nothing. We glassed down into the valley and he was gone. Russ assured me that we would find another bear.

For a change of pace, Russ suggested that we try our luck at caribou hunting. Not feeling the best, I did agree and we went scouting behind the camp. After two or three hours, we found a herd of caribou with four or five good bulls that appeared to be trophy-sized. After careful scoping, I picked one that seemed to be the best. We stalked the caribou and when we were within 200 yards, I shot and killed it. Just one shot, well-placed in the front shoulder. Was it a beauty! Heavy beams, long points on top, and a very big shovel. Getting this trophy, I forgot my aches and pains from the strenuous walking and the disappointment of missing the grizzly. After two days of packing-out the meat and taking care of the hide and cape, it was time to move on to get that moose, or bear, whichever came first.

On the ninth day, we decided to pick a high spot on the mountain near our tent site to watch the valley for moose. We found a nice location to observe the valley below, and we were in luck. Russ said, "Tom, your bear has returned." I could hardly believe our luck. There, approximately 1,000 yards away, was the bear I had missed a week ago. As we watched his progress, we knew what we had to do. Staying on top and moving so that we would be ahead of him, we stayed low so that he could not see us. We calculated that I should be prepared to shoot at 150 yards or so when we got over the next ridge. But to our surprise, when we topped the ridge, there was no bear in sight. We could not believe that we miscalculated his progress, and we could not believe that he had spotted us. But in a split second I saw a movement out of the corner of my eye that is hard to describe. There, within 30 yards of us, came this huge bear.

In a low voice, Russ told me to shoot and to make it a good one. In that instant, the bear spotted us, but he was too close to retreat. Being excited, with the bear so close, I aimed for the shoulder, hitting him a little high. He started to roll down the hill, with me shooting until my gun was empty (total of three shots). However, when he stopped rolling, we saw that he was dead. When we got to him, Russ knew that I had killed a records book grizzly. After 4,000 miles of flying, many miles on foot, and several days of rain, fog, wind, and sleet, I had my grizzly, and a record one at that. What a feeling! After many pictures and six hours of skinning, it was time to go back to camp. The next day, we prepared the skull and also fleshed the hide.

On the 12th day, with time remaining in the hunt, we knew that there was a chance to find a moose and complete the hunt with four trophies. We returned to the location where the grizzly had been sighted and, to our surprise, we spotted a couple of moose in the valley. After a careful stalk, I picked one that seemed to be the largest and, would you believe it, a 67-inch spread. What a way to end my hunt.

When we got back to the main lodge, we were the talk of the camp. We returned with a black bear, a large moose, a records-book caribou, and a records-book grizzly. Curly Warren told me that not only had I the good fortune to get four animals, but they were exceptional trophies. As it turned out, the caribou and grizzly are in the Boone and Crockett Club records book, with the moose just missing by an inch.

Yes, it was truly a "DREAM COME TRUE."

Photograph Courtesy of Vincent A. Pisani

Vincent A. Pisani and grizzly bear he shot in 1986 near Tsayta Lake, British Columbia. Pisani's bear scores 24-12/16 points.

Photograph Courtesy of Brenton Morgenstern

Brenton Morgenstern with the stretched hide of the grizzly bear he shot in 1988 along the Nulato River in Alaska. It scores 23 points to place in the Awards records book.

GRIZZLY BEAR 26

SECOND AWARD

Peter Martinson

It was May 18th. Our first day was spent glassing slides, which generally are the first areas to green-up in the spring. We saw one sow bear with three cubs, but it is illegal to shoot any grizzly in a family unit, so we passed on them.

The next morning we awoke to another clear, windy, sunny day and immediately started glassing. We saw lots of goats but not much else. By this time, I must admit that I felt a little discouraged. Mornings and evenings are generally the best time for spotting game, so with the approach of the afternoon, we stopped for a bite to eat. After some discussion, we decided to drive to Meziadin Lake and glass the slides on the other side. We had been glassing for two hours when I suddenly saw a grizzly walking across a patch of snow. The distance across the lake is at least a mile, so to get a better look, we launched our canoe and paddled to the other side. The first attempt to cross the lake proved fruitless, since there were two-foot waves and it was too dangerous. We had to turn back, my hopes diminished.

Time wore on while I helplessly glassed the bear. The sun started setting, and it was approximately 45 minutes until dark, when we thought we would try again. The waves were smaller now, and before we knew it, we were 500-600 yards closer. Now we could see that there were two bears. The smaller I presumed to be a sow, but it had a beautiful, straw-colored coat. The larger grizzly was soaking wet from dipping-in-and-out of the lake, so it was hard to tell the condition of his hide. Since there was still a fair bit of snow in places, and since I assumed this was a large bear, I decided to go for him.

I loaded my .300 Winchester Mag and took aim. The sound seemed to be a deafening intrusion in the breathtaking scenery. I felt sorry for this magnificent beast. Thankfully, this sorrow didn't last long. When I approached the bear, I realized this was no average grizzly. He was huge. We skinned until well past dark and were greatly relieved to make it back across the lake to more familiar scenes.

A few days later, we returned to the lake to retrieve the carcass for proper measurements. When we arrived home with the carcass and weighed it, we were surprised to find that it weighed 955 pounds, with hide. With aid of my measurements, it was later mounted life-size by my firm, Bornite Mountain Taxidermy, to remember for many more years.

Photograph Courtesy of William A. Brooks, Sr.

GRIZZLY BEAR
THIRD AWARD
SCORE: 25-15/16

Locality: Tubutulik River, Alaska   Date: April 1986
Hunter: William A. Brooks, Sr.

GRIZZLY BEAR 25-15/16

William A. Brooks, Sr.

I have always wanted to go grizzly hunting, but the opportunity never arose until my wife, Mary, and I attended the annual Sportsman's Show in Harrisburg, Pennsylvania. It was there that we met outfitter Bob Hannon. Mary and I were impressed with Bob's grizzly hunting success rates, and the longer we talked to him, the more I wanted to go bear hunting. After the show, Mary and I talked about the hunt for weeks. I really wanted to go but couldn't see how we could swing it financially. Mary finally said, "You're not getting any younger." I called Bob and made reservations. The next few months were spent shopping for warm clothes and getting in shape. I realized that being in shape would be the most important factor in having a successful hunt.

When the day finally arrived, I flew to Nome, Alaska, where I purchased my hunting license and grizzly tag. Then it was on to Koyuk, where I spent the next day-and-a-half learning how to walk in snowshoes. Bob showed up late the next day, and we flew-out the following morning. On the plane, Bob said he had talked to some Eskimos who said they had seen a big bear in our hunting area.

The following day my guide, Barry, and I began hunting. There was over three feet of snow on the ground and I kept tripping on what I thought were twigs. They turned out to be the tops of small pine trees. When you fall in such deep snow, the natural tendency is to put your hand out to break your fall. Trouble is, your hand breaks right through and you bury your face in the snow. After a day-and-a-half of this, I kept asking myself if I really wanted a bear that bad. The answer was always yes.

We finally found the bear's trail and started playing catch-up. We went up one ridge and down another, putting on mile after mile. My legs were really starting to ache when I spotted the bear walking up the ridge. The bear must have smelled or heard us, because all-of-a-sudden he turned around. I knew he wouldn't stand there for long, so I immediately slid a round into the chamber of my .308 Norma Mag, aimed, and fired. The grizzly didn't even flinch! He just turned and walked up the ridge like nothing had happened. I didn't have time to shoot again.

I began to doubt that I had hit him, but my hold was steady and all the shooting practice I had over the summer told me I did. Barry and I started up the ridge after the bear. When we reached the top, we stopped to glass the pines below us to see if the bear was anywhere in sight. When 30 minutes of waiting and glassing failed to turn up anything, we decided to go after the bear.

While following the bear's tracks down the ridge, Barry told me not to look for the whole bear because he had probably already made his "chute." Barry said a wounded grizzly will walk back and forth to pack down the snow to make it easier for him to attack. (I was really glad he told me that at the time.) The tracks led us through some dense pines and alders. Visibility was very poor. I constantly searched for the bear, watching for movement or his blonde coat.

Suddenly, a humped back and two beady eyes appeared over a snow mound only 20 yards away. The bear was going to charge! I quickly shouldered my gun, put the scope a few inches under his chin so I wouldn't ruin his skull, and fired. The bear dropped when the magnum roared. There was no growling, thrashing, or charge. He just dropped dead. When Barry reached me, all he could say was, "I thought you would never shoot." Barry, who was behind and above me, had spotted the bear before I had and had watched everything.

After taking a bunch of photos, we skinned the bear. We found that my first shot had entered the chest and exited the arm pit area without hitting any vital organs. It was then I realized that I had just walked up to a healthy grizzly. That night, while lying in the tent, I went over the day's events. I couldn't get out of my mind how close I had gotten to the grizzly. Just thinking about what could have happened made my body start to shake. Needless to say, I didn't sleep at all that night.

Later, back home in Pennsylvania, I had my bear scored for the records book. I was happy to learn that he entry scored 26-3/16, enough to make the records book with room to spare. He was 17-1/2 years old, as verified by biologists in Nome, Alaska, after scanning an extracted lower tooth. He squared-out at 9 feet, 6 inches. His live weight was estimated to be about 1,200 pounds.

Photograph Courtesy of William O. West

William O. West's Alaska brown bear trophy was buried in an avalanche for three days before he could claim it. Taken on Kodiak Island, Alaska, in 1988, it scores 26-14/16 points.

Photograph Courtesy of Alan O'Neil

This Alaska brown bear was killed by Alan O'Neil in 1988 on Kodiak Island. It scores 28-15/16 points and qualifies for the all-time records book.

Photograph Courtesy of W. Ted Burger

ALASKA BROWN BEAR
FIRST AWARD
SCORE: 29-13/16

Locality: Kodiak Island, Alaska   Date: November 1985
Hunter: W. Ted Burger

ALASKA BROWN BEAR 29-13/16

W. Ted Burger

Ted Burger raised his rifle and aimed well-over a patch of Kodiak Island alders. Maybe, he hoped, the sudden crack of his .375 Mag would spook the huge Kodiak brown bear out of the alder patch and into the open. Or maybe, he feared, this bear had slipped away as the others had. His hopes were sagging. He'd been hunting 14 days.

The last time Burger and his guide, Joe Want, had seen the animal, it was 2-1/2 miles from them, in the same alders that Burger now guarded, a patch only slightly larger than a football field. But in the time it took to reach the thicket, the bear had disappeared. Burger fired into the air. The bear didn't show. "More lousy luck," Burger mumbled. When would it end, the bad luck?

Burger cradled the rifle in his arms and, still watching the alder for any sign of bear movement, turned his back against the raw afternoon wind. There he was, hunkered on an island hummock on November 8, 1985, the day he and his twin brother, Bud, had planned to be returning home to Minneapolis. But the Burger brothers had quickly learned that on Alaska's Kodiak Island, the best-laid plans often go astray. What was supposed to have been a 14 day hunt for the two well-known sportsmen now was going on three weeks because of inclement weather.

For three days they had waited on the mainland for suitable flying weather to reach Joe Want's outfitter's cabin on the south end of Kodiak. Then, after reaching main camp via floatplane, the start of their hunt was held up another two days while 60 to 80 mile-per-hour winds battered the island. Want, a veteran Kodiak bear guide, said he'd never seen such horrible November weather on the island. The two brothers had decided that Ted would take the first trophy bear and Bud would take the second, if they were so lucky.

While Want led the way, the two hunters, joined by a packer, hiked toward the island's midsection, carrying all their supplies in 75 pound backpacks. When the wind wasn't blowing, it was raining, or both. Sometimes it snowed. For footgear, they wore hip boots. They discovered the island abounded with wildlife, particularly Sitka blacktail deer and bald eagles. The sea coast bays teemed with waterfowl. Ptarmigan, the grouse of the arctic, were an abundant meal for the hunters.

For three days, the four men backpacked into the island maze of ridges and valleys in search of the giant bears. The daily routine started with a hot breakfast made in a pressure cooker, followed by a two-hour hike to a high point to glass for bear on the far hillsides, or below in the creek bottoms.

Want liked to concentrate his hunting time in the afternoon, particularly late when the big brownies would begin to move. As a result, it was always dark when the four men returned to camp. "One night we spooked a bear while we were hiking back to camp," Bud Burger said. "It ran the other way but it gave you something to think about."

For three days they hunted and for three days they saw nothing. On the fourth day, the first brown bear was spotted, but it quickly disappeared. Eventually, more bears were seen but most were judged too small to stalk. The days wore on. Sometimes the wind and fog made it impossible to search the far slopes.

This bear hunt was turning into a physical ordeal. For two weeks, they had camped without the luxury of a wood fire or its heat. (There wasn't any wood.) Meals were cooked on a single-burner kerosene stove. Life had become simple: eat, sleep, hike, climb, and glass the slopes and alder thickets.

It was dark and overcast that afternoon, but something was in the air. By 2:30 p.m., they had already spotted four bears feeding on salmon in the stream below. Such a high amount of bear activity was unusual. "It means a change of weather is coming," Want said. They kept scanning the faraway slope. The day before, Bud had seen what he figured was a large boar roaming in the general area until it disappeared in darkness. Maybe, they hoped, it would show up again.

Joe Want suddenly pointed. The huge bear had reappeared in a small alder thicket, some 2-1/2 miles away and across a valley. It didn't take the veteran guide long to judge the trophy, "It's gonna be a SOB. Let's go." Burger, along with Want and the packer, began the long hike toward the unsuspecting bear while Bud stayed behind on the knob to keep watch in the event the animal moved out of the alder clumps.

Reaching the lower end of the alder thicket, Burger positioned himself where he could see open terrain. The plan was to use human scent to spook the big brown into the open. Mark (the packer) climbed the hillside, staying upwind of the alder thicket. The bear didn't show. Maybe the wind switched. Mark climbed the other side of the bear's hideaway. The bear didn't show. Maybe a loud noise would work. Burger fired his rifle. Nothing.

Want said he had one more idea. He would walk through the center of the alder patch. "I remember thinking a coupla things," Burger says, "If the bear came out I wanted to make sure I didn't wound it. I also wondered if my guide would be in front or behind the bear if it did come out." Want disappeared into the alders. In the meantime, Bud Burger knew from his high vantage point what no one else knew. The big boar had bedded down and was still in the alder thicket. The guide soon discovered the same thing, as did Ted Burger.

From the edge of the alders, the big bear bolted into the open, about 200 yards from where Burger was waiting. Burger fired three shots. It was over. "I knew it was big, but not that big," Burger says. He couldn't lift the bear's massive head. Its hide stretched flat was about 12 feet wide and 10 feet long. Burger figures the animal weighed between 1,200 and 1,500 pounds and stood nine feet tall. It took five days to haul the bear's hide the 14 miles back to main camp. A total of eight other brown bear was seen. Bud Burger never fired a shot, but he lost 14 pounds and had a great time.

Photographs Courtesy of Philip L. Iverson and Robert D. Hancock, Jr.

(l) Philip L. Iverson was especially pleased with this unusually dark Alaska brown bear that he shot in 1986 near Red Shirt Lake, Alaska. It scores 26-12/16 points. (r) Deadman Bay, Alaska, is the area where Robert D. Hancock, Jr., killed this Alaska brown bear in 1987 that scores 27 points.

Photograph Courtesy of Edward H. Dobler

Edward H. Dobler took this Alaska brown bear on the eighth day of his 10 day hunt on the Alaska Peninsula in 1987. It scores 26-3/16 points.

Photograph Courtesy of John L. Largura

ALASKA BROWN BEAR
SECOND AWARD
SCORE: 29
Locality: Kiavak Bay, Alaska   Date: May 1987
Hunter: John L. Largura

ALASKA BROWN BEAR 29

John L. Largura

This hunt became a reality about a year after my friend Bob Welsh said, "Let's go to Kodiak Island and hunt for brown bear." We decided to contact Jack Jonas of Jonas Inc. in Denver to see if he could recommend a good outfitter to us. Jack suggested that we contact J&B Safaris in Denver. They said they were having excellent success with a guide named Andy Runyan. His success rate was nearly 100 percent. Andy had been hunting bears for over 20 years, and we had an excellent chance of getting a trophy bear in his area. We decided to book our hunt with Andy for the following spring, May 1 to May 14, 1987.

Not really sure of what I had gotten myself into, I did not think of this hunt until February of 1987 when it came time to purchase a rifle. We both decided on a .375 Sako equipped with a 1.5x5 power scope.

When the day finally arrived, Bob and I boarded a United Airlines plane to Anchorage, Alaska. The next day, we flew Alaska Air to Kodiak Island where we waited for our Penn Air flight to our hunting camps. This gave us an opportunity to visit the city of Kodiak and see the large commercial fishing fleet based there. Approximately 1,000 fishing boats were in port, preparing for the Halibut season. This season lasts just one day, but it would generate a great deal of income for the fishermen.

About 4:30 p.m. on April 30, our charter floatplane was ready to take us to our camps. Bob and I flipped a coin to see who would go to the tent camp and who would go to the cabin at Kiavak Bay. When I won the flip, I decided that since Bob had done all the planning of this trip, I would let him hunt with Andy Runyan from the cabin and I would go to the tent camp. As this turned-out, it was a good decision. The flight from Kodiak to our hunting area took about 40 minutes, with parts of the flight below the mountain tops. We landed in a beautiful bay with a mountain range on three sides.

Here, we finally met Andy Runyan, my guide Steve Berg, and two hunters who were leaving. One hunter had shot a trophy bear during their 14 day hunt, while the other hunter passed many small bears in search of a 10 foot bear. After a short introduction and getting the necessary paper work filled-out, I again boarded a plane with Steve for our trip to camp. The two camps were approximately 15 miles apart and separated by a large mountain range. After the short flight, we circled a small "visqueen" plastic tent off the shore of the Gulf of Alaska. After landing and taxiing to shore, we said good-by to our pilot. This would be the beginning of an 11 day stay.

We moved supplies to a supply tent, and then our sleeping bags, guns, and clothes to the main tent. This tent was eight feet wide by 12 feet long, and very comfortable with two cots, a small table, and a Coleman stove to cook on. Steve wanted to be sure my rifle was still on, so we took a couple of practice shots on the beach. After a quick dinner and a short session on placement of various shots on bears in different positions, it was time for bed. The excitement of the hunt made deep sleep difficult.

When morning came, we had a rushed breakfast, packed our lunch, and hurried-off to a lookout on a hill a mile away. Hunting, walking, and climbing in hip boots was a new experience for me. The weather on Kodiak Island changed continually, with sunshine, rain, sleet, snow, and fog all possible on the same day. After we reached our lookout, Steve began to glass the immediate area and mountains in search of a bear. After an explanation of what to look for, I also began to glass with my 10x40 Zeiss binoculars. I was a little unsure of what a bear would appear like in the surroundings though. About 1 p.m., Steve shouted that he could see a bear, but it was over two miles away and moving away from us. I now had my first glimpse of a Kodiak bear through a spotting scope. Over the next seven days, 31 bears were seen but were either not huntable, with cubs, or they disappeared after a stalk.

It was during these sessions that much wildlife could be seen such as: bald eagles, otters, seals, whales, Sitka blacktail deer, ducks, swans, ptarmigans, and fox. Probably my favorite was an arctic fox, just changing from silver to red, that came to camp each night for a handout. He became so tame that you could approach within five feet of him, and at times he would follow us to a location many miles from camp.

On the eighth day we began our hunt as usual and chose to try an area where many bears had been seen. This area was a lowland between a large peninsula and a mountain range. Here we had great visibility and hoped to find a bear somewhere in this large area. About 8:30 a.m., I called to Steve that I had found a bear that was just beginning to cross the lowlands. Steve watched the bear for about five minutes through his spotting scope and said it was a nice bear, but it was moving fast toward the mountain range. If we were to have any chance of bagging him, we would have to move fast and try to get between the bear and the mountain range. He added that after we left our lookout, we would have to cross over a mile-and-a-half of tundra as quickly as possible, and we still might not see the bear. My reply was, "Nothing ventured, nothing gained. Let's go."

We picked up our backpacks, after putting our jackets into them, and took off on an intercept course for the bear. The area we had to cover was complicated by the soft tundra. The only way we could make any real progress was to follow a bear or deer trail. These had been walked on for years by these animals. The trails, however, did not always go in the direction you wanted, so you were still required to walk on the tundra much of the time. After 45 minutes of hard going, we were fast closing-in on the Gulf of Alaska and we hoped that the bear was still in the lowlands and had not reached the mountain range. Steve occasionally stopped to glass the area ahead. On one of these stops he said he could see a bear looking down from the mountain but he was sure it was not the bear we were hunting. After watching it for a while, he decided it was a female and she was watching our bear. Since she was about 500 yards ahead and 200 yards up the mountain, we felt we still had a excellent chance for my bear. Steve said to move quickly, talk softly, and chamber a shell.

We again moved to try to cut-off my bear before it followed the female up the mountain. Steve, being a lot younger and no doubt in better shape, moved faster than me. Since we could no longer see the female, we could only hope that we had our bear trapped between us and the water. Then all at once, out of the corner of my eye, I caught some movement in the alder bushes directly on my left and about 45 yards away. I had stopped for a better look when a huge head, and then the complete bear, stood looking at me. I immediately called to Steve that the bear was "right here." Upon hearing my voice, the bear dropped to all fours and began to move away from us, still trying to follow the female up the mountain. Steve said as soon as the bear cleared the heavy alders, to take him. I waited until that time (the bear was about 65 yards away) before I fired from a standing position. To my surprise, the bear dropped in its tracks with the single shot.

It was then that the real impact of this great bear made my legs a little weak. Steve watched the bear for a while before approaching, very cautiously. When he got near the bear, he remarked that it was a very large bear. After a picture-taking session, Steve began to skin the animal, which took 3-1/2 hours. After the skinning process was completed, Steve put the skin in his backpack, the skull in one hand and his rifle in the other, and started for camp. Due to the weight of the hide and the distance from camp, it was 7:30 p.m. before we finally arrived. This brought to an end one of the greatest experiences any man could ever have in hunting.

ALASKA BROWN BEAR 28-15/16

THIRD AWARD

Ron D. King

I started hunting for Alaska brown bears in the spring of 1986 when Bruce Rogers, a hunting buddy of mine, took me to a little bay along the south coast of the Alaska Peninsula, out of King Salmon, Alaska. On that trip, Bruce bagged a nice blond brown bear, but I came up empty. I knew that I would return in two years when the brown bear season would be open again on the peninsula. So as the spring 1988 bear season approached, Randy Bridwell (whom I do most of my hunting with) and I began to make our plans. After going over maps of the area, we decided to pack-in five miles from the beach, up a river valley that would take us to a huge bowl in the mountains. Having made this decision, we planned to set up a base camp at the beach and a spike camp in the bowl.

We got all the gear we would need together, then set-out to buy our food. Since we were going to be there for two weeks, we knew we couldn't take any fresh meat and the food had to be light since we would have to pack it to the spike camp. We ended-up buying a few canned hams, with the rest consisting of ramen noodles, oatmeal, "cup-of-soups," and lots of granola bars and trail mix for snacks.

The morning of May 7, 1988, along with all our gear, we boarded a plane at Anchorage International Airport and flew to King Salmon. There, we loaded into a Cessna 180 that would land us on the beach of the bay we were to hunt. We touched-down on the beach at 5 p.m. and began to set up the base camp. After the base camp was completed, we loaded our packs with the spike camp. The spike camp consisted of a Moss two-man tent, our guns, some extra clothes, a small stove, and five days worth of food.

The next morning, we got up at 6 a.m., strapped the packs to our backs, grabbed the guns, and headed up the river valley. As it turned-out, the valley was covered with several streams that meandered back and forth across the valley, forcing us to cross the same streams several different times. Having elected not to carry our hip boots with us, we tied our rain pants at the ankles with nylon cord, which worked rather well. After we had gone about 2-1/2 miles, we decided to camp there for the night and do some glassing of the surrounding mountains to make sure we hadn't missed anything.

As soon as we got the spike tent set up, we grabbed our spotting scopes and set out for a small hill. We hadn't gone 20 feet from the tent when I spotted a large set of bear tracks in the mud. From the top of a small hill, we spotted a couple of bear trails crossing the snow covered peaks but no bears. Since it was still early, we decided to hike further up the valley to try to get a look at the bowl we were planning on hunting. As we made it to the bowl, the view was stunning and we knew we had picked a good spot to hunt brown bear. We made our way back to the spike camp and then headed for the bowl.

Once we reached the bowl, we set the spike camp up in the middle so that we could glass the surrounding mountains for a full 360 degrees. We still had two days until the season opened, so we figured we would just relax and spend the next day glassing the mountains. But the weather changed from clear and sunny to gusting wind and rain, with clouds dropping down around the mountains until we couldn't see more than 50 yards up the hills. The weather stayed bad, pinning us to our tent as opening day came and went. Then, around noon on May 11, the clouds began to move out of the valley, so we decided to crawl out of the tent and roam around the bowl a little. Being that the day was half-gone, we didn't plan on embarking on any serious hunting and, since I had my gun, Randy left his at the tent.

We started on a short walk, but the further we went, the more we wanted to see. About an hour later we ended-up on a small hill, three-fourths of a mile from the tent, glassing the mountains. As we sat there glassing, the wind died down; when it did, the biting flies appeared in swarms around our faces, making it hard to concentrate on glassing the mountains. We were studying the brown spots on the snow-covered slopes, most of which were rocks that the snow had melted from. After a few minutes, Randy spotted a brown spot that looked odd to him, so he kept his binoculars on it. Suddenly, it began to move and he said to me, "I see one." He pointed it out to me and we both studied it. Sure enough, it was a bear, a light blond one. Then, as we were watching the bear, Randy caught some movement out of the corner of his binoculars; it was another bear, dark-chocolate color and about 200 yards up the hill from the first one. We decided that Randy should get his gun and backpack.

Full of excitement, Randy ran all the way to the tent and back. When he got back, we used the spotting scope to get a better look at the two bears. Suddenly, the blond bear got up and started walking up the hill toward the other bear. When he got about half-way, the dark bear jumped up and started down toward the blond one. They met each other and began to fight, rolling through the snow as they bit and clawed at each other. Suddenly they rolled apart and stood up on their hind legs and then clashed again, biting at each other's neck. Then, one of them let out a roar that echoed down the mountain; the sound was enough to make the hair on the back of your neck stand up, to say the least. They then fell to the ground, still locked together, and rolled through the snow, coming up on all fours. Facing each other, they stared at one another for a couple of minutes, then both turned and walked back to their beds and lay back down.

At this point, we decided it was time for us to make our move. We were about 1,200 yards from the bears, across a small valley with two streams to cross to get to the base of the mountain the bears were on. We grabbed our gear and headed down the hill and crossed the first stream. Then, as we came to the second one, we decided to take our packs and rain gear off to cut down on noise. Then we crossed the last stream and made our way to the base of the mountain. There I suddenly realized that in the excitement I had left my extra shells in the pocket of my rain coat. We decided we didn't want to waste any more time, so instead of going back to the stream to get them, Randy gave me two of his four extra shells, so now we each had four in our gun and two in our pockets.

Randy was concerned that two shells in the same pocket might rattle and spook the bears, so we put one in each pocket, something I will never do again as I soon found out it makes it awful hard to get at both shells in a hurry. Now that we were all set, we headed up the mountain, following a trail along the edge of the hill where the bears had worn the snow down to the dirt. On our left was four feet of snow, and on the right a cliff that dropped off into a valley. We crawled along the trail, at times on our bellies, to get through the alder branches without making too much noise. As we went higher, the valley got to be about 80 feet below us. Having spotted the bears, Randy got first shot. So when we got to within about 100 yards of the blond bear, Randy decided that was the one he wanted. I stayed in the trail and he moved over, into the snow, to get a clear shot through the alder bushes.

When he got situated, Randy looked through his scope at the bear that was facing down hill at us. At that point, Randy realized that this was a huge animal. He then looked over at me and said, "OK, I'm going to take him, but if he gets up you start shooting right away, don't wait." I got myself positioned so that I could watch the other bear to see what it was going to do, and still be able to swing my gun back to the blond bear if need be. Just as Randy was ready to shoot, the blond bear raised his head to look around, as he had been doing periodically. Randy took the opportunity to get a chest shot. Just as he pulled the trigger, the bear dropped his head and Randy's 180 grain Nosler struck the bear just above the right eye, shattering the skull and penetrating the brain. The bear didn't even wiggle.

When Randy fired, the dark bear didn't even look up. We guessed that since there were avalanches going off all around us, the bear figured it was just another avalanche and continued to sleep. At this point, it was all Randy could do to keep from whooping it up over his kill, but he knew we had a rare chance to bag another big bear, so he didn't. We decided to move up the hill to his bear to get a better shot at the dark bear. On our way up, Randy thought it would be neat for me to shoot my bear off his bear, but as we approached the dead bear, I found a good rest and a clear shot through the small bushes from about 15 yards below the dead bear. So I got situated there as Randy moved on to his bear. When I looked through my scope, I could see the dark bear was lying in a depression in the snow, on his side, with his head covering his chest. I told Randy that I didn't like the angle of the shot. He said that if I hit the bear with the first shot, he would stand up, giving me a good second shot, which made sense at the time. I aimed for the shoulder area over his head and squeezed the trigger. The bullet struck the bear high in the back, only serving to get his adrenalin pumping. He sprang to his feet, walking broadside to us, so I quickly worked my bolt to load another shell and aimed for his neck. The bullet hit the bear in the neck, damaging the artery, and when it hit, he roared and headed straight down the steep slope toward the blond bear and Randy.

The bear took about four steps, then he lost his balance and rolled head-over-heels toward the bottom of the hill. While he rolled, I fired my last two shots. But when the bear reached the bottom, he came to his feet, still heading for the blond bear. I stood up to reload and Randy asked if I would mind if he started shooting. I replied, "Hell no, go ahead." Randy pulled up his gun to shoot and just as he pulled the trigger, the bear disappeared in a gully. Knowing that the bear was heading right for him, Randy came running down the trail toward me. As he ran past me, I angrily yelled at him not to run but to stay here and shoot. Just as I got one shell in my gun, the bear reappeared about 40 yards away. I slammed my bolt shut and pulled my gun to my shoulder. Looking through my Leupold scope (set on seven power), I could see the bear's bottom jaw hanging open, with all his teeth and his tongue hanging out of the corner of his mouth as he approached. I put the cross hairs on his shoulder and pulled the trigger. The hair just behind the shoulder exploded, the bullet pierced the lungs, but the bear kept coming. Randy had stopped about 10 feet behind me, so I ducked down and turned back toward him, reaching into my pocket for my last shell as Randy raised his gun and put another 180 grains of lead into the huge bear. As he reached the blond bear, the brown bear rolled on his back right next to the blond bear.

Not yet knowing that the bear was down for good, I asked Randy where the bear was, thinking he might be about on top of us. Randy said the bear was dead. I was relieved that it was over and I started to head to the bears. Randy said he had to sit down for a few minutes as his legs were trembling too much to walk, so we sat down. Randy told me he had always wanted to have a bear charge him so that he could see what it would be feel like; but now, he never wanted it to happen again. I had to agree with him on that one, even though the bear was obviously going for the blond bear and didn't realize we were there. He must have thought that his old sparring partner was somehow responsible for the trouble he was in. To this day, I'm glad the bear wasn't aware of our presence. Who knows, it might have given him enough inspiration to cover that last 20 yards down to where we were standing.

After a few minutes, we went to look at the two bears. They were both big bears with nice hides. As Randy went back down to get the packs and the camera, I retraced the path the bear had taken. I was amazed that he had lasted that long, as the path in the snow was about three feet wide and bright red from the shot to the neck. It really showed the power of a bear pumped with adrenalin.

After Randy returned, we took some pictures. We then spent the rest of that day and half of the next getting the two bears skinned. The deep snow made it impossible to carry the hides down, so we drug them to the bottom where we loaded them on the packs. Then, we found that we couldn't pick the pack up high enough for one of us to get it on, so we both carried it to a stream bank where we could lean into it without having to bend our knees. Estimating the weight of each hide at about 150 pounds, it was more than one could carry very far, so we traded-off. We ferried them first to spike camp and then spent the next three days getting them and our gear back to the base camp. Once back at the base camp, we were both very sore and stiff. We still had a week before we would be picked up, so we spent the time fleshing and salting the hides. Both bears were about the same size, with mine measuring 10 feet, 3 inches from nose to tail and 8 feet, 11 inches from claw to claw. When we got back, we had both skulls measured. My bear made Boone and Crockett and Randy's just missed, confirming that they were both dandy bears.

ALASKA BROWN BEAR 28-12/16

FOURTH AWARD

Joe B. Brewster

I think Murphy's Law and Lady Luck go head to head with each other when I decide to do almost anything! This particular situation happened when my friend and hunting partner, Hunter Henderson, along with friend Pete Thompson, and I drew for Kodiak brown bear. We drew Unit 211 for a partner hunt, and Pete drew a connecting unit to the West. Therefore, we all decided to go together. Our arrival in Kodiak was less than pleasing to us. We've been around enough in 8-10 years to know that 12 inches of snow at the airport isn't good. Then add winds of 50 mph plus. We thought we might be sightseeing for a while in downtown Kodiak! What we didn't know is that it was to snow and blow like this for three straight days.

We occupied our time while in Kodiak by touring the Old Russian Orthodox Church, the downtown square, and the boat harbor. On the third day, Pete borrowed Hunter's new 35 mm camera to photograph the numerous boats and the historical church. Little did he know that "Mr. Murphy's Law" was working on him for the third day. He'd later find out that Lady Luck was with us the next day for an early a.m. scheduled flight. The 80-100 mph winds for the previous three days had started to calm.

Island Air told us we'd be loading in one to two hours due to weather information stating the winds were dying. Contrary to the weather report, we loaded our gear into the plane in 50-60 mph winds. The ice was building-up on the dock walkway as we transported load after load to the "Beaver." We finished around 11 p.m. and scheduled a 7 a.m. departure. Lady Luck was on our side this time, since we finally got out of town. Arriving safely at Red Lake, we set out to find our week-long home. We'd asked about the status of a cabin at the end of the lake. We were told the old white cabin at the old fish-weir site was not available for rent, due to its run-down condition. The only other cabin at that end of the lake belonged to the guides Pennell and Talifson.

Folks find what cover they can in this weather and both cabins were occupied. Pennell and Talifson had clients for hunting brown bear and the "old cabin" was occupied by deer hunters. We set up camp close by the old fish cabin, since our neighbors were leaving the next day. Lady Luck must have been with us again at this point. The guides, as well as we, didn't know what to think about this weather. It was 5 to 15 degrees the whole time we were there! A kerosene heater inside the tent worked wonders compared to anything outside. We didn't expect quite this low temperature, since Kodiak is usually a lot warmer in October.

We spotted bear the first day, but were restricted from shooting. (You cannot shoot the same day you fly in Alaska, with the exception of waterfowl and deer.) We also spotted a few deer meandering in the alders, but we refrained from shooting. We'd wait until tomorrow and see what the day would bring. In the early morning of the 26th, we went northwest of camp and saw three or four bears at a long distance. We then saw a big sow that Hunter shot. It turned out to be a nice, 8 foot, 8 inch bear with a beautiful hide. Packing and fleshing took up the remainder of the day and most of the night. Lady Luck seemed to be with us again for this part of the trip.

The next day, we hiked northeast of our camp. (We'd since moved into the old fish cabin next door, in which the prior occupants had skinned and quartered two deer the previous night.) Evidently, the bears didn't like deer that night, and Lady Luck was with us one more time, since they didn't come to the powerful odor. We hiked to the top of a big mountain where we spotted two bears eating salmon to the west of our location. Since Hunter had taken a bear the day before, he became the coordinator with the 50-yard-line view. Pete Thompson and I headed down the mountain toward the two bears we'd spotted earlier.

Before we left the mountain top, we had been watching a large bear approach to the north. He was a half-mile or more away, so I thought I'd go after the other two to the west. One seemed to be a large framed bear, at least compared to the other bear feeding at the stream. Pete would go with me and back me up on the stalk. I think "Mr. Murphy" entered the scene about now! Some things were planned and others were not.

Pete and I headed down toward the bears to the west. After what I'd estimate as 10-15 minutes of downhill walking and looking back at Hunter motioning us to go on as we were, Hunter suddenly changed signals to tell us to return to the top of the mountain we'd just descended. At the time, Pete and I didn't know what to think. We'd later learn that the big brown we'd spotted earlier was now coming into the canyon to the east.

Hunter was sure it was a large bear and he wanted us to come stalk it. We started back up the mountain, and about half-way up, we saw signals to go back to the original route. Anyone who's been here starts to wonder, "What has the altitude done to my partner!" At this point, I took off down the mountain and Pete decided to walk parallel to the slope and head north. The next thing I know, I'm still watching the bear's movement from below and I decide to check with my "mountain top" friend, but now I have two "mountain toppers." Pete had circled around and ended-up back at the top of the mountain with Hunter. Two bears at the bottom, two companions at the top, and I'm nearly in the middle but closer to the bottom, so I decide I'll have the lone stalk.

I'm going to quote my two hunting partners as they later told me the story, but first I'll tell how they got their "50-yard-line seat."

The wind was right for my stalk as I lowered myself parallel to the ground (as much as a 6-foot, 5-inch frame can be lowered.) I knew this big bear was to my right, so I kept going straight to keep downwind. Before long, I ran into a stream and made the choice of turning into the wind and hoping the bear hadn't gotten past me. Little did I know the bear had gone in the opposite direction, turned around and was now headed toward me on the same side of the stream. I should now relate the sight my hunting partners saw and later related.

"It was like having a 50-yard-line seat at the stadium," said Pete. (Remember, Pete was supposed to have been with me as a backup.) Pete and Hunter were watching through their binoculars as the meeting was progressing between me and the bear. I was downwind heading up the stream, and the bear was headed with the wind and straight toward me. Neither one of us knew the other was in such close proximity. As the bear and I were approaching each other, the conversation between Pete and Hunter became quite excited, according to Hunter. He thought I'd be all right, but Pete was worried. As the bear and I got closer and closer, Hunter stated, "He'd better see him soon, real soon!"

Suddenly, the big brown bear was only 50 yards away and you can bet my adrenalin was flowing! I spotted him over a big mound of grass and quickly shed my pack. I prepared to fire, but I thought I'd wait until the bear walked around the grass because I didn't think he'd spotted me yet. I knelt and took aim. The big bruin came over the mound and I fired my .338 Winchester Mag (with 200 grain bullet), burying it in the bear's chest. I raised from my kneeling position to chamber another shell and the bear met every movement. He raised his right paw and roared his disapproval. I shot again and was met with the same gesture. The third bullet finally quieted him. I knew he was a large bear, and I took my time approaching him.

Not long after, my hunting partners arrived to detail what they'd seen from their "50-yard-line seat." Hunter then commented "You should have heard him roar after the first shot!" All I could say was that I did hear it, very well, thank you, and I will never forget it. I had taken a 10 foot, 1 inch bear with a large skull. Lady Luck was with me for sure on this one! I've often thought of the other possible outcomes on a confrontation like this. I'm just glad "Mr. Murphy" waited till later to show his stuff; he weathered-us-in for two extra days!

TABULATIONS OF RECORDED TROPHIES
20TH AWARDS ENTRY PERIOD
1986 - 1988

The trophy data shown herein have been taken from score charts in the Records Archives of the Boone and Crockett Club for the 20th Awards entry period, 1986-1988. Trophies listed are those that meet minimum score and other stated requirements of trophy entry for the period. The final scores and rank shown are official, except for trophies shown with an asterisk. The asterisk is assigned to trophies whose entry scores are subject to certification by an Awards Panel of Judges. The asterisk can be removed (except in case of a potential World's Record) by the submitting of two additional, independent scorings by Official Measurers of the Boone and Crockett Club. The Records Committee of the Club will review the three scorings available (original, plus two additional) and determine which, if any, will be accepted in lieu of the Judges Panel measurement. When the score has been accepted as final by the Records Committee, the asterisk will be removed in future editions of the all-time records book, *Records of North American Big Game*, and other publicatons. In the case of a potential World's Record, the trophy must come before a Judges Panel at the end of an entry period. Only a Judges Panel can certify a World's Record and finalize its score.

Asterisked trophies are shown at the end of the listings for their category. They are not ranked, as their final score is subject to revision by a Judges Panel or by the submission of additional official scorings, as described above. Note that "pr" preceding date of kill indicates "prior to" the date shown for kill.

The scientific and vernacular names, and the sequence of presentation, follows that suggested in the *Revised Checklist of North American Mammals North of Mexico, 1979* (J. Knox Jones, et al; Texas Tech University, 14 December 1979.)

TROPHY BOUNDARIES

Many of the categories recognized in the records keeping are based upon subspecies differences. In nature, subspecies freely interbreed where their ranges overlap, thus necessitating the setting of geographic boundaries to keep them separate for records keeping purposes.

Geographic boundaries are described for a number of categories. These include: brown and grizzly bear; American and Roosevelt's elk; mule, Columbia, and Sitka blacktail deer; whitetail and Coues' deer; moose; and caribou. Pertinent information is included in the trophy data listings that follow, but the complete, detailed description for each is to be found in the latest editon (9th. Ed., 1988) of the all-time records book, *Records of North American Big Game*, and also in the "how-to" book, *Measuring and Scoring North American Big Game Trophies*.

In addition to category specific boundaries, all trophies must be from North America, north of the south border of Mexico, to be eligible. For pelagic trophies, such as walrus and polar bear, they must be from the U.S. side of the International Date Line to be eligible.

Trophy boundaries are set by the Boone and Crockett Club's Records of North American Big Game Committee, working with the latest and best available information from scientific researchers, guides, hunters, and other parties with serious interest in our big game resources. In general, boundaries are set so that it is highly unlikely that specimens of the larger category can be taken within the boundaries set for the smaller category, thus upsetting the rankings of the smaller category. Trophy boundaries are revised as necessary to maintain this separation of the categories.

Black Bear

Ursus americanus americanus and related subspecies

Minimum Score 20 World's Record 23-10/16

Score	Greatest Length of Skull Without Lower Jaw	Greatest Width of Skull	Locality Killed	By Whom Killed	Owner	Date Killed	Rank
23 7/16	14 8/16	8 15/16	Lycoming Co., Pa.	William H. Slater	Pennsylvania Game Comm.	1987	1
22 9/16	14 6/16	8 3/16	Greenlee Co., Ariz.	William H. Slater	William H. Slater	1987	2
22 3/16	13 13/16	8 6/16	Frog Lake, Alta.	Darren Daniel	Darren Daniel	1983	3
22 2/16	13 11/16	8 7/16	Sanpete Co., Utah	Larry W. Cox	Larry W. Cox	1987	4
22	13 11/16	8 3/16	Maknak, Man.	Cory A. Pardon	Cory A. Pardon	1986	5
22	13 10/16	8 6/16	Hamilton Co., N.Y.	Samuel A. Johnson	Samuel A. Johnson	1986	5
22	13 11/16	8 5/16	Carbon Co., Utah	Michael J. Hreinson	Michael J. Hreinson	1987	5
22	13 7/16	8 9/16	Prince of Wales Island, Alaska	John W. Simons	John W. Simons	1987	5
22	13 7/16	8 9/16	Roscommon Co., Mich.	Matthew A. Gettler	Matthew A. Gettler	1987	5
21 15/16	13 9/16	8 6/16	Russell, Man.	Gerry Mushumanski	Gerry Mushumanski	1987	10
21 13/16	14 6/16	7 7/16	St. Johns Co., Fla.	Picked Up	Florida Game & Fresh Water Fish Comm.	1985	11
21 12/16	13 14/16	7 14/16	California Creek, Alaska	Boyd J. Blair	Boyd J. Blair	1976	12
21 12/16	13 11/16	8 1/16	Greenwater Lake, Sask.	John Woulfe	John Woulfe	1987	12
21 11/16	13 5/16	8 6/16	Kern Co., Calif.	George H. Hershberger	George H. Hershberger	1985	14
21 11/16	13 7/16	8 4/16	Karta Bay, Alaska	Douglas A. McNeil	Douglas A. McNeil	1985	14
21 11/16	13 6/16	8 5/16	Cass Co., Minn.	Anne M. Zahalka	Anne M. Zahalka	1986	14
21 11/16	13 15/16	7 12/16	Hyde Co., N.C.	Gurnwood L. Radcliff, Jr.	Gurnwood L. Radcliff, Jr.	1986	14
21 11/16	13 11/16	8	Prairie River, Sask.	Gregory Stabrylla	Gregory Stabrylla	1987	14
21 9/16	13 9/16	8	Tioga Co., Pa.	Thomas B. Gamble	Thomas B. Gamble	1987	19
21 9/16	13 3/16	8 6/16	Pelican Lake, Man.	Rick D. Oliphant	Rick D. Oliphant	1987	19
21 8/16	13 7/16	8 1/16	Rossburn, Man.	Unknown	Randy Bean	1980	21
21 8/16	13 11/16	7 13/16	Douglas Co., Wisc.	Picked Up	Wisconsin Dept. of Natl. Resc.	1984	21
21 8/16	12 15/16	8 9/16	Mesa Co., Colo.	Rem B. Bennett, Jr.	Rem B. Bennett, Jr.	1986	21
21 8/16	13 6/16	8 2/16	Navajo Co., Ariz.	Fred Peters	Fred Peters	1987	21
21 7/16	13 3/16	8 4/16	Greenlee Co., Ariz.	Robin W. Bechtel	Robin W. Bechtel	1985	25
21 7/16	13 4/16	8 3/16	Tokeen, Alaska	Terry D. Denmon	Terry D. Denmon	1986	25
21 7/16	13 6/16	8 1/16	Loon Lake, Sask.	Wyatt Barnes	Wyatt Barnes	1988	25
21 5/16	13	8 5/16	Mendocino Co., Calif.	John Jacobs	John Jacobs	1985	28
21 5/16	13 2/16	8 3/16	Navajo Co., Ariz.	D. Howard Mullins	D. Howard Mullins	1986	28
21 5/16	13 4/16	8 1/16	Gila Co., Ariz.	Neil L. Sullivan	Neil L. Sullivan	1986	28
21 5/16	12 13/16	8 9/16	Rio Blanco Co., Colo.	Jason Steiner	Jason Steiner	1987	28

Black Bear - Continued

Score	Greatest Length of Skull Without Lower Jaw	Greatest Width of Skull	Locality Killed	By Whom Killed	Owner	Date Killed	Rank
21 5/16	13 2/16	8 3/16	Prince of Wales Island, Alaska	Mark S. Rodin	Mark S. Rodin	1987	28
21 4/16	13	8 4/16	Marquette Co., Mich.	David L. Pietro	David L. Pietro	1975	33
21 4/16	13 4/16	8	Vanderhoof, B.C.	William Stanley	William Stanley	1985	33
21 4/16	13 7/16	7 13/16	Navajo Co., Ariz.	Fred Peters	Fred Peters	1988	33
21 3/16	13 1/16	8 2/16	Graham Co., Ariz.	O. Dale Porter	O. Dale Porter	1970	36
21 3/16	12 15/16	8 4/16	Slave Lake, Alta.	Dwight E. Diehl	Dwight E. Diehl	1982	36
21 3/16	13 5/16	7 14/16	McBride Lake, Sask.	Maurice Maurer	Maurice Maurer	1984	36
21 3/16	12 19/16	8 9/16	Chuwhels Mt., B.C.	Ronald J. Couture	Ronald J. Couture	1986	36
21 3/16	13 1/16	8 2/16	Valleyview, Alta.	Alfred Heschl	Alfred Heschl	1986	36
21 3/16	13	7 12/16	Minitonas, Man.	Scott Ward	Scott Ward	1986	36
21 3/16	13 3/16	8	Mesa Co., Colo.	Marilyn J. Scott	Marilyn J. Scott	1987	36
21 3/16	13	8 3/16	Eaglehead Lake, Ont.	Ty Sweeney	Ty Sweeney	1987	36
21 3/16	13 2/16	8 1/16	Whiteshell Lake, Man.	Paul D. Pauls	Paul D. Pauls	1987	36
21 3/16	13 6/16	7 13/16	Washington Co., Maine	John S. Barmby	John S. Barmby	1987	36
21 3/16	13 6/16	8 1/16	Lincoln Co., Wisc.	Daniel L. Lemke	Daniel L. Lemke	1987	36
21 3/16	13 8/16	7 11/16	Jim Lake, Sask.	James A. Lynn	James A. Lynn	1988	36
21 2/16	13	8	Fox Creek, Alta.	Brent E. Eeles	Brent E. Eeles	1982	48
21 2/16	12 15/16	8 3/16	Gallatin Co., Mont.	Steven M. Steele	Steven M. Steele	1986	48
21 2/16	13 2/16	8	Montmorency Co., Mich.	Kenneth R. Reed	Kenneth R. Reed	1986	48
21 2/16	13	8 2/16	Caribou Co., Idaho	Ronald J. Thompson	Ronald J. Thompson	1986	48
21 2/16	13 9/16	7 9/16	Gila Co., Ariz.	Jesse L. Enterkin, Jr.	Jesse L. Enterkin, Jr.	1987	48
21 2/16	13 3/16	7 15/16	Beltrami Co., Minn.	Douglas P. Budensiek	Douglas P. Budensiek	1987	48
21 2/16	13 8/16	7 10/16	Marco, Man.	Erwin Weidenfeld	Erwin Weidenfeld	1987	48
21 2/16	13 2/16	8	Kuiu Island, Alaska	Robert M. Teskey	Robert M. Teskey	1988	48
21 1/16	12 15/16	8 2/16	Menominee Co., Mich.	Manfred L. Pfitzer	Manfred L. Pfitzer	1986	56
21 1/16	13 5/16	7 12/16	Valley River, Man.	Craig Kozak	Craig Kozak	1987	56
21 1/16	13 4/16	7 13/16	Gila Co., Ariz.	Daniel G. Robinett	Daniel G. Robinett	1987	56
21 1/16	12 13/16	8 4/16	Klakas Inlet, Alaska	Stephen P. Harvey	Stephen P. Harvey	1988	56
21 1/16	12 15/16	8 2/16	Eagle Lake, Sask.	Randall N. Olejnik	Randall N. Olejnik	1988	56
21	13 2/16	7 14/16	Santa Barbara Co., Calif.	Picked Up	Marshall Munger	1984	61
21	13 1/16	7 15/16	Garfield Co., Colo.	Gordon L. Haxton	Gordon L. Haxton	1985	61
21	13 3/16	7 13/16	Graham Co., Ariz.	Mark J. Bensley	Mark J. Bensley	1986	61
21	13 1/16	7 15/16	Carrot River, Sask.	Demetry Procyk	Demetry Procyk	1987	61
21	13 6/16	7 19/16	Ogemaw Co., Mich.	William D. Massey	William D. Massey	1987	61

		Location	Hunter	Owner	Year		Rank
20 15/16	13 1/16	7 14/16	Prince of Wales Island, Alaska	Donald E. King	Donald E. King	1986		66
20 14/16	12 8/16	8 6/16	Eagle Co., Colo.	Willis D. Bassett	Willis D. Bassett	1987		67
20 13/16	12 9/16	8 4/16	Price Co., Wisc.	William J. Straveler	William J. Straveler	1987		68
20 11/16	13	7 11/16	Klamath Co., Oreg.	Alan R. Cain	Alan R. Cain	1986		69
20 11/16	12 14/16	7 13/16	Cook Co., Minn.	Dana W. Haagenson	Dana W. Haagenson	1986		69
20 11/16	12 14/16	7 13/16	Threemile Creek, Alaska	George P. Mann	George P. Mann	1987		69
20 11/16	13 3/16	7 9/16	Wasilla, Alaska	Michael R. Lutes	Michael R. Lutes	1988		69
20 10/16	13	7 10/16	Neck Lake, Alaska	Cheryl A. Capps	Cheryl A. Capps	1988		73
20 9/16	12 14/16	7 11/16	Piwei River, Sask.	Lloyd B. Pistone	Lloyd B. Pistone	1988		74
20 9/16	13 1/16	7 8/16	Lac la Plonge, Sask.	Danny D. Turner	Danny D. Turner	1988		74
20 8/16	12 12/16	7 12/16	Cass Co., Minn.	Samuel F. Smith	Samuel F. Smith	1985		76
20 8/16	12 14/16	7 10/16	Sundre, Alta.	Ronald A. Bowers	Ronald A. Bowers	1987		76
20 7/16	12 9/16	7 14/16	Sheridan Co., Wyo.	Mike D. Janich	Mike D. Janich	1970		78
20 6/16	12 8/16	7 14/16	Duchesne Co., Utah	Jeffrey K. Kummer	Jeffrey K. Kummer	1986		79
20 6/16	12 12/16	7 10/16	Maricopa Co., Ariz.	Charles A. Grimmett	Charles A. Grimmett	1986		79
20 6/16	12 5/16	8 1/16	Spiritwood, Sask.	Robert W. Peet	Robert W. Peet	1987		79
20 5/16	12 8/16	7 13/16	Kuiu Island, Alaska	Alvin C. Lundell	Alvin C. Lundell	1985		82
20 5/16	12 7/16	7 14/16	Dore Lake, Sask.	Lloyd B. Pistone	Lloyd B. Pistone	1986		82
20 5/16	12 12/16	7 9/16	Garfield Co., Colo.	Paul H. Prather	Paul H. Prather	1988		82
20 5/16	12 10/16	7 11/16	Umatilla Co., Oreg.	Kerry A. Fann	Kerry A. Fann	1988		82
20 4/16	12 8/16	7 12/16	Greenlee Co., Ariz.	Robin W. Bechtel	Robin W. Bechtel	1979		86
20 4/16	12 9/16	7 11/16	Kuiu Island, Alaska	Walter R. Michael	Walter R. Michael	1986		86
20 3/16	12 5/16	7 14/16	Aroostook Co., Maine	Peter R. Cole	Peter R. Cole	1988		88
20 2/16	12 8/16	7 10/16	Renfrew, Ont.	Daniel A. Cea	Daniel A. Cea	1986		89
20 2/16	12 10/16	7 8/16	Gallants, Nfld.	Melvin Locklyn	Melvin Locklyn	1986		89
20 2/16	12 11/16	7 7/16	Garfield Co., Colo.	Terry L. Smalec	Terry L. Smalec	1987		89
20 2/16	12 6/16	7 12/16	Teton Co., Wyo.	R. Bryan Williams	R. Bryan Williams	1988		89
20 1/16	12 3/16	7 14/16	Gila Co., Ariz.	Richard L. Wolfel	Richard L. Wolfel	1987		93
20 1/16	12 6/16	7 11/16	Sublette Co., Wyo.	W. Frank Chapman, Jr.	W. Frank Chapman, Jr.	1988		93
20	12 4/16	7 12/16	Piscataquis Co., Maine	Michael J. Delfino, Sr.	Michael J. Delfino, Sr.	1978		95
20	12 14/16	7 2/16	Canyon Creek, B.C.	Bruce F. Gilbert	Bruce F. Gilbert	1986		95
20	12 4/16	7 12/16	Duchesne Co., Utah	Jet C. Abegglen	Jet C. Abegglen	1986		95
20	12 10/16	7 6/16	Durban, Man.	Russell Topp	Russell Topp	1986		95
20	12 7/16	7 9/16	Gila Co., Ariz.	Gordon A. Grimmis	Gordon A. Grimmis	1987		95
22 8/16*	14 3/16	8 5/16	Crane River, Man.	Joe's Taxidermy	Unknown	1981	pr	
22 7/16*	14 1/16	8 6/16	Sevier Co., Utah	Richard A. Fillmore	Richard A. Fillmore	1967		

* Final Score subject to revision by additional verifying measurements.

Grizzly Bear
Ursus arctos horribilis

Minimum Score 23 World's Record 27-2/16

Score	Greatest Length of Skull Without Lower Jaw	Greatest Width of Skull	Locality Killed	By Whom Killed	Owner	Date Killed	Rank
26 1/16	16 4/16	9 13/16	Camelback Mt., Alaska	Thomas E. Smith	Thomas E. Smith	1985	1
26	16 2/16	9 14/16	Meziadin Lake, B.C.	Peter Martinson	Peter Martinson	1987	2
25 15/16	15 15/16	10 5/16	Tubukutulik River, Alaska	William A. Brooks, Sr.	William A. Brooks, Sr.	1986	3
25 9/16	16 1/16	9 8/16	Klinaklini River, B.C.	Homer Harvey	Homer Harvey	1987	4
25 8/16	16 2/16	9 6/16	Iskut River, B.C.	Robin Buchanan	Robin Buchanan	1987	5
25 8/16	15 15/16	9 9/16	Ospika River, B.C.	Frank H. Gunther	Frank H. Gunther	1987	5
25 6/16	15 13/16	9 9/16	Liard River, B.C.	Norman F. Schenk	Norman F. Schenk	1986	7
25 6/16	16 2/16	9 4/16	Bella Coola, B.C.	G. Thierbach & F. Rad	George Thierbach	1987	7
25 3/16	15 9/16	9 9/16	Anahim Lake, B.C.	Lloyd E. Nygaard	Lloyd E. Nygaard	1973	9
25 3/16	16	9 3/16	Nunakogok River, Alaska	Randy Jackson	Randy Jackson	1984	9
25 3/16	15 14/16	9 5/16	Boston Creek, Alaska	Sigurd E. Murphy	Sigurd E. Murphy	1987	9
25 3/16	15 8/16	9 11/16	Salcha River, Alaska	Danny E. Walker	Danny E. Walker	1987	9
25 2/16	15 2/16	10	Kemano River, B.C.	Victor L. Sensenig	Victor L. Sensenig	1983	13
25 2/16	15 12/16	9 6/16	Toklat River, Alaska	Marvin Carkhuff	Marvin Carkhuff	1987	13
25 1/16	15 12/16	9 5/16	Euchiniko Lakes, B.C.	Indian	Mark J. Simonson	1986	15
24 15/16	15 5/16	9 10/16	Tetsa River, B.C.	John J. Belous	John J. Belous	1985	16
24 13/16	15 8/16	9 5/16	Noatak River, Alaska	Dave R. Cerenzia	Dave R. Cerenzia	1987	17
24 13/16	15 5/16	9 8/16	Bear River, Alaska	Richard M. Cowles	Richard M. Cowles	1987	17
24 12/16	15 6/16	9 6/16	Norton Sound, Alaska	Lewis E. Henyon	Lewis E. Henyon	1984	19
24 12/16	16 2/16	8 10/16	Tsayta Lake, B.C.	Vincent A. Pisani	Vincent A. Pisani	1986	19
24 11/16	15 9/16	9 2/16	American Creek, Alaska	Marvin H. Hanebuth	Marvin H. Hanebuth	1986	21
24 11/16	15 6/16	9 5/16	Cadomin, Alta.	Pemble Davis	Pemble Davis	1987	21
24 8/16	15 9/16	8 15/16	Brazeau Mts., Alta.	Richard F. Edmonds, Jr.	Richard F. Edmonds, Jr.	1986	23
24 8/16	15 5/16	8 15/16	Kuskokwim River, Alaska	Jerome D. Melbinger	Jerome D. Melbinger	1986	23
24 8/16	14 14/16	9 10/16	Greyling Creek, Yukon	Lee A. Hickey, Sr.	Lee A. Hickey, Sr.	1987	23
24 7/16	14 15/16	9 8/16	Wulik River, Alaska	Peter W. Dress	Bill Dress	1986	26
24 7/16	14 15/16	8 9/16	Nation River, Alaska	Robert W. Stenehjem	Robert W. Stenehjem	1987	26
24 6/16	15 10/16	8 12/16	Macoun Creek, B.C.	Martin McIlroy	Martin McIlroy	1984	28
24 5/16	15 4/16	9 1/16	Stikine River, B.C.	Frederick L. Wood III	Frederick L. Wood III	1986	29
24 5/16	15	9 5/16	Mt. Fairplay, Alaska	David G. Kelleyhouse	David G. Kelleyhouse	1987	29
24 4/16	14 12/16	9 8/16	Luwa Mt., B.C.	Joel B. Benner	Joel B. Benner	1985	31
24 3/16	14 15/16	9 4/16	Monashee Mts., B.C.	Georg Frisch	Georg Frisch	1986	32

24 3/16	14 15/16	9 4/16	Squirrel River, Alaska	Bob L. Eubank	Bob L. Eubank	1986	32
24 3/16	14 14/16	9 5/16	Sinclair Mills, B.C.	Steven L. Gingras	Steven L. Gingras	1986	32
24 2/16	15 19/16	8 8/16	Deep Valley Creek, Alta.	Gerald Desjardins	Gerald Desjardins	1984	35
24 2/16	15	9 2/16	Casadepaga River, Alaska	Richard L. Hoffman	Richard L. Hoffman	1987	35
24 1/16	15 7/16	8 19/16	California Creek, Alaska	Boyd J. Blair	Boyd J. Blair	1975	37
24	14 11/16	9 5/16	Kelly River, Alaska	Thomas W. Becker	Thomas W. Becker	1986	38
24	14 12/16	9 4/16	Stikine River, B.C.	Lynn F. Greenlee	Lynn F. Greenlee	1987	38
23 7/16	14 4/16	9 3/16	Hirschfield Creek, B.C.	J. Mark Hanger	J. Mark Hanger	1987	40
23	14 13/16	8 3/16	Nulato River, Alaska	Brenton Morgenstern	Brenton Morgenstern	1988	41
26 9/16*	16 10/16	9 15/16	Bella Coola, B.C.	Aivars O. Berkis	Aivars O. Berkis	1986	
25 19/16*	16 4/16	9 6/16	Oldhouse Creek, Alta.	Picked Up	Roderick R. Hallam	1986	

* Final Score subject to revision by additional verifying measurements.

Alaska Brown Bear

Ursus arctos middendorffi and certain related subspecies

Minimum Score 26 — World's Record 30-12/16

Score	Greatest Length of Skull Without Lower Jaw	Greatest Width of Skull	Locality Killed	By Whom Killed	Owner	Date Killed	Rank
29 13/16	17 14/16	11 15/16	Kodiak Island, Alaska	W. Ted Burger	W. Ted Burger	1985	1
29	17 12/16	11 4/16	Shearwater Bay, Alaska	Chester E. Chellman	Chester E. Chellman	1987	2
29	17 12/16	11 4/16	Kiavak Bay, Alaska	John L. Largura	John L. Largura	1987	2
29	17 14/16	11 2/16	Amber Bay, Alaska	Richard M. Welch	Richard M. Welch	1988	4
28 15/16	17 9/16	11 7/16	Olga Bay, Alaska	Alan O'Neil	Alan O'Neil	1988	5
28 15/16	18 7/16	10 9/16	Alaska Pen., Alaska	Ron D. King	Ron D. King	1988	5
28 13/16	17 14/16	10 15/16	Beaver Bay, Alaska	Jesse T. Kirk	Jesse T. Kirk	1988	7
28 12/16	17 5/16	11 7/16	Kodiak Island, Alaska	Joe B. Brewster	Joe B. Brewster	1985	8
28 12/16	17 14/16	10 14/16	Lilly Lake, Alaska	Darryl W. Indvik	Darryl W. Indvik	1987	8
28 11/16	17 12/16	10 15/16	Cold Bay, Alaska	John F. Bermen	John F. Bermen	1988	10
28 10/16	17 5/16	11 5/16	Kodiak, Alaska	Larry L. Stephens	Larry L. Stephens	1984	11
28 8/16	17 4/16	11 4/16	Kiavak Bay, Alaska	Robert J. Welsh, Jr.	Robert J. Welsh, Jr.	1987	12
28 8/16	17 12/16	10 12/16	Ash Creek, Alaska	Phil N. Alward	Phil N. Alward	1988	12
28 7/16	17 8/16	10 15/16	Uganik River, Alaska	Donald W. Baxter	Donald W. Baxter	1985	14
28 7/16	17 7/16	10 14/16	Stuyahok River, Alaska	William S. Greene, Jr.	William S. Greene, Jr.	1985	15
28 5/16	16 12/16	11 9/16	Kodiak Island, Alaska	Roy F. Bain	Roy F. Bain	1988	15
28 4/16	17 5/16	10 15/16	Alaska Pen., Alaska	H. Blake Allen	H. Blake Allen	1986	17
28 2/16	17 19/16	10 9/16	Cold Bay, Alaska	George A. Bettas	George A. Bettas	1986	18
28 2/16	17 12/16	10 6/16	Kiavak Bay, Alaska	Wayne E. Clark	Wayne E. Clark	1987	18
28 2/16	17 5/16	10 13/16	Pumice Creek, Alaska	Tony E. Jorgenson	Tony E. Jorgenson	1988	18
28 1/16	18	10 1/16	Alaska Pen., Alaska	Kurt R. Clark	Kurt R. Clark	1986	21
28 1/16	17 5/16	10 12/16	Sturgeon River, Alaska	Michael R. Dullen	Michael R. Dullen	1987	21
28 1/16	17 9/16	10 8/16	Canoe Bay, Alaska	John E. Hoye	John E. Hoye	1987	21
28	17 4/16	10 12/16	Afognak Lake, Alaska	Picked Up	Leon A. Metz	1984	24
27 15/16	17 3/16	10 12/16	Sturgeon River, Alaska	Timothy W. Lawrence	Timothy W. Lawrence	1988	25
27 11/16	17 13/16	9 14/16	Windy Bay, Alaska	William H. Crawford	William H. Crawford	1987	26
27 11/16	17 2/16	10 9/16	Sturgeon River, Alaska	Stephan A. Parks	Stephan A. Parks	1987	26
27 8/16	17	10 8/16	Kodiak Island, Alaska	Jeffrey K. Flaming	Jeffrey K. Flaming	1986	28
27 7/16	17 7/16	10	Beaver Bay, Alaska	Pierre A. Fontaine	Pierre A. Fontaine	1988	29
27 7/16	16 6/16	11 1/16	Karluk Lake, Alaska	Roger H. Rosin	Roger H. Rosin	1988	29
27 2/16	17 3/16	9 15/16	Kodiak Island, Alaska	Arlo J. Spiess	Arlo J. Spiess	1987	31
27	16 10/16	10 6/16	Deadman Bay, Alaska	Robert D. Hancock, Jr.	Robert D. Hancock, Jr.	1987	32

27	16 4/16	10 12/16	Kaiugnak Bay, Alaska	Robert D. Rich II	1988	32
26 15/16	16 14/16	10 1/16	Uganik Bay, Alaska	Randy S. Shumate	1988	34
26 14/16	16 14/16	10	Kodiak Island, Alaska	F.J. Farmer III	1986	35
26 14/16	16 6/16	10 8/16	Zachar Bay, Alaska	Ronald G. Danner	1987	35
26 14/16	16 9/16	10 5/16	Karluk Lake, Alaska	William O. West	1988	35
26 12/16	16 13/16	9 15/16	Red Shirt Lake, Alaska	Philip L. Iverson	1986	38
26 11/16	16 5/16	10 6/16	Painter Creek, Alaska	Mark D. Nuessle	1986	39
26 4/16	16 15/16	9 5/16	Halibut Bay, Alaska	Robert D. Boutang	1986	40
26 3/16	16 10/16	9 9/16	Alinchak Bay, Alaska	Edward H. Dobler	1987	41
26	16 2/16	9 14/16	Terror Bay, Alaska	Gary L. Simpson	1987	42
26	15 7/16	10 9/16	Kodiak Island, Alaska	Bobby W. Hill	1987	42
29 5/16*	18 3/16	11 2/16	Kodiak Island, Alaska	Antonin Fabriger	1986	
29 4/16*	18 6/16	10 14/16	Stepovak Bay, Alaska	Kurt A. Haskin	1986	

* Final Score subject to revision by additional verifying measurements.

Cougar or Mountain Lion

Felis concolor hippolestes and related subspecies

Minimum Score 14-8/16   World's Record 16-4/16

Score	Greatest Length of Skull Without Lower Jaw	Greatest Width of Skull	Locality Killed	By Whom Killed	Owner	Date Killed	Rank
16 3/16	9 9/16	6 11/16	Idaho Co., Idaho	Gene R. Alford	B&C National Collection	1988	1
15 11/16	9 4/16	6 7/16	Idaho Co., Idaho	Richard C. Farthing	Richard C. Farthing	1988	2
15 10/16	9	6 19/16	Tatla Lake, B.C.	Harold J. Coult	Harold J. Coult	1986	3
15 9/16	9 2/16	6 7/16	Elko Co., Nev.	Joel C. Brown	Joel C. Brown	1986	4
15 9/16	9 2/16	6 7/16	Flathead Co., Mont.	Rusby Seabaugh	Brad Seabaugh	1986	4
15 8/16	9 3/16	6 5/16	Robbins Range, B.C.	R.J. Petrie & G. Schweitzer	Robert J. Petrie	1987	6
15 8/16	9	6 8/16	Wallowa Co., Oreg.	Robin D. Dickenson	Robin D. Dickenson	1987	6
15 7/16	9	6 7/16	Columbia Co., Wash.	Curtis D. Neal	Curtis D. Neal	1986	8
15 7/16	9 2/16	6 5/16	Idaho Co., Idaho	Harold A. Kottre	Harold A. Kottre	1988	8
15 7/16	9 1/16	6 6/16	Lewis & Clark Co., Mont.	Mike Barthelmess	M. Barthelmess & D. Wilson	1987	8
15 6/16	9 1/16	6 5/16	Clearwater Co., Idaho	Daniel J. Greve	Daniel J. Greve	1985	11
15 6/16	9	6 6/16	Idaho Co., Idaho	Ralph L. Hatter	Ralph L. Hatter	1987	11
15 6/16	8 15/16	6 7/16	Mineral Co., Mont.	James E. Miller III	James E. Miller III	1988	11
15 5/16	8 13/16	6 8/16	Okanogan Co., Wash.	Clyde A. Paul	Clyde A. Paul	1965	14
15 5/16	9	6 5/16	Rio Blanco Co., Colo.	Rocky O. Alburtiss	Rocky O. Alburtiss	1987	14
15 5/16	9 1/16	6 4/16	Beaverhead Co., Mont.	R.C. Carlson & O.D. Perala	R.C. Carlson & O.D. Perala	1987	14
15 4/16	9	6 4/16	Rio Arriba Co., N.M.	Ray B. Bailey	Ray B. Bailey	1986	17
15 4/16	9	6 4/16	Uintah Co., Utah	Albert L. Farace	Albert L. Farace	1986	17
15 4/16	9	6 4/16	Madison Co., Mont.	Stephen P. Connell	Stephen P. Connell	1986	17
15 4/16	9	6 4/16	Columbia Co., Wash.	Gregory P. Leid	Gregory P. Leid	1987	17
15 4/16	9 1/16	6 3/16	Porcupine Hills, Alta.	Lyle Czember	Lyle Czember	1988	17
15 3/16	8 13/16	6 6/16	Silver Creek, Alta.	John E. Cassidy	John E. Cassidy	1981	22
15 3/16	8 14/16	6 5/16	Plumbob Mt., B.C.	Andreas Felber	Andreas Felber	1985	22
15 3/16	8 14/16	6 5/16	Hot Springs Co., Wyo.	Dan B. Artery	Dan B. Artery	1986	22
15 3/16	8 14/16	6 5/16	Idaho Co., Idaho	Steve C. Ryan	Richard Farthing	1987	22
15 2/16	8 12/16	6 6/16	Little White Mt., B.C.	Thomas M. Lavelle	Thomas M. Lavelle	1986	26
15 2/16	8 13/16	6 5/16	Latah Co., Idaho	Terry L. Watkins	Terry L. Watkins	1986	26
15 2/16	8 13/16	6 5/16	Castle River, Alta.	Duane B. Schultz	Duane B. Schultz	1988	26
15 2/16	8 12/16	6 5/16	Utah Co., Utah	Brent M. Taylor	Brent M. Taylor	1988	26
15 1/16	8 14/16	6 3/16	Idaho Co., Idaho	Elliot V. Nelson	Elliot V. Nelson	1965	30
15 1/16	8 14/16	6 3/16	Idaho Co., Idaho	Roy M. Schumacher	Roy M. Schumacher	1984	30
15 1/16	8 13/16	6 4/16	Garfield Co., Colo.	Jay H. Kneasel	Jay H. Kneasel	1985	30

		Location	Hunter	Owner	Date	Rank
15 1/16	9 1/16	Lincoln Co., Mont.	Gary C. Cargill	Gary C. Cargill	1986	30
15 1/16	8 15/16	Clearwater Co., Idaho	Charles C. Smith	Charles C. Smith	1987	30
15 1/16	8 14/16	Garfield Co., Colo.	Joseph S. Arrain	Joseph S. Arrain	1987	30
15 1/16	8 13/16	Newington Creek, B.C.	James W. Anderson	James W. Anderson	1987	30
15 1/16	8 14/16	Apache Co., Ariz.	John F. Peters	John F. Peters	1988	30
15	8 15/16	Millard Co., Utah	William J. Alldredge	William J. Alldredge	1982	38
15	8 13/16	San Miguel Co., Colo.	Jerry J. Jergins	Jerry J. Jergins	1985	38
15	8 14/16	Idaho Co., Idaho	John G. Klauss	John G. Klauss	1986	38
15	9	Rio Grande Co., Colo.	Richard J. Dugas	Richard J. Dugas	1986	38
15	8 15/16	Dolores Co., Colo.	Ray E. Ables	Ray E. Ables	1986	38
15	8 12/16	Dolores Co., Colo.	Richard S. Inman	Richard S. Inman	1987	38
15	8 15/16	Lewis & Clark Co., Mont.	Jim Foster	Jim Foster	1987	38
15	8 14/16	Deadeye Creek, B.C.	Claude W. Rohrbaugh	Claude W. Rohrbaugh	1987	38
15	8 13/16	Ferry Co., Wash.	Arthur E. Crate	Arthur E. Crate	1988	38
14 15/16	9 1/16	Jeff Davis Co., Texas	Clint L. Siddons	Clint L. Siddons	1986	47
14 15/16	8 11/16	Garfield Co., Colo.	Oliver G. McCutchan, Jr.	Oliver G. McCutchan, Jr.	1987	47
14 14/16	8 14/16	Chaffee Co., Colo.	Paul F. Gabel	Paul F. Gabel	1965	49
14 14/16	8 13/16	Castle River, Alta.	Grant L. Jasman	Grant L. Jasman	1987	49
14 14/16	8 11/16	Wayne Co., Utah	Ron Morrill	Ron Morrill	1987	49
14 13/16	8 11/16	Millard Co., Utah	Dee J. Burnett	Dee J. Burnett	1987	52
14 13/16	8 11/16	Lemhi Co., Idaho	George L. Kudrick	George L. Kudrick	1987	52
14 12/16	8 10/16	Lemhi Co., Idaho	Dan F. Holleman	Dan F. Holleman	1978	54
14 12/16	8 12/16	Mesa Co., Colo.	Joe B. Owen	Joe B. Owen	1987	54
14 12/16	8 6/16	Greenlee Co., Ariz.	Thomas D. Suedmeier	Thomas D. Suedmeier	1987	54
14 11/16	5 14/16	Washington Co., Utah	Eldon L. Buckner	Eldon L. Buckner	1986	57
14 10/16	8 9/16	Box Elder Co., Utah	Jerry E. Mason	Jerry E. Mason	1982	58
14 10/16	8 11/16	Lincoln Co., N.M.	Humberto Garcia	Humberto Garcia	1986	58
14 9/16	8 8/16	Wigwam River, B.C.	William D. Hutchens	William D. Hutchens	1982	60
14 9/16	8 10/16	Rio Arriba Co., N.M.	Larry J. Steeley, Jr.	Larry J. Steeley, Jr.	1985	60
14 9/16	8 7/16	Lewis & Clark Co., Mont.	Ellen Merganthal	Ellen Merganthal	1986	60
14 9/16	8 9/16	Missoula Co., Mont.	Nelson L. Cole	Nelson L. Cole	1987	60
14 9/16	8 9/16	Montezuma Co., Colo.	Eric M. Stevens	Eric M. Stevens	1988	60
14 8/16	8 7/16	Utah Co., Utah	Dell J. Christensen	Dell J. Christensen	1982	65
14 8/16	8 9/16	Rio Blanco Co., Colo.	Albert A. Meyers	Albert A. Meyers	1985	65
14 8/16	8 12/16	Fremont Co., Colo.	Terry L. Ellison	Terry L. Ellison	1986	65
14 8/16	8 8/16	Yavapai Co., Ariz.	Mark D. Nuessle	Mark D. Nuessle	1987	65
16 *	9 15/16	Wallowa Co., Oreg.	Gary R. Maki	Gary R. Maki	1982	

* Final Score subject to revision by additional verifying measurements.

Pacific Walrus

Odobenus rosmarus divergens

Minimum Score 100

World's Record 145-6/8

Score	Entire Length of Loose Tusk R.	L.	Circumference of Base R.	L.	Circumference at Third Quarter R.	L.	Locality Killed	By Whom Killed	Owner	Date Killed	Rank
116 4/8	28 4/8	29	8 4/8	8	6	6	Nunivak Island, Alaska	Darrell D. Wells	Darrell D. Wells	1978	1
110	27 6/8	28 6/8	7 1/8	7 3/8	5 2/8	5 2/8	Nelson Island, Alaska	Picked Up	Brent R. Akers	1987	2

American Elk, Typical Antlers
Cervus elaphus nelsoni and related subspecies

Minimum Score 360   World's Record 442-3/8

Score	Length of Main Beam R.	L.	Inside Spread	Circumference at Smallest Place Between First and Second Points R.	L.	Number of Points R.	L.	Locality Killed	By Whom Killed	Owner	Date Killed	Rank
402 3/8	59 4/8	62 1/8	47 7/8	8 2/8	8 6/8	8	7	San Miguel Co., Colo.	Lewis Fredrickson	Jay Scott	1954	1
401 7/8	55 3/8	54 4/8	45 3/8	9 6/8	9 4/8	6	6	Kootenay Lake, B.C.	Picked Up	Rick D. Armstrong	1986	2
401 7/8	57 4/8	58 4/8	42 4/8	9 4/8	9 2/8	6	7	Apache Co., Ariz.	Bruce R. Keller	Bruce R. Keller	1987	2
400 4/8	59 4/8	61	48 4/8	8 2/8	8 5/8	8	7	Routt Co., Colo.	Lewis Fredrickson	Lewis Fredrickson	1953	4
392 3/8	53 4/8	54 4/8	46 3/8	8 3/8	8 6/8	6	6	Umatilla Co., Oreg.	Picked Up	Robert L. Brown	1982	5
388 6/8	50 4/8	47 7/8	45 4/8	10	9 4/8	7	6	Larimer Co., Colo.	John Zimmerman	Ft. Collins Mus.	pr 1890	6
388 2/8	56 1/8	54 7/8	40	9 2/8	9 1/8	7	6	Sentinel Mt., B.C.	Martin Braun	Martin Braun	1986	7
388 2/8	59 1/8	59	54	7 5/8	7 7/8	7	6	Cutoff Creek, Alta.	Joe A. Riveira	Joe A. Riveira	1986	7
385 5/8	52 7/8	54 7/8	46 7/8	9 3/8	9 1/8	6	6	Wheeler Co., Oreg.	Ronny E. Rhoden	Ronny E. Rhoden	1986	9
385 3/8	56 3/8	57 3/8	37 4/8	8 2/8	8 2/8	6	6	Emery Co., Utah	Neville L. Wimmer	Russell N. Wimmer	1939	10
384 5/8	57 5/8	56 6/8	40 5/8	8 7/8	8 7/8	6	6	Graham Co., Ariz.	Laura R. Williams	Laura R. Williams	1986	11
383 5/8	54 6/8	55 3/8	54 4/8	8 3/8	8	6	7	Apache Co., Ariz.	Randall S. Ulmer	Randall S. Ulmer	1987	12
381 6/8	50 3/8	49 7/8	42	9 1/8	8 7/8	8	6	Madison Co., Mont.	Allan L. Mintken	Allan L. Mintken	1986	13
381 5/8	59 6/8	58	39 7/8	9 5/8	9 2/8	6	6	Coconino Co., Ariz.	George E. Long	George E. Long	1985	14
380 3/8	56 3/8	58	44 1/8	7 5/8	7 5/8	6	7	Catron Co., N.M.	Donald Parks, Jr.	Donald Parks, Jr.	1988	15
380 2/8	53 2/8	55 6/8	55 5/8	9 6/8	9 2/8	7	7	Las Animas Co., Colo.	Picked Up	Crawford Ranch	1987	16
379 7/8	56 7/8	56 2/8	42	8 1/8	8 4/8	8	6	Graham Co., Ariz.	Gerald Williams	Gerald Williams	1985	17
379 3/8	51 2/8	47	42 3/8	9 4/8	9 1/8	6	6	Otero Co., N.M.	Hubert R. Kennedy	Hubert R. Kennedy	1985	18
379 3/8	52 3/8	53 6/8	40 1/8	11 1/8	12	6	6	Sierra Co., N.M.	James D. Wagner	James D. Wagner	1986	18
379 2/8	53 2/8	52 3/8	44	8	8 4/8	6	6	Yakima Co., Wash.	Donald G. Stein	Donald G. Stein	1985	20
378 7/8	53 3/8	54 7/8	52 5/8	7 5/8	7 5/8	7	7	Navajo Co., Ariz.	Stanford H. Atwood, Jr.	Stanford H. Atwood, Jr.	1987	21
376 5/8	46 3/8	45 5/8	42 2/8	10	9 6/8	6	7	Flotten Lake, Sask.	Garry G. Ronald	Garry G. Ronald	1987	22
376 3/8	55 5/8	55 5/8	39 1/8	9	9	6	6	Gunnison Co., Colo.	Gerald J. Obertino	Gerald J. Obertino	1986	23
375 2/8	47 3/8	52 5/8	34 1/8	7 5/8	8 1/8	8	6	Powell Co., Mont.	Allan F. Kruse	Allan F. Kruse	1977	24
375	57 1/8	58 1/8	42 6/8	9 1/8	8 6/8	6	6	Wheeler Co., Oreg.	William K. Bartlett	William K. Bartlett	1986	25
374 4/8	53 2/8	54 2/8	40 2/8	7 2/8	8 2/8	6	6	Garfield Co., Utah	Brett R. Nybo	Brett R. Nybo	1984	26
368 2/8	50 5/8	50 4/8	42 4/8	8	9 1/8	6	6	Carbon Co., Wyo.	Larry J. Thoney	Larry J. Thoney	1978	27
365 3/8	56 7/8	55 5/8	43 6/8	8 6/8	7 4/8	7	8	Barrier Mt., Alta.	James A. Bauer	James A. Bauer	1985	28
365 7/8	50 4/8	53 3/8	39 3/8	10	9 6/8	7	7	Navajo Co., Ariz.	Joe B. Reynolds	Joe B. Reynolds	1987	29

American Elk, Typical Antlers - *Continued*

Score	Length of Main Beam R.	Length of Main Beam L.	Inside Spread	Circumference at Smallest Place Between First and Second Points R.	Circumference at Smallest Place Between First and Second Points L.	Number of Points R.	Number of Points L.	Locality Killed	By Whom Killed	Owner	Date Killed	Rank
365 1/8	51 4/8	51 2/8	38 5/8	10	10 5/8	7	7	Sandoval Co., N.M.	John C. McClendon	John C. McClendon	1985	30
363 6/8	47 4/8	49 1/8	40 1/8	8 3/8	8 3/8	7	6	Custer Co., S.D.	Todd Craig	Todd Craig	1986	31
360 7/8	53 6/8	52 4/8	41 6/8	9 6/8	9	6	7	Catron Co., N.M.	Robert H. Pickett, Jr.	Robert H. Pickett, Jr.	1987	32
389 6/8 *	56 3/8	55 7/8	39 4/8	8 5/8	8 5/8	6	7	Navajo Co., Ariz.	Fred Fortier	Fred Fortier	1985	

* Final Score subject to revision by additional verifying measurements.

American Elk, Non-Typical Antlers

Cervus elaphus nelsoni and related subspecies

Minimum Score 385   New World's Record 445-5/8

Score	Length of Main Beam R.	L.	Inside Spread	Circumference at Smallest Place Between First and Second Points R.	L.	Number of Points R.	L.	Locality Killed	By Whom Killed	Owner	Date Killed	Rank
445 5/8	58	57 7/8	41 6/8	9 2/8	10	8	8	Apache Co., Ariz.	Jerry J. Davis	Jerry J. Davis	1984	1
423	53 4/8	52 3/8	40	8 2/8	8 6/8	8	10	Coconino Co., Ariz.	James L. Ludvigson	James L. Ludvigson	1985	2
414	48 2/8	48 2/8	46 7/8	7 3/8	6 5/8	9	10	Taos Co., N.M.	Lou A. DePaolis	Lou A. DePaolis	1974	3
406 2/8	48 1/8	47 2/8	34 7/8	8 2/8	7 4/8	7	8	Apache Co., Ariz.	Joe W. Carroll	Joe W. Carroll	1982	4
405 3/8	59 4/8	58 1/8	40 2/8	8 4/8	8 2/8	7	8	Vermillion River, Man.	Ernie M. Bernat	Ernie M. Bernat	1986	5
403 7/8	46 5/8	52	32 4/8	10 3/8	10 6/8	8	9	Shoshone Co., Idaho	Fred S. Scott	Mannie Moore	1964	6
402 7/8	48 6/8	50	39	8 2/8	8 3/8	8	9	Powell Co., Mont.	Donald A. Roberson	Donald A. Roberson	1987	7
402	51 7/8	46 3/8	38 3/8	8 6/8	8 2/8	8	9	Lundar, Man.	Picked Up	Fred Thorkelson	1980	8
401 7/8	51 6/8	50	49 2/8	9 4/8	9 2/8	9	7	Beaverhead Co., Mont.	Ben C. Holland	Ben C. Holland	1953	9
398 4/8	52 7/8	51 4/8	42 3/8	10 1/8	10 1/8	7	9	Morton Co., Kan.	Camron Paxton	Camron Paxton	1987	10
398 1/8	52 2/8	55	44 2/8	8 5/8	8 3/8	8	7	Park Co., Mont.	Picked Up	O. Cline Stelzig	1972	11
397 2/8	53 2/8	51 6/8	45 4/8	9 2/8	8 6/8	8	8	Powell Co., Mont.	Rex Sorenson	Univ. of Mont. Zool. Mus.	1952	12
386 5/8	51 7/8	50 6/8	45 7/8	8 4/8	8 4/8	8	7	Beaverhead Co., Mont.	Unknown	William H. Flesch	pr 1962	13
385 1/8	50 5/8	48 6/8	40 4/8	7 5/8	7 4/8	9	8	Latah Co., Idaho	James A. Carpenter	James A. Carpenter	1985	14
408 *	53 5/8	53	40 6/8	9	9 1/8	7	8	Apache Co., Ariz.	J.G. Brittingham & W. Dale	Jack G. Brittingham	1987	
407 6/8 *	54 6/8	54 2/8	46 6/8	9	8	8	8	Granite Co., Mont.	Scott Hicks	Scott Hicks	1971	
402 2/8 *	55 5/8	55 3/8	50 1/8	9 3/8	10 1/8	7	7	Dogrib Creek, Alta.	Robert H. Jochim	Robert H. Jochim	1984	

* Final Score subject to revision by additional verifying measurements.

Roosevelt's Elk

Cervus elaphus roosevelti

Minimum Score 275 | World's Record 384-3/8

Roosevelt's elk includes trophies from: west of Highway I-5 in Oregon and Washington; Del Norte and Humboldt Counties of California; Afognak and Raspberry Islands of Alaska; and Vancouver Island, British Columbia.

Score	Length of Main Beam R.	L.	Inside Spread	Circumference at Smallest Place Between First and Second Points R.	L.	Number of Points R.	L.	Locality Killed	By Whom Killed	Owner	Date Killed	Rank
376 2/8	53 2/8	52 3/8	41 5/8	10 3/8	10 3/8	8	7	Clallam Co., Wash.	Picked Up	Roy C. Ewen	1912	1
362 6/8	45 7/8	45 3/8	37 3/8	9 4/8	9 1/8	7	7	Lincoln Co., Oreg.	James H. Flescher	James H. Flescher	1955	2
341 2/8	45 1/8	42 4/8	44 6/8	9 6/8	9 3/8	8	8	Josephine Co., Oreg.	Robert Veatch	Cass E. Raymond	pr 1890	3
339 6/8	45 5/8	45 4/8	42 6/8	8 3/8	8	8	7	Gold River, B.C.	William H. Taylor	William H. Taylor	1987	4
338	43 5/8	44 1/8	41 1/8	9 7/8	9 1/8	7	7	Tillamook Co., Oreg.	Tony W. Hancock	Tony W. Hancock	1985	5
336 2/8	46	48 3/8	40	8 3/8	9 1/8	7	7	Clallam Co., Wash.	Howard M. Cameron	Lawrence C. Cameron	1936	6
326 4/8	54 1/8	54 2/8	40	7 5/8	7 5/8	7	7	Pacific Co., Wash.	Donald Beasley	Donald Beasley	1963	7
324 7/8	50 1/8	47 4/8	36 5/8	8 3/8	8 6/8	8	7	Ucona River, B.C.	Norman W. Dougan	Norman W. Dougan	1986	8
324 3/8	40 6/8	44 2/8	43 6/8	7 7/8	7 6/8	7	7	Jefferson Co., Wash.	Newton P. Morris	Newton P. Morris	1975	9
322 6/8	44 6/8	45 2/8	41 3/8	8 5/8	9 1/8	7	7	Lincoln Co., Oreg.	James R. Goodwin	James R. Goodwin	1960	10
322 1/8	45 3/8	45 3/8	42 2/8	11 1/8	11	6	6	Polk Co., Oreg.	R.L. Stamps	R.L. Stamps	1985	11
320 2/8	49 6/8	48 7/8	42 4/8	8 4/8	8 1/8	6	6	Mason Co., Wash.	Tony J. Bogachus	Tony J. Bogachus	1955	12
318 5/8	48	49 2/8	40	8 2/8	8	6	6	Del Norte Co., Calif.	Richard K. Armas	Richard K. Armas	1988	13
311 2/8	47 6/8	40 3/8	41 2/8	8 6/8	8 6/8	6	7	Jefferson Co., Wash.	Walter L. Campbell	Walter L. Campbell	1987	14
309 1/8	47 3/8	43 7/8	37 7/8	9 2/8	8 2/8	6	6	Clatsop Co., Oreg.	Valentine T. Mueller	John A. Mueller	1938	15
308 3/8	48	48.8	41 5/8	9 7/8	9 2/8	6	7	Coos Co., Oreg.	Dean Dunson	Dean Dunson	1986	16
302 5/8	41	39 6/8	44	9 7/8	9 5/8	9	9	Lincoln Co., Oreg.	Michael Kosydar	Michael Kosydar	1985	17
299 6/8	48 7/8	49 1/8	37 2/8	8 2/8	7 7/8	6	6	Lincoln Co., Oreg.	Jullian Smallwood	Gerald Smallwood	1945	18
299 4/8	42 2/8	40 7/8	39	8 2/8	7 7/8	6	7	Lincoln Co., Oreg.	Gene Nyhus	Gene Nyhus	1950	19
298 3/8	43 5/8	44 1/8	38 3/8	8	8 1/8	6	6	White River, B.C.	Harvey J. King	Harvey J. King	1987	20
298 2/8	47	44 3/8	37 4/8	7 6/8	7 4/8	8	8	Columbia Co., Oreg.	Nicholas A. Berg	Nicholas A. Berg	1963	21
298 2/8	42 5/8	43 1/8	40 6/8	8 4/8	8 3/8	6	7	Polk Co., Oreg.	R.L. Stamps	R.L. Stamps	1981	21
297 6/8	46	45 3/8	42 3/8	7 3/8	7 3/8	6	6	Clallam Co., Wash.	Arnold J. LaGambina	Arnold J. LaGambina	1988	23
297 1/8	47 2/8	45 3/8	36 3/8	9	9	7	7	Clallam Co., Wash.	Ronald W. Sanchez	Ronald W. Sanchez	1988	24
296 1/8	39	39 3/8	35 2/8	8 2/8	7 7/8	7	7	Jefferson Co., Wash.	Max E. Graves	Max E. Graves	1970	25
296	46	46 5/8	36 5/8	7 7/8	7 7/8	7	7	Yamhill Co., Oreg.	Steven E. Anderson	Steven E. Anderson	1983	26
295 7/8	44 3/8	44 1/8	41 5/8	8 3/8	7 5/8	7	7	Jefferson Co., Wash.	Newton P. Morris	Newton P. Morris	1970	27
293 1/8	42	42 1/8	41 3/8	8 2/8	8 3/8	6	6	Jefferson Co., Wash.	William H. Boatman	William H. Boatman	1951	28

291 4/8	38 2/8	38 7/8	33 7/8	8 2/8	8 1/8	8	7	Tillamook Co., Oreg.	Picked Up	Tim J. Christensen	1975	29
290 7/8	44 1/8	44 3/8	42 5/8	7 7/8	8 7/8	6	6	Jefferson Co., Wash.	William A. Harrison	William A. Harrison	1984	30
283 4/8	42 7/8	44 1/8	35 2/8	6 7/8	6 7/8	7	6	Columbia Co., Oreg.	Thomas E. Eilertsen	Thomas E. Eilertsen	1968	31
279 7/8	47 1/8	45	39 3/8	8 3/8	8 2/8	6	5	Tillamook Co., Oreg.	Denis Schmitz	Denis Schmitz	1987	32
378 5/8 *	53 2/8	51 3/8	37	8 7/8	8 5/8	7	9	Clatsop Co., Oreg.	Fred M. Williamson	Charles R. Lindburg	1947	
373 3/8 *	50 4/8	50	34 3/8	8 7/8	9 2/8	6	8	Memekay River, B.C.	Shane Jamieson	Shane Jamieson	1987	

* Final Score subject to revision by additional verifying measurements.

Mule Deer, Typical Antlers

Minimum Score 185 — *Odocoileus hemionus hemionus* and certain related subspecies — World's Record 225-6/8

Score	Length of Main Beam	Inside Spread	Circumference at Smallest Place Between Burr and First Point	Number of Points	Locality Killed	By Whom Killed	Owner	Date Killed	Rank
209 5/8	27 5/8 26 5/8	30 6/8	4 7/8 5 2/8	6 8	Coconino Co., Ariz.	Unknown	John C. McClendon	pr 1985	1
208	29 26 4/8	34 3/8	5 5 1/8	5 5	Utah Co., Utah	Ned H. Losser	Ned H. Losser	1972	2
207 4/8	27 4/8 26	24	4 7/8 4 7/8	5 5	Washington Co., Utah	John K. Frei	John K. Frei	1987	3
206 7/8	29 29 2/8	29 7/8	5 3/8 5 3/8	5 5	Washington Co., Idaho	E. Jack Raby	E. Jack Raby	1968	4
206 2/8	26 5/8 27 5/8	23 4/8	5 5/8 5 7/8	5 5	Mesa Co., Colo.	Picked Up	James S. Bennett	1974	5
206 1/8	24 7/8 25 1/8	25 2/8	5 1/8 5 1/8	5 5	Idaho Co., Idaho	William B. Joyner	William B. Joyner	1965	6
205 2/8	27 1/8 27 5/8	28 1/8	4 5/8 5	5 5	Carbon Co., Wyo.	Shelly R. Risner	Shelly R. Risner	1986	7
204 3/8	29 2/8 30 1/8	35	4 4/8 4 5/8	5 5	Sonora, Mexico	David V. Collis	David V. Collis	1986	8
203 4/8	27 5/8 28 3/8	25	4 5/8 4 4/8	5 5	Garfield Co., Colo.	John T. Sewell	John T. Sewell	1985	9
202	26 7/8 27 2/8	27 7/8	6 3/8 6 3/8	6 6	Lincoln Co., Mont.	William E. Hubbard	William E. Hubbard	1963	10
201 5/8	26 2/8 27 3/8	24 3/8	5 4/8 5 4/8	5 5	Baker Co., Oreg.	Terry Williams	Terry Williams	1988	11
201 3/8	26 5/8 25 7/8	23 3/8	5 2/8 5 2/8	6 7	Sublette Co., Wyo.	Jerry C. Lopez	Jerry C. Lopez	1985	12
200 7/8	28 7/8 29	36 5/8	5 4/8 5 5/8	5 5	Sonora, Mexico	Toby J. Johnson	Toby J. Johnson	1986	13
200 2/8	25 7/8 24 1/8	19 2/8	4 4/8 4 5/8	5 5	Montrose Co., Colo.	Nelson Harding	Nelson Harding	1985	14
200 2/8	25 2/8 27 1/8	25 1/8	4 7/8 4 7/8	5 6	Sevier Co., Utah	Mayben J. Crane	Mayben J. Crane	1987	14
199 6/8	29 7/8 29	21 5/8	5 2/8 5 2/8	8 8	Montrose Co., Colo.	James O. McCleary	John E. McCleary	1951	16
199 5/8	25 4/8 24 2/8	21 7/8	6 1/8 6	5 5	Humboldt Co., Nev.	Robert L. Swinney	Robert L. Swinney	1982	17
199 2/8	26 4/8 26 2/8	27 4/8	5 6/8 5 5/8	5 5	Grand Co., Utah	Picked Up	Jon P. Leatham	1976	18
199 1/8	25 4/8 25 3/8	23 3/8	5 5/8 6	5 5	Morgan Co., Utah	H. Ritman Jons	H. Ritman Jons	1987	19
198 4/8	29 5/8 30	28 4/8	4 4/8 4 5/8	6 7	LaPlata Co., Colo.	Pauline J. Bostic	Pauline J. Bostic	1971	20
198 2/8	28 2/8 28 3/8	27	5 4/8 5 3/8	5 7	Bonneville Co., Idaho	Thomas N. Thiel	Thomas N. Thiel	1987	21
198	25 1/8 25 2/8	22 4/8	5 1/8 5	4 4	Davis Co., Utah	Carl D. Craig	Jay D. Craig	1939	22
197 5/8	26 7/8 27 3/8	26	5 4 7/8	5 6	Uintah Co., Utah	Robert C. Chapoose, Jr.	Robert C. Chapoose, Jr.	1987	23
197 2/8	24 4/8 24 7/8	23 3/8	4 4/8 4 4/8	5 6	Flathead Co., Mont.	James E. Betters	James E. Betters	1986	24
197 1/8	28 1/8 27 3/8	22 7/8	5 5	5 5	Mesa Co., Colo.	Willis A. Kinsey	Willis A. Kinsey	1978	25
196 6/8	24 24 1/8	23 6/8	5 7/8 6 1/8	5 5	Coconino Co., Ariz.	James D. Wagner	James D. Wagner	1986	26
196 5/8	26 3/8 26 7/8	23 3/8	6 1/8 5 3/8	8 8	Moffat Co., Colo.	Tran Canton	Tran Canton	1960	27
196 4/8	26 3/8 27 5/8	27 5/8	5 4 7/8	6 6	North Dakota	Unknown	Robert L. Klisares	pr 1958	28
196 4/8	26 2/8 26 1/8	25 2/8	5 2/8 5 5/8	6 6	Morgan Co., Utah	Elwood Williams	Elwood Williams	1968	28
196 2/8	26 26 4/8	26	5 4/8 5 4/8	5 5	Dawes Co., Neb.	Terry L. Sandstrom	Terry L. Sandstrom	1968	30
196 2/8	27 1/8 27 5/8	26	5 2/8 5	5 5	Baker Co., Oreg.	Vivian M. Zikmund	Vivian M. Zikmund	1986	30
195 7/8	27 5/8 25 7/8	26 4/8	4 5/8 4 6/8	5 7	Lassen Co., Calif.	Sulo E. Lakso	Tracy A. Jenkins	1943	32

Score							Locality	Hunter	Date	Rank
195 7/8	27	28 4/8	28 4/8	5 3/8	5 4/8	7	Franklin Co., Idaho	Melvin S. Thomson	1987	32
195 6/8	25 6/8	25 3/8	24 1/8	6 2/8	6 2/8	6	Eagle Co., Colo.	James B. Mesecke	1985	34
195 5/8	26 6/8	27	24 3/8	5 2/8	5 4/8	9	Archuleta Co., Colo.	Matthew J. Arkins	1986	35
195 4/8	26	26 1/8	25 4/8	5	5	5	Bear Lake Co., Idaho	Joseph R. Given	1985	36
195 3/8	25	25 2/8	25 1/8	4 4/8	4 4/8	6	Wallowa Co., Oreg.	Michael R. Shirley	1986	37
195 2/8	28 5/8	29 7/8	29	5 4/8	5 7/8	5	Niobrara Co., Wyo.	David E. Pauna	1976	38
195 1/8	27 3/8	28 2/8	27 1/8	5 5/8	5 5/8	5	Kane Co., Utah	Cecil Hunt	1987	39
194 6/8	28	27 5/8	26 7/8	4 5/8	4 7/8	6	Grand Co., Utah	Richard V. Beesley	1986	40
194	23 3/8	25 1/8	22 4/8	4 6/8	4 7/8	5	Sublette Co., Wyo.	James J. McBride	1979	41
193 3/8	26 7/8	27 1/8	23 3/8	4 7/8	4 7/8	5	Washoe Co., Nev.	Barbara M. Conley	1987	42
192	26 4/8	25 2/8	27 1/8	5 3/8	5 3/8	5	Delta Co., Colo.	James W. Arellano	1977	43
191 1/8	26 5/8	24 6/8	24 3/8	4 7/8	4 7/8	5	Uintah Co., Utah	Robert B. Keel	1986	44
190 7/8	27 4/8	27 7/8	27	4 5/8	5	6	Elmore Co., Idaho	Michael H. Felton	1980	45
189 6/8	23 5/8	24 2/8	27 6/8	4 7/8	4 6/8	5	Sonora, Mexico	Joseph J. Luterbach	1986	46
189 4/8	25 2/8	25 1/8	27 7/8	4 4/8	4 5/8	5	Emery Co., Utah	Marvin H. Christensen	1974	47
189 3/8	24 7/8	25 1/8	24 3/8	5 1/8	5 3/8	5	San Juan Co., Utah	Keele Johnson	1986	48
189 1/8	25	28 4/8	21	5	5 2/8	7	LaPlata Co., Colo.	James L. Leyshon	1986	49
188 7/8	26 4/8	27	23 6/8	4 6/8	4 4/8	8	Sublette Co., Wyo.	George Shuleshko	1986	50
188 5/8	24 4/8	23 7/8	24 4/8	5 2/8	5 2/8	5	Rio Arriba Co., N.M.	George R. Payne	1973	51
188 5/8	26 4/8	26 2/8	23 5/8	5	5	8	Washoe Co., Nev.	Christine L. Matley	1986	51
188 3/8	21 1/8	21 6/8	18 6/8	4 3/8	4 3/8	5	Larimer Co., Colo.	Fred W. Loy	1965	53
188 2/8	23	23 2/8	16 2/8	4 7/8	4 7/8	5	Daggett Co., Utah	Roy D. Sessions	1979	54
187 7/8	23 6/8	23 6/8	23 1/8	5 5/8	5 3/8	5	Kane Co., Utah	Theo J. McAllister	1985	55
187 5/8	25 6/8	26 1/8	24 1/8	5 4/8	5	5	Flathead Co., Mont.	Jeffrey A. Bechtel	1983	56
187	25 2/8	24 6/8	26 3/8	4 6/8	4 7/8	5	Bonneville Co., Idaho	Rockie L. Walker	1986	57
187	24 6/8	25	28 1/8	5	5 1/8	5	Moffat Co., Colo.	Warren C. Nuzum	1987	57
186 7/8	24	24 6/8	23	4 5/8	4 6/8	6	Garfield Co., Colo.	Gary L. Hecht	1986	59
186 7/8	24 6/8	22 3/8	19 7/8	4 4/8	4 4/8	5	Idaho Co., Idaho	Tom M. Schachten	1987	59
186 6/8	23 6/8	23 6/8	24	5 4/8	5 3/8	5	Routt Co., Colo.	Willie Jones	1976	61
186 6/8	24	22 7/8	18 2/8	5 5/8	5 2/8	6	Grant Co., Oreg.	Leslie M. Brady	1986	61
186 5/8	25	23 2/8	26	4 6/8	4 7/8	5	Fremont Co., Colo.	Donald B. Anderson, Jr.	1986	63
186 4/8	24 5/8	25 5/8	25	5 2/8	5 2/8	4	Routt Co., Colo.	William A. S. Heuer	1981	64
186 1/8	24 6/8	26 4/8	25 1/8	5 6/8	5 5/8	7	Sanpete Co., Utah	Deland G. James	1935	65
185 7/8	24 3/8	24 3/8	22 1/8	4 6/8	4 7/8	6	Lincoln Co., Wyo.	James P. Speck	1987	66
185 7/8	25 2/8	25	23 6/8	4 6/8	4 4/8	5	Juab Co., Utah	Chris J. Carter	1987	66
185 5/8	26 2/8	26 2/8	20 7/8	5 5/8	5 5/8	8	Franklin Co., Idaho	R. Ashley Lyman III	1964	68
185 4/8	24 2/8	24 2/8	23 6/8	4 7/8	4 7/8	6	Brule Co., S.D.	Kenny E. Yeaton	1985	69

Mule Deer, Non-Typical Antlers

Odocoileus hemionus hemionus and certain related subspecies

Minimum Score 225 World's Record 355-2/8

Score	Length of Main Beam R.	L.	Inside Spread	Circumference at Smallest Place Between Burr and First Point R.	L.	Number of Points R.	L.	Locality Killed	By Whom Killed	Owner	Date Killed	Rank
305 6/8	23 7/8	24 1/8	21 3/8	6 1/8	6 4/8	17	17	Shasta Co., Calif.	Artie McGram	Artie McGram	1987	1
302	26 7/8	26 2/8	21 5/8	6 3/8	6 5/8	21	15	Iron Co., Utah	Darwin Hulett	Rocky Mt. Antler Mus.	1950	2
300 7/8	24	22 6/8	29 4/8	5 5/8	5 3/8	17	16	Bonneville Co., Idaho	Brett J. Sauer	Brett J. Sauer	1985	3
296 6/8	30 1/8	30 2/8	26 5/8	5 7/8	5 7/8	12	14	Mesa Co., Colo.	Unknown	Homer Saye	1981 pr	4
286 1/8	27	26 6/8	26 1/8	5 2/8	5 3/8	12	20	Utah Co., Utah	Joe Allen	Todd L. Johnson	1950 pr	5
282 6/8	24 4/8	24 3/8	25 4/8	5 4/8	5 2/8	14	16	Cabri, Sask.	Robert Comba	Homer Saye	1962	6
267 1/8	23 7/8	25 3/8	24 3/8	5 3/8	5 4/8	15	11	Eagle Co., Colo.	Josef Langegger	Josef Langegger	1969	7
265 7/8	23 5/8	24 1/8	22 7/8	5 5/8	5 5/8	20	15	Powder River Co., Mont.	Michael A. Siewert	Michael A. Siewert	1987	8
265	24	24 2/8	19 4/8	4 7/8	5	13	15	Custer Co., Idaho	John L. Simmons	John L. Simmons	1986	9
263 2/8	24	24	20 3/8	5 2/8	5 2/8	15	10	Rio Arriba Co., N.M.	Kenneth Campbell	Kenneth Campbell	1970	10
258 1/8	27 1/8	25 1/8	23 2/8	5 7/8	5 7/8	11	13	Morgan Co., Utah	Martin Harris	Rodney D. Layton	1935	11
257 4/8	23 6/8	24 1/8	20 4/8	5 5/8	5 4/8	12	10	Sanpete Co., Utah	Dan J. Keller	Dan J. Keller	1986	12
255 7/8	26 5/8	26 7/8	26 5/8	5 2/8	5 2/8	11	9	Cache Co., Utah	Roland Leishman	Roland Leishman	1980	13
255 3/8	23 3/8	23 5/8	25 5/8	5 5/8	5 7/8	12	12	Coconino Co., Ariz.	Glenn A. Hunt	Glenn A. Hunt	1985	14
251 1/8	28 1/8	27 7/8	26 3/8	6	6 1/8	10	9	Iron Co., Utah	James C. Howard	James C. Howard	1987	15
249 2/8	24 3/8	23 6/8	27	4 6/8	4 6/8	10	10	Lincoln Co., Wyo.	Robert J. Stallone	Robert J. Stallone	1986	16
247 5/8	25 4/8	25 4/8	22 4/8	6 1/8	6	12	16	Mohave Co., Ariz.	Brad L. Johnson	Brad L. Johnson	1986	17
247 1/8	25 1/8	25	23 7/8	5 5/8	5 4/8	7	10	Carbon Co., Utah	Ralph A. Sanich	Ralph A. Sanich	1986	18
244 2/8	23 1/8	25 1/8	23 6/8	5 2/8	5 1/8	12	11	Mesa Co., Colo.	Thomas S. Hundley	Thomas S. Hundley	1986	19
244 1/8	24 2/8	23 7/8	27	4 2/8	4 6/8	14	9	Mesa Co., Colo.	Edward B. Walsh	Mrs. Edward B. Walsh	1960	20
243 7/8	23 6/8	23 2/8	26	4 4/8	4 6/8	10	11	Utah Co., Utah	Zenneth K. Chamberlain	Zenneth K. Chamberlain	1956	21
243 5/8	23 6/8	23 2/8	26 6/8	4 4/8	4 5/8	7	9	Cache Co., Utah	Albert C. Steffenhagen	A. Ladell Atkinson	1924	22
243 4/8	22 2/8	18 2/8	23 3/8	4 4/8	4 5/8	14	11	Cibola Co., N.M.	Fred R. Valdez, Jr.	Fred R. Valdez, Jr.	1986	23
243 2/8	28 4/8	28 1/8	25 3/8	4 4/8	4 7/8	10	10	Colorado	Unknown	Brad A. Bauer	1954	24
242 1/8	26	25 3/8	28	5 3/8	5 2/8	12	10	Hinsdale Co., Colo.	Bill Crose	Bill Crose	1973	25
241 3/8	27 1/8	26 7/8	26 1/8	5 5/8	5 4/8	13	11	Kane Co., Utah	Aivars O. Berkis	Aivars O. Berkis	1987	26
238 2/8	23 5/8	24 1/8	26 5/8	5 1/8	5	16	11	Walsh, Alta.	Rick M. MacDonald	Rick M. MacDonald	1987	27
237 3/8	23 5/8	23 3/8	23 3/8	5 5/8	5 7/8	11	12	Bonneville Co., Idaho	Bert L. Freed	Bert L. Freed	1987	28
232 5/8	24 4/8	25 7/8	17 7/8	4 3/8	4 3/8	13	10	Teton Co., Wyo.	Bruce K. McRae	Bruce K. McRae	1986	29

232	23 1/8	24	18 3/8	5 3/8	5 3/8	10	17	Grand Co., Colo.	William L. Henry	William L. Henry	1986	30
231 7/8	25 3/8	30 2/8	25 2/8	5	4 7/8	11	9	Rio Arriba Co., N.M.	Dan F. Holleman	Vernon D. Holleman	1966	31
227 1/8	27 3/8	26	22 4/8	4 7/8	4 4/8	8	7	Nez Perce Co., Idaho	Richard S. Lowe	Richard S. Lowe	1986	32
268 1/8 *	27 7/8	27 7/8	30 3/8	5 2/8	5 5/8	14	14	Elbow, Sask.	Allan J. Selzler	Allan J. Selzler	1986	

* Final Score subject to revision by additional verifying measurements.

Columbia Blacktail Deer
Odocoileus hemionus columbianus

Minimum Score 120   World's Record 182-2/8

Score	Length of Main Beam R.	L.	Inside Spread	Circumference at Smallest Place Between Burr and First Point R.	L.	Number of Points R.	L.	Locality Killed	By Whom Killed	Owner	Date Killed	Rank
163 7/8	21 7/8	21 7/8	19 5/8	4 5/8	4 5/8	5	5	Lincoln Co., Oreg.	Picked Up	Bruce & Scott Wales	1987	1
162 6/8	25	25 2/8	23 2/8	4 5/8	4 5/8	7	7	Pierce Co., Wash.	Dick Allen	Craig Allen	1952	2
159 6/8	24 3/8	24 1/8	16 1/8	4 5/8	4 5/8	5	8	Jackson Co., Oreg.	Douglas L. Milburn	Douglas L. Milburn	1985	3
158 2/8	22 6/8	24 4/8	18 6/8	5 2/8	4 5/8	5	5	Lewis Co., Wash.	Keith A. Heldreth	Keith A. Heldreth	1984	4
156 4/8	22 4/8	21 6/8	17	3 5/8	3 6/8	5	5	King Co., Wash.	Byron Gusa	Byron Gusa	1980	5
156 4/8	19 6/8	19 7/8	16 6/8	4 3/8	4 2/8	5	6	Lincoln Co., Oreg.	Bruce G. Wales	Bruce G. Wales	1985	5
156 1/8	22 3/8	22	20 2/8	4 4/8	4 4/8	5	6	Lincoln Co., Oreg.	Robert G. Biron	Robert G. Biron	1963	7
154	24 3/8	24 3/8	19 5/8	4 7/8	4 4/8	5	5	Josephine Co., Oreg.	Wayne H. Breeze	Wayne H. Breeze	1986	8
150	20 4/8	21 7/8	16 6/8	4 2/8	4 2/8	5	5	Tehama Co., Calif.	Marion F. Foster	Barbara J. Foster	1971	9
148 1/8	23 4/8	22 4/8	15 5/8	5 1/8	5 1/8	5	5	Clackamas Co., Oreg.	Steven C. Oaks	Steven C. Oaks	1986	10
147 5/8	22 3/8	22 7/8	22 3/8	4 5/8	4 5/8	6	6	Mendocino Co., Calif.	Richard Sterling	Richard Sterling	1986	11
145 5/8	22 5/8	20 5/8	17	4 2/8	4 2/8	5	4	King Co., Wash.	Terry Flowers	Terry Flowers	1959	12
145 5/8	20 4/8	21	16 4/8	3 7/8	4	5	5	Siskiyou Co., Calif.	Wallace D. Barlow	Wallace D. Barlow	1985	13
145 2/8	23	23 6/8	22 7/8	5 4/8	5 2/8	5	5	Marion Co., Oreg.	James J. Edgell	James J. Edgell	1979	14
145 2/8	23 5/8	23 4/8	23 3/8	4 3/8	4 4/8	5	5	Josephine Co., Oreg.	Jim Breeze	Jim Breeze	1986	14
145	22 4/8	21 4/8	21 2/8	5 1/8	5 2/8	6	7	Tehama Co., Calif.	Lamar G. Hanson	Lamar G. Hanson	1972	16
144 2/8	20 4/8	19 6/8	20 3/8	5 1/8	5 1/8	5	5	Josephine Co., Oreg.	Ralph I. Sibley	Ralph I. Sibley	1986	17
143 7/8	20 5/8	19 5/8	20 3/8	3 6/8	3 6/8	6	5	Humboldt Co., Calif.	Clinton Moore	Clinton Moore	1975	18
143 6/8	19 5/8	19 4/8	15 4/8	5	5 1/8	5	5	Mendocino Co., Calif.	Lois C. Miller	Lois C. Miller	1986	19
143 5/8	20 5/8	19 3/8	18 5/8	4 3/8	4 6/8	6	5	Mendocino Co., Calif.	Mark Ciancio	Mark Ciancio	1986	20
142 6/8	20 4/8	20 1/8	20 2/8	4 1/8	4 2/8	5	5	Trinity Co., Calif.	Kenneth L. Cogle, Jr.	Kenneth L. Cogle, Jr.	1985	21
141 5/8	23	22 5/8	15 7/8	4 4/8	3 7/8	5	4	Josephine Co., Oreg.	Reginald P. Breeze	Reginald P. Breeze	1986	22
141 4/8	21 2/8	21 1/8	16 2/8	5 2/8	4 7/8	5	5	Skamania Co., Wash.	E. Gerald Tikka	E. Gerald Tikka	1987	23
141 4/8	20 7/8	20 4/8	20	4 2/8	4 2/8	5	5	Del Norte Co., Calif.	Greg Rocha	Greg Rocha	1985	24
141 2/8	21 4/8	20 6/8	18 2/8	4 3/8	4 4/8	5	5	Marion Co., Oreg.	Les Johnson	Les Johnson	1986	24
141 1/8	23 3/8	23 2/8	17 5/8	4 2/8	4 4/8	6	6	Jackson Co., Oreg.	Arthur L. Schmidt	Arthur L. Schmidt	1986	26
140 4/8	21 1/8	21 3/8	14 4/8	4 1/8	4 1/8	6	5	Mendocino Co., Calif.	Harold R. Embury	Harold R. Embury	1985	27
140 1/8	21 2/8	20 2/8	16 3/8	3 7/8	4	4	4	Siskiyou Co., Calif.	Jay M. Gates III	Jay M. Gates III	1986	28
140 1/8	21 6/8	21	17 1/8	4	4 4/8	5	6	Trinity Co., Calif.	Rickford M. Fisher	Rickford M. Fisher	1986	29
140 1/8	21 6/8	21	17 1/8	4	4 4/8	5	6	Trinity Co., Calif.	Wayne Sorensen	C.W. Sorensen	1986	29
140	22 2/8	22 2/8	18	5 5/8	5 2/8	5	5	Mendocino Co., Calif.	Nick Deffterios	Nick Deffterios	1970	31

Score							Locality	Owner	Hunter	Year	Rank
139 7/8	20 7/8	20 1/8	18 7/8	5	5	5	Jackson Co., Oreg.	Dale E. Hoskins	Dale E. Hoskins	1946	32
139 5/8	21 2/8	21 1/8	14 4/8	4 2/8	4 2/8	6	Cowlitz Co., Wash.	David A. Martin	David A. Martin	1962	33
139 4/8	20 7/8	22 3/8	19 4/8	4 5/8	4 5/8	6	Jackson Co., Oreg.	Everett B. Music, Jr.	Everett B. Music, Jr.	1985	34
139 2/8	21	21	16 7/8	3 7/8	3 7/8	5	Trinity Co., Calif.	Terry H. Walker	Terry H. Walker	1986	35
139 2/8	21 7/8	23 3/8	17 1/8	5 1/8	4 3/8	7	Josephine Co., Oreg.	David L. Teasley	David L. Teasley	1986	35
139 1/8	22	21 2/8	18 5/8	4 2/8	4 2/8	5	Humboldt Co., Calif.	George E. Watson	George E. Watson	1933	37
139 1/8	20 4/8	20 5/8	16 5/8	4 2/8	4 2/8	5	Tillamook Co., Oreg.	Henry Naegeli	Henry Naegeli	1970	38
138 7/8	20 5/8	21 3/8	15 5/8	4 5/8	4 5/8	5	Chipmunk Creek, B.C.	Larri H. Woodrow	Larri H. Woodrow	1987	39
138 6/8	22 2/8	21 1/8	22 2/8	4 1/8	4	5	Mendocino Co., Calif.	Gordon O. Hanson	Gordon O. Hanson	1988	39
138 2/8	21 1/8	21 2/8	17 4/8	5	5 1/8	4	Linn Co., Oreg.	Douglas J. Morehead	Douglas J. Morehead	1984	41
138	22 3/8	21 7/8	21 1/8	4 7/8	5	6	Mendocino Co., Calif.	Brian K. Isaac	Brian K. Isaac	1985	42
137 6/8	20 2/8	20 7/8	19 6/8	3 6/8	3 7/8	5	Trinity Co., Calif.	Kevin Clair	Kevin Clair	1986	43
136 6/8	19 3/8	20	14 3/8	4 5/8	5	6	Lewis Co., Wash.	Mark G. Frohmader	Mark G. Frohmader	1969	44
136 2/8	21 6/8	22	21 4/8	5	4 7/8	5	Siskiyou Co., Calif.	Wayne G. Rose	Wayne G. Rose	1977	45
136 1/8	20 4/8	20	15 5/8	4 3/8	4 2/8	5	Jackson Co., Oreg.	Nancy J. Eden	Nancy J. Eden	1971	46
136	20 4/8	19 5/8	19 2/8	4	4	5	Trinity Co., Calif.	John P. Morton	John P. Morton	1987	47
135 7/8	19 2/8	19 3/8	16 1/8	4 2/8	4 2/8	4	Tehama Co., Calif.	John A. Crockett	John A. Crockett	1982	48
135 5/8	20	20 2/8	17 2/8	4 5/8	4 5/8	5	Cowlitz Co., Wash.	William R. Gottfryd	William R. Gottfryd	1986	49
135 5/8	22 4/8	23 2/8	20 1/8	4 3/8	4 3/8	4	Pierce Co., Wash.	Mark A. Dye	Mark A. Dye	1987	50
135	18 6/8	18 6/8	15 5/8	4 3/8	5	5	Trinity Co., Calif.	Andrew M. Felt	Andrew M. Felt	1986	51
134 4/8	22 4/8	22 5/8	16	5 1/8	5 1/8	6	Thurston Co., Wash.	George W. Sharrow	George W. Sharrow	1946	52
134 3/8	22 5/8	22 5/8	22 3/8	4 7/8	4 7/8	4	Tehama Co., Calif.	Bob C. Haase	Bob C. Haase	1987	53
134 2/8	19 3/8	19 5/8	20 2/8	4 7/8	4 7/8	5	Mendocino Co., Calif.	Sebastian D. Carrasco	Sebastian D. Carrasco	1986	54
133 7/8	21 2/8	21 1/8	16	3 7/8	4 6/8	6	Mendocino Co., Calif.	Terence K. Prechter	Terence K. Prechter	1986	55
133 5/8	21 1/8	19 5/8	15	4 6/8	4 7/8	6	Columbia Co., Oreg.	Duane M. Bernard	Duane M. Bernard	1952	56
133 5/8	18 6/8	18 1/8	13 5/8	4 4/8	4 3/8	5	Josephine Co., Oreg.	Jack D. Chambers	Jack D. Chambers	1985	56
133 4/8	21 3/8	20 6/8	13 6/8	4 4/8	5	5	Clallam Co., Wash.	Tony M. Rickel	Tony M. Rickel	1987	58
133 3/8	20 4/8	21 6/8	12 5/8	4 4/8	4 6/8	5	Clallam Co., Wash.	Glen W. Gooding	Glen W. Gooding	1957	59
133	18 3/8	18 7/8	15 5/8	3 7/8	4	5	Lane Co., Oreg.	Karl R. Rymer	Karl R. Rymer	1969	60
132 7/8	21 6/8	22 5/8	18 5/8	3 6/8	4 2/8	4	Jackson Co., Oreg.	Lorin C. Bosch	Lorin C. Bosch	1986	61
132 7/8	20 5/8	21 4/8	19 2/8	4 2/8	4 3/8	5	Humboldt Co., Calif.	Dennis R. Lake	Dennis R. Lake	1988	61
132 6/8	20 5/8	21 5/8	17 6/8	4 4/8	4 4/8	5	Siskiyou Co., Calif.	Paul J. Bruno	Paul J. Bruno	1985	63
132 6/8	21 4/8	20 3/8	15 2/8	4	4	5	Jackson Co., Oreg.	Brad B. Brown	Brad B. Brown	1985	63
132 5/8	20 5/8	20 1/8	17 7/8	4 4/8	4 2/8	6	Mason Co., Wash.	Brian L. Martin	Brian L. Martin	1984	65
132 3/8	21 4/8	22 4/8	15 1/8	4	3 7/8	4	Tillamook Co., Oreg.	Greg E. Myers	Greg E. Myers	1977	66
132 2/8	20	20	16 3/8	4 1/8	4 2/8	5	Mendocino Co., Calif.	Richard L. Moore	Richard L. Moore	1987	67
131 5/8	22	21 6/8	17 3/8	4 2/8	4 2/8	5	Pierce Co., Wash.	Lyle O. Brateng	Lyle O. Brateng	1984	68
131 4/8	19 5/8	19 6/8	17 3/8	3 6/8	3 6/8	6	Mendocino Co., Calif.	James J. McBride	James J. McBride	1982	69
131 4/8	18 2/8	17 5/8	14 4/8	4 6/8	5	5	Snohomish Co., Wash.	Philip C. Thompson	Philip C. Thompson	1986	69
131 3/8	20	19 6/8	14 4/8	4	4	5	Linn Co., Oreg.	Boyd Iverson	Boyd Iverson	1985	71
131 3/8	19 6/8	19 6/8	17 3/8	4	3 7/8	5	Trinity Co., Calif.	L. Irvin Barnhart	L. Irvin Barnhart	1986	72
130 5/8	19 7/8	20 5/8	14 5/8	4	4 7/8	5	Josephine Co., Oreg.	Raymond D. Dodge	Raymond D. Dodge	1987	73

Columbia Blacktail Deer - Continued

Score	Length of Main Beam R.	L.	Inside Spread	Circumference at Smallest Place Between Burr and First Point R.	L.	Number of Points R.	L.	Locality Killed	By Whom Killed	Owner	Date Killed	Rank
130 4/8	21	21 5/8	17 2/8	5 1/8	4 7/8	6	4	Multnomah Co., Oreg.	Dennis R. Thorud	Dennis R. Thorud	1985	74
130 4/8	22 5/8	22 1/8	21 1/8	4 2/8	4 1/8	4	5	Trinity Co., Calif.	Wayne Erickson	Wayne Erickson	1985	74
130 1/8	19 2/8	19 5/8	17 1/8	4 7/8	5 1/8	5	6	Thurston Co., Wash.	Gano S. Hayes	Gano S. Hayes	1985	76
130 1/8	20 3/8	20 1/8	20 1/8	4 2/8	4 5/8	4	4	San Mateo Co., Calif.	Dan Caughey III	Dan Caughey III	1988	76
130	22 1/8	22 2/8	15 6/8	3 5/8	3 5/8	5	3	Trinity Co., Calif.	Terry H. Walker	Terry H. Walker	1979	78
128 5/8	18 4/8	18 4/8	13 7/8	4	4 2/8	4	5	Lincoln Co., Oreg.	Ken E. Bernet	Ken E. Bernet	1986	79
128 2/8	20 4/8	20 2/8	14 4/8	4 1/8	4 2/8	5	5	Clallam Co., Wash.	James W. Fatherson	James W. Fatherson	1983	80
127 5/8	20 3/8	21	19 5/8	5 1/8	5 2/8	6	7	Clallam Co., Wash.	Harry E. Reed, Jr.	Harry E. Reed, Jr.	1977	81
127 1/8	21	21 1/8	20 1/8	4 2/8	4 3/8	4	5	Marion Co., Oreg.	John E. Williams	John E. Williams	1974	82
126 3/8	20 7/8	16 4/8	17 3/8	4	4 4/8	4	4	Columbia Co., Oreg.	Charles Lindberg	Charles Lindberg	1971	83
125 5/8	18 2/8	19 5/8	22 5/8	3 5/8	3 5/8	4	4	Humboldt Co., Calif.	Lodewijk J. Wurfbain	Lodewijk J. Wurfbain	1986	84
123 5/8	21 3/8	21 6/8	18 1/8	3 5/8	3 5/8	3	3	King Co., Wash.	Gene D. Collecchi	Gene D. Collecchi	1987	85
123 3/8	20 5/8	21	18 6/8	4 4/8	4 3/8	7	8	Lewis Co., Wash.	Unknown	Robert E. Shirer	pr 1960	86
123 1/8	22 1/8	21 2/8	18 3/8	4 3/8	4 2/8	5	4	Pierce Co., Wash.	Robert J. Keeley	Robert J. Keeley	1968	87
122 6/8	21 2/8	19 5/8	16	4 4/8	4 4/8	4	5	San Mateo Co., Calif.	Daniel R. Caughey, Jr.	Daniel R. Caughey, Jr.	1964	88
122 6/8	19 6/8	20 1/8	14 4/8	3 5/8	3 6/8	4	5	Jefferson Co., Wash.	Ralph E. Wean	Ralph E. Wean	1987	88
122 3/8	19 4/8	21	16 1/8	4 3/8	4 1/8	4	4	San Mateo Co., Calif.	Daniel R. Caughey, Jr.	Daniel R. Caughey, Jr.	1986	90
122 2/8	19	18 7/8	16 2/8	4 2/8	4	5	4	Yamhill Co., Oreg.	Picked Up	Mike McQuaw	1980	91
122 2/8	22	21 5/8	16 6/8	4 1/8	4 1/8	4	4	King Co., Wash.	Russell L. McKinnon	Russell L. McKinnon	1987	91
122 1/8	20 2/8	19 5/8	17 1/8	4	4	4	4	Trinity Co., Calif.	Terry H. Walker	Terry H. Walker	1976	93
121	18 5/8	18 5/8	18 3/8	4	4	4	4	San Mateo Co., Calif.	Daniel R. Caughey, Jr.	Daniel R. Caughey, Jr.	1971	94
169 3/8 *	23 2/8	22 7/8	18 3/8	5 7/8	6 1/8	6	6	Lewis Co., Wash.	Larry V. Taylor	Thomas Gogan	1941	

* Final Score subject to revision by additional verifying measurements.

Sitka Blacktail Deer

Odocoileus hemionus sitkensis

Minimum Score 100
New World's Record 128

Sitka blacktail deer includes trophies from coastal Alaska and Queen Charlotte Islands of British Columbia.

Score	Length of Main Beam R.	L.	Inside Spread	Circumference at Smallest Place Between Burr and First Point R.	L.	Number of Points R.	L.	Locality Killed	By Whom Killed	Owner	Date Killed	Rank
128	19 6/8	19	19 4/8	4 7/8	4 7/8	5	5	Kodiak Island, Alaska	Unknown	Craig Allen	1985	1
126 3/8	18 5/8	19 4/8	14 5/8	4	4 1/8	5	5	Sunny Hay Mt., Alaska	Harry R. Horner	Harry R. Horner	1987	2
126 2/8	19 6/8	20 3/8	16 3/8	4 5/8	4 4/8	6	5	Control Lake, Alaska	William B. Steele, Jr.	William B. Steele, Jr.	1987	3
125 7/8	17 7/8	18 6/8	13 5/8	4	4	4	4	Tenakee Inlet, Alaska	Donald E. Thompson	Donald E. Thompson	1964	4
124 2/8	19 1/8	18 2/8	14 4/8	4 3/8	4	5	5	Exchange Cove, Alaska	Daniel J. Leo	Daniel J. Leo	1986	5
123 3/8	18 3/8	18 3/8	14 4/8	4 3/8	4 1/8	5	5	Prince of Wales Island, Alaska	Kenneth W. Twitchell	Kenneth W. Twitchell	1987	6
120 4/8	18 3/8	16 1/8	14 6/8	3 7/8	4 1/8	5	5	Cleveland Pen., Alaska	Dennis E. Northrup	Dennis E. Northrup	1986	7
120 1/8	17 7/8	17 3/8	16 3/8	4 5/8	4 4/8	5	5	Halibut Bay, Alaska	James W. Bickman	James W. Bickman	1987	8
118 5/8	17	16 6/8	15 1/8	3 7/8	3 7/8	5	5	Uganik Lake, Alaska	Larry D. Leuenberger	Larry D. Leuenberger	1985	9
117 4/8	17	16 6/8	15 2/8	3 3/8	3 7/8	5	5	Shrubby Island, Alaska	Alfred Oglend	Alfred Oglend	1986	10
114 7/8	17 7/8	19 1/8	17 5/8	4 2/8	4	5	5	Dall Island, Alaska	Picked Up	Lynn W. Merrill	1987	11
114	15 7/8	16	13 6/8	4	3 7/8	5	5	Olga Bay, Alaska	Frank E. Entsminger	Frank E. Entsminger	1986	12
113 6/8	17 5/8	19 1/8	16 2/8	3 3/8	3 2/8	4	4	Long Island, Alaska	Picked Up	Allan C. Merrill	1987	13
112 3/8	18 2/8	17 7/8	17 5/8	3 5/8	4	6	7	Alder Creek, Alaska	Richard L. Reeves	Richard L. Reeves	1988	14
112 2/8	19	19 2/8	16 4/8	4 3/8	4 2/8	4	4	Olga Bay, Alaska	John D. Frost	John D. Frost	1987	15
112 1/8	17	16 2/8	15 5/8	4 1/8	4	5	5	Alitak Bay, Alaska	Dale J. Bunnage	Dale J. Bunnage	1988	16
111 7/8	18 5/8	18 6/8	15 5/8	4 2/8	4 1/8	5	4	Uganik Bay, Alaska	Jeff A. Buffum	Jeff A. Buffum	1987	17
111 3/8	18	17 7/8	16 3/8	4	3 7/8	4	5	Spiridon Lake, Alaska	David H. Raskey	David H. Raskey	1986	18
111	16 3/8	16 5/8	14 2/8	3 5/8	3 7/8	5	5	Karluk Lake, Alaska	Ted H. Spraker	Ted H. Spraker	1983	19
110 3/8	16 5/8	17	13 7/8	3 3/8	3 4/8	5	5	Hidden Basin, Alaska	Don J. Edwards	Don J. Edwards	1987	20
110 1/8	19	18 5/8	15 4/8	3 7/8	4	6	6	Outlet Cape, Alaska	Henry T. Hamelin	Henry T. Hamelin	1981	21
109 5/8	17 1/8	17	15 1/8	3 5/8	3 3/8	5	5	Terror Bay, Alaska	Christopher L. Linford	Christopher L. Linford	1987	22
109 2/8	18 2/8	18 3/8	15 2/8	4	4	4	4	Olga Bay, Alaska	David G. Kelleyhouse	David G. Kelleyhouse	1987	23
109 1/8	18 4/8	18 7/8	14 7/8	3 7/8	3 7/8	5	5	Kupreanof Pen., Alaska	John B. Murray	John B. Murray	1982	24
109	17	17 4/8	15 4/8	4	4	5	5	Kodiak Island, Alaska	D. Roger Liebner	D. Roger Liebner	1983	25
109	17 7/8	18	15	4 1/8	4	5	5	Dall Island, Alaska	Sharla L. Merrill	Sharla L. Merrill	1985	25
109	15 5/8	16	15 5/8	3 5/8	3	5	5	Terror Bay, Alaska	John R. Odom III	John R. Odom III	1985	25
108 4/8	19 3/8	19 6/8	15	4	4	4	4	Cleveland Pen., Alaska	Dennis E. Northrup	Dennis E. Northrup	1985	28

Sitka Blacktail Deer - Continued

Score	Length of Main Beam R.	Length of Main Beam L.	Inside Spread	Circumference at Smallest Place Between Burr and First Point R.	Circumference at Smallest Place Between Burr and First Point L.	Number of Points R.	Number of Points L.	Locality Killed	By Whom Killed	Owner	Date Killed	Rank
108	16 6/8	17 3/8	14 4/8	3 6/8	3 6/8	5	5	Kizhuyak Bay, Alaska	Gene D. Carter	Gene D. Carter	1987	29
107 2/8	17	17 1/8	16	3 7/8	4	4	5	Uganik Bay, Alaska	Robert C. Jones	Robert C. Jones	1987	30
107	17	17	16 6/8	3 6/8	4	5	5	Kodiak Island, Alaska	Andrew G. Johnson	Andrew G. Johnson	1986	31
104 4/8	16 6/8	15 5/8	15 4/8	3 5/8	3 4/8	5	4	Malina Bay, Alaska	Thomas A. Ray	Thomas A. Ray	1981	32
104	17 3/8	17 2/8	15 6/8	3 3/8	3 5/8	5	5	Uganik Bay, Alaska	Robert C. Jones	Robert C. Jones	1987	33
103	17 6/8	17 6/8	17 6/8	3 7/8	3 5/8	4	4	Viekoda Bay, Alaska	Forrest E. Weiant	Forrest E. Weiant	1984	34
102 6/8	17	16 7/8	15 4/8	3 5/8	3 6/8	4	4	Browns Lagoon, Alaska	Charles R. Price	Charles R. Price	1986	35
102 3/8	17 7/8	16 2/8	14 5/8	3 7/8	3 4/8	5	5	Uyak Bay, Alaska	Toby J. Johnson	Toby J. Johnson	1987	36
102 2/8	16	16 1/8	15 4/8	3 4/8	3 4/8	6	5	Kodiak Island, Alaska	John H. Saunby	John H. Saunby	1983	37
101 6/8	18	17 3/8	15	3 5/8	3 5/8	5	4	Karluk Lake, Alaska	Randy S. Shumate	Randy S. Shumate	1988	38
100 1/8	16 3/8	16 5/8	13 5/8	4	4 3/8	4	4	Viekoda Bay, Alaska	Forrest E. Weiant	Forrest E. Weiant	1985	39
131 5/8 *	19 2/8	20 5/8	16 5/8	5	4 5/8	7	6	Luck Lake, Alaska	Picked Up	Ronald L. Sowards	1982	
119 6/8 *	18 7/8	19 6/8	14 7/8	3 5/8	4 2/8	4	5	Coffman Cove, Alaska	Gary R. Dilley	Gary R. Dilley	1987	
112 6/8 *	17 6/8	17 3/8	16	3 5/8	4 1/8	5	5	Prince of Wales Island, Alaska	William H. Welton	William H. Welton	1988	
112 4/8 *	17 5/8	17 2/8	16 4/8	4 1/8	3 7/8	5	5	Uganik Lake, Alaska	George W. Gozelski	George W. Gozelski	1983	
111 3/8 *	18	17 5/8	15 5/8	4	4 1/8	5	4	Uyak Bay, Alaska	Charlie W. Hastings	Charlie W. Hastings	1986	
110 5/8 *	19 1/8	18 2/8	15 5/8	3 5/8	3 7/8	4	5	Afognak Island, Alaska	Dale W. Grove	Dale W. Grove	1987	
109 7/8 *	16	17 6/8	15 2/8	3 5/8	3 5/8	6	5	Uyak Bay, Alaska	Bradley A. Pope	Bradley A. Pope	1986	

* Final Score subject to revision by additional verifying measurements.

Whitetail Deer, Typical Antlers

Minimum Score 160 *Odocoileus virginianus virginianus* and certain related subspecies World's Record 206-1/8

Score	Length of Main Beam R.	Length of Main Beam L.	Inside Spread	Circumference at Smallest Place Between Burr and First Point R.	Circumference at Smallest Place Between Burr and First Point L.	Number of Points R.	Number of Points L.	Locality Killed	By Whom Killed	Owner	Date Killed	Rank
197 7/8	27 4/8	27 2/8	19 4/8	4 6/8	4 6/8	8	9	Assiniboine River, Man.	Larry H. MacDonald	Larry H. MacDonald	1980	1
197 5/8	27 7/8	27 5/8	21 6/8	5 2/8	5 2/8	7	8	Wood Co., Wisc.	Joe Haske	Goldie Haske	1945	2
196 1/8	27 1/8	26 4/8	24 5/8	4 6/8	4 4/8	8	9	McMullen Co., Texas	Milton P. George	John L. Stein	1906	3
195 4/8	25 3/8	25 2/8	19	4 7/8	4 7/8	9	7	Porcupine Plain, Sask.	Philip Philipowich	Philip Philipowich	1985	4
195 1/8	28 6/8	28 4/8	20 3/8	4 7/8	5	5	5	Parke Co., Ind.	B. Dodd Porter	B. Dodd Porter	1985	5
194 7/8	26 7/8	27 7/8	23 1/8	6 1/8	5 5/8	7	7	Leavenworth Co., Kan.	William R. Mikijanis	William R. Mikijanis	1985	6
193 2/8	28 3/8	27 7/8	22 2/8	5 2/8	5 2/8	8	6	Jackson Co., Mich.	Craig Calderone	Craig Calderone	1986	7
192	27 1/8	27 2/8	19	4 5/8	4 5/8	6	6	Pine Co., Minn.	Frank Worlickey	Robert Worlickey	1952	8
192	24 3/8	23 5/8	17	4 7/8	4 6/8	7	7	Clay Co., Minn.	Mark L. Peterson	Mark L. Peterson	1984	8
191 5/8	26	26 1/8	21 7/8	5	5 1/8	5	7	Goodhue Co., Minn.	David C. Klatt	Joel Hilgendorf	1985	10
191 5/8	25 5/8	25	22 7/8	4 3/8	4 4/8	5	6	Albany Co., Wyo.	Robert D. Ross	Robert D. Ross	1986	10
189 7/8	29 4/8	29 6/8	19 5/8	5	4 7/8	9	6	Trempealeau Co., Wisc.	Emil Stelmach	Emil Stelmach	1959	12
189	25 1/8	25 4/8	17 2/8	4 5/8	4 4/8	6	6	Crawford Co., Ark.	Tom Sparks, Jr.	Tom Sparks, Jr.	1975	13
189	25 4/8	25 4/8	23 2/8	5 1/8	5 1/8	8	8	Red Deer Lake, Man.	Will Bigelow	Will Bigelow	1986	13
188 6/8	25 3/8	25 3/8	16 2/8	5 2/8	5 3/8	6	6	Shenandoah Co., Va.	Gene W. Wilson	Gene W. Wilson	1985	15
188 4/8	27 1/8	27 7/8	20 5/8	6 6/8	6 2/8	5	5	Souris River, Man.	Wes Todoruk	Wes Todoruk	1986	16
188 3/8	24 2/8	26 4/8	18 5/8	5 5/8	5 5/8	8	7	Sanford, Man.	Picked Up	Manitoba Wildl. Branch	1982	17
187 7/8	25 5/8	26 1/8	21 3/8	4 5/8	4 4/8	7	6	Zavala Co., Texas	Donald Rutledge	Frank Rutledge	1946	18
187 6/8	28	28 4/8	20 6/8	5 5/8	6 1/8	6	5	Houston Co., Minn.	Donald M. Grant	Donald M. Grant	1978	19
187 6/8	25 5/8	23 2/8	17 2/8	6	5 5/8	6	8	Mantagao Lake, Man.	Picked Up	Mel Podaima	1988	19
187 4/8	25 2/8	25	18 3/8	5 2/8	5 3/8	7	6	Frio Co., Texas	Kenneth Campbell	Kenneth Campbell	1987	21
187 2/8	25 1/8	25 5/8	19 1/8	4 3/8	4 3/8	6	7	Atchison Co., Mo.	Unknown	John L. Stein	1984	22
187 1/8	26 3/8	25	18 6/8	5 1/8	5 1/8	7	7	McLean Co., N.D.	Frank O. Bauman	Donald Bauman	1986	22
187 1/8	27 7/8	28 3/8	18 7/8	5 5/8	5 2/8	5	5	Mercer Co., Mo.	Picked Up	Bob Summers	1986	24
186 3/8	28	28	23 1/8	4 6/8	4 4/8	5	6	Lee Co., Ala.	Picked Up	George P. Mann	1986	25
186	30	29 4/8	22	6	5 4/8	6	5	Warren Co., Ky.	Arnold M. Bush	Arnold M. Bush	1986	26
185 5/8	28 5/8	28 3/8	20 5/8	5 2/8	5 2/8	5	5	Beltrami Co., Minn.	Picked Up	Jerome D. Erdahl	1987	27
185 5/8	25 2/8	25 4/8	19 2/8	4 5/8	4 3/8	6	7	Dallas Co., Mo.	James E. Headings	James E. Headings	1986	28
185 1/8	29 2/8	29 2/8	25 5/8	5	5 1/8	7	6	Warren Co., Iowa	Joyce McCormick	Joyce McCormick	1968	29
185	25 7/8	25 1/8	19	4 7/8	4 7/8	7	7	Winona Co., Minn.	Ronald Bunke	B., S., & B. Bunke	1973	30
185	27 1/8	27 2/8	18 6/8	5 3/8	5 4/8	6	8	Putnam Co., Ind.	Earl G. McCammack	Earl G. McCammack	1985	30

Whitetail Deer, *Typical Antlers* - Continued

Score	Length of Main Beam R.	L.	Inside Spread	Circumference at Smallest Place Between Burr and First Point R.	L.	Number of Points R.	L.	Locality Killed	By Whom Killed	Owner	Date Killed	Rank
185	26 7/8	27	17 5/8	5 7/8	6	10	8	Seward Co., Kan.	Michael D. Gatlin	Michael D. Gatlin	1987	30
184 7/8	25 1/8	24 4/8	17 7/8	5 1/8	5 1/8	6	7	Yellowstone Co., Mont.	Picked Up	Dennis Helmey	1984	33
184 7/8	28	28	23 4/8	6	6	9	8	Vermilion, Alta.	C. Letawsky & B. Myshak	C. Letawsky & B. Myshak	1986	33
184 7/8	26 3/8	26 3/8	21	6	5 7/8	6	6	Baraga Co., Mich.	Louis J. Roy	Louis J. Roy	1987	33
184 6/8	28 5/8	28 6/8	21 6/8	5 6/8	5 4/8	6	6	Madison Parish, La.	John Lee	Don R. Broadway	1943	36
184 5/8	28 5/8	28 2/8	22	4 5/8	4 4/8	6	6	Washington Co., Maine	Unknown	Chuck P. Vose	1944	37
184 5/8	26	25 1/8	21 7/8	5 3/8	5 3/8	5	5	Polk Co., Neb.	Keith Houdersheldt	Keith Houdersheldt	1985	37
184 5/8	24 4/8	24 4/8	19 3/8	5 3/8	5 2/8	5	5	Hudson Bay, Sask.	Picked Up	Wade Hersikorn	1986	37
184 4/8	26 7/8	26 3/8	19 7/8	4 4/8	4 4/8	7	7	Missoula Co., Mont.	Jack Greenwood	Jack Greenwood	1985	40
184 4/8	29 1/8	28 2/8	18 6/8	4 7/8	5	6	7	Hardin Co., Iowa	Robert D. Imsland	Robert D. Imsland	1985	41
184 4/8	31 3/8	29	24	6	6	8	8	Waldo Co., Maine	Christopher Ramsey	Christopher Ramsey	1983	42
184	28 1/8	27 6/8	20 5/8	5 2/8	5 1/8	6	6	Saline Co., Kan.	James R. Bell	James R. Bell	1985	43
184	25	24 4/8	17 4/8	4 1/8	4	6	6	Hart Co., Ga.	Kenton L. Adams	Kenton L. Adams	1986	43
184	28 6/8	27 6/8	20 4/8	4 5/8	4 5/8	6	6	Grayson Co., Ky.	Floyd Stone	Floyd Stone	1987	43
183	26 1/8	26 1/8	19 3/8	5	5	6	8	Lorne, Man.	Alain G. Comte	Alain G. Comte	1987	46
182 7/8	27 1/8	27 3/8	19 2/8	5	5 3/8	7	7	Noxubee Co., Miss.	Glen R. Jourdon	Glen R. Jourdon	1986	47
182 7/8	22	23 1/8	19 5/8	5	4 7/8	8	7	Rock Island Co., Ill.	Clifton C. Webster	Clifton C. Webster	1986	47
182 5/8	28 3/8	28 4/8	24 1/8	5 2/8	5 1/8	5	6	Jefferson Co., Iowa	William J. Waugh	William J. Waugh	1985	49
182 2/8	28 1/8	27	20	5 3/8	5 5/8	5	5	Champaign Co., Ill.	Tom Babb	Tom Babb	1985	50
182 2/8	29 3/8	29	19 4/8	5 7/8	6	5	5	Forest Co., Wisc.	Richard J. Moore	Richard J. Moore	1987	50
182 2/8	27 4/8	26 6/8	24	5 1/8	5	5	6	Frontier Co., Neb.	Robert G. Bortner	Robert G. Bortner	1985	52
181 7/8	26 5/8	27 3/8	21 5/8	4 4/8	4 4/8	5	5	Clearwater Co., Idaho	Richard E. Carver	Richard E. Carver	1985	53
181 7/8	24 4/8	25 2/8	17 1/8	5 4/8	5 4/8	5	7	Lesser Slave Lake, Alta.	Picked Up	Jerry Napier	1985	53
181 7/8	28 5/8	27 4/8	22 1/8	4 4/8	4 4/8	5	5	Coahuila, Mexico	German L. Flores	German L. Flores	1986	53
181 7/8	25 3/8	25 4/8	23 5/8	5 3/8	5	5	5	Guilford Co., N.C.	Terry E. Daffron	Terry E. Daffron	1987	53
181 6/8	26 5/8	25 5/8	24	4 6/8	4 4/8	6	6	Nuevo Leon, Mexico	J.P. Davis	J.P. Davis	1985	57
181 6/8	25 5/8	26 6/8	23 6/8	5	4 7/8	7	6	Montgomery Co., Md.	Gary F. Menso	Gary F. Menso	1985	57
181 5/8	28 2/8	27 6/8	19 7/8	3 7/8	4 1/8	6	6	Pierce Co., Wisc.	Raymond G. Miller, Sr.	Raymond G. Miller, Sr.	1960	59
181 5/8	26 6/8	27 6/8	21 5/8	6 1/8	6 3/8	6	6	Wabash Co., Ill.	Mike Drone	Mike Drone	1987	59
181 4/8	26 6/8	27 6/8	20 6/8	4 4/8	4 6/8	6	6	Trempealeau Co., Wisc.	Randy A. Hoff	Randy A. Hoff	1987	61
181 3/8	24 1/8	24	20 4/8	5 1/8	5 3/8	6	6	Harding Co., S.D.	Cregg Else	Cregg Else	1985	62
181 2/8	26 5/8	26	21 1/8	5 3/8	5 3/8	8	7	Sheridan Co., Mont.	Arthur M. Hagan, Sr.	Ken Hagan	1957	63

Score						L	R	Location	Hunter	Owner	Year	Rank
180 7/8	26 5/8	28	17 7/8	4 4/8	4 4/8	5	5	Marinette Co., Wisc.	Albert Giese	Kenneth J. Giese	1938	64
180 7/8	28 5/8	27 7/8	22 1/8	5 2/8	5 2/8	5	6	Polk Co., Minn.	Daniel Omdahl	Daniel Omdahl	1987	64
180 6/8	25 4/8	25 5/8	19	5 2/8	5 2/8	5	5	Marshall Co., Minn.	Scott T. Rabehl	Scott T. Rabehl	1987	66
180 5/8	28 3/8	28 4/8	22 6/8	5 1/8	5 2/8	6	4	Nuevo Leon, Mexico	Charles H. Priess	Charles H. Priess	1985	67
180 4/8	27 6/8	26 2/8	20	4 6/8	4 6/8	6	7	Madison Parish, La.	Buford Perry	Buford Perry	1961	68
180 4/8	25 4/8	26 2/8	17 4/8	4 3/8	4 3/8	6	6	Carver Co., Minn.	Stephen M. Polston	Stephen M. Polston	1985	68
180 3/8	26 6/8	25 5/8	20 1/8	6 3/8	6 2/8	7	7	Aikin Co., Minn.	Donald J. Sorenson	Donald J. Sorenson	1963	70
180 3/8	30 4/8	29 2/8	22 3/8	5 1/8	5 1/8	4	4	Hand Co., S.D.	Vernon Winter	J.D. Andrews	1965	70
180 3/8	27	28 1/8	17 6/8	4 5/8	4 5/8	6	6	Huron Co., Mich.	Picked Up	Ray W. Hatfield	1985	70
180	26 4/8	27 1/8	18 2/8	5 3/8	5 5/8	9	6	Edwards Co., Kan.	David R. Cross	David R. Cross	1985	73
180	25 2/8	25 5/8	22 7/8	5 4/8	4 7/8	7	8	Pulaski Co., Ill.	Picked Up	Pat Kearny	1988	73
179 7/8	27 6/8	26 3/8	19 7/8	5 4/8	5 4/8	5	6	Hamiota, Man.	Alan J. Sheridan	Alan J. Sheridan	1984	75
179 7/8	26 1/8	26 5/8	19 1/8	5 5/8	5 4/8	6	5	Nicollet Co., Minn.	Joe Welter	Joe Welter	1987	75
179 6/8	26 7/8	26 5/8	21 4/8	4 4/8	4 4/8	6	7	Woodbury Co., Iowa	Harlan L. Allison	Harlan L. Allison	1979	77
179 4/8	26 2/8	26 2/8	19 5/8	5 5/8	5 3/8	6	5	Whitemud River, Man.	L. Greg Fehr	L. Greg Fehr	1985	78
179 4/8	27 3/8	27 2/8	20 2/8	5	5	5	5	Cremona, Alta.	E. Roger Jackson	E. Roger Jackson	1985	78
179 2/8	28 1/8	28 4/8	25 2/8	4 4/8	4 5/8	5	5	Webster Co., Iowa	Douglas W. Baedke	Douglas W. Baedke	1982	80
179 1/8	27 3/8	27 7/8	21 3/8	5 2/8	5 1/8	6	6	Renville Co., Minn.	Todd Swartz	Todd Swartz	1984	81
179	27 6/8	29 2/8	20 7/8	5 4/8	5 5/8	8	11	Perry Co., Ill.	Roy A. Smith	Roy A. Smith	1987	82
178 6/8	27	27	19 3/8	4 6/8	4 5/8	6	6	Webb Co., Texas	M.J. Satcher	M.J. Satcher	1987	83
178 5/8	27 3/8	27 1/8	24 1/8	5	5 2/8	6	5	Crawford Co., Wisc.	Dale Check, Jr.	Dale Check, Jr.	1985	84
178 5/8	24 7/8	25 1/8	18 1/8	5	4 7/8	6	6	Grant Co., Wisc.	I. James Meng	I. James Meng	1985	84
178 5/8	25 2/8	26 1/8	20 1/8	5 4/8	5 3/8	6	7	Caldwell Co., Mo.	Jack L. Murray	Jack L. Murray	1986	84
178 5/8	25 2/8	24 7/8	21 3/8	5	5	5	5	Flat Lake, Alta.	Paul Franchuk	Paul Franchuk	1987	84
178 4/8	26 6/8	26 1/8	28 4/8	4 7/8	4 7/8	5	5	Beltrami Co., Minn.	Arthur I. Hill	Arthur A. Hill	1954	88
178 4/8	28 1/8	25 4/8	21 4/8	5 2/8	5 4/8	5	6	Riley Co., Kan.	Stan E. Christiansen	Stan E. Christiansen	1973	88
178 4/8	25 1/8	25 4/8	19 4/8	5 3/8	5 3/8	5	5	Firdale, Man.	Randall J. Bean	Randall J. Bean	1988	88
178 3/8	25 1/8	26 1/8	21 2/8	4 6/8	4 7/8	5	6	Clinton Co., Ill.	Richard V. Spihlmann	Richard V. Spihlmann	1961	91
178 3/8	26 4/8	25	19	4 7/8	4 7/8	6	7	Jo Daviess Co., Ill.	Gary J. Flynn	Gary J. Flynn	1986	91
178 2/8	26 6/8	28 1/8	19 6/8	5 4/8	5 4/8	7	7	Ohio Co., Ky.	Earl R. Trogden	Earl R. Trogden	1986	93
178 1/8	28 5/8	29	21 6/8	5 5/8	5 5/8	5	5	Aroostook Co., Maine	Gary G. Saucier	Gary G. Saucier	1987	94
178	24 1/8	25 3/8	16 6/8	4 6/8	4 7/8	6	6	Hillsdale Co., Mich.	Dudley N. Spade	Dudley N. Spade	1972	95
178	25 4/8	25 1/8	18 5/8	4 1/8	4 1/8	7	7	Caswell Co., N.C.	Picked Up	Jimmy Koger	1988	95
177 7/8	29 5/8	29 5/8	18 2/8	5	5	7	7	Burnett Co., Wisc.	John Backlund	Lester Thor	1916	97
177 7/8	26 6/8	26 6/8	18 2/8	4 3/8	4 3/8	6	6	Penobscot Co., Maine	Andrew B. Alexander	Andrew B. Alexander	1985	97
177 7/8	22 4/8	23 3/8	17 7/8	5 2/8	5 2/8	7	8	Cass Co., N.D.	Joe D. Chesley	Joe D. Chesley	1987	97
177 6/8	24 3/8	23 5/8	19	4 6/8	4 6/8	5	5	Clark Co., Mo.	Billie G. Noble	Billie G. Noble	1985	100
177 5/8	26	25 5/8	19 3/8	4 4/8	4 4/8	5	5	Idaho Co., Idaho	Donna M. Knight	Donna M. Knight	1986	101
177 4/8	28 5/8	29 2/8	18 3/8	5 5/8	5 5/8	6	9	Otter Tail Co., Minn.	Larry K. Sherman	Larry K. Sherman	1964	102
177 4/8	28 3/8	28 4/8	23 5/8	4 3/8	4 3/8	8	5	Krydor, Sask.	Robert J. Perszyk	Robert J. Perszyk	1985	102
177 4/8	26	28	21 6/8	5 5/8	5 3/8	7	6	Krydor, Sask.	Julian Shewchuk	Julian Shewchuk	1985	102
177 4/8	29 7/8	28 7/8	21 1/8	4 7/8	4 7/8	5	5	Grayson Co., Ky.	David W. Mercer	David W. Mercer	1986	102

Whitetail Deer, Typical Antlers - Continued

Score	Length of Main Beam R.	L.	Inside Spread	Circumference at Smallest Place Between Burr and First Point R.	L.	Number of Points R.	L.	Locality Killed	By Whom Killed	Owner	Date Killed	Rank
177 3/8	27 1/8	26 3/8	20 3/8	5 4/8	5 2/8	6	5	Greene Co., Iowa	Roger V. Carlson	Roger V. Carlson	1983	106
177 3/8	27 3/8	28	16 5/8	5	5 1/8	5	5	Claiborne Parish, La.	Steven L. Morton	Steven L. Morton	1986	106
177 3/8	29 1/8	30 1/8	24 7/8	6 4/8	6 2/8	9	9	Menominee Co., Wisc.	Jeff N. Dixon	Jeff N. Dixon	1987	106
177 2/8	24 1/8	24 5/8	22 2/8	4 2/8	4 1/8	5	5	LaSalle Co., Texas	T.H. Barker	Michael R. Barker	1939	109
177 2/8	27	26 7/8	20 6/8	5	5	5	5	Belmont Co., Ohio	Kevin A. Grimes	Kevin A. Grimes	1987	109
177 1/8	27	27	18 1/8	4 6/8	4 7/8	5	5	Gregory Co., S.D.	Harold Deering	Harold Deering	1969	111
177 1/8	25 5/8	25 5/8	22 3/8	4 7/8	4 6/8	6	5	Thorsby, Alta.	Unknown	Adam Tomaszewski	1985	111
177 1/8	28	26 7/8	21 1/8	5 3/8	5 3/8	5	5	Kittson Co., Minn.	Dan Haskins	George W. Flaim	1987	114
177	28 3/8	28 6/8	22 3/8	4 1/8	4	6	5	Jasper Co., Ind.	Bruce A. Crofton	Douglas R. Plourde	1975	114
177	24 7/8	25	16 3/8	5 1/8	5 1/8	8	9	Daly, Man.	Fred Thorkelson	Bruce A. Crofton	1984	114
177	23 7/8	25 1/8	14 3/8	5 2/8	5 1/8	11	7	Lundar, Man.	Jack Van Nice	Fred Thorkelson	1986	114
177	26 2/8	26 1/8	20 4/8	4 3/8	4 5/8	6	6	Muscatine Co., Iowa	Fred W. Collins	Jack Van Nice	1986	114
176 7/8	25 5/8	27 4/8	22 4/8	5	5 1/8	9	6	Prince George Co., Va.	Richard F. Krohe	Fred W. Collins	1949	118
176 7/8	25 5/8	25 2/8	18 1/8	4 5/8	4 7/8	7	7	McDonough Co., Ill.	Thomas A. Bridenstine	Richard F. Krohe	1986	118
176 7/8	27 4/8	28	25 3/8	5 6/8	5 5/8	7	5	Marion Co., Ohio	Thomas A. Bridenstine	Thomas A. Bridenstine	1987	118
176 7/8	30	28	29 5/8	5 4/8	5 4/8	4	4	Unknown	Unknown	R. Rogers & R. Scott	1988 pr	118
176 6/8	26 3/8	26	19 2/8	4 4/8	4 4/8	6	6	Winona Co., Minn.	Harry M. Timm	Harry M. Timm	1964	122
176 6/8	27	27 7/8	22 2/8	5 5/8	5 7/8	5	5	Buffalo, Wisc.	Dean Broberg	Dean Broberg	1985	122
176 6/8	24 4/8	24 5/8	19 4/8	5	5 3/8	6	6	Miami Co., Kan.	Richard T. Hale	Richard T. Hale	1985	122
176 6/8	25 1/8	23 3/8	19 2/8	5 4/8	5 2/8	8	9	Saskatchewan	Unknown	D. Ross Sayrs	1986	122
176 6/8	22 3/8	23 3/8	16 2/8	4 1/8	4 1/8	7	7	Idaho Co., Idaho	Edward D. Moore	Edward D. Moore	1986	122
176 6/8	26 1/8	25	20 5/8	6 2/8	5 7/8	6	6	Adams Co., Wisc.	Mark R. Faber	Mark R. Faber	1987	122
176 6/8	26 5/8	25 5/8	17	5 3/8	5 1/8	7	7	Idaho Co., Idaho	Frank J. Loughran	Frank J. Loughran	1987	122
176 6/8	27 4/8	26	22 7/8	4 5/8	5 1/8	7	5	McHenry Co., Ill.	Eugene Melby	Eugene Melby	1988	122
176 5/8	23 7/8	26 1/8	21 1/8	5 1/8	5	7	7	Rusk Co., Wisc.	Ercel Dustin	Ercel Dustin	1966	130
176 5/8	28	28 7/8	19 1/8	5 2/8	5 3/8	6	7	Dickinson Co., Kan.	Robert L. Aldrich	Robert L. Aldrich	1986	132
176 3/8	25 5/8	25 3/8	20 2/8	4 4/8	5 2/8	7	5	Wright Co., Mo.	Mike Napier	Mike Napier	1986	132
176 3/8	25 5/8	25 4/8	20 1/8	4 4/8	4 4/8	6	6	Logan Co., Ohio	Larry D. Hyzer	Larry D. Hyzer	1987	134
176 2/8	28 2/8	27 5/8	21	4 6/8	4 4/8	7	5	Houston Co., Minn.	John W. Zahrte	John W. Zahrte	1981	134
176 2/8	26 3/8	26 3/8	20 4/8	4 6/8	5	5	7	Litchfield Co., Conn.	Frederick H. Clymer	Frederick H. Clymer	1987	134
176 1/8	25 7/8	25 5/8	19 1/8	4 4/8	4 4/8	5	6	Grunthal, Man.	Edwin Froese	Edwin Froese	1986	136
176	26	26	18 4/8	5 7/8	6 2/8	6	6	Racine Co., Wisc.	Daniel P. Cramer	Daniel P. Cramer	1985	137
176	26 4/8	27	18 4/8	4	4 4/8	5	7	Nemaha Co., Kan.	Joseph L. Schmelzle	Joseph L. Schmelzle	1985	137

Score						Location	Hunter	Hunter	Date	Rank
176	26 3/8	26 2/8	20	5 1/8	5 1/8	5	Goodhue Co., Minn.	Martin H. Bollum	Martin H. Bollum	1986	137
175 7/8	26 1/8	26 4/8	20 3/8	4 3/8	4 3/8	7	Lewis Co., N.Y.	Andrew Lustyik	Andrew F. Lustyik	1942	140
175 7/8	27 5/8	27 1/8	22 5/8	6 5/8	6 2/8	9	Pouce Coupe River, B.C.	Dale Callahan	Dale Callahan	1986	140
175 6/8	26 5/8	27 2/8	19 6/8	4 6/8	4 7/8	6	Cypress River, Man.	Murray Jones	Murray Jones	1973	142
175 6/8	26 4/8	27 6/8	20 3/8	5 2/8	5 2/8	5	Nine Mile Brook, N.B.	Leopold Leblanc	Jim Oickle	1973	142
175 5/8	26 3/8	25	21 4/8	5 3/8	5 5/8	6	Crawford Co., Wisc.	David R. Kluesner	David R. Kluesner	1985	145
175 5/8	26 5/8	26 7/8	18 5/8	4 6/8	4 6/8	5	Rock Co., Wisc.	Neil Laube	Neil Laube	1965	145
175 5/8	27 5/8	27 3/8	19 5/8	4 6/8	4 7/8	6	Goodhue Co., Minn.	Ellsworth Ramseier	Chuck Ramseier	1972	145
175 5/8	26 6/8	26	20 6/8	4 5/8	4 4/8	6	Warren Co., Iowa	Art L. Daniels	Art L. Daniels	1986	145
175 4/8	25 5/8	25 5/8	20 1/8	4 7/8	4 7/8	5	Buffalo Co., Wisc.	Picked Up	Charles G. Dienger	1983	148
175 4/8	26 2/8	26 3/8	16 5/8	5 3/8	5 4/8	8	Canaan, N.B.	Marcel Poirier	Marcel Poirier	1985	148
175 4/8	24 5/8	25 5/8	16 2/8	4 7/8	5 2/8	7	Macon Co., Ga.	Charles W. Haynie	Charles W. Haynie	1987	148
175 3/8	25 7/8	26 3/8	19 5/8	5 1/8	5 2/8	6	Wabasha Co., Minn.	Ronald V. Hurlburt	Ronald V. Hurlburt	1987	148
175 3/8	26	25 4/8	17 7/8	5 1/8	5 3/8	10	Clark Co., Ill.	Gary L. Lovell	Gary L. Lovell	1986	152
175 3/8	26	25 5/8	18 7/8	5 6/8	5 7/8	5	Carberry, Man.	H. & B. Calvert	H. & B. Calvert	1987	152
175 2/8	25 5/8	25 5/8	19 4/8	4 3/8	4 6/8	5	Bayfield Co., Wisc.	Bill Holiday	Douglas R. Plourde	1920	154
175 2/8	24 2/8	24 6/8	20	4 2/8	4 2/8	6	Aitkin Co., Minn.	Terry Kullhem	Terry Kullhem	1958	154
175 2/8	25	24 3/8	17	4 3/8	5	6	Russell, Man.	Emile DeCorby	Emile DeCorby	1986	154
175 2/8	25 3/8	26 3/8	23 3/8	5 3/8	5 7/8	6	Krydor, Sask.	Lorne M. Shewchuk	Lorne M. Shewchuk	1986	154
175 2/8	23 3/8	24 1/8	19 3/8	4 5/8	4 5/8	5	Mayerthorpe, Alta.	Gregory Graff	Gregory Graff	1987	154
175 1/8	26 7/8	25 3/8	17 4/8	5 1/8	5 1/8	6	Taylor Co., Wisc.	Jack L. Dittrich	Jack L. Dittrich	1945	159
175 1/8	25 6/8	25 2/8	16 7/8	5 3/8	5 4/8	7	Howard Co., Iowa	Russell L. Stevenson, Jr.	Russell L. Stevenson, Jr.	1971	159
175 1/8	25 5/8	25 1/8	24 3/8	4 7/8	4 7/8	6	Lincoln Co., Minn.	Robert R. Bushman	Robert R. Bushman	1973	159
175 1/8	23 7/8	24 4/8	17 3/8	4 5/8	4 4/8	6	Kings Co., N.B.	Wayne F. Anderson	Wayne F. Anderson	1987	159
175 1/8	27 5/8	27 1/8	19 6/8	5 3/8	5 5/8	7	Marquette Co., Mich.	Andrew E. Cook II	Andrew E. Cook II	1987	159
175 1/8	24 5/8	25 4/8	17 5/8	5 5/8	5 4/8	5	Witchekan Lake, Sask.	Brent A. Smith	Brent A. Smith	1987	159
175	26	26	18 4/8	4 5/8	4 4/8	6	Webb Co., Texas	Leslie G. Fisher	Leslie G. Fisher, Jr.	1935	165
175	28 5/8	27 5/8	18 1/8	5	4 7/8	5	Louisa Co., Iowa	Glen D. Brandt	Glen D. Brandt	1974	165
174 7/8	24 3/8	24 2/8	23 6/8	4 7/8	4 7/8	7	Delta Co., Mich.	Will Willman	Delor J. Willman	1930	167
174 7/8	25 5/8	25 5/8	16 5/8	4 4/8	5	6	Fillmore Co., Minn.	Daniel M. Hansen	Daniel M. Hansen	1979	167
174 7/8	25 1/8	25 1/8	20 6/8	4 1/8	4 3/8	8	Polk Co., Texas	Charlie L. Albertson	Charlie L. Albertson	1984	167
174 6/8	24 7/8	24 2/8	18 2/8	4 4/8	4 4/8	6	Isanti Co., Minn.	Larry Roos	Larry Roos	1971	170
174 6/8	25 5/8	24	18	4 7/8	5	5	Fisher Branch, Man.	Paul Sanduliak	Paul Sanduliak	1985	170
174 6/8	26 5/8	26 1/8	20 1/8	4 4/8	4 6/8	7	Talbot Co., Ga.	Harold Cole, Sr.	Harold Cole, Sr.	1985	170
174 5/8	29 4/8	28 3/8	21 7/8	6	6	8	Otter Tail Co., Minn.	James C. Vonderbruggen	James C. Vonderbruggen	1976	173
174 5/8	25 1/8	25	16 5/8	5 3/8	5 1/8	9	Livingston Co., Mich.	Nicholas S. Converse	Nicholas S. Converse	1987	173
174 4/8	28 3/8	28	22 5/8	5 3/8	5 3/8	5	Johnson Co., Mo.	Thomas E. White	Thomas E. White	1987	173
174 3/8	27 5/8	25 2/8	23 5/8	5 1/8	5	6	Geary Co., Kan.	James Brethour	James Brethour	1984	176
174 3/8	24	24	17 4/8	5 4/8	5 4/8	8	Sawyer Co., Wisc.	Patrick E. Jasper	Patrick E. Jasper	1985	176
174 3/8	28	28 3/8	21 2/8	4 6/8	4 7/8	5	LaCrosse Co., Wisc.	Kevin M. Kastenschmidt	Kevin M. Kastenschmidt	1986	176
174 3/8	26 4/8	26 4/8	23 3/8	5 2/8	5 2/8	6	Trempealeau Co., Wisc.	Laverne Killian, Jr.	Laverne Killian, Jr.	1986	176
174 3/8	28 3/8	26 7/8	23 1/8	4 3/8	4 4/8	7	Dimmit Co., Texas	Steven W. Vaughn	Steven W. Vaughn	1987	176

Whitetail Deer, Typical Antlers - Continued

Score	Length of Main Beam R.	L.	Inside Spread	Circumference at Smallest Place Between Burr and First Point R.	L.	Number of Points R.	L.	Locality Killed	By Whom Killed	Owner	Date Killed	Rank
174 2/8	26 1/8	26 5/8	22 6/8	5	4 6/8	7	6	Clearwater Co., Idaho	Douglas B. Crockett	Douglas B. Crockett	1983	181
174 2/8	27 6/8	26 5/8	19 4/8	5 2/8	6 1/8	5	5	Butler Co., Pa.	Ralph Stoltenberg, Jr.	Ralph Stoltenberg, Jr.	1986	181
174 2/8	27 7/8	27	21 2/8	5 2/8	5 1/8	5	5	Ashland Co., Wisc.	Kelly J. McClaire	Kelly J. McClaire	1986	181
174 1/8	27 1/8	28 1/8	24 7/8	5 1/8	5	6	6	Mahnomen Co., Minn.	Rolland Agnew	James Frazee	1941	184
174 1/8	25 3/8	25 5/8	19 2/8	5 4/8	5 4/8	6	6	Pierson, Man.	Art Minshull	Brad Minshull	pr	184
174 1/8	25 6/8	26	18 5/8	4 6/8	4 4/8	6	6	Iowa Co., Iowa	Ronald L. Brecht	Ronald L. Brecht	1973	184
174 1/8	27	26 1/8	20 7/8	6 5/8	6 7/8	6	7	Tuscarawas Co., Ohio	Dennis J. May, Jr.	Dennis J. May, Jr.	1985	184
174 1/8	25 5/8	25 5/8	19 6/8	5	4 7/8	6	6	McDonough Co., Ill.	Jack C. Icenogle	Jack C. Icenogle	1986	184
174 1/8	26 3/8	26 4/8	20 7/8	4 7/8	4 7/8	5	5	Amherstview, Ont.	Tony H. Stranak	Tony H. Stranak	1987	184
174	28 1/8	27 1/8	21 3/8	6 1/8	6 1/8	6	6	Reno Co., Kan.	Stan E. Christiansen	Stan E. Christiansen	1987	190
174	27 5/8	28	24	5	4 7/8	5	5	Mills Co., Iowa	Rick W. Elliott	Rick W. Elliott	1987	190
173 7/8	25 5/8	24 2/8	20 1/8	5 1/8	5 2/8	7	6	Ohio Co., Ky.	Rolly Tichenor	Rolly Tichenor	1982	192
173 7/8	28 6/8	27 5/8	18 5/8	5 3/8	5 3/8	6	7	Penobscot Co., Maine	Gregory A. York	Gregory A. York	1986	192
173 6/8	26 4/8	25 4/8	18 6/8	4 2/8	4 2/8	7	6	Stephens Co., Texas	Robert L. Murphy	Robert L. Murphy	1986	194
173 6/8	26 1/8	26 2/8	18 7/8	5 3/8	5 3/8	6	8	Schoolcraft Co., Mich.	Thomas J. Haas	Thomas J. Haas	1987	194
173 5/8	24	22 2/8	19 1/8	5	5	6	6	Morris Co., Kan.	Wayne Kasten	Wayne Kasten	1985	196
173 5/8	28	26 4/8	20 3/8	4 4/8	4 4/8	5	5	Fillmore Co., Minn.	Kelly J. McQuay	Kelly J. McQuay	1986	196
173 4/8	28	27 6/8	18 2/8	5	5	5	5	Winona Co., Minn.	Raymond A. Manion	Raymond A. Manion	1950	198
173 4/8	28 3/8	29 3/8	18	4 4/8	4 3/8	6	6	Livingston Co., Mich.	Paul M. Peckens	Paul M. Peckens	1959	198
173 4/8	23	23 6/8	18 4/8	5	4 6/8	5	5	Fulton Co., Ill.	Locie L. Murphy	Locie L. Murphy	1985	198
173 4/8	28 4/8	27 1/8	22 1/8	5 5/8	5 2/8	5	5	Ellsworth Co., Kan.	Monte Hudson	Monte Hudson	1986	198
173 4/8	24 2/8	24 7/8	20 4/8	4 4/8	4 7/8	7	7	Tamaulipas, Mexico	John F. Sontag, Jr.	John F. Sontag, Jr.	1987	198
173 4/8	25 7/8	27	23	5	5 1/8	5	5	McHenry Co., Ill.	Gordon R. Sunderlage	Gordon R. Sunderlage	1987	198
173 3/8	26 4/8	26 6/8	20 1/8	5	4 7/8	6	5	St. George, N.B.	Gilbert Leavitt	Gilbert Leavitt	1962	204
173 3/8	27 3/8	26 5/8	19 3/8	4 6/8	4 6/8	6	5	Pend Oreille Co., Wash.	Tom R. Lentz	Tom R. Lentz	1987	204
173 2/8	25 5/8	25 4/8	19	4 6/8	4 6/8	6	5	Battle River, Alta.	Steven M. Cooper	Steven M. Cooper	1984	206
173 2/8	25 3/8	25 4/8	21 2/8	5 3/8	5 2/8	6	8	Webb Co., Texas	Frank J. Sitterle	Frank J. Sitterle	1987	206
173 1/8	28	28 2/8	21 5/8	4 6/8	4 6/8	7	7	Dunn Co., Wisc.	Jack K. Dodge	Jack K. Dodge	1987	208
173	29 1/8	28 7/8	21	4 7/8	4 6/8	8	6	Bayfield Co., Wisc.	Unknown	Eagle Knob Lodge	1930 pr	209
173	28 2/8	27	21 2/8	5 5/8	5 5/8	6	7	Oconto Co., Wisc.	Donald P. Wimmer	Donald P. Wimmer	1969	209
173	26 5/8	25 3/8	19 4/8	4 7/8	5 1/8	8	6	Owen Co., Ky.	Roger Breeden	Roger Breeden	1978	209
173	26 4/8	25 7/8	18 4/8	4 4/8	4 4/8	5	5	Becker Co., Minn.	Albert E. Jahnke	Albert E. Jahnke	1985	209
173	28 1/8	29 4/8	24 4/8	4 4/8	4 4/8	6	5	Jefferson Co., Ohio	Adam Firm	Adam Firm	1987	209

Score							Locality	Hunter	Owner	Date	Rank
172 7/8	25 7/8	26 5/8	19 7/8	5 5/8	5	6	Williamson Co., Ill.	Picked Up	John L. Roseberry	1975	214
172 7/8	25 7/8	26 5/8	20 5/8	4 7/8	4 7/8	5	Pike Co., Ill.	Robert L. Hubbell	Robert L. Hubbell	1987	214
172 7/8	26 6/8	27 3/8	19 6/8	4	4 2/8	6	Jefferson Co., Ind.	Chet A. Nolan	Chet A. Nolan	1987	214
172 6/8	26 1/8	23 6/8	19	4 6/8	4 6/8	6	Somerset Co., Pa.	Edward B. Stutzman	Edward B. Stutzman, Jr.	1945	217
172 6/8	25 6/8	23 2/8	21 4/8	4 6/8	4 6/8	6	Trempealeau Co., Wisc.	Henry M. Hoff	Henry M. Hoff	1956	217
172 6/8	27	27 1/8	23 7/8	6 6/8	6 6/8	7	Powder River Co., Mont.	Picked Up	George A. Bettas	1974	217
172 6/8	24 5/8	25 1/8	22	5 3/8	5 5/8	6	Surry Co., Va.	Edward B. Jones	Edward B. Jones	1984	217
172 5/8	27 6/8	27 4/8	20 2/8	5 7/8	6 2/8	5	Fayette Co., Iowa	Greg P. Bordignon	Greg P. Bordignon	1987	222
172 5/8	25 3/8	25 6/8	18 3/8	5	5 2/8	6	Sauk Co., Wisc.	Terry A. Diske	Terry A. Diske	1987	222
172 4/8	25 1/8	27	20 1/8	5 5/8	5 2/8	5	Surry Co., Va.	Picked Up	Virginia L. Logan	1987	224
172 3/8	29 5/8	29 1/8	20 3/8	4 2/8	4 4/8	6	Snider Mt., N.B.	Jack W. Brown	Jack W. Brown	1975	224
172 2/8	27 1/8	26 5/8	16	4	4	5	Dane Co., Wisc.	Randy L. Letlebo	Randy L. Letlebo	1987	226
172 2/8	26 7/8	27	20 6/8	4 4/8	4 4/8	5	St. Louis Co., Minn.	Everett Larson	George W. Flaim	1942	226
172 2/8	24 6/8	25 3/8	18 2/8	5 1/8	5 1/8	5	Trego Co., Kan.	Alan Baldwin	Alan Baldwin	1982	226
172 2/8	27 2/8	30	20 4/8	5 4/8	5 4/8	7	Minnedosa River, Man.	Eric W. C. Abel	Eric W. C. Abel	1986	226
172 2/8	24 2/8	25	18 1/8	4 2/8	4 3/8	5	Minnesota	Unknown	Jeff A. Puhl	1987 pr	226
172 1/8	26 1/8	26 2/8	19 3/8	4 4/8	4 4/8	5	St. Louis Co., Minn.	Luke Schoeppner	Ted Schoeppner	1955	230
172 1/8	24 7/8	24	18 6/8	4 4/8	4	6	Clinton Co., Ill.	James D. Rueter	James D. Rueter	1984	230
172 1/8	26 1/8	25	18 5/8	5 5/8	5 5/8	8	Clinton Co., Iowa	R. Dean Grimes	R. Dean Grimes	1984	230
172 1/8	27 3/8	27 1/8	19 4/8	4 5/8	4 6/8	7	Granville Co., N.C.	Dudley Barnes	Dudley Barnes	1985	230
172 1/8	27 1/8	25 7/8	20 3/8	4 2/8	4 3/8	5	Buffalo Co., Wisc.	Aaron Comero	Aaron Comero	1986	230
172 1/8	25	25 5/8	18 3/8	5 4/8	5 5/8	5	Lac Emilien, Alta.	Dennis Ewanec	Dennis Ewanec	1987	230
172	26 1/8	26 3/8	17 4/8	5	4	6	Dodge Co., Wisc.	Dennis E. Schulteis	Dennis E. Schulteis	1985	236
172	27	27	17 1/8	4 6/8	5 2/8	5	Caroline Co., Md.	Garey N. Brown	Garey N. Brown	1986	236
172	25 4/8	25 4/8	17 4/8	4 6/8	4 4/8	6	Coahuila, Mexico	Picked Up	Carl Kallina	1986	236
171 7/8	26	26 1/8	20 3/8	5 1/8	5	5	Clayton Co., Iowa	Michael A. Roussel	Michael A. Roussel	1986	239
171 6/8	26 3/8	26 1/8	26 1/8	5 5/8	5 1/8	5	St. Louis Co., Minn.	Unknown	George W. Flaim	1970 pr	240
171 6/8	27 5/8	25 6/8	18 2/8	5 2/8	5 1/8	6	Rice Co., Kan.	Stan E. Christiansen	Stan E. Christiansen	1981	240
171 6/8	28 3/8	29 2/8	23 7/8	6	6	8	Taylor Co., Ga.	Picked Up	Charles L. Childree	1985	240
171 5/8	25	25 5/8	16 2/8	4 3/8	4 3/8	5	Koochiching Co., Minn.	Ray W. Bastin	Ray W. Bastin	1930	243
171 5/8	27 1/8	25 7/8	20	4 7/8	5	6	Pocahontas Co., Iowa	Larry G. Almond	Larry G. Almond	1983	243
171 5/8	24 2/8	23 6/8	16 1/8	4 4/8	4 4/8	6	Carlton Co., Minn.	Charles Ditmarsen	Charles Ditmarsen	1985	243
171 5/8	26 3/8	25	19 3/8	5 2/8	5 2/8	5	Logan Co., Ky.	Alan M. Scott	Alan M. Scott	1987	243
171 4/8	25 5/8	24	17 4/8	5 2/8	5 2/8	7	Wood Co., Wisc.	Unknown	Joe Hutwagner	1918	247
171 4/8	25 3/8	26 6/8	22	5 3/8	5 1/8	8	Lac qui Parle Co., Minn.	Wayne A. Hegland	Wayne A. Hegland	1977	247
171 4/8	24 7/8	25 2/8	19 4/8	4 7/8	5 2/8	6	Latah Co., Idaho	Darwin L. Baker	Darwin L. Baker	1986	247
171 4/8	25 6/8	26 7/8	17 2/8	4 2/8	5	6	Unknown	Unknown	Jerry L. Johnson	1987 pr	247
171 4/8	26 1/8	26	20 1/8	4 4/8	4 5/8	8	Rocky Mt. House, Alta.	Lloyd Cadrain	Lloyd Cadrain	1987	247
171 4/8	25 1/8	24 3/8	18 6/8	4 7/8	4 6/8	6	Elliott Co., Ky.	George Stafford	George Stafford	1987	247
171 3/8	26 7/8	26 6/8	17 7/8	4 7/8	4 6/8	6	Turner Co., Ga.	Jerry S. Cook	Jerry S. Cook	1986	253
171 3/8	23 1/8	23	18	5	5	6	Washington Co., Mo.	Jerry D. Bouse	Jerry D. Bouse	1987	253
171 3/8	23 3/8	23 7/8	18 3/8	4 5/8	4 7/8	5	Stonewall Co., Texas	Jay W. Knorr	Jay W. Knorr	1987	253

Whitetail Deer, Typical Antlers - Continued

Score	Length of Main Beam R.	L.	Inside Spread	Circumference at Smallest Place Between Burr and First Point R.	L.	Number of Points R.	L.	Locality Killed	By Whom Killed	Owner	Date Killed	Rank
171 2/8	26 7/8	25 5/8	18 2/8	5 2/8	5 1/8	5	5	Beltrami Co., Minn.	Mickey Ewing	Mickey Ewing	1981	256
171 2/8	21 1/8	21	16 5/8	5	5 1/8	8	7	Yuma Co., Colo.	John O. Cletcher	John O. Cletcher	1985	256
171 2/8	24	23 7/8	19 4/8	5 4/8	5 5/8	5	5	Pembina Co., N.D.	Lee Einarson	Lee Einarson	1985	256
171 2/8	23 1/8	24	16 6/8	4 2/8	4 2/8	5	5	Lake Co., Mont.	Del A. Niemeyer	Del A. Niemeyer	1986	256
171 2/8	26 3/8	24 4/8	18 6/8	4 4/8	4 4/8	5	5	Oyen, Alta.	Daryl Peers	Daryl Peers	1986	256
171 2/8	27 3/8	27	21	4 5/8	4 5/8	5	5	Randolph Co., Ill.	Steven R. Thompson	Steven R. Thompson	1986	262
171 1/8	24 7/8	25 3/8	21 1/8	4 4/8	4 4/8	5	5	Sanders Co., Mont.	William Brox	Henry C. Bennett	1948	262
171 1/8	27	27	20 3/8	4 7/8	4 6/8	6	6	Polk Co., Wisc.	Harold Dau	Harold Dau	1966	262
171 1/8	23 6/8	24 7/8	15 7/8	4	4	7	7	Jackson Co., S.D.	Dale Jarman	Dale Jarman	1966	262
171 1/8	25 5/8	26 7/8	16 1/8	4 3/8	4 4/8	7	7	Menominee Co., Wisc.	Vyron N. Dixon, Sr.	Vyron N. Dixon, Sr.	1968	262
171 1/8	26 6/8	26 6/8	19 3/8	4 2/8	4 4/8	5	5	Unknown	Unknown	Keith Spencer	pr	262
171 1/8	27 7/8	27 3/8	21 5/8	5 5/8	5 4/8	5	4	Fulton Co., N.Y.	Kenneth R. Mowrey, Jr.	Kenneth R. Mowrey, Jr.	1985	262
171 1/8	23 7/8	23 5/8	17 1/8	5 2/8	5 1/8	8	8	Otter Tail Co., Minn.	Thomas E. Berger	Thomas E. Berger	1985	262
171 1/8	28 5/8	26 6/8	20 1/8	5	5	6	6	Livingston Co., Mo.	Richard L. West	Richard L. West	1986	262
171 1/8	25 2/8	25	17 6/8	4 7/8	5 1/8	8	8	Hubbard Co., Minn.	Merald D. Folkestad	Merald D. Folkestad	1987	262
171	26	24 4/8	19 6/8	5 2/8	5	5	5	Wabasha Co., Minn.	John W. Mussell	John W. Mussell	1966	271
171	26 1/8	26 1/8	17 2/8	5 5/8	6	6	5	Pierce Co., Wisc.	Picked Up	Roger Hines	1975	271
171	28 5/8	30 4/8	22 5/8	5 2/8	5 1/8	7	5	Penobscot Co., Maine	Samuel C. Hands	Samuel C. Hands	1985	271
171	23 3/8	24 3/8	19	4 3/8	4 4/8	7	8	Independence Co., Ark.	Frankie Felton	Frankie Felton	1986	271
171	24 3/8	23 7/8	20 6/8	5	4 4/8	6	6	Pike Co., Ind.	Phil Lemond	Phil Lemond	1986	271
171	25 7/8	26 2/8	20 2/8	5 1/8	5	7	7	Comanche Co., Kan.	Robert Jensen	Robert Jensen	1986	271
170 7/8	29	29	20 1/8	4 4/8	4 2/8	8	8	Marinette Co., Wisc.	Charles Rader	Thomas W. Goddard	1909	277
170 7/8	24 5/8	24 3/8	16 6/8	5 3/8	5 4/8	5	7	Delta Co., Mich.	Jim Lawson	Mary Jo Wellman	1939	277
170 7/8	27 1/8	26 3/8	20 3/8	4 1/8	4	5	5	Bayfield Co., Wisc.	John Kavajecz	John Kavajecz	1964	277
170 7/8	30 4/8	30 2/8	24 7/8	4 2/8	4 2/8	5	5	Alexander Co., Ill.	Kenneth L. Karhliker	Kenneth L. Karhliker	1986	277
170 7/8	27 4/8	28 4/8	21 4/8	4 7/8	5	7	8	Leavenworth Co., Kan.	Jacob W. Dragieff	Jacob W. Dragieff	1987	277
170 6/8	24 7/8	23 7/8	19 2/8	5 6/8	6 5/8	6	5	Aitkin Co., Minn.	Unknown	George W. Flaim	pr	282
170 6/8	25 5/8	26 7/8	19 1/8	4 6/8	4 4/8	6	5	Bayfield Co., Wisc.	Sigurd A. Sandstrom	Sigurd A. Sandstrom	1955	282
170 6/8	24 6/8	25 6/8	19	4 7/8	4 5/8	5	5	Guysborough Co., N.S.	Roy B. Simpson	Roy B. Simpson	1968	282
170 6/8	28	28	21 3/8	5 3/8	5 3/8	5	5	Penobscot Co., Maine	William Stratton	William Stratton	1974	282
170 5/8	27	26 7/8	19 5/8	5	5 1/8	7	5	St. Louis Co., Minn.	Unknown	George W. Flaim	pr	286
170 5/8	25 2/8	27 1/8	16	4 7/8	4 4/8	7	6	Big Stone Co., Minn.	Jeffrey A. Thielke	Jeffrey A. Thielke	1985	286
170 5/8	22 3/8	24 6/8	16 6/8	4 6/8	4 4/8	7	7	Webster Parish, La.	Henry G. Gregory	Henry G. Gregory	1985	286

Score					L	R	Locality	Hunter	Owner	Date	Rank
170 5/8	24 1/8	24 5/8	16 7/8	4 6/8	4 5/8	5	5 Kings Co., N.B.	Allen MacDonald	Allen MacDonald	1986	286
170 4/8	23 5/8	26 1/8	22 1/8	5 6/8	5 2/8	5	5 Kittson Co., Minn.	Unknown	George W. Flaim	1950	290 pr
170 4/8	26 6/8	26 3/8	17 3/8	4	4	5	6 Houston Co., Minn.	Kenneth Carlson	Kenneth Carlson	1983	290
170 4/8	26 2/8	25 4/8	18 4/8	5 3/8	5 3/8	9	7 Keya Paha Co., Neb.	Michael L. LeZotte	Michael L. LeZotte	1986	290
170 4/8	26 3/8	26	22 4/8	5 3/8	5 3/8	5	5 Oak Mts., N.B.	Michael E. Mertz	Michael E. Mertz	1986	290
170 4/8	23 4/8	24 1/8	18 4/8	4 4/8	4 5/8	5	6 Logan Co., N.D.	Jon M. Midthun	Jon M. Midthun	1986	290
170 3/8	25 3/8	25 3/8	18 2/8	5	5 1/8	7	5 Lesser Slave Lake, Alta.	Adriaan Mik	Adriaan Mik	1985	296
170 3/8	25 7/8	25 5/8	18 7/8	5 1/8	5 2/8	6	6 Beltrami Co., Minn.	Floyd Hlucny	Floyd Hlucny	1985	296
170 3/8	26 1/8	26 4/8	19 5/8	4 4/8	4 2/8	6	7 Haskell Co., Okla.	Loyd Long	Loyd Long	1985	296
170 3/8	23 7/8	23 7/8	19 4/8	4 4/8	4 4/8	5	5 Emmet Co., Mich.	Jeffrey A. Phillips	Jeffrey A. Phillips	1986	296
170 3/8	25 2/8	24	16 4/8	4 4/8	4 4/8	8	9 Cow Lake, Alta.	Edward J. Burns	Edward J. Burns	1987	296
170 3/8	25 5/8	25 3/8	15 7/8	4 3/8	4 4/8	5	5 Baraga Co., Mich.	Howard D. Musick	Howard D. Musick	1945	301
170 2/8	24 6/8	23 6/8	18	4 3/8	4 3/8	6	8 Polk Co., Wisc.	Robert G. Overman	Robert G. Overman	1950	301
170 2/8	24 3/8	25 2/8	16 6/8	5 2/8	5 3/8	6	5 Carlton Co., Minn.	Unknown	George W. Flaim	1972	301
170 2/8	27 4/8	25 5/8	18	4	4	5	5 Houston Co., Minn.	Randy J. Benson	Randy J. Benson	1979	301
170 2/8	25 2/8	24 6/8	19 4/8	5 1/8	5 2/8	6	6 Bradley Co., Ark.	Brad J. Davis	Brad J. Davis	1981	301
170 2/8	25	25	16 4/8	4 3/8	4 4/8	5	5 Olmsted Co., Minn.	James L. Miller	James L. Miller	1987	301
170 2/8	24 4/8	26 1/8	18	5	5	5	5 Pembina River, Man.	Bernie Thiessen	Bernie Thiessen	1987	301
170 1/8	26 1/8	26	21 1/8	4 6/8	4 6/8	6	6 Lake Co., Minn.	Ed Gregorich	George W. Flaim	1969	307
170 1/8	27 1/8	27 1/8	20 3/8	5 6/8	5 6/8	5	5 Essex Co., Ver.	Kevin A. Brockney	Kevin A. Brockney	1986	307
170 1/8	26 4/8	27	20 3/8	4 4/8	4 7/8	5	7 Vermilion River, Alta.	Vince V. Philipps	Vince V. Philipps	1986	307
170 1/8	22 3/8	22 3/8	15 5/8	5 3/8	5 2/8	5	5 Greene Co., Iowa	Charles Gunn	Charles Gunn	1986	307
170 1/8	26 7/8	26	20 7/8	4 6/8	4 6/8	5	6 Harford Co., Md.	Edward C. Garrison	Edward C. Garrison	1987	307
170 1/8	27 3/8	26	22 1/8	4 7/8	4 7/8	8	5 Coahuila, Mexico	Rodolfo F. Barrera	Rodolfo F. Barrera	1988	307
170	28 4/8	27 3/8	21 1/8	4 7/8	5	5	7 Latah Co., Idaho	Lewis L. Turcott	Lewis L. Turcott	1974	313
170	29 1/8	27 5/8	23 7/8	5 4/8	5 4/8	6	6 Penobscot Co., Maine	Picked Up	Tad D. Proudlove	1985	313
170	27 5/8	27 5/8	21 5/8	5 5/8	5 2/8	5	5 Jefferson Co., Wisc.	Robert L. Becker	Robert L. Becker	1987	313
169 7/8	25 1/8	25 4/8	19 4/8	4 2/8	4 3/8	8	8 Crawford Co., Ga.	Alan R. Williams	Alan R. Williams	1975	316
169 3/8	26 3/8	25 5/8	20 6/8	4 2/8	4 2/8	6	6 Coleman Co., Texas	Steven C. Fails	Steven C. Fails	1986	317
168 6/8	25 2/8	25 2/8	20 4/8	4 6/8	4 4/8	7	7 Charles Mix Co., S.D.	Gary D. DeJong	Gary D. DeJong	1985	318
168 4/8	28 4/8	28 2/8	22 3/8	5	4 7/8	5	5 Oneida Co., Wisc.	Raymond Lorbetske, Jr.	Raymond Lorbetske, Jr.	1985	319
168 3/8	26 6/8	26	17 6/8	4	4	7	5 Houston Co., Minn.	Robert J. Nontelle	Robert J. Nontelle	1984	320
168 2/8	24 3/8	23 6/8	17 6/8	4 6/8	5	6	6 Marengo Co., Ala.	William L. Wright	William L. Wright	1979	321
168	25 2/8	25	18 4/8	5 6/8	5 6/8	6	5 Warren Co., Miss.	Frank Dorroh	Martha Dorroh	1952	322
167 7/8	28 3/8	27 4/8	16 5/8	5	4 6/8	6	9 Chautauqua Co., Kan.	Dan E. Hadley	Dan E. Hadley	1984	323
167 6/8	26	26	19 7/8	5 6/8	5 5/8	5	6 Concordia Parish, La.	Gary L. Kinsland	Gary L. Kinsland	1978	324
167 5/8	27	26 5/8	20	5 3/8	5 3/8	5	6 Sangamon Co., Ill.	Bruce D. Horne	Bruce D. Horne	1986	325
167 4/8	26	26 2/8	18 3/8	5 7/8	5 4/8	6	6 Platte Co., Mont.	Michael J. Brown	Michael J. Brown	1987	325
167	23 6/8	24 4/8	15 5/8	4 4/8	4 2/8	6	7 Acadia Valley, Alta.	Joseph H. Niwa	Joseph H. Niwa	1979	327
167	24 7/8	24 2/8	18 4/8	4 6/8	4 4/8	12	5 Sarpy Co., Neb.	William B. Dillon III	William B. Dillon III	1970	328
166 7/8	24	23 6/8	20 7/8	5	4 7/8	5	5 McHenry Co., Ill.	David A. McGinnis	David A. McGinnis	1986	329
166 5/8	25 7/8	27 3/8	17 3/8	5	5	6	6 Somerset Co., Maine	Walter B. Rusak	Walter B. Rusak	1986	330

Whitetail Deer, Typical Antlers - Continued

Score	Length of Main Beam		Inside Spread	Circumference at Smallest Place Between Burr and First Point		Number of Points		Locality Killed	By Whom Killed	Owner	Date Killed	Rank
	R.	L.		R.	L.	R.	L.					
166 5/8	26 2/8	26 1/8	19 7/8	5	4 7/8	4	4	Adair Co., Mo.	Daniel C. Elfrink	Daniel C. Elfrink	1987	330
166 5/8	25 1/8	24 3/8	18 6/8	4 7/8	4 6/8	6	6	Elliott Co., Ky.	George Stafford	George Stafford	1987	330
166 3/8	27 1/8	26 2/8	18 4/8	5	4 6/8	8	8	Lowndes Co., Ga.	Jack D. Knight	Jack D. Knight	1981	333
166 3/8	26 1/8	24 6/8	20 1/8	5 4/8	5 1/8	6	5	Portage Bay, Man.	Dan Hill	Dan Hill	1986	333
166 2/8	27 7/8	28	21	4 7/8	4 5/8	5	7	Fillmore Co., Minn.	Richard C. Bjortomt	Richard C. Bjortomt	1972	335
166 1/8	24 7/8	25 4/8	20 5/8	4	4 1/8	6	5	Lenawee Co., Mich.	Gerb Portenga	Gerb Portenga	1969	336
165 7/8	23 5/8	24 1/8	18 1/8	4 7/8	4 6/8	5	5	Rusk Co., Wisc.	Fredric P. Burak	Fredric P. Burak	1976	337
165 7/8	25	26 1/8	21 1/8	4 4/8	4 5/8	5	5	Wilkin Co., Minn.	Brian Arnhalt	Brian Arnhalt	1982	337
165 6/8	25 3/8	26 1/8	19 4/8	4 4/8	4 3/8	6	6	Nelson Co., Va.	Larry W. Toms	Larry W. Toms	1986	339
165 5/8	27	26 1/8	19 7/8	4 4/8	4 3/8	5	5	Cass Co., Minn.	Ronald A. Peterson	Ronald A. Peterson	1987	340
165 3/8	26 3/8	26 3/8	17 7/8	5 5/8	5	8	8	Forest Co., Wisc.	Virgil J. Gueths	Virgil J. Gueths	1987	341
165 3/8	25 2/8	26 4/8	20 5/8	4 4/8	4 3/8	6	6	Preble Co., Ohio	Robert L. Mason	Robert L. Mason	1988	341
165 2/8	24 6/8	25 4/8	20	5	4 7/8	5	5	Lyon Co., Ky.	James Chambers	James Chambers	1974	343
165 2/8	25 1/8	25 5/8	28 6/8	5 1/8	5	5	5	Accomack Co., Va.	John W. Smith, Jr.	John W. Smith, Jr.	1986	343
164 7/8	26	25 7/8	22 4/8	5 3/8	5 2/8	5	6	Piscataquis Co., Maine	Robert J. Fortunati	Robert J. Fortunati	1987	345
164 6/8	26 1/8	26 1/8	18 6/8	4 2/8	4 3/8	6	6	Concordia Parish, La.	Joseph L. Landry	Joseph L. Landry	1969	346
164 6/8	27 3/8	26 3/8	22	4 7/8	4 6/8	5	5	Fillmore Co., Minn.	Russell Ristau	Russell Ristau	1973	346
164 5/8	25 1/8	25 4/8	20 7/8	5	5	5	5	Jefferson Co., Wisc.	Jerald Behling	Jerald Behling	1975	348
164 5/8	24 2/8	24 2/8	17 7/8	4 3/8	4 5/8	5	5	Jones Co., Ga.	Larry Scarborough	Larry Scarborough	1981	348
164 5/8	27 4/8	27 6/8	22 7/8	5	4 7/8	5	5	Waldo Co., Maine	Timothy A. Reilly	Timothy A. Reilly	1985	348
164	27 1/8	26 3/8	22 5/8	5	5	7	8	Roseau Co., Minn.	George Rinde	George Rinde	1972	351
164	23	23	18 4/8	4 4/8	4 4/8	6	6	Latah Co., Idaho	Gary Esser	Michael J. Stewart	1979	351
164	25 5/8	25 1/8	16 4/8	4 7/8	5 1/8	5	5	Bienville Parish, La.	Charles R. Carr	Charles R. Carr	1983	351
163 7/8	26 2/8	25 4/8	18 2/8	5 5/8	5 5/8	5	5	Goodhue Co., Minn.	James N. Reuter	James N. Reuter	1986	354
163 7/8	26 5/8	26 6/8	23	4 2/8	4 7/8	6	6	Aitkin Co., Minn.	John P. Falteisek	David A. Vomela	1945	355
163 7/8	25 5/8	25 4/8	25 4/8	4 2/8	4 2/8	5	5	Brandon, Man.	Conrad McClure	Conrad McClure	1982	355
163 7/8	25 5/8	25 4/8	19 4/8	4 3/8	4 3/8	6	6	Wilcox Co., Ga.	Danny Luke	Danny Luke	1987	355
163 1/8	27 3/8	27 1/8	21 7/8	5 4/8	5 2/8	7	7	Piscataquis Co., Maine	Irwin A. Ridley	Irwin A. Ridley	1985	358
163 1/8	24 7/8	24 5/8	14 7/8	4 2/8	4 2/8	6	6	Wilcox Co., Ga.	Roy Bloodworth	Roy Bloodworth	1986	358
162 7/8	26 1/8	24 7/8	18 3/8	4 2/8	5 1/8	6	6	Perry Co., Ala.	Rodney A. Pilot	Rodney A. Pilot	1987	360
162 6/8	24 3/8	24 1/8	21 6/8	4 4/8	4 4/8	5	5	Calhoun Co., Ark.	Vernon Evans	Vernon Evans	1962	361
162 6/8	24 4/8	24 3/8	22 4/8	4 5/8	4 4/8	6	6	Latah Co., Idaho	Larry Stohs	Larry Stohs	1986	361
162 5/8	30 7/8	26 5/8	23	5 2/8	5 2/8	6	5	Oxford Co., Maine	Chester A. Coolidge	Chester A. Coolidge	1930	363

Score						Location	Hunter	Owner	Year	Rank
162 5/8	28 7/8	25 7/8	23 7/8	5 1/8	4	Kennebec Co., Maine	James E. Greene	James E. Greene	1985	363
162 5/8	25 4/8	25 3/8	16 5/8	4 3/8	7	Hubbard Co., Minn.	Nick J. Thill, Jr.	Nick J. Thill, Jr.	1987	363
162 3/8	25 1/8	24 7/8	20 5/8	5 2/8	8	Buffalo Co., Wisc.	Michael J. Lurndal	Michael J. Lurndal	1987	366
162	26 1/8	26 3/8	18 2/8	4	5	Daniels Co., Mont.	John F. Hrimnak, Jr.	John F. Hrimnak, Jr.	1985	367
162	24 7/8	24 2/8	21	4 5/8	7	Winona Co., Minn.	Jeffrey B. Bunke	Jeffrey B. Bunke	1986	367
162	23 6/8	22 7/8	19 6/8	4 3/8	5	Steward Co., Ga.	Judge W. Lanneau	Judge W. Lanneau	1986	367
161 6/8	25 6/8	25	19 2/8	4 6/8	6	Greene Co., Ala.	William H. Fincher	William H. Fincher	1982	370
161 6/8	25 2/8	25 3/8	17 7/8	4 2/8	5	Loudoun Co., Va.	Gary C. Smith	Gary C. Smith	1986	370
161 5/8	22 4/8	22 7/8	20 5/8	5	7	Penobscot Co., Maine	John D. Hughes	John D. Hughes	1987	372
161 4/8	24 5/8	24 7/8	17 4/8	5 2/8	5	Barbour Co., Ala.	Craig Thompson	Craig Thompson	1979	373
161 3/8	25	23 3/8	20 5/8	4 7/8	5	Pipestone, Man.	Homer Perreault	Homer Perreault	1985	374
161 2/8	24 7/8	25	19	3 7/8	6	Faulk Co., S.D.	Robert Knadle	Robert Knadle	1986	375
161 1/8	25 7/8	27 1/8	17 3/8	4 7/8	5	Franklin Co., Maine	James L. Harding	James L. Harding	1983	376
161 1/8	27 4/8	27 1/8	20 3/8	4 6/8	6	Carroll, Man.	Wayne Rudneski	Wayne Rudneski	1984	376
161 1/8	24 3/8	25 4/8	21 5/8	4 3/8	5	Lake Co., Ill.	John W. Schnider, Jr.	John W. Schnider, Jr.	1987	376
161	27 1/8	26	22 2/8	5 4/8	4	Lucas Co., Iowa	Gary Goering	Gary Goering	1987	379
161	25 3/8	26 1/8	15	4 7/8	7	Koochiching Co., Minn.	Bradlee Karan	Bradlee Karan	1987	379
161	24 1/8	23 4/8	18 5/8	5	5	Butler Co., Ohio	Fred S. Spurlin	Fred S. Spurlin	1987	379
160 5/8	21 2/8	21 4/8	14 7/8	4	3 7/8	Kenedy Co., Texas	Cal Adger	Cal Adger	1987	382
160 5/8	27 5/8	26 4/8	15 5/8	4 3/8	4 6/8	Montgomery Co., Mo.	Dennis E. Alvarez	Dennis E. Alvarez	1987	382
160 5/8	25	24 6/8	20 5/8	5	5	Redwood Co., Minn.	John C. Dunn	John C. Dunn	1987	382
160 5/8	22 1/8	22 5/8	19	4 6/8	6	Rush Co., Ind.	James D. Moffett	James D. Moffett	1987	382
160 4/8	25 5/8	25 5/8	20 4/8	5	6	Washington Co., Minn.	James A. Thurmes	James A. Thurmes	1973	386
160 4/8	28 4/8	28 4/8	21 4/8	4 6/8	6	Penobscot Co., Maine	David P. Chinn	David P. Chinn	1986	386
160 2/8	24 1/8	23 4/8	18	4 4/8	6	Early Co., Ga.	Todd Bell	Todd Bell	1985	388
160 2/8	23 5/8	23 6/8	20 6/8	4 1/8	5	Coahuila, Mexico	Jesus H. Garza Villarreal	Jesus H. Garza Villarreal	1988	388
160 1/8	24 1/8	24 7/8	18 5/8	4 6/8	7	Sidney, Man.	Tony Kranjc	Tony Kranjc	1987	390
160	25 4/8	23 7/8	18 5/8	4 1/8	5	Le Flore Co., Okla.	Carl E. Hale	Carl E. Hale	1978	391
160	26 1/8	25 4/8	20 2/8	4 5/8	5	Virden, Man.	Dan Olafson	Dan Olafson	1986	391
201 1/8 *	28 5/8	29 7/8	19 7/8	5 3/8	7 8	Clark Co., Ohio	William D. Kontras	William D. Kontras	1986	
200 2/8 *	29 3/8	28 7/8	22	5 3/8	5 4/8 6	Harrison Co., Iowa	Harold H. Dickman, Sr.	Harold H. Dickman, Sr.	1964	
198 7/8 *	30 2/8	29 3/8	18 7/8	5 1/8	5 1/8 7	Aitkin Co., Minn.	Glen Johnstone	Unknown	1965	pr
197 5/8 *	29 2/8	30	20 2/8	5 5/8	5 7/8 6	Wright Co., Minn.	Curtis F. Van Lith	Curtis F. Van Lith	1986	

* Final Score subject to revision by additional verifying measurements.

Whitetail Deer, Non-Typical Antlers

Odocoileus virginianus virginianus and certain related subspecies

Minimum Score 185 — World's Record 333-7/8

Score	Length of Main Beam R.	L.	Inside Spread	Circumference at Smallest Place Between Burr and First Point R.	L.	Number of Points R.	L.	Locality Killed	By Whom Killed	Owner	Date Killed	Rank
267 4/8	26 6/8	27 6/8	29 6/8	5 1/8	5 1/8	16	23	Idaho	Unknown	Jack Brittingham	pr 1923	1
264 5/8	27	26 5/8	20 6/8	6 1/8	6 1/8	19	15	West Afton River, N.S.	Alexander C. MacDonald	Sup Museum	1960	2
259 5/8	26 7/8	26 5/8	20 3/8	6	5 4/8	14	13	Chariton Co., Mo.	Duane R. Linscott	Duane R. Linscott	1985	3
256 1/8	28 7/8	26 5/8	23 3/8	7 5/8	7 2/8	18	13	Marshall Co., S.D.	Francis Fink	J.D. Andrews	1948	4
250 6/8	25 3/8	25 4/8	15 1/8	5	5 3/8	19	13	South Dakota	Howard Eaton	Jack Brittingham	1870	5
250 6/8	27 2/8	25 2/8	23 4/8	5 4/8	5 2/8	12	12	Richland Co., Ohio	David D. Dull	David D. Dull	1987	5
249 7/8	26 5/8	25 5/8	23 2/8	4 1/8	4 2/8	12	22	Kings Co., N.B.	Ronald Martin	Ronald Martin	1946	7
249 2/8	29 6/8	28 7/8	21 3/8	5 2/8	5 2/8	10	14	Fillmore Co., Minn.	Dallas R. Henn	Dallas R. Henn	1961	8
245 2/8	25 5/8	25 2/8	24 2/8	5 2/8	5 3/8	12	12	Itasca Co., Minn.	Peter Rutkowski	John L. Stein	1942	9
245 3/8	24	24 4/8	17 4/8	5 7/8	6 1/8	14	14	Itasca Co., Minn.	Mike Hammer	Mike Hammer	1956	10
241 5/8	25 2/8	27 3/8	26 7/8	5 3/8	5 5/8	15	20	Idaho Co., Idaho	Johnnie W. Nickel	Jerry Rodriguez	1960	11
241 5/8	25	24 4/8	21 3/8	6 2/8	6 2/8	19	18	Manitoba	Unknown	Jack Brittingham	1984	11
239	28	29 2/8	22 5/8	5 7/8	5 5/8	13	13	Lyon Co., Kan.	Don E. Roberts	Don E. Roberts	1987	13
238 3/8	28	26 5/8	22 7/8	6	5 5/8	12	10	Assiniboine River, Man.	Doug Hawkins	Doug Hawkins	1981	14
238 1/8	26 4/8	27 5/8	27	5 3/8	5 5/8	12	17	Madison Co., Ill.	Joe Bardill	Patrick Bardill	1985	15
236 5/8	27 2/8	26 1/8	20 1/8	7 1/8	6 6/8	11	9	Pike Co., Ill.	Floyd Pursley	Floyd Pursley	1987	16
233 5/8	28 2/8	27	21 1/8	5	5 4/8	13	13	Custer Co., Neb.	Lonnie E. Poland	Lonnie E. Poland	1986	17
233 1/8	29 2/8	29	20 4/8	5 5/8	5 5/8	14	9	Condon Lakes, N.S.	Don McDonnell	Don McDonnell	1987	18
232 5/8	28 3/8	29	23 6/8	5 2/8	5 3/8	9	9	Wabasha Co., Minn.	Robert R. Friese	Robert R. Friese	1948	19
232 5/8	23 2/8	23 7/8	18 2/8	7	6 5/8	15	11	Winfield, Alta.	Harry O. Hueppelshevser	Harry O. Hueppelshevser	1986	19
232 4/8	29 2/8	28 6/8	18 7/8	5	5	14	18	Buckingham Co., Va.	James R. Shumaker	James R. Shumaker	1986	21
232 2/8	23 3/8	22 7/8	17 2/8	5 5/8	5 4/8	12	18	Thorsby, Alta.	Robert G. MacRae	Robert G. MacRae	1987	22
231 4/8	29 4/8	29 4/8	18 6/8	6 2/8	6 1/8	14	13	Perry Co., Ill.	Unknown	John L. Stein	1968	23
231 1/8	28 3/8	28 4/8	24 2/8	5 1/8	5 3/8	12	9	Winona Co., Minn.	Robert E. Bains	Robert E. Bains	1973	24
230 1/8	27 2/8	27 1/8	18	5 3/8	5 3/8	15	11	Pope Co., Minn.	Harvey J. Erickson	Harvey J. Erickson	1974	25
229 2/8	26 1/8	26	21 5/8	5 1/8	5 1/8	12	13	Decatur Co., Iowa	Edgar Shields	Edgar Shields	1986	26
229 4/8	28 5/8	28 4/8	20 4/8	5 5/8	5 3/8	9	8	Dewey Co., Okla.	Ricky C. Watt	Ricky C. Watt	1987	27
229 3/8	27 7/8	26 6/8	23 6/8	5 3/8	5 4/8	8	8	Wapello Co., Iowa	Robert D. Harding	Robert D. Harding	1985	28
228 4/8	24	26	20 6/8	5 7/8	5 2/8	10	13	Montgomery Co., Md.	John W. Poole	John W. Poole	1987	29

Score							Locality	Hunter	Owner	Date	Rank
226 7/8	30 2/8	28 1/8	20 7/8	5	5	13	Dimmitt Co., Texas	Lake Webb	Warren N. Webb	1937	30
226 4/8	26	26 6/8	24 7/8	4 6/8	5	11	La Salle Co., Texas	A.L. Lipscomb, Sr.	James O. Lipscomb	1909	31
226 3/8	27 7/8	26 2/8	22 7/8	5 4/8	5 4/8	8	Clark Co., Ind.	Robert L. Bromm, Sr.	Robert L. Bromm, Sr.	1985	32
225 1/8	30 6/8	31	23 4/8	5 5/8	5 5/8	9	Nodaway Co., Mo.	Ken Barcus	John L. Stein	1982	33
224 4/8	25 3/8	27 6/8	20 4/8	5 5/8	5 4/8	9	Cass Co., Minn.	Roy K. Blowers, Sr.	Roy K. Blowers, Sr.	1947	34
223 3/8	28 4/8	27 5/8	24 1/8	5 4/8	5 5/8	10	Maine	Frank Maxwell	David G. Cordray	1900	35
222 4/8	25 1/8	24 1/8	18 5/8	6 1/8	6 2/8	13	Davis Co., Iowa	James L. Fine	James L. Fine	1987	36
222 1/8	26 2/8	25 7/8	17 3/8	4 5/8	4 4/8	14	Hancock Co., Iowa	Jerry M. Monson	William H. Lilienthal	1977	37
222 1/8	27 1/8	28 1/8	22 3/8	4 6/8	4 4/8	12	Cass Co., Minn.	Marvel R. Utke	Marvel R. Utke	1977	37
221 7/8	26 6/8	26	21 3/8	5	5 1/8	11	Tama Co., Iowa	Charles Upah	Richard Upah	1959	39
221 3/8	26 3/8	25	19 7/8	6 3/8	7 1/8	13	Louisa Co., Va.	Picked Up	James T. Rapalee	1981	40
221	29 1/8	29	23 4/8	4 5/8	4 4/8	9	Pike Co., Ill.	Frank C. Skelton	Frank C. Skelton	1987	41
220 7/8	23 1/8	23 7/8	14 4/8	6 7/8	6 6/8	17	Pembina Co., N.D.	Gary F. Bourbanis	Gary F. Bourbanis	1985	42
220 7/8	27 6/8	27 7/8	22 6/8	5 5/8	5 1/8	9	Sauk Co., Wisc.	Bryan J. McGann	Bryan J. McGann	1986	42
220 5/8	29 1/8	28 2/8	20 6/8	5 4/8	5 5/8	13	Kittson Co., Minn.	Todd J. Porter	George W. Flaim	1986	44
220	28 1/8	26 5/8	18 5/8	4 7/8	4 5/8	15	Wayne Co., Iowa	Dallas Patterson	Dallas Patterson	1975	45
219 5/8	28 1/8	27 5/8	20 5/8	4 4/8	4 4/8	12	Webster Co., Iowa	David Propst	David Propst	1987	46
219 2/8	23 6/8	23 3/8	23 3/8	4 4/8	4 4/8	12	Mud Creek, Alta.	Hank Stainbrook	Caroline Supplies Ltd.	1971	47
218 7/8	22 2/8	23 3/8	15 4/8	7 3/8	7 1/8	16	Bay of Fundy, N.S.	Basil S. Lewis	Basil S. Lewis	1983	48
218 6/8	23 5/8	24 7/8	19 7/8	6 2/8	5 4/8	14	Morrison Co., Minn.	Wilfred LeBlanc	George W. Flaim	1938	49
218 5/8	25	25 4/8	14 4/8	5 1/8	5 1/8	13	Itasca Co., Minn.	John W. Pierson, Sr.	John W. Pierson, Sr.	1945	50
218 5/8	25 3/8	24 6/8	18	6 5/8	6 3/8	17	Otter Tail Co., Minn.	Gerald P. Lucas	Gerald P. Lucas	1985	50
218 4/8	23 1/8	22 7/8	20 5/8	7 1/8	7 1/8	9	Logan Co., Ky.	Robert L. Schrader, Jr.	Robert L. Schrader, Jr.	1987	52
218 3/8	23	26	16 7/8	5 4/8	5 4/8	15	Itasca Co., Minn.	Unknown	George W. Flaim	1983	53
217 7/8	29 5/8	29 5/8	25 3/8	5 2/8	5 2/8	8	Mills Co., Iowa	Rick W. Elliott	Rick W. Elliott	1976	54
217 2/8	24 5/8	24 2/8	17 4/8	5 3/8	6 3/8	5	Dallas Co., Ala.	Robert Tate	Robert Tate	1988	54
216 6/8	24 1/8	24 1/8	17	7	7 1/8	11	Lake of the Woods Co., Minn.	Andy Streiff	Andy Streiff	1974	56
216 4/8	25 2/8	27 3/8	23	5	5	12	Surry Co., Va.	Stanley M. Hall	Stanley M. Hall	1986	57
215 5/8	28 2/8	29 2/8	18 6/8	4 6/8	4 5/8	9	Wise Co., Va.	Edison Holcomb	Edison Holcomb	1987	58
215 2/8	29 1/8	29 4/8	23 4/8	6 1/8	6 2/8	11	Wayne Co., Ind.	Clyde L. Day	Clyde L. Day	1986	59
214 7/8	24 4/8	26 6/8	17	5 2/8	5 1/8	15	St. John Co., N.B.	T. Emery	New Brunswick Museum	1968	60
214 4/8	25 2/8	27 6/8	22 2/8	7 2/8	6	13	Hitchcock Co., Neb.	David W. Oates	David W. Oates	1985	61
214	23 2/8	24 5/8	17 3/8	5 4/8	5 5/8	13	Atchison Co., Mo.	Warren E. Davis	Warren E. Davis	1983	62
213 5/8	18 5/8	18 1/8	17 5/8	4 1/8	4	14	Washington Co., Texas	Thomas N. Holle	Thomas N. Holle	1987	63
213 4/8	25 4/8	26	22	6 2/8	6 1/8	11	Pike Co., Ill.	Donald L. Roseberry	Michael R. Roseberry	1984	64
213	27	27 7/8	15 5/8	4 5/8	4 4/8	14	St. Louis Co., Minn.	Walfred Olson	Erling H. Olson	1935	65
212 7/8	25 5/8	29 1/8	20 6/8	5 3/8	5 2/8	10	Otter Tail Co., Minn.	Harold L. Collins	Harold L. Collins	1985	66
212 2/8	28 2/8	28 6/8	24 4/8	5 3/8	5	9	Madison Co., Iowa	Larry D. Bain	Larry D. Bain	1984	67
212 2/8	26 5/8	25 6/8	20	4 7/8	5	9	Stevens Co., Minn.	Ronald J. Mohr	Ronald J. Mohr	1963	68
212 2/8	23 3/8	23	20 3/8	5	5 5/8	8	Minnedosa, Man.	Albert Pfau	Albert Pfau	1966	68
212 1/8	28 1/8	28	18 1/8	5 4/8	5 4/8	9	Winona Co., Minn.	Donald J. Mehren	Donald J. Mehren	1985	68

Whitetail Deer, Non-Typical Antlers - Continued

Score	Length of Main Beam R.	L.	Inside Spread	Circumference at Smallest Place Between Burr and First Point R.	L.	Number of Points R.	L.	Locality Killed	By Whom Killed	Owner	Date Killed	Rank
211 6/8	26 3/8	26	24 7/8	5 3/8	5 2/8	11	6	Marion Co., Iowa	Paul J. Pearson	Paul J. Pearson	1964	71
211 5/8	26 3/8	23 3/8	20 2/8	5 1/8	6 1/8	9	12	Adams Co., Ohio	William J. DeCamp	William J. DeCamp	1987	72
210 1/8	23 4/8	24	18 5/8	5 1/8	5	9	7	Harris, Sask.	Kenneth M. Lepp	Kenneth M. Lepp	1985	73
210	28 3/8	26	26 5/8	4 7/8	4 7/8	7	13	Calvert Co., Md.	Robert E. Barnett	Robert E. Barnett	1984	74
209 1/8	26 3/8	26 3/8	19 1/8	5 4/8	5 4/8	10	8	Keweenaw Co., Mich.	Nathan E. Ruonavaara	Nathan E. Ruonavaara	1946	75
209	26 4/8	25 6/8	20 5/8	4 7/8	5	11	10	Hughes Co., Okla.	Lane Grimes	Lane Grimes	1987	76
208 7/8	29 4/8	27 5/8	18 4/8	4 6/8	4 4/8	14	10	Washington Co., Maine	Robert E. Cooke	Robert E. Cooke	1972	77
208 5/8	27 1/8	26 5/8	22 4/8	4 4/8	5	9	12	St. Francis Co., Ark.	George W. Hobson	George W. Hobson	1987	78
208 4/8	30 5/8	29 2/8	17 3/8	5 1/8	5 1/8	7	9	Day Co., S.D.	Unknown	J.D. Andrews	pr 1950	79
208 3/8	25 2/8	28 2/8	18 7/8	5 1/8	4 7/8	13	13	St. Louis Co., Minn.	Unknown	George W. Flaim	pr 1940	80
208 3/8	27 5/8	28 1/8	21 7/8	5	4 7/8	11	7	Decatur Co., Ga.	James L. Darley	James L. Darley	1964	80
208 1/8	30	31 2/8	23 6/8	5 3/8	5 4/8	8	8	Hancock Co., Maine	Hollis Staples	Doug Scott	1922	82
207 7/8	24 4/8	23 5/8	20 3/8	5 1/8	5 3/8	10	12	Fond du Lac Co., Wisc.	Henry Theisen	Henry Theisen	1956	83
207 7/8	23 3/8	23 5/8	23 4/8	5 5/8	5 4/8	11	10	Assiniboine River, Man.	Terry L. Simcox	Terry L. Simcox	1987	83
207 5/8	30 1/8	29 3/8	20 1/8	5 1/8	5 2/8	10	9	Webster Co., Iowa	Larry E. Iles	Larry E. Iles	1979	85
207 4/8	28 7/8	27 6/8	19 5/8	4 7/8	4 4/8	10	9	Barron Co., Wisc.	Charles Slayton	Gordon Lee	pr 1920	86
207 3/8	30 1/8	29 5/8	21	5 5/8	5 4/8	8	7	Andrew Co., Mo.	Frank Kelso	Delores C. Kelso	1981	87
207	26 4/8	27 1/8	25	5 4/8	5 2/8	10	8	Stark Co., Ohio	Tad E. Crawford	Tad E. Crawford	1987	88
206 5/8	25 5/8	25 5/8	21 5/8	5 5/8	5 5/8	10	9	Pine Lake, Alta.	Richard D. Doan	Leila R. Doan	1979	89
206 5/8	25 1/8	27 1/8	22 4/8	5 1/8	4 4/8	11	9	Maple Creek, Sask.	Theodore Reierson	Theodore Reierson	1984	89
206 3/8	20 4/8	21 3/8	14 5/8	5 3/8	5	11	9	Whitemouth River, Man.	Tom Clarke, Jr.	Tom Clarke, Jr.	1987	89
206 3/8	28 3/8	27 7/8	20 1/8	5 2/8	5 1/8	9	6	Stearns Co., Minn.	Steven J. Sperl	Steven J. Sperl	1987	89
206 3/8	24 6/8	20 6/8	18 3/8	5	5	12	12	Menard Co., Ill.	Frank C. Pickett	Frank C. Pickett	1985	93
206 2/8	24 4/8	24 1/8	19	6	5 3/8	10	13	Lincoln Co., Mont.	Larry H. Beller	Larry H. Beller	1985	94
206 1/8	26 3/8	26 2/8	17 4/8	6	6	12	12	Osage Co., Okla.	Wesley D. Coldren	Wesley D. Coldren	1986	95
205 7/8	24 7/8	23 5/8	20	6	6	14	11	Battle River, Alta.	Bryan Champagne	Bryan Champagne	1987	96
205 5/8	23 5/8	23	19 6/8	5 5/8	5 5/8	12	16	St. Louis Co., Minn.	Picked Up	George W. Flaim	1985	97
205 5/8	26	25 4/8	20 2/8	5 4/8	5 4/8	8	8	Washington Co., Minn.	Lonnie J. Diethert	Lonnie J. Diethert	1987	97
205 1/8	26 6/8	25 4/8	20 3/8	5 5/8	5 5/8	11	9	Rat River, Man.	Ken L. Maxymowich	Ken L. Maxymowich	1987	99
205 1/8	24 5/8	24 4/8	20 2/8	5	4 7/8	13	11	Antler, Sask.	Regina K. V. Ross	Regina K. V. Ross	1987	99
204 7/8	25 2/8	25 2/8	21 2/8	5	5 3/8	13	12	Roseau Co., Minn.	Andy Streiff	Andy Streiff	1967	101
204 7/8	25 4/8	26 3/8	21 2/8	5 5/8	5 4/8	13	9	Bentley, Alta.	Stanley A. Anderson	Stanley A. Anderson	1968	101
204 5/8	23 1/8	24 2/8	19 7/8	5 5/8	5 5/8	8	12	Saskatchewan River, Man.	Dieter Boehner	Dieter Boehner	1973	103

Score								Locality	Hunter	Owner	Date Killed	Rank
204 6/8	28 4/8	27 5/8	26 1/8	4 4/8	4 5/8	8	7	Stearns Co., Minn.	Curt Fettig	Curt Fettig	1975	103
204 3/8	24 5/8	25 5/8	19 3/8	5 3/8	5 3/8	10	8	Nanton, Alta.	Barry Flipping	Barry Flipping	1986	105
204 2/8	26 2/8	26 4/8	22 2/8	4 6/8	4 6/8	5	8	Boone Co., Mo.	Calvin E. Brown	Calvin E. Brown	1985	106
204 2/8	27 3/8	27 7/8	21 4/8	6 2/8	6	9	8	Yuma Co., Colo.	Jeff L. Mekelburg	Jeff L. Mekelburg	1986	106
204 1/8	28	27 3/8	24 5/8	5 2/8	5 2/8	8	11	Pope Co., Minn.	LeRoy D. Hausmann	LeRoy D. Hausmann	1967	108
204 1/8	26 5/8	26 2/8	22	5	4 7/8	7	9	Dubuque Co., Iowa	Joe J. Rettenmeier	Joe J. Rettenmeier	1987	108
203 7/8	22	22 5/8	19	5 1/8	5 1/8	10	10	Pope Co., Minn.	Irwin E. Strangeland	Irwin E. Strangeland	1980	110
203 5/8	28	27 3/8	17 5/8	6 2/8	5 1/8	14	9	Page Co., Iowa	Picked Up	Rodney S. Brooks	1981	111
203 3/8	25 1/8	25 1/8	17 5/8	5 2/8	5	9	11	Warren Co., Iowa	Ted Miller	Ted Miller	1986	111
203 3/8	23	24 1/8	20 2/8	6 4/8	6 2/8	10	13	Dunn Co., Wisc.	Terry J. Evenson	Terry J. Evenson	1987	113
203 2/8	27 1/8	26 6/8	16 6/8	5 5/8	5 5/8	10	10	Marinette Co., Wisc.	Marvin E. Holmgren	Marvin E. Holmgren	1986	114
203 3/8	24 5/8	25 1/8	18 7/8	5 3/8	5 1/8	12	11	McHenry Co., N.D.	Garry L. Heizelman	Garry L. Heizelman	1987	114
203 3/8	25 2/8	25 5/8	16 1/8	5 1/8	5 1/8	13	9	Scott Co., Iowa	Marv A. Schmidt, Jr.	Marv A. Schmidt, Jr.	1987	114
203 2/8	24	23 5/8	19 5/8	6 1/8	7 5/8	7	14	Ross Co., Ohio	Scott Zurmehly	Scott Zurmehly	1987	114
203 1/8	23 7/8	24 3/8	17 5/8	4 4/8	4 4/8	13	9	Kootenai Co., Idaho	William M. Ziegler	William M. Ziegler	1965	118
202 5/8	22 5/8	23 4/8	18 4/8	4 6/8	4 4/8	16	9	Carroll Co., Miss.	George Galey	Terry Galey	1960	119
202 3/8	26 1/8	26 6/8	26 1/8	6 4/8	6 2/8	13	13	Washington Co., Ill.	Richard C. Keller	Richard C. Keller	1986	120
202 3/8	23 1/8	26 3/8	20 1/8	6	5 3/8	11	6	Lake Co., Minn.	Lawrence J. Simonich	Lawrence J. Simonich	1987	120
202 2/8	27 5/8	26 2/8	19 3/8	5 5/8	5 5/8	12	7	Louisa Co., Iowa	Robert L. McFadden	Robert L. McFadden	1986	122
201 7/8	26 1/8	25 2/8	17 4/8	5 2/8	5 1/8	8	7	Louisa Co., Iowa	Jason Gapinski	Jason Gapinski	1987	123
201 1/8	23 3/8	23 4/8	19 5/8	4 4/8	4 4/8	10	10	Custer Co., S.D.	Unknown	Kenny Spring	1940 pr	124
201 1/8	24	24	17 5/8	6	6	17	15	Wilkinson Co., Miss.	Jimmy Ashley	Jimmy Ashley	1985	124
201 3/8	24 2/8	24 7/8	21	5	5	8	8	Brown Co., S.D.	Wallace Labisky	J.D. Andrews	1962	126
201 1/8	24 5/8	25 2/8	15 7/8	5 3/8	5 5/8	15	17	Pushmataha Co., Okla.	Maurice Jackson	Maurice Jackson	1975	127
201 2/8	30 6/8	28	17 5/8	4 7/8	4 6/8	8	8	Cumberland Co., Ky.	Ewing Groce	Ewing Groce	1968	128
201	28	27	21 3/8	4 7/8	5	11	8	Empress, Alta.	David Booker	David Booker	1979	129
200 6/8	24 4/8	24	18 2/8	5 1/8	5	10	8	Morrison Co., Minn.	Elmer J. Hollenkamp	Elmer J. Hollenkamp	1977	130
200 6/8	23 5/8	21 5/8	21 1/8	4 5/8	4 4/8	8	9	Uvalde Co., Texas	W.S. Gordon	First State Bank of Uvalde	1923	131
200 4/8	27	26 2/8	22	5 5/8	5 5/8	8	8	Clearwater Co., Minn.	Ronald O. Halvorson	Ronald O. Halvorson	1987	131
200 3/8	25	26 4/8	17 4/8	4 6/8	4 7/8	11	10	Nez Perce Co., Idaho	Tim C. Baldwin	Tim C. Baldwin	1987	133
200 1/8	27	26 4/8	21 7/8	5 5/8	5 5/8	9	9	Itasca Co., Minn.	Clyde Sucher	James Davidson	1926	134
200	26 3/8	25 3/8	21 1/8	5 4/8	5 7/8	12	12	Todd Co., Minn.	James J. Carr	James J. Carr	1978	135
199 7/8	24 1/8	23 3/8	19	4 7/8	4 4/8	6	10	Queens Lake, N.B.	Wendell Lacey	George Lacey	1915	136
199 7/8	29 2/8	28 3/8	18 2/8	5 3/8	5 1/8	10	9	Cheyenne Co., Kan.	William H. Lilienthal	Picked Up	1986	136
199 6/8	26 5/8	27 2/8	18 5/8	5 2/8	4 2/8	7	7	Harris Co., Ga.	Kenneth H. Brown	Kenneth H. Brown	1974	138
199 4/8	23 5/8	22 5/8	15 5/8	6 3/8	6	13	12	Duck Mt., Man.	Jim Whitt	Picked Up	1986 pr	138
199 5/8	27 7/8	27 3/8	23 2/8	5 2/8	5 5/8	8	9	Labette Co., Kan.	John L. Bryant	John L. Bryant	1987	140
199 1/8	21 7/8	24 6/8	20	4 6/8	4 7/8	12	10	Clinton Co., N.Y.	Unknown	William F. Mathieson	1971 pr	141
199	25 1/8	26	19 2/8	5 5/8	5 5/8	9	6	Grattan Creek, Alta.	Torleif A. Larson	Torleif A. Larson	1968	142
199	24 2/8	24 7/8	19 4/8	5	5 1/8	13	8	Penobscot Co., Maine	Picked Up	Todd Africano	1971	142
198 7/8	24	25 2/8	22 3/8	5 5/8	5 5/8	9	7	Morse River, Alta.	Leo M. Schmaus	Leo M. Schmaus	1985	144

Whitetail Deer, Non-Typical Antlers - Continued

Score	Length of Main Beam R.	L.	Inside Spread	Circumference at Smallest Place Between Burr and First Point R.	L.	Number of Points R.	L.	Locality Killed	By Whom Killed	Owner	Date Killed	Rank
198 6/8	28 6/8	28 4/8	21 4/8	4 3/8	4 3/8	8	9	Crow Wing Co., Minn.	Unknown	George W. Flaim	1965	145
198 6/8	25 1/8	27 1/8	15 4/8	5	5	10	8	Buffalo Co., Wisc.	Rod Buck	Rod Buck	1984	145
198 6/8	26 2/8	25 2/8	17 3/8	6 1/8	5 3/8	10	8	James River, Alta.	Hans Van Vlaanderen	Hans Van Vlaanderen	1986	145
198 4/8	27 2/8	27	22 2/8	5 3/8	5 1/8	6	9	Kanabec Co., Minn.	Unknown	George W. Flaim	1927	148
198 3/8	27	25 5/8	21 6/8	5	4 7/8	10	9	Clark's Brook, N.B.	Bernard V. Sharp	Bernard V. Sharp	1985	149
198 2/8	27	26 2/8	21	4 7/8	4 5/8	8	9	Cass Co., Minn.	Timothy L. Anderson	Timothy L. Anderson	1987	150
198 2/8	24 6/8	24 6/8	16 3/8	5 5/8	5 7/8	10	15	Rock Co., Neb.	Picked Up	Dan L. Sandall	1987	150
198	25 7/8	23 4/8	17 5/8	5	5	8	8	Assiniboine River, Man.	James A. Roberts	James A. Roberts	1980	152
198	28 5/8	27 3/8	21 7/8	5 2/8	5 4/8	8	10	Christian Co., Ill.	Jack B. Hartwig	Jack B. Hartwig	1987	152
197 5/8	28	25 2/8	21 5/8	5 5/8	5 5/8	9	11	Adams Co., Ill.	Daniel J. Schlosser	Daniel J. Schlosser	1987	154
197 3/8	24 5/8	22 5/8	18 5/8	6 2/8	5 5/8	9	12	Buffalo Co., Wisc.	Walter Mengelt	Timothy W. Trones	1957	155
197 3/8	26 5/8	27 1/8	16 5/8	5 1/8	5 1/8	8	14	Kittson Co., Minn.	Unknown	George W. Flaim	pr 1988	155
197 3/8	26 3/8	26 7/8	17 3/8	5 1/8	5 2/8	10	12	Douglas Co., Wisc.	Unknown	Wayne G. Nevar	pr 1988	155
197 1/8	27 5/8	27 2/8	21 4/8	4 5/8	4 7/8	9	9	Becker Co., Minn.	Unknown	George W. Flaim	1924	158
197	27 5/8	27 5/8	22 7/8	5 1/8	5 3/8	8	8	Houghton Co., Mich.	Edward Heinonen	Edward Heinonen	1970	159
197	23 5/8	23 4/8	20 4/8	6 2/8	6	9	14	Barber Co., Kan.	Lewis M. Mull	Lewis M. Mull	1986	159
197	24 3/8	24 1/8	18	5	5	7	8	Souris River, Man.	Picked Up	T. Allan Good	1986	159
196 7/8	26 5/8	26 7/8	19 2/8	5 1/8	5 3/8	7	8	Pepin Co., Wisc.	Jerry R. Breitung	Jerry R. Breitung	1985	162
196 6/8	26 7/8	27 7/8	21 4/8	5 2/8	5 3/8	13	10	Lake Co., Minn.	Unknown	George W. Flaim	pr 1984	163
196 5/8	26 5/8	25 7/8	23 6/8	5 5/8	5 7/8	10	10	Buffalo Co., Wisc.	Bill Black, Sr.	Tom Black	1956	164
196 4/8	24 1/8	23 3/8	18 2/8	5 1/8	5 2/8	9	8	Trigg Co., Ky.	Jeffery Taylor	Jeffery Taylor	1983	165
196 3/8	24 7/8	25 2/8	15 3/8	4 6/8	4 7/8	10	12	Lee Co., Iowa	Douglas W. Hopp	Douglas W. Hopp	1984	166
196 3/8	26 3/8	25 7/8	18 3/8	4 4/8	4 5/8	11	8	Price Co., Wisc.	John R. Lemke	John R. Lemke	1986	166
196 3/8	23 7/8	25 5/8	17 3/8	6 3/8	6 1/8	10	8	Otter Tail Co., Minn.	William J. Klyve	William J. Klyve	1987	168
196 3/8	25 5/8	23 2/8	22 3/8	5 5/8	6	11	9	Webster Co., Ky.	Timothy J. Shelton	Timothy J. Shelton	1987	168
196 1/8	25 5/8	24 4/8	16 7/8	5	4 7/8	11	10	Wyoming Co., N.Y.	Eric D. Baney	Eric D. Baney	1985	170
196	25 2/8	25 4/8	19 6/8	4 6/8	4 4/8	13	9	Missoula Co., Mont.	James D. Pladson	James D. Pladson	1987	171
195 7/8	25 1/8	25 1/8	18 6/8	4 7/8	5 5/8	7	9	Allamakee Co., Iowa	John L. Cahalan	John L. Cahalan	1953	172
195 7/8	24 5/8	23 7/8	18 2/8	6	5 5/8	7	7	Monroe Co., Miss.	Kenneth A. Dye	Kenneth A. Dye	1986	172
195 5/8	23 2/8	22 2/8	19 2/8	4 4/8	4 4/8	12	10	Florence Co., Wisc.	Joseph R. Szczepanski, Jr.	Terry J. Baranczyk	pr 1945	174
195 5/8	25 5/8	24 2/8	19 1/8	5 4/8	5 5/8	8	16	Carlton Co., Minn.	Nick Rukovina	George W. Flaim	1960	174
195 1/8	28	27 7/8	24 3/8	4 4/8	4 4/8	9	11	La Salle Co., Texas	Unknown	John L. Stein	1952	176

406

Score								Locality	Hunter	Owner	Date Killed	Rank
195 4/8	25 3/8	24 3/8	21 6/8	4 3/8	4 4/8	7	10	Worth Co., Ga.	Shane Calhoun	Shane Calhoun	1985	176
195 4/8	28 6/8	27 7/8	18 7/8	4 7/8	5 3/8	10	15	Hamilton Co., Ill.	Douglas P. Collins	Douglas P. Collins	1985	176
195 4/8	21 6/8	23 7/8	22 1/8	4 7/8	5 1/8	9	13	St. Louis Co., Minn.	LeRoy N. Nelson	LeRoy N. Nelson	1987	176
195 3/8	23 7/8	24 2/8	18 3/8	4 3/8	4 3/8	11	11	Pope Co., Minn.	Kenneth M. Besonen	Kenneth M. Besonen	1975	180
195 2/8	28 3/8	28 3/8	21	6	5 4/8	9	8	Somerset Co., Maine	David A. McAllister	David A. McAllister	1985	181
195 1/8	20 3/8	20	15 3/8	4 3/8	5 4/8	6	17	Carlton Co., Minn.	Unknown	George W. Flaim	1910	182
195 1/8	27 7/8	27 6/8	20 7/8	5 5/8	5 2/8	7	7	Buffalo Co., Wisc.	Maynard Trones	Maynard Trones	1958	182
195 1/8	26 7/8	27 4/8	19 4/8	5	5	8	10	Holmes Co., Ohio	Randy J. Strohminger	Randy J. Strohminger	1987	182
195	27 2/8	25 5/8	21 5/8	5 3/8	5 4/8	9	7	Windham Co., Conn.	Harold Tanner	Warren W. Rogers	1970	185
194 1/8	24 4/8	24 2/8	19 5/8	4 7/8	5	8	7	Portage Co., Wisc.	Wendell A. Krogwold	Wendell A. Krogwold	1950	186
193 5/8	27	26 6/8	16 2/8	5 4/8	5 5/8	8	9	Henry Co., Ga.	Jason J. Patrick	Jason J. Patrick	1986	187
192 4/8	23 5/8	25 3/8	19 5/8	6 1/8	6 3/8	12	10	Jones Co., Ga.	Fred H. Maxwell	Fred H. Maxwell	1962	188
191 7/8	25 7/8	25 4/8	16 2/8	4 6/8	4 6/8	11	9	Florence Co., Wisc.	Lloyd Conger	Lloyd Conger	1959	189
191 2/8	22 4/8	22 4/8	14 6/8	7 4/8	7 6/8	8	14	Delaware Co., Ind.	Robert D. McFarland	Robert D. McFarland	1986	190
190 3/8	24 3/8	24 3/8	20 2/8	4 7/8	4 5/8	6	8	Lyon Co., Kan.	Wayne F. Redeker	Wayne F. Redeker	1987	191
190 2/8	26	27 1/8	16 3/8	7	7	10	6	Concordia Parish, La.	John T. Lincecum	John T. Lincecum	1986	192
189 7/8	22 7/8	23 7/8	17 7/8	5 4/8	5 5/8	12	10	Saskatchewan	Unknown	D. Ross Sayrs	1986 pr	193
189 3/8	28 3/8	27 1/8	17 4/8	5 2/8	5	9	11	Itasca Co., Minn.	James S. Bischoff	James S. Bischoff	1973	194
188 7/8	26 7/8	26 1/8	21 1/8	5 5/8	5 5/8	6	7	Stevens Co., Minn.	Edward Wilson	Edward Wilson	1965	195
188 2/8	25	24 1/8	18 2/8	4 7/8	4 7/8	7	8	Cass Co., Mich.	Robert H. Watson	Robert H. Watson	1983	196
188 2/8	25 7/8	27 4/8	23	5 5/8	5 5/8	8	8	Becker Co., Minn.	Kenneth R. Ringstad	Kenneth R. Ringstad	1987	196
188 1/8	24 1/8	23 3/8	16 6/8	5 5/8	5 7/8	6	11	Hamiota, Man.	Cecil Epp	Cecil Epp	1985	198
187 6/8	24 4/8	26	18 1/8	4 7/8	4 7/8	8	9	Custer Co., Okla.	Ricky E. Johnson	Ricky E. Johnson	1987	199
187 3/8	23 2/8	23 1/8	17 1/8	4 5/8	4 3/8	11	10	Vernon Co., Wisc.	Darrell A. Bendel	Darrell A. Bendel	1986	200
187	27 7/8	26 1/8	21	5 5/8	5 5/8	6	8	Greene Co., Ala.	William H. Fincher	William H. Fincher	1976	201
187	27 7/8	28 1/8	23 6/8	6 3/8	6 2/8	6	9	Putnam Co., Mo.	Josh Rennells	Josh Rennells	1987	201
186 1/8	23 7/8	23 7/8	18 3/8	4 6/8	5	17	12	Jackson Co., Fla.	Henry Brinson	T.L. Brinson	1959	203
186 1/8	26 7/8	24 7/8	20 6/8	5 4/8	5 5/8	8	8	Eaton Co., Mich.	John A. Serniak, Jr.	John A. Serniak, Jr.	1985	203
186	21 5/8	23 6/8	16 3/8	5 4/8	5 4/8	13	12	Marinette Co., Wisc.	James Sanborn	Michael Brissette	1945 pr	205
185 7/8	25 5/8	24 2/8	22 3/8	4 2/8	4 1/8	10	8	Charles Co., Md.	Robert Sparks	Robert Sparks	1980	206
185 1/8	27 5/8	27 7/8	21 2/8	5 2/8	5 2/8	8	7	Fillmore Co., Minn.	Calvin Anderson	Calvin Anderson	1986	206
185 3/8	20 6/8	22 4/8	21 6/8	4 2/8	4 2/8	10	9	Maverick Co., Texas	John N. Garner	Richard H. Bennett	1954	208
269 3/8 *	24 2/8	24 5/8	19 6/8	6 2/8	6 3/8	16	13	Shawnee Co., Kan.	Joseph H. Waters	Joseph H. Waters	1987	
244 1/8 *	25 5/8	26 6/8	22 7/8	6	5 7/8	13	10	Meeting Lake, Sask.	Greg Brataschuk	Greg Brataschuk	1987	
243 *	23	21 7/8	18 3/8	5 3/8	5 1/8	18	16	Mahoning Co., Ohio	Ronald K. Osborne	Ronald K. Osborne	1986	

* Final Score subject to revision by additional verifying measurements.

Coues' Whitetail Deer, Typical Antlers
Odocoileus virginianus couesi

Minimum Score 100   World's Record 143

Score	Length of Main Beam R.	Length of Main Beam L.	Inside Spread	Circumference at Smallest Place Between Burr and First Point R.	Circumference at Smallest Place Between Burr and First Point L.	Number of Points R.	Number of Points L.	Locality Killed	By Whom Killed	Owner	Date Killed	Rank
126 5/8	21 6/8	19 6/8	14	4	4 4/8	6	5	Cochise Co., Ariz.	Mike Kasun	Mike Kasun, Jr.	1959	1
126 1/8	19 5/8	19 7/8	16 2/8	3 7/8	4	6	6	Pima Co., Ariz.	Robert G. McDonald	Robert G. McDonald	1986	2
123 6/8	18 2/8	17 7/8	14 2/8	4 4/8	4 4/8	6	6	Cochise Co., Ariz.	Larry Vance, Jr.	Larry Vance, Jr.	1985	3
119 1/8	19 6/8	19	14 3/8	3 5/8	3 3/8	4	4	Cochise Co., Ariz.	James A. Leiendecker	James A. Leiendecker	1986	4
116 6/8	17 7/8	18 3/8	14	4 7/8	5	4	4	Coconino Co., Ariz.	Clay McDonald	Clay McDonald	1985	5
116 2/8	16 2/8	16 5/8	14	4	4	4	4	Graham Co., Ariz.	Dale J. Holladay	Dale J. Holladay	1984	6
116	19	18 7/8	14	3 5/8	3 5/8	5	5	Santa Cruz Co., Ariz.	Jeffrey C. Lichtenwalter	Jeffrey C. Lichtenwalter	1982	7
115 7/8	19 3/8	18 6/8	14 1/8	4	4	4	5	Yavapai Co., Ariz.	Robert W. Gaylor	Robert W. Gaylor	1987	8
115 4/8	18	17 1/8	15 1/8	4 2/8	4 2/8	4	4	Gila Co., Ariz.	Doug J. Althoff	Doug J. Althoff	1985	9
115 3/8	19 1/8	19 5/8	19 5/8	3 7/8	3 6/8	4	4	Pima Co., Ariz.	William H. Taylor	William H. Taylor	1986	10
115	18 5/8	18	17 7/8	4	4 2/8	5	5	Pinal Co., Ariz.	George Martin	George Martin	1983	11
114 6/8	17 1/8	17 4/8	16 2/8	4 2/8	4	4	4	Cochise Co., Ariz.	Rudy Alvarez	Rudy Alvarez	1960	12
114 4/8	19 6/8	18 3/8	14 4/8	3 6/8	3 6/8	4	4	Pima Co., Ariz.	James M. Machac	James M. Machac	1985	13
113 4/8	17 1/8	17 1/8	12 2/8	4 1/8	4	5	5	Santa Cruz Co., Ariz.	Robert A. Smith	Robert A. Smith	1985	14
113 2/8	18	17	14 2/8	4 1/8	4 1/8	5	5	Santa Cruz Co., Ariz.	Hector Guglielmo	Hector Guglielmo	1984	15
113 1/8	15 5/8	16 2/8	13 7/8	4 4/8	4 5/8	5	5	Grant Co., N.M.	Andrew A. Musacchio	Andrew A. Musacchio	1985	16
112 5/8	17 6/8	17 4/8	15 3/8	5	4 7/8	4	4	Greenlee Co., Ariz.	John W. Barber	John W. Barber	1985	17
112 1/8	17 3/8	18 6/8	14 4/8	3 7/8	3 7/8	7	6	Cochise Co., Ariz.	Edwin L. Hawkins	Edwin L. Hawkins	1977	18
112 1/8	18 2/8	17 1/8	10 7/8	3 7/8	3 7/8	4	5	Pima Co., Ariz.	David J. Vancas	David J. Vancas	1985	18
111 4/8	17 6/8	17 7/8	15 4/8	4 6/8	4 4/8	5	4	Coconino Co., Ariz.	Dennis L. Campbell	Dennis L. Campbell	1987	20
111 3/8	18 5/8	18 3/8	12 5/8	3 6/8	3 6/8	5	5	Pima Co., Ariz.	Picked Up	Ruel Holt	pr 1974	21
110 1/8	16 1/8	16 3/8	11 5/8	4 4/8	4 3/8	4	4	Hidalgo Co., N.M.	Unknown	Neuman Sanford	1981	22
107 4/8	16 4/8	16 5/8	10 6/8	3 6/8	3 6/8	5	5	Santa Cruz Co., Ariz.	William W. Sharp	William W. Sharp	1986	23
106 4/8	17 4/8	17 4/8	16	3 4/8	3 6/8	4	4	Maricopa Co., Ariz.	Jerry E. Mason	Jerry E. Mason	1983	24
106	17 3/8	17 1/8	13 2/8	3 5/8	3 5/8	4	5	Sonora, Mexico	David V. Collis	David V. Collis	1985	25
105 3/8	16 4/8	15 5/8	13 7/8	3 4/8	3 5/8	4	4	Pima Co., Ariz.	James J. McBride	James J. McBride	1973	26
104 7/8	16 2/8	16	13	3 6/8	3 7/8	5	6	Pima Co., Ariz.	William W. Sharp	William W. Sharp	1985	27
102 2/8	18 6/8	19 1/8	15 2/8	3 6/8	3 5/8	4	4	Cochise Co., Ariz.	Kenneth D. Rupkalvis	Kenneth D. Rupkalvis	1985	28
101	17 7/8	17 7/8	13 2/8	3 6/8	3 7/8	4	5	Pima Co., Ariz.	Keith L. Miller	Keith L. Miller	1984	29

Coues' Whitetail Deer, Non-Typical Antlers

Odocoileus virginianus couesi

Minimum Score 105 — New World's Record 158-4/8

Score	Length of Main Beam R.	L.	Inside Spread	Circumference at Smallest Place Between Burr and First Point R.	L.	Number of Points R.	L.	Locality Killed	By Whom Killed	Owner	Date Killed	Rank
158 4/8	17 1/8	16 7/8	12 6/8	3 7/8	4 1/8	11	11	Santa Cruz Co., Ariz.	Picked Up by Walter H. Pollock	Loaned to B&C National Collection	1988	1
134 2/8	17 7/8	16 5/8	13 1/8	4 5/8	4 5/8	6	7	Sonora, Mexico	Unknown	Ronald D. Hyatt	pr 1986	2
134 2/8	20 6/8	20 4/8	13 5/8	4 2/8	4 3/8	7	8	Yavapai Co., Ariz.	William B. Bullock	William B. Bullock	1986	2
132	20	19 7/8	14 5/8	3 6/8	3 6/8	5	5	Sonora, Mexico	Picked Up	Harry P. Samarin	pr 1988	4
131 3/8	19 1/8	18 1/8	14 7/8	3 7/8	4 1/8	6	6	Cochise Co., Ariz.	Erik M. Thorsrud	Erik M. Thorsrud	1986	5
122 4/8	15 7/8	16 5/8	12	4 1/8	4	9	7	Cochise Co., Ariz.	Randy D. Goll	Randy D. Goll	1984	6
120 1/8	16 5/8	17 5/8	15	3 5/8	3 5/8	7	8	Pima Co., Ariz.	Eugene S. Robinson	Eugene S. Robinson	1985	7
117	17 1/8	17	13 1/8	4 1/8	4 1/8	9	7	Pima Co., Ariz.	William W. Sharp	William W. Sharp	1976	8
114 6/8	17	17 1/8	15 1/8	4 2/8	4	6	5	Graham Co., Ariz.	Robin W. Bechtel	Robin W. Bechtel	1985	9
111 6/8	16 5/8	16 2/8	17 5/8	3 5/8	3 7/8	6	5	Cochise Co., Ariz.	Frank E. Safford	Frank E. Safford	1982	10
105 6/8	16 1/8	16 1/8	13 3/8	4 4/8	4 3/8	5	5	Graham Co., Ariz.	Robin W. Bechtel	Robin W. Bechtel	1985	11

Canada Moose

Minimum Score 185   *Alces alces americana* and *Alces alces andersoni*   World's Record 242

Three categories of moose are recognized for the records keeping, with boundaries based on geographic lines. Canada moose includes trophies from Canada (except for the Yukon and Northwest Territories), Minnesota, Maine, and North Dakota.

Score	Greatest Spread	Length of Palm R.	Length of Palm L.	Width of Palm R.	Width of Palm L.	Circumference of Beam at Smallest Place R.	Circumference of Beam at Smallest Place L.	Number of Normal Points R.	Number of Normal Points L.	Locality Killed	By Whom Killed	Owner	Date Killed	Rank
227 4/8	58 4/8	44	43 4/8	17 3/8	17 5/8	7 6/8	7 5/8	19	16	Cook Co., Minn.	Donald F. Blake	Donald F. Blake	1985	1
218	58 4/8	43 2/8	43 3/8	17	16 4/8	7	7 1/8	13	15	Wellman Lake, Man.	Clifford S. Henderson	Bernie P. Nemetchek	1964	2
215 3/8	53 1/8	43 7/8	43 4/8	18	14	7 6/8	7 5/8	16	20	Meekwap Lake, Alta.	Russell S. Watts, Sr.	Russell G. Watts, Jr.	1960	3
214 6/8	56 2/8	45 5/8	42 3/8	17 4/8	19 4/8	7 3/8	7 4/8	14	12	Kennicott Lake, B.C.	Robert G. Burkhouse	Robert G. Burkhouse	1988	4
209 4/8	57 7/8	40 3/8	44 2/8	16 1/8	15	7 5/8	7 5/8	13	13	Hasler Creek, B.C.	Mike Nussbaumer	Mike Nussbaumer	1984	5
208	62	40 7/8	40 5/8	13 4/8	11 6/8	7 6/8	7 5/8	15	13	Hotchkiss River, Alta.	Andy G. Petkus	Andy G. Petkus	1985	6
206 2/8	61 2/8	44 2/8	40 4/8	13 4/8	14 1/8	8 4/8	8 7/8	10	13	Piscataquis Co., Maine	Vernon Knott	Vernon Knott	1987	7
206 2/8	66 4/8	38 7/8	41 6/8	13 5/8	13 6/8	8 5/8	8 2/8	12	9	Manning, Alta.	Nick Denecky	Nick Denecky	1988	7
205 7/8	64 3/8	41 2/8	38 5/8	12 2/8	14 1/8	6 4/8	6 5/8	13	16	Cook Co., Minn.	H. Chapman, C. Chapman, M. Chapman, & J. Anderson	H. Chapman, C. Chapman, M. Chapman, & J. Anderson	1987	9
205 5/8	65 1/8	38 2/8	39 7/8	13 4/8	13 4/8	7 4/8	7 4/8	11	13	Bottineau Co., N.D.	Lloyd E. Burgard	Lloyd E. Burgard	1985	10
205 3/8	60 7/8	43 4/8	42 2/8	13 4/8	15 4/8	7	7 4/8	9	11	Cassiar Mts., B.C.	George R. Weeks	George R. Weeks	1985	11
204 3/8	56 5/8	43	41	15 2/8	14 4/8	7 3/8	7 4/8	11	11	Prophet River, B.C.	Daniel L. Rafferty	Daniel L. Rafferty	1986	12
203 6/8	52 5/8	43	43 4/8	13 4/8	12 1/8	8	7 5/8	13	13	Turnagain River, B.C.	Larry R. Zilinski	Larry R. Zilinski	1986	13
203 4/8	55 5/8	43 4/8	41	14 1/8	14 1/8	7	7 1/8	13	12	Dease Lake, B.C.	John W. Goodwin	John W. Goodwin	1986	14
203	59	42 2/8	44	12 5/8	12 2/8	7	7	11	11	Bloodvein River, Man.	R. Stearns, R. Sigurdson, R. Blowers, & L. Walters	R. Stearns, R. Sigurdson, R. Blowers, & L. Walters	1988	15
202 6/8	60 4/8	42	43 1/8	12	12 3/8	7 2/8	7 1/8	12	11	Chinchaga River, Alta.	Oliver Travers	Oliver Travers	1985	16
202 4/8	58	38 1/8	35 5/8	15 4/8	17 3/8	7 1/8	7 3/8	14	15	Margaree Valley, N.S.	Leo C. Horne	Leo C. Horne	1986	17
202 2/8	59 4/8	38 1/8	37 4/8	12 4/8	15 4/8	7 4/8	7 3/8	14	14	King Brook, N.B.	Glen Gilks	Glen Gilks	1972	18
201 4/8	56 6/8	41 4/8	44	12 4/8	14 1/8	6 5/8	6 6/8	12	15	Bougie Mt., B.C.	Dennis R. Mitchell	Dennis R. Mitchell	1987	19
201	53 4/8	44 4/8	42 4/8	15 4/8	14 4/8	7 5/8	8	10	9	Wallace River, B.C.	Victor R. Tessier	Victor R. Tessier	1985	20
200 7/8	61 5/8	36 7/8	40 3/8	16 6/8	14 5/8	7 5/8	7 7/8	11	13	Muskwa River, B.C.	Stan Longyear	Stan Longyear	1984	21
200 5/8	56 6/8	39	38 5/8	15	14 4/8	7	6 7/8	12	15	Turnagain River, B.C.	Kenneth M. Brown	Kenneth M. Brown	1986	22

Score								Location	Hunter	Year	Rank
200 7/8	60	40	14 2/8	12 5/8	7 4/8	7 1/8	11	Adsit Lake, B.C.	Morris R. Nadeau	1986	23
199 6/8	59	36 1/8	14 3/8	13 3/8	7 2/8	7	14	Cassiar Mts., B.C.	James D. Hoekstra	1986	24
199 3/8	57 7/8	40 1/8	12 3/8	12 3/8	7 2/8	7 3/8	11	Sand River, Alta.	Douglas R. Lowe	1977	25
199 3/8	69 3/8	33 7/8	12 3/8	14 3/8	7 6/8	7 6/8	11	Blanchard River, B.C.	James T. Walter	1987	25
199	58 6/8	36 7/8	7 6/8	7 6/8	14 1/8	13 5/8	13	Otter Lake, Man.	Horace R. Cockerill	1985	27
198 7/8	60 2/8	45 6/8	11 4/8	11 6/8	7 7/8	7	7	Copper River, B.C.	J. William Hofsink	1985	28
198 4/8	58	39 2/8	13 7/8	16	7 1/8	7 3/8	13	Spatsizi Plateau, B.C.	Gordon J. Birgbauer, Jr.	1986	29
197 5/8	57 5/8	44	14 1/8	11 6/8	7 4/8	7 4/8	9	Simeon Lake, Ont.	Craig L. Chandonnet	1986	30
197 4/8	63 2/8	39 5/8	15	15 2/8	7	7	8	Cassiar Mts., B.C.	Michael J. Jacobson	1986	31
197 4/8	49 4/8	40 3/8	13 2/8	13 5/8	7 3/8	7 3/8	13	Albany River, Ont.	Lee H. Monge	1986	31
197	58	42 2/8	12	13 1/8	7 5/8	8	9	Chinchaga River, Alta.	Glen Mulzet	1986	33
196 7/8	55 7/8	40 1/8	12 2/8	13 7/8	7 2/8	7 1/8	11	Polk Co., Minn.	William H. Vollbrecht, Jr.	1985	34
196 7/8	50 1/8	42 2/8	14 4/8	14 2/8	6 7/8	7	12	Christina Falls, B.C.	David V. Collis	1987	34
195 6/8	48 5/8	42 4/8	12	13 7/8	8 1/8	8 2/8	11	Pasquia Hills, Sask.	Ray Eros	1985	36
195 4/8	52 2/8	39	13	13 1/8	6 5/8	6 5/8	13	Spatsizi Wilderness, B.C.	J.D. O'Rear	1985	37
195 3/8	55 7/8	39	37 1/8	16	15 5/8	6 5/8	6 6/8	Metsantan Lake, B.C.	Dwight L. Boettcher	1986	38
195 1/8	55 3/8	36 7/8	36 1/8	12 4/8	13 3/8	7 2/8	7 4/8	Goodwin Lake, B.C.	Delmar W. Welch	1986	39
194 5/8	53 5/8	41 5/8	41 1/8	13 5/8	12	7 5/8	8	Drayton Valley, Alta.	Dale R. Leschert	1985	40
194 1/8	52 7/8	45 5/8	43 2/8	15	12 5/8	7 1/8	7 5/8	Kakwa River, B.C.	Jack E. Garner	1986	41
192 6/8	57 5/8	39 3/8	39 5/8	16	11 1/8	7 2/8	7	Penobscot Co., Maine	Arthur J. Travers	1985	42
191 1/8	64 7/8	37 5/8	41	9 5/8	10 3/8	7 3/8	7 4/8	Washington Co., Maine	Charles D. Hamlyn	1988	43
190 7/8	49 7/8	40 7/8	38	18 5/8	15 5/8	6 5/8	7	Taku River, B.C.	Bernard Sippin	1987	44
189 5/8	54 7/8	37 7/8	40 3/8	13 4/8	14 3/8	7 5/8	7 5/8	Klastline River, B.C.	Bert Baumbach	1986	45
187 4/8	52 4/8	38 4/8	40 1/8	12	13 4/8	7	7 3/8	Drayton Valley, Alta.	Howard McMullen	1985	46
187	54	38 2/8	34 5/8	13 5/8	13 4/8	7 5/8	7 1/8	Muskwa River, B.C.	Ralph A. Shoberg	1988	47
186 5/8	57 5/8	35 5/8	39 3/8	13 5/8	12 1/8	7	7 1/8	Pink Mt., B.C.	Charles P. Turco, Sr.	1988	48
186 4/8	60 5/8	33 5/8	36	12	16 1/8	7 1/8	7 1/8	Nakina Lake, B.C.	Larry G. Shuey	1988	49
186 3/8	53 3/8	36 4/8	37 1/8	11 1/8	13 5/8	7	6 5/8	Halfway River, B.C.	Clifford J. Verheyen	1987	50
186 2/8	59	31	31 5/8	15	15 7/8	7 5/8	7 5/8	Telescope Lake, Ont.	Frank J. Bosanic	1985	51
185 7/8	58 5/8	35 1/8	38 3/8	15 5/8	16 7/8	6 3/8	6 3/8	Simonhouse Lake, Man.	Roy W. Johnson	1970	52
220 7/8 *	58 3/8	44 3/8	45 2/8	15 4/8	19 3/8	8 3/8	8 3/8	Athabasca River, Alta.	Bob Bugera	1984	

* Final Score subject to revision by additional verifying measurements.

Alaska-Yukon Moose

Alces alces gigas

Minimum Score 210 World's Record 255

Alaska-Yukon moose includes trophies from Alaska, the Yukon Territory, and the Northwest Territories.

Score	Greatest Spread	Length of Palm R.	Length of Palm L.	Width of Palm R.	Width of Palm L.	Circumference of Beam at Smallest Place R.	Circumference of Beam at Smallest Place L.	Number of Normal Points R.	Number of Normal Points L.	Locality Killed	By Whom Killed	Owner	Date Killed	Rank
248 3/8	68 5/8	49 7/8	50 3/8	17 2/8	17 4/8	7 6/8	7 6/8	15	17	Natla River, N.W.T.	Myron A. Peterson	Myron A. Peterson	1988	1
247 5/8	73 1/8	46	46 1/8	19 6/8	21 1/8	9 6/8	9	15	15	Bering River, Alaska	Vol S. Davis, Jr.	Vol S. Davis, Jr.	1984	2
239 6/8	74 2/8	45 2/8	42 2/8	22 2/8	24 2/8	8 3/8	9 2/8	11	21	Tustumena Lake, Alaska	Richard R. Sawyer	Richard R. Sawyer	1988	3
235 5/8	69 1/8	46 3/8	47 3/8	14 6/8	15 6/8	7 1/8	7 3/8	15	15	Nowitna River, Alaska	Brian C. Ziegenfuss	Brian C. Ziegenfuss	1988	4
233 4/8	72 6/8	40 6/8	47 3/8	25 5/8	25 2/8	8	7 6/8	11	9	Kenai Pen., Alaska	Picked Up	Shawn T. Brown	1972 pr	5
232	65	47 5/8	46	17	15	9 4/8	9 6/8	15	13	King Salmon, Alaska	P.J. Grady	J. Michael Conoyer	1979	6
231 3/8	66 3/8	47 3/8	49 3/8	21 3/8	19 3/8	8 4/8	8 3/8	9	13	Kenai Pen., Alaska	Paula Rak	Paula Rak	1987	7
230	72	44 7/8	45 3/8	16 3/8	16 2/8	8	7 5/8	12	10	Maclaren River, Alaska	Ronald D. Hocking	Ronald D. Hocking	1988	8
229 6/8	61 2/8	43 1/8	45 3/8	16 3/8	25 4/8	7 3/8	7 7/8	17	20	Yanert Fort, Alaska	Marvin H. Breitkreutz	Marvin H. Breitkreutz	1988	9
228 6/8	69	49 4/8	47 3/8	14 2/8	13 2/8	7 7/8	8 1/8	13	11	Koyukuk River, Alaska	David W. Doner	David W. Doner	1988	10
228	63 2/8	47 3/8	46 3/8	15 3/8	14 4/8	7 4/8	7 2/8	16	14	Koyukuk River, Alaska	Michael J. Harlin	Michael J. Harlin	1988	11
227 5/8	63 1/8	47 1/8	43 4/8	15 4/8	17 1/8	7 2/8	7 2/8	15	22	Divide Lake, N.W.T.	Joseph L. Bell	Joseph L. Bell	1986	12
227	66 2/8	43	41 1/8	16 1/8	17	8 1/8	8 1/8	15	19	Wood River, Alaska	Wayne G. Elwood	Wayne G. Elwood	1986	13
227	67 4/8	45 2/8	45 3/8	14 5/8	17 6/8	7 3/8	8 3/8	12	14	Iliamna River, Alaska	David S. Haeg	David S. Haeg	1987	13
226 5/8	72 5/8	46 4/8	43 5/8	16	15 5/8	7 5/8	8	13	10	King Salmon River, Alaska	Daniel E. Farr	Daniel E. Farr	1986	15
226	65	44 5/8	47 3/8	13 4/8	14 1/8	8	8 1/8	15	17	Alagnak River, Alaska	John H. Webster	John H. Webster	1985	16
225 7/8	68 7/8	50 3/8	45 3/8	19 1/8	14 4/8	7 5/8	8	12	11	Melozitna River, Alaska	John E. Stenehjem	John E. Stenehjem	1985	17
225 4/8	71	44 2/8	46 6/8	15 4/8	18 3/8	7 4/8	7 7/8	10	10	Stony River, Alaska	Leland R. McFarland	Leland R. McFarland	1969	18
225 3/8	65 3/8	43 3/8	41 1/8	15	15 1/8	7 5/8	7 4/8	18	16	Tustumena Lake, Alaska	Harley E. Johnson	Harley E. Johnson	1983	19
225 1/8	73 1/8	43 3/8	44 3/8	17 4/8	15 6/8	8 2/8	8 2/8	12	11	Alagnak River, Alaska	Jack & James Hertel	Jack & James Hertel	1987	20
225 1/8	61 5/8	47 4/8	47 3/8	15 4/8	15 7/8	7	7	12	13	June Lake, N.W.T.	Bertha E. Thompson	Bertha E. Thompson	1987	20
225	61 2/8	46 2/8	46 1/8	15 3/8	15 7/8	7 4/8	7 3/8	13	17	Pelly River, Yukon	Glen H. Taylor	Glen H. Taylor	1985	22
224 7/8	67 7/8	45 5/8	41 5/8	19 3/8	19 3/8	8 5/8	8 2/8	10	13	Fifteenmile River, Yukon	Joel B. Benner	Joel B. Benner	1986	23
224 7/8	72 3/8	40	38 1/8	17 7/8	17 4/8	6 5/8	6 7/8	14	17	Yuki River, Alaska	Steven B. Spaulding	Steven B. Spaulding	1986	23
224 4/8	67	46 3/8	44 5/8	17 7/8	14 6/8	8 5/8	8 3/8	15	11	Cook's Inlet, Alaska	Dall Dew	Colorado Outdoor Jour.	1898 pr	25
224 4/8	65 6/8	44 4/8	47	17 3/8	16 3/8	8 1/8	8	13	10	Iliamna Lake, Alaska	Norbert A. Prokosch	Norbert A. Prokosch	1986	25
224 2/8	58	49 6/8	49 4/8	13 5/8	13 6/8	7 2/8	7 2/8	12	12	Wood River Mts., Alaska	F. Jay Riley	F. Jay Riley	1987	27
224 1/8	68 7/8	45 4/8	44 4/8	15 2/8	13 1/8	7 4/8	7 6/8	14	12	Bear Lake, Alaska	Earl K. Wahl, Jr.	Earl K. Wahl, Jr.	1987	28

Score								Locality	Hunter	Owner	Date Killed	Rank
223 5/8	63 3/8	47 2/8	47 2/8	16 6/8	15 1/8	8	10	12	Shotgun Hills, Alaska	Vernon Scott	Vernon Scott	1985	29
223 3/8	62 6/8	43 5/8	43 5/8	19	16 3/8	8 2/8	17	12	Dry Creek, Alaska	P. Andrew Timperlake	P. Andrew Timperlake	1988	30
221 7/8	64 5/8	46 2/8	46 3/8	17	16 6/8	7 5/8	12	8	Innoko River, Alaska	Dennis H. DiBetta	Dennis H. DiBetta	1988	31
219 6/8	69 4/8	42 6/8	41	16	16 2/8	8	10	13	Iliamna River, Alaska	Jerry D. Delker	Jerry D. Delker	1985	32
218 7/8	65 3/8	44 4/8	43 5/8	15 5/8	14 4/8	7 5/8	11	12	Innoko River, Alaska	William D. Furlong	William D. Furlong	1988	33
216 6/8	70 5/8	38 6/8	47 5/8	15 2/8	16 6/8	8 1/8	13	11	Lower Ugashik Lake, Alaska	George H. Pidgeon, Jr.	George H. Pidgeon, Jr.	1987	34
216 5/8	66 2/8	46 5/8	44 3/8	15 1/8	13 2/8	7 4/8	12	10	Mulchatna River, Alaska	Darold L. Gere	Darold L. Gere	1988	34
216	62 4/8	45 2/8	45 5/8	16 7/8	16 2/8	7 6/8	10	8	Seward Pen., Alaska	Robert L. Lindsey	Robert L. Lindsey	1986	36
215 7/8	67 3/8	47 3/8	41 5/8	12 6/8	13 5/8	8 2/8	12	13	Long Lake, Yukon	Alfred Klumph	Alfred Klumph	1967	37
215 5/8	63 2/8	47 2/8	43 4/8	15 7/8	18 6/8	7 3/8	10	10	Wind River, Alaska	Dan F. Holleman	Dan F. Holleman	1971	38
215 2/8	65 2/8	41 1/8	40 2/8	14 3/8	15	7 3/8	13	14	Innoko River, Alaska	Denis R. Douglas	Denis R. Douglas	1988	39
215	69 4/8	46 4/8	40 6/8	13	14 2/8	7 7/8	12	12	Beluga Lake, Alaska	C. Cornell Hunt	C. Cornell Hunt	1987	40
214 3/8	57 1/8	45	44 6/8	15 4/8	15 2/8	7 1/8	12	12	Totatlanika River, Alaska	V.D. & D.F. Holleman	V.D. & D.F. Holleman	1969	41
213 1/8	63 5/8	43 7/8	41 1/8	15	15 7/8	7 6/8	13	12	Chilikadrotna River, Alaska	Curtis J. Trahan	Curtis J. Trahan	1987	42
212 6/8	60 2/8	47 3/8	42 2/8	17	16	7 4/8	14	11	Copper River, Alaska	James W. Wennerlind	James W. Wennerlind	1967	43
212 2/8	62 2/8	40 6/8	39	16 3/8	14 6/8	8 1/8	17	14	Dall Mt., Yukon	Richard L. Jolly	Richard L. Jolly	1985	43
212 3/8	61 3/8	43 1/8	45	14 6/8	13 6/8	7 5/8	15	11	Iliamna Lake, Alaska	K. James Malady III	K. James Malady III	1987	45
211 7/8	72 1/8	39	38 1/8	13 6/8	15 1/8	7	11	12	Mother Goose Lake, Alaska	Don T. Simon	Don T. Simon	1985	46
211	71	41 1/8	39 2/8	14 2/8	14 2/8	7 4/8	9	9	Alaska Range, Alaska	Charles H. Rohrer	Charles H. Rohrer	1970	47
210 7/8	65 7/8	43 7/8	42 2/8	12.4	14 3/8	8 3/8	9	10	Lake Creek, Alaska	Kenneth J. Broussard	Kenneth J. Broussard	1987	48
210 1/8	60 1/8	42 6/8	43	14.4	13 5/8	7 5/8	14	11	Koyukuk River, Alaska	David L. Rogers	David L. Rogers	1987	49
238 2/8 *	73 5/8	47 2/8	45 7/8	19 2/8	20 3/8	7 3/8	12	10	Lower Ugashik Lake, Alaska	Bert A. McLay	Bert A. McLay	1986	

* Final Score subject to revision by additional verifying measurements.

413

Wyoming or Shiras Moose

Alces alces shirasi

Minimum Score 140　　　　　　　　　　　　　　　　World's Record 205-4/8

Wyoming moose includes trophies taken in Utah, Idaho, Montana, Wyoming, and Washington.

Score	Greatest Spread	Length of Palm R.	Length of Palm L.	Width of Palm R.	Width of Palm L.	Circumference of Beam at Smallest Place R.	Circumference of Beam at Smallest Place L.	Number of Normal Points R.	Number of Normal Points L.	Locality Killed	By Whom Killed	Owner	Date Killed	Rank
199	48 4/8	40 4/8	42 1/8	12 1/8	11	7 7/8	7 7/8	17	16	Park Co., Wyo.	Amos E. Hand	B. & M. Smith	1946	1
185 6/8	54	42 2/8	42	9 3/8	8 4/8	7 5/8	7 3/8	8	11	Sheridan Co., Wyo.	Richard E. Jones, Jr.	Richard E. Jones, Jr.	1987	2
179 1/8	49 7/8	36	38 4/8	11 6/8	11	6 5/8	6 5/8	12	11	Teton Co., Wyo.	Marion J. Fonville	Marion J. Fonville	1987	3
178 5/8	46 3/8	33 5/8	31 2/8	16 6/8	14 6/8	6 4/8	6 1/8	20	14	Cache Co., Utah	Barton R. Critchlow	Barton R. Critchlow	1985	4
178	51 2/8	37 2/8	37 4/8	10 2/8	9 5/8	7	7 1/8	11	11	Madison Co., Idaho	Kevin W. Nichols	Kevin W. Nichols	1987	5
176 1/8	50 5/8	31 4/8	31 1/8	13	12 3/8	6 2/8	6 2/8	14	13	Cache Co., Utah	Richard E. Green	Richard E. Green	1988	6
174 7/8	45 3/8	35 4/8	36 3/8	11 1/8	11 1/8	7 2/8	7 1/8	11	13	Teton Co., Wyo.	John W. Whalen, Jr.	John W. Whalen, Jr.	1988	7
174 6/8	50 5/8	36	36 5/8	9 5/8	10 4/8	6 3/8	6 7/8	11	11	Park Co., Mont.	Picked Up	Duane A. Ferrell	1973	8
174 2/8	46 5/8	35 6/8	34 4/8	13 2/8	13 1/8	7	7 3/8	9	12	Sheridan Co., Wyo.	Toby J. Johnson	Toby J. Johnson	1988	9
173 5/8	47 7/8	40 1/8	35 5/8	11 7/8	10 6/8	7 3/8	7 5/8	12	9	Weber Co., Utah	C. Brent Morgan	C. Brent Morgan	1985	10
173 4/8	45 2/8	37 2/8	39 4/8	11 1/8	11 2/8	6 7/8	6 1/8	9	9	Sheridan Co., Wyo.	Picked Up	D.V. Collis & R.R. Smith	1987	11
173	46	33 4/8	34	12 3/8	13	6 5/8	6 5/8	11	11	Cache Co., Utah	Michael C. Leonhardt	Michael C. Leonhardt	1987	12
170 4/8	45 3/8	32 4/8	31	13 5/8	12 5/8	5 5/8	5 3/8	13	13	Flathead Co., Mont.	Arthur M. Nelson	Arthur M. Nelson	1987	13
170	48 3/8	35 4/8	35	10 3/8	11 5/8	6 4/8	6 3/8	9	10	Bonneville Co., Idaho	Dean L. Brown	Dean L. Brown	1987	14
169 2/8	53 5/8	33 2/8	34 7/8	10 5/8	10 5/8	5 7/8	6 1/8	8	10	Lincoln Co., Mont.	Frank J. O'Connor	Frank J. O'Connor	1982	15
169 1/8	48 1/8	33 4/8	33	12	13 3/8	6 4/8	6 4/8	9	11	Bonneville Co., Idaho	Picked Up	Michael J. Zwicker	1986	16
168 6/8	51 6/8	31 5/8	37 2/8	9 7/8	10	7	7 2/8	10	13	Sheridan Co., Wyo.	James W. Owens	James W. Owens	1987	17
167 7/8	52	31 1/8	31 6/8	10 5/8	10	6 5/8	6 5/8	11	10	Summit Co., Utah	L. Irvin Barnhart	L. Irvin Barnhart	1985	18
167 1/8	46 7/8	30 5/8	31 3/8	12 1/8	12 4/8	6 3/8	6 4/8	11	12	Clearwater Co., Idaho	Richard E. Hardy	Richard E. Hardy	1987	19
167	44 2/8	35 1/8	35 2/8	12 3/8	10 5/8	6 5/8	6 5/8	12	9	Sheridan Co., Wyo.	David V. Collis	David V. Collis	1987	20
166 7/8	48 3/8	32 7/8	32 6/8	10 1/8	9	6 4/8	6 4/8	11	11	Gallatin Co., Mont.	Albert D. Williams	Albert D. Williams	1986	21
166 6/8	47 2/8	33	32 7/8	13 5/8	12 2/8	6 5/8	6 5/8	8	8	Lincoln Co., Wyo.	Nancy J. Combs	Nancy J. Combs	1986	22
166 4/8	51 2/8	30 3/8	33 3/8	13 1/8	13 3/8	6 1/8	6 3/8	11	8	Caribou Co., Idaho	Diane G. Hall	Diane G. Hall	1985	23
165 6/8	45	34 3/8	33 3/8	12 3/8	13 3/8	6	5 5/8	12	9	Weber Co., Utah	Wayne J. Yamashita	Wayne J. Yamashita	1985	24
165 1/8	45 1/8	29 3/8	31	10 3/8	11	5 5/8	5 5/8	14	14	Teton Co., Wyo.	Joseph M. Griset	Joseph M. Griset	1969	25
165 1/8	48 3/8	32	36	9 5/8	11 3/8	6 4/8	6 4/8	11	10	Lincoln Co., Wyo.	Kenneth Madsen	Kenneth Madsen	1974	25
164 7/8	47 3/8	38 1/8	31 4/8	11 3/8	11	7 3/8	7 4/8	9	10	Sheridan Co., Wyo.	John D. Frost	John D. Frost	1988	27
164 4/8	49	32 7/8	32	11 2/8	13	6 4/8	6 3/8	8	9	Morgan Co., Utah	Craig S. Engelke	Craig S. Engelke	1987	28

164 3/8	48 5/8	31	36 1/8	9 5/8	10	6 3/8	6 2/8	11	12	Uinta Co., Wyo.	Richard J. Gilmore	Richard J. Gilmore	1986	29
164 2/8	41 6/8	34 4/8	38 2/8	11 5/8	10 7/8	6 7/8	6 7/8	9	10	Morgan Co., Utah	S. Kim Bonnett	S. Kim Bonnett	1986	30
164 2/8	51 6/8	32 3/8	30	10 3/8	11 3/8	6 7/8	7	9	10	Cache Co., Utah	Karl E. Engelke	Karl E. Engelke	1987	30
163 2/8	41 6/8	40 2/8	38 1/8	9 2/8	7 1/8	6 4/8	6 4/8	9	10	Fremont Co., Idaho	Lavonne A. Crews	Lavonne A. Crews	1985	32
163	44 4/8	32	31 6/8	9 6/8	11 3/8	5 6/8	6	12	12	Morgan Co., Utah	Archie J. Nesbitt	Archie J. Nesbitt	1987	33
162 4/8	42	32 1/8	31 5/8	12 6/8	11 4/8	6 1/8	6 1/8	13	11	Lincoln Co., Wyo.	Gayle E. Hubert	Gayle E. Hubert	1987	34
161 5/8	49 3/8	29 2/8	27 6/8	10 3/8	10 1/8	6 2/8	6 2/8	12	12	Cache Co., Utah	Lloyd M. Owens	Lloyd M. Owens	1987	35
161	51 4/8	31 6/8	33 4/8	8 4/8	10 3/8	6 4/8	6 5/8	11	8	Rich Co., Utah	Picked Up	Robert G. Petersen	1984	36
160 6/8	43 4/8	32	33 7/8	11	11	6 5/8	7 3/8	10	9	Sanders Co., Mont.	Ray E. Wolff	Ray E. Wolff	1987	37
159 6/8	49	32 4/8	31 3/8	7 3/8	8 3/8	6 5/8	6 7/8	10	11	Madison Co., Idaho	Max Bosworth	Max Bosworth	1985	38
159 4/8	45 6/8	33 1/8	32 6/8	10 2/8	10 4/8	6 7/8	7 1/8	7	12	Jackson Co., Colo.	Donald I. Poeschl	Donald I. Poeschl	1987	39
158 7/8	47 1/8	31 3/8	33	9 2/8	9 2/8	6 2/8	6 3/8	9	11	Weber Co., Utah	Donald E. Franklin	Donald E. Franklin	1985	40
158 2/8	46 2/8	33 1/8	31 6/8	10 7/8	10 1/8	6 2/8	6 1/8	10	8	Cache Co., Utah	Scott W. Crosbie	Scott W. Crosbie	1987	41
157 7/8	52 3/8	32	30 3/8	8 4/8	10 6/8	5 7/8	6 1/8	8	8	Lincoln Co., Wyo.	Patrick H. Roberts	Patrick H. Roberts	1988	42
157 3/8	49 7/8	37 5/8	25 5/8	13 6/8	14	6 7/8	7	11	8	Bonneville Co., Idaho	George L. Vivian	George L. Vivian	1987	43
157	47 2/8	29 1/8	26 7/8	11 6/8	11 6/8	6 3/8	6 2/8	10	10	Beaverhead Co., Mont.	Jason W. Roylance	Jason W. Roylance	1986	44
156 3/8	48 1/8	33 1/8	30 5/8	11	10 6/8	6 6/8	7	6	8	Idaho Co., Idaho	Max D. Hunsaker	Max D. Hunsaker	1986	45
156 2/8	41 6/8	30	32	10 4/8	9 7/8	6 3/8	6 4/8	11	11	Teton Co., Wyo.	James A. Kent	James A. Kent	1988	46
156 1/8	40 1/8	33 2/8	32 5/8	12 3/8	13 6/8	6	6 2/8	7	8	Idaho Co., Idaho	John R. Lewinski	John R. Lewinski	1986	47
155 4/8	47 6/8	30 2/8	31 4/8	9 3/8	10 1/8	6 2/8	6 4/8	8	10	Morgan Co., Utah	Michael C. Allen	Michael C. Allen	1987	48
155 1/8	45 3/8	30 7/8	31	9 6/8	10 1/8	6 2/8	6 4/8	10	8	Madison Co., Mont.	Shawn G. Stewart	Shawn G. Stewart	1987	49
153 5/8	54 1/8	29 1/8	28 6/8	8	9 2/8	6	6 1/8	7	9	Gallatin Co., Mont.	Roger N. Olmstead	Roger N. Olmstead	1985	50
151 1/8	50 7/8	28	30 5/8	8 5/8	10	6	6 1/8	8	11	Morgan Co., Utah	David V. Collis	David V. Collis	1985	51
150 7/8	45 3/8	36 7/8	31 3/8	8 7/8	8 5/8	6	5 6/8	7	8	Cache Co., Utah	Joddy S. Bodrero	Joddy S. Bodrero	1987	52
150 4/8	48 6/8	27	31 6/8	9 3/8	8 7/8	6	6 3/8	9	10	Rich Co., Utah	Blake Poppleton	Blake Poppleton	1987	53
150	39 4/8	30 2/8	30	9 6/8	13 3/8	6 4/8	6 5/8	9	11	Bonneville Co., Idaho	Darren L. Wolz	Darren L. Wolz	1985	54
147 4/8	45 4/8	25 2/8	39 5/8	13 5/8	13 4/8	6 4/8	6 2/8	6	7	Lincoln Co., Wyo.	William H. Moyer	William H. Moyer	1981	55
144 5/8	42 7/8	28 1/8	30 6/8	10 3/8	11 3/8	6 3/8	6 6/8	7	6	Idaho Co., Idaho	R. Ashley Lyman III	R. Ashley Lyman III	1987	56
144 1/8	47 3/8	30 5/8	29	9 4/8	9 2/8	6 3/8	6 1/8	4	7	Teton Co., Wyo.	Virgil E. Ningen	Virgil E. Ningen	1986	57
143 2/8	45 2/8	25	25 7/8	9 1/8	9 3/8	6	5 7/8	9	10	Sublette Co., Wyo.	Michaelangelo P. Ripepi	Michaelangelo P. Ripepi	1988	58
202 4/8 *	55	37 4/8	40	16 3/8	16 3/8	6 7/8	6 7/8	13	13	Idaho Co., Idaho	Linda M. Mort	Linda M. Mort	1987	

* Final Score subject to revision by additional verifying measurements.

Mountain Caribou
Rangifer tarandus caribou

Minimum Score 360　　　　　　　　　　　　　　　　　　　　　　　　　　　World's Record 452

Mountain caribou includes trophies from Alberta, British Columbia, southern Yukon Territory, and the Mackenzie Mountains of the Northwest Territories.

Score	Length of Main Beam R.	L.	Inside Spread	Circumference at Smallest Place Between Brow and Bez Points R.	L.	Length of Brow Points R.	L.	Width of Brow Points R.	L.	Number of Points R.	L.	Locality Killed	By Whom Killed	Owner	Date Killed	Rank
444	42	43 1/8	35	6 4/8	6 5/8	15 5/8	17	8 1/8	7 3/8	20	23	Kechika Range, B.C.	James C. Johnson	James C. Johnson	1988	1
423 4/8	55 5/8	53 4/8	41 5/8	7	7 1/8	19 2/8	17 2/8	10 1/8	1 6/8	15	16	Divide Lake, N.W.T.	Les Jacobson	Les Jacobson	1988	2
423 1/8	51 6/8	50 6/8	32 3/8	7 1/8	7 2/8	20 7/8	18	6 3/8	11 2/8	16	18	Twitya River, N.W.T.	Carol S. Kraft	Carol S. Kraft	1987	3
422 2/8	50 6/8	52 2/8	28 3/8	6 1/8	6 1/8	22 4/8	9 6/8	18 6/8	1/8	23	14	Mountain River, N.W.T.	Leroy A. Schommer	Leroy A. Schommer	1985	4
417 6/8	51	51 2/8	29 4/8	6 5/8	6 4/8	15 7/8	20 1/8	12 1/8	4 1/8	16	16	Fire Lake, Yukon	Marvin E. Egger	Marvin E. Egger	1986	5
413	51 3/8	50 7/8	49 2/8	7 2/8	7 4/8	18 2/8	2 2/8	11 7/8	1/8	15	16	Kechika Range, B.C.	John J. Ottman	John J. Ottman	1988	6
412 6/8	48	47	47	7 3/8	7 2/8	16 5/8	17 4/8	10 6/8	10 3/8	14	18	Grass Lake, Yukon	Carol A. Domes	Carol A. Domes	1987	7
412 6/8	42 1/8	45 1/8	30 7/8	6 4/8	6	16 3/8	16 3/8	14 2/8	12 1/8	20	17	Black Fox Creek, B.C.	Norman L. Meints	Norman L. Meints	1987	7
412 3/8	50 4/8	49 6/8	38 3/8	6 3/8	6 4/8	17 3/8	18	1/8	12 2/8	16	18	Mackenzie Mts., N.W.T.	James F. Willoughby	James F. Willoughby	1988	9
410 6/8	57 2/8	57 7/8	42 5/8	7	6 4/8	18 3/8	1 7/8	12 2/8	1/8	17	15	Keele Lake, Yukon	Robert L. Gilkey	Robert L. Gilkey	1986	10
410 3/8	48 5/8	47 1/8	34	6 5/8	6 2/8	17 3/8	5 4/8	16 1/8	1/8	27	19	Level Mt., B.C.	Stephen Sipes, Jr.	Stephen Sipes, Jr.	1985	11
410	47	49 6/8	37 6/8	6 2/8	6 4/8	18 4/8	18 1/8	11 5/8	1 6/8	14	10	Deadwood Lake, B.C.	Joseph Mannino	Joseph Mannino	1986	12
409 7/8	51 7/8	51 1/8	40 1/8	6 1/8	6 2/8	16 3/8	17 1/8	4	9 2/8	19	16	Divide Lake, N.W.T.	Eldon L. Thompson	Eldon L. Thompson	1986	13
408 4/8	50 3/8	49 6/8	36 2/8	6 5/8	7	4 4/8	18	1/8	12 3/8	20	25	Mackenzie Mts., N.W.T.	Janet R. Johnson	Janet R. Johnson	1987	14
408 2/8	46 6/8	47	29	5 7/8	5 4/8	13 5/8	14 1/8	7 4/8	13 6/8	16	18	Spatsizi Plateau, B.C.	Michael M. Golightly	Michael M. Golightly	1985	15
407 5/8	42 7/8	45 5/8	40 6/8	6 5/8	6 5/8	17 4/8	16	9 6/8	1/8	16	14	Finlayson Lake, Yukon	Ken N. Booker	Ken N. Booker	1985	16
406	55 6/8	56 1/8	47	7 2/8	6 7/8	18 4/8		15		26	16	Jennings River, B.C.	R.D. Thomas, Jr.	R.D. Thomas, Jr.	1986	17
404 1/8	52 5/8	53 3/8	36 5/8	7 3/8	7 4/8	5 2/8	22 2/8	1/8	16 5/8	12	17	Keele Peak, Yukon	Robert L. Gilkey	Robert L. Gilkey	1987	18
403 6/8	55	54 7/8	44 5/8	5 2/8	5 2/8	18 5/8	18 5/8	15	3 5/8	18	12	Carcajou River, N.W.T.	Julian B. White, Jr.	Julian B. White, Jr.	1988	19
403 2/8	50	52 2/8	41 5/8	7 3/8	7 2/8	20 1/8	17 7/8	12 6/8	11 1/8	16	14	Mountain River, N.W.T.	Reginald Zebedee	Reginald Zebedee	1986	20
402 4/8	50 2/8	49 6/8	36 5/8	6 3/8	6 1/8	8 2/8	17 1/8	1	13 4/8	13	21	Mountain River, N.W.T.	Charles J. Gagliano	Charles J. Gagliano	1988	21
402 3/8	45	43 1/8	40 1/8	6 5/8	7 3/8	12 6/8	16 3/8	7 5/8	9	20	25	Glenlyon Range, Yukon	Louis A. Rupp	Louis A. Rupp	1985	22
401 1/8	48	47 3/8	37 5/8	6 4/8	6 4/8	10 4/8	17 1/8	1/8	14	12	18	Arctic Red River, N.W.T.	Picked Up	L.M. Schmaus & S. Bowick	1986	23
401	47 5/8	48 4/8	28 5/8	6 4/8	7	20 4/8	18 4/8	19 5/8	3 5/8	22	18	Mackenzie Mts., N.W.T.	James O. White	James O. White	1988	24
400 6/8	42 4/8	43 7/8	33 2/8	6 6/8	7	19	7 3/8	15 4/8	1/8	25	22	Aishihik Lake, Yukon	Armando J. Garcia	Armando J. Garcia	1987	25
398 7/8	48 5/8	52 1/8	40 4/8	6 4/8	6 5/8	6 5/8	15 5/8	1/8	12 5/8	14	19	Mackenzie Mts., N.W.T.	Craig R. Johnson	Craig R. Johnson	1987	26
396 6/8	46 4/8	47 6/8	34 4/8	7 1/8	6 7/8	18 4/8		13 4/8		18	15	Mackenzie Mts., N.W.T.	Mark Cook	Mark Cook	1988	27
396 2/8	47 1/8	44 3/8	38	7	7 1/8	20 1/8	2 5/8	13 5/8	1/8	15	14	Dease Lake, B.C.	David A. Smith	David A. Smith	1987	28

416

Score												Locality	Hunter	Year	Rank
396 1/8	52 7/8	52 7/8	41 5/8	6	6 7/8	19 5/8	9 5/8	14 5/8	18	16		Drury Lake, Yukon	Ostell G. Penner	1985	29
394 6/8	52 2/8	48 5/8	39 2/8	6 2/8	6 2/8	22 1/8	7 5/8	20	12	14		Divide Lake, N.W.T.	Richard A. Belotti	1987	30
394 4/8	44 5/8	44 5/8	39 1/8	5 7/8	6 1/8	18 3/8	9 1/8	10 1/8	20	14		Ruby Range, Yukon	John R. Bloise	1985	31
392 5/8	46 7/8	48 4/8	30 2/8	7 1/8	7 3/8	2 4/8	16 5/8	1/8	21	23		Arctic Red River, N.W.T.	Leo M. Schmaus	1986	32
391 7/8	49 4/8	49 4/8	44 1/8	6 7/8	6 7/8	18 5/8	13 5/8	14 2/8	15	13		Twitya River, N.W.T.	Melvin E. Kraft	1987	33
391	49 5/8	50 7/8	42 7/8	6 3/8	6 3/8	16 2/8	15 2/8	6 5/8	15	15		Blue River, B.C.	Aldo Guglielmini	1976	34
390 5/8	50 5/8	51 7/8	43	6 7/8	6 6/8	5	15	1/8	9 5/8	17	20	Semenot Hills, Yukon	Thomas F. Jeffcote	1975	35
390 5/8	43 3/8	39 4/8	27 5/8	6 2/8	6 6/8	16 3/8	15 5/8	8 1/8	9 5/8	20	17	Drury Lake, Yukon	Robert D. Day	1986	36
387 1/8	55 5/8	52	34 2/8	7	7 1/8	19 1/8	8	10	1/8	14	14	Logan Mts., Yukon	W.G. Hawes	1970	37
386 7/8	45 7/8	45 2/8	30 4/8	7 3/8	7 7/8	16 2/8	15 5/8	4 3/8	10 2/8	14	16	Fire Lake, Yukon	Gerald E. Hellwig	1973	38
384 1/8	49	48	37 2/8	7 5/8	7 5/8	4 2/8	17 5/8	1/8	14 5/8	13	16	Keele River, N.W.T.	William E. Stafford	1985	39
381 6/8	53 6/8	51 5/8	47 5/8	6 4/8	6 4/8	15	8 1/8			14	14	Stikine River, B.C.	Christopher Theodor	1987	40
381 1/8	48 6/8	47 3/8	29	5 5/8	5 7/8	19 5/8	20 4/8	3 3/8	17 4/8	15	19	Mackenzie Mts., N.W.T.	James R. Cook	1988	41
377 2/8	46 7/8	48 6/8	35 5/8	9 5/8	9 7/8	7 3/8	18 1/8	2 2/8	16	13	17	Mackenzie Mts., N.W.T.	C. Randall Byers	1988	42
370 7/8	50 5/8	49 1/8	43 5/8	6 7/8	6 3/8	2 5/8	15 5/8	1/8	9 5/8	12	14	Divide Lake, N.W.T.	John T. Wenders	1988	43
364 6/8	48 3/8	48 7/8	40 5/8	6 5/8	6 7/8	4 3/8	16 5/8	1/8	13 5/8	18	18	Nuthinaw Mt., B.C.	Ross H. Mann	1987	44
361	45 5/8	46 6/8	24 2/8	6 4/8	6 6/8	18 5/8	2 5/8	11 5/8	6/8	17	12	Keele River, N.W.T.	Thomas C. White	1984	45
458 3/8*	51 7/8	48 5/8	40	7 1/8	7 2/8	21	21 5/8	14 5/8	3 5/8	18	19	Pelly Mts., Yukon	Paul T. Deuling	1988	
436 1/8*	44	41 5/8	42 5/8	7 5/8	7 3/8	20 4/8	9 5/8	16 2/8	2 5/8	25	20	Ludwig Lake, B.C.	Gary D. Lloyd	1987	
428 2/8*	50 5/8	52 5/8	42 5/8	7	7 5/8	16 5/8	19 5/8	2 5/8	18 1/8	17	19	Big Campbell Creek Yukon	Leonard J. Derringer	1987	
427*	42 5/8	40 5/8	26	6 5/8	6 4/8	15 5/8	15 5/8	7 5/8	8 5/8	25	22	Nelson Lake, B.C.	Charlie D. Todd	1985	

* Final Score subject to revision by additional verifying measurements.

Woodland Caribou

Rangifer tarandus caribou

Minimum Score 265

World's Record 419-5/8

Woodland caribou includes trophies from Nova Scotia, New Brunswick, and Newfoundland.

Score	Length of Main Beam		Inside Spread	Circumference at Smallest Place Between Brow and Bez Points		Length of Brow Points		Width of Brow Points		Number of Points		Locality Killed	By Whom Killed	Owner	Date Killed	Rank
	R.	L.		R.	L.	R.	L.	R.	L.	R.	L.					
341 2/8	38 7/8	38 6/8	38 1/8	5 6/8	6 1/8	17	17 1/8	7 4/8	13 2/8	13	15	Barachois Brook, Nfld.	Harry L. Gunter	Harry L. Gunter	1986	1
336 1/8	40 6/8	40 4/8	26 7/8	5 3/8	6	22 7/8	16 3/8	19 4/8	1/8	15	9	Barachois Brook, Nfld.	Thomas W. Triplett	Thomas W. Triplett	1986	2
322 6/8	40 7/8	41 4/8	33 3/8	5 6/8	5 6/8	2 5/8	16 1/8	1/8	12 2/8	10	18	Rocky Pond, Nfld.	Wayne Karlin	Wayne Karlin	1988	3
320 6/8	38 1/8	38 1/8	30 6/8	5	5	16 5/8	15 3/8	14 7/8	10 7/8	20	19	Long Range Mts., Nfld.	Gary L. Benner	Gary L. Benner	1983	4
319	32 2/8	32 2/8	27 4/8	4 6/8	5	11 5/8	12 7/8	8 5/8	10 4/8	18	24	Fishels Brook, Nfld.	Fred Waite	Fred Waite	1986	5
318 6/8	39 5/8	39 3/8	25 1/8	5 2/8	5 2/8	15 4/8	12 5/8	13 5/8	19	15	16	Mouse Pond, Nfld.	C.T. Barnett	C.T. Barnett	1987	6
314	34 1/8	34 6/8	29 3/8	5 1/8	4 7/8	14 5/8	14 2/8	13 1/8	12 2/8	10	21	Long Range Mts., Nfld.	Gordon J. Birgbauer, Jr.	Gordon J. Birgbauer, Jr.	1986	7
311 6/8	35 5/8	40 4/8	28	5 7/8	5 5/8	19 5/8	18 3/8	6 4/8	8	19	14	Grey River, Nfld.	Edward R. Janas	Edward R. Janas	1986	8
310 3/8	42	42	29 5/8	5 4/8	5 5/8	12 3/8	12	9 3/8	8 7/8	13	14	Port aux Basques, Nfld.	George C. Thompson, Jr.	George C. Thompson, Jr.	1987	9
307 1/8	38	37 2/8	30 5/8	5 3/8	5 2/8	17 1/8	16 4/8	11 6/8	14 1/8	16	17	Buchans Plateau, Nfld.	Gary A. Laatsch	Gary A. Laatsch	1986	10
307 1/8	35 4/8	37 1/8	29 3/8	5 1/8	4 7/8	12 4/8	10 5/8	11 7/8	6 2/8	13	11	Conne River, Nfld.	Michael J. Park	Michael J. Park	1987	10
303 7/8	44	45	33 4/8	4 6/8	5 1/8	16 5/8	16 3/8	9	10 2/8	12	12	Blue Hills, Nfld.	Charlie D. Todd	Charlie D. Todd	1986	12
302 5/8	40 6/8	41 3/8	29 5/8	5 4/8	5 4/8	15 5/8	15	9 4/8	11 3/8	11	11	La Poile, Nfld.	L. Dale Gaugler	L. Dale Gaugler	1986	13
301 3/8	29 3/8	31 5/8	32 4/8	5	5	11 3/8	11 2/8	7 5/8	6 1/8	14	13	Buchans Plateau, Nfld.	Robert C. Kaufman	Robert C. Kaufman	1988	14
300 5/8	41 3/8	40	37 7/8	6 1/8	5 3/8	11 4/8	18	2 4/8	14 6/8	15	13	Long Range Mts., Nfld.	John L. Van Horn	John L. Van Horn	1983	15
299 7/8	43 7/8	42 3/8	36 2/8	5 2/8	5 3/8	12 1/8	12 3/8	9 3/8	8 2/8	12	14	Long Range Mts., Nfld.	Edwin J. Tichy, Jr.	Edwin J. Tichy, Jr.	1985	16
299	36 3/8	37 4/8	35 4/8	4 4/8	4 5/8	12 6/8	10 6/8	9	9 7/8	15	15	La Poile, Nfld.	Newton F. Moyer	Newton F. Moyer	1986	17
298 4/8	40 5/8	37 3/8	33 5/8	4 6/8	5	17 7/8	14 6/8	9 2/8	7 3/8	11	14	Lloyds River, Nfld.	William A. Shaw	William A. Shaw	1987	18
281 5/8	37 7/8	39	31 2/8	6 4/8	6 2/8	18 7/8	18 5/8	16 3/8	1/8	14	10	Buchans Plateau, Nfld.	Gary C. Davis	Gary C. Davis	1985	19
278 7/8	39 6/8	39 6/8	38 4/8	4 7/8	4 7/8	7 4/8	12 1/8	1/8	7 1/8	11	11	Buchans Plateau, Nfld.	David V. Collis	David V. Collis	1985	20
269 5/8	32 3/8	36 4/8	28 1/8	5 3/8	5 2/8	10 3/8	10 3/8	8	5 5/8	12	12	Saddlers Lake, Nfld.	David G. Noble	David G. Noble	1988	21
355 7/8 *	45 3/8	45 1/8	35	5 4/8	5 4/8	19 1/8	17 5/8	14 4/8	14	18	17	Middle Ridge, Nfld.	Wayne A. Pennell	Wayne A. Pennell	1985	
327 5/8 *	43 1/8	40 5/8	38 7/8	6 1/8	6 1/8	10 3/8	14 1/8	1/8	11 2/8	12	15	South Branch, Nfld.	Mark L. Johansen	Mark L. Johansen	1986	

* Final Score subject to revision by additional verifying measurements.

Barren Ground Caribou

Rangifer tarandus granti

Minimum Score 375 New World's Record 465-1/8

Barren ground caribou includes trophies from Alaska, northern Yukon Territory, Saskatchewan, Manitoba, and Ontario.

Score	Length of Main Beam R.	L.	Inside Spread	Circumference at Smallest Place Between Brow and Bez Points R.	L.	Length of Brow Points R.	L.	Width of Brow Points R.	L.	Number of Points R.	L.	Locality Killed	By Whom Killed	Owner	Date Killed	Rank
465 1/8	50 5/8	49 7/8	40 1/8	7	7	19	20 4/8	9 7/8	14 5/8	24	23	Mosquito Creek, Alaska	Roger Hedgecook	Loaned to B&C National Collection	1987	1
450 6/8	58 1/8	59 4/8	55 5/8	6 1/8	6 2/8	19 4/8	21 6/8	11 5/8	11 4/8	15	16	Bonanza Hills, Alaska	David A. Fulbright	David A. Fulbright	1987	2
448 3/8	56 5/8	59	45 3/8	6 5/8	6 2/8	20 3/8	20 5/8	8 1/8	14 1/8	15	19	Stoney River, Alaska	Picked Up	William O. West	1987	3
443 1/8	53 4/8	50 3/8	41	5 5/8	5 4/8	17 5/8	22	13 4/8	11 4/8	20	24	Kobuk River, Alaska	Ralph G. Colas	Ralph G. Colas	1988	4
441 2/8	43 3/8	46 6/8	41 1/8	6 7/8	7 1/8	19 2/8	21 1/8	1	15 4/8	17	23	Tonzona River, Alaska	Dean W. Coffman	Dean W. Coffman	1964	5
440 3/8	54 2/8	56 5/8	38 5/8	7 3/8	7 7/8	15 3/8	14 4/8	11 3/8	4 6/8	23	19	Lake Clark, Alaska	James W. Vorhease	James W. Vorhease	1988	6
440 1/8	54	57	48 1/8	7 3/8	6 5/8	18 3/8	17 7/8	12 6/8	9 3/8	18	17	Wood River, Alaska	David A. Schuller	David A. Schuller	1982	7
438 1/8	58 3/8	58 6/8	53 6/8	6 4/8	6 2/8	23 3/8	23	17	2 2/8	18	12	Iliamna Lake, Alaska	Jerry L. Peterson	Jerry L. Peterson	1986	8
437 4/8	48 5/8	50 7/8	37 1/8	5 1/8	5 1/8	21 4/8	22 3/8	18 1/8	16 5/8	18	16	Port Heiden, Alaska	Joyce A. Houston	Joyce A. Houston	1987	9
436 1/8	55 3/8	55	47 2/8	7 3/8	7 5/8	21 4/8	6 3/8	15 1/8	1/8	19	14	Iliamna Lake, Alaska	Robert S. Marvin	Robert S. Marvin	1987	10
432 2/8	52 5/8	56	48 1/8	6	5 7/8	19	17 3/8	9 5/8	10 6/8	19	18	Iliamna Lake, Alaska	Thomas R. Reed, Jr.	Thomas R. Reed, Jr.	1988	11
431 3/8	53 3/8	54 2/8	43	6 5/8	7 1/8	17 5/8	16 7/8	6 3/8	11 4/8	20	19	Mulchatna River, Alaska	Valerie E. King	Valerie E. King	1984	12
430 7/8	51 2/8	49 4/8	36 5/8	7 2/8	7 1/8	16 4/8	18 2/8	6 3/8	11	12	15	Mulchatna River, Alaska	Ted M. Labedz	Ted M. Labedz	1987	13
429 5/8	56 5/8	48 4/8	39 5/8	6 3/8	6 6/8	18 3/8	11 7/8	10 6/8	5 4/8	17	14	Mulchatna River, Alaska	Jerry D. Downing	Jerry D. Downing	1986	14
428 1/8	53	55 3/8	38 1/8	6 2/8	6 1/8	19 4/8	19 7/8	3 7/8	12 4/8	19	20	Ivishak River, Alaska	Joseph A. Renfrow, Jr.	Joseph A. Renfrow, Jr.	1987	15
428 1/8	62 6/8	62	49 1/8	6 5/8	6 4/8	23 1/8	11 4/8	14 6/8	1/8	12	9	Mulchatna River, Alaska	Ricky A. Beauchamp	Ricky A. Beauchamp	1987	15
426 7/8	59	56 6/8	44 5/8	6 1/8	6 1/8	21 4/8	11 5/8	13	1 7/8	20	16	Alaska Pen., Alaska	John S. Rohrer	John S. Rohrer	1987	17
426 3/8	50 3/8	56 4/8	37 4/8	7 6/8	7	1 5/8	26 6/8	1/8	22	18	22	Lake Clark, Alaska	Mark E. Carda	Mark E. Carda	1986	18
422 5/8	55 2/8	55 5/8	45 4/8	6 3/8	7 1/8	20 6/8	18 6/8	4 4/8	15 6/8	16	18	Mother Goose Lake, Alaska	James B. Bloomer	James B. Bloomer	1987	19
422 1/8	49	49 2/8	36 1/8	6 6/8	8 1/8	19 7/8	17 6/8	16 7/8	14	21	20	Mulchatna River, Alaska	Thomas N. Govin	Thomas N. Govin	1987	20
421 2/8	52 6/8	50 5/8	43 2/8	6 4/8	6 4/8	4 3/8	21 3/8	1/8	16 7/8	14	20	Boulder Creek, Alaska	Neal E. Osgood	Neal E. Osgood	1986	21
421	55 5/8	57	44 7/8	7 1/8	6 6/8	18	9 2/8	10 7/8	1/8	20	14	Ugashik Lake, Alaska	John M. Hangar	John M. Hangar	1988	22
420 5/8	53 7/8	49 1/8	40 2/8	6 1/8	5 7/8	18 1/8	19 3/8	11 3/8	11 2/8	12	13	Mulchatna River, Alaska	Ronald K. Hodges	Ronald K. Hodges	1986	23
419 7/8	49 7/8	49 2/8	37 3/8	6 5/8	6 4/8	14 7/8	18 5/8	1 4/8	14 2/8	16	23	Alaska Pen., Alaska	Kenneth E. Hess	Kenneth E. Hess	1987	24
419 4/8	57 3/8	57 3/8	46 6/8	6 4/8	6 1/8	17 4/8	19 3/8	9 6/8	7 5/8	17	16	King Salmon, Alaska	David C. Smith	David C. Smith	1987	25
419 2/8	49 7/8	49 4/8	35 5/8	6 6/8	6 1/8	22 4/8	21 5/8	15 1/8	4 6/8	15	11	Iliamna Lake, Alaska	Roy F. Smith	Roy F. Smith	1987	26
419 1/8	44 3/8	44 4/8	31 1/8	7 4/8	6 6/8	20	20 3/8	5	13	19	25	Ugashik River, Alaska	Ronald W. Madsen	Ronald W. Madsen	1987	27

Barren Ground Caribou - Continued

Score	Length of Main Beam R.	Length of Main Beam L.	Inside Spread	Circumference at Smallest Place Between Brow and Bez Points R.	Circumference at Smallest Place Between Brow and Bez Points L.	Length of Brow Points R.	Length of Brow Points L.	Width of Brow Points R.	Width of Brow Points L.	Number of Points R.	Number of Points L.	Locality Killed	By Whom Killed	Owner	Date Killed	Rank
417 7/8	56 5/8	58 5/8	46 5/8	6 1/8	6 3/8	19 1/4	10 7/8	18 3/8	1/8	17	10	Tyone Creek, Alaska	Edward D. Hull	Quint Hull	1987	28
417 7/8	54 2/8	52 3/8	40 4/8	6 3/8	6 5/8	20 1/8	3 5/8	15 2/8	1/8	18	13	White River, Alaska	Gary L. Todd	Gary L. Todd	1984	29
417	59 6/8	60 2/8	38 3/8	6 3/8	6 2/8	20	23 4/8	13 1/8	9	14	16	Mulchatna River, Alaska	Mark H. Young	Mark H. Young	1987	30
416 7/8	61 3/8	60 2/8	42 6/8	5 6/8	6	2 5/8	17 4/8	1/8	12 4/8	13	20	Mulchatna River, Alaska	Q.D. Edwards	Q.D. Edwards	1987	31
416 1/8	50	46	39 2/8	5 5/8	6 2/8	18 3/8	17	14	13 4/8	21	16	Lake Clark, Alaska	Rainer H. Unger	Rainer H. Unger	1987	32
416 1/8	54 1/8	54 4/8	37 3/8	7 3/8	6 3/8	5	19 2/8	1/8	14 1/8	21	24	Becharof Lake, Alaska	Todd Rice	Todd Rice	1987	32
414 6/8	54	57 2/8	39 2/8	7 3/8	7 4/8	11 6/8	21 5/8	1/8	20	13	22	Yanert Fork, Alaska	Russell W. McInnis	Russell W. McInnis	1988	34
414 3/8	50 1/8	50 6/8	40	5 5/8	5 5/8	15 3/8	16 4/8	11 6/8	10 6/8	16	18	Lake Clark, Alaska	Stanley J. Leger	Stanley J. Leger	1986	35
414 1/8	43 2/8	43 4/8	35 3/8	6 4/8	6 4/8	16	10 2/8	13	1 4/8	27	23	Snake River, Yukon	Leslie Kish	Leslie Kish	1985	36
412 7/8	58 5/8	58 3/8	47 2/8	5 5/8	5 7/8	16 4/8	10 7/8	12 1/8	1/8	28	20	Tutna Lake, Alaska	Ernest C. Noble	Ernest C. Noble	1987	37
412 3/8	59	60 2/8	40 5/8	5 5/8	5 5/8	21 4/8	23 3/8	15	7 5/8	15	13	Dog Salmon River, Alaska	John S. Alley	John S. Alley	1987	38
412 1/8	44	46	44	6 4/8	6 1/8	8	19 2/8	1/8	16 6/8	17	26	Hoholitna River, Alaska	Daniel E. Lunde	Daniel E. Lunde	1986	39
411 7/8	53 6/8	51 1/8	39 1/8	7 4/8	6 5/8	3	17 3/8	1/8	14	16	20	Billy Creek, Alaska	David L. Richards	David L. Richards	1987	40
411 7/8	53 3/8	55	41 2/8	6 4/8	6 4/8	12 3/8	20 6/8	1 5/8	16 3/8	14	19	Lake Becharof, Alaska	Douglas G. Bonetti	Douglas G. Bonetti	1987	40
411 4/8	51 4/8	49 5/8	34 3/8	5 7/8	6	15 5/8	19 3/8	2 2/8	15 4/8	15	21	Hartman River, Alaska	Robert B. Hancock	Robert B. Hancock	1988	42
411	59 5/8	55 3/8	54	6 4/8	8	13 1/8	16 3/8	3 3/8	9	13	16	Tutna Lake, Alaska	Joseph M. Negri	Joseph M. Negri	1986	43
411	53 2/8	49 4/8	36 4/8	6 7/8	7 2/8	22	7 1/8	14 2/8	1/8	20	14	Mt. Harper, Alaska	Gary L. Truitt	Gary L. Truitt	1987	43
410 6/8	55 5/8	56 5/8	41 1/8	6 1/8	6 3/8	13 2/8	18 7/8	1/8	15 3/8	12	22	Talkeetna Mts., Alaska	Melissa A. Everett	Melissa A. Everett	1988	45
410 5/8	57 5/8	57 5/8	48 3/8	5 7/8	6 1/8	4	20 3/8	1/8	11 6/8	11	19	Becharof Lake, Alaska	Marcus C. Deede	Marcus C. Deede	1987	46
410 5/8	53 4/8	52	43 1/8	7 2/8	7 5/8	17 3/8	21 5/8	1/8	21 3/8	13	20	Haines Lake, Alaska	Len F. Onorato	Len F. Onorato	1987	46
409 5/8	46 2/8	47 1/8	46 6/8	6 3/8	6 4/8	13 7/8	17 1/8	4 5/8	9 3/8	13	15	Whitefish Lake, Alaska	Thomas M. Krueger	Thomas M. Krueger	1987	48
409 1/8	56 6/8	60	44 4/8	6 4/8	6 2/8	19 4/8	2	15 5/8	1/8	18	15	Nikabuna Lakes, Alaska	Stephen E. Warner	Stephen E. Warner	1986	49
409 1/8	57	51	47 2/8	6 5/8	7 1/8	18 3/8	19 3/8	15	12 2/8	20	21	King Salmon, Alaska	Robert E. Deis	Robert E. Deis	1986	49
409	55 1/8	51 5/8	40 2/8	7 5/8	7 7/8	19	13 2/8	9 3/8	9 5/8	15	11	Kuskokwim River, Alaska	Thomas B. May	Thomas B. May	1987	51
408 3/8	48 5/8	50 6/8	38 4/8	5 7/8	5 5/8	15 5/8	18 5/8	6 2/8	14 3/8	18	23	Port Heiden, Alaska	Harold L. Moore, Jr.	Harold L. Moore, Jr.	1985	52
407 7/8	49 6/8	51	42 2/8	6 2/8	6 3/8	7 6/8	18 6/8	1/8	14 4/8	15	22	Whitefish Lake, Alaska	Robert R. King	Robert R. King	1986	53
406 7/8	51 4/8	54	50 3/8	6 6/8	6 6/8	5 1/8	19 6/8	1/8	15 2/8	14	19	Hoholitna River, Alaska	Shawn T. Brown	Shawn T. Brown	1988	54
405 4/8	57 6/8	56 7/8	40 4/8	5 5/8	5 5/8	21 1/8	19 5/8	18 1/8	1/8	18	11	Mesa Mt., Alaska	Robert E. Lieberum	Robert E. Lieberum	1988	55
405 3/8	43	47 4/8	42	5 5/8	5 3/8	20 3/8	1 7/8	15 4/8	1/8	22	16	Becharof Lake, Alaska	Roy Ruiz	Roy Ruiz	1987	56
405 1/8	56	53 3/8	37 4/8	5 3/8	5 3/8	16 2/8	19	4 2/8	8 1/8	10	10	Iliamna, Alaska	Fred W. Amyotte	Fred W. Amyotte	1987	57
405	52 3/8	53	36 1/8	6 6/8	6 4/8	18	20 3/8	12 2/8	16 4/8	18	16	Stevens Creek, Alaska	John T. Lunenschloss	John T. Lunenschloss	1987	58
404 3/8	50 5/8	51	47 1/8	4 5/8	4 7/8	14 1/8	13 4/8	14 1/8	6 6/8	25	18	Brooks Range, Alaska	Dwight C. Davis	Dwight C. Davis	1984	59
403 5/8	57 6/8	57 7/8	46 3/8	5 5/8	6	20 4/8	19 3/8	11 2/8	14 3/8	15	15	King Salmon, Alaska	Gary A. Markofer	Gary A. Markofer	1986	60

Score												Location	Hunter	Owner	Year	Rank
403 5/8	44 5/8	45 1/8	27 5/8	6 7/8	6 7/8	19 5/8	3 3/8	14 2/8	2 1/8	15	12	Mulchatna River, Alaska	William H. Basil	William H. Basil	1987	60
403 4/8	49 1/8	45 7/8	32 1/8	6 7/8	6	19 1/8	18 2/8	4 7/8	12 1/8	15	21	Kotsetna River, Alaska	Kevin J. Bores	Kevin J. Bores	1987	62
403 1/8	54 5/8	45 5/8	45 5/8	6	6	22 4/8	16 6/8	14 6/8	1 7/8	14	14	Becharof Lake, Alaska	Linda J. McBride	Linda J. McBride	1988	63
403	48 4/8	47 4/8	47 5/8	6 2/8	5 5/8	15 3/8	15 2/8	10 3/8	13 3/8	21	23	Brooks Range, Alaska	Jerry Imperial	Jerry Imperial	1985	64
402 7/8	53 4/8	51 4/8	37	6 3/8	6 6/8	19 6/8	13 4/8	16 4/8	1/8	19	13	Sheep Creek, Alaska	David J. Palonis	David J. Palonis	1987	65
402 6/8	53 6/8	51 6/8	51	5 5/8	5 5/8	2 3/8	19 1/8	1/8	15 3/8	19	19	King Salmon, Alaska	Daniel R. Nilles	Daniel R. Nilles	1985	66
402 6/8	59 5/8	58 3/8	54 6/8	5 5/8	5 5/8	21 2/8	14 2/8	15 2/8	1 4/8	14	19	Egegik, Alaska	Michael D. Odegard	Michael D. Odegard	1985	66
402 5/8	53	54 2/8	41 3/8	6 2/8	6 4/8	5 5/8	17 3/8	1/8	4 6/8	17	13	Pilot Point, Alaska	Joseph P. Sebo, Jr.	Joseph P. Sebo, Jr.	1987	68
402 5/8	51 5/8	50 1/8	34 5/8	5 2/8	6 2/8	18 5/8	19 2/8	12 1/8	14 5/8	19	21	Lake Clark, Alaska	Gene Thoney	Gene Thoney	1987	68
402 2/8	50 5/8	47 3/8	35 5/8	6 2/8	6 2/8	18 2/8	20	1 2/8	13	14	18	Cathedral Bluff, Alaska	John H. Harvey, Jr.	John H. Harvey, Jr.	1987	70
402 1/8	53 4/8	54 6/8	49 7/8	5 7/8	5 5/8	15 5/8	16 5/8	6	13 2/8	16	21	Dago Creek, Alaska	John M. Gillette	John M. Gillette	1987	71
402	51 3/8	57 3/8	45 6/8	5 2/8	5 1/8	5	18 3/8	1/8	15 4/8	17	25	Ivishak River, Alaska	Vernon D. Holleman	Vernon D. Holleman	1986	72
402	49	49 6/8	32 5/8	6	6 2/8	17 7/8	19	12 3/8	10 7/8	20	22	Tundra Lake, Alaska	Clyde A. James	Clyde A. James	1986	72
402	53 6/8	52 5/8	51 2/8	6 2/8	6	21 5/8	21	9 4/8	12 7/8	11	17	Groundhog Mt., Alaska	James B. Haynes III	J.B. Haynes & Q.T. Hardtner	1988	72
401 7/8	53 7/8	50 4/8	36 4/8	5 5/8	5 5/8	18 3/8	4 2/8	11 7/8	1/8	22	18	Stony River, Alaska	Richard Berry	Richard Berry	1986	75
401 7/8	51 5/8	51 7/8	37 5/8	7 5/8	7	18 4/8	18	13 4/8	3 5/8	14	13	Whitefish Lake, Alaska	Wesley W. Siegrist	Wesley W. Siegrist	1986	75
401 6/8	50 1/8	52 2/8	32 3/8	6 1/8	6 5/8	14 5/8	18 6/8	5 6/8	11 6/8	14	21	Deadman Lake, Alaska	Richard W. Dean	Richard W. Dean	1986	77
401 3/8	51 7/8	52 5/8	26 3/8	7 3/8	8	19 6/8	19	11 3/8	15 1/8	15	13	Little Nelchina River, Alaska	Francis M. Thistle	Francis M. Thistle	1957	78
401	53 5/8	56 5/8	46 7/8	5	5 2/8	20	17 7/8	10 2/8	11 7/8	17	16	Whitefish Lake, Alaska	Joe C. Simmons	Joe C. Simmons	1986	79
401	49 2/8	49 2/8	41 6/8	7 4/8	8 2/8	12 3/8	9 6/8	4 4/8	1/8	18	16	Iliamna Lake, Alaska	Thomas R. Reed III	Thomas R. Reed III	1988	79
400 5/8	54 3/8	51	47 4/8	5 6/8	5 5/8	25 4/8	20 7/8	18 2/8	8 2/8	13	12	Port Heiden, Alaska	H. Bruce Freeman	Picked Up	1984	81
400 5/8	57 2/8	55 4/8	44 3/8	6 6/8	7	4	19 4/8	1/8	14 7/8	15	21	Iliamna Lake, Alaska	K. James Malady III	K. James Malady III	1987	81
400 3/8	59 5/8	58 3/8	43	6 1/8	6	19 4/8	2 1/8	14 7/8	1/8	16	10	Hook Lake, Alaska	James L. Horneck	James L. Horneck	1983	83
400 3/8	52 6/8	56 7/8	46	6 1/8	5 7/8	10 5/8	18 2/8	4 2/8	15 4/8	15	21	Painter Creek, Alaska	Stephen R. Hurt	Stephen R. Hurt	1987	83
400	49 5/8	48 3/8	39 5/8	6 1/8	6 1/8	21 1/8	19 1/8	14 1/8	2 1/8	19	11	Lake Aleknagik, Alaska	Monty D. McCormick	Monty D. McCormick	1987	85
398 7/8	54 3/8	59 2/8	38 2/8	6 6/8	6 3/8	3 2/8	17 7/8	1/8	11 4/8	13	13	Chilikadrotna River, Alaska	Bruce E. Bartels	Bruce E. Bartels	1987	86
397 4/8	53	52 5/8	40 4/8	6 3/8	6 3/8	17 1/8	17 4/8	10 4/8	11 4/8	16	19	Iliamna Lake, Alaska	Daniel R. Fisher	Daniel R. Fisher	1987	87
396 3/8	48 3/8	47	37 3/8	7 1/8	7 1/8	11 5/8	15 4/8	1/8	8 4/8	14	14	Tonzona River, Alaska	Jack A. McCloskey, Jr.	Jack A. McCloskey, Jr.	1986	88
394 4/8	51 6/8	49 6/8	34 4/8	6 6/8	6 4/8	14 7/8	1 1/8	11 7/8	1/8	20	17	Mulchatna River, Alaska	R. Douglas Isbell	R. Douglas Isbell	1988	89
394 3/8	50 5/8	50 6/8	42 4/8	6 6/8	6 6/8	1 3/8	18 3/8	1/8	13	14	16	Portage Creek, Alaska	Joe E. Schaefer	Joe E. Schaefer	1987	90
394	57 3/8	59 2/8	49 1/8	6 3/8	6 1/8		17 7/8		11 1/8	17	22	Chignik Lake, Alaska	Alden A. Johnson	Alden A. Johnson	1977	91
393 7/8	56 5/8	54	45 5/8	5 3/8	5 4/8	19 4/8	20 3/8	9 6/8	14 5/8	17	18	Talkeetna River, Alaska	Stephen F. Wells	Stephen F. Wells	1987	92
392 2/8	50 3/8	51 7/8	39 5/8	5 1/8	5 3/8	17 1/8	15 7/8	7 1/8	10 1/8	18	18	Holitna River, Alaska	Clark M. Smith, Jr.	Clark M. Smith, Jr.	1987	93
392 1/8	53 3/8	56 1/8	47 7/8	6 1/8	6 1/8	20 2/8	3 2/8	15 1/8	1/8	17	12	Alaska Pen., Alaska	Larry G. Sanders	Larry G. Sanders	1986	94
391 7/8	52 7/8	50 6/8	42 5/8	5 4/8	6	10 6/8	21	1/8	16 2/8	13	28	Iliamna Lake, Alaska	William E. Butler	William E. Butler	1986	95
390 5/8	53 3/8	53 4/8	39 5/8	5 7/8	6 3/8	8 2/8	16 6/8	1/8	9 3/8	12	13	Lake Clark, Alaska	Frederick E. Slyfield	Frederick E. Slyfield	1988	96
390	46 3/8	49 1/8	41 4/8	7 4/8	7	18 4/8	18 4/8	4	15 4/8	13	20	Talkeetna Mts., Alaska	Paul A. Dubsky	Paul A. Dubsky	1986	97
389 6/8	51 1/8	50 5/8	37 5/8	5	5	19 1/8	16 1/8	15 1/8	3 1/8	20	16	Brooks Range, Alaska	James F. Arnold	James F. Arnold	1986	98
388 4/8	58 6/8	54 2/8	38 2/8	7 4/8	7	21 7/8	1 5/8	17 7/8	1/8	14	11	Wood River, Alaska	Walter L. Goas III	Walter L. Goas III	1986	99

Barren Ground Caribou - Continued

Score	Length of Main Beam R	L	Inside Spread	Circumference at Smallest Place Between Brow and Bez Points R	L	Length of Brow Points R	L	Width of Brow Points R	L	Number of Points R	L	Locality Killed	By Whom Killed	Owner	Date Killed	Rank
388 3/8	48 2/8	51 1/8	37 2/8	5 4/8	5 5/8	15 7/8	17 5/8	10 4/8	15 1/8	15	13	Charley River, Alaska	Ernest M. Krueger	Ernest M. Krueger	1986	100
385 4/8	57 5/8	56 5/8	44	6	6 7/8	16 4/8	2 1/8	8	1/8	13	13	Talkeetna Mts., Alaska	Donald W. Graham	Donald W. Graham	1985	101
384	52 4/8	49 1/8	39 6/8	10	9 2/8	15 5/8	14 7/8	7 7/8	10 1/8	15	15	Alaska Pen., Alaska	Charles H. Rohrer	Charles H. Rohrer	1987	102
383 6/8	51	50 6/8	37 7/8	5 6/8	8 7/8	15 4/8	14 5/8	12 4/8	6	21	21	Alaska Pen., Alaska	James J. McBride	James J. McBride	1983	103
383 3/8	52 4/8	50 7/8	34 1/8	5 1/8	5 4/8	20 4/8	21 4/8	11 3/8	10 7/8	18	17	Alaska Pen., Alaska	Richard A. Fording	Richard A. Fording	1984	104
383 3/8	51 5/8	53 3/8	40 6/8	7 6/8	7 2/8	18 3/8	17 5/8	13 6/8	1/8	11	9	Camelback Mt., Alaska	Thomas E. Smith	Thomas E. Smith	1985	104
383	52 4/8	50 1/8	31	6	6 3/8	19 5/8	15	13 7/8	4 6/8	20	16	Watana Lake, Alaska	Kenneth J. Broussard	Kenneth J. Broussard	1987	106
382 5/8	48 7/8	46 3/8	32 4/8	7 3/8	6 7/8	14 5/8	14 7/8	7 2/8	9 3/8	18	18	Nishlik Lake, Alaska	Robert J. Lucurell	Robert J. Lucurell	1985	107
382 3/8	48 6/8	50 6/8	37 5/8	6 4/8	6 4/8	15 5/8	16	1/8	12 2/8	13	16	Mulchatna River, Alaska	Richard W. Isbell	Richard W. Isbell	1988	108
381 1/2	51 3/8	53 3/8	42 1/8	7 2/8	8 3/8	19 1/8	1 1/8	14	1/8	14	15	Mesa Mt., Alaska	Douglas R. Plourde	Douglas R. Plourde	1987	109
380 3/8	53 1/8	53 3/8	37 5/8	5 1/8	5 4/8	16 5/8	15 3/8	11 1/8	8 5/8	13	15	Lake Clark, Alaska	James L. Butterfield	James L. Butterfield	1986	110
380 3/8	53 3/8	52 7/8	34 6/8	6 7/8	6	17 2/8	4 6/8	11 4/8	1/8	16	13	Wood River, Alaska	Ronald R. Roberts	Ronald R. Roberts	1986	110
380 1/8	53 6/8	54 1/8	41 1/8	6 1/8	5	21 4/8	13	14	1/8	15	10	Ugashik Lakes, Alaska	Joseph M. Harner	Joseph M. Harner	1988	112
379 7/8	47 5/8	46 5/8	42	7 2/8	8	15	15 5/8	5 2/8	9 4/8	16	16	California Creek, Alaska	Stan W. Hughes	Stan W. Hughes	1987	113
379 3/8	47 4/8	47 7/8	32 4/8	6 3/8	6 3/8	16 2/8	13 3/8	11 4/8	4 4/8	16	15	Cairn Mt., Alaska	Darold L. Gere	Darold L. Gere	1987	114
378 4/8	50	54	43 4/8	5 5/8	5 2/8	17 2/8	22 2/8	1/8	15 3/8	11	19	Whale Mt., Alaska	James Bowden, Jr.	James Bowden, Jr.	1987	115
378 2/8	53 4/8	55 1/8	38 5/8	8 3/8	6 1/8	19	6 4/8	14 5/8	1/8	21	13	Alaska Pen., Alaska	Donald Anderson	Donald Anderson	1984	116
378	56 3/8	53 3/8	41 5/8	5 5/8	5 4/8	16 7/8	11 3/8	14 5/8	2 4/8	15	13	Ugashik Lakes, Alaska	Barry F. Dugosh	Barry F. Dugosh	1985	117
376 7/8	51 6/8	53 3/8	46 1/8	6 1/8	6	17 3/8	2	12 2/8	1/8	11	10	Hoholitna River, Alaska	Mary L. Brooks	Mary L. Brooks	1987	118
376 7/8	50	50 3/8	33 3/8	6 3/8	6 6/8	17 4/8	16 1/8	8 4/8	11 3/8	16	16	Hoholitna River, Alaska	Aaron E. Malone	Aaron E. Malone	1987	118
462 5/8 *	59 3/8	59 5/8	55	6	6 3/8	19 3/8	21 3/8	14 4/8	11 6/8	20	21	Becharof Lake, Alaska	Picked Up	E.L. Brown & J. Feightner	pr 1986	
448 1/8 *	55	57 1/8	58 5/8	6 7/8	7 2/8	22 5/8	19 3/8	17 3/8	2	21	15	Brooks Range, Alaska	Jerrell A. Friz, Jr.	Jerrell A. Friz, Jr.	1985	

* Final Score subject to revision by additional verifying measurements.

Central Canada Barren Ground Caribou

Rangifer tarandus groenlandicus

Minimum Score 330 — New World's Record 416

Central Canada barren ground caribou occur on Baffin Island and the mainland of N.W.T., with geographic boundaries of the Mackenzie River to the west; the north edge of the continent to the north (excluding any islands except Baffin Island); Hudson's Bay to the east; and the southern boundary of N.W.T. to the south.

Score	Length of Main Beam R.	L.	Inside Spread	Circumference at Smallest Place Between Brow and Bez Points R.	L.	Length of Brow Points R.	L.	Width of Brow Points R.	L.	Number of Points R.	L.	Locality Killed	By Whom Killed	Owner	Date Killed	Rank
416	52	52	43 5/8	6 5/8	5 3/8	17 4/8	16 5/8	13 1/8	10 7/8	20	14	Courageous Lake, N.W.T.	Toby J. Johnson	Toby J. Johnson	1987	1
408 3/8	47 1/8	46 2/8	31 5/8	4 7/8	5 1/8	18 1/8	13 6/8	12 3/8	9	15	14	Courageous Lake, N.W.T.	Jon Vanderhoef	Jon Vanderhoef	1987	2
400 6/8	51 2/8	50	27 2/8	4 6/8	5 5/8	12 6/8	20 5/8	1/8	14 2/8	19	26	Rendez-vous Lake, N.W.T.	Dale L. Zeigler	Dale L. Zeigler	1986	3
398 4/8	46 3/8	44 1/8	31 3/8	5 5/8	5 5/8	17 5/8	18 3/8	13 7/8	7 7/8	23	23	Rendez-vous Lake, N.W.T.	Robert M. Hazlewood	Robert M. Hazlewood	1986	4
393 2/8	47 3/8	48 3/8	24 6/8	5 4/8	5 3/8	19	21 3/8	4 2/8	18 7/8	19	25	Courageous Lake, N.W.T.	Robert G. Koffman	Robert G. Koffman	1987	5
391 1/8	47 1/8	50 6/8	25	5 3/8	5	20 6/8	16 7/8	11 2/8	11 2/8	27	23	MacKay Lake, N.W.T.	Grady E. Maggard, Jr.	Grady E. Maggard, Jr.	1988	6
390 4/8	43 5/8	44 2/8	28	4 5/8	4 7/8	16	17	5 3/8	15 5/8	20	24	Courageous Lake, N.W.T.	Joseph Pinkas	Joseph Pinkas	1987	7
390 3/8	55 5/8	54 1/8	43 5/8	5	4 7/8	18 3/8	16 5/8	9 5/8	9 3/8	19	8	Courageous Lake, N.W.T.	Patrick H. Ackerman	Patrick H. Ackerman	1988	8
387 1/8	47 4/8	49	38 5/8	5 2/8	5 3/8		15 5/8		13 4/8	13	20	Courageous Lake, N.W.T.	James J. McBride	James J. McBride	1987	9
386 3/8	52 4/8	52 1/8	28 3/8	5	5 3/8	16	16 5/8	9 4/8	12 2/8	24	25	Rendez-vous Lake, N.W.T.	Jerome T. Loendorf	Jerome T. Loendorf	1988	10
386	48 6/8	48 1/8	33 5/8	5 4/8	5 4/8	15 4/8	15 5/8	11	4 1/8	16	18	Parry Pen., N.W.T.	Bernard Sippin	Bernard Sippin	1988	11
385 1/8	57 5/8	57 4/8	41	4 3/8	4 4/8	20 5/8	3 3/8	18 2/8	1/8	18	11	Lake Providence, N.W.T.	Paul Wisness	Paul Wisness	1987	12
382 2/8	47 4/8	50 1/8	30 7/8	8 2/8	6 2/8	13 6/8	14 1/8	4 2/8	11 1/8	19	20	Paulatuk, N.W.T.	William H. Taylor	William H. Taylor	1986	13
380 4/8	52 1/8	52 5/8	36 1/8	4 3/8	4 4/8	18 5/8	15 4/8	13 1/8	12	17	18	Lac de Gras, N.W.T.	James R. Crawford	James R. Crawford	1987	14
376 5/8	55 5/8	54	38 2/8	5 5/8	5 3/8	15 4/8	1 4/8	10 5/8	1/8	14	15	Snare Lake, N.W.T.	Gary L. Temple	Gary L. Temple	1987	15
373	53 2/8	55 3/8	23 3/8	4 4/8	4 5/8	20 2/8	16 6/8	15 5/8	11 4/8	21	16	Providence Lake, N.W.T.	Dean G. Fletcher	Dean G. Fletcher	1987	16
369 7/8	52 3/8	50	28 4/8	5 5/8	5 5/8	19 4/8	19 4/8	5	15 4/8	16	19	Rendez-vous Lake, N.W.T.	Philip L. Wright	Philip L. Wright	1986	17
368 5/8	55 5/8	56	41 6/8	5 5/8	5	18	14 7/8	12 3/8	11 1/8	15	17	Point Lake, N.W.T.	Douglas G. Kirchhoff	Douglas G. Kirchhoff	1987	18

Central Canada Barren Ground Caribou - *Continued*

Score	Length of Main Beam R.	L.	In-side Spread	Circumference at Smallest Place Between Brow and Bez Points R.	L.	Length of Brow Points R.	L.	Width of Brow Points R.	L.	Number of Points R.	L.	Locality Killed	By Whom Killed	Owner	Date Killed	Rank
368 2/8	54	55 4/8	39 7/8	5	4 5/8	17 5/8	14 3/8	11	10 5/8	15	11	Rendez-vous Lake, N.W.T.	David P. Jacobson	David P. Jacobson	1988	19
366	45 3/8	47 1/8	32 5/8	4 5/8	4 4/8	13 3/8	10 4/8	8 7/8	7 7/8	18	23	Courageous Lake, N.W.T.	Arthur C. Peckham, Jr.	Arthur C. Peckham, Jr.	1987	20
365 5/8	48	47 7/8	31 1/8	9 3/8	8 7/8	15 5/8		5 4/8		14	12	Coppermine River, N.W.T.	David P. Jacobson	David P. Jacobson	1975	21
350 7/8	47 1/8	48 6/8	31 1/8	5 1/8	4 7/8	16 5/8	16 7/8	13 1/8	11 7/8	14	13	Courageous Lake, N.W.T.	Daryl W. Schreiner	Daryl W. Schreiner	1986	22
348 3/8	54 6/8	53 5/8	34	5	5	10 4/8	16 3/8	3 6/8	6 4/8	13	16	Courageous Lake, N.W.T.	Thomas A. McIntyre	Thomas A. McIntyre	1987	23
347 3/8	46 3/8	48 6/8	34 3/8	6 1/8	7 2/8	12 3/8	13 2/8	9 2/8	6 3/8	20	14	Paulatuk, N.W.T.	Don L. Corley	Don L. Corley	1985	24
347 1/8	41 6/8	44 5/8	25 5/8	6	5 3/8	13	13 2/8	8	12 5/8	17	15	Courageous Lake, N.W.T.	Harold B. Van Hoy	Harold B. Van Hoy	1986	25
346 2/8	50	53	38 3/8	5 2/8	5 7/8	16	10 7/8	12 5/8	1/8	13	15	Obstruction Rapids, N.W.T.	Fred H. Palmer	Fred H. Palmer	1988	26
346 1/8	47 3/8	49 7/8	42 1/8	4 4/8	4 6/8	14	1 7/8	9 1/8	1/8	17	17	Courageous Lake, N.W.T.	Glenn St. Charles	Glenn St. Charles	1987	27
345 3/8	49	52 5/8	37 3/8	5 5/8	5 5/8	19 1/8	2 7/8	14 1/8	1/8	13	14	Rendez-vous Lake, N.W.T.	David P. Jacobson	David P. Jacobson	1988	28
398 1/8 *	52 3/8	52 1/8	34 3/8	5	5	16 5/8	16 5/8	12 4/8	12 5/8	20	19	Lac de Gras, N.W.T.	Glen P. Rupe	Glen P. Rupe	1987	
395 5/8 *	52 7/8	51 5/8	33 3/8	5 4/8	5 4/8	16 4/8	18 4/8	12	9 3/8	16	20	Lac de Gras, N.W.T.	David H. Christman, Jr.	David H. Christman Jr.	1987	
394 3/8 *	49 3/8	49 6/8	28 1/8	5 5/8	5 2/8	14 4/8	18 5/8	13 3/8	19 1/8	23	22	Rendez-vous Lake, N.W.T.	John P. Poston	John P. Poston	1986	
392 1/8 *	50 5/8	53	45 1/8	5 1/8	5 1/8	17 2/8	18	2 6/8	14 4/8	15	18	MacKay Lake, N.W.T.	Alfred E. Journey	Alfred E. Journey	1988	
391 7/8 *	54 2/8	52 6/8	41 4/8	5 5/8	6 1/8	16 6/8	17 7/8	2	15	14	17	Providence Lake, N.W.T.	Bert Varkonyi	Bert Varkonyi	1986	
391 5/8 *	50 7/8	48	34	5 3/8	5 2/8	14 2/8	16 5/8	7 5/8	8 2/8	17	22	Lac de Gras, N.W.T.	Donald P. Lamm	Donald P. Lamm	1987	
390 5/8 *	54 2/8	55 5/8	37 1/8	5 3/8	5 3/8	14 2/8	13 2/8	9	8 2/8	18	17	Cape Dorset, N.W.T.	Randall J. Kiessel	Randall J. Kiessel	1986	
382 1/8 *	51 5/8	50 5/8	32 2/8	5 1/8	5	16 1/8	17 4/8	13 1/8	14 4/8	19	16	Courageous Lake, N.W.T.	Kevin J. McCormick	Kevin J. McCormick	1983	
376 5/8 *	49 5/8	48 4/8	35 5/8	5 3/8	6	6 5/8	13 3/8	1 5/8	11 4/8	20	22	Lac de Gras, N.W.T.	Raymond C. Hunt	Raymond C. Hunt	1987	
375 *	46 5/8	46 1/8	40 4/8	5 5/8	5 3/8	15 4/8	16	8 5/8	12 3/8	16	17	Courageous Lake, N.W.T.	Toby J. Johnson	Toby J. Johnson	1988	

371 7/8 *	45 1/8	44 5/8	28 1/8	5 4/8	6	15 2/8	12 4/8	12 2/8	2 6/8	15	15	Courageous Lake, N.W.T.	Robert C. Kaufman	Robert C. Kaufman	1984
366 2/8 *	43 4/8	43 5/8	28 6/8	4 6/8	4 6/8	15 2/8	16	13 3/8	12 3/8	24	20	Courageous Lake, N.W.T.	Toby J. Johnson	Toby J. Johnson	1987
365 3/8 *	44 3/8	44 3/8	27 5/8	5 2/8	5 2/8	13 4/8	12 7/8	10 5/8	10 4/8	23	23	Courageous Lake, N.W.T.	Lilly Pinkas	Lilly Pinkas	1987
365 1/8 *	47	49 4/8	32 1/8	5 1/8	5 1/8		18 2/8	15 4/8		16	20	Courageous Lake, N.W.T.	Frederick E. Haskell	Frederick E. Haskell	1987
364 7/8 *	46 3/8	44 5/8	34 5/8	5	4 6/8	13	15 4/8	6 6/8	11 1/8	12	13	Providence Lake, N.W.T.	Bert Varkonyi	Bert Varkonyi	1986
361 5/8 *	47 2/8	47 3/8	32 6/8	4 4/8	4 6/8	12	15 1/8	1 2/8	10 4/8	17	23	Courageous Lake, N.W.T.	Jack Lamb	Jack Lamb	1986
361 1/8 *	44 5/8	43	31 2/8	4 2/8	4 2/8	15 4/8	13 2/8	12 7/8	7 4/8	22	17	Lake Providence, N.W.T.	Grant M. St. Germaine	Grant M. St. Germaine	1988
358 5/8 *	45 6/8	46 6/8	31 2/8	6 3/8	6 4/8	13 1/8	2 7/8	10	1/8	13	15	Cape Dorset, N.W.T.	Ronald E. Gray	Ronald E. Gray	1985
356 2/8 *	49	48	31 5/8	7	7 5/8		13		10 5/8	17	23	Arctic Bay, N.W.T.	James E. Mockerman	James E. Mockerman	1987
356 2/8 *	52 4/8	52 5/8	38 1/8	4 7/8	4 5/8	13 3/8	16	1 3/8	12 5/8	13	13	Coppermine River, N.W.T.	Duane Schroh	Duane Schroh	1987
355 6/8 *	47	48 6/8	40 3/8	5 4/8	5 7/8	4	16 4/8	1/8	13 2/8	16	16	Warburton Bay, N.W.T.	Stanley Godfrey	Stanley Godfrey	1988
354 3/8 *	47 2/8	49	40 1/8	4 6/8	5 2/8	15 4/8	5 6/8	11 5/8	1/8	15	14	Lac de Gras, N.W.T.	Brooks Carmichael	Brooks Carmichael	1987
353 3/8 *	45 7/8	45 6/8	27 7/8	5	5	19 5/8	1 5/8	16 3/8	1/8	18	14	Courageous Lake, N.W.T.	Collins F. Kellogg	Collins F. Kellogg	1987
351 7/8 *	46 7/8	48 6/8	33 1/8	5 2/8	5 2/8	14 7/8	15 7/8	1 4/8	9 3/8	13	12	Point Lake, N.W.T.	Jeffrey M. Turner	Jeffrey M. Turner	1987

* Final Score subject to revision by additional verifying measurements.

Quebec-Labrador Caribou

Rangifer tarandus from Quebec and Labrador

Minimum Score 365   World's Record 474-6/8

Score	Length of Main Beam R.	L.	Inside Spread	Circumference at Smallest Place Between Brow and Bez Points R.	L.	Length of Brow Points R.	L.	Width of Brow Points R.	L.	Number of Points R.	L.	Locality Killed	By Whom Killed	Owner	Date Killed	Rank
433 2/8	46 5/8	44 2/8	41 1/8	5 1/8	5 5/8	20 1/8	20 3/8	14 5/8	17 7/8	22	24	Lake Otelnuk, Que.	Robert E. McNeill	Robert E. McNeill	1986	1
431 5/8	53 1/8	56	46 1/8	5 5/8	5 5/8	16 5/8	20 5/8	3 5/8	15 1/8	19	18	Tunulik River, Que.	Carol A. Mauch	Carol A. Mauch	1984	2
427	56 1/8	57 5/8	48 2/8	6 5/8	6 5/8	16 5/8	14 7/8	14 6/8	2 7/8	21	13	Ungava Bay, Que.	David Walker	David Walker	1984	3
408	55 7/8	55 1/8	44 6/8	5	5 3/8	18 3/8	19 1/8	17 7/8	16 6/8	20	23	Caniapiscau River, Que.	Bernard W. Masino	Bernard W. Masino	1987	4
406 2/8	49	49	48 7/8	4 6/8	4 6/8	5 2/8	22 2/8	1/8	16 6/8	20	22	Caniapiscau River, Que.	Michael R. Miggins	Michael R. Miggins	1987	5
406	45 6/8	44 3/8	43 2/8	4 6/8	4 5/8	16 3/8	19 3/8	14 5/8	15 5/8	25	18	Narcy Lake, Que.	Thomas A. Rue	Thomas A. Rue	1988	6
403 3/8	54 3/8	54 2/8	41 5/8	5 5/8	5 3/8	18 3/8	11 3/8	14 7/8	1/8	20	17	Caniapiscau River, Que.	Bernard W. Masino	Bernard W. Masino	1987	7
403	47 7/8	45 1/8	35 5/8	5 5/8	5 2/8	11 6/8	17 4/8	3 5/8	14 6/8	21	28	Caniapiscau River, Que.	Barbara A. Shuler	Barbara A. Shuler	1985	8
402 6/8	56 4/8	54	47	5	5	1	19 7/8	1/8	16 6/8	28	20	Kuujjuaq, Que.	John T. Richards, Jr.	John T. Richards, Jr.	1986	9
401 3/8	57 1/8	57 5/8	48 5/8	5 2/8	5 3/8	20	19	15 3/8	9 2/8	19	17	Koksoak River, Que.	Arthur J. Pelon	Arthur J. Pelon	1986	10
400 3/8	56 5/8	53 1/8	47 3/8	6	9 1/8	17 3/8	16 6/8	9 3/8	11	21	18	Pons River, Que.	Charles E. Putt	Charles E. Putt	1988	11
400 1/8	51 1/8	51 1/8	51 1/8	5	5	18 5/8	19 2/8	15 5/8	15 7/8	22	22	Pons River, Que.	Ronald L. Boucher	Ronald L. Boucher	1986	12
400	53	50 4/8	54	5 3/8	5 2/8	12 4/8	18 4/8	1/8	13 7/8	11	21	Fort Chimo, Que.	Elwood Larsen	Elwood Larsen	1986	13
399 3/8	55 7/8	53 5/8	48 6/8	6 1/8	6 4/8	17 7/8	15 7/8	5 7/8	8 4/8	27	20	Pons River, Que.	Robert L. Smock	Gary R. Smock	1986	14
398 3/8	54 7/8	53	49	5 2/8	5 2/8	19 4/8	17 5/8	16 2/8	1 7/8	18	17	Tunulik River, Que.	Anthony L. Pinnavaia, Sr.	Anthony L. Pinnavaia, Sr.	1987	15
397 7/8	53 3/8	54 4/8	49 3/8	5 4/8	5 5/8	18			14 3/8	14	21	Caniapiscau River, Que.	John R. Connelly	John R. Connelly	1988	16
397 4/8	48 1/8	51 2/8	38 5/8	5 6/8	5 7/8	19 2/8	17 7/8	8	12 6/8	20	22	Serigny River, Que.	Gary A. Perin	Gary A. Perin	1987	17
396 3/8	53 1/8	52	38 5/8	5 1/8	5 1/8	19 3/8	16 3/8	14 2/8	1	21	18	Pons River, Que.	Glenn M. Smith	Glenn M. Smith	1986	18
394	54 2/8	51 6/8	48	6	5 5/8	5	18	4/8	15 2/8	13	21	Ungava Bay, Que.	Nancy J. Alward	Nancy J. Alward	1988	19
392 4/8	52 4/8	53 4/8	44 7/8	5 2/8	5 2/8	18 5/8	17 3/8	12 2/8	1/8	16	14	Caniapiscau River, Que.	Michael E. Ingold	Michael E. Ingold	1988	20
392 3/8	51 4/8	51 2/8	44 6/8	4 6/8	4 6/8	1 5/8	14 6/8	1/8	12 6/8	19	19	Baleine River, Que.	John D. Sheaffer	John D. Sheaffer	1988	21
389 1/8	51 2/8	50 6/8	40 4/8	7 4/8	6 7/8	4	14 2/8		10 5/8	16	16	Tunulic River, Que.	George Dempsey	George Dempsey	1987	22
388 4/8	52 7/8	52 5/8	58 1/8	5 5/8	5 5/8	17 4/8	14 4/8	12 1/8	10	18	17	Koksoak River, Que.	Charlie D. Todd	Charlie D. Todd	1987	23
388	55	54 5/8	53	5 2/8	5 2/8	21 5/8	18 3/8	6 5/8	1/8	15	12	Caniapiscau River, Que.	Henry O. Fromm	Henry O. Fromm	1987	24
387 7/8	52 2/8	51 4/8	42 2/8	6 2/8	6 1/8	12 5/8	17 4/8	1	13 1/8	21	17	George River, Que.	Michael Yeck	Michael Yeck	1985	25
387 6/8	53 4/8	52 1/8	55 1/8	5 3/8	5 3/8	2 5/8	15	1/8	17	17	22	George River, Que.	John Downing	John Downing	1987	25
387 6/8	52 1/8	53 3/8	37 4/8	5 5/8	5 5/8	18	18 2/8	13	6 2/8	23	23	Ungava Bay, Que.	Fred N. Huston, Sr.	Fred N. Huston, Sr.	1987	27
387 5/8	53 2/8	56	53	5 2/8	5 2/8		14 5/8		12 6/8	14	19	Ungava Bay, Que.	Phil N. Alward	Phil N. Alward	1988	28
387 4/8	42 2/8	39 5/8	47 1/8	5 4/8	5 4/8	15 5/8	17 2/8	11 7/8	13 2/8	27	18	Delay River, Que.	Larry E. Smith	Larry E. Smith	1987	29
387 3/8	54 2/8	53 4/8	61 1/8	5 5/8	5 1/8	17 5/8		14 6/8		17	12	Tunulik Lake, Que.	Jay G. St. Charles	Jay G. St. Charles	1986	30

Score												Locality	Hunter	Date	Rank
385 5/8	46 5/8	48	48 1/8	5 1/8	5 1/8	19 3/8	18 5/8	10 3/8	11 5/8	20	14	George River, Que.	David G. Noble	1986	31
384 4/8	50 4/8	52 1/8	48	5 5/8	5 4/8		12 5/8		7 5/8	19	19	Abloviak Fiord, Que.	Brian L. Dam	1986	32
384 4/8	46 5/8	46 5/8	42 4/8	4 7/8	5	16	17 5/8	7	10 5/8	18	19	Baleine River, Que.	Elmer R. Luce, Jr.	1987	32
384 2/8	45 2/8	46 6/8	49	5 5/8	5 4/8		15 1/8		8 5/8	19	23	Baleine River, Que.	Elmer R. Luce, Jr.	1987	34
383 5/8	51 4/8	52 5/8	53 6/8	5 1/8	5 3/8	18 5/8	15 1/8	13 4/8	1 1/8	16	13	Ungava Bay, Que.	Fred S. DeHaan	1986	35
382 3/8	48 1/8	50 5/8	45 5/8	6 5/8	5 7/8	15 5/8	17 5/8	12 3/8	13 5/8	16	24	Wayne Lake, Que.	Timothy D. Gildersleeve	1987	36
381 7/8	59	55 7/8	53 5/8	5 1/8	5 1/8	1 7/8	19 5/8	1/8	16 1/8	13	16	Nullualuk Lake, Que.	Walter J. Manning	1988	37
381 6/8	47 5/8	48 2/8	45 5/8	5 2/8	5 2/8	16 5/8	16 3/8	6 4/8	8	23	22	Indian Lake, Que.	Donald A. Lawrence	1987	38
381 6/8	51 2/8	51 1/8	41 5/8	5 1/8	5 2/8	18 5/8	14 2/8	11 4/8	10	19	18	Ungava Bay, Que.	James B. Wessinger	1987	38
381 2/8	51 5/8	54 4/8	45 5/8	5 4/8	5 4/8	9	17 5/8	1	12 5/8	19	25	Caniapiscau River, Que.	Donald P. Travis	1986	40
381 1/8	48 3/8	49 1/8	53 2/8	4 4/8	4 5/8	19 4/8	18 2/8	13 2/8	15	17	21	Tudor Lake, Que.	Collins F. Kellogg, Jr.	1970	41
381 1/8	56	53 3/8	47 2/8	6	5 5/8	16 4/8	2	8 4/8	1/8	17	15	Koksoak River, Que.	Arthur J. Pelon	1984	41
380 7/8	54 4/8	55 5/8	49 4/8	5 7/8	5 3/8	15 1/8	19 4/8	1/8	15 3/8	16	18	Tunulik River, Que.	Joseph P. Toth	1986	43
380 5/8	51 7/8	51 3/8	47 5/8	5 4/8	5 3/8	14 4/8	18 5/8	4 4/8	12 5/8	18	19	Lake Gerido, Que.	Dan D. Boy	1987	44
379 7/8	49 7/8	46 5/8	44 7/8	5 1/8	5	14	18 3/8	13 7/8	1/8	11	17	Serigny River, Que.	Gary A. Perin	1987	45
379 6/8	49 4/8	49 5/8	42 5/8	5 5/8	5 2/8	19 6/8	19 4/8	10	11 1/8	17	14	Long Lake, Que.	Ted K. Jaycox	1986	46
379 5/8	45 6/8	47	44 4/8	5 1/8	5 1/8	18 5/8	2 2/8	13	1/8	18	19	Caniapiscau River, Que.	John W. Czerwinski	1987	46
378 4/8	54 5/8	53 5/8	40	6	5 5/8	19	17 3/8	17 7/8	3 4/8	18	12	Ungava Bay, Que.	James B. Wessinger	1987	48
377 7/8	51	49 7/8	40 4/8	5 3/8	5 5/8	19 5/8	11 2/8	17 4/8	1 2/8	16	14	Ungava Bay, Que.	Joseph Mannino	1985	49
377 3/8	51 4/8	49 5/8	43 1/8	5 7/8	5 7/8	3 4/8	15 1/8	1/8	12 4/8	13	14	Ungava Bay, Que.	Arlo J. Spiess	1985	50
376	50 3/8	50 3/8	44	5 4/8	5 5/8	18	16	13 5/8	6	19	15	Lake Patu, Que.	Burnell R. Kauffman	1985	51
375 1/8	56 4/8	56 1/8	55 3/8	5 1/8	5 4/8	14 4/8		15 5/8		23	16	Ungava Bay, Que.	Ronald R. Pomery	1986	52
375	48 7/8	52 7/8	40	5 2/8	5	17	16 4/8	14 4/8	16	23	20	Ungava Bay, Que.	Glenn M. Smith	1986	53
375	50 4/8	50 7/8	52 2/8	5 1/8	5 2/8	16 2/8	18 2/8	6 4/8	13 2/8	11	11	Caniapiscau River, Que.	Ronald Hurlburt	1987	53
373 3/8	46 5/8	46 4/8	41 5/8	5 2/8	5 1/8	16 7/8	16 5/8	11	10 1/8	16	14	Serigny River, Que.	Gary R. Lawrence	1987	55
371	55 5/8	57 2/8	43 2/8	5 4/8	5 5/8		17 5/8		15 1/8	13	21	Ungava Bay, Que.	Brenton Morgenstern	1986	56
366 3/8	56 2/8	58	44	5 3/8	5 3/8	19 4/8		15 5/8		16	10	Doreen Lake, Que.	Douglas D. Meier	1987	57
365 5/8	50	51 1/8	41	5	5 1/8	15	17 5/8	9 1/8	11	16	14	Ungava Bay, Que.	David G. Kidder	1987	58
365 2/8	56	54 3/8	43 1/8	5 4/8	5 5/8	2 3/8	16 5/8	1/8	10 3/8	14	16	Ford Lake, Que.	William H. Moyer	1986	58
427 1/8 *	61	61 3/8	54 2/8	6 4/8	5 2/8	21 4/8	22 2/8	12	10 4/8	15	15	Lake Nachicapau, Que.	Charles L. Buechel, Jr.	1987	59

* Final Score subject to revision by additional verifying measurements.

Pronghorn

Antilocapra americana americana and related subspecies

Minimum Score 80   World's Record 93-4/8

Score	Length of Horn R.	Length of Horn L.	Circumference of Base R.	Circumference of Base L.	Circumference at Third Quarter R.	Circumference at Third Quarter L.	Inside Spread	Tip to Tip Spread	Length of Prong R.	Length of Prong L.	Locality Killed	By Whom Killed	Owner	Date Killed	Rank
90 6/8	17 5/8	17 5/8	7 1/8	6 7/8	3 4/8	3 4/8	9 5/8	3 4/8	5 4/8	5 2/8	Catron Co., N.M.	John P. Grimmett	John P. Grimmett	1986	1
89 6/8	18 2/8	18	7	6 7/8	3	2 7/8	9 7/8	3 3/8	6 3/8	6 3/8	Coconino Co., Ariz.	James W. Barrett	James W. Barrett	1987	2
89 4/8	17 7/8	17 7/8	7 7/8	8 1/8	3 3/8	3 2/8	10 4/8	5	5 3/8	5 4/8	Uintah Co., Utah	Charles A. Grimmett	Charles A. Grimmett	1988	3
89 2/8	17 2/8	17 2/8	6 6/8	6 6/8	2 7/8	3	12 2/8	4 4/8	5 7/8	5 5/8	Cochise Co., Ariz.	Rene J. Dube, Jr.	Rene J. Dube, Jr.	1985	4
89 2/8	16 3/8	16 3/8	7	6 7/8	3	2 7/8	9 5/8	6 6/8	7 5/8	6 7/8	Hudspeth Co., Texas	Jack E. Beal	Jack E. Beal	1987	4
89	16 1/8	16	7 3/8	7 4/8	3	2 7/8	11 2/8	8	6 5/8	7 1/8	Sweetwater Co., Wyo.	Willis E. Haines	Willis E. Haines	1985	6
88 5/8	18	17 7/8	6 6/8	6 5/8	2 5/8	2 4/8	15 4/8	11 5/8	6 7/8	6 3/8	Washoe Co., Nev.	Bruce L. Zeller	Bruce L. Zeller	1986	7
88 5/8	16 4/8	16 5/8	7 5/8	7 4/8	2 6/8	3	8 4/8	4 7/8	5 6/8	5 5/8	White Pine Co., Nev.	William W. Diekmann	William W. Diekmann	1987	7
88 5/8	18 4/8	18 4/8	7 7/8	7 6/8	2 5/8	2 5/8	12	12	4 6/8	4 4/8	Brewster Co., Texas	John W. Houchins	John W. Houchins	1988	7
88 4/8	18	17 5/8	6 4/8	6 4/8	2 5/8	2 5/8	13 2/8	8	6 4/8	6 2/8	Coconino Co., Ariz.	Randall W. Smith	Randall W. Smith	1985	10
88 4/8	16 5/8	16 2/8	7	6 7/8	3 4/8	3 2/8	8	2 1/8	5 5/8	5 7/8	Catron Co., N.M.	Doug W. Kasey	Doug W. Kasey	1987	10
88 4/8	17 7/8	17 7/8	6 6/8	6 6/8	2 7/8	3	13 7/8	8	5 5/8	5	Yavapai Co., Ariz.	Arthur C. Savoini	Arthur C. Savoini	1988	10
88	17 1/8	16 1/8	7 4/8	6 5/8	3	2 7/8	8 3/8	6 6/8	7 4/8	7 3/8	Hudspeth Co., Texas	Gibson D. Lewis	Gibson D. Lewis	1986	13
88	17 1/8	17 4/8	7 1/8	7	2 6/8	2 6/8	14 1/8	9	5 7/8	6 1/8	Chaves Co., N.M.	Grant L. Perry	Grant L. Perry	1988	13
87 7/8	17 3/8	17 5/8	6 6/8	6 6/8	2 5/8	2 4/8	14 4/8	9 5/8	5 5/8	6	Coconino Co., Ariz.	Thomas R. Roberts	Thomas R. Roberts	1986	15
87 5/8	16 2/8	16 3/8	7	6 7/8	3 2/8	3	8 3/8	4 1/8	5 4/8	5 4/8	Socorro Co., N.M.	Enoch D. Brandenburg	Enoch D. Brandenburg	1987	16
87 4/8	16 7/8	16 5/8	6 6/8	6 6/8	2 6/8	2 7/8	11 7/8	7 2/8	6 1/8	6 1/8	Mora Co., N.M.	Anthony J. Garrett	Anthony J. Garrett	1987	16
87 2/8	16 5/8	17	7	7	2 7/8	3	13 6/8	10	5 5/8	5 5/8	Chaves Co., N.M.	Charles A. Grimmett	Charles A. Grimmett	1988	18
86 7/8	16 5/8	17 3/8	6 7/8	6 7/8	2 4/8	2 4/8	15 3/8	9 6/8	6 6/8	6 6/8	South Dakota	Unknown	Daniel E. McBride	1940 pr	19
86 6/8	17 1/8	17	7	7	2 6/8	2 7/8	12 4/8	11 2/8	5 1/8	5 1/8	Catron Co., N.M.	John H. Bevel	John H. Bevel	1986	19
86 6/8	15 5/8	15 5/8	7 7/8	7 7/8	2 7/8	2 6/8	11	7 7/8	6 2/8	6 1/8	Carbon Co., Wyo.	Troy T. Hall	Troy T. Hall	1987	19
86 6/8	16 7/8	16 7/8	6 6/8	6 7/8	3 2/8	3 1/8	8 5/8	4 3/8	5	5 5/8	Hudspeth Co., Texas	Peter L. Bright	Peter L. Bright	1988	19
86 4/8	15 7/8	15 7/8	7 2/8	7 2/8	2 5/8	2 5/8	12 6/8	9	5 5/8	5 3/8	Catron Co., N.M.	H. James Tonkin, Jr.	H. James Tonkin, Jr.	1987	23
86 2/8	15 1/8	15 1/8	7 5/8	7 4/8	2 5/8	2 5/8	10 6/8	10 1/8	7	6 6/8	Sweetwater Co., Wyo.	Kurt A. Mari	Kurt A. Mari	1988	24
86	16	16	6 5/8	6 7/8	2 4/8	2 4/8	10 4/8	7	6 7/8	6 6/8	McCone Co., Mont.	Danny L. Curtiss	Danny L. Curtiss	1983	25
86	17	17 1/8	6 3/8	6 4/8	2 4/8	2 3/8		7 4/8	6 3/8	6 2/8	De Baca Co., N.M.	Bennie F. Hromadka	Bennie F. Hromadka	1985	25
86	15 2/8	15	7 3/8	7 4/8	2 7/8	2 6/8	12 6/8	8 1/8	6 2/8	6 3/8	Coconino Co., Ariz.	John S. Harrison	John S. Harrison	1986	25
85 7/8	16 3/8	16 3/8	6 6/8	6 6/8	3	3	17	15 3/8	6 2/8	6 1/8	Yavapai Co., Ariz.	Vincent J. Conti	Vincent J. Conti	1986	28
85 5/8	15 7/8	16 1/8	7 7/8	7 6/8	3	2 6/8	12 6/8	9 3/8	6 2/8	6 2/8	Navajo Co., Ariz.	C. Boyd Austin	C. Boyd Austin	1987	29
85 4/8	16 5/8	16 5/8	6 7/8	7 2/8	2 6/8	2 6/8	9 3/8	4 1/8	5 4/8	6 1/8	Yavapai Co., Ariz.	Steven C. Dunn	Steven C. Dunn	1987	30
85 4/8	17 2/8	17 2/8	6 6/8	6 7/8	2 7/8	2 7/8	17 2/8	13 4/8	5 1/8	5 3/8	Washoe Co., Nev.	Peter K. Beers	Peter K. Beers	1988	30
85 2/8	17 1/8	17 2/8	6 6/8	6 4/8	2 7/8	2 6/8	7 1/8	2 2/8	6 4/8	6 2/8	Emery Co., Utah	Marvin L. Thayn	Marvin L. Thayn	1986	32

Score							Location	Hunter	Owner	Date	Rank
85 2/8	16	18	6 6/8	6 6/8	2 7/8	2 7/8	13	9 2/8	5 7/8	6	Socorro Co., N.M.	L. Steve Waide	L. Steve Waide	1986	32
85	16 5/8	16 2/8	7 3/8	7	3 2/8	3 2/8	16 3/8	14 3/8	5	4 2/8	Carbon Co., Wyo.	Toby J. Johnson	Toby J. Johnson	1988	34
85	17 3/8	18	6	5 7/8	2 6/8	2 6/8	17	13 7/8	5 5/8	5 5/8	Hudspeth Co., Texas	Ronnie L. Hinze	Ronnie L. Hinze	1988	34
84 7/8	15 1/8	16 1/8	7 7/8	7 4/8	2 7/8	3	18 2/8	17 1/8	5 4/8	5 4/8	Ochiltree Co., Texas	Wayne Blue	Wayne Blue	1988	36
84 6/8	16 3/8	16 2/8	6 4/8	6 4/8	3	3	9 3/8	4 2/8	5 2/8	5 3/8	Carbon Co., Wyo.	Paul Herring	Paul Herring	1983	37
84 6/8	16 7/8	17 2/8	6 5/8	6 3/8	3	3 2/8	16 5/8	11 3/8	7 1/8	5	Hudspeth Co., Texas	Charles E. Davis	Charles E. Davis	1986	37
84 6/8	16	16 1/8	6 6/8	6 6/8	3 1/8	3 1/8	8 6/8	6	4 7/8	5	Hudspeth Co., Texas	Charles D. Tuttle	Charles D. Tuttle	1986	37
84 6/8	15 4/8	16 2/8	7 2/8	7 1/8	2 6/8	2 4/8	11 7/8	7 7/8	6	6 3/8	Mora Co., N.M.	William P. Boone	William P. Boone	1987	37
84 4/8	16	16 7/8	7 2/8	7 4/8	2 4/8	2 5/8	8 4/8	4 4/8	5 5/8	5 5/8	Natrona Co., Wyo.	Joe L. Ficken	Joe L. Ficken	1985	41
84 4/8	17 3/8	17 3/8	6 1/8	6 2/8	2 5/8	2 4/8	7 3/8	1 7/8	5 1/8	5 5/8	Emery Co., Utah	Bruce Gordon	Bruce Gordon	1986	41
84 4/8	16 4/8	16 5/8	6 7/8	6 7/8	2 6/8	2 7/8	8 3/8	4	5 1/8	5 7/8	Sweetwater Co., Wyo.	Mike D. McKell	Mike D. McKell	1986	41
84 4/8	16 1/8	16 5/8	7	7	2 6/8	2 6/8	7 3/8	2 5/8	4 6/8	5 1/8	Prairie Co., Mont.	Duane R. Pisk	Duane R. Pisk	1988	41
84 2/8	16	16	7 4/8	7 3/8	2 5/8	2 5/8	13 5/8	12	4 6/8	4 2/8	Washoe Co., Nev.	Eugene E. Belli	Eugene E. Belli	1986	45
84 2/8	16 3/8	16 2/8	7	7	2 3/8	2 5/8	12	7 2/8	6 2/8	6 6/8	Yellowstone Co., Mont.	Jim B. Cherpeski	Jim B. Cherpeski	1986	45
84 2/8	14 5/8	14 2/8	6 7/8	6 7/8	2 6/8	2 6/8	7 2/8	6 7/8	6 6/8	6 6/8	Carter Co., Mont.	Robert Cunningham	Robert Cunningham	1986	45
84 2/8	15 2/8	15 1/8	6 1/8	6	2 1/8	2 2/8	11 3/8	7 2/8	5 5/8	6 1/8	Baker Co., Oreg.	Paul W. Schon	Paul W. Schon	1987	45
84 2/8	16 4/8	18 2/8	6 2/8	6 1/8	2 5/8	2 6/8	11 1/8	6 5/8	6 1/8	6 1/8	Coconino Co., Ariz.	Kevin B. Call	Kevin B. Call	1987	45
84 2/8	17	16 7/8	6 2/8	6 1/8	2 7/8	2 6/8	13 1/8	7 3/8	6 1/8	6 1/8	Hudspeth Co., Ariz.	Sam H. Gann IV	Sam H. Gann IV	1988	45
84	15 2/8	15 3/8	6 2/8	6 3/8	2 4/8	2 6/8	12 3/8	8	7 1/8	7 2/8	Campbell Co., Wyo.	Unknown	J. Michael Conoyer	1986	51
84	16 3/8	16 1/8	7 2/8	7 2/8	2 6/8	2 6/8	10	6 3/8	5 7/8	5 3/8	Lake Co., Oreg.	Del J. Desart	Del J. Desart	1986	51 pr
84	16 3/8	16 1/8	6 7/8	6 6/8	2 5/8	2 4/8	11	5 4/8	6	6	Lassen Co., Calif.	Al J. Accurso, Jr.	Al J. Accurso, Jr.	1986	51
84	16 3/8	16 3/8	6 5/8	6 6/8	2 7/8	3 1/8	14 7/8	16 6/8	5 5/8	6 1/8	Yavapai Co., Ariz.	James K. McCasland	James K. McCasland	1987	51
84	14 2/8	14 4/8	7	7 1/8	3 1/8	3 2/8	11 1/8	7 3/8	5 4/8	5 3/8	Colfax Co., N.M.	Ruel T. Holt	Ruel T. Holt	1988	51
84	16 1/8	16 3/8	6 2/8	6 2/8	2 4/8	2 4/8	16 5/8	13	6	7	Hudspeth Co., Texas	W. Wayne Spahn	W. Wayne Spahn	1988	51
83 6/8	15 4/8	15 4/8	7 3/8	7 4/8	2 2/8	2 2/8	13 1/8	9 6/8	6 2/8	5 5/8	Colfax Co., N.M.	LeGrand C. Kirby III	LeGrand C. Kirby III	1986	57
83 6/8	16 1/8	15 7/8	6 5/8	6 4/8	2 5/8	2 4/8	15 2/8	11 5/8	6 3/8	6	Catron Co., N.M.	Charles A. Grimmett	Charles A. Grimmett	1986	57
83 6/8	16 6/8	16 5/8	6 6/8	6 4/8	2 5/8	2 6/8	13 3/8	10	5 5/8	5 2/8	De Baca Co., N.M.	Ben L. Mueller	Ben L. Mueller	1986	57
83 6/8	14 7/8	15	7 5/8	7 5/8	2 7/8	2 6/8	9 4/8	7	6 2/8	6 6/8	Fremont Co., Wyo.	Carl N. Anderson	Carl N. Anderson	1987	57
83 6/8	14 3/8	14 3/8	6 1/8	6 4/8	2 7/8	2 6/8	7	3 3/8	5 7/8	5 5/8	Carbon Co., Wyo.	Thomas D. Widiker	Thomas D. Widiker	1987	57
83 4/8	16 4/8	16 5/8	6 1/8	6	3 2/8	3 2/8	12 4/8	9 1/8	5 2/8	5 2/8	Mora Co., N.M.	Brent Arrant	Brent Arrant	1986	62
83 2/8	16	16 2/8	6 4/8	6 3/8	3 1/8	3 1/8	9 5/8	3 3/8	4 4/8	4 3/8	Lincoln Co., Nev.	Linda P. Allen	Linda P. Allen	1985	63
83 2/8	18	17 7/8	6 3/8	6 3/8	2 3/8	3	10 3/8	3 4/8	4 2/8	6	Cochise Co., Ariz.	Neil G. Sutherland II	Neil G. Sutherland II	1986	63
83 2/8	16 5/8	16 7/8	6 3/8	6 3/8	3 1/8	3	9 3/8	3 1/8	4 7/8	4 1/8	Sweetwater Co., Wyo.	Rob M. Knight	Rob M. Knight	1987	63
83	15 5/8	15 4/8	7 1/8	7 1/8	2 6/8	2 6/8	6 6/8	1 2/8	5 4/8	5 5/8	Sweetwater Co., Wyo.	Clifford Rockhold	Clifford Rockhold	1985	66
83	15 5/8	15 4/8	6 6/8	6 5/8	3	2 7/8	11 7/8	7 7/8	5 5/8	5 5/8	Fremont Co., Wyo.	Thomas A. Dremel	Thomas A. Dremel	1985	66
83	16 5/8	17 2/8	7 1/8	7 2/8	2 6/8	3	15 3/8	13 5/8	4 5/8	4 5/8	Humboldt Co., Nev.	Lenda Z. Azcarate	Lenda Z. Azcarate	1986	66
83	15 5/8	16	7 5/8	7 2/8	2 4/8	2 4/8	13 4/8	10 4/8	4 7/8	5	Baker Co., Oreg.	Richard R. Mason	Richard R. Mason	1986	66
83	16 5/8	16 5/8	6 6/8	6 6/8	2 6/8	2 6/8	11 7/8	7 7/8	5 2/8	5 5/8	Manyberries, Alta.	Richard Bishop	Richard Bishop	1986	66
83	15 5/8	15 3/8	6 6/8	6 6/8	2 5/8	2 5/8	13 3/8	10 1/8	5 3/8	5 5/8	Modoc Co., Calif.	Rae E. Cervo	Rae E. Cervo	1986	66
83	15 5/8	15 7/8	7 2/8	7	2 6/8	2 6/8	11 7/8	9 4/8	5 7/8	5 5/8	Natrona Co., Wyo.	Gerald Utrup	Gerald Utrup	1986	66
83	15 1/8	15	7	7 1/8	2 6/8	2 6/8	9 3/8	7	5 5/8	5 4/8	Washoe Co., Nev.	Christopher T. Rores	Christopher T. Rores	1987	66
83	15 3/8	15 2/8	6 4/8	6 4/8	3 1/8	3	8	3	5 5/8	5	Washoe Co., Nev.	Edward J. Smith	Edward J. Smith	1987	66

Pronghorn - *Continued*

Score	Length of Horn R.	Length of Horn L.	Circumference of Base R.	Circumference of Base L.	Circumference at Third Quarter R.	Circumference at Third Quarter L.	Inside Spread	Tip to Tip Spread	Length of Prong R.	Length of Prong L.	Locality Killed	By Whom Killed	Owner	Date Killed	Rank
83	17 2/8	17 5/8	6	6	2 4/8	2 3/8	12 6/8	9	5 7/8	5 7/8	Catron Co., N.M.	Dan L. Harper	Dan L. Harper	1987	66
83	16 4/8	16 6/8	6 6/8	7	2 4/8	2 3/8	10 1/8	6	6 1/8	5 6/8	Emery Co., Utah	Dennis G. McElvain	Dennis G. McElvain	1987	66
83	17 1/8	17	6 4/8	6 4/8	3 2/8	3 2/8	12 1/8	8 6/8	3 7/8	4 4/8	Graham Co., Ariz.	Marvin R. Selke	Marvin R. Selke	1987	66
83	17 2/8	16 2/8	6 6/8	6 4/8	3 2/8	2 5/8	11 3/8	9 6/8	5 2/8	5 7/8	Moffat Co., Colo.	Marvin L. Shepard	Marvin L. Shepard	1987	66
83	15 7/8	15 6/8	7	7 1/8	2 6/8	2 6/8	8 5/8	4 2/8	5 2/8	5 1/8	Albany Co., Wyo.	Robert J. Miller	Robert J. Miller	1987	66
82 6/8	15 4/8	15 3/8	6 6/8	6 5/8	2 4/8	2 3/8	10 5/8	4 3/8	6 4/8	7 1/8	Yavapai Co., Ariz.	Roy T. Hume	Roy T. Hume	1985	80
82 6/8	15 7/8	15 5/8	7 2/8	7 3/8	2 2/8	2 3/8	14 5/8	10 6/8	6 2/8	6	Natrona Co., Wyo.	Michael L. Brownell	Michael L. Brownell	1985	80
82 6/8	16 6/8	16 7/8	7	6 7/8	2 5/8	2 5/8	13 3/8	8 4/8	5 3/8	5 5/8	Lake Co., Oreg.	Wayne W. Wingert	Wayne W. Wingert	1986	80
82 6/8	16 2/8	16 4/8	6 5/8	6 3/8	2 6/8	2 6/8	12 4/8	9 3/8	6 1/8	5 6/8	Larimer Co., Colo.	James D. Brink	James D. Brink	1986	80
82 6/8	15 2/8	15 3/8	7	7	2 5/8	2 6/8	8 5/8	3 2/8	5 7/8	6 1/8	Natrona Co., Wyo.	Tom Covert	Tom Covert	1987	80
82 6/8	16 2/8	16	6 3/8	6 4/8	2 4/8	2 5/8	10 7/8	8 1/8	6	6 2/8	Malheur Co., Oreg.	Terrence L. Vaughan	Terrence L. Vaughan	1988	80
82 6/8	16 1/8	15 4/8	6 2/8	6 2/8	2 5/8	2 4/8	12 4/8	8 2/8	6 2/8	6 6/8	Sweetwater Co., Wyo.	Roy D. Sessions	Roy D. Sessions	1988	80
82 4/8	16 4/8	16 4/8	6 3/8	6 3/8	2 6/8	2 6/8	11 2/8	5 6/8	5	5 4/8	Humboldt Co., Nev.	Frank K. Azcarate, Jr.	Frank K. Azcarate, Jr.	1985	87
82 4/8	16 4/8	16 6/8	6 5/8	6 3/8	3 1/8	3 2/8	12 1/8	7	4 7/8	4 7/8	Lassen Co., Calif.	Bob Freed	Bob Freed	1985	87
82 4/8	16	15 5/8	6 6/8	6 6/8	2 7/8	2 6/8	9	4	5 3/8	5 3/8	Rosebud Co., Mont.	Robert B. DeLattre	Robert B. DeLattre	1985	87
82 4/8	15	15	6 6/8	7	2 5/8	2 5/8	13 3/8	10 5/8	6 6/8	6 3/8	Saguache Co., Colo.	Michael J. Atwood, Sr.	Michael J. Atwood, Sr.	1986	87
82 4/8	15 3/8	15 3/8	7 1/8	7 2/8	2 4/8	2 6/8	11 5/8	7 4/8	5 2/8	4 7/8	Colfax Co., N.M.	John A. Jones	John A. Jones	1987	87
82 4/8	15 5/8	15 5/8	7	7	2 5/8	2 4/8	9 3/8	5	5 6/8	5 7/8	Campbell Co., Wyo.	Robert J. Anderson	Robert J. Anderson	1987	87
82 4/8	15 3/8	15 3/8	6 3/8	6 2/8	3	3	11	6 2/8	5 3/8	5 5/8	Yellowstone Co., Mont.	Jon J. Wilson	Jon J. Wilson	1988	87
82 2/8	18 2/8	18 7/8	6 3/8	6 2/8	2 2/8	2 5/8	9 5/8	5 5/8	5 2/8	4 7/8	Humboldt Co., Nev.	David E. Boyles, Sr.	David E. Boyles, Sr.	1984	94
82 2/8	15 4/8	16	6 6/8	6 4/8	2 5/8	2 6/8	13 4/8	12	6 4/8	6 4/8	Sweetwater Co., Wyo.	Carl Holland	William Holland	1984	94
82 2/8	15 2/8	15	7 1/8	7 1/8	3	2 7/8		5	5 2/8	4 7/8	Humboldt Co., Nev.	Andrew S. Burnett	Andrew S. Burnett	1986	94
82 2/8	15 2/8	15	7 3/8	7 4/8	2 7/8	2 7/8	10 2/8	7 6/8	5 4/8	4 6/8	Natrona Co., Wyo.	Steven N. Levin	Steven N. Levin	1986	94
82 2/8	16	15 7/8	6 5/8	6 4/8	3 1/8	3	11 1/8	9 3/8	4 7/8	4 4/8	Fergus Co., Mont.	Patricia M. Dreeszen	Patricia M. Dreeszen	1986	94
82 2/8	17	17 2/8	6 2/8	6 2/8	3 2/8	3 2/8	8 6/8	3 4/8	4 4/8	4 4/8	Torrance Co., N.M.	Michael F. Killoy	Michael F. Killoy	1987	94
82 2/8	16 5/8	16 4/8	6	6	2 6/8	2 6/8	11	6 7/8	5 5/8	5 6/8	Catron Co., N.M.	Harry J. Turiello	Harry J. Turiello	1987	94
82	16 2/8	16 1/8	6 1/8	6	2 6/8	2 7/8	8 2/8	5	6	5 6/8	Lake Co., Oreg.	Calvin M. Auvil	Calvin M. Auvil	1976	101
82	15 5/8	16 1/8	6 7/8	6 6/8	2 5/8	2 7/8	8 4/8	3	5 6/8	5 6/8	Carbon Co., Wyo.	James A. Rademacher	James A. Rademacher	1986	101
82	16 4/8	17	6 3/8	6 4/8	2 5/8	2 5/8	10 2/8	7 4/8	5 3/8	5	Johnson Co., Wyo.	Thomas F. Williams	Thomas F. Williams	1986	101
82	17 4/8	18	5 6/8	5 6/8	2 6/8	2 7/8	18	16 2/8	4 6/8	4 5/8	Graham Co., Ariz.	James P. Kniffin	James P. Kniffin	1987	101
82	16 1/8	16	6 6/8	6 5/8	2 4/8	2 4/8	11 6/8	7 5/8	6	5 3/8	Apache Co., Ariz.	Leonard J. Imperial	Leonard J. Imperial	1987	101
82	16 4/8	16 2/8	6 4/8	6 4/8	2 4/8	2 3/8	7 5/8	3 2/8	5 7/8	5 7/8	Sweetwater Co., Wyo.	Jeffrey A. Schalow	Jeffrey A. Schalow	1987	101
82	15 4/8	15 4/8	6 6/8	6 6/8	2 6/8	2 5/8	8 4/8	5 7/8	5 6/8	4 6/8	Alberta	Peter M. Parkyn	Peter M. Parkyn	1987	101
82	15 3/8	15 3/8	6 6/8	6 5/8	2 2/8	2 2/8	7 2/8	3 4/8	6 2/8	6 2/8	Elko Co., Nev.	Roger L. Curry	Roger L. Curry	1988	101

Score											Locality	Hunter	Year	Rank
82	14 2/8	14 3/8	7 2/8	7 2/8	2 5/8	2 6/8	9 3/8	5 4/8	5 7/8	5 3/8	Carbon Co., Wyo.	Donald L. Soderberg	1988	101
81 1/8	14 1/8	14 5/8	7 3/8	7 5/8	2 5/8	2 6/8	15 5/8	14 2/8	6 1/8	6	Converse Co., Wyo.	Barbara Moore	1987	110
81	15 4/8	15 4/8	6 3/8	6 2/8	2 4/8	2 3/8	11 7/8	7 6/8	6 6/8	6 1/8	Socorro Co., N.M.	Donald Reuter	1985	111
81	15 6/8	15 5/8	6 5/8	6 4/8	2 4/8	2 4/8	13 4/8	9	5 5/8	5	Colfax Co., N.M.	John J. Doherty	1987	111
80 6/8	16 4/8	16 2/8	6 5/8	6 4/8	3	2 5/8	17 2/8	17 2/8	4 7/8	4 7/8	Carbon Co., Wyo.	Harry G. Flock, Jr.	1981	113
80 6/8	17	16 3/8	6 2/8	6 1/8	2 6/8	2 5/8	12 1/8	6 7/8	5	5 1/8	Hudspeth Co., Texas	Mel Reichert	1986	113
80 6/8	15 4/8	15 4/8	7	6 6/8	2 6/8	2 5/8	11 7/8	9 5/8	5 2/8	5	Socorro Co., N.M.	Mark D. Nuessle	1987	113
80 6/8	16 3/8	16 3/8	6 4/8	6 3/8	2 7/8	2 7/8	11 7/8	8	5	5	Powder River Co., Mont.	John J. Landa	1988	113
80 4/8	16 4/8	16 5/8	6	5 6/8	2 5/8	2 4/8	9 1/8	2 5/8	6	6	Mohave Co., Ariz.	Charles A. Grimmett	1984	117
80 4/8	15	15	6 2/8	6 5/8	3 1/8	3	12 1/8	8	5 4/8	5 2/8	Catron Co., N.M.	Charles A. Grimmett	1987	117
80 4/8	15 3/8	15 2/8	6 4/8	6 4/8	2 5/8	2 5/8	10 4/8	6	6	5 5/8	Natrona Co., Wyo.	Richard O. Burns, Jr.	1979	119
80 2/8	16 1/8	16 3/8	6 2/8	6 2/8	2 7/8	3	10 5/8	6 4/8	3 3/8	3 7/8	Baker Co., Oreg.	Patrick M. Bruce	1988	119
80 2/8	14 6/8	14 3/8	6 4/8	6 4/8	2 6/8	2 5/8	11 2/8	7 6/8	5 5/8	5 5/8	Fergus Co., Mont.	Patricia M. Dreeszen	1988	119
80	17	16 7/8	6 4/8	6 4/8	2 3/8	2 3/8	12 3/8	9	4 6/8	5	Carbon Co., Wyo.	Stanley K. Ash	1987	122
80	17 3/8	16 7/8	6 2/8	6 2/8	2 7/8	2 7/8	9 5/8	3 7/8	3 5/8	3 7/8	Mora Co., N.M.	Michael E. Bailey	1987	122
80	15 6/8	15 5/8	6 2/8	6 2/8	3 1/8	3	9 2/8	2 7/8	4 5/8	4 4/8	Tooele Co., Utah	Jack F. Newman	1987	122
80	15 5/8	15 7/8	5 5/8	6	2 4/8	2 5/8	9 1/8	4 2/8	5 5/8	5 5/8	Chaves Co., N.M.	William T. Simmons	1987	122
91 2/8 *	16 2/8	16 4/8	7 4/8	7 4/8	3	3	13 4/8	9	6 6/8	6 4/8	Fremont Co., Wyo.	Bill E. Boatman	1988	

* Final Score subject to revision by additional verifying measurements.

Bison

Minimum Score 115 *Bison bison bison* and *Bison bison athabascae* World's Record 136-4/8

Trophies from the lower 48 states are acceptable only for records, not awards, and only from states that recognize bison as wild and free-ranging and for which a hunting license and/or big-game tag is required for hunting.

Score	Length of Horn R.	Length of Horn L.	Circumference of Base R.	Circumference of Base L.	Circumference at Third Quarter R.	Circumference at Third Quarter L.	Greatest Spread	Tip to Tip Spread	Locality Killed	By Whom Killed	Owner	Date Killed	Rank
125 4/8	19 6/8	19 5/8	14 7/8	14 6/8	6 3/8	5 7/8	31 5/8	25	Custer Co., S.D.	C. Brent Morgan	C. Brent Morgan	1986	1
124 2/8	19	18 4/8	14 4/8	14 4/8	6 6/8	6 7/8	30 6/8	24 4/8	Custer Co., S.D.	Robert D. Taylor	Robert D. Taylor	1986	2
123 6/8	19	17 7/8	16	16 1/8	5 4/8	5 6/8	29	22 3/8	Calais Lake, N.W.T.	Warren D. St. Germaine	Warren D. St. Germaine	1988	3
123 2/8	18 3/8	18 1/8	13 6/8	14 2/8	7 6/8	7 5/8	28	22 1/8	Garfield Co., Utah	Carl R. Albrecht	Carl R. Albrecht	1986	4
123 2/8	19	18 5/8	15 2/8	14 7/8	6 1/8	5 5/8	32	26 4/8	Chitina River, Alaska	Gerald H. Phillips	Gerald H. Phillips	1987	4
122 2/8	18 1/8	20 1/8	15 3/8	15 5/8	5 5/8	6 1/8	31 5/8	27	Lawrence Co., S.D.	Kenneth H. Jones	Kenneth H. Jones	1986	6
121	17 2/8	17 5/8	14 4/8	15 1/8	7	7 2/8	29 6/8	23 3/8	Park Co., Mont.	Dale K. Jackson	Dale K. Jackson	1986	7
120 4/8	17 5/8	17 2/8	14 6/8	15	7 4/8	7 3/8	30 4/8	26 3/8	Custer Co., S.D.	Dale L. Martin	Dale L. Martin	1983	8
120	18 4/8	19 3/8	15 3/8	15 5/8	5	5 3/8	31 2/8	27 6/8	Park Co., Mont.	Luke G. Eighorn	Luke G. Eighorn	1986	9
120	19 5/8	19 4/8	14 4/8	14 2/8	5	5	28 4/8	22 3/8	Wayne Co., Utah	Bryant S. Furness	Bryant S. Furness	1986	9
119 6/8	18 4/8	19 4/8	14 2/8	13 7/8	6 2/8	6 2/8	23 1/8	30 6/8	Custer Co., S.D.	Charles E. Ferguson	Charles E. Ferguson	1985	11
119 2/8	16 7/8	17 4/8	14 5/8	14 6/8	6 2/8	6 2/8	29 5/8	24 6/8	Custer Co., S.D.	Merlynn K. Jones	Merlynn K. Jones	1986	12
119 2/8	18 5/8	19	14 6/8	14 2/8	6 4/8	6 5/8	28 7/8	21 3/8	Custer Co., S.D.	John L. Van Horn	John L. Van Horn	1986	12
118 6/8	17 5/8	17 7/8	13 5/8	13 2/8	7	7 1/8	29 1/8	22 3/8	Copper River, Alaska	G. Michael Miller	G. Michael Miller	1988	14
118 4/8	20	19 4/8	14 5/8	14 3/8	5 1/8	4 6/8	27 5/8	20 2/8	Garfield Co., Utah	Robert B. Williams	Robert B. Williams	1986	15
118 2/8	20 2/8	20 2/8	14 2/8	14 3/8	4 6/8	5	26	14 6/8	Davis Co., Utah	Ronald J. Dallin	Ronald J. Dallin	1987	15
117 7/8	17 7/8	17 7/8	14 1/8	14 1/8	5 5/8	6	28 5/8	24 6/8	Park Co., Mont.	Donald E. Franklin	Donald E. Franklin	1986	17
117 6/8	16 6/8	16 3/8	15	14 6/8	6 1/8	5 1/8	27 3/8	23 1/8	Garfield Co., Utah	L. Scot Jenkins	L. Scot Jenkins	1987	17
117 2/8	19 1/8	18 6/8	14 2/8	14 6/8	5	4 7/8	27 5/8	18 4/8	Wayne Co., Utah	Tony K. Cross	Tony K. Cross	1987	17
117	19	18 4/8	13 6/8	14	6	6	28 4/8	19 6/8	Custer Co., S.D.	William E. Butler	William E. Butler	1986	20
115 6/8	19 6/8	19 4/8	13 4/8	13 3/8	5	5 1/8	32 1/8	25 7/8	Gerstle River, Alaska	Robert F. Wiese	Robert F. Wiese	1987	21
115 2/8	17	17 4/8	13 7/8	14	5 4/8	5 5/8	28 4/8	24 1/8	Garfield Co., Utah	Marsha Nickle	Marsha Nickle	1986	22
115	18 2/8	17 7/8	14	14	5 1/8	5	26	18	Garfield Co., Utah	LaMar K. Cox	LaMar K. Cox	1985	23

Rocky Mountain Goat

Oreamnos americanus americanus and related subspecies

Minimum Score 47 World's Record 56-6/8

Score	Length of Horn R.	L.	Circumference of Base R.	L.	Circumference at Third Quarter R.	L.	Greatest Spread	Tip to Tip Spread	Locality Killed	By Whom Killed	Owner	Date Killed	Rank
53 6/8	10 6/8	10 6/8	5 7/8	6	2	2	8 6/8	8	Sheslay River, B.C.	Dan Stobbe	Dan Stobbe	1987	1
53 4/8	10 4/8	10 6/8	6 2/8	6 1/8	2	2	8 5/8	8 1/8	Beggerlay Creek, B.C.	Joe Hamelink	Joe Hamelink	1986	2
53 2/8	10 3/8	10 3/8	5 7/8	6	2 1/8	2 1/8	7 6/8	7 2/8	Skeena River, B.C.	Robin B. Freeman	Robin B. Freeman	1985	3
53	11	10 7/8	5 7/8	5 5/8	2	1 7/8	10 1/8	9 3/8	Sheslay Mt., B.C.	Wallace E. Sills	Wallace E. Sills	1985	4
53	10 4/8	10 4/8	5 4/8	5 4/8	2	2	9 5/8	9 3/8	Tagish Lake, B.C.	Larry W. White	Larry W. White	1987	4
52 6/8	10 5/8	10 5/8	6	6	1 7/8	1 7/8	7 5/8	6	Foch Lake, B.C.	A.S. Griffin, Jr.	A.S. Griffin, Jr.	1985	6
52 6/8	11 3/8	11 2/8	5 5/8	5 5/8	1 7/8	1 6/8	8 5/8	7 3/8	Park Co., Colo.	Lyle K. Willmarth	Lyle K. Willmarth	1988	6
52 2/8	10 6/8	10 2/8	5 5/8	5 5/8	2	2	7 5/8	7 1/8	Bradfield Canal, Alaska	C. Wayne Treadway	C. Wayne Treadway	1988	8
52 2/8	10 6/8	10 5/8	5 5/8	5 5/8	1 7/8	1 7/8	7	6 3/8	Telegraph Creek, B.C.	Britt W. Wilson	Britt W. Wilson	1986	9
52	10 6/8	10 4/8	5 5/8	5 5/8	2	2	7 4/8	7 4/8	Old Tom Creek, B.C.	Dusty R. Cooper	Dusty R. Cooper	1986	9
51 6/8	10 3/8	10 2/8	5 5/8	5 5/8	1 7/8	1 7/8	7 3/8	7 1/8	Spatsizi Plateau, B.C.	Gary R. Schneider	Gary R. Schneider	1986	11
51 6/8	10 4/8	10 4/8	5 4/8	6	1 7/8	1 7/8	8	6 6/8	McGavin Creek, B.C.	Charles H. Menzer	Charles H. Menzer	1987	11
51 4/8	10 1/8	10 1/8	5 4/8	5 4/8	2 1/8	2 1/8	7 5/8	7 5/8	Little Oliver Creek, B.C.	JoAnn F. Flemming	JoAnn F. Flemming	1985	13
51 4/8	10 1/8	10 1/8	5 5/8	5 5/8	1 7/8	1 7/8	7 5/8	7 4/8	Gallatin Co., Mont.	Jack D. Yadon	Jack D. Yadon	1986	13
51 4/8	10 3/8	10 3/8	5 5/8	5 5/8	1 7/8	1 7/8	8 1/8	7 5/8	Taku River, B.C.	Bernard Sippin	Bernard Sippin	1987	13
51 4/8	11	10 6/8	5 5/8	5 5/8	2	1 7/8	7	6 3/8	Nass River, B.C.	Scott McDonald	Scott McDonald	1988	13
51 2/8	10	10 3/8	5 7/8	5 7/8	1 7/8	1 7/8	8 3/8	8 3/8	Tahltan River, B.C.	Wayne H. Kingsley	Wayne H. Kingsley	1988	13
51 2/8	10 6/8	10 3/8	5 4/8	5 4/8	2	2 1/8	8 4/8	8 3/8	Nass River, B.C.	Larry Zilinski	Larry Zilinski	1982	18
51 2/8	10 4/8	10 2/8	5 4/8	5 4/8	2	2	7	6 3/8	Mt. Guanton, B.C.	Charles R. McKinley	Charles R. McKinley	1986	18
51 2/8	10 1/8	10 1/8	5 6/8	5 4/8	1 7/8	1 7/8	6 1/8	6 6/8	Crown Mt., Alaska	Robert L. Hales	Robert L. Hales	1986	18
51	8 4/8	8 6/8	6	5 5/8	2 3/8	2 2/8	7 5/8	7 2/8	Salt Lake Co., Utah	Andrea L. Shaffer	Andrea L. Shaffer	1987	21
51	10 4/8	10 4/8	5 5/8	5 5/8	1 7/8	1 6/8	8 3/8	8 2/8	Skilak Glacier, Alaska	Mark A. Gaede	Mark A. Gaede	1988	21
51	10 3/8	10 3/8	5 5/8	5 5/8	2	1 7/8	7	6 3/8	Clear Creek Co., Colo.	Janice L. Hemingson	Janice L. Hemingson	1988	21
50 6/8	9 6/8	9 7/8	5 7/8	6	1 7/8	1 7/8	5 7/8	5 7/8	Salt Lake Co., Utah	Picked Up	Utah Div. of Wildl. Resc.	1985	24
50 6/8	10 5/8	10 5/8	5 7/8	5 5/8	1 7/8	1 7/8	6 6/8	6 5/8	Chelan Co., Wash.	David L. Metzler	David L. Metzler	1986	24
50 6/8	10 1/8	10 1/8	5 5/8	5 5/8	1 7/8	1 7/8	6 2/8	5 5/8	Williams Lake, B.C.	Norwood N. Kern	Norwood N. Kern	1988	24
50 6/8	9 5/8	9 5/8	5 5/8	5 5/8	1 7/8	1 7/8	6 6/8	6 3/8	Salt Lake Co., Utah	Macie J. Manire	Macie J. Manire	1988	24
50 6/8	10 5/8	10 5/8	5 5/8	5 5/8	1 6/8	1 6/8	7 2/8	7 1/8	Kootenay Mt., B.C.	Ted A. Trout	Ted A. Trout	1988	24
50 4/8	10 6/8	10 6/8	5 3/8	5 3/8	1 7/8	1 7/8	8	7 5/8	Icy Bay, Alaska	David W. Dillard	David W. Dillard	1985	29
50 4/8	10 1/8	10 1/8	5 5/8	5 5/8	1 7/8	1 5/8	6 4/8	5	Missoula Co., Mont.	Bill R. Tillerson	Bill R. Tillerson	1985	29

Rocky Mountain Goat - Continued

Score	Length of Horn R.	Length of Horn L.	Circumference of Base R.	Circumference of Base L.	Circumference at Third Quarter R.	Circumference at Third Quarter L.	Greatest Spread	Tip to Tip Spread	Locality Killed	By Whom Killed	Owner	Date Killed	Rank
50 4/8	9 7/8	10	5 5/8	5 5/8	1 6/8	1 7/8	6 2/8	5 5/8	Lewis & Clark Co., Mont.	Don St. Clair	Don St. Clair	1986	29
50 4/8	10	10 1/8	5 5/8	5 5/8	1 7/8	1 7/8	5 5/8	5	Madison Co., Mont.	Corey M. Halvorson	Corey M. Halvorson	1986	29
50 4/8	11	11	5 5/8	5 4/8	1 6/8	1 6/8	5 5/8	4 4/8	Beaver Lake, B.C.	Richard G. Henke	Richard G. Henke	1986	29
50 4/8	10	10 1/8	5 5/8	5 5/8	1 7/8	1 7/8	6 2/8	6 4/8	Bonneville Co., Idaho	William D. Stoddard	William D. Stoddard	1986	29
50 2/8	10 2/8	10 2/8	5 4/8	5 6/8	1 7/8	1 7/8	6 5/8	5 4/8	Eagle Lake, Alaska	Dale E. Gibbons	Dale E. Gibbons	1982	35
50 2/8	9 4/8	9 5/8	5 6/8	5 6/8	1 7/8	2	7	6 5/8	Snohomish Co., Wash.	Wayne E. Ritter	Wayne E. Ritter	1985	35
50 2/8	9 5/8	9 5/8	5 6/8	5 5/8	1 7/8	1 7/8	7	6 4/8	Kudwat Creek, B.C.	William R. Orth	William R. Orth	1986	35
50	10	10	5 6/8	5 5/8	1 6/8	1 6/8	7 1/8	7	Kodiak Island, Alaska	Terry R. Stockman	Terry R. Stockman	1986	38
50	9 5/8	9 7/8	5 7/8	5 7/8	1 7/8	1 7/8	6 5/8	6 1/8	Yohetta Creek, B.C.	Terry R. Wagner	Terry R. Wagner	1986	38
50	10 2/8	10 2/8	5 5/8	5 6/8	2	2	8 1/8	7 4/8	Rapid River, B.C.	Michael D. Rowe	Michael D. Rowe	1988	38
50	9 7/8	9 7/8	5 5/8	5 5/8	1 7/8	1 7/8	7 7/8	7 4/8	Nass River, B.C.	Murray McDonald	Murray McDonald	1988	38
50	10 3/8	10 3/8	5 5/8	5 5/8	1 6/8	1 6/8	6 5/8	6 1/8	Lincoln Co., Mont.	Wayne Hill	Wayne Hill	1988	38
49 6/8	10 3/8	10 3/8	5 5/8	5 4/8	1 6/8	1 6/8	6 5/8	6	Quash Creek, B.C.	Anthony Gioffre	Anthony Gioffre	1985	43
49 6/8	10	10	5 5/8	5 5/8	1 6/8	1 6/8	7 2/8	6 4/8	Johnstone Bay, Alaska	Stephen K. Karcz	Stephen K. Karcz	1988	43
49 2/8	10 3/8	10 4/8	5 2/8	5 2/8	1 6/8	1 6/8	5 5/8	5 3/8	Purcell Mts., B.C.	Robert G. Helming	Robert G. Helming	1986	45
48 7/8	9 2/8	9 2/8	5 3/8	5 2/8	2	2	8 2/8	7 7/8	Kenai Mts., Alaska	Daniel G. Detert	Daniel G. Detert	1978	46
48 5/8	10 1/8	9 5/8	5 4/8	5 4/8	1 7/8	1 7/8	6 2/8	5 7/8	Zaggodetchino Mt., B.C.	Wyatt W. Dawson, Jr.	Wyatt W. Dawson, Jr.	1985	46
48 2/8	9 5/8	9 4/8	5 3/8	5 3/8	1 7/8	1 7/8	5 5/8	4 4/8	Whatcom Co., Wash.	Greg J. Bullene	Greg J. Bullene	1986	48
48 2/8	9 7/8	10 1/8	5 2/8	5 3/8	1 6/8	1 6/8	7 2/8	6 5/8	Day Harbor, Alaska	Danny W. Pankoski	Danny W. Pankoski	1987	48
48	9 7/8	9 7/8	5 4/8	5 3/8	1 6/8	1 6/8	7 4/8	7 4/8	Wild Creek, Alaska	Charles H. Rohrer	Charles H. Rohrer	1984	50
47 7/8	10	9 7/8	5 2/8	5 2/8	1 7/8	1 6/8	7 4/8	6 7/8	Okanogan Co., Wash.	Mark Cook	Mark Cook	1987	51
47 7/8	9 4/8	9 7/8	5 1/8	5 1/8	1 6/8	1 6/8	6 4/8	5 5/8	Allison Creek, Alaska	Ron W. Biggs	Ron W. Biggs	1987	51
47 2/8	9 2/8	9 1/8	5 4/8	5 4/8	1 7/8	1 7/8	8 1/8	8	Ice Mt., B.C.	Jerald E. Mason	Jerald E. Mason	1966	53
47 2/8	9 4/8	9 5/8	5 3/8	5 3/8	1 5/8	1 5/8	6 6/8	6 2/8	Bonneville Co., Idaho	Stephen W. Deiro	Stephen W. Deiro	1985	53
47 2/8	10 1/8	10 2/8	5 2/8	5 2/8	1 5/8	1 5/8	6 6/8	6 2/8	Saunders Co., Mont.	Byron E. Wates, Jr.	Byron E. Wates, Jr.	1987	53
47	9 7/8	10	5 2/8	5 2/8	1 6/8	1 6/8	7 2/8	7	Poutang Creek, B.C.	Reg R. Smith	Reg R. Smith	1977	56
55 5/8 *	10 6/8	11	6 1/8	6 2/8	2	2 1/8	8 5/8	8 5/8	Skeena Mts., B.C.	William E. Gourlie	William E. Gourlie	1985	
54 4/8 *	11	10 7/8	6	6	2	2 1/8	7	6 7/8	Stikine River, Alaska	Patrick Flanary	Patrick Flanary	1986	

* Final Score subject to revision by additional verifying measurements.

Muskox

Ovibos moschatus moschatus and certain related subspecies

Minimum Score 90   New World's Record 125-2/8

Score	Length of Horn R.	Length of Horn L.	Width of Boss R.	Width of Boss L.	Circumference at Third Quarter R.	Circumference at Third Quarter L.	Greatest Spread	Tip to Tip Spread	Locality Killed	By Whom Killed	Owner	Date Killed	Rank
125 2/8	27 2/8	27 1/8	10 5/8	10 2/8	6 5/8	6 4/8	30 4/8	30 1/8	Bay Chimo, N.W.T.	Donald Nicholson	Donald Nicholson	1988	1
124 2/8	30 1/8	29 6/8	9 2/8	9	6	5 7/8	31 1/8	31	Perry River, N.W.T.	Robert D. Jones	Robert D. Jones	1988	2
121 6/8	28 2/8	29	9 7/8	9 6/8	5 5/8	6 2/8	32 4/8	32 2/8	Cambridge Bay, N.W.T.	Tom Gross	Tom Gross	1986	3
115 2/8	27 3/8	27 2/8	9 1/8	9 3/8	5 3/8	5 2/8	31 5/8	30 7/8	Perry Island, N.W.T.	Richard A. Jones	Richard A. Jones	1988	4
114 7/8	28 1/8	27 7/8	9 2/8	9 1/8	5	4 7/8	25 5/8	22 5/8	Banks Island, N.W.T.	Don L. Corley	Don L. Corley	1985	5
113 4/8	29	28	8 7/8	9 3/8	5 5/8	5 1/8	28 6/8	28 4/8	Ellice River, N.W.T.	Steve Munier	Steve Munier	1988	6
111 7/8	28 1/8	26 5/8	10 1/8	10 1/8	5 5/8	4 4/8	28 1/8	26 7/8	Perry River, N.W.T.	Douglas G. Williams	Douglas G. Williams	1987	7
109 6/8	27 2/8	27 2/8	8 4/8	8 1/8	5 1/8	5 1/8	26	26 2/8	Nelson Island, Alaska	Brent R. Akers	Brent R. Akers	1986	8
109 6/8	26 1/8	25 4/8	9 7/8	10 1/8	5 3/8	5	26	25 1/8	Victoria Island, N.W.T.	Virgil R. Graber	Virgil R. Graber	1987	8
109 6/8	27 5/8	27 4/8	9	9	5 1/8	4 6/8	27 3/8	26	Nunivak Island, Alaska	Scott Hebertson	Scott Hebertson	1988	8
109 4/8	26 2/8	26 4/8	8 6/8	8 4/8	5 3/8	5 4/8	27	26 1/8	Nelson Island, Alaska	Jeff C. Rogers	Jeff C. Rogers	1986	11
109	27 1/8	27	8 1/8	7 6/8	5	5	30 5/8	27 1/8	Nunivak Island, Alaska	Ron D. King	Ron D. King	1986	12
108 7/8	24 7/8	26 1/8	10 5/8	10 4/8	5	5 2/8	27	24 2/8	Sachs Harbour, N.W.T.	Charles D. Lein	Charles D. Lein	1986	13
108 4/8	26 5/8	26	8 2/8	8 2/8	4 7/8	5	24 4/8	24 4/8	Nunivak Island, Alaska	Lloyd E. Laborde	Lloyd E. Laborde	1986	14
108 4/8	27	26 7/8	8 3/8	8 4/8	5 1/8	5	27 1/8	26 3/8	Nunivak Island, Alaska	Jaci A. Crace	Jaci A. Crace	1986	14
108	26 5/8	25 3/8	9	9 1/8	5	5 1/8	28 3/8	27 1/8	Perry River, N.W.T.	Robert D. Jones	Robert D. Jones	1988	16
107 7/8	26 2/8	26 2/8	9 6/8	9 7/8	4 7/8	5 1/8	26	24 1/8	Pellatt Lake, N.W.T.	Robert A. Skrzypek	Robert A. Skrzypek	1988	17
107 4/8	26 2/8	26 4/8	9	9 1/8	4 4/8	5 2/8	24 6/8	21 1/8	Banks Island, N.W.T.	Karen K. Jacobsen	Karen K. Jacobsen	1987	18
106 7/8	26 2/8	26 3/8	7 7/8	8 1/8	5	5	26 1/8	25 4/8	Nunivak Island, Alaska	Jerald M. Finney	Jerald M. Finney	1987	19
106 4/8	25 7/8	25 7/8	8 1/8	8 4/8	5 1/8	4 7/8	28 1/8	28	Karon Lake, Alaska	R. Kim Francisco	R. Kim Francisco	1985	20
106 2/8	24 6/8	25 2/8	9	8 6/8	6	5 2/8	27	26 4/8	Nunivak Island, Alaska	Frank N. Rome	Frank N. Rome	1985	21
106 2/8	25 2/8	25 3/8	9 3/8	9 4/8	5 7/8	4 7/8	25	21 2/8	Victoria Island, N.W.T.	Lawrence T. Epping	Lawrence T. Epping	1986	21
106 2/8	26 4/8	25 7/8	7 7/8	8 1/8	4 7/8	5 3/8	27 6/8	26 7/8	Perry River, N.W.T.	Jack Downing	Jack Downing	1988	21
106	25 1/8	25 2/8	8 6/8	8 6/8	5	4	26	26 1/8	Rendez-vous Lake, N.W.T.	Lanny L. Walker	Lanny L. Walker	1988	24
105 7/8	25 2/8	25	9	8 7/8	4 6/8	5 1/8	23 6/8	21 5/8	Coronation Gulf, N.W.T.	James A. Hale	James A. Hale	1987	25
105 7/8	25	24 7/8	9 4/8	9 6/8	4 6/8	4 6/8	27 5/8	25 6/8	Sachs Harbour, N.W.T.	Donald J. Craite	Donald J. Craite	1987	25
105 7/8	26 2/8	26 6/8	7 7/8	7 6/8	5	5 2/8	29 6/8	29 6/8	Nunivak Island, Alaska	Henry M. Hills III	Henry M. Hills III	1987	25
105 7/8	25	26	9 7/8	9 5/8	4 3/8	5 2/8	27 1/8	26 6/8	Banks Island, N.W.T.	Bernard Sippin	Bernard Sippin	1988	25
105 5/8	26 4/8	26 7/8	7 7/8	8	4 5/8	4 7/8	27 3/8	26 3/8	Nunivak Island, Alaska	John D. Frost	John D. Frost	1986	29
105 3/8	25 6/8	25 5/8	8 3/8	8 3/8	4 6/8	5	27 2/8	26 6/8	Nunivak Island, Alaska	David A. Schuller	David A. Schuller	1982	30
105 2/8	24 5/8	24 7/8	9 6/8	9 6/8	4 6/8	5 2/8	25 1/8	23 7/8	Richardson River, N.W.T.	Ronald L. Fuller	Ronald L. Fuller	1988	30

Muskox - Continued

Score	Length of Horn R.	Length of Horn L.	Width of Boss R.	Width of Boss L.	Circumference at Third Quarter R.	Circumference at Third Quarter L.	Greatest Spread	Tip to Tip Spread	Locality Killed	By Whom Killed	Owner	Date Killed	Rank
104 6/8	24 5/8	25	9 4/8	9 2/8	4 4/8	4 5/8	25	23	Banks Island, N.W.T.	Susan D. Sherer	Susan D. Sherer	1986	32
104 4/8	25 4/8	25 2/8	9	9 1/8	5 1/8	4 4/8	25 4/8	24 2/8	Banks Island, N.W.T.	Ronald L. Sherer	Ronald L. Sherer	1986	33
104 2/8	25 3/8	25 2/8	8 2/8	8 5/8	4 7/8	4 7/8	30	29 6/8	Nunivak Island, Alaska	George J. Elledge, Jr.	George J. Elledge, Sr.	1987	34
104 2/8	25 2/8	23 6/8	9 6/8	9 7/8	5 4/8	4 1/8	26 3/8	25 5/8	Victoria Island, N.W.T.	Charles W. Selby	Charles W. Selby	1987	34
104	25 2/8	25 3/8	8 4/8	8 2/8	4 4/8	4 7/8	27 6/8	27 1/8	Nunivak Island, Alaska	Tim D. Hiner	Tim D. Hiner	1988	36
103 6/8	24 7/8	23 7/8	9 5/8	9 4/8	5 1/8	4 3/8	26 3/8	25 1/8	Resolute Bay, N.W.T.	William F. Jury	William F. Jury	1986	37
103 6/8	26 1/8	27	7 7/8	8	4 4/8	5	28 4/8	28 3/8	Nunivak Island, Alaska	Jack F. Campbell	Jack F. Campbell	1987	37
103 4/8	25 5/8	26 3/8	8 8/8	8 2/8	4 4/8	5 1/8	26 1/8	25 3/8	Nunivak Island, Alaska	Bonnie L. Scott	Bonnie L. Scott	1987	39
103 2/8	25 3/8	25 5/8	8 2/8	8	4 5/8	4 7/8	27 4/8	27 6/8	Nunivak Island, Alaska	George J. Elledge, Sr.	George J. Elledge, Sr.	1987	40
103 2/8	25 7/8	25	8 1/8	8 2/8	5	4 6/8	25 7/8	25 4/8	Nunivak Island, Alaska	Allan L. Howard	Allan L. Howard	1988	40
103	22 7/8	23 5/8	8 2/8	8 4/8	5 6/8	5 5/8	24 7/8	24	Ellesmere Island, N.W.T.	Picked Up	Warren St. Germaine	pr 1986	42
102 6/8	23 7/8	26 6/8	9 1/8	8 6/8	5 7/8	4 6/8	26	24 7/8	Banks Island, N.W.T.	Picked Up	Randy Forsyth	1983	43
102 6/8	26 5/8	25 3/8	8 1/8	8 2/8	4 6/8	4 3/8	27 7/8	27 5/8	Nunivak Island, Alaska	Alan J. Quimby	Alan J. Quimby	1987	43
102 4/8	24 1/8	25 2/8	8 6/8	8 5/8	4 6/8	5 3/8	25 3/8	24	Sachs Harbour, N.W.T.	Charlie D. Todd	Charlie D. Todd	1986	45
102 4/8	25 3/8	25 7/8	8	7 5/8	5	4 7/8	25 2/8	24 6/8	Nunivak Island, Alaska	Stanley N. Steffensen	Stanley N. Steffensen	1988	45
102	24	24 3/8	9 2/8	9 3/8	4 4/8	4 7/8	25 1/8	24 2/8	Banks Island, N.W.T.	James W. Hearn	James W. Hearn	1985	47
102	25 5/8	24 3/8	8 5/8	9	5 1/8	4 7/8	27 1/8	23 7/8	Parry Pen. N.W.T.	Terry Jackson	Terry Jackson	1986	47
101 6/8	25 3/8	24 4/8	9 2/8	9 3/8	4 4/8	4 5/8	25 3/8	23 6/8	Victoria Island, N.W.T.	Robert T. Mullis	Robert T. Mullis	1987	49
101 6/8	24 6/8	25 2/8	8 3/8	8 6/8	4 3/8	4 4/8	27 3/8	26 6/8	Nunivak Island, Alaska	Donavon K. Lee	Donavon K. Lee	1988	49
101	23 7/8	25	8 1/8	8 4/8	4 7/8	5	26	25	Nunivak Island, Alaska	Robert E. Barndt	Robert E. Barndt	1987	51
100 6/8	24 7/8	26	8	7 5/8	4 3/8	5 2/8	26 7/8	26 6/8	Nunivak Island, Alaska	Lee R. Ellenburg	Lee R. Ellenburg	1987	52
100 4/8	24	25	9 6/8	10	4	4 4/8	27 5/8	27	Banks Island, N.W.T.	Craig Leerberg	Craig Leerberg	1983	53
100 4/8	24 2/8	24 1/8	8	7 5/8	4 3/8	4 5/8	27 3/8	23 5/8	Banks Island, N.W.T.	Picked Up	Evan Saugstad	1986	53
100 2/8	25 1/8	25 2/8	7 3/8	7 4/8	5 1/8	4 6/8	26 6/8	26 1/8	Canning River, Alaska	Jerry D. Lees	Jerry D. Lees	1988	55
99	22 7/8	24 7/8	9 3/8	9 2/8	4 2/8	5	25 1/8	24 1/8	Banks Island, N.W.T.	Mark B. Sippin	Mark B. Sippin	1988	56
98 6/8	24 6/8	24 5/8	9 2/8	9 1/8	4 3/8	4 3/8	25 5/8	24 5/8	Holman Island, N.W.T.	Wayne E. Ballantine	Wayne E. Ballantine	1985	57
98 6/8	24 6/8	25 5/8	9 3/8	9 2/8	3 6/8	4 5/8	26 4/8	26	Coppermine, N.W.T.	Paul E. Robey	Paul E. Robey	1987	57
98	25	24 6/8	7 5/8	7 4/8	4 4/8	4 2/8	25 7/8	21 7/8	Nunivak Island, Alaska	Darrell D. Wells	Darrell D. Wells	1977	59
98	22 5/8	25	9 4/8	9 1/8	4 1/8	5 5/8	26	24 7/8	Victoria Island, N.W.T.	John L. Van Horn	John L. Van Horn	1987	59
97 7/8	24 6/8	27 7/8	8 3/8	8 3/8	2 7/8	5 2/8	28 4/8	28 1/8	Nunivak Island, Alaska	Tim J. Crace	Tim J. Crace	1986	61
97 6/8	24 4/8	25	7 5/8	7 6/8	5 1/8	6	25 7/8	24 6/8	Coronation Gulf, N.W.T.	Gary L. Benner	Gary L. Benner	1987	61
97 4/8	24 4/8	25 3/8	9	8 7/8	4 2/8	4 4/8	19 1/8	16 3/8	Coronation Gulf, N.W.T.	William W. McQuerry	William W. McQuerry	1987	61
97 2/8	24 1/8	25 3/8	8 5/8	8 2/8	4	4 5/8	25 2/8	23 3/8	Victoria Island, N.W.T.	John R. Rains	John R. Rains	1987	61
96	23 5/8	23 5/8	9 1/8	8 7/8	4 3/8	4 4/8	24 4/8	22 2/8	Raddi Lake, N.W.T.	John E. Hoye	John E. Hoye	1988	65

Score									Location	Hunter	Owner	Date Killed	Rank
95 6/8	25 1/8	23 1/8	8 6/8	9 4/8	4 5/8	3 5/8	26 2/8	24 5/8	Holman Island, N.W.T.	David G. Ballantine	David G. Ballantine	1985	66
95 5/8	24 3/8	23 4/8	8 5/8	8 7/8	4 3/8	3 7/8	25 2/8	20 5/8	Surrey Lake, N.W.T.	Lawrence T. Epping	Lawrence T. Epping	1986	66
95 2/8	24 1/8	25 5/8	8 1/8	8	3 7/8	4 2/8	26 2/8	26	Coronation Gulf, N.W.T.	William J. Scheg, Jr.	William J. Scheg, Jr.	1987	68
93 6/8	24	23 5/8	7 6/8	7 4/8	4 3/8	4 2/8	21 3/8	19 1/8	Coronation Gulf, N.W.T.	Donald R. Boerschlein	Donald R. Boerschlein	1987	69
121 *	29 2/8	29 2/8	10 3/8	10	5 2/8	5 5/8	26 5/8	24 5/8	King William Island, N.W.T.	Picked Up	Emile R. Stanley	1986	
118 6/8 *	29 1/8	30 7/8	9 6/8	10 1/8	4 1/8	5	31 7/8	31	Ellice River, N.W.T.	Robert M. Juneau	Robert M. Juneau	1987	
115 5/8 *	28 1/8	28 4/8	9 1/8	8 7/8	5 2/8	5 4/8	31 7/8	31 7/8	Perry Island, N.W.T.	William M. Cobb	William M. Cobb	1987	
114 4/8 *	26 7/8	28 7/8	10 1/8	10 1/8	4 5/8	6 4/8	29	28	Perry River, N.W.T.	Jerry Imperial	Jerry Imperial	1986	
113 4/8 *	26 3/8	27 1/8	10 1/8	10 3/8	5 2/8	5 1/8	25 5/8	24 1/8	Rendez-vous Lake, N.W.T.	John T. Blaine	John T. Blaine	1988	
112 2/8 *	27	26 7/8	9 4/8	9 4/8	5 2/8	5 1/8	26 3/8	24 4/8	Banks Island, N.W.T.	Robert L. Jacobsen	Robert L. Jacobsen	1987	
111 6/8 *	24 7/8	26 1/8	9	9 1/8	6 3/8	7 4/8	27 7/8	26 1/8	Perry River, N.W.T.	Robert H. Hanson	Robert H. Hanson	1987	
111 4/8 *	28	28	8 6/8	8 4/8	5	5	26 6/8	25 4/8	Nunivak Island, Alaska	Todd A. Sneesby	Todd A. Sneesby	1988	
110 4/8 *	26 3/8	25 3/8	9	9 2/8	5 4/8	5 5/8	26 1/8	25 7/8	Thelon River, N.W.T.	Picked Up	H.P.L. Kiliaan	1982	

* Final Score subject to revision by additional verifying measurements.

Note: Beginning with 21st Awards entry period (began on January 1, 1989) the minimum entry score for muskox is 105.

Bighorn Sheep

Ovis canadensis canadensis and certain related subspecies

Minimum Score 175   World's Record 208-1/8

Score	Length of Horn R.	L.	Circumference of Base R.	L.	Circumference at Third Quarter R.	L.	Greatest Spread	Tip to Tip Spread	Locality Killed	By Whom Killed	Owner	Date Killed	Rank
197 7/8	43 2/8	42 7/8	14 7/8	15	11 4/8	11 5/8	21 6/8	21 2/8	Wallowa Co., Oreg.	Picked Up	Oreg. Dept. Fish & Wildl.	1986	1
193 5/8	40 4/8	39 6/8	16 6/8	16 4/8	9 7/8	9	23 7/8	22 7/8	Granite Co., Mont.	Michael L. Girard	Michael L. Girard	1986	2
192 1/8	42 7/8	42 4/8	16	16 2/8	9 1/8	8 6/8	22 4/8	19 1/8	Deer Lodge Co., Mont.	Mitchell A. Thorson	Mitchell A. Thorson	1987	3
191 4/8	44 3/8	39 3/8	15 7/8	16	9 6/8	9 3/8	23 6/8	20 3/8	Wallowa Co., Oreg.	Sam Jaksick, Jr.	Sam Jaksick, Jr.	1987	4
191	40	39 2/8	16 5/8	16 5/8	9 1/8	9	24	22 2/8	Granite Co., Mont.	Harry W. Miller	Harry W. Miller	1985	5
190 5/8	40 4/8	42 5/8	15 5/8	16 1/8	9 2/8	9 2/8	24 2/8	23 2/8	Missoula Co., Mont.	Chris L. Mostad	Chris L. Mostad	1986	6
190 1/8	41 5/8	40 3/8	15 7/8	16 1/8	9 2/8	9 2/8	23 4/8	21	Missoula Co., Mont.	Joseph C. Turner	Joseph C. Turner	1987	7
189 3/8	40 1/8	41 4/8	16 6/8	16 6/8	8 5/8	8	23 2/8	21 6/8	Asotin Co., Wash.	Edwin L. Harris	Edwin L. Harris	1987	8
189 1/8	37 3/8	38	15 7/8	15 6/8	11	11 1/8	19	20 7/8	Sheep River, Alta.	Patrick J. Downey	Patrick J. Downey	1986	9
188 7/8	40 5/8	40 4/8	14 6/8	14 7/8	10 6/8	10 5/8	20 4/8	22	Wallowa Co., Oreg.	Nick J. Gianopoulos	Nick J. Gianopoulos	1986	10
188 6/8	40	40	15 1/8	15 1/8	11	10 7/8	20 4/8	16 4/8	Onion Lake, Alta.	Martin M. Reddy	Martin M. Reddy	1985	11
188 3/8	40	40 7/8	15 5/8	15 5/8	9 6/8	9 7/8	24	23 1/8	Deer Lodge Co., Mont.	Paul J. Druyvestein	Paul J. Druyvestein	1986	12
188 2/8	43	42 2/8	15 5/8	15 5/8	7 7/8	8 1/8	24 3/8	24 3/8	Deer Lodge Co., Mont.	Walter F. Smith	Walter F. Smith	1986	13
188	41 1/8	39 5/8	15	15	10 4/8	10 5/8	20 5/8	16 4/8	Cardinal River, Alta.	Lawrence N. Baraniuk	Lawrence N. Baraniuk	1986	14
187 5/8	39 6/8	39 7/8	15 5/8	15 5/8	9 3/8	9 3/8	22	20 5/8	El Paso Co., Colo.	Picked Up	Michael D. Swanson	1988	15
187 2/8	41 1/8	38 3/8	17	17	7 7/8	7 4/8	24 2/8	20 1/8	Asotin Co., Wash.	Roger S. Brazier	Roger S. Brazier	1986	16
187 2/8	39 2/8	40 4/8	15 7/8	15 7/8	8 6/8	8 6/8	23 1/8	22 6/8	Granite Co., Mont.	Donald A. Chamberlain	Donald A. Chamberlain	1987	16
187 2/8	42 4/8	39 4/8	15 7/8	15 6/8	8 3/8	8 1/8	22 2/8	21 5/8	Granite Co., Mont.	Chuck Houtz	Chuck Houtz	1988	16
187	39 6/8	38	16 7/8	17	8 1/8	8 1/8	20	21 7/8	Highwood Range, Alta.	Sten B. Lundberg	Sten B. Lundberg	1984	19
187	40 6/8	40 4/8	16 4/8	16 4/8	7 5/8	8	21 6/8	21 6/8	Deer Lodge Co., Mont.	Wayne E. Bousfield	Wayne E. Bousfield	1985	19
185 4/8	39 2/8	38 3/8	16 6/8	16 3/8	8 2/8	8 2/8	27 3/8	27 3/8	Granite Co., Mont.	Lawrence R. Simkins	Lawrence R. Simkins	1986	21
184 3/8	41	41 1/8	14 2/8	14 3/8	10	10	21 4/8	18 2/8	Burnt Timber Creek, Alta.	Terry S. Marcum	Terry S. Marcum	1988	22
183 6/8	37 5/8	36 5/8	16 5/8	16 6/8	9	9	23 4/8	23 4/8	Ravalli Co., Mont.	Sandra L. Gann	Les Towner	1985	23
183 6/8	37 4/8	37 4/8	16	16	9 3/8	9 4/8	24	22 4/8	Silver Bow Co., Mont.	Emmett O. Riordan	Emmett O. Riordan	1986	23
183 4/8	38 2/8	39 2/8	16 1/8	16 2/8	8 6/8	8 1/8	18	13 7/8	Granite Co., Mont.	Karen Throckmorton	Karen Throckmorton	1987	25
183 3/8	42 7/8	42 4/8	15 2/8	15 2/8	7 4/8	6 5/8	27 4/8	27 1/8	Sanders Co., Mont.	Edward W. Blackwood	Rocky Mtn. Elk Found.	1985	26
183 3/8	40 4/8	41 1/8	15 4/8	15 4/8	7 5/8	7 4/8	21 4/8	21 5/8	Sanders Co., Mont.	Ilse R. Knight	Ilse R. Knight	1986	26
183 2/8	38 2/8	38 6/8	15 5/8	16	8 5/8	8 5/8	20 5/8	20 5/8	Bow River, Alta.	Guy R. Woods	Guy R. Woods	1985	28
183 2/8	41 4/8	40 2/8	16 2/8	16 4/8	7 5/8	7 6/8	22 7/8	21 1/8	Sanders Co., Mont.	Alma E. Arnold	Alma E. Arnold	1986	28
183 2/8	40 2/8	40 2/8	15 7/8	15 4/8	8 1/8	8 1/8	23 6/8	23 3/8	Sanders Co., Mont.	Thorne R. Johnson	Thorne R. Johnson	1987	28
182 3/8	38 7/8	38 3/8	15 4/8	15 3/8	9 1/8	9 5/8	20	18 1/8	Montana	Unknown	Joseph P. Scurti	pr 1949	31

Score							Locality	Hunter	Owner	Date	Rank
182	39 7/8	40 1/8	15 5/8	15 3/8	8	8 1/8	20 4/8	20 6/8	Murray Creek, B.C.	Nancy J. Koopman	Nancy J. Koopman	1986	32
182	40 7/8	39 5/8	16 3/8	16 3/8	7 1/8	7 3/8	22 5/8	22 2/8	Wallowa Co., Oreg.	Dale R. Dotson	Dale R. Dotson	1988	32
182	37	38 5/8	15 3/8	15 1/8	10 4/8	9 6/8	22 1/8	20 2/8	Deer Lodge Co., Mont.	George A. Kovacich	George A. Kovacich	1988	32
181 6/8	38 2/8	36 4/8	17	16 7/8	8 4/8	8 4/8	23 6/8	20 6/8	Gunnison Co., Colo.	Paula D. Darner	Paula D. Darner	1986	35
181 5/8	39	38 1/8	15 5/8	15 2/8	9 7/8	9 2/8	22 6/8	20	Lemhi Co., Idaho	David Freel	David Freel	1986	36
181 5/8	39	37 7/8	15 7/8	16	9	8 3/8	19 5/8	13 4/8	Kootenay River, B.C.	Arthur V. Parsons	Arthur V. Parsons	1986	36
181 4/8	38 7/8	41 3/8	16 2/8	16 3/8	6 7/8	6 7/8	24	24	Granite Co., Mont.	Michael B. Murphy	Michael B. Murphy	1987	38
181 4/8	38 6/8	36 4/8	16 6/8	16 5/8	7 5/8	7 3/8	19 4/8	11 7/8	Mt. Evans-Thomas, Alta.	William E. MacDougall	William E. MacDougall	1988	38
181 3/8	38 4/8	39 5/8	14 4/8	14 7/8	9 3/8	9	20 6/8	20 3/8	Lake Co., Mont.	Picked Up	J. Michael Conoyer	1978	40
181 3/8	39	38 3/8	15 4/8	15 5/8	8 2/8	8 5/8	21 2/8	20 5/8	Lewis & Clark Co., Mont.	Elmer T. Crawford	Elmer T. Crawford	1986	40
181 2/8	39 2/8	40 2/8	14 1/8	14	10	10 2/8	20 5/8	16 5/8	Timber Creek, Alta.	Jason G. Hindes	Jason G. Hindes	1985	42
181 2/8	40 3/8	40 2/8	14 3/8	14 3/8	8 7/8	9	23 7/8	23 7/8	Lewis & Clark Co., Mont.	Brandon C. Johns	Brandon C. Johns	1987	42
181 1/8	38 2/8	40 3/8	15	15 3/8	8 5/8	8 3/8	17 3/8	21	Scalp Creek, Alta.	James Mills	James Mills	1984	44
181 1/8	39	38 5/8	15 4/8	15 3/8	8 5/8	8 3/8	20 6/8	17 7/8	Mt. Inflexible, Alta.	Carl Gallant	Carl Gallant	1987	44
180 5/8	41 4/8	41 7/8	14 7/8	14 7/8	7 5/8	7 6/8	27 7/8	27 1/8	Sanders Co., Mont.	Raymond J. Baenen	Raymond J. Baenen	1986	46
180 3/8	37 5/8	41 4/8	15 2/8	15 3/8	7 7/8	8 3/8	23 4/8	23 7/8	Silverbow Co., Mont.	Scott A. Shuey	Scott A. Shuey	1985	47
180 3/8	37 1/8	38	15 4/8	15 5/8	9	8 6/8	21	19	Sanders Co., Mont.	Calvin L. Pomrenke	Calvin L. Pomrenke	1986	47
180 1/8	39 6/8	39 7/8	14	14 1/8	9 4/8	9 4/8	22 7/8	17 4/8	Kootenay Mts., B.C.	Picked Up	Gary E. Brown	1963	49
180 1/8	38 5/8	42 6/8	15 7/8	15 7/8	6 3/8	6 3/8	24 3/8	24 3/8	Granite Co., Mont.	Leonard W. Bowen	Leonard W. Bowen	1985	49
180 1/8	38	37 1/8	16 6/8	16 4/8	7 6/8	7 5/8	19 3/8	19 3/8	Sanders Co., Mont.	Bruce P. Allen	Bruce P. Allen	1986	49
180 1/8	39 4/8	38 5/8	15	15	8 5/8	8 2/8	23 1/8	20 7/8	Custer Co., Idaho	Leland S. Speakes, Jr.	Leland S. Speakes, Jr.	1987	49
180	39 7/8	40 1/8	15 5/8	15 5/8	7 5/8	7 4/8	22 2/8	22 2/8	Granite Co., Mont.	Jim A. Crepeau	Jim A. Crepeau	1986	53
179 4/8	38 3/8	38 3/8	15 2/8	15 3/8	8 4/8	8 2/8	20 4/8	12 3/8	Park Co., Wyo.	Michael S. Messenger	Michael S. Messenger	1986	54
177 5/8	39 1/8	36 6/8	14 4/8	14 4/8	9	8 7/8	22 5/8	20	Park Co., Wyo.	William B. Hickman III	William B. Hickman III	1987	55
177 1/8	37 2/8	37 3/8	16	16	7 3/8	7 3/8	21 4/8	20	Pincher Creek, Alta.	Stephen Taylor	Stephen Taylor	1977	56
176 4/8	38 3/8	38 3/8	15	15 1/8	8 1/8	8 4/8	20 7/8	19 1/8	Sanders Co., Mont.	Dino V. Seppi	Dino V. Seppi	1987	57
195 4/8 *	46 2/8	41	16 1/8	16 3/8	9	9	29 6/8	29 6/8	Deer Lodge Co., Mont.	Thomas J. Matosich	Thomas J. Matosich	1986	
194 3/8 *	42 3/8	43 2/8	16	16 2/8	9 1/8	9	26 5/8	26 6/8	Deer Lodge Co., Mont.	Norman F. Lesh	Norman F. Lesh	1987	

* Final Score subject to revision by additional verifying measurements.

Desert Sheep

Minimum Score 165   *Ovis canadensis nelsoni* and certain related subspecies   World's Record 205-1/8

Score	Length of Horn R.	L.	Circumference of Base R.	L.	Circumference at Third Quarter R.	L.	Greatest Spread	Tip to Tip Spread	Locality Killed	By Whom Killed	Owner	Date Killed	Rank
186	37	36	15 7/8	16	11 7/8	11 7/8	21 7/8	19	Arizona	Unknown	J. Michael Conoyer	1960	1
184 2/8	40 4/8	37 2/8	15 4/8	15 4/8	9 2/8	9 3/8	22 1/8	22 1/8	Pinal Co., Ariz.	Everett A. Hodge	Everett A. Hodge	1988	2
183 2/8	37 6/8	37	14 7/8	14 7/8	10 7/8	11 1/8	14 2/8	14 2/8	Pima Co., Ariz.	Picked Up	LeRoy Van Buggenum	1987	3
182 2/8	39 3/8	39 5/8	15 3/8	15 3/8	9 3/8	9	22 3/8	21 5/8	Graham Co., Ariz.	Beverly M. Nuessle	Beverly M. Nuessle	1986	4
180 3/8	37 2/8	38 5/8	15 2/8	15 1/8	9 4/8	9 3/8	21 6/8	19 1/8	Baja Calif., Mexico	Emory C. Thompson	Emory C. Thompson	1985	5
180 2/8	36 2/8	36 4/8	15 5/8	15 4/8	9 7/8	10 1/8	22 4/8	21 1/8	Baja Calif., Mexico	Hector Aguilar Parada	Hector Aguilar Parada	1988	6
180 2/8	41 2/8	39 6/8	14 4/8	14 4/8	8 7/8	9 7/8	22 6/8	22 2/8	Baja Calif., Mexico	Bernard Sippin	Bernard Sippin	1988	6
180 1/8	36 5/8	35 4/8	16 5/8	16 5/8	9 1/8	8 5/8	22 4/8	21 5/8	Pima Co., Ariz.	Robert A. Christy	Robert A. Christy	1986	8
179 4/8	38 1/8	37 1/8	15 5/8	15 4/8	8 7/8	8 5/8	26 6/8	26	Baja Calif., Mexico	Ronald J. Wade	Ronald J. Wade	1987	9
178 4/8	40 4/8	39 3/8	14 1/8	13 7/8	9 6/8	10	25 7/8	25 7/8	Clark Co., Nev.	Stephen E. Aiazzi	Stephen E. Aiazzi	1985	10
176 4/8	36 7/8	38 3/8	16	16	7 7/8	7 7/8	20 6/8	18 4/8	Pinal Co., Ariz.	Robbie A. Brown	Robert L. Brown	1985	11
176 1/8	37 7/8	38 2/8	15 1/8	15 4/8	8 3/8	8	21 1/8	21 1/8	Clark Co., Nev.	Tim L. Iverson	Tim L. Iverson	1985	12
176 1/8	36 5/8	36 4/8	14 6/8	14 6/8	9 3/8	9 4/8	21 6/8	20	Pinal Co., Ariz.	Warren A. Adams	Warren A. Adams	1985	12
176	36 2/8	35 6/8	14 6/8	14 6/8	10 2/8	10	19 1/8	16 1/8	Baja Calif., Mexico	Pedro S. Montano	Pedro S. Montano	1986	14
174 2/8	34 2/8	33 4/8	15 2/8	15 5/8	9 4/8	9 3/8	24 1/8	21 6/8	Maricopa Co., Ariz.	Debi L. Adair	Debi L. Adair	1987	15
174	31 6/8	34 4/8	15 6/8	15 6/8	9 5/8	9 5/8	22	20	Pima Co., Ariz.	George Martin	George Martin	1978	16
173 5/8	37 3/8	36 2/8	14 4/8	14 4/8	8 5/8	8 3/8	22	21 3/8	Baja Calif., Mexico	Patrick C. Allen	Patrick C. Allen	1987	17
173 5/8	37 5/8	36 6/8	14 6/8	14 5/8	8 2/8	8 3/8	21 6/8	20	Clark Co., Nev.	Dale O. Millerin	Dale O. Millerin	1987	17
173 1/8	37 5/8	32 2/8	14 6/8	14 6/8	9	11	25 1/8	25 1/8	Lincoln Co., Nev.	Picked Up	Billy D. Stoddard	1965	19
173	35 1/8	35 3/8	16	16 1/8	8 1/8	8 1/8	20 2/8	19 4/8	Baja Calif., Mexico	Tom W. Housh	Tom W. Housh	1988	20
172 7/8	41 1/8	37 2/8	14 2/8	14 3/8	9 4/8	8 2/8	24 5/8	24 3/8	Gila Co., Ariz.	Byron Wiley	Byron Wiley	1986	21
172 4/8	37 7/8	35 4/8	15 4/8	15 4/8	8	8	25 5/8	23	Yuma Co., Ariz.	William J. Paul	William J. Paul	1987	22
172 3/8	33 5/8	34	16 1/8	16 1/8	8 6/8	9	20 2/8	16 2/8	Pima Co., Ariz.	Loren G. Pederson, Jr.	Loren G. Pederson, Jr.	1985	23
172 2/8	35	35 5/8	15 3/8	15 3/8	8 6/8	8 5/8	22 6/8	18 5/8	Baja Calif., Mexico	Ralph A. Shoberg	Ralph A. Shoberg	1986	24
172 1/8	35 5/8	36 6/8	14 5/8	14 4/8	9 5/8	9 3/8	22 4/8	21 4/8	Clark Co., Nev.	Robert F. Sievert	Robert F. Sievert	1985	25
172	36 4/8	36	14 2/8	14 4/8	9 2/8	9 2/8	22 4/8	22 2/8	Clark Co., Nev.	Mike W. Steele	Mike W. Steele	1986	26
172	34	36 4/8	14 5/8	14 4/8	9 4/8	9 3/8	23 3/8	22 5/8	Clark Co., Nev.	Jerry J. Long	Jerry J. Long	1987	26
171 7/8	35 3/8	36 2/8	15	15	9	9 1/8	20 2/8	18 2/8	Graham Co., Ariz.	Roger J. Stolp	Roger J. Stolp	1985	28
171 7/8	34 7/8	33 3/8	15 5/8	15 4/8	8 7/8	9 6/8	21 5/8	18 4/8	La Paz Co., Ariz.	Robert M. H. Gray	Robert M. H. Gray	1987	28
171 3/8	35 3/8	35 4/8	14 1/8	13 7/8	9 1/8	9 5/8	23 6/8	24 1/8	Mojave Co., Ariz.	Picked Up	Dan Priest	1985	30
171	36 4/8	35 2/8	14 5/8	14 6/8	9 2/8	9 3/8	23 1/8	21 1/8	Clark Co., Nev.	Richard A. Bell	Richard A. Bell	1986	31
171	37 1/8	37 1/8	14 5/8	14 2/8	7 7/8	8 1/8	24 4/8	24 4/8	Clark Co., Nev.	Toni M. Venturacci	Toni M. Venturacci	1986	31

Score								Location	Hunter	Year	Rank
171	35 5/8	36 1/8	14 7/8	14 7/8	8 5/8	8 5/8	17	Pima Co., Ariz.	Don J. Parks, Jr.	1986	31
170 7/8	33	35 7/8	15 3/8	15 3/8	8	8 7/8	18 7/8	Pima Co., Ariz.	Barbara J. Ridgeway	1984	34
170 7/8	37	36 1/8	15 2/8	14 6/8	8 1/8	8 2/8	23 1/8	Mohave Co., Ariz.	Dale A. Kelling	1987	34
170 6/8	36 4/8	35 4/8	14 2/8	14 2/8	9 2/8	9 4/8	24	Nye Co., Nev.	Donald A. Leveille	1986	36
170 6/8	34 1/8	36 7/8	15	15 1/8	8 1/8	8 2/8	17 4/8	Yuma Co., Ariz.	Bryan L. Rogers	1986	36
170 4/8	32 5/8	34 2/8	16 2/8	16 2/8	8	8 3/8	24	Baja Calif., Mexico	Stephen P. Connell	1986	38
170 2/8	37 5/8	37 2/8	15 3/8	15 2/8	7	7 4/8	24 7/8	Clark Co., Nev.	Raymond B. Graber II	1987	39
170 2/8	34 2/8	35	14 4/8	14 5/8	9 4/8	10	21 6/8	Yuma Co., Ariz.	Lance K. Parks	1987	39
170 2/8	33	33	14 7/8	14 7/8	10 1/8	10 1/8	21	Yuma Co., Ariz.	Valentino J. Pugnea	1987	39
170	35 5/8	35 7/8	14 2/8	14	9 2/8	9	20 1/8	Clark Co., Nev.	Roy A. Walker	1985	42
169 6/8	36 4/8	36 6/8	15 3/8	15	7 7/8	7 3/8	21	Baja Calif., Mexico	Richard L. Larson	1985	43
169 6/8	33 5/8	34 1/8	14	14 2/8	10	10 2/8	22	Yuma Co., Ariz.	Gary S. Sitton	1986	43
169 2/8	36 2/8	34 4/8	14 2/8	14 4/8	8 4/8	8 1/8	23 1/8	Clark Co., Nev.	Richard M. McDrew	1986	45
169 1/8	36	36 7/8	14 7/8	15	7	7 1/8	23 5/8	Clark Co., Nev.	Vernon C. Tays	1987	46
169	36 1/8	35 4/8	15 2/8	15 2/8	7 6/8	7 6/8	25 5/8	Clark Co., Nev.	Charles E. Sibley	1986	47
168 4/8	35 5/8	35 5/8	15 3/8	15 3/8	7 3/8	7 5/8	23 5/8	Clark Co., Nev.	James M. Machac	1987	48
168 3/8	34 6/8	34 3/8	15 1/8	15	9	8 4/8	21 6/8	Maricopa Co., Ariz.	Peter C. Knagge	1985	49
168 3/8	35 4/8	37 1/8	13 6/8	13 5/8	9 3/8	9 4/8	24	Clark Co., Nev.	Leonard C. Lerg	1985	49
168 2/8	37	36	13 6/8	13 6/8	10 2/8	9 3/8	19 4/8	Lincoln Co., Nev.	Lee A. Raine	1982	51
168 2/8	34 6/8	36	13 5/8	14	8 7/8	9 1/8	23	Yuma Co., Ariz.	Ralph C. Stayner	1985	51
168	35 5/8	35 5/8	14 6/8	14 6/8	8 3/8	8 2/8	24 1/8	Mojave Co., Ariz.	Picked Up	1984	53
168	34	34 5/8	15 5/8	15 1/8	8 1/8	8 1/8	18 2/8	Pinal Co., Ariz.	Peter A. Inorio	1986	53
168	36 7/8	36 3/8	14 1/8	14 2/8	8 1/8	8 1/8	20 1/8	Yuma Co., Ariz.	Alan D. Maynard	1987	53
189 *	41	40 2/8	16 2/8	16 2/8	8 7/8	8 7/8	23 2/8	Gila Co., Ariz.	Samuel S. Jaksick, Jr.	1988	
183 2/8 *	40 5/8	41 5/8	15 7/8	15 2/8	8 3/8	8 8/8	27 2/8	Clark Co., Nev.	Alan G. Means	1988	
182 6/8 *	36	38 2/8	16	16 1/8	9 4/8	9 3/8	18 2/8	Pima Co., Ariz.	Richard F. Morin	1987	

* Final Score subject to revision by additional verifying measurements.

Dall's Sheep

Ovis dalli dalli and Ovis dalli kenaiensis

Minimum Score 165　　　　　　　　　　　　　　　　　　World's Record 189-6/8

Score	Length of Horn R.	Length of Horn L.	Circumference of Base R.	Circumference of Base L.	Circumference at Third Quarter R.	Circumference at Third Quarter L.	Greatest Spread	Tip to Tip Spread	Locality Killed	By Whom Killed	Owner	Date Killed	Rank
171 7/8	42 7/8	43	13 1/8	13 1/8	6 7/8	6 6/8	25 7/8	25 1/8	Robertson River, Alaska	David C. Sharp	David C. Sharp	1987	1
171 6/8	44 2/8	40 2/8	13 7/8	13 7/8	6 2/8	6 3/8	30 3/8	30 3/8	Ivishak River, Alaska	Charles W. Troutman	Charles W. Troutman	1987	2
171 3/8	42 1/8	42 4/8	14	13 6/8	5 4/8	5 5/8	22 2/8	22 2/8	Chugach Mts., Alaska	Anthony R. Russ	Anthony R. Russ	1988	3
171 2/8	39	39 6/8	14 3/8	14 3/8	7	7 1/8	19 6/8	19 6/8	Kluane River, Yukon	Phil Temple	Phil Temple	1972	4
171 1/8	43 2/8	42 7/8	13 2/8	13 1/8	6	6	26 4/8	26 2/8	Chugach Mts., Alaska	Emil V. Nelson	Emil V. Nelson	1988	5
171	40 6/8	40 6/8	14 2/8	14 2/8	6 1/8	6 2/8	29	29	Greyling Creek, Alaska	Michael M. Stitzel	Michael M. Stitzel	1986	6
170 7/8	41 5/8	41 6/8	14 1/8	14	6 1/8	6	29	29	Wrangell Mts., Alaska	Unknown	J. Michael Conoyer	1980	7
170 4/8	41 3/8	41 3/8	13 5/8	13 5/8	6 5/8	6 7/8	26 3/8	26 3/8	Ogilvie River, Yukon	Charles L. Baldridge	Charles L. Baldridge	1987	8
170	38 7/8	40 7/8	14	14 1/8	6 6/8	6 5/8	24	24	Snake River, Yukon	Clark Johnson	Clark Johnson	1988	9
170	40 5/8	37 7/8	14	13 6/8	7 2/8	7 2/8	22 1/8	22 1/8	Chugach Mts., Alaska	Russell Scribner	Russell Scribner	1988	9
168 6/8	42 2/8	43 6/8	13 2/8	13 6/8	5 3/8	5 3/8	25 1/8	25 1/8	Iron Creek, Alaska	Robert M. Pepper, Jr.	Robert M. Pepper, Jr.	1985	11
168 6/8	40	40 6/8	13 7/8	13 7/8	5 7/8	6 1/8	25 2/8	24 5/8	Talkeetna Mts., Alaska	Jeffrey D. Wallis	Jeffrey D. Wallis	1988	11
168 1/8	40 3/8	40	12 5/8	12 7/8	8	7 5/8	24 1/8	24 1/8	Big River, Alaska	Floyd R. Lunde	Floyd R. Lunde	1986	13
167 1/8	45 4/8	43 3/8	12 2/8	12 3/8	5 5/8	6	29 4/8	29 2/8	Alaska Range, Alaska	Robert W. Cassell	Robert W. Cassell	1985	14
165 7/8	38 6/8	38 3/8	14 1/8	14 1/8	6 2/8	6 3/8	24 4/8	23 4/8	Mackenzie Mts., N.W.T.	Lynn B. Jackson	Lynn B. Jackson	1986	15
165 4/8	40 7/8	38 3/8	13 3/8	13 3/8	6 1/8	6 1/8	22 3/8	22 3/8	Mackenzie Mts., N.W.T.	Frank Moryle	W. & V. St. Germaine	1946	16
165	40 4/8	41 1/8	13 6/8	13 6/8	5 5/8	5 5/8	28 4/8	28 4/8	Nahanni Butte, N.W.T.	Gary T. Laya	Gary T. Laya	1986	17
165	39 3/8	40 5/8	13 7/8	13 6/8	6 2/8	5 7/8	24 1/8	24	Mackenzie Mts., N.W.T.	Vicki St. Germaine	Vicki St. Germaine	1987	17
172 2/8 *	43 1/8	43 3/8	13 5/8	13 4/8	6 2/8	6 3/8	26 6/8	26 4/8	Chugach Mts., Alaska	Michael L. Kasterin	Michael L. Kasterin	1986	
172 2/8 *	42 3/8	41 3/8	13 4/8	13 5/8	6 5/8	6 5/8	23	22 7/8	Chugach Mts., Alaska	Ethan Williams	Ethan Williams	1988	

* Final Score subject to revision by additional verifying measurements.

Stone's Sheep
Ovis dalli stonei

Minimum Score 165 — World's Record 196-6/8

Score	Length of Horn R.	L.	Circumference of Base R.	L.	Circumference at Third Quarter R.	L.	Greatest Spread	Tip to Tip Spread	Locality Killed	By Whom Killed	Owner	Date Killed	Rank
182 4/8	42 5/8	41 7/8	14 6/8	14 6/8	7 7/8	7 7/8	24	24	Chlotapecta Creek, B.C.	Gary F. Bogner	Gary F. Bogner	1987	1
179 1/8	41 7/8	42 7/8	15	15 1/8	7	6 5/8	26 6/8	26	Muskwa River, B.C.	Cliff C. Cory	Cliff C. Cory	1987	2
176	39	41 7/8	15 2/8	15 1/8	6 5/8	6 4/8	23 6/8	23 5/8	Tetsa River, B.C.	Ron Sedor	Ron Sedor	1988	3
173 5/8	41 3/8	41 5/8	14 4/8	14 2/8	6 2/8	6 2/8	26 4/8	26 4/8	Coldfish Lake, B.C.	Roger Britton	Roger Britton	1986	4
170 6/8	42 2/8	42 2/8	13 7/8	13 6/8	6 1/8	6 2/8	32	32	Pink Mt., B.C.	Unknown	J. Michael Conoyer	1960	5
170 2/8	39 5/8	40 7/8	14 2/8	14 2/8	6 6/8	6 6/8	27 1/8	27 1/8	Cutbank Creek, B.C.	Brett M. Moore	Brett M. Moore	1987	6
170 1/8	40	40 1/8	14 1/8	14 1/8	6 4/8	6 4/8	24 2/8	24 1/8	Rabbit River, B.C.	Frank F. Azcarate	Frank F. Azcarate	1985	7
169 2/8	40 1/8	40 7/8	15 3/8	15 3/8	5 5/8	5 5/8	27 5/8	27 6/8	Richards Creek, B.C.	Dan E. McBride	Dan E. McBride	1986	8
166 4/8	42 1/8	35 5/8	14 2/8	14 2/8	6 1/8	5 1/8	27 3/8	27 3/8	Richards Creek, B.C.	S. Randy Archibald	S. Randy Archibald	1987	9
166 4/8	38 5/8	37 7/8	14 1/8	14 2/8	6 5/8	7 1/8	21 2/8	21 2/8	Prophet River, B.C.	Keith Martin	Keith Martin	1988	9
178 *	44 7/8	44 1/8	13 5/8	13 5/8	6 6/8	6 6/8	29 5/8	29 6/8	Rose Mt., Yukon	William P. Williamson	William P. Williamson	1987	
177 1/8 *	42 1/8	41 5/8	15 3/8	15 4/8	6 4/8	6	27 4/8	27	Muskwa River, B.C.	Gerald A. Paille	Gerald A. Paille	1986	
177 *	36	40 4/8	15 1/8	15	8 3/8	8 1/8	21 6/8	18 6/8	Sikanni Chief River, B.C.	Don R. Hughes	Don R. Hughes	1988	
176 3/8 *	45	38 7/8	14 4/8	14 4/8	7 3/8	6 5/8	23	23	Wokkpash Creek, B.C.	H. Robert Grounds	H. Robert Grounds	1987	

* Final Score subject to revision by additional verifying measurements.

Score Charts
of the
Official Scoring System
for
North American
Big Game Trophies

OFFICIAL SCORING SYSTEM FOR NORTH AMERICAN BIG GAME TROPHIES

Records of North American Big Game

BOONE AND CROCKETT CLUB

P.O. Box 547
Dumfries, VA 22026

Minimum Score:	Awards	All-time
Alaska brown	26	28
black	20	21
grizzly	23	24
polar	27	27

BEAR

Kind of Bear: Alaska brown
Sex: Male

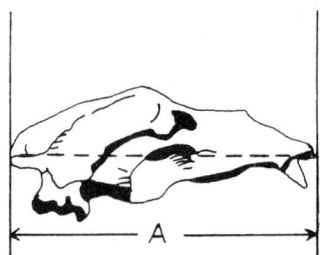
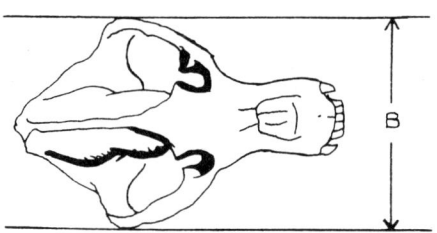

SEE OTHER SIDE FOR INSTRUCTIONS	Measurements
A. Greatest Length Without Lower Jaw	17 14/16
B. Greatest Width	11 15/16
FINAL SCORE	29 13/16

Exact Locality Where Killed: Kodiak Island, Alaska
Date Killed: 11/08/85 By Whom Killed: W. Ted Burger
Present Owner: W. Ted Burger
Address:
Guide Name and Address: Joe Want
Remarks: (Mention Any Abnormalities or Unique Qualities)

I certify that I have measured the above trophy on _____ 29 April _____ 19 89
at (Address) New Mexico Museum of Natural History (City) Albuquerque (State) NM
and that these measurements and data are, to the best of my knowledge and belief, made in accordance with the instructions given.

Witness: Dennis L. Shirley   Signature: William C. MacCarty III
                                              B&C OFFICIAL MEASURER
                                              I.D. Number

INSTRUCTIONS FOR MEASURING BEAR

Measurements are taken with calipers or by using parallel perpendiculars, to the nearest one-sixteenth of an inch, without reduction of fractions. Official measurement cannot be taken until skull has dried for at least sixty days after the animal was killed. All adhering flesh, membrane and cartilage must be completely removed before official measurements are taken.

A. Greatest Length is measured between perpendiculars parallel to the long axis of the skull, without the lower jaw and excluding malformations.

B. Greatest Width is measured between perpendiculars at right angles to the long axis.

* * * * * * * * * * * * * * * * * *

FAIR CHASE STATEMENT FOR ALL HUNTER-TAKEN TROPHIES

To make use of the following methods shall be deemed as UNFAIR CHASE and unsportsmanlike, and any trophy obtained by use of such means is disqualified from entry.

I. Spotting or herding game from the air, followed by landing in its vicinity for pursuit;

II. Herding or pursuing game with motor-powered vehicles;

III. Use of electronic communications for attracting, locating or observing game, or guiding the hunter to such game;

IV. Hunting game confined by artificial barriers, including escape-proof fencing; or hunting game transplanted solely for the purpose of commercial shooting.

* * * * * * * * * * * * * * * * * *

I certify that the trophy scored on this chart was not taken in UNFAIR CHASE as defined above by the Boone and Crockett Club. I further certify that it was taken in full compliance with local game laws of the state, province, or territory.

Date: _____ Signature of Hunter: _____

(Have Signature Notarized by a Notary Public)

Copyright © 1988 by Boone and Crockett Club
(Reproduction strictly forbidden without express, written consent)

OFFICIAL SCORING SYSTEM FOR NORTH AMERICAN BIG GAME TROPHIES

Records of North American Big Game

BOONE AND CROCKETT CLUB

P.O. Box 547
Dumfries, VA 22026

Minimum Score: Awards   All-time
  cougar   14-8/16 15
  jaguar   14-8/16 14-8/16

COUGAR AND JAGUAR

Kind of Cat __cougar__

Sex __male__

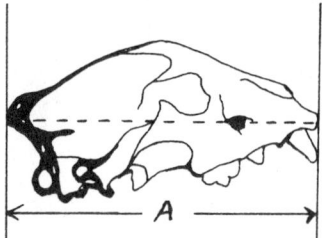 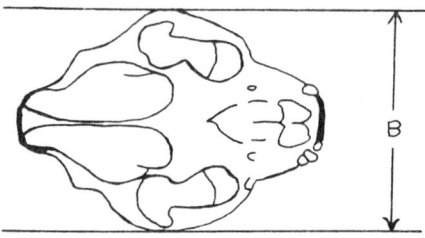

SEE OTHER SIDE FOR INSTRUCTIONS	Measurements
A. Greatest Length Without Lower Jaw	9 8/16
B. Greatest Width	6 11/16
FINAL SCORE	16 3/16

Exact Locality Where Killed: Idaho Co., Idaho
Date Killed: 02/26/88   By Whom Killed: Gene R. Alford
Present Owner: B&C National Collection
Address:
Guide Name and Address:
Remarks: (Mention Any Abnormalities or Unique Qualities)

I certify that I have measured the above trophy on _____ 30 April 19 89
at (Address) New Mexico Museum of Natural History (City) Albuquerque (State) NM
and that these measurements and data are, to the best of my knowledge and belief, made in accordance with the instructions given.

Witness: Dennis L. Shirley   Signature: C. Randall Byers
                                          B&C OFFICIAL MEASURER
                                                                    I.D. Number

INSTRUCTIONS FOR MEASURING COUGAR AND JAGUAR

Measurements are taken with calipers or by using parallel perpendiculars, to the nearest one-sixteenth of an inch, without reduction of fractions. Official measurements cannot be taken until the skull has dried for at least sixty days after the animal was killed. All adhering flesh, membrane and cartilage must be completely removed before official measurements are taken.

A. Greatest Length is measured between perpendiculars parallel to the long axis of the skull, without the lower jaw and excluding malformations.

B. Greatest Width is measured between perpendiculars at right angles to the long axis.

* * * * * * * * * * * * * * * * * *

FAIR CHASE STATEMENT FOR ALL HUNTER-TAKEN TROPHIES

To make use of the following methods shall be deemed as UNFAIR CHASE and unsportsmanlike, and any trophy obtained by use of such means is disqualified from entry.

I. Spotting or herding game from the air, followed by landing in its vicinity for pursuit;

II. Herding or pursuing game with motor-powered vehicles;

III. Use of electronic communications for attracting, locating or observing game, or guiding the hunter to such game;

IV. Hunting game confined by artificial barriers, including escape-proof fencing; or hunting game transplanted solely for the purpose of commercial shooting.

* * * * * * * * * * * * * * * * * *

I certify that the trophy scored on this chart was not taken in UNFAIR CHASE as defined above by the Boone and Crockett Club. I further certify that it was taken in full compliance with local game laws of the state, province, or territory.

Date: _____ Signature of Hunter: _____

(Have Signature Notarized by a Notary Public)

Copyright © 1988 by Boone and Crockett Club
(Reproduction strictly forbidden without express, written consent)

OFFICIAL SCORING SYSTEM FOR NORTH AMERICAN BIG GAME TROPHIES

Records of North American Big Game

BOONE AND CROCKETT CLUB

P.O. Box 547
Dumfries, VA 22026

Minimum Score: Awards All-time
Atlantic 95 95
Pacific 100 100

WALRUS

Kind of Walrus: Pacific

Sex: male

SEE OTHER SIDE FOR INSTRUCTIONS		Column 1	Column 2	Column 3
A. Greatest Spread	10 6/8	Right Tusk	Left Tusk	Difference
B. Tip to Tip Spread	9 7/8			
C. Entire Length of Loose Tusk		28 4/8	29	4/8
D-1. Circumference of Base		8 4/8	8	4/8
D-2. Circumference at First Quarter		8 5/8	8 3/8	2/8
D-3. Circumference at Second Quarter		7 5/8	7 3/8	2/8
D-4. Circumference at Third Quarter		6	6	
TOTALS		59 2/8	58 6/8	1 4/8
Enter Total of Columns 1 and 2	118	Exact Locality Where Killed: Nunivak Island, Alaska		
Subtract Column 3	1 4/8	Date Killed: 05/06/78 By Whom Killed: Darrell D. Wells		
FINAL SCORE	116 4/8	Present Owner: Darrell D. Wells		
		Guide Name and Address:		
		Remarks:		

I certify that I have measured the above trophy on _____ 30 November _____ 19 87

at (Address) P.O. Box 2534 (City) Soldotna (State) AK

and that these measurements and data are, to the best of my knowledge and belief, made in accordance with the instructions given.

Witness: David L. Waltenger   Signature: Ted H. Spraker

B&C OFFICIAL MEASURER

I.D. Number

INSTRUCTIONS FOR MEASURING WALRUS

All measurements must be made with a 1/4-inch, flexible steel tape to the nearest one-eighth of an inch. Wherever it is necessary to change direction of measurement, mark a control point and swing tape at this point. Enter fractional figures in eighths, without reduction. Tusks must be removed from mounted specimens for measuring. Official measurement cannot be taken until tusks have dried for at least sixty days after the animal was killed.

A. Greatest Spread is measured between perpendiculars at a right angle to the center line of the skull.

B. Tip to Tip Spread is measured between tips of tusks.

C. Entire Length of Loose Tusk is measured over outer curve from base to a point in line with tip.

D-1 Circumference of Base is measured at a right angle to axis of tusk. Do not follow edge of contact between tusk and skull.

D. 2-3-4 Divide measurement C of longer tusk by four. Starting at base, mark both tusks at these quarters (even though the other tusk is shorter) and measure circumferences at these marks.

* * * * * * * * * * * * * * * * * *

FAIR CHASE STATEMENT FOR ALL HUNTER-TAKEN TROPHIES

To make use of the following methods shall be deemed as UNFAIR CHASE and unsportsmanlike, and any trophy obtained by use of such means is disqualified from entry.

I. Spotting or herding game from the air, followed by landing in its vicinity for pursuit;

II. Herding or pursuing game with motor-powered vehicles;

III. Use of electronic communications for attracting, locating or observing game, or guiding the hunter to such game;

IV. Hunting game confined by artificial barriers, including escape-proof fencing; or hunting game transplanted solely for the purpose of commercial shooting.

* * * * * * * * * * * * * * * * * *

I certify that the trophy scored on this chart was not taken in UNFAIR CHASE as defined above by the Boone and Crockett Club. I further certify that it was taken in full compliance with local game laws of the state, province, or territory.

Date: _____ Signature of Hunter: _____

(Have Signature Notarized by a Notary Public)

Copyright © 1988 by Boone and Crockett Club
(Reproduction strictly forbidden without express, written consent)

OFFICIAL SCORING SYSTEM FOR NORTH AMERICAN BIG GAME TROPHIES

Records of North American Big Game

BOONE AND CROCKETT CLUB

P.O. Box 547
Dumfries, VA 22026

Minimum Score: Awards 360 All-time 375

TYPICAL AMERICAN ELK (WAPITI)

DETAIL OF POINT MEASUREMENT

Abnormal Points	
Right Antler	Left Antler
	2 7/8

| E. Total of Lengths of Abnormal Points | 2 7/8 |

SEE OTHER SIDE FOR INSTRUCTIONS				Column 1	Column 2	Column 3	Column 4
A. No. Points on Right Antler	6	No. Points on Left Antler	7	Spread Credit	Right Antler	Left Antler	Difference
B. Tip to Tip Spread	35 7/8	C. Greatest Spread	48 4/8				
D. Inside Spread of Main Beams	42 4/8	(Credit May Equal But Not Exceed Longer Antler)		42 4/8			
F. Length of Main Beam					57 4/8	58 4/8	1
G-1. Length of First Point					21 3/8	20 6/8	5/8
G-2. Length of Second Point					22 7/8	22 6/8	1/8
G-3. Length of Third Point					17 7/8	15 2/8	2 5/8
G-4. Length of Fourth (Royal) Point					19 4/8	19 5/8	1/8
G-5. Length of Fifth Point					15 3/8	14 6/8	5/8
G-6. Length of Sixth Point, If Present							
G-7. Length of Seventh Point, If Present							
H-1. Circumference at Smallest Place Between First and Second Points					9 4/8	9 2/8	2/8
H-2. Circumference at Smallest Place Between Second and Third Points					7 1/8	7 3/8	2/8
H-3. Circumference at Smallest Place Between Third and Fourth Points					7 4/8	8	4/8
H-4. Circumference at Smallest Place Between Fourth and Fifth Points					6 6/8	6 7/8	1/8
TOTALS				42 4/8	185 3/8	183 1/8	6 2/8

Enter Total of Columns 1, 2, and 3	411	Exact Locality Where Killed:	Apache Co., Ariz.
Subtract Column 4	6 2/8	Date Killed: 09/22/87	By Whom Killed: Bruce R. Keller
Subtotal	404 6/8	Present Owner:	Bruce R. Keller
Subtract (E) Total of Lengths of Abn. Points	2 7/8	Guide Name and Address:	Tom Caddo
FINAL SCORE	401 7/8	Remarks:	

I certify that I have measured the above trophy on _____ 30 April ____ 19 89 ___

at (address) New Mexico Museum of Natural History   City Albuquerque   State NM

and that these measurements and data are, to the best of my knowledge and belief, made in accordance with the instructions given.

Witness: Eldon Buckner   Signature Tim Kelly

B&C OFFICIAL MEASURER

I.D. Number

INSTRUCTIONS FOR MEASURING TYPICAL AMERICAN ELK (WAPITI)

All measurements must be made with a 1/4-inch flexible steel tape to the nearest one-eighth of an inch. Wherever it is necessary to change direction of measurement, mark a control point and swing tape at this point. (Note: a flexible steel cable can be used to measure points and main beams only.) Enter fractional figures in eighths, without reduction. Official measurements cannot be taken until the antlers have dried for at least 60 days after the animal was killed.

A. **Number of Points on Each Antler:** to be counted a point, the projection must be at least one inch long, with length exceeding width at one inch or more of length. All points are measured from tip of point to nearest edge of beam as illustrated. Beam tip is counted as a point but not measured as a point.

B. **Tip to Tip Spread** is measured between tips of main beams.

C. **Greatest Spread** is measured between perpendiculars at a right angle to the center line of the skull at widest part, whether across main beams or points.

D. **Inside Spread of Main Beams** is measured at a right angle to the center line of the skull at widest point between main beams. Enter this measurement again as Spread Credit if it is less than or equal to the length of longer antler; if longer, enter longer antler length for Spread Credit.

E. **Total of Lengths of all Abnormal Points:** Abnormal Points are those non-typical in location (such as points originating from a point or from bottom or sides of main beam) or pattern (extra points, not generally paired). Measure in usual manner and record in appropriate blanks.

F. **Length of Main Beam** is measured from lowest outside edge of burr over outer curve to the most distant point of what is, or appears to be, the main beam. The point of beginning is that point on the burr where the center line along the outer curve of the beam intersects the burr, then following generally the line of the illustration.

G. 1-2-3-4-5-6-7 **Length of Normal Points:** Normal points project from the top or front of the main beam in the general pattern illustrated. They are measured from nearest edge of main beam over outer curve to tip. Lay the tape along the outer curve of the beam so that the top edge of the tape coincides with the top edge of the beam on both sides of point to determine the baseline for point measurement. Record point length in appropriate blanks.

H. 1-2-3-4 Circumferences are taken as detailed for each measurement.

* * * * * * * * * * * * * * * * *

FAIR CHASE STATEMENT FOR ALL HUNTER-TAKEN TROPHIES

To make use of the following methods shall be deemed as UNFAIR CHASE and unsportsmanlike, and any trophy obtained by use of such means is disqualified from entry.

  I. Spotting or herding game from the air, followed by landing in its vicinity for pursuit;

  II. Herding or pursuing game with motor-powered vehicles;

  III. Use of electronic communications for attracting, locating or observing game, or guiding the hunter to such game;

  IV. Hunting game confined by artificial barriers, including escape-proof fencing; or hunting game transplanted solely for the purpose of commercial shooting.

* * * * * * * * * * * * * * * * *

I certify that the trophy scored on this chart was not taken in UNFAIR CHASE as defined above by the Boone and Crockett Club. I further certify that it was taken in full compliance with local game laws of the state, province, or territory.

Date _____   Signature of Hunter _____

(Have signature notarized by a Notary Public)

Copyright © 1988 by Boone and Crockett Club
(Reproduction strictly forbidden without express, written consent)

OFFICIAL SCORING SYSTEM FOR NORTH AMERICAN BIG GAME TROPHIES

Records of North American Big Game

BOONE AND CROCKETT CLUB

P.O. Box 547
Dumfries, VA 22026

Minimum Score: Awards 385 All-time 385

NON-TYPICAL AMERICAN ELK (WAPITI)

Abnormal Points	
Right Antler	Left Antler
6 5/8	16 3/8
15	11 5/8
E. Total of Lengths of Abnormal Points	49 5/8

SEE OTHER SIDE FOR INSTRUCTIONS				Column 1 Spread Credit	Column 2 Right Antler	Column 3 Left Antler	Column 4 Difference
A. No. Points on Right Antler	8	No. Points on Left Antler	8				
B. Tip to Tip Spread	31 2/8	C. Greatest Spread	60 3/8				
D. Inside Spread of Main Beams	41 6/8	(Credit May Equal But Not Exceed Longer Antler)		41 6/8			
F. Length of Main Beam					58	57 7/8	1/8
G-1. Length of First Point					19 4/8	17 7/8	1 5/8
G-2. Length of Second Point					18 4/8	15 4/8	3
G-3. Length of Third Point					18 7/8	17 4/8	1 3/8
G-4. Length of Fourth (Royal) Point					22 6/8	22 7/8	1/8
G-5. Length of Fifth Point					14 6/8	17 1/8	2 3/8
G-6. Length of Sixth Point, If Present							
G-7. Length of Seventh Point, If Present							
H-1. Circumference at Smallest Place Between First and Second Points					9 2/8	10	6/8
H-2. Circumference at Smallest Place Between Second and Third Points					7 2/8	7 3/8	1/8
H-3. Circumference at Smallest Place Between Third and Fourth Points					7 2/8	7 6/8	4/8
H-4. Circumference at Smallest Place Between Fourth and Fifth Points					7 2/8	7 1/8	1/8
TOTALS				41 6/8	183 3/8	181	10 1/8

Enter Total of Columns 1, 2, and 3	406 1/8	Exact Locality Where Killed: Apache Co., Ariz.
Subtract Column 4	10 1/8	Date Killed: 10/01/84 By Whom Killed: Jerry J. Davis
Subtotal	396	Present Owner: Jerry J. Davis
Add (E) Total of Lengths of Abnormal Points	49 5/8	Guide Name and Address: Phil Stago, Jr.
FINAL SCORE	445 5/8	Remarks:

454

I certify that I have measured the above trophy on _____ 30 April _____ 19 89 _____

at (address) New Mexico Museum of Natural History   City Albuquerque   State NM
and that these measurements and data are, to the best of my knowledge and belief, made in accordance with the instructions given.

Witness: Eldon Buckner _____   Signature Tim Kelly _____

B&C OFFICIAL MEASURER | | | |

I.D. Number

INSTRUCTIONS FOR MEASURING NON-TYPICAL AMERICAN ELK (WAPITI)

All measurements must be made with a 1/4-inch flexible steel tape to the nearest one-eighth of an inch. Wherever it is necessary to change direction of measurement, mark a control point and swing tape at this point. (Note: a flexible steel cable can be used to measure points and main beams only.) Enter fractional figures in eighths, without reduction. Official measurements cannot be taken until the antlers have dried for at least 60 days after the animal was killed.

A. Number of Points on Each Antler: to be counted a point, the projection must be at least one inch long, with length exceeding width at one inch or more of length. All points are measured from tip of point to nearest edge of beam as illustrated. Beam tip is counted as a point but not measured as a point.

B. Tip to Tip Spread is measured between tips of main beams.

C. Greatest Spread is measured between perpendiculars at a right angle to the center line of the skull at widest part, whether across main beams or points.

D. Inside Spread of Main Beams is measured at a right angle to the center line of the skull at widest point between main beams. Enter this measurement again as the Spread Credit if it is less than or equal to the length of longer antler; if longer, enter longer antler length for Spread Credit.

E. Total of Lengths of all Abnormal Points: Abnormal Points are those non-typical in location (such as points originating from a point or from bottom or sides of main beam) or pattern (extra points, not generally paired). Measure in usual manner and record in appropriate blanks.

F. Length of Main Beam is measured from lowest outside edge of burr over outer curve to the most distant point of what is, or appears to be, the main beam. The point of beginning is that point on the burr where the center line along the outer curve of the beam intersects the burr, then following generally the line of the illustration.

G. 1-2-3-4-5-6-7 Length of Normal Points: Normal points project from the top or front of the main beam in the general pattern illustrated. They are measured from nearest edge of main beam over outer curve to tip. Lay the tape along the outer curve of the beam so that the top edge of the tape coincides with the top edge of the beam on both sides of point to determine the baseline for point measurement. Record point length in appropriate blanks.

H. 1-2-3-4 Circumferences are taken as detailed for each measurement.

* * * * * * * * * * * * * * * * * *

FAIR CHASE STATEMENT FOR ALL HUNTER-TAKEN TROPHIES

To make use of the following methods shall be deemed as UNFAIR CHASE and unsportsmanlike, and any trophy obtained by use of such means is disqualified from entry.

  I. Spotting or herding game from the air, followed by landing in its vicinity for pursuit;
 II. Herding or pursuing game with motor-powered vehicles;
III. Use of electronic communications for attracting, locating or observing game, or guiding the hunter to such game;
 IV. Hunting game confined by artificial barriers, including escape-proof fencing; or hunting game transplanted solely for the purpose of commercial shooting.

* * * * * * * * * * * * * * * * * *

I certify that the trophy scored on this chart was not taken in UNFAIR CHASE as defined above by the Boone and Crockett Club. I further certify that it was taken in full compliance with local game laws of the state, province, or territory.

Date _____   Signature of Hunter _____

(Have signature notarized by a Notary Public)

Copyright © 1988 by Boone and Crockett Club
(Reproduction strictly forbidden without express, written consent)

OFFICIAL SCORING SYSTEM FOR NORTH AMERICAN BIG GAME TROPHIES

Records of North American Big Game

BOONE AND CROCKETT CLUB

P.O. Box 547
Dumfries, VA 22026

Minimum Score: Awards 275 All-time 290

ROOSEVELT'S ELK

Crown Points	
Right Antler	Left Antler
12 5/8	2 3/8

I. Add to Total	15

Abnormal Points	
Right Antler	Left Antler

E. Total of Lengths of Abnormal Points

SEE OTHER SIDE FOR INSTRUCTIONS			Column 1 Spread Credit	Column 2 Right Antler	Column 3 Left Antler	Column 4 Difference
A. No. Points on Right Antler	7	No. Points on Left Antler	7			
B. Tip to Tip Spread	36 6/8	C. Greatest Spread	43 4/8			
D. Inside Spread of Main Beams	37 4/8	(Credit May Equal But Not Exceed Longer Antler)	37 4/8			
F. Length of Main Beam				45 7/8	45 5/8	2/8
G-1. Length of First Point				19 1/8	17 5/8	1 4/8
G-2. Length of Second Point				17 6/8	17 7/8	1/8
G-3. Length of Third Point				19 4/8	19	4/8
G-4. Length of Fourth (Royal) Point				16 5/8	18	1 3/8
G-5. Length of Fifth Point				9 2/8	8 6/8	
G-6. Length of Sixth Point, If Present						
G-7. Length of Seventh Point, If Present						
H-1. Circumference at Smallest Place Between First and Second Points				9 4/8	9 1/8	3/8
H-2. Circumference at Smallest Place Between Second and Third Points				7 3/8	7 5/8	2/8
H-3. Circumference at Smallest Place Between Third and Fourth Points				7 1/8	7 4/8	3/8
H-4. Circumference at Smallest Place Between Fourth and Fifth Points				5 7/8	6	1/8
TOTALS			37 4/8	158	157 1/8	4 7/8

Enter Total of Columns 1, 2, 3 and (I)	367 5/8	Exact Locality Where Killed:	Lincoln Co., Oreg.
SUBTRACT Column 4	4 7/8	Date Killed: 11/55	By Whom Killed: James H. Flescher
Subtotal	362 6/8	Present Owner:	James H. Flescher
SUBTRACT (E) Abn. Pts.		Guide Name and Address:	
FINAL SCORE	362 6/8	Remarks:	

I certify that I have measured the above trophy on _____ 29 April _____ 19 89 ____

at (address) __New Mexico Museum of Natural History__ City __Albuquerque__ State __NM__
and that these measurements and data are, to the best of my knowledge and belief, made in accordance with the instructions given.

Witness: __Dennis L. Shirley__ Signature __William C. MacCarty III__

B&C OFFICIAL MEASURER

I.D. Number

INSTRUCTIONS FOR MEASURING ROOSEVELT'S ELK

All measurements must be made with a 1/4-inch flexible steel tape to the nearest one-eighth of an inch. Wherever it is necessary to change direction of measurement, mark a control point and swing tape at this point. (Note: a flexible steel cable can be used to measure points and main beams only.) Enter fractional figures in eighths, without reduction. Official measurements cannot be taken until the antlers have dried for at least 60 days after the animal was killed.

A. Number of Points on Each Antler: to be counted a point, the projection must be at least one inch long, with length exceeding width at one inch or more of length. All points are measured from tip of point to nearest edge of beam as illustrated. Beam tip is counted as a point but not measured as a point.
B. Tip to Tip Spread is measured between tips of main beams.
C. Greatest Spread is measured between perpendiculars at a right angle to the center line of the skull at widest part, whether across main beams or points.
D. Inside Spread of Main Beams is measured at a right angle to the center line of the skull at widest point between main beams. Enter this measurement again as the Spread Credit if it is less than or equal to the length of longer antler; if longer, enter longer antler length for Spread Credit.
E. Total of Lengths of all Abnormal Points: Abnormal Points are those non-typical in location (such as points originating from a point or from bottom or sides of main beam) or pattern (extra points, not generally paired). Measure in usual manner and record in appropriate blanks. **Note: do not confuse with Crown Point that may occur at base of Royal.**
F. Length of Main Beam is measured from lowest outside edge of burr over outer curve to the most distant point of what is, or appears to be, the main beam. The point of beginning is that point on the burr where the center line along the outer curve of the beam intersects the burr, then following generally the line of the illustration.
G. 1-2-3-4-5-6-7 Length of Normal Points: Normal points project from the top or front of the main beam in the general pattern illustrated. They are measured from nearest edge of main beam over outer curve to tip. Lay the tape along the outer curve of the beam so that the top edge of the tape coincides with the top edge of the beam on both sides of point to determine the baseline for point measurement. Record point length in appropriate blanks.
H. 1-2-3-4 Circumferences are taken as detailed for each measurement.
I. Crown Points: From the well-defined Royal on out to end of beam, all points other than the normal points in their typical locations are Crown Points. This includes points occurring on the Royal, on other normal points, and on Crown Points. Measure and record in appropriate blanks provided and add to score below.

* * * * * * * * * * * * * * * * * *

FAIR CHASE STATEMENT FOR ALL HUNTER-TAKEN TROPHIES

To make use of the following methods shall be deemed as UNFAIR CHASE and unsportsmanlike, and any trophy obtained by use of such means is disqualified from entry.

I. Spotting or herding game from the air, followed by landing in its vicinity for pursuit;

II. Herding or pursuing game with motor-powered vehicles;

III. Use of electronic communications for attracting, locating or observing game, or guiding the hunter to such game;

IV. Hunting game confined by artificial barriers, including escape-proof fencing; or hunting game transplanted solely for the purpose of commercial shooting.

* * * * * * * * * * * * * * * * * *

I certify that the trophy scored on this chart was not taken in UNFAIR CHASE as defined above by the Boone and Crockett Club. I further certify that it was taken in full compliance with local game laws of the state, province, or territory.

Date _____ Signature of Hunter _____

(Have signature notarized by a Notary Public)

Copyright © 1988 by Boone and Crockett Club
(Reproduction strictly forbidden without express, written consent)

OFFICIAL SCORING SYSTEM FOR NORTH AMERICAN BIG GAME TROPHIES

Records of North American Big Game

BOONE AND CROCKETT CLUB

P.O. Box 547
Dumfries, VA 22026

Minimum Score:	Awards	All-time
mule	185	195
Columbia	120	130
Sitka	100	108

TYPICAL MULE AND BLACKTAIL DEER

Kind of Deer: Sitka blacktail

DETAIL OF POINT MEASUREMENT

Abnormal Points	
Right Antler	Left Antler

E. Total of Lengths of Abnormal Points

SEE OTHER SIDE FOR INSTRUCTIONS			Column 1	Column 2	Column 3	Column 4
A. No. Points on Right Antler	5	No. Points on Left Antler	5	Spread Credit	Right Antler	Left Antler	Difference
B. Tip to Tip Spread	4 6/8	C. Greatest Spread	16 5/8				
D. Inside Spread of Main Beams	14 5/8	(Credit May Equal But Not Exceed Longer Antler)		14 5/8			
F. Length of Main Beam					18 5/8	19 4/8	7/8
G-1. Length of First Point, If Present					1 4/8	1 7/8	3/8
G-2. Length of Second Point					10	10 2/8	2/8
G-3. Length of Third Point, If Present					5 5/8	5 4/8	1/8
G-4. Length of Fourth Point, If Present					6 1/8	6 4/8	3/8
H-1. Circumference at Smallest Place Between Burr and First Point					4	4 1/8	1/8
H-2. Circumference at Smallest Place Between First and Second Points					3 5/8	3 6/8	1/8
H-3. Circumference at Smallest Place Between Main Beam and Third Point					3 1/8	3 3/8	2/8
H-4. Circumference at Smallest Place Between Second and Fourth Points					3 3/8	3 6/8	3/8
TOTALS				14 5/8	56	58 5/8	2 7/8

Enter Total of Columns 1, 2, and 3	129 2/8	Exact Locality Where Killed:	Sunny Hay Mt., Alaska
Subtract Column 4	2 7/8	Date Killed: 10/17/87	By Whom Killed: Harry R. Horner
Subtotal	126 3/8	Present Owner:	Harry R. Horner
Subtract (E) Total of Lengths of Abn. Points		Guide Name and Address:	
FINAL SCORE	126 3/8	Remarks:	

458

I certify that I have measured the above trophy on **30 April 1989**
at (address) **New Mexico Museum of Natural History** City **Albuquerque** State **NM**
and that these measurements and data are, to the best of my knowledge and belief, made in accordance with the instructions given.

Witness: **Dennis L. Shirley** Signature: **Eldon Buckner**
B&C OFFICIAL MEASURER   I.D. Number

INSTRUCTIONS FOR MEASURING TYPICAL MULE AND BLACKTAIL DEER

All measurements must be made with a 1/4-inch flexible steel tape to the nearest one-eighth of an inch. Wherever it is necessary to change direction of measurement, mark a control point and swing tape at this point. (Note: a flexible steel cable can be used to take point and beam length measurements only.) Enter fractional figures in eighths, without reduction. Official measurements cannot be taken until antlers have dried for at least 60 days after the animal was killed.

A. Number of Points on Each Antler: to be counted a point, the projection must be at least one inch long, with length exceeding width at one inch or more of length. All points are measured from tip of point to nearest edge of beam as illustrated. Beam tip is counted as a point but not measured as a point.

B. Tip to Tip Spread is measured between tips of main beams.

C. Greatest Spread is measured between perpendiculars at a right angle to the center line of the skull at widest part, whether across main beams or points.

D. Inside Spread of Main Beams is measured at a right angle to the center line of the skull at widest point between main beams. Enter this measurement again as Spread Credit if it is less than or equal to the length of longer antler; if longer, enter longer antler length for Spread Credit.

E. Total of Lengths of all Abnormal Points: Abnormal Points are those non-typical in location such as points originating from a point (exception: G-3 originates from G-2 in perfectly normal fashion) or from bottom or sides of main beam, or any points beyond the normal pattern of five (including beam tip) per antler. Measure each abnormal point in usual manner and enter in appropriate blanks.

F. Length of Main Beam is measured from lowest outside edge of burr over outer curve to the most distant point of what is, or appears to be, the Main Beam. The point of beginning is that point on the burr where the center line along the outer curve of the beam intersects the burr, then following generally the line of the illustration.

G. 1-2-3-4 Length of Normal Points: Normal points are the brow and the upper and lower forks as shown in the illustration. They are measured from nearest edge of beam over outer curve to tip. Lay the tape along the outer curve of the beam so that the top edge of the tape coincides with the top edge of the beam on both sides of point to determine the baseline for point measurement. Record point lengths in appropriate blanks.

H. 1-2-3-4 Circumferences are taken as detailed for each measurement. If brow point is missing, take H-1 and H-2 at smallest place between burr and G-2. If G-3 is missing, take H-3 halfway between the base and tip of second point. If G-4 is missing, take H-4 halfway between second point and tip of main beam.

* * * * * * * * * * * * * * * * *

FAIR CHASE STATEMENT FOR ALL HUNTER-TAKEN TROPHIES

To make use of the following methods shall be deemed as UNFAIR CHASE and unsportsmanlike, and any trophy obtained by use of such means is disqualified from entry.

I. Spotting or herding game from the air, followed by landing in its vicinity for pursuit;

II. Herding or pursuing game with motor-powered vehicles;

III. Use of electronic communications for attracting, locating or observing game, or guiding the hunter to such game;

IV. Hunting game confined by artificial barriers, including escape-proof fencing; or hunting game transplanted solely for the purpose of commercial shooting.

* * * * * * * * * * * * * * * * *

I certify that the trophy scored on this chart was not taken in UNFAIR CHASE as defined above by the Boone and Crockett Club. I further certify that it was taken in full compliance with local game laws of the state, province, or territory.

Date: _____ Signature of Hunter: _____
(Have signature notarized by a Notary Public)

Copyright © 1988 by Boone and Crockett Club
(Reproduction strictly forbidden without express, written consent)

OFFICIAL SCORING SYSTEM FOR NORTH AMERICAN BIG GAME TROPHIES

Records of North American Big Game

BOONE AND CROCKETT CLUB

P.O. Box 547
Dumfries, VA 22026

Minimum Score: Awards 225 All-time 240

NON-TYPICAL MULE DEER

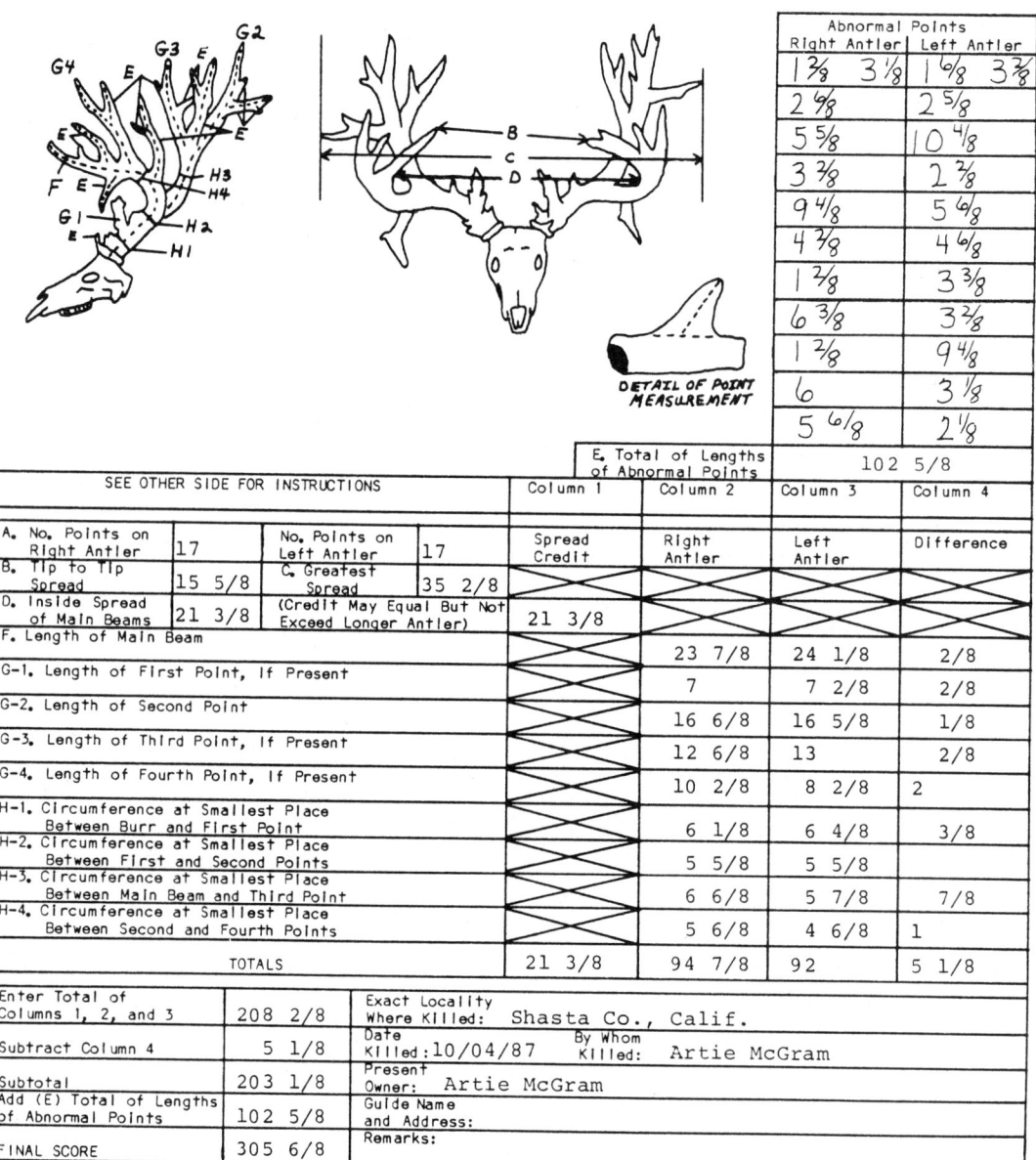

Abnormal Points			
Right Antler		Left Antler	
1. 7/8	3 1/8	1. 6/8	3 7/8
2. 6/8		2 5/8	
5 5/8		10 4/8	
3 7/8		2 7/8	
9 4/8		5 6/8	
4 7/8		4 6/8	
1 7/8		3 3/8	
6 3/8		3 7/8	
1 7/8		9 4/8	
6		3 1/8	
5 6/8		2 1/8	

E. Total of Lengths of Abnormal Points: 102 5/8

SEE OTHER SIDE FOR INSTRUCTIONS

				Column 1 Spread Credit	Column 2 Right Antler	Column 3 Left Antler	Column 4 Difference
A. No. Points on Right Antler	17	No. Points on Left Antler	17				
B. Tip to Tip Spread	15 5/8	C. Greatest Spread	35 2/8				
D. Inside Spread of Main Beams	21 3/8	(Credit May Equal But Not Exceed Longer Antler)		21 3/8			
F. Length of Main Beam					23 7/8	24 1/8	2/8
G-1. Length of First Point, If Present					7	7 2/8	2/8
G-2. Length of Second Point					16 6/8	16 5/8	1/8
G-3. Length of Third Point, If Present					12 6/8	13	2/8
G-4. Length of Fourth Point, If Present					10 2/8	8 2/8	2
H-1. Circumference at Smallest Place Between Burr and First Point					6 1/8	6 4/8	3/8
H-2. Circumference at Smallest Place Between First and Second Points					5 5/8	5 5/8	
H-3. Circumference at Smallest Place Between Main Beam and Third Point					6 6/8	5 7/8	7/8
H-4. Circumference at Smallest Place Between Second and Fourth Points					5 6/8	4 6/8	1
TOTALS				21 3/8	94 7/8	92	5 1/8

Enter Total of Columns 1, 2, and 3	208 2/8	Exact Locality Where Killed: Shasta Co., Calif.
Subtract Column 4	5 1/8	Date Killed: 10/04/87 By Whom Killed: Artie McGram
Subtotal	203 1/8	Present Owner: Artie McGram
Add (E) Total of Lengths of Abnormal Points	102 5/8	Guide Name and Address:
FINAL SCORE	305 6/8	Remarks:

460

I certify that I have measured the above trophy on _____1 May_____ 19_89_

at (address) _New Mexico Museum of Natural History_ City _Albuquerque_ State _NM_
and that these measurements and data are, to the best of my knowledge and belief, made in accordance with the instructions given.

Witness: _Walter H. White_   Signature: _Eldon Buckner_

B&C OFFICIAL MEASURER   I.D. Number

INSTRUCTIONS FOR MEASURING NON-TYPICAL MULE DEER

All measurements must be made with a 1/4-inch flexible steel tape to the nearest one-eighth of an inch. Wherever it is necessary to change direction of measurement, mark a control point and swing tape at this point. (Note: a flexible steel cable can be used to measure points and main beams only.) Enter fractional figures in eighths, without reduction. Official measurements cannot be taken until antlers have dried for at least 60 days after the animal was killed.

A. Number of Points on Each Antler: to be counted a point, the projection must be at least one inch long, with the length exceeding width at one inch or more of length. All points are measured from tip of point to nearest edge of beam as illustrated. Beam tip is counted as a point but is not measured as a point.

B. Tip to Tip Spread is measured between tips of main beams.

C. Greatest Spread is measured between perpendiculars at a right angle to the center line of the skull at widest part, whether across main beams or points.

D. Inside Spread of Main Beams is measured at a right angle to the center line of the skull at widest point between main beams. Enter this measurement again as the Spread Credit if it is less than or equal to the length of longer antler; if longer, enter longer antler length for Spread Credit.

E. Total of Lengths of all Abnormal Points: Abnormal Points are those non-typical in location such as points originating from a point (exception: G-3 originates from G-2 in perfectly normal fashion) or from bottom or sides of main beam, or any points beyond the normal pattern of five (including beam tip) per antler. Measure each abnormal point in usual manner and enter in appropriate blanks.

F. Length of Main Beam is measured from lowest outside edge of burr over outer curve to the most distant point of what is, or appears to be, the main beam. The point of beginning is that point on the burr where the center line along the outer curve of the beam intersects the burr, then following generally the line of the illustration.

G. 1-2-3-4 Length of Normal Points: Normal points are the brow and the upper and lower forks, as shown in the illustration. They are measured from nearest edge of main beam over outer curve to tip. Lay the tape along the outer curve of the beam so that the top edge of the tape coincides with the top edge of the beam on both sides of point to determine the baseline for point measurement. Record point lengths in appropriate blanks.

H. 1-2-3-4 Circumferences are taken as detailed for each measurement. If brow point is missing, take H-1 and H-2 at smallest place between burr and G-2. If G-3 is missing, take H-3 halfway between the base and tip of second point. If G-4 is missing, take H-4 halfway between second point and tip of main beam.

* * * * * * * * * * * * * * * * *

FAIR CHASE STATEMENT FOR ALL HUNTER-TAKEN TROPHIES

To make use of the following methods shall be deemed as UNFAIR CHASE and unsportsmanlike, and any trophy obtained by use of such means is disqualified from entry.

I. Spotting or herding game from the air, followed by landing in its vicinity for pursuit;

II. Herding or pursuing game with motor-powered vehicles;

III. Use of electronic communications for attracting, locating or observing game, or guiding the hunter to such game;

IV. Hunting game confined by artificial barriers, including escape-proof fencing; or hunting game transplanted solely for the purpose of commercial shooting.

* * * * * * * * * * * * * * * * *

I certify that the trophy scored on this chart was not taken in UNFAIR CHASE as defined above by the Boone and Crockett Club. I further certify that it was taken in full compliance with local game laws of the state, province, or territory.

Date: _____   Signature of Hunter: _____

(Have signature notarized by a Notary Public)

Copyright © 1988 by Boone and Crockett Club
(Reproduction strictly forbidden without express, written consent)

OFFICIAL SCORING SYSTEM FOR NORTH AMERICAN BIG GAME TROPHIES

Records of North American Big Game

BOONE AND CROCKETT CLUB

P.O. Box 547
Dumfries, VA 22026

Minimum Score: Awards All-time
  whitetail   160   170
  Coues'   100   110

TYPICAL
WHITETAIL AND COUES' DEER

Kind of Deer: whitetail

DETAIL OF POINT MEASUREMENT

Abnormal Points	
Right Antler	Left Antler
1 4/8	1 3/8

				E. Total of Lengths of Abnormal Points	2 7/8	
SEE OTHER SIDE FOR INSTRUCTIONS				Column 1	Column 2	Column 3	Column 4

				Spread Credit	Right Antler	Left Antler	Difference
A. No. Points on Right Antler	7	No. Points on Left Antler	8				
B. Tip to Tip Spread	13 3/8	C. Greatest Spread	24 1/8				
D. Inside Spread of Main Beams	21 6/8	(Credit May Equal But Not Exceed Longer Antler)		21 6/8			
F. Length of Main Beam					27 2/8	27 5/8	3/8
G-1. Length of First Point, If Present					3 5/8	4 1/8	4/8
G-2. Length of Second Point					12 7/8	11 4/8	1 3/8
G-3. Length of Third Point					12 1/8	12	1/8
G-4. Length of Fourth Point, If Present					10 7/8	10 2/8	5/8
G-5. Length of Fifth Point, If Present					4 1/8	6 4/8	2 3/8
G-6. Length of Sixth Point, If Present						1 5/8	1 5/8
G-7. Length of Seventh Point, If Present							
H-1. Circumference at Smallest Place Between Burr and First Point					5 2/8	5 4/8	2/8
H-2. Circumference at Smallest Place Between First and Second Points					5 1/8	5	1/8
H-3. Circumference at Smallest Place Between Second and Third Points					5 1/8	5 2/8	1/8
H-4. Circumference at Smallest Place Between Third and Fourth Points					5 2/8	5 2/8	
TOTALS				21 6/8	91 5/8	94 5/8	7 4/8

Enter Total of Columns 1, 2, and 3	208
Subtract Column 4	7 4/8
Subtotal	200 4/8
Subtract (E) Total of Lengths of Abn. Points	2 7/8
FINAL SCORE	197 5/8

Exact Locality Where Killed: Wood Co., Wisc.
Date Killed: 11/24/45   By Whom Killed: Joe Haske
Present Owner: Goldie Haske
Guide Name and Address:
Remarks:

I certify that I have measured the above trophy on _____1 May___1989_____

at (address) _New Mexico Museum of Natural History_ City _Albuquerque_ State _NM_
and that these measurements and data are, to the best of my knowledge and belief, made in accordance with the instructions given.

Witness: _Bob Estes_ Signature: _John M. Graham_

B&C OFFICIAL MEASURER

I.D. Number

INSTRUCTIONS FOR MEASURING TYPICAL WHITETAIL AND COUES' DEER

All measurements must be made with a 1/4-inch flexible steel tape to the nearest one-eighth of an inch. Wherever it is necessary to change direction of measurement, mark a control point and swing tape at this point. (Note: a flexible steel cable can be used to measure points and main beams only.) Enter fractional figures in eighths, without reduction. Official measurements cannot be taken until antlers have dried for at least 60 days after the animal was killed.

A. Number of Points on Each Antler: to be counted a point, the projection must be at least one inch long, with the length exceeding width at one inch or more of length. All points are measured from tip of point to nearest edge of beam as illustrated. Beam tip is counted as a point but not measured as a point.

B. Tip to Tip Spread is measured between tips of main beams.

C. Greatest Spread is measured between perpendiculars at a right angle to the center line of the skull at widest part, whether across main beams or points.

D. Inside Spread of Main Beams is measured at a right angle to the center line of the skull at widest point between main beams. Enter this measurement again as the Spread Credit if it is less than or equal to the length of longer antler; if longer, enter longer antler length for Spread Credit.

E. Total of Lengths of all Abnormal Points: Abnormal Points are those non-typical in location (such as points originating from a point or from bottom or sides of main beam) or extra points beyond the normal pattern of points. Measure in usual manner and enter in appropriate blanks.

F. Length of Main Beam is measured from lowest outside edge of burr over outer curve to the most distant point of what is, or appears to be, the main beam. The point of beginning is that point on the burr where the center line along the outer curve of the beam intersects the burr, then following generally the line of the illustration.

G. 1-2-3-4-5-6-7 Length of Normal Points: Normal points project from the top of the main beam. They are measured from nearest edge of main beam over outer curve to tip. Lay the tape along the outer curve of the beam so that the top edge of the tape coincides with the top edge of the beam on both sides of the point to determine the baseline for point measurements. Record point lengths in appropriate blanks.

H. 1-2-3-4 Circumferences are taken as detailed for each measurement. If brow point is missing, take H-1 and H-2 at smallest place between burr and G-2. If G-4 is missing, take H-4 halfway between G-3 and tip of main beam.

* * * * * * * * * * * * * * * * *

FAIR CHASE STATEMENT FOR ALL HUNTER-TAKEN TROPHIES

To make use of the following methods shall be deemed as UNFAIR CHASE and unsportsmanlike, and any trophy obtained by use of such means is disqualified from entry.

I. Spotting or herding game from the air, followed by landing in its vicinity for pursuit;

II. Herding or pursuing game with motor-powered vehicles;

III. Use of electronic communications for attracting, locating or observing game, or guiding the hunter to such game;

IV. Hunting game confined by artificial barriers, including escape-proof fencing; or hunting game transplanted solely for the purpose of commercial shooting.

* * * * * * * * * * * * * * * * *

I certify that the trophy scored on this chart was not taken in UNFAIR CHASE as defined above by the Boone and Crockett Club. I further certify that it was taken in full compliance with local game laws of the state, province, or territory.

Date: _____ Signature of Hunter: _____

(Have signature notarized by a Notary Public)

Copyright © 1988 by Boone and Crockett Club
(Reproduction strictly forbidden without express, written consent)

OFFICIAL SCORING SYSTEM FOR NORTH AMERICAN BIG GAME TROPHIES

Records of North American Big Game

BOONE AND CROCKETT CLUB

P.O. Box 547
Dumfries, VA 22026

Minimum Score: Awards All-time
whitetail 185 195
Coues' 105 120

NON-TYPICAL WHITETAIL AND COUES' DEER

Kind of Deer: Coues'

Abnormal Points	
Right Antler	Left Antler
1 7/8	3 1/8
1 7/8	6 2/8
6 1/8	3 5/8
2 6/8	2 2/8
1 6/8	2 4/8
2	2 1/8
4 5/8	1 3/8

E. Total of Lengths of Abnormal Points: 42 2/8

SEE OTHER SIDE FOR INSTRUCTIONS

				Column 1 Spread Credit	Column 2 Right Antler	Column 3 Left Antler	Column 4 Difference
A. No. Points on Right Antler	11	No. Points on Left Antler	11				
B. Tip to Tip Spread	6 3/8	C. Greatest Spread	18 1/8				
D. Inside Spread of Main Beams	12 6/8	(Credit May Equal But Not Exceed Longer Antler)		12 6/8			
F. Length of Main Beam					17 1/8	16 7/8	2/8
G-1. Length of First Point, If Present					7 1/8	7 1/8	
G-2. Length of Second Point					9	8 2/8	6/8
G-3. Length of Third Point					5 3/8	6 3/8	1
G-4. Length of Fourth Point, If Present							
G-5. Length of Fifth Point, If Present							
G-6. Length of Sixth Point, If Present							
G-7. Length of Seventh Point, If Present							
H-1. Circumference at Smallest Place Between Burr and First Point					3 7/8	4 1/8	2/8
H-2. Circumference at Smallest Place Between First and Second Points					4 3/8	4 1/8	2/8
H-3. Circumference at Smallest Place Between Second and Third Points					3 5/8	3 7/8	2/8
H-4. Circumference at Smallest Place Between Third and Fourth Points					2 4/8	2 5/8	1/8
TOTALS				12 6/8	53	53 3/8	2 7/8

Enter Total of Columns 1, 2, and 3	119 1/8	Exact Locality Where Killed: Santa Cruz Co., Ariz.
Subtract Column 4	2 7/8	Date Killed: Prior 1988 By Whom Killed: Picked up by Walter Pollock
Subtotal	116 2/8	Present Owner: Loaned to B&C National Collection
Add (E) Total of Lengths of Abnormal Points	42 2/8	Guide Name and Address:
FINAL SCORE	158 4/8	Remarks:

I certify that I have measured the above trophy on ___29 April___ 19_89_

at (address) __New Mexico Museum of Natural History__ City __Albuquerque__ State __NM__
and that these measurements and data are, to the best of my knowledge and belief, made in accordance with the instructions given.

Witness: __John G. Stelfox__   Signature: __Bob Estes__

B&C OFFICIAL MEASURER   I.D. Number

INSTRUCTIONS FOR MEASURING NON-TYPICAL WHITETAIL AND COUES' DEER

All measurements must be made with a 1/4-inch flexible steel tape to the nearest one-eighth of an inch. Wherever it is necessary to change direction of measurement, mark a control point and swing tape at this point. (Note: a flexible steel cable can be used to measure points and main beams only.) Enter fractional figures in eighths, without reduction. Official measurements cannot be taken until antlers have dried for at least 60 days after the animal was killed.

A. Number of Points on Each Antler: to be counted a point, the projection must be at least one inch long, with the length exceeding width at one inch or more of length. All points are measured from tip of point to nearest edge of beam as illustrated. Beam tip is counted as a point but not measured as a point.

B. Tip to Tip Spread is measured between tips of main beams.

C. Greatest Spread is measured between perpendiculars at a right angle to the center line of the skull at widest part, whether across main beams or points.

D. Inside Spread of Main Beams is measured at a right angle to the center line of the skull at widest point between main beams. Enter this measurement again as the Spread Credit if it is less than or equal to the length of longer antler; if longer, enter longer antler length for Spread Credit.

E. Total of Lengths of all Abnormal Points: Abnormal Points are those non-typical in location (such as points originating from a point or from bottom or sides of main beam) or extra points beyond the normal pattern of points. Measure in usual manner and enter in appropriate blanks.

F. Length of Main Beam is measured from lowest outside edge of burr over outer curve to the most distant point of what is, or appears to be, the main beam. The point of beginning is that point on the burr where the center line along the outer curve of the beam intersects the burr, then following generally the line of the illustration.

G. 1-2-3-4-5-6-7 Length of Normal Points: Normal points project from the top of the main beam. They are measured from nearest edge of main beam over outer curve to tip. Lay the tape along the outer curve of the beam so that the top edge of the tape coincides with the top edge of the beam on both sides of the point to determine the baseline for point measurement. Record point lengths in appropriate blanks.

H. 1-2-3-4 Circumferences are taken as detailed for each measurement. If brow point is missing, take H-1 and H-2 at smallest place between burr and G-2. If G-4 is missing, take H-4 halfway between G-3 and tip of main beam.

* * * * * * * * * * * * * * * * *

FAIR CHASE STATEMENT FOR ALL HUNTER-TAKEN TROPHIES

To make use of the following methods shall be deemed as UNFAIR CHASE and unsportsmanlike, and any trophy obtained by use of such means is disqualified from entry.

  I. Spotting or herding game from the air, followed by landing in its vicinity for pursuit;

  II. Herding or pursuing game with motor-powered vehicles;

  III. Use of electronic communications for attracting, locating or observing game, or guiding the hunter to such game;

  IV. Hunting game confined by artificial barriers, including escape-proof fencing; or hunting game transplanted solely for the purpose of commercial shooting.

* * * * * * * * * * * * * * * * *

I certify that the trophy scored on this chart was not taken in UNFAIR CHASE as defined above by the Boone and Crockett Club. I further certify that it was taken in full compliance with local game laws of the state, province, or territory.

Date: _____ Signature of Hunter: _____

(Have signature notarized by a Notary Public)

Copyright © 1988 by Boone and Crockett Club
(Reproduction strictly forbidden without express, written consent)

OFFICIAL SCORING SYSTEM FOR NORTH AMERICAN BIG GAME TROPHIES

Records of North American Big Game
BOONE AND CROCKETT CLUB
P.O. Box 547
Dumfries, VA 22026

MOOSE

Kind of Moose: Alaska-Yukon

Minimum Score:
	Awards	All-time
Alaska-Yukon	210	224
Canada	185	195
Wyoming	140	155

DETAIL OF POINT MEASUREMENT

SEE OTHER SIDE FOR INSTRUCTIONS	Column 1	Column 2	Column 3	Column 4
A. Greatest Spread	68 5/8	Right Antler	Left Antler	Difference
B. Number of Abnormal Points on Both Antlers				
C. Number of Normal Points		15	17	2
D. Width of Palm		17 2/8	17 4/8	2/8
E. Length of Palm Including Brow Palm		49 7/8	50 4/8	5/8
F. Circumference of Beam at Smallest Place		7 6/8	7 6/8	
TOTALS	68 5/8	89 7/8	92 6/8	2 7/8

Enter Total of Columns 1, 2, and 3	251 2/8
Subtract Column 4	2 7/8
FINAL SCORE	248 3/8

Exact Locality Where Killed: Natla River, N.W.T.
Date Killed: 09/17/88
By Whom Killed: Myron A. Peterson
Present Owner: Myron A. Peterson
Guide Name and Address: Duane Nelson
Remarks:

I certify that I have measured the above trophy on 30 April 1989
at (Address) New Mexico Museum of Natural History (City) Albuquerque (State) NM
and that these measurements and data are, to the best of my knowledge and belief, made in accordance with the instructions given.

Witness: Bob Hults
Signature: Dennis L. Shirley
B&C OFFICIAL MEASURER
I.D. Number

INSTRUCTIONS FOR MEASURING MOOSE

All measurements must be made with a 1/4-inch flexible steel tape to the nearest one-eighth of an inch. Enter fractional figures in eighths, without reduction. Official measurements cannot be taken until antlers have dried for at least sixty days after animal was killed.

A. Greatest Spread is measured between perpendiculars in a straight line at a right angle to the center line of the skull.

B. Number of Abnormal Points on Both Antlers: Abnormal points are those projections originating from normal points or from the upper or lower palm surface, or from the inner edge of palm (see illustration). Abnormal points must be at least one inch long, with length exceeding width at one inch or more of length.

C. Number of Normal Points: Normal points originate from the outer edge of palm. To be counted a point, a projection must be at least one inch long, with the length exceeding width at one inch or more of length.

D. Width of Palm is taken in contact with the under surface of palm, at a right angle to the length of palm measurement line. The line of measurement should begin and end at the midpoint of the palm edge, which gives credit for the desirable character of palm thickness.

E. Length of Palm Including Brow Palm is taken in contact with the surface along the underside of the palm, parallel to the inner edge, from dips between points at the top to dips between points (if present) at the bottom. If a bay is present, measure across the open bay if the proper line of measurement, parallel to inner edge, follows this path. The line of measurement should begin and end at the midpoint of the palm edge, which gives credit for the desirable character of palm thickness.

F. Circumference of Beam at Smallest Place is taken as illustrated.

* * * * * * * * * * * * * * * * * * *

FAIR CHASE STATEMENT FOR ALL HUNTER-TAKEN TROPHIES

To make use of the following methods shall be deemed as UNFAIR CHASE and unsportsmanlike, and any trophy obtained by use of such means is disqualified from entry.

I. Spotting or herding game from the air, followed by landing in its vicinity for pursuit;

II. Herding or pursuing game with motor-powered vehicles;

III. Use of electronic communications for attracting, locating or observing game, or guiding the hunter to such game;

IV. Hunting game confined by artificial barriers, including escape-proof fencing; or hunting game transplanted solely for the purpose of commercial shooting.

* * * * * * * * * * * * * * * * * * *

I certify that the trophy scored on this chart was not taken in UNFAIR CHASE as defined above by the Boone and Crockett Club. I further certify that it was taken in full compliance with local game laws of the state, province, or territory.

Date: _____ Signature of Hunter: _____

(Have Signature Notarized by a Notary Public)

Copyright © 1988 by Boone and Crockett Club
(Reproduction strictly forbidden without express, written consent)

OFFICIAL SCORING SYSTEM FOR NORTH AMERICAN BIG GAME TROPHIES

Records of North American Big Game

BOONE AND CROCKETT CLUB

P.O. Box 547
Dumfries, VA 22026

CARIBOU

Kind of Caribou: **barren ground**

Minimum Score:	Awards	All-time
barren ground	375	400
mountain	360	390
Quebec-Labrador	365	375
woodland	265	295
Central Canada barren ground	330	345

DETAIL OF POINT MEASUREMENT

SEE OTHER SIDE FOR INSTRUCTIONS		Column 1 Spread Credit	Column 2 Right Antler	Column 3 Left Antler	Column 4 Difference
A. Tip to Tip Spread	42 2/8				
B. Greatest Spread	42 6/8				
C. Inside Spread of Main Beams	40 1/8	(Credit May Equal But Not Exceed Longer Antler)	40 1/8		
D. Number of Points on Each Antler Excluding Brows			18	17	1
Number of Points on Each Brow			6	6	
E. Length of Main Beam			50 6/8	49 7/8	7/8
F-1. Length of Brow Palm or First Point			19	20 4/8	
F-2. Length of Bez or Second Point			30	25 3/8	4 5/8
F-3. Length of Rear Point, If Present			22 6/8	20	2 6/8
F-4. Length of Second Longest Top Point			10 7/8	19 1/8	8 2/8
F-5. Length of Longest Top Point			19 2/8	20 7/8	1 5/8
G-1. Width of Brow Palm			9 7/8	14 5/8	
G-2. Width of Top Palm			5	8	3
H-1. Circumference at Smallest Place Between Brow and Bez Points			7	7	
H-2. Circumference at Smallest Place Between Bez and Rear Point, If Present			5 5/8	5 4/8	1/8
H-3. Circumference at Smallest Place Before First Top Point			4 6/8	5 2/8	4/8
H-4. Circumference at Smallest Place Between Two Longest Top Palm Points			9 7/8	15 3/8	5 4/8
TOTALS		40 1/8	218 6/8	234 4/8	28 2/8

Enter Total of Columns 1, 2, and 3	493 3/8	Exact Locality Where Killed: Mosquito Creek, Alaska
Subtract Column 4	28 2/8	Date Killed: 09/25/87 By Whom Killed: Roger Hedgecock
FINAL SCORE	465 1/8	Present Owner: Loaned to B&C National Collection
		Guide Name and Address: Bob Tracy
		Remarks:

I certify that I have measured the above trophy on _____/_____ 2 May 19 89

at (address) New Mexico Museum of Natural History City Albuquerque State NM
and that these measurements and data are, to the best of my knowledge and belief, made in accordance with the instructions given.

Witness: Dennis L. Shirley Signature Elvin Hawkins

B&C OFFICIAL MEASURER

I.D. Number

INSTRUCTIONS FOR MEASURING CARIBOU

All measurements must be made with a 1/4-inch flexible steel tape to the nearest one-eighth of an inch. Wherever it is necessary to change direction of measurement, mark a control point and swing tape at this point. (Note: a flexible steel cable can be used to measure points and main beams only.) Enter fractional figures in eighths, without reduction. Official measurements cannot be taken until antlers have dried for at least 60 days after the animal was killed.

A. Tip to Tip Spread is measured between tips of main beams.
B. Greatest Spread is measured between perpendiculars at a right angle to the center line of the skull at widest part, whether across main beams or points.
C. Inside Spread of Main Beams is measured at a right angle to the center line of the skull at widest point between main beams. Enter this measurement again as Spread Credit if it is less than or equal to the length of longer antler; if longer, enter longer antler length for Spread Credit.
D. Number of Points on Each Antler: To be counted a point, a projection must be at least one-half inch long, with length exceeding width at the point of measurement. Beam tip is counted as a point but not measured as a point. There are no "abnormal" points in caribou.
E. Length of Main Beam is measured from lowest outside edge of burr over outer curve to the most distant point of what is, or appears to be, the main beam. The point of beginning is that point on the burr where the center line along the outer curve of the beam intersects the burr.
F. 1-2-3 Length of Points are measured from nearest edge of beam on the shortest line over outer curve to tip. Lay the tape along the outer curve of the beam so that the top edge of the tape coincides with the top edge of the beam on both sides of point to determine the baseline for point measurement. Record point lengths in appropriate blanks.
F. 4-5 Length of Points are measured from the tip of the point to the top of the beam, then at a right angle to the lower edge of beam. The Second Longest Top Point cannot be a point branch of the Longest Top Point.
G-1 Width of Brow is measured in a straight line from top edge to lower edge, as illustrated, with measurement line at a right angle to main axis of brow.
G-2 Width of Top Palm is measured from midpoint of lower rear edge of main beam to midpoint of a dip between points, at widest part of palm. The line of measurement begins and ends at midpoints of palm edges, which gives credit for palm thickness.
H. 1-2-3-4 Circumferences are taken as described for measurements. If brow point is missing, take H-1 at smallest point between burr and bez point. If rear point is missing, take H-2 and H-3 measurements at smallest place between bez and first top point. Do not depress the tape into any dips of the palm or main beam.

* * * * * * * * * * * * * * * * *

FAIR CHASE STATEMENT FOR ALL HUNTER-TAKEN TROPHIES

To make use of the following methods shall be deemed as UNFAIR CHASE and unsportsmanlike, and any trophy obtained by use of such means is disqualified from entry.

I. Spotting or herding game from the air, followed by landing in its vicinity for pursuit;

II. Herding or pursuing game with motor-powered vehicles;

III. Use of electronic communications for attracting, locating or observing game, or guiding the hunter to such game;

IV. Hunting game confined by artificial barriers, including escape-proof fencing; or hunting game transplanted solely for the purpose of commercial shooting.

* * * * * * * * * * * * * * * * *

I certify that the trophy scored on this chart was not taken in UNFAIR CHASE as defined above by the Boone and Crockett Club. I further certify that it was taken in full compliance with local game laws of the state, province, or territory.

Date _____ Signature of Hunter _____

(Have signature notarized by a Notary Public)

Copyright © 1988 by Boone and Crockett Club
(Reproduction strictly forbidden without express, written consent)

OFFICIAL SCORING SYSTEM FOR NORTH AMERICAN BIG GAME TROPHIES

Records of North American Big Game

BOONE AND CROCKETT CLUB

P.O. Box 547
Dumfries, VA 22026

Minimum Score: Awards 80 All-time 82

PRONGHORN

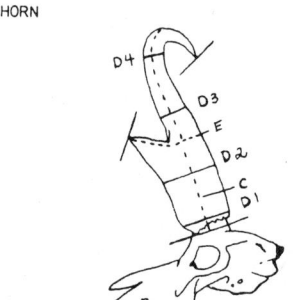

SEE OTHER SIDE FOR INSTRUCTIONS		Column 1	Column 2	Column 3
A. Tip to Tip Spread	3 4/8	Right Horn	Left Horn	Difference
B. Inside Spread of Main Beams	9 5/8			
IF Inside Spread Exceeds Longer Horn, Enter Difference		✕	✕	
C. Length of Horn		17 5/8	17 5/8	
D-1. Circumference of Base		7	6 7/8	1/8
D-2. Circumference at First Quarter		7 1/8	7 2/8	1/8
D-3. Circumference at Second Quarter		5	5	
D-4. Circumference at Third Quarter		3 4/8	3 4/8	
E. Length of Prong		5 4/8	5 2/8	2/8
TOTALS		45 6/8	45 4/8	4/8

Enter Total of Columns 1 and 2	91 2/8	Exact Locality Where Killed: Catron Co., N.M.
Subtract Column 3	4/8	Date Killed: 09/27/86 By Whom Killed: John P. Grimmett
FINAL SCORE	90 6/8	Present Owner: John P. Grimmett
		Guide Name and Address:
		Remarks:

I certify that I have measured the above trophy on _____ 3 May _____ 19 89

at (Address) New Mexico Museum of Natural History (City) Albuquerque (State) NM

and that these measurements and data are, to the best of my knowledge and belief, made in accordance with the instructions given.

Witness: James J. McBride   Signature: George K. Tsukamoto

B&C OFFICIAL MEASURER

I.D. Number

INSTRUCTIONS FOR MEASURING PRONGHORN

All measurements must be made with a 1/4-inch, flexible steel tape to the nearest one-eighth of an inch. Wherever it is necessary to change direction of measurement, mark a control point and swing tape at this point. Enter fractional figures in <u>eighths</u>, without reduction. Official measurement cannot be taken until horns have dried for at least sixty days <u>after</u> the animal was killed.

A. Tip to Tip Spread is measured between tips of horns.

B. Inside Spread of Main Beams is measured at a right angle to the center line of the skull, at widest point between main beams.

C. Length of Horn is measured on the outside curve on the general line illustrated. The line taken will vary with different heads, depending on the direction of their curvature. Measure along the center of the outer curve from tip of horn to a point in line with the lowest edge of the base, using a straight edge to establish the line end.

D-1 Measure around base of horn at a right angle to long axis. Tape must be in contact with the lowest circumference of the horn in which there are no serrations.

D. 2-3-4 Divide measurement C of longer horn by four. Starting at base, mark <u>both</u> horns at these quarters (even though the other horn is shorter) and measure circumferences at these marks. If the prong interferes with D-2, move the measurement down to just below the swelling of the prong. If the prong interferes with D-3, move the measurement up to just above the swelling of the prong.

E. Length of Prong: Measure from the tip of the prong along the upper edge of the outer curve to the horn; then continue around the horn to a point at the rear of the horn where a straight edge across the back of both horns touches the horn, with the latter part being at a right angle to the long axis of horn.

* * * * * * * * * * * * * * * * * *

FAIR CHASE STATEMENT FOR ALL HUNTER-TAKEN TROPHIES

To make use of the following methods shall be deemed as UNFAIR CHASE and unsportsmanlike, and any trophy obtained by use of such means is disqualified from entry.

I. Spotting or herding game from the air, followed by landing in its vicinity for pursuit;

II. Herding or pursuing game with motor-powered vehicles;

III. Use of electronic communications for attracting, locating or observing game, or guiding the hunter to such game;

IV. Hunting game confined by artificial barriers, including escape-proof fencing; or hunting game transplanted solely for the purpose of commercial shooting.

* * * * * * * * * * * * * * * * * *

I certify that the trophy scored on this chart was not taken in UNFAIR CHASE as defined above by the Boone and Crockett Club. I further certify that it was taken in full compliance with local game laws of the state, province, or territory.

Date: _____ Signature of Hunter: _____

(Have Signature Notarized by a Notary Public)

Copyright © 1988 by Boone and Crockett Club
(Reproduction strictly forbidden without express, written consent)

OFFICIAL SCORING SYSTEM FOR NORTH AMERICAN BIG GAME TROPHIES

Records of North American Big Game

BOONE AND CROCKETT CLUB

P.O. Box 547
Dumfries, VA 22026

Minimum Score: Awards 115 All-time 115

Sex male

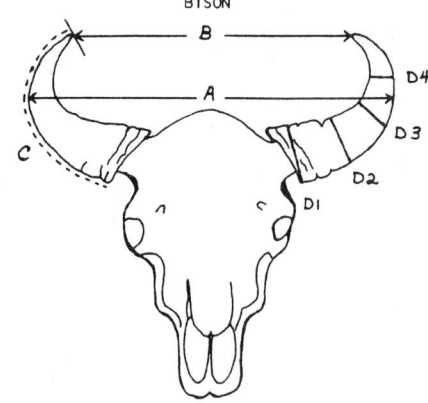

BISON

SEE OTHER SIDE FOR INSTRUCTIONS		Column 1	Column 2	Column 3
A. Greatest Spread	32	Right Horn	Left Horn	Difference
B. Tip to Tip Spread	26 4/8			
C. Length of Horn		19	18 5/8	3/8
D-1. Circumference of Base		15 2/8	14 7/8	3/8
D-2. Circumference at First Quarter		12 3/8	12 2/8	1/8
D-3. Circumference at Second Quarter		10	10	
D-4. Circumference at Third Quarter		6 1/8	5 7/8	2/8
TOTALS		62 6/8	61 5/8	1 1/8

Enter Total of Columns 1 and 2	124 3/8	Exact Locality Where Killed:	Chitina River, Alaska
Subtract Column 3	1 1/8	Date Killed: 09/29/87	By Whom Killed: Gerald H. Phillips
FINAL SCORE	123 2/8	Present Owner:	Gerald H. Phillips
		Guide Name and Address:	Paul Claus
		Remarks:	

I certify that I have measured the above trophy on _____ 1 May 1989
at (Address) New Mexico Museum of Natural History (City) Albuquerque (State) NM.
and that these measurements and data are, to the best of my knowledge and belief, made in accordance with the instructions given.

Witness: Dennis L. Shirley   Signature: Jesse E. Williams

B&C OFFICIAL MEASURER

I.D. Number

INSTRUCTIONS FOR MEASURING BISON

All measurements must be made with a 1/4-inch, flexible steel tape to the nearest one-eighth of an inch. Wherever it is necessary to change direction of measurement, mark a control point and swing tape at this point. Enter fractional figures in eighths, without reduction. Official measurement cannot be taken until horns have dried for at least sixty days after the animal was killed.

A. **Greatest Spread** is measured between perpendiculars at a right angle to the center line of the skull.

B. **Tip to Tip Spread** is measured between tips of horns.

C. **Length of Horn** is measured from the lowest point on underside over outer curve to a point in line with tip. Use a straight edge, perpendicular to horn axis, to end the measurement, if necessary.

D-1 **Circumference of Base** is measured at a right angle to axis of horn. Do not follow the irregular edge of horn; the line of measurement must be entirely on horn material, not the jagged edge often noted.

D. 2-3-4 Divide measurement C of longer horn by four. Starting at base, mark both horns at these quarters (even though the other horn is shorter) and measure circumferences at these marks, with measurements taken at right angles to horn axis.

* * * * * * * * * * * * * * * * *

FAIR CHASE STATEMENT FOR ALL HUNTER-TAKEN TROPHIES

To make use of the following methods shall be deemed as UNFAIR CHASE and unsportsmanlike, and any trophy obtained by use of such means is disqualified from entry.

I. Spotting or herding game from the air, followed by landing in its vicinity for pursuit;

II. Herding or pursuing game with motor-powered vehicles;

III. Use of electronic communications for attracting, locating or observing game, or guiding the hunter to such game;

IV. Hunting game confined by artificial barriers, including escape-proof fencing; or hunting game transplanted solely for the purpose of commercial shooting.

* * * * * * * * * * * * * * * * *

I certify that the trophy scored on this chart was not taken in UNFAIR CHASE as defined above by the Boone and Crockett Club. I further certify that it was taken in full compliance with local game laws of the state, province, or territory.

Date: _____ Signature of Hunter: _____

(Have Signature Notarized by a Notary Public)

Copyright © 1988 by Boone and Crockett Club
(Reproduction strictly forbidden without express, written consent)

OFFICIAL SCORING SYSTEM FOR NORTH AMERICAN BIG GAME TROPHIES

Records of North American Big Game

BOONE AND CROCKETT CLUB

P.O. Box 547
Dumfries, VA 22026

Minimum Score: Awards 47 All-time 50

ROCKY MOUNTAIN GOAT

Sex: male

SEE OTHER SIDE FOR INSTRUCTIONS		Column 1	Column 2	Column 3
A. Greatest Spread	8 6/8	Right Horn	Left Horn	Difference
B. Tip to Tip Spread	8			
C. Length of Horn		10 6/8	10 6/8	
D-1. Circumference of Base		5 7/8	6	1/8
D-2. Circumference at First Quarter		4 6/8	5	2/8
D-3. Circumference at Second Quarter		3 4/8	3 5/8	1/8
D-4. Circumference at Third Quarter		2	2	
TOTALS		26 7/8	27 3/8	4/8

Enter Total of Columns 1 and 2	54 2/8	Exact Locality Where Killed: Sheslay River, B.C.
Subtract Column 3	4/8	Date Killed: 09/05/87 By Whom Killed: Dan Stobbe
FINAL SCORE	53 6/8	Present Owner: Dan Stobbe
		Guide Name and Address:
		Remarks:

I certify that I have measured the above trophy on _____ 1 May 1989

at (Address) New Mexico Museum of Natural History (City) Albuquerque (State) NM

and that these measurements and data are, to the best of my knowledge and belief, made in accordance with the instructions given.

Witness: James J. McBride Signature: George K. Tsukamoto

B&C OFFICIAL MEASURER

I.D. Number

INSTRUCTIONS FOR MEASURING ROCKY MOUNTAIN GOAT

All measurements must be made with a 1/4-inch, flexible steel tape to the nearest one-eighth of an inch. Wherever it is necessary to change direction of measurement, mark a control point and swing tape at this point. Enter fractional figures in eighths, without reduction. Official measurement cannot be taken until horns have dried for at least sixty days after the animal was killed.

A. Greatest Spread is measured between perpendiculars at a right angle to the center line of the skull.

B. Tip to Tip Spread is measured between tips of horns.

C. Length of Horn is measured from the lowest point in front over outer curve to a point in line with tip.

D-1 Circumference of Base is measured at a right angle to axis of horn. Do not follow irregular edge of horn.

D. 2-3-4 Divide measurement C of longer horn by four. Starting at base, mark both horns at these quarters (even though the other horn is shorter) and measure circumferences at these marks.

* * * * * * * * * * * * * * * * * *

FAIR CHASE STATEMENT FOR ALL HUNTER-TAKEN TROPHIES

To make use of the following methods shall be deemed as UNFAIR CHASE and unsportsmanlike, and any trophy obtained by use of such means is disqualified from entry.

   I. Spotting or herding game from the air, followed by landing in its vicinity for pursuit;

   II. Herding or pursuing game with motor-powered vehicles;

   III. Use of electronic communications for attracting, locating or observing game, or guiding the hunter to such game;

   IV. Hunting game confined by artificial barriers, including escape-proof fencing; or hunting game transplanted solely for the purpose of commercial shooting.

* * * * * * * * * * * * * * * * * *

I certify that the trophy scored on this chart was not taken in UNFAIR CHASE as defined above by the Boone and Crockett Club. I further certify that it was taken in full compliance with local game laws of the state, province, or territory.

Date: _____ Signature of Hunter: _____

(Have Signature Notarized by a Notary Public)

Copyright © 1988 by Boone and Crockett Club
(Reproduction strictly forbidden without express, written consent)

OFFICIAL SCORING SYSTEM FOR NORTH AMERICAN BIG GAME TROPHIES

Records of North American Big Game

BOONE AND CROCKETT CLUB

P.O. Box 547
Dumfries, VA 22026

Minimum Score: Awards 105 All-time 105

MUSKOX

Sex _male_

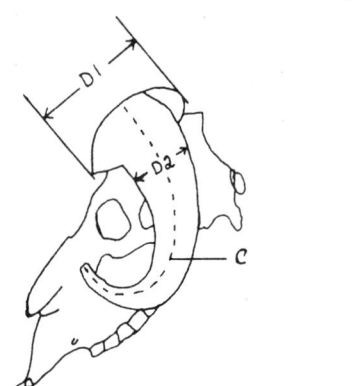

SEE OTHER SIDE FOR INSTRUCTIONS		Column 1	Column 2	Column 3
A. Greatest Spread	30 4/8	Right Horn	Left Horn	Difference
B. Tip to Tip Spread	30 1/8			
C. Length of Horn		27 2/8	27 1/8	1/8
D-1. Width of Boss		10 5/8	10 2/8	3/8
D-2. Width at First Quarter		7	7 5/8	5/8
D-3. Circumference at Second Quarter		11 6/8	12	2/8
D-4. Circumference at Third Quarter		6 5/8	6 4/8	1/8
TOTALS		63 2/8	63 4/8	1 4/8

Enter Total of Columns 1 and 2	126 6/8	Exact Locality Where Killed: Bay Chimo, N.W.T.
Subtract Column 3	1 4/8	Date Killed: 08/21/88 By Whom Killed: Donald Nicholson
FINAL SCORE	125 2/8	Present Owner: Donald Nicholson
		Guide Name and Address: Phillip Kadlun
		Remarks:

I certify that I have measured the above trophy on _____ 30 April 19 89
at (Address) New Mexico Museum of Natural History (City) Albuquerque (State) NM
and that these measurements and data are, to the best of my knowledge and belief, made in accordance with the instructions given.

Witness: Walter H. White   Signature: John G. Stelfox
                                        B&C OFFICIAL MEASURER

I.D. Number

INSTRUCTIONS FOR MEASURING MUSKOX

All measurements must be made with a 1/4-inch, flexible steel tape and adjustable calipers to the nearest one-eighth of an inch. Wherever it is necessary to change direction of measurement, mark a control point and swing tape at this point. Enter fractional figures in eighths, without reduction. Official measurement cannot be taken until horns have dried for at least sixty days after the animal was killed.

A. Greatest Spread is measured between perpendiculars at a right angle to the center line of the skull.

B. Tip to Tip Spread is measured between tips of horns by using large calipers, which are then read against a yardstick.

C. Length of Horn is measured along center of upper horn surface, staying within curve of horn as illustrated, to a point in line with tip. Attempt to free the connective tissue between the horns at the center of the boss to determine the lowest point of horn material on each side, near the top center of the skull. Hook the tape under the lowest point of the horn and measure the length of horn, with the measurement line maintained in the center of the upper surface of horn following the converging lines to the horn tip.

D-1 Width of Boss is measured with calipers at greatest width of base, with measurement line forming a right angle with horn axis. It is often helpful to measure D-1 before C, marking the midpoint of the boss as the correct path of C.

D. 2-3-4 Divide measurement C of longer horn by four. Starting at base, mark both horns at these quarters (even though the other horn is shorter). Then, using calipers, measure width of boss at D-2, making sure the measurement is at a right angle to horn axis and in line with the D-2 mark. Circumferences are then measured at D-3 and D-4, with measurements being taken at right angles to horn axis.

* * * * * * * * * * * * * * * * *

FAIR CHASE STATEMENT FOR ALL HUNTER-TAKEN TROPHIES

To make use of the following methods shall be deemed as UNFAIR CHASE and unsportsmanlike, and any trophy obtained by use of such means is disqualified from entry.

  I. Spotting or herding game from the air, followed by landing in its vicinity for pursuit;

  II. Herding or pursuing game with motor-powered vehicles;

  III. Use of electronic communications for attracting, locating or observing game, or guiding the hunter to such game;

  IV. Hunting game confined by artificial barriers, including escape-proof fencing; or hunting game transplanted solely for the purpose of commercial shooting.

* * * * * * * * * * * * * * * * *

I certify that the trophy scored on this chart was not taken in UNFAIR CHASE as defined above by the Boone and Crockett Club. I further certify that it was taken in full compliance with local game laws of the state, province, or territory.

Date: _____ Signature of Hunter: _____

(Have Signature Notarized by a Notary Public)

Copyright © 1988 by Boone and Crockett Club
(Reproduction strictly forbidden without express, written consent)

OFFICIAL SCORING SYSTEM FOR NORTH AMERICAN BIG GAME TROPHIES

Records of North American Big Game

BOONE AND CROCKETT CLUB

P.O. Box 547
Dumfries, VA 22026

Minimum Score:	Awards	All-time
bighorn	175	180
desert	165	168
Dall's	165	170
Stone's	165	170

SHEEP

Kind of Sheep desert

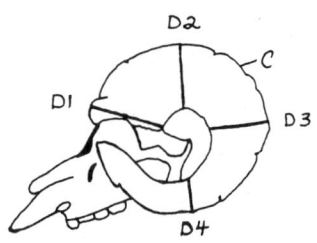 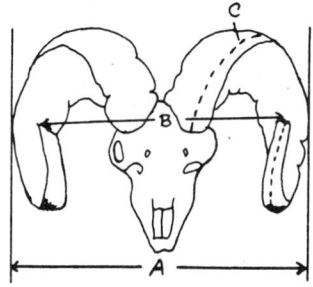 

MEASURE TO A POINT IN LINE WITH HORN TIP

SEE OTHER SIDE FOR INSTRUCTIONS		Column 1	Column 2	Column 3
A. Greatest Spread (Is Often Tip to Tip Spread)	22 3/8	Right Horn	Left Horn	Difference
B. Tip to Tip Spread	21 5/8			
C. Length of Horn		39 3/8	39 5/8	✗
D-1. Circumference of Base		15 3/8	15 3/8	
D-2. Circumference at First Quarter		14 7/8	14 5/8	2/8
D-3. Circumference at Second Quarter		13 3/8	12 5/8	6/8
D-4. Circumference at Third Quarter		9 3/8	9	3/8
TOTALS		92 3/8	91 2/8	1 3/8

Enter Total of Columns 1 and 2	183 5/8	Exact Locality Where Killed: Graham Co., Ariz.
Subtract Column 3	1 3/8	Date Killed: 12/11/86 By Whom Killed: Beverly M. Nuessle
FINAL SCORE	182 2/8	Present Owner: Beverly M. Nuessle
		Guide Name and Address: Floyd Krank
		Remarks:

I certify that I have measured the above trophy on _____ 2 May 1989
at (Address) New Mexico Museum of Natural History (City) Albuquerque (State) NM
and that these measurements and data are, to the best of my knowledge and belief, made in accordance with the instructions given.

Witness: John G. Stelfox   Signature: Jesse E. Williams
                                    B&C OFFICIAL MEASURER
                                                                    I.D. Number

INSTRUCTIONS FOR MEASURING SHEEP

All measurements must be made with a 1/4-inch, flexible steel tape to the nearest one-eighth of an inch. Wherever it is necessary to change direction of measurement, mark a control point and swing tape at this point. Enter fractional figures in eighths, without reduction. Official measurement cannot be taken until horns have dried for at least sixty days after the animal was killed.

A. Greatest Spread is measured between perpendiculars at a right angle to the center line of the skull.

B. Tip to Tip Spread is measured between tips of horns.

C. Length of Horn is measured from the lowest point in front on outer curve to a point in line with tip. Do not press tape into depressions. The low point of the outer curve of the horn is considered to be the low point of the frontal portion of the horn, situated above and slightly medial to the eye socket (not the outside edge). Use a straight edge, perpendicular to horn axis, to end measurement on "broomed" horns.

D-1 Circumference of Base is measured at a right angle to axis of horn. Do not follow irregular edge of horn; the line of measurement must be entirely on horn material, not the jagged edge often noted.

D. 2-3-4 Divide measurement C of longer horn by four. Starting at base, mark both horns at these quarters (even though the other horn is shorter) and measure circumferences at these marks, with measurements taken at right angles to horn axis.

* * * * * * * * * * * * * * * * * *

FAIR CHASE STATEMENT FOR ALL HUNTER-TAKEN TROPHIES

To make use of the following methods shall be deemed as UNFAIR CHASE and unsportsmanlike, and any trophy obtained by use of such means is disqualified from entry.

  I. Spotting or herding game from the air, followed by landing in its vicinity for pursuit;

  II. Herding or pursuing game with motor-powered vehicles;

  III. Use of electronic communications for attracting, locating or observing game, or guiding the hunter to such game;

  IV. Hunting game confined by artificial barriers, including escape-proof fencing; or hunting game transplanted solely for the purpose of commercial shooting.

* * * * * * * * * * * * * * * * * *

I certify that the trophy scored on this chart was not taken in UNFAIR CHASE as defined above by the Boone and Crockett Club. I further certify that it was taken in full compliance with local game laws of the state, province, or territory.

Date: _____ Signature of Hunter: _____

(Have Signature Notarized by a Notary Public)

Copyright © 1988 by Boone and Crockett Club
(Reproduction strictly forbidden without express, written consent)

This book was:

Compiled with able assistance of:
                                  Eugene C. Harter 3rd
                                  Geri B. Nesbitt
                                  Carol A. Palmerino
                                  Margaret E. Sefchick

Book design and layout by: Wm. H. Nesbitt

Typesetting by systems designed by: Wm. H. Nesbitt
   With a fraction font designed by: Eugene C. Harter 3rd

Printed and bound by: Haddon Craftsmen
                            Scranton, Pennsylvania